THE DREAMLAND CHRONICLES

BOOK TWO

D1374224

DEC 2008

LI

THE DREAMLAND CHRONICLES: BOOK TWO

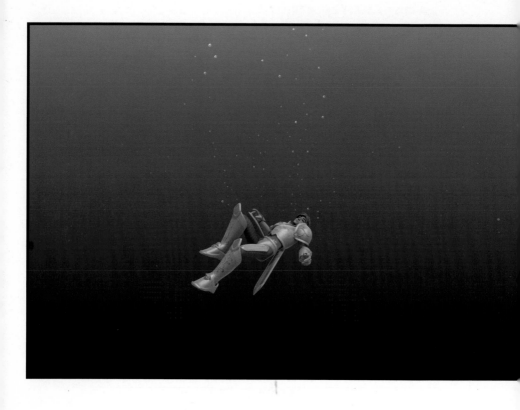

FOR MORE INFORMATION, PLEASE GO TO:
WWW.THEDREAMLANDCHRONICLES.COM

ISBN: 0-9789168-3-2
ISBN13: 978-0-9789168-3-1
LIBRARY OF CONGRESS CONTROL NUMBER:
2007932090

FOR BRENDAN DANIEL AND LOGAN ALEXANDER...
MAY GOD BLESS YOUR ADVENTURES
AS YOU DISCOVER DREAMLAND
FOR YOURSELVES.

CHAPTER FIVE

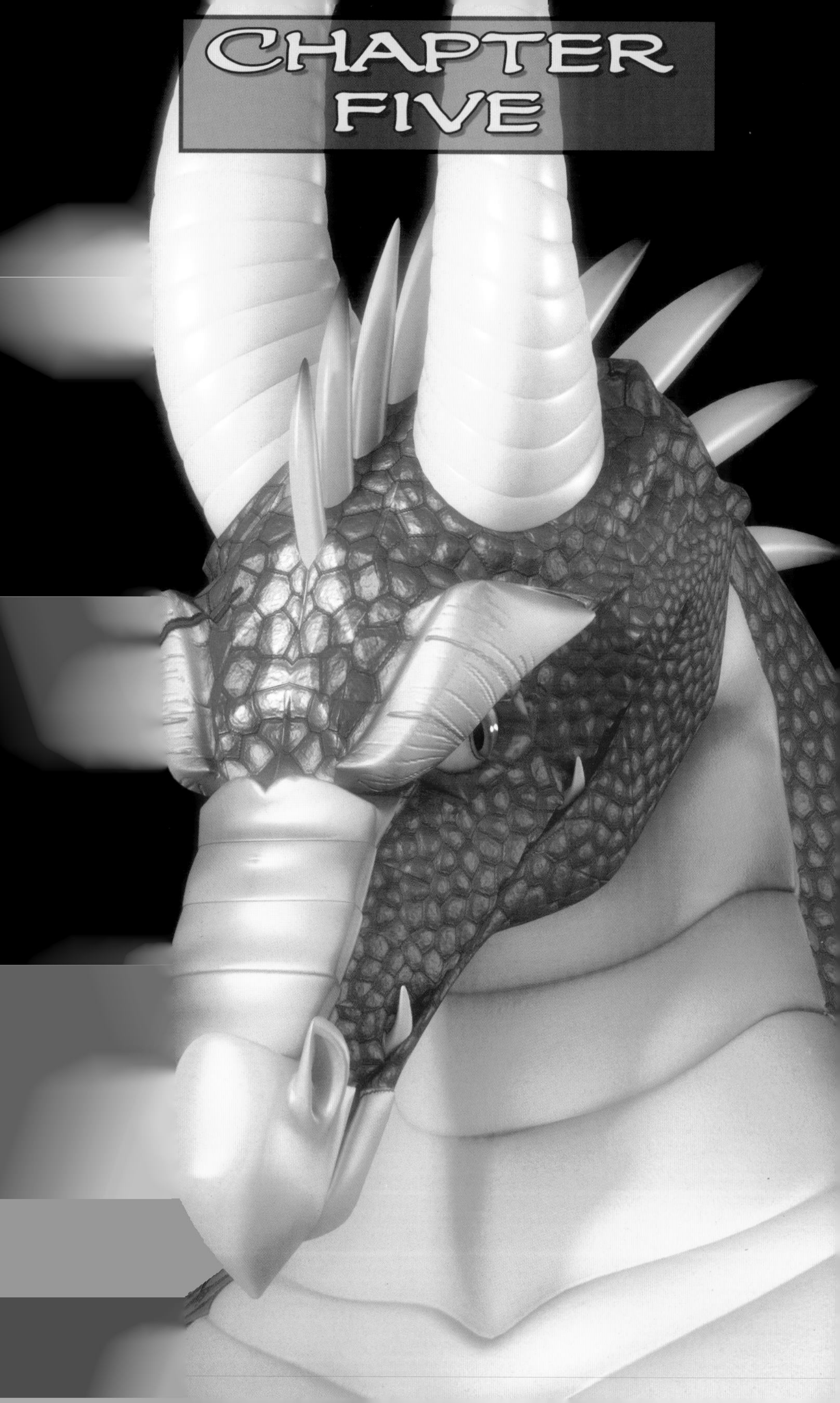

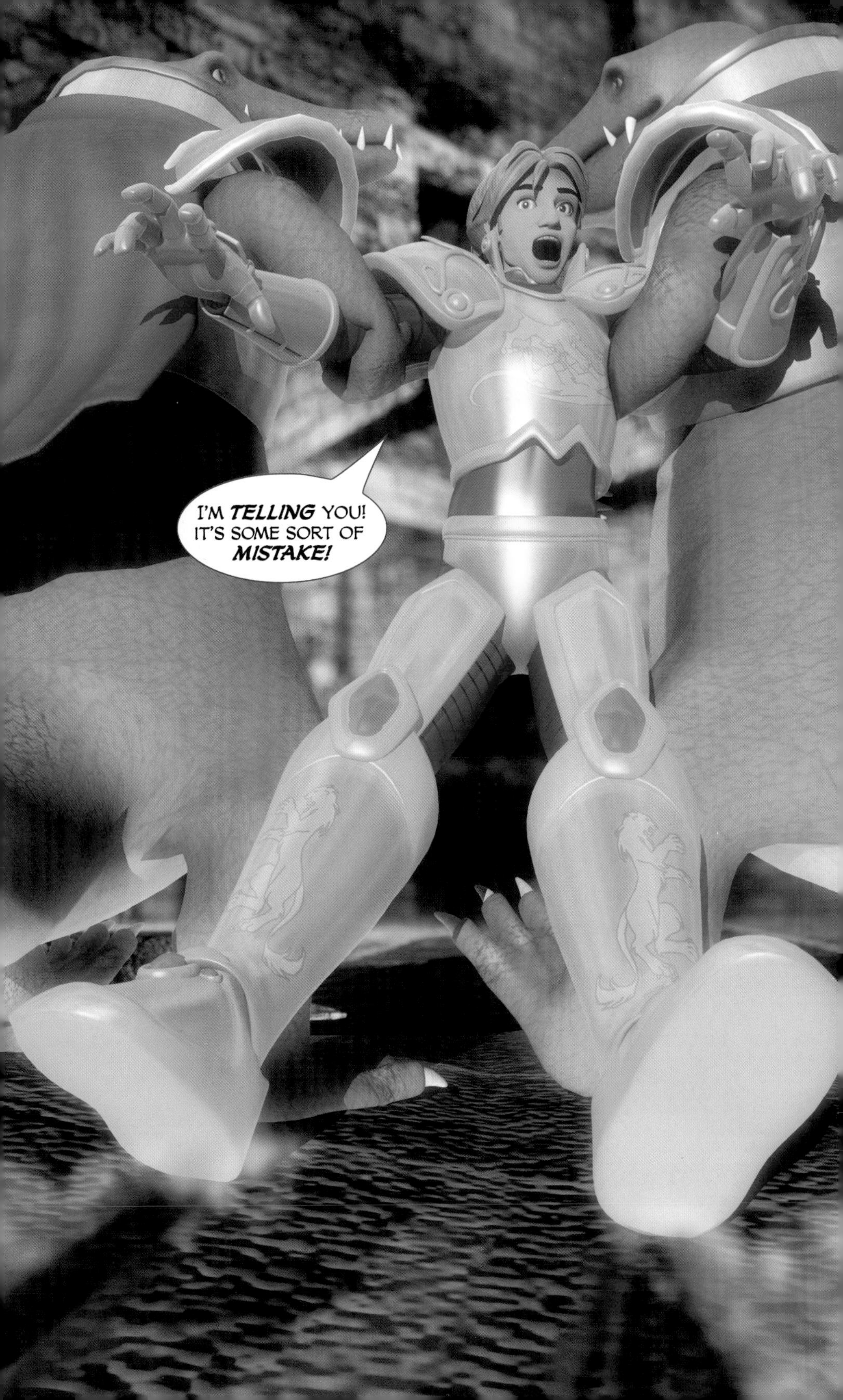
I'M **TELLING** YOU! IT'S SOME SORT OF **MISTAKE!**

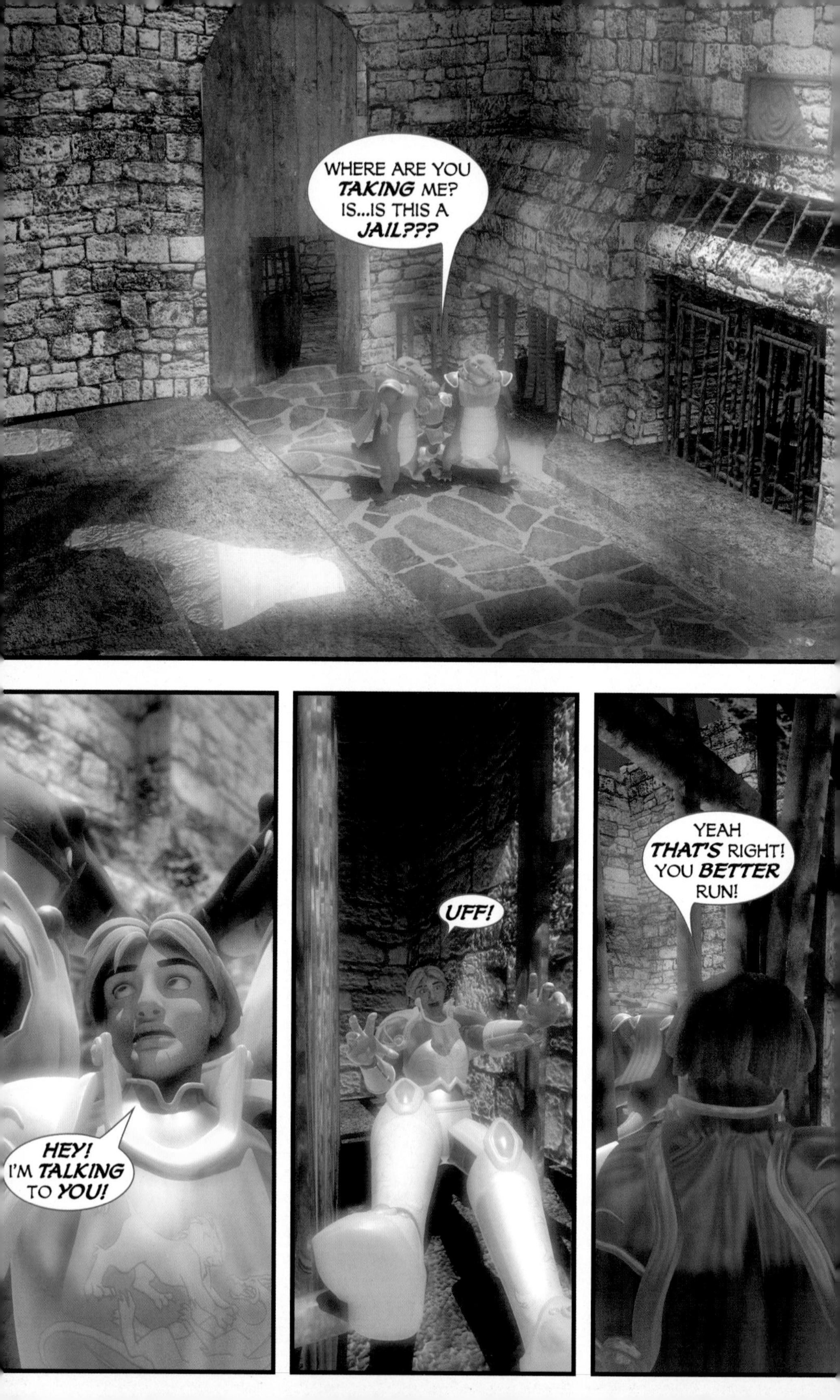
WHERE ARE YOU TAKING ME? IS...IS THIS A JAIL???
HEY! I'M TALKING TO YOU!
UFF!
YEAH THAT'S RIGHT! YOU BETTER RUN!

CRUD.

WELL *HELLO!* LOOKS LIKE I'VE GOT *COMPANY.*

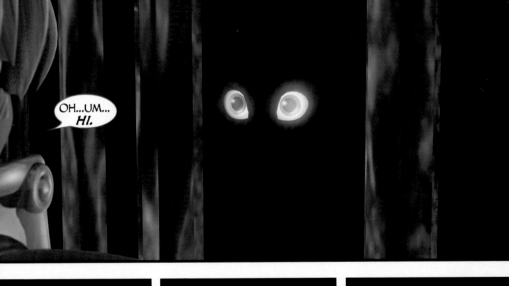

OH...UM... *HI.*

WHAT ARE YOU *IN* FOR, NEW GUY?

UH... I *THINK* I *TICKED* OFF *NICODEMUS* AS A KID.

HA HA! AND HE'S *STILL* HOLDING A GRUDGE? YEAH...*THAT* SOUNDS LIKE *OL' NICK.*

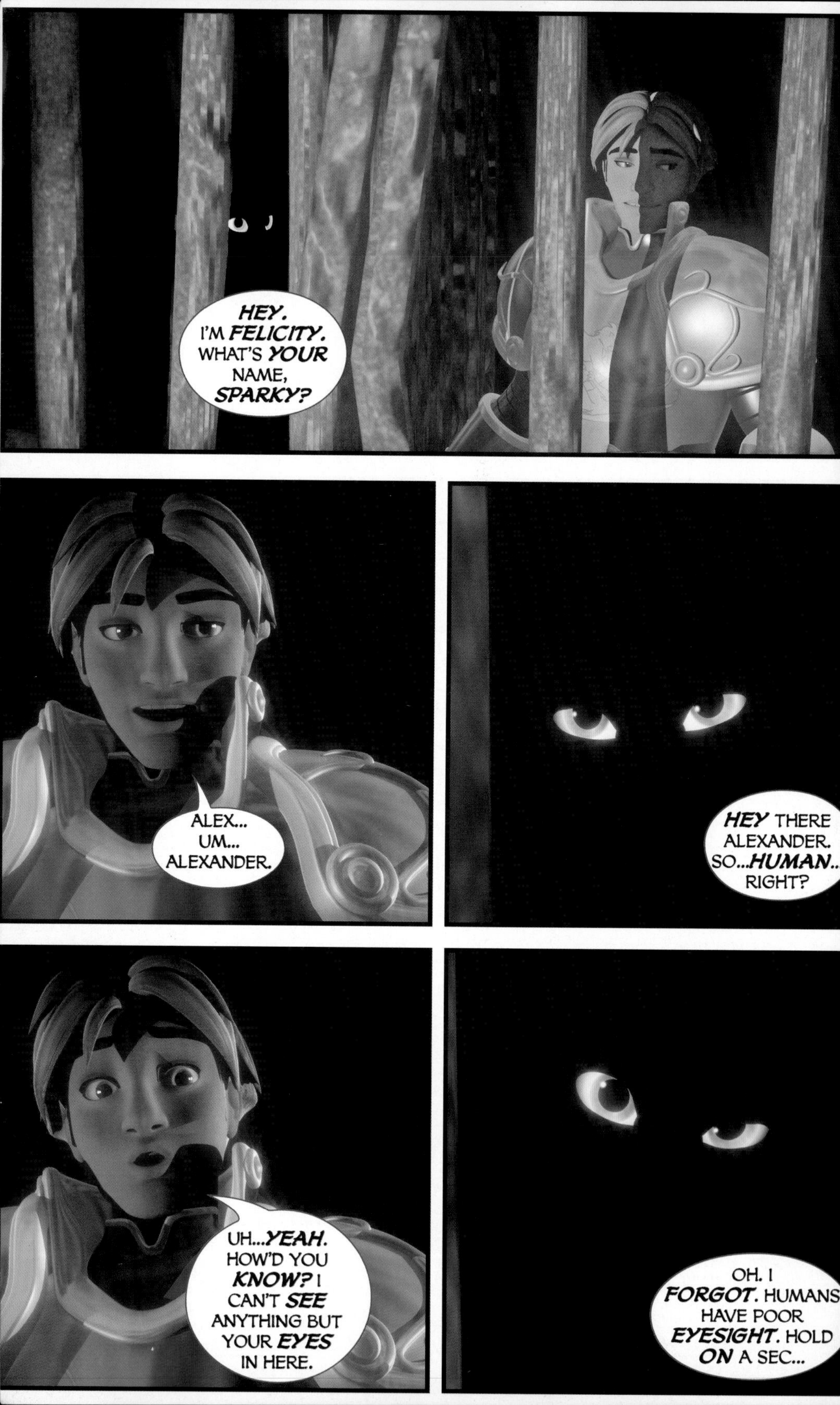
HEY. I'M FELICITY. WHAT'S YOUR NAME, SPARKY?
ALEX... UM... ALEXANDER.
HEY THERE ALEXANDER. SO...HUMAN... RIGHT?
UH...YEAH. HOW'D YOU KNOW? I CAN'T SEE ANYTHING BUT YOUR EYES IN HERE.
OH. I FORGOT. HUMANS HAVE POOR EYESIGHT. HOLD ON A SEC...

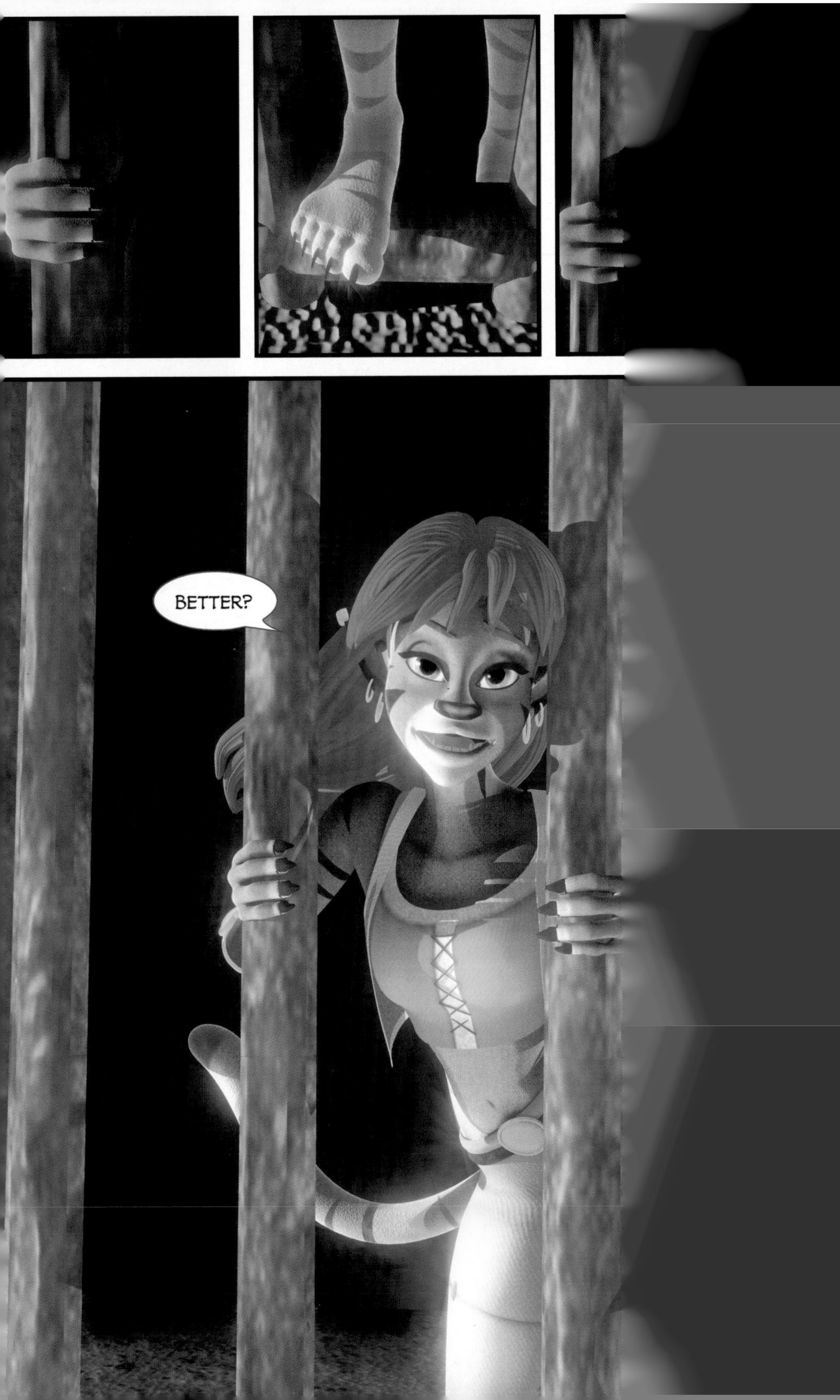
BETTER?

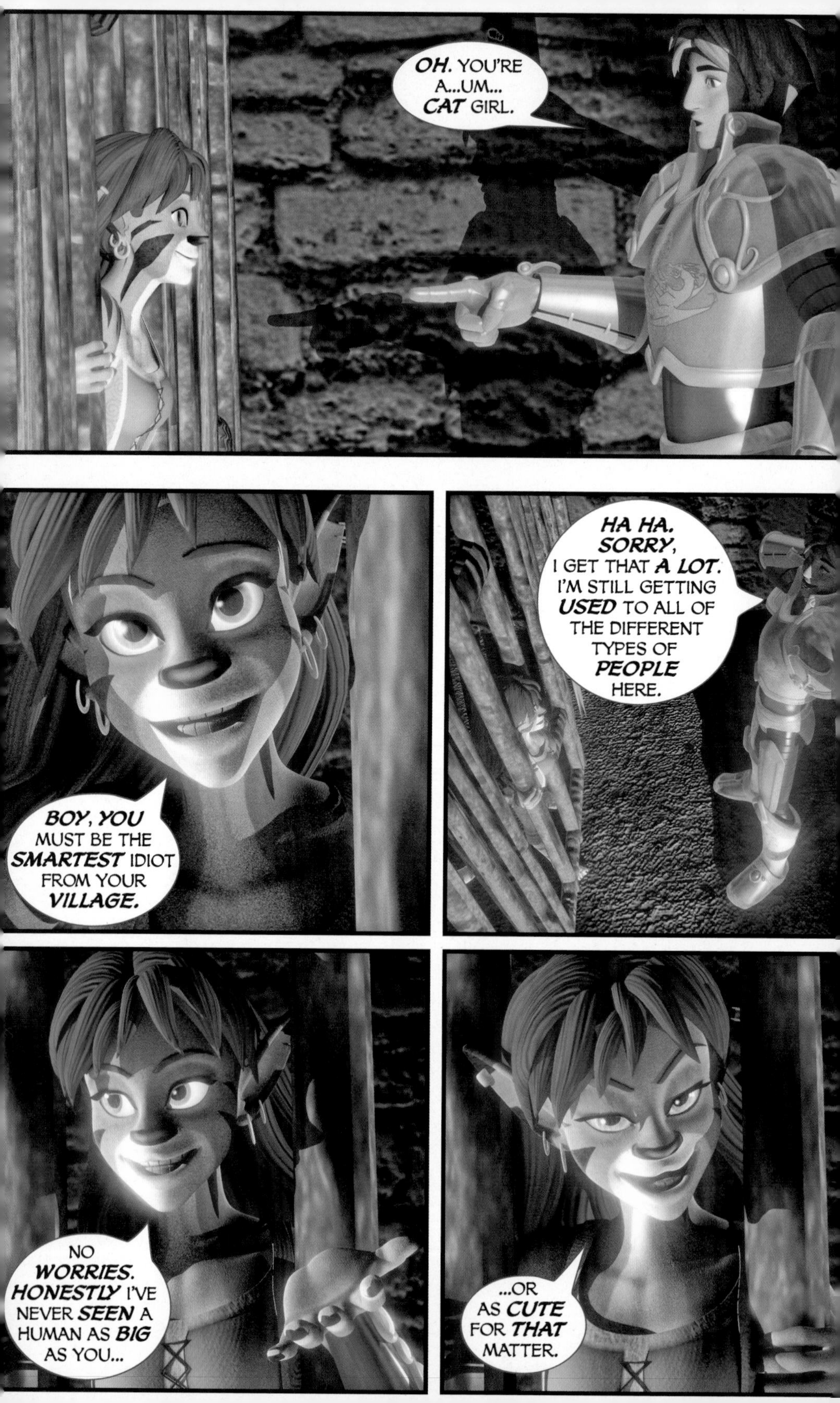
OH. YOU'RE A...UM... CAT GIRL.
BOY, YOU MUST BE THE SMARTEST IDIOT FROM YOUR VILLAGE.
HA HA. SORRY, I GET THAT A LOT. I'M STILL GETTING USED TO ALL OF THE DIFFERENT TYPES OF PEOPLE HERE.
NO WORRIES. HONESTLY I'VE NEVER SEEN A HUMAN AS BIG AS YOU...
...OR AS CUTE FOR THAT MATTER.

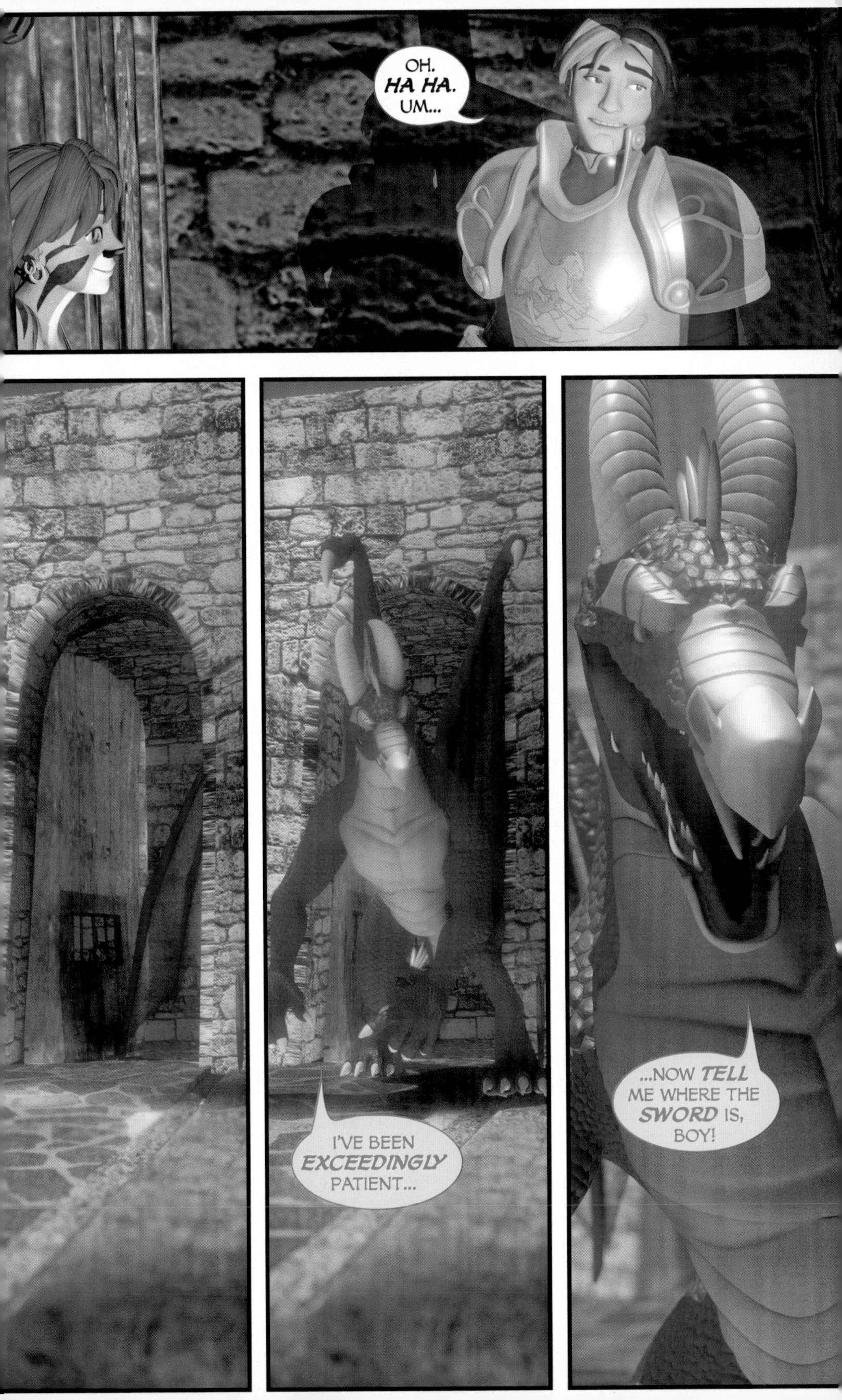
OH.
HA HA.
UM...
I'VE BEEN EXCEEDINGLY PATIENT...
...NOW TELL ME WHERE THE SWORD IS, BOY!

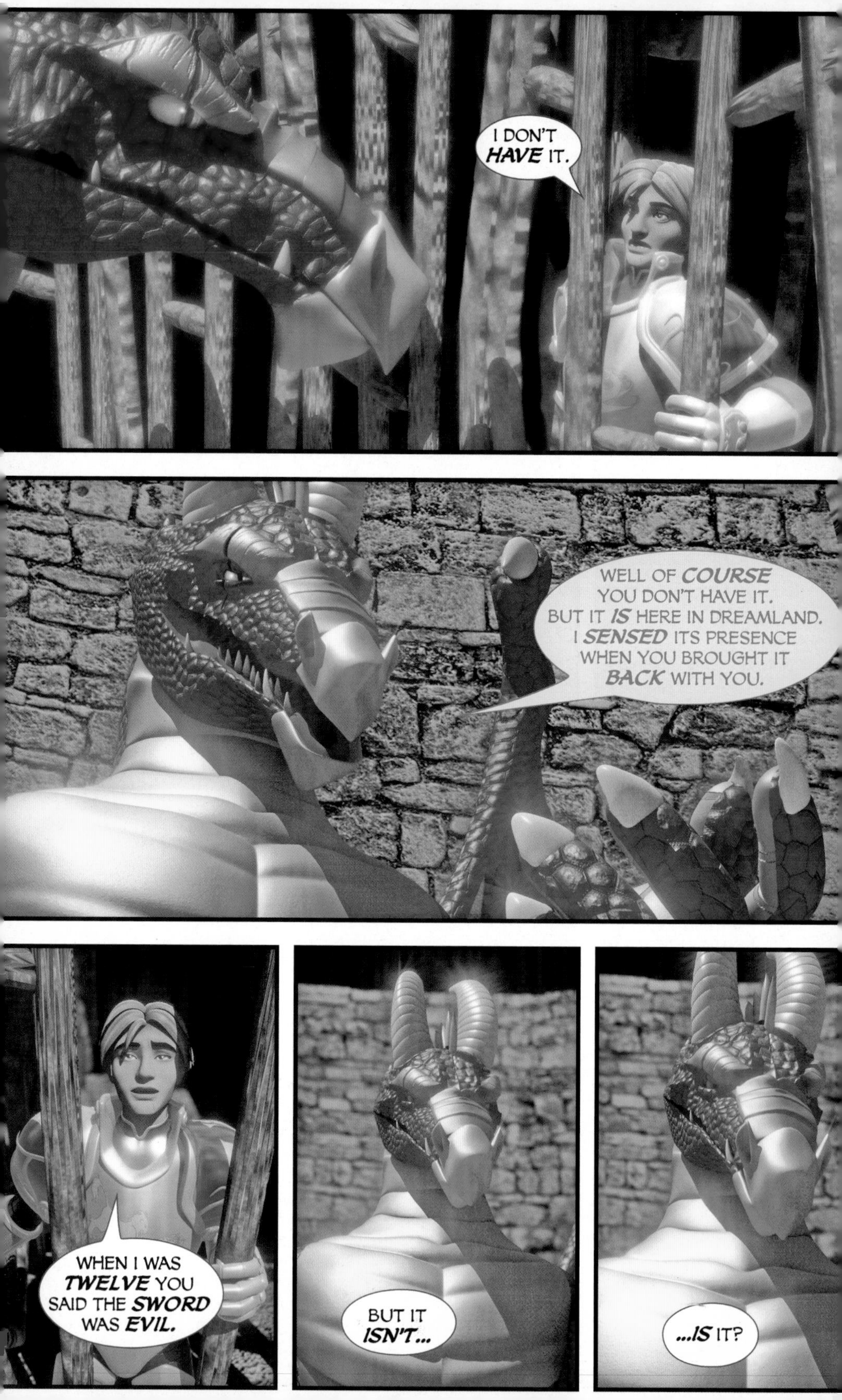
I DON'T *HAVE* IT.
WELL OF *COURSE* YOU DON'T HAVE IT. BUT IT *IS* HERE IN DREAMLAND. I *SENSED* ITS PRESENCE WHEN YOU BROUGHT IT *BACK* WITH YOU.
WHEN I WAS *TWELVE* YOU SAID THE *SWORD* WAS *EVIL.*
BUT IT *ISN'T...*
...IS IT?

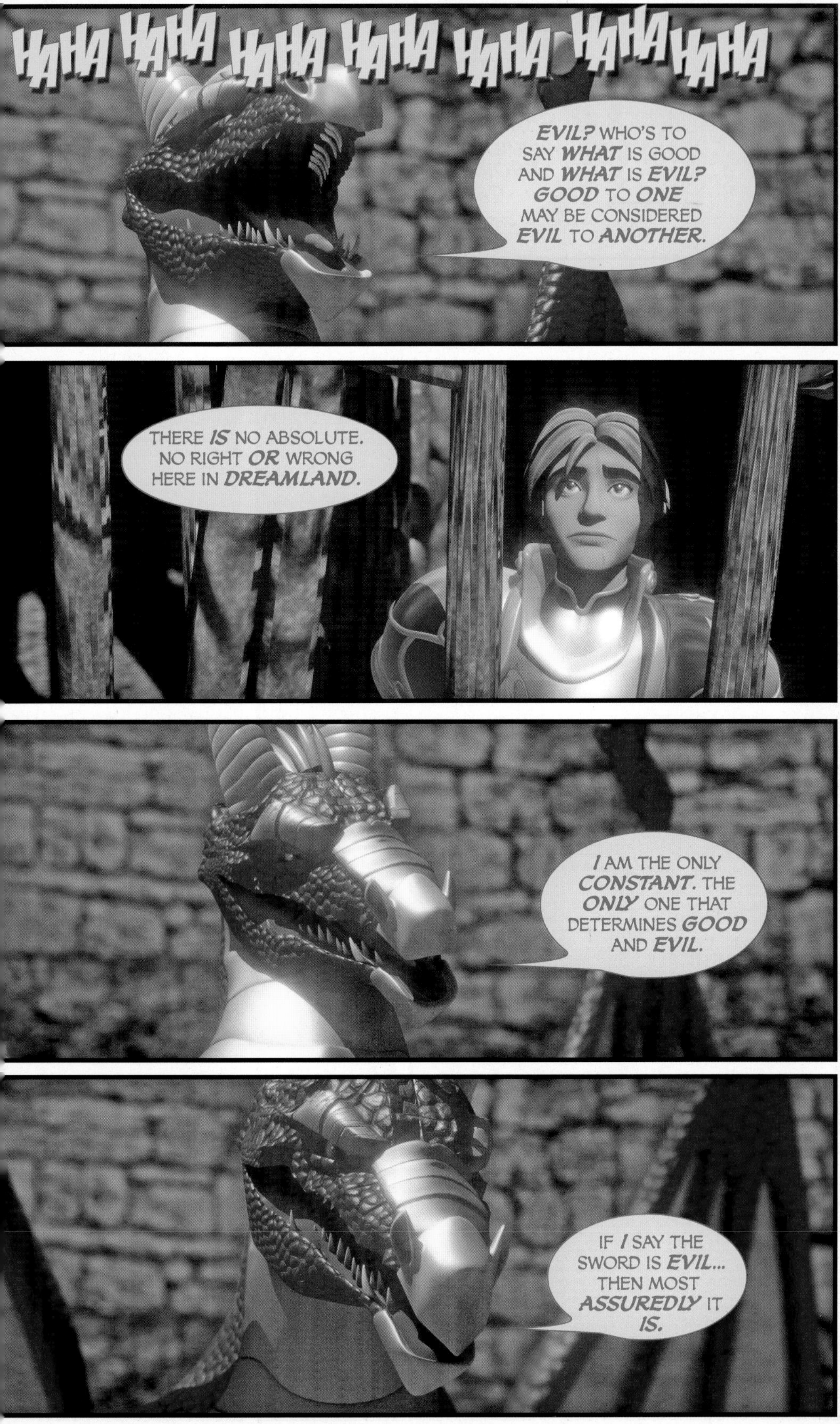
HAHA HAHA HAHA HAHA HAHA HAHA HAHA
EVIL? WHO'S TO SAY WHAT IS GOOD AND WHAT IS EVIL? GOOD TO ONE MAY BE CONSIDERED EVIL TO ANOTHER.
THERE IS NO ABSOLUTE. NO RIGHT OR WRONG HERE IN DREAMLAND.
I AM THE ONLY CONSTANT. THE ONLY ONE THAT DETERMINES GOOD AND EVIL.
IF I SAY THE SWORD IS EVIL... THEN MOST ASSUREDLY IT IS.

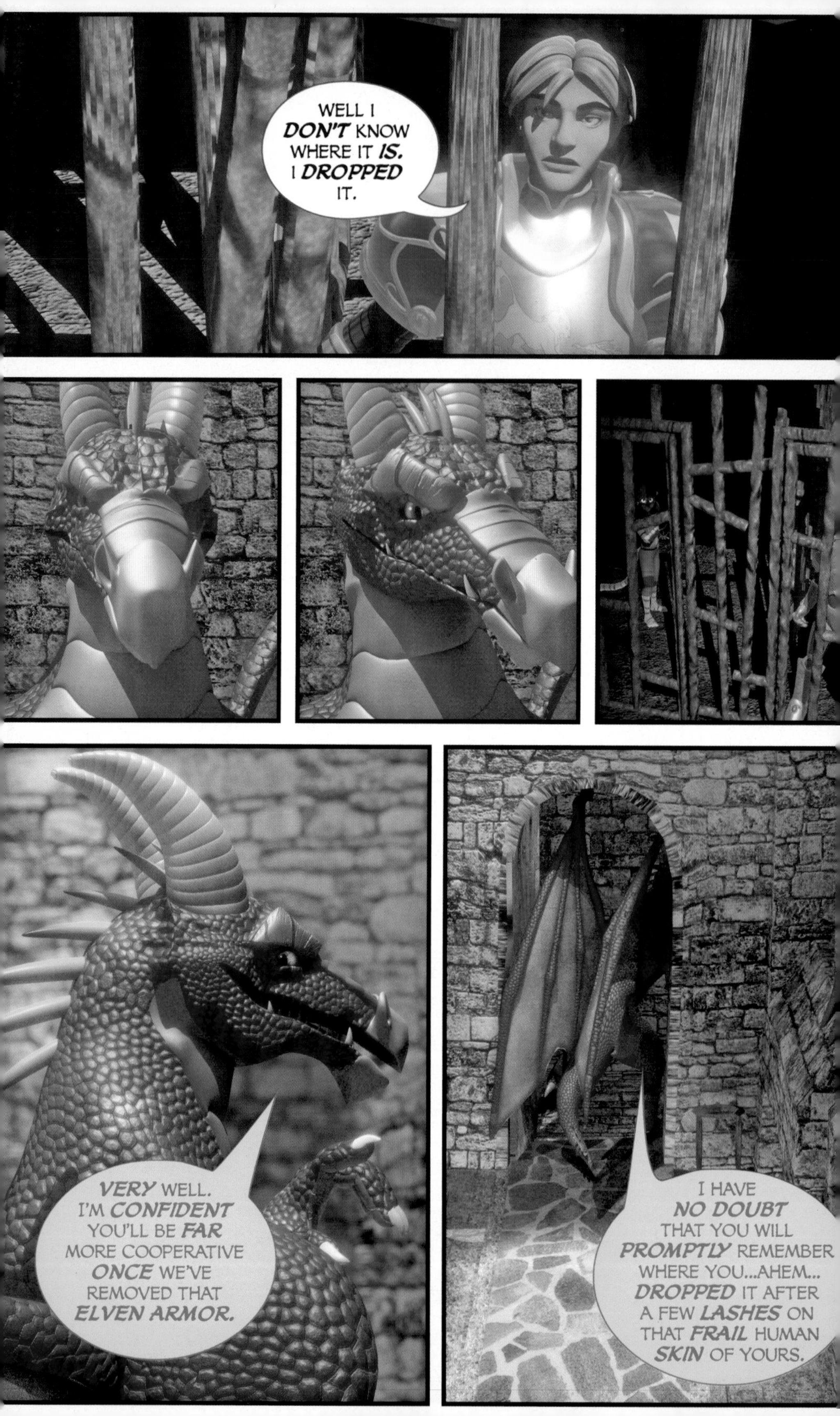
WELL I DON'T KNOW WHERE IT IS. I DROPPED IT.
VERY WELL. I'M CONFIDENT YOU'LL BE FAR MORE COOPERATIVE ONCE WE'VE REMOVED THAT ELVEN ARMOR.
I HAVE NO DOUBT THAT YOU WILL PROMPTLY REMEMBER WHERE YOU...AHEM... DROPPED IT AFTER A FEW LASHES ON THAT FRAIL HUMAN SKIN OF YOURS.

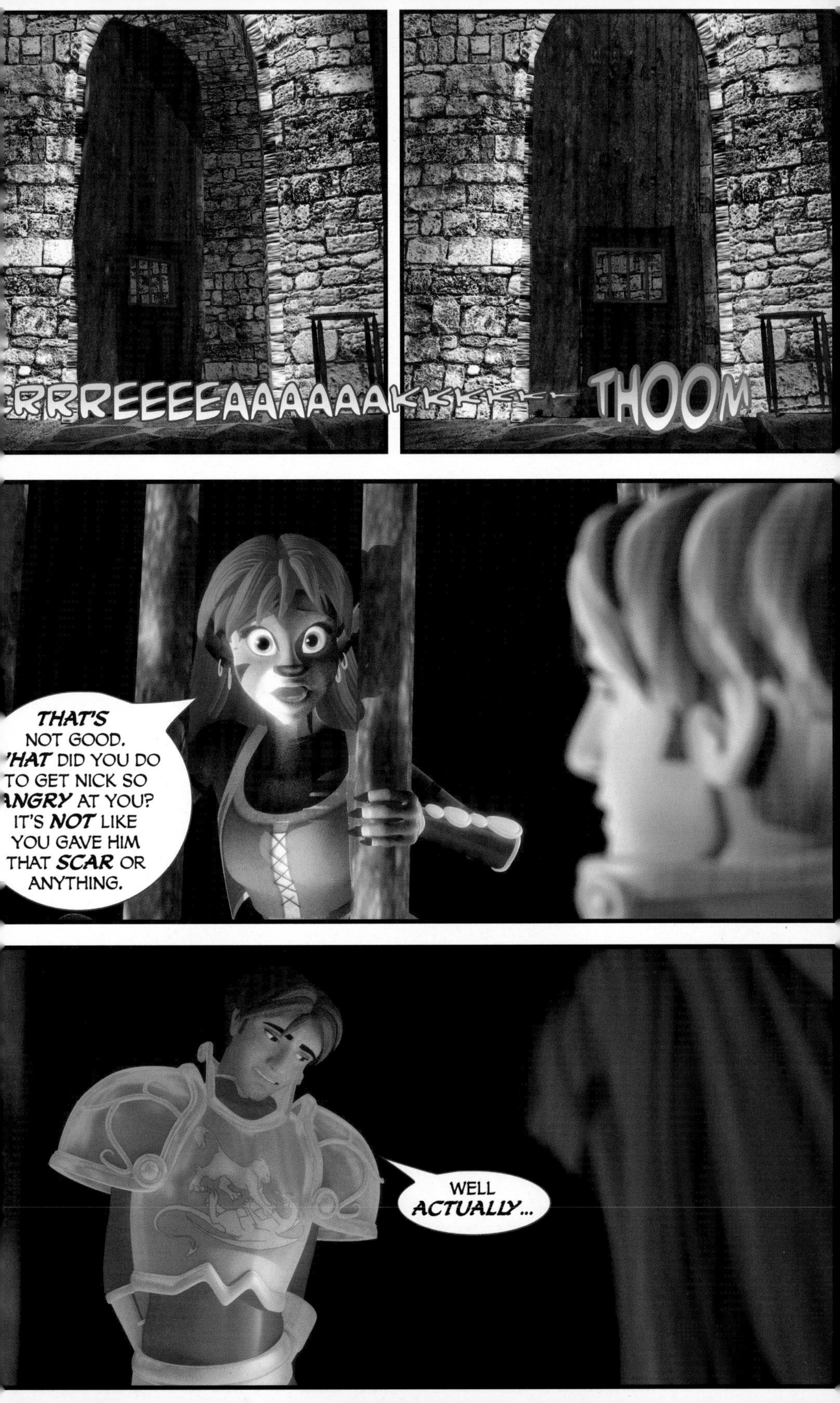
RRREEEEEAAAAAAKKKKK
THOOM
THAT'S NOT GOOD. HAT DID YOU DO TO GET NICK SO NGRY AT YOU? IT'S NOT LIKE YOU GAVE HIM THAT SCAR OR ANYTHING.
WELL ACTUALLY...

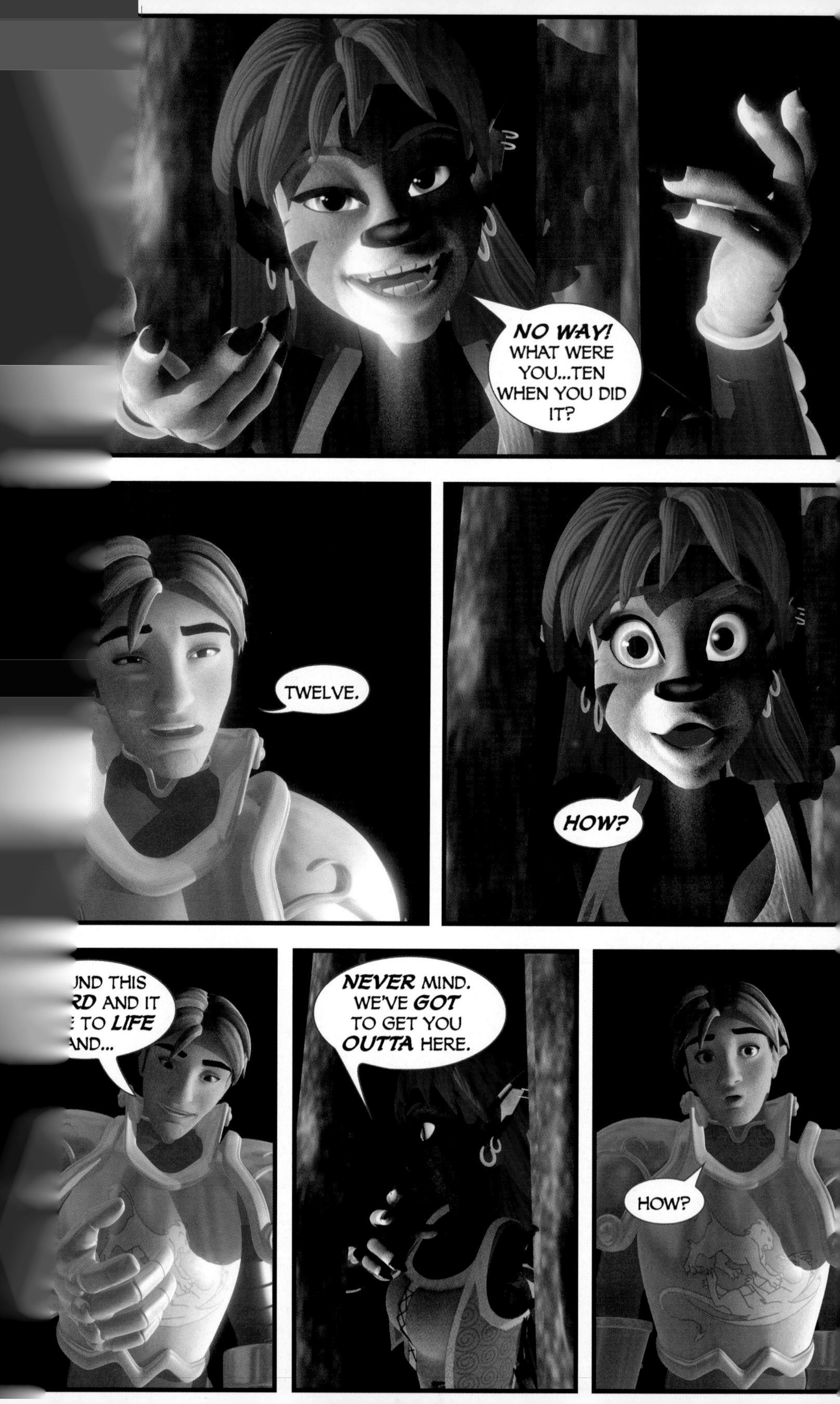
NO WAY! WHAT WERE YOU...TEN WHEN YOU DID IT?
TWELVE.
HOW?
UND THIS RD AND IT E TO LIFE AND...
NEVER MIND. WE'VE GOT TO GET YOU OUTTA HERE.
HOW?

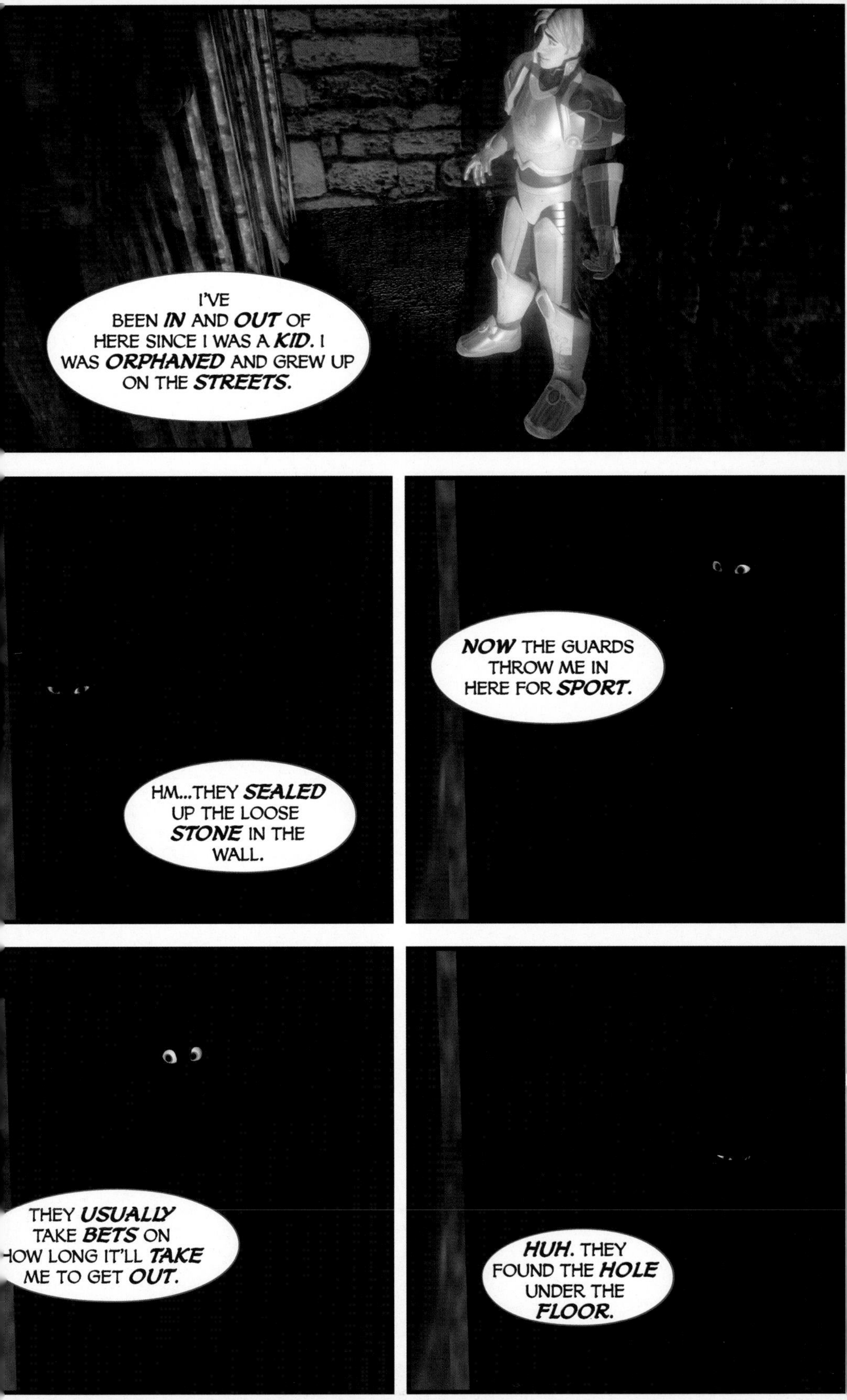
I'VE BEEN IN AND OUT OF HERE SINCE I WAS A KID. I WAS ORPHANED AND GREW UP ON THE STREETS.
HM...THEY SEALED UP THE LOOSE STONE IN THE WALL.
NOW THE GUARDS THROW ME IN HERE FOR SPORT.
THEY USUALLY TAKE BETS ON HOW LONG IT'LL TAKE ME TO GET OUT.
HUH. THEY FOUND THE HOLE UNDER THE FLOOR.

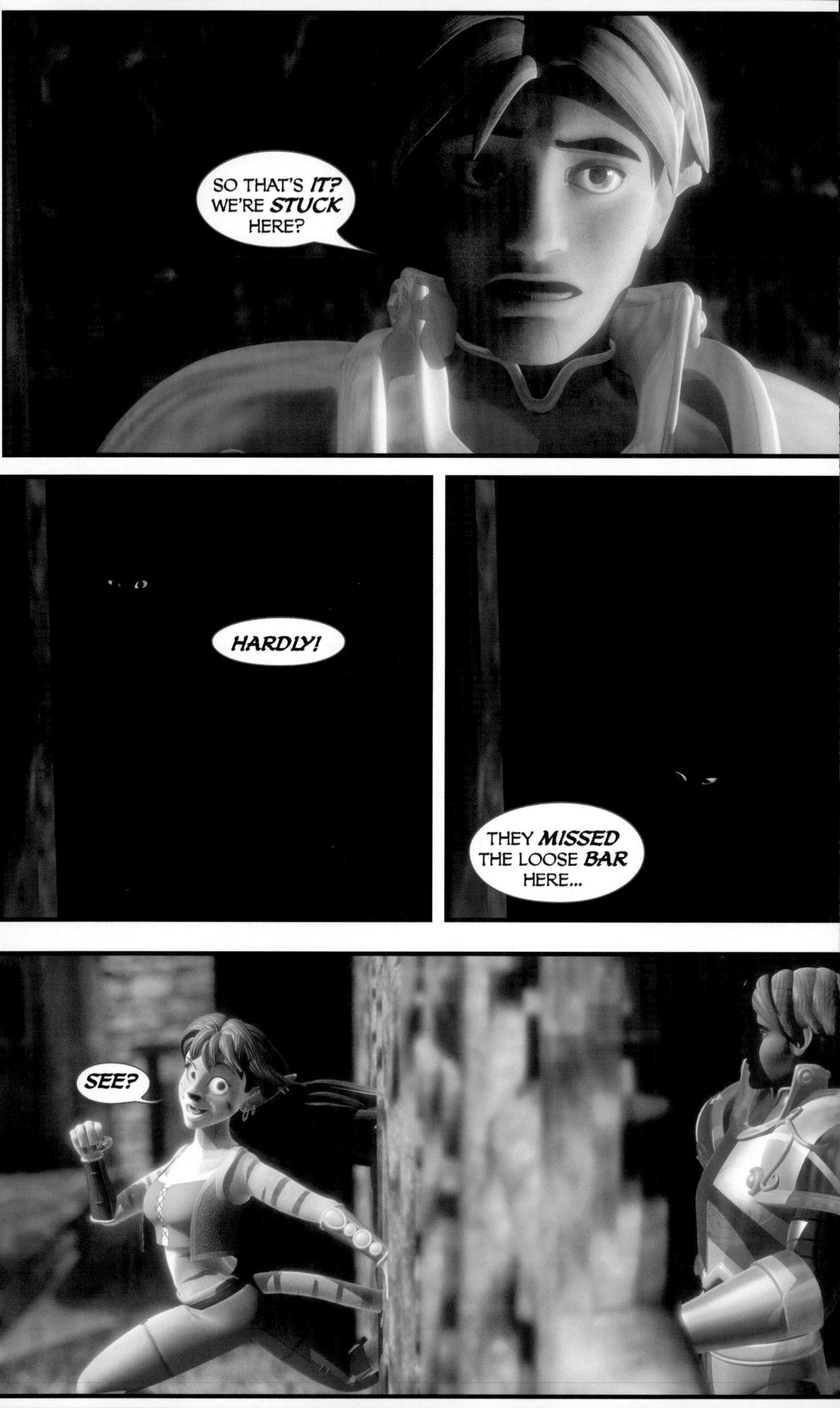
SO THAT'S *IT?* WE'RE *STUCK* HERE?
HARDLY!
THEY *MISSED* THE LOOSE *BAR* HERE...
SEE?

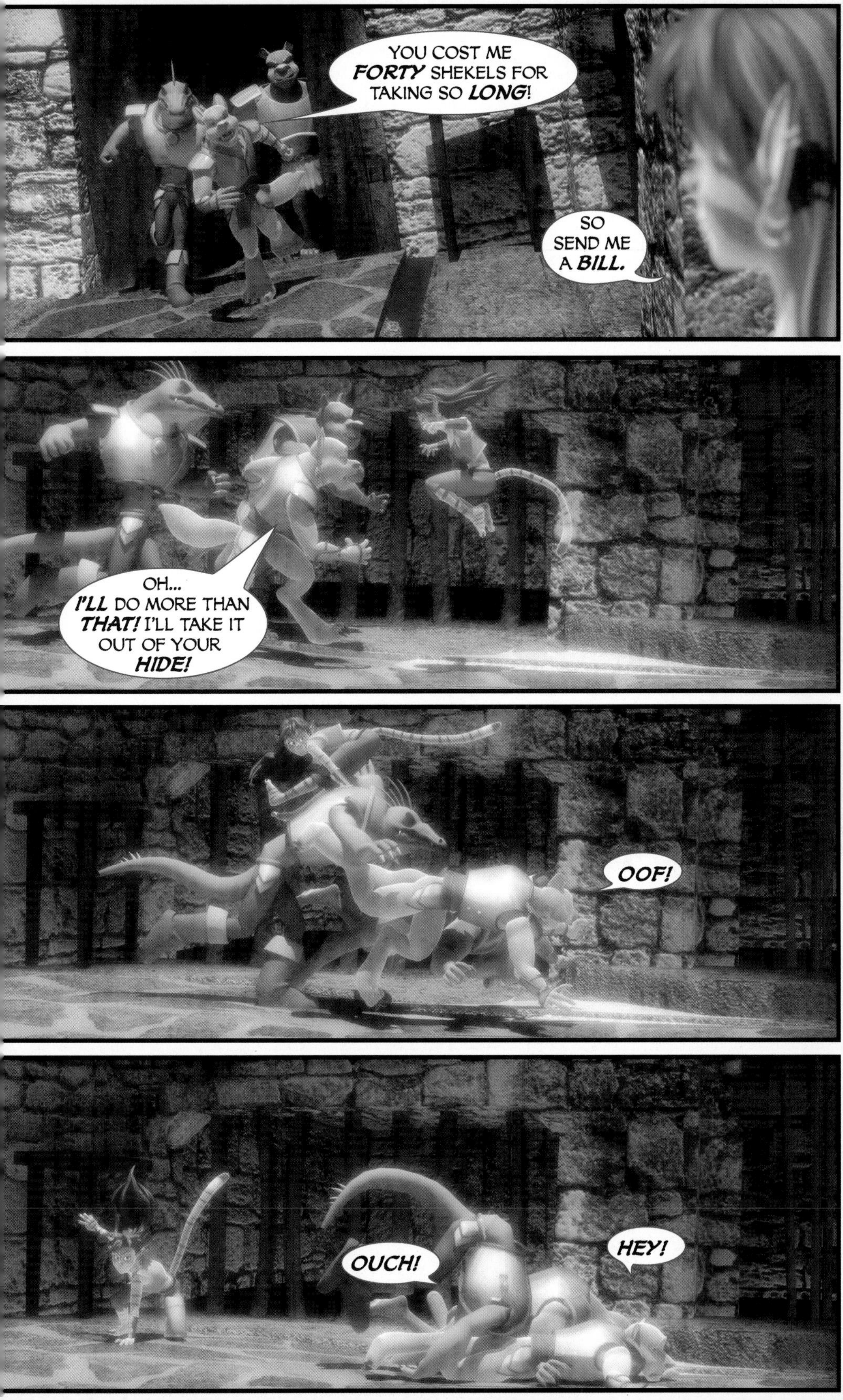
YOU COST ME FORTY SHEKELS FOR TAKING SO LONG!
SO SEND ME A BILL.
OH... I'LL DO MORE THAN THAT! I'LL TAKE IT OUT OF YOUR HIDE!
OOF!
OUCH!
HEY!

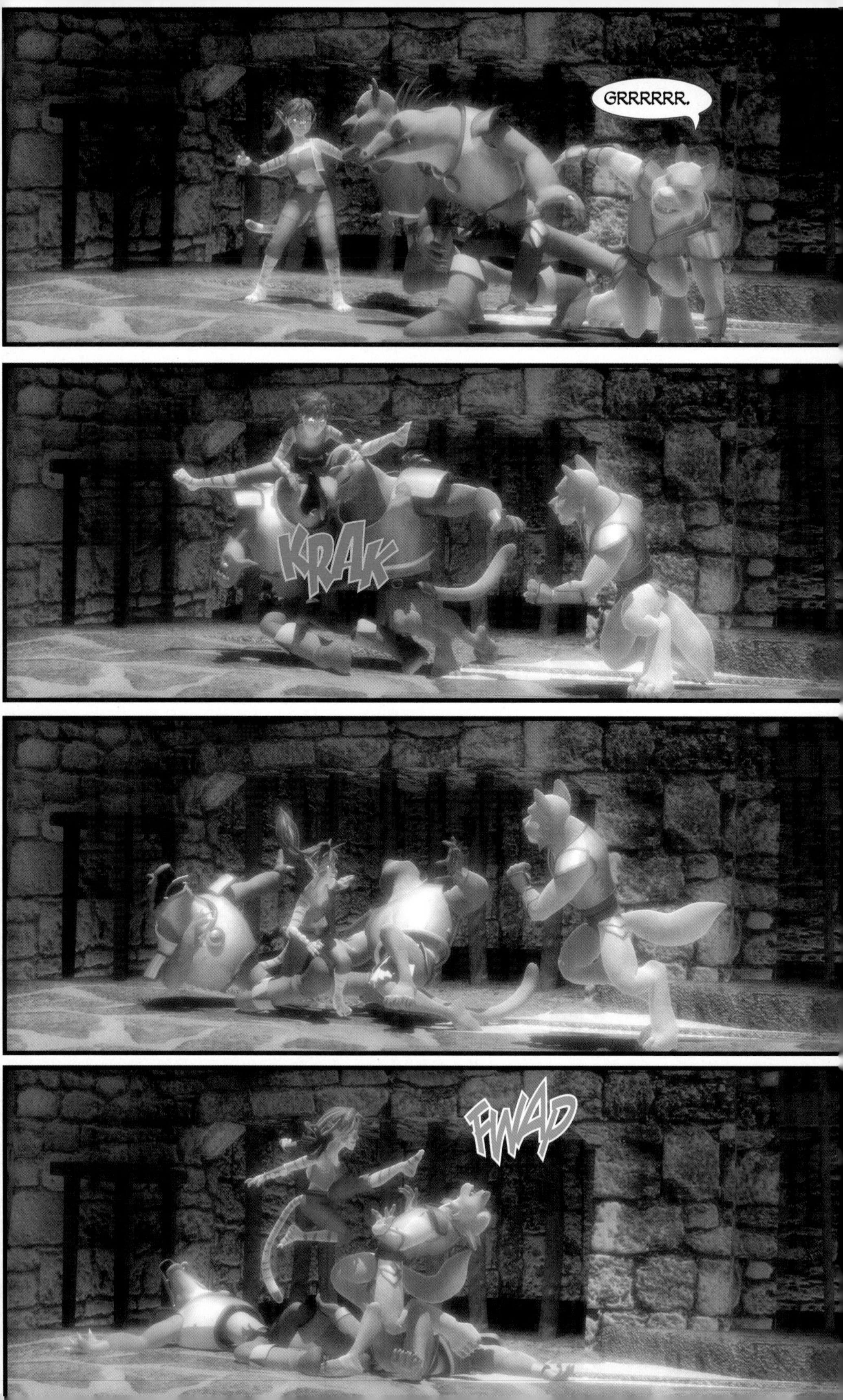
GRRRRRR.
KRAK
FWAP

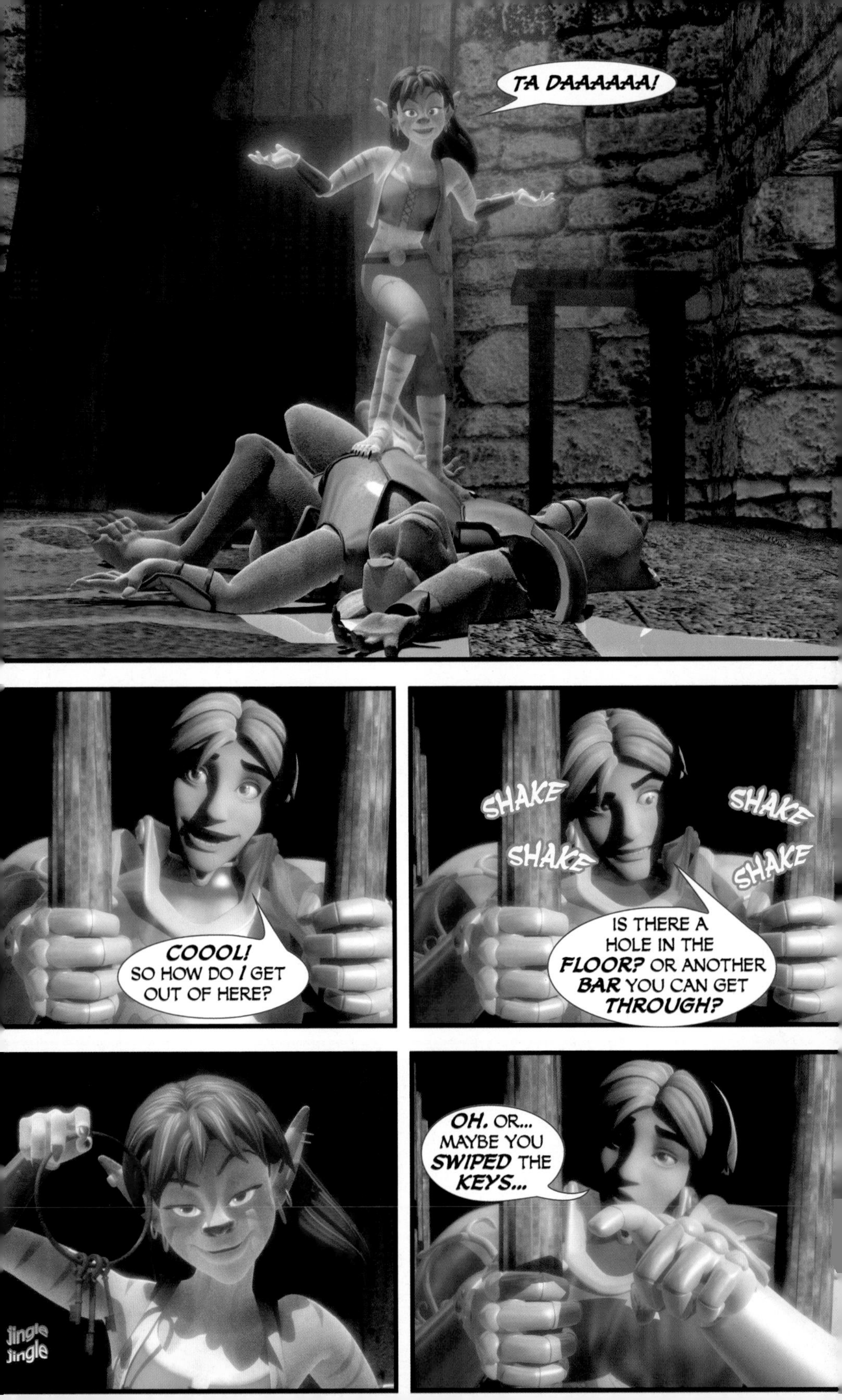

TA DAAAAAAA!
COOOL! SO HOW DO I GET OUT OF HERE?
SHAKE
SHAKE
SHAKE
SHAKE
IS THERE A HOLE IN THE FLOOR? OR ANOTHER BAR YOU CAN GET THROUGH?
jingle jingle
OH. OR... MAYBE YOU SWIPED THE KEYS...

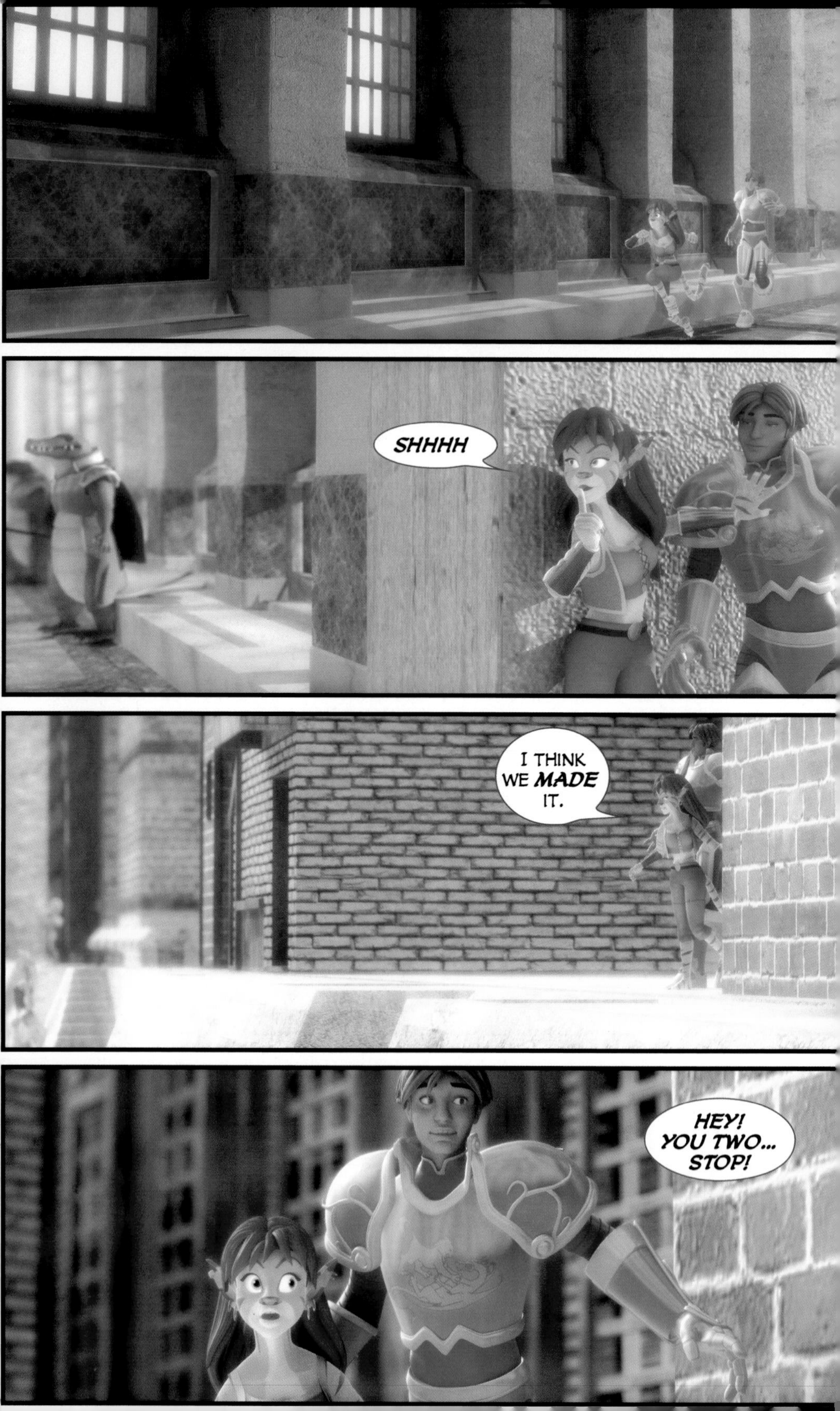
SHHHH
I THINK WE MADE IT.
HEY! YOU TWO... STOP!

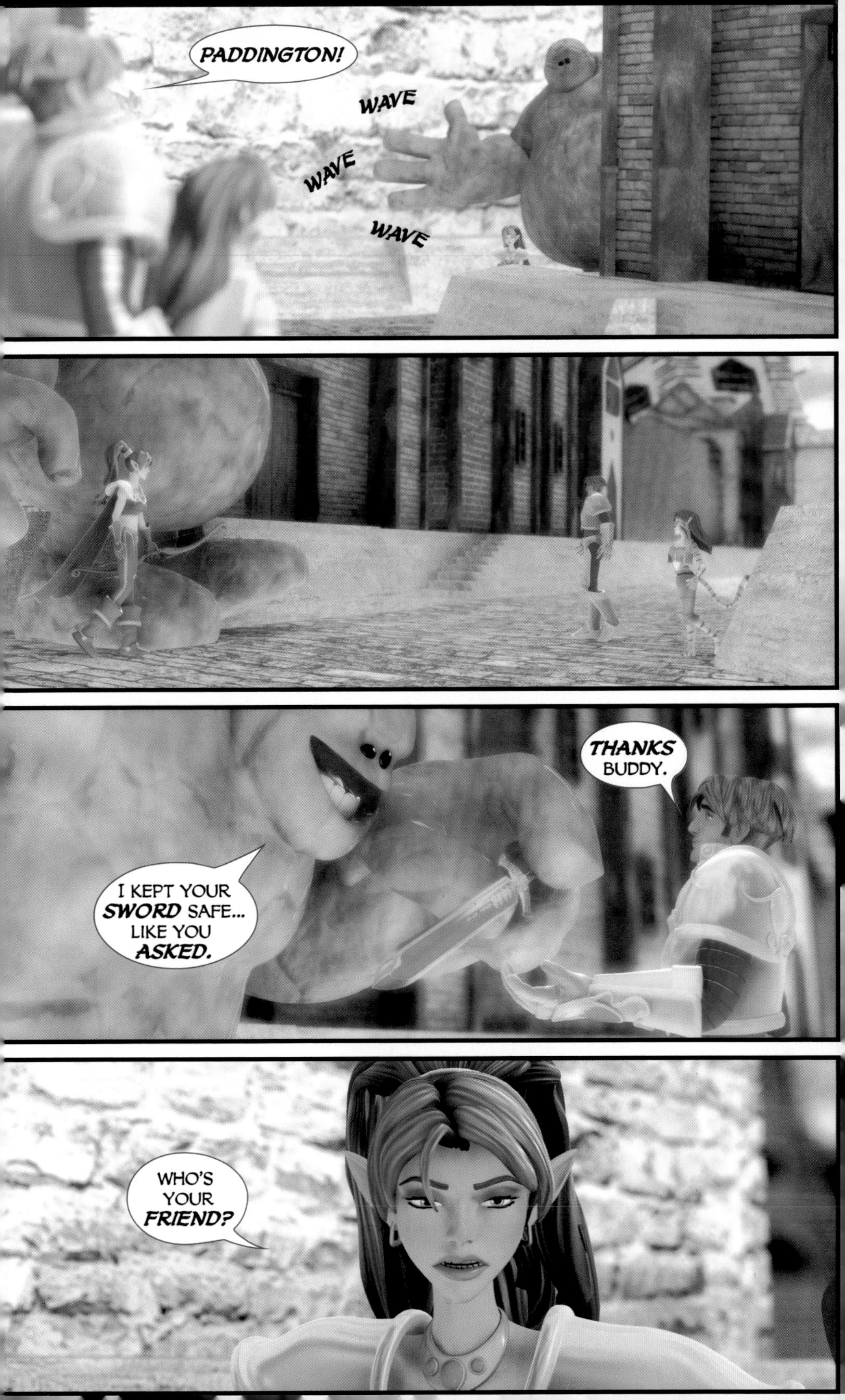
PADDINGTON!
WAVE
WAVE
WAVE
THANKS BUDDY.
I KEPT YOUR SWORD SAFE... LIKE YOU ASKED.
WHO'S YOUR FRIEND?

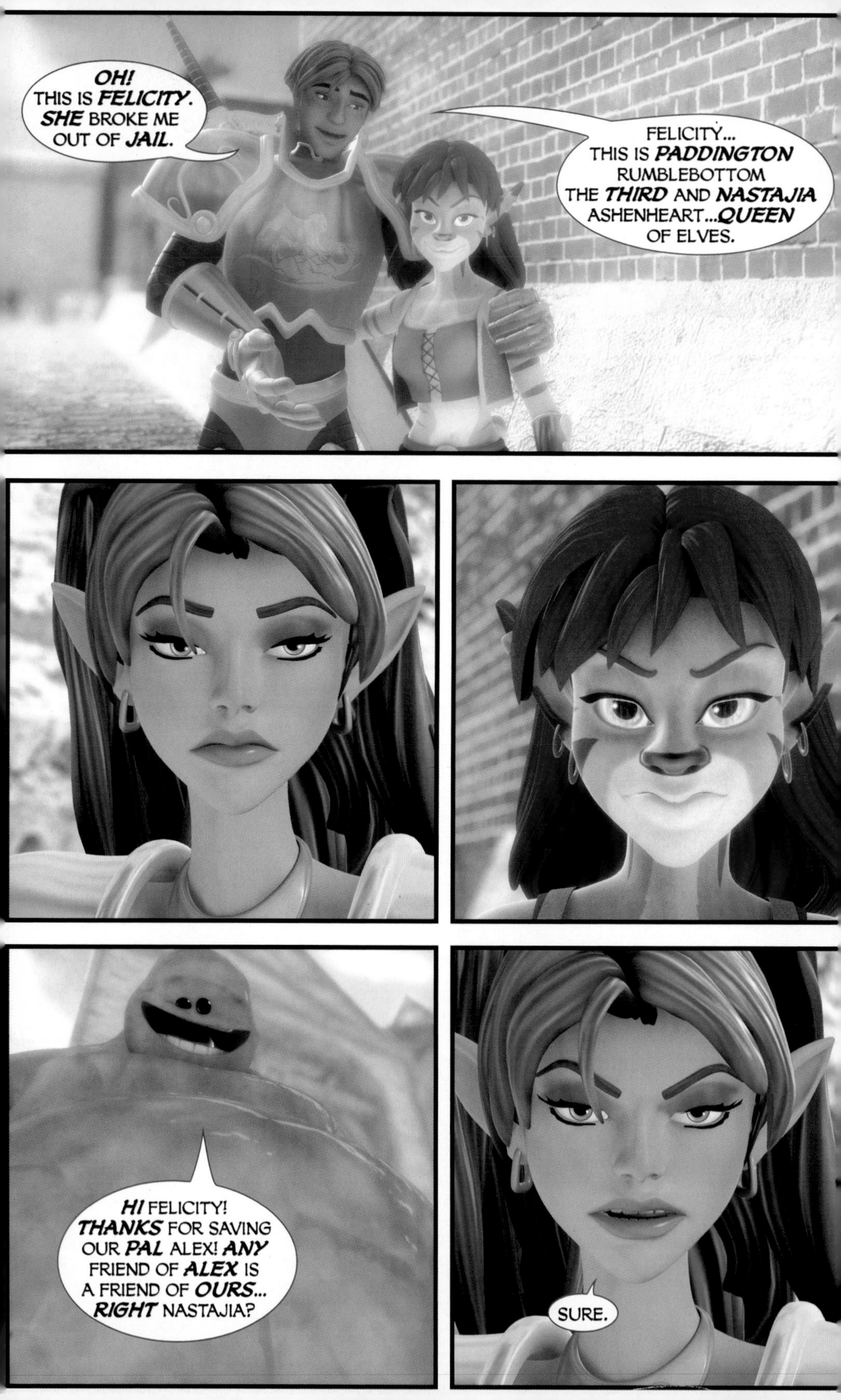
OH! THIS IS FELICITY. SHE BROKE ME OUT OF JAIL.
FELICITY... THIS IS PADDINGTON RUMBLEBOTTOM THE THIRD AND NASTAJIA ASHENHEART...QUEEN OF ELVES.
HI FELICITY! THANKS FOR SAVING OUR PAL ALEX! ANY FRIEND OF ALEX IS A FRIEND OF OURS... RIGHT NASTAJIA?
SURE.

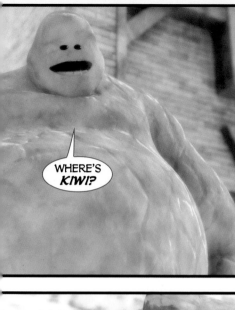

WHERE'S KIWI?

OH NO! SHE'S STILL A PRISONER!

CAN'T YOU DO SOMETHING, NASTAJIA? YOU ARE ROYALTY AND ALL.

ROYALTY TO MY PEOPLE, PADDINGTON... NOT IN NICODEMUS' EYES.

HE DOESN'T RECOGNIZE ANY POWER BUT HIS OWN. HE ENTERTAINS MY POSITION AMONG MY PEOPLE BECAUSE IT SUITS HIS GOALS.

WELL WE'VE GOT TO GET HER OUT OF THERE.

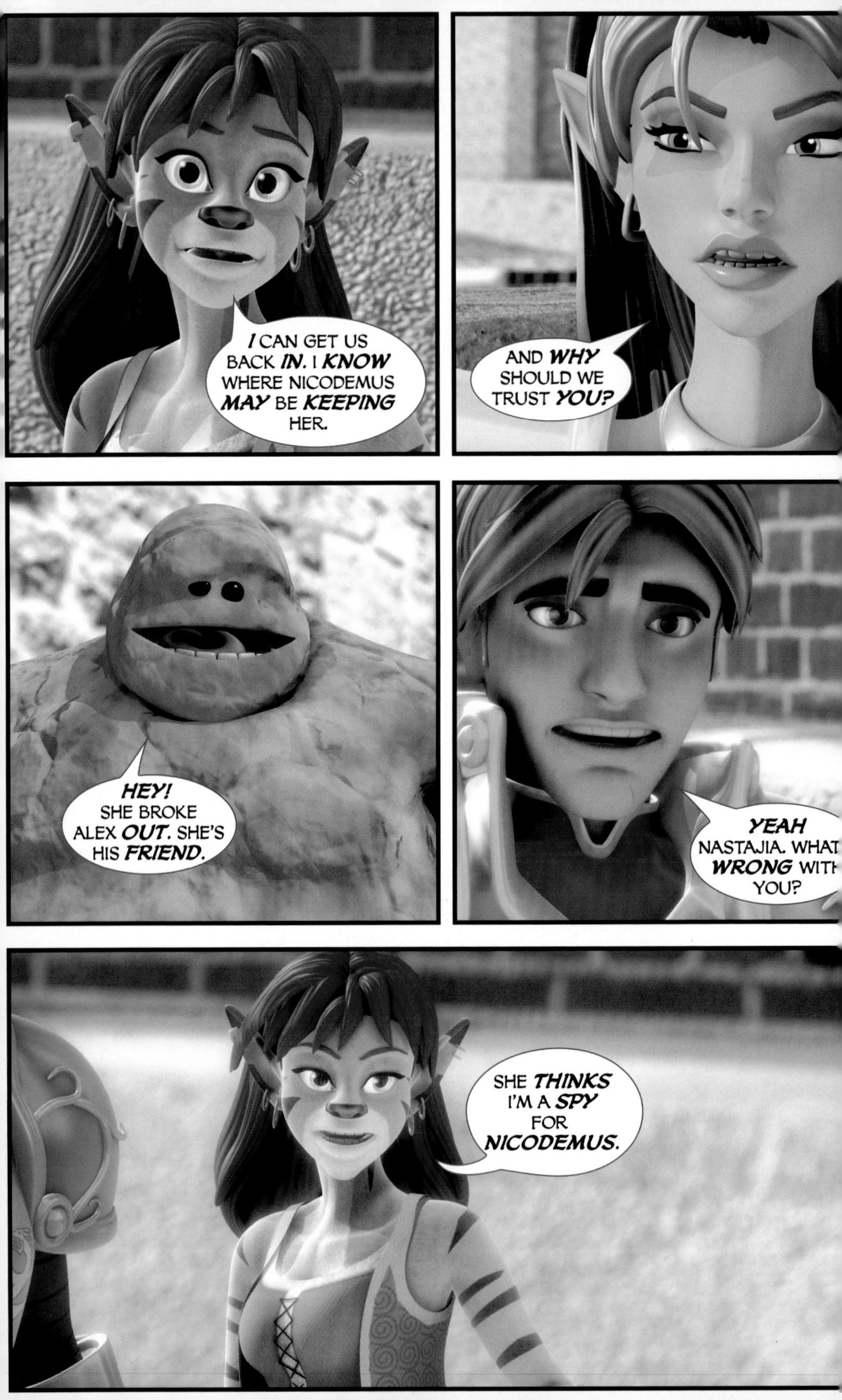

I CAN GET US BACK IN. I KNOW WHERE NICODEMUS MAY BE KEEPING HER.
AND WHY SHOULD WE TRUST YOU?
HEY! SHE BROKE ALEX OUT. SHE'S HIS FRIEND.
YEAH NASTAJIA. WHAT WRONG WITH YOU?
SHE THINKS I'M A SPY FOR NICODEMUS.

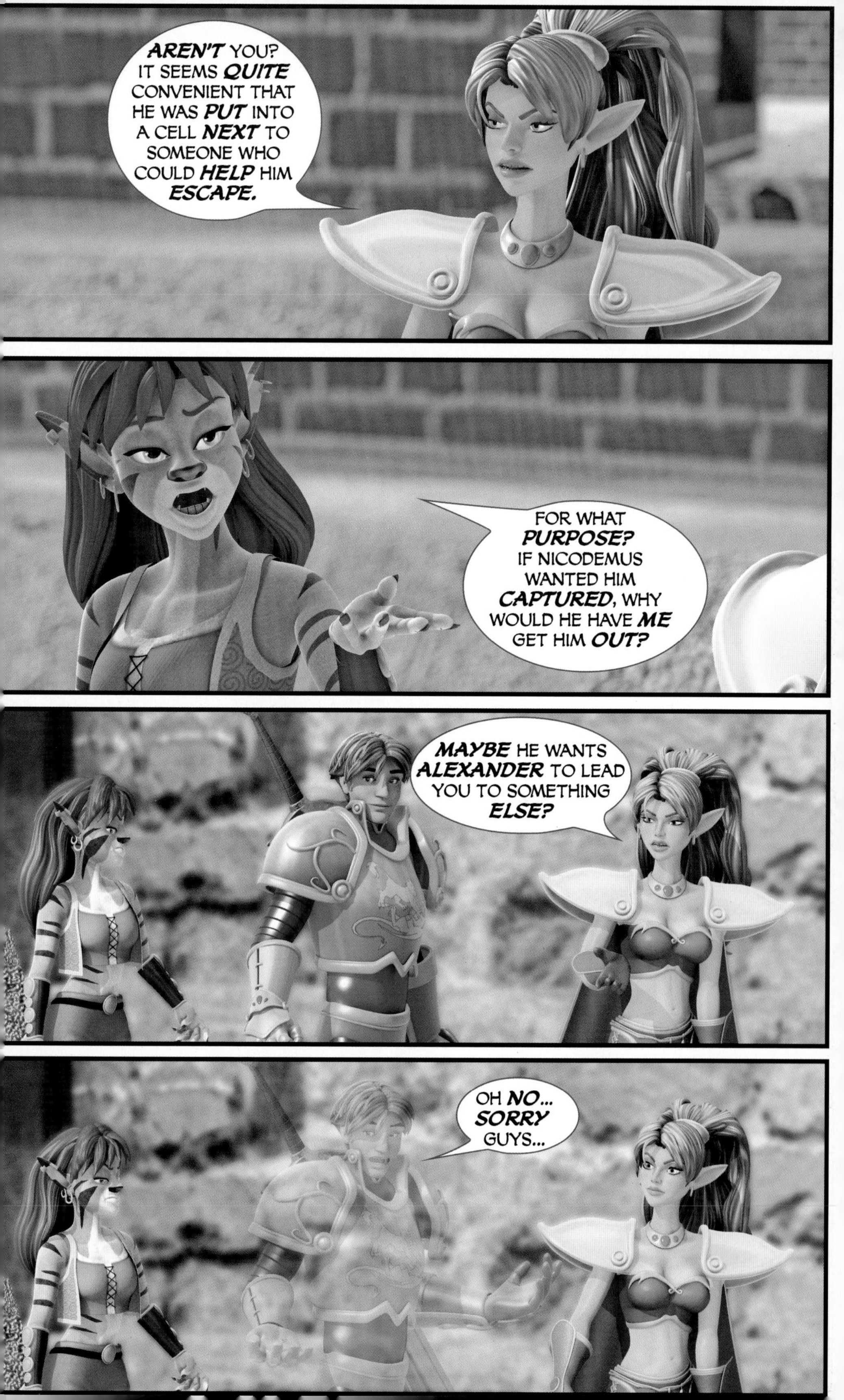
AREN'T YOU? IT SEEMS QUITE CONVENIENT THAT HE WAS PUT INTO A CELL NEXT TO SOMEONE WHO COULD HELP HIM ESCAPE.
FOR WHAT PURPOSE? IF NICODEMUS WANTED HIM CAPTURED, WHY WOULD HE HAVE ME GET HIM OUT?
MAYBE HE WANTS ALEXANDER TO LEAD YOU TO SOMETHING ELSE?
OH NO... SORRY GUYS...

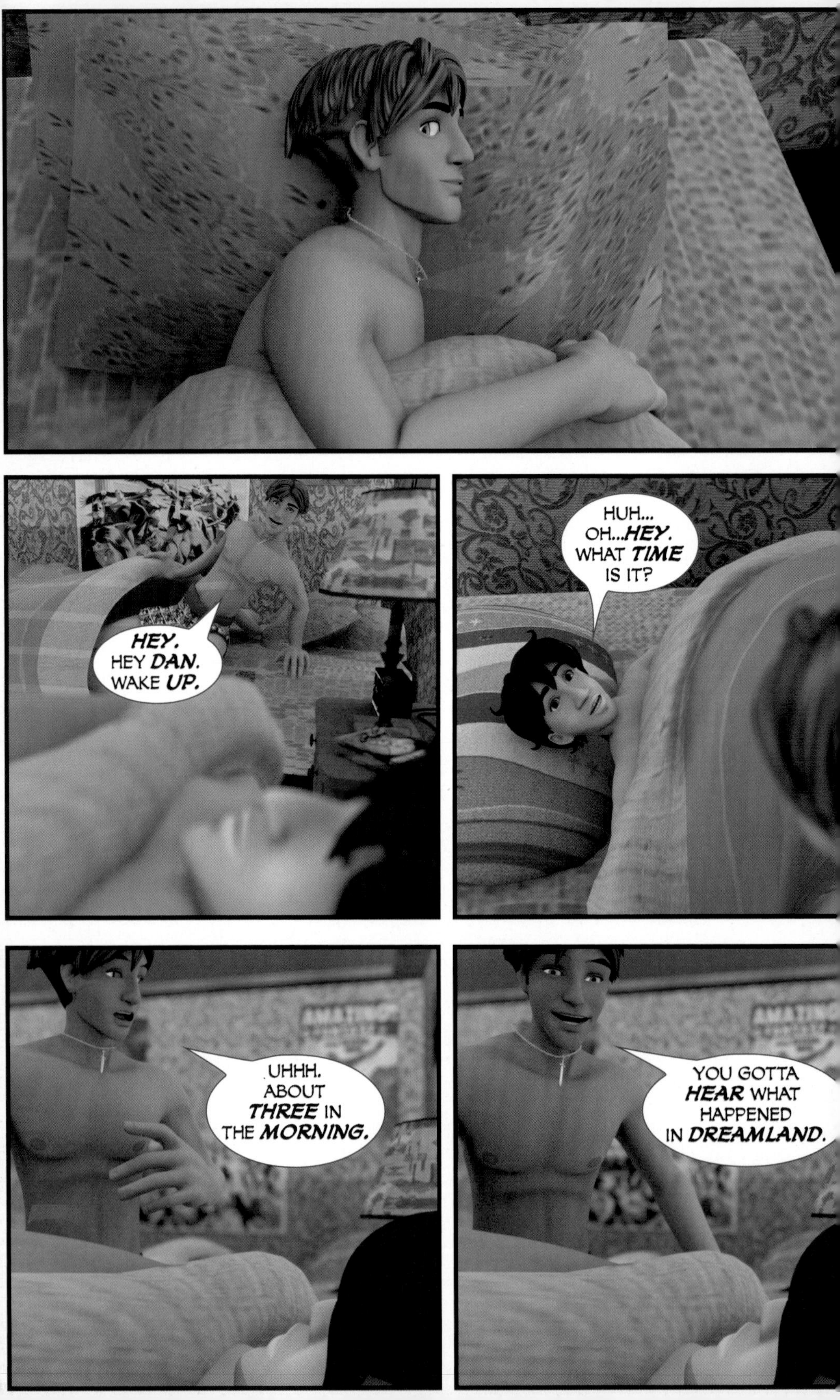

HEY. HEY DAN. WAKE UP.
HUH... OH...HEY. WHAT TIME IS IT?
UHHH. ABOUT THREE IN THE MORNING.
YOU GOTTA HEAR WHAT HAPPENED IN DREAMLAND.

WHAT *HAPPENED?*

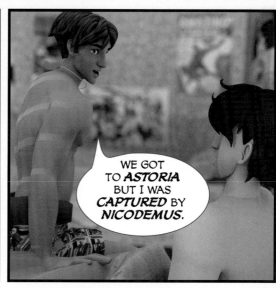

WE GOT TO *ASTORIA* BUT I WAS *CAPTURED* BY *NICODEMUS.*

NICODEMUS THE *RULER* OF *DREAMLAND* EVERYONE KEEPS *TALKING* ABOUT? WHAT'S HE *LIKE?*

HE'S THE *DRAGON.* THE ONE THAT I *CUT* WITH THE *SWORD!*

NO WAY!

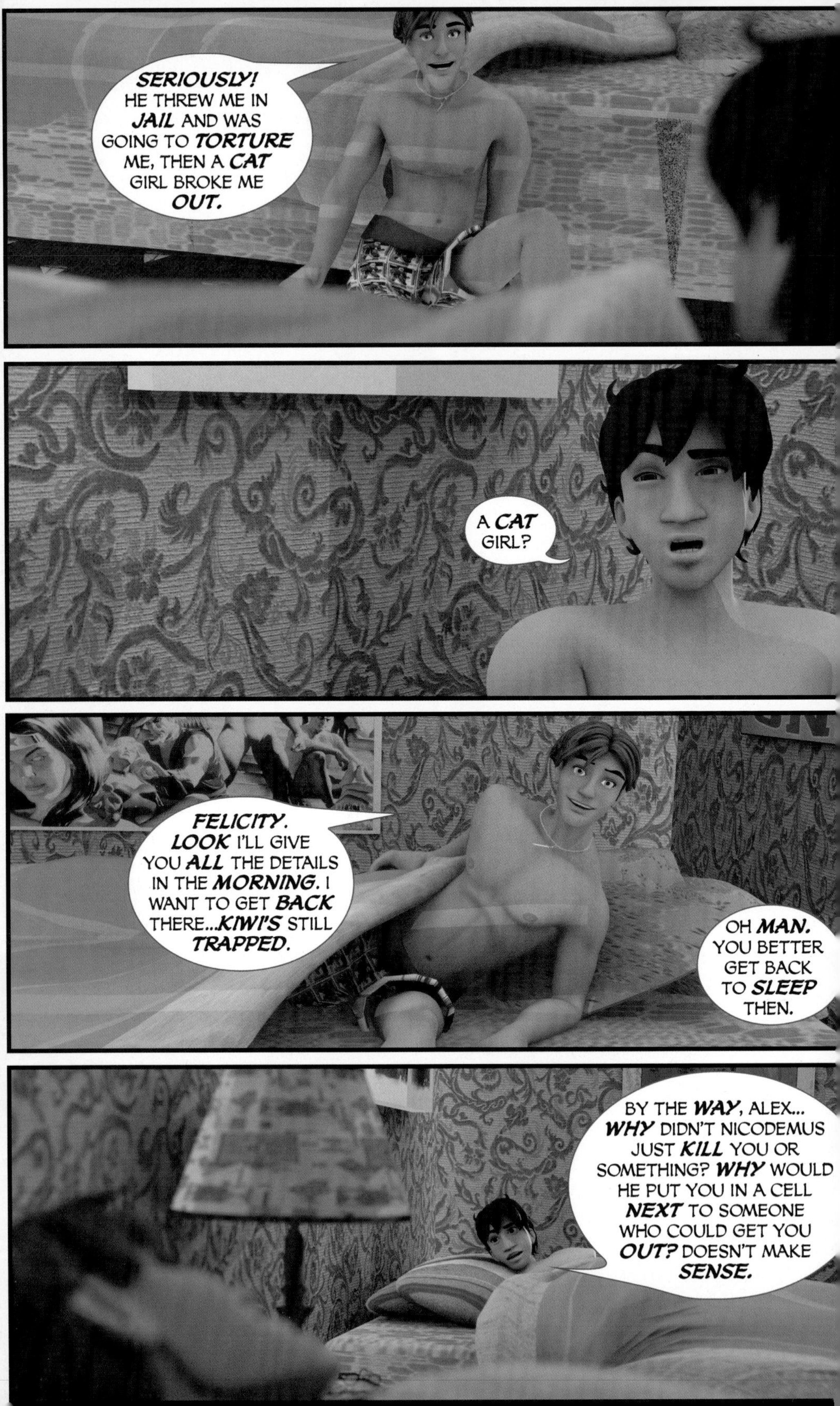
SERIOUSLY! HE THREW ME IN JAIL AND WAS GOING TO TORTURE ME, THEN A CAT GIRL BROKE ME OUT.
A CAT GIRL?
FELICITY. LOOK I'LL GIVE YOU ALL THE DETAILS IN THE MORNING. I WANT TO GET BACK THERE...KIWI'S STILL TRAPPED.
OH MAN. YOU BETTER GET BACK TO SLEEP THEN.
BY THE WAY, ALEX... WHY DIDN'T NICODEMUS JUST KILL YOU OR SOMETHING? WHY WOULD HE PUT YOU IN A CELL NEXT TO SOMEONE WHO COULD GET YOU OUT? DOESN'T MAKE SENSE.

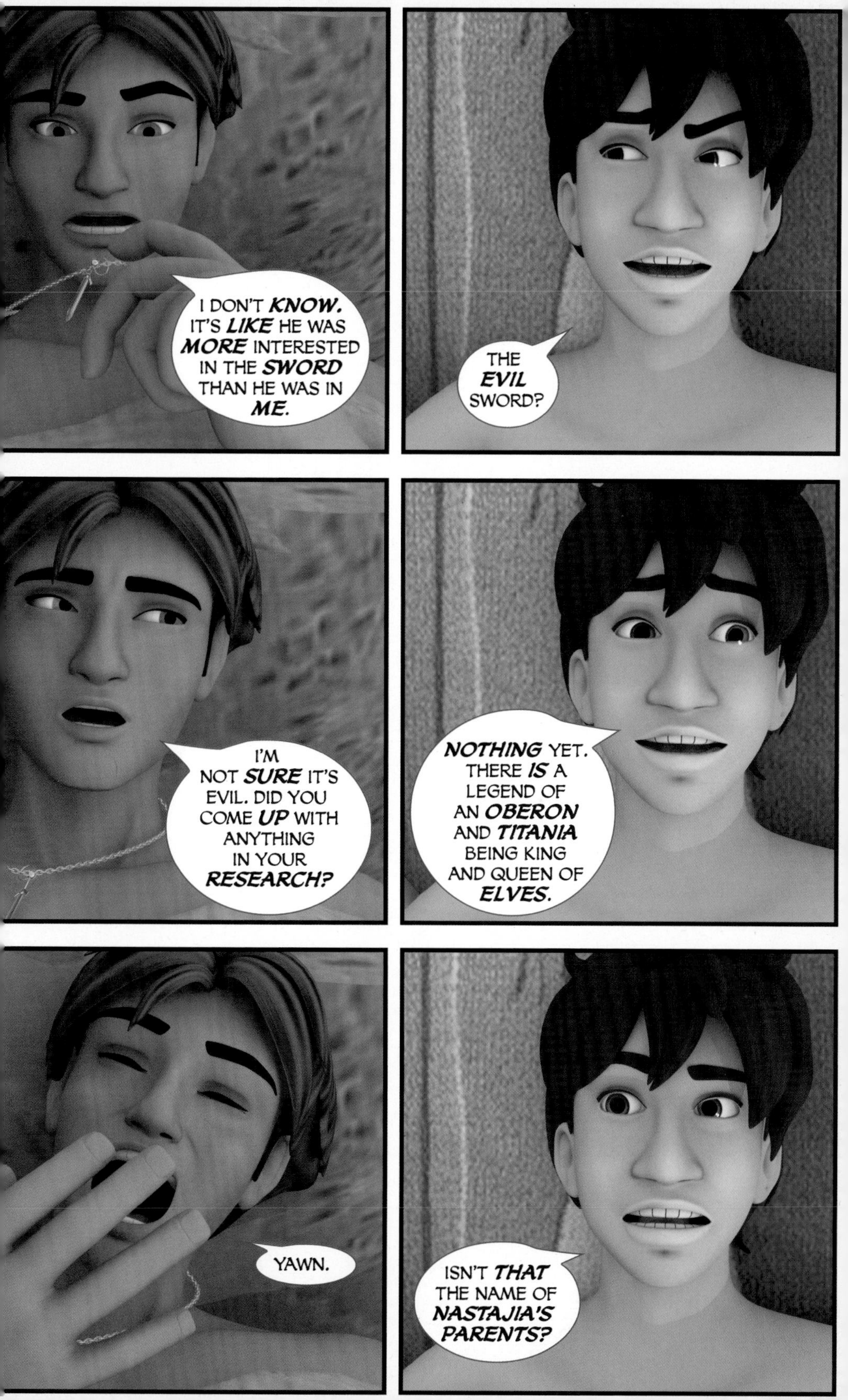
I DON'T KNOW. IT'S LIKE HE WAS MORE INTERESTED IN THE SWORD THAN HE WAS IN ME.
THE EVIL SWORD?
I'M NOT SURE IT'S EVIL. DID YOU COME UP WITH ANYTHING IN YOUR RESEARCH?
NOTHING YET. THERE IS A LEGEND OF AN OBERON AND TITANIA BEING KING AND QUEEN OF ELVES.
YAWN.
ISN'T THAT THE NAME OF NASTAJIA'S PARENTS?

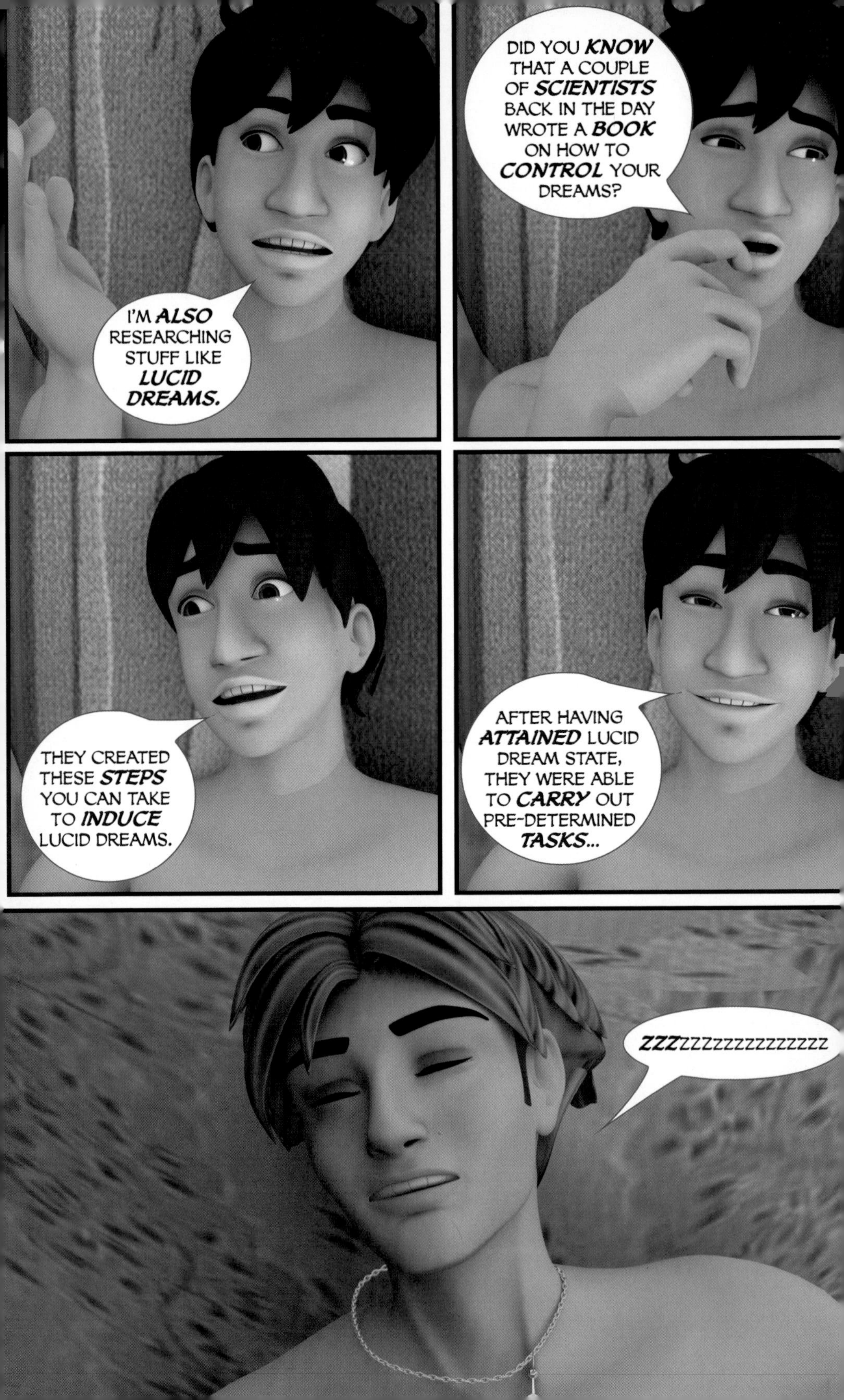
I'M ALSO RESEARCHING STUFF LIKE LUCID DREAMS.
DID YOU KNOW THAT A COUPLE OF SCIENTISTS BACK IN THE DAY WROTE A BOOK ON HOW TO CONTROL YOUR DREAMS?
THEY CREATED THESE STEPS YOU CAN TAKE TO INDUCE LUCID DREAMS.
AFTER HAVING ATTAINED LUCID DREAM STATE, THEY WERE ABLE TO CARRY OUT PRE-DETERMINED TASKS...
ZZZZZZZZZZZZZZZZZ

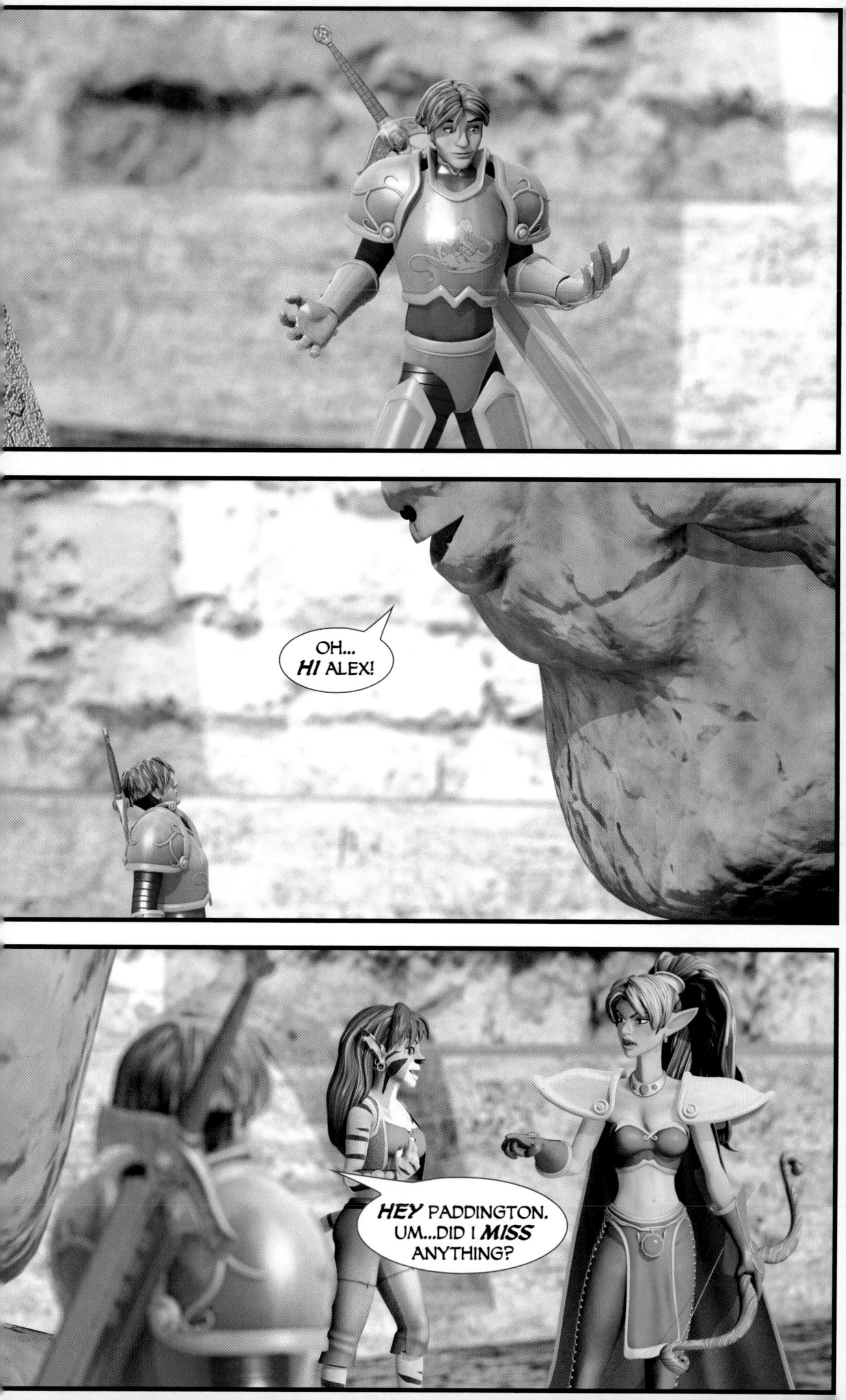
OH...
HI ALEX!
HEY PADDINGTON.
UM...DID I MISS
ANYTHING?

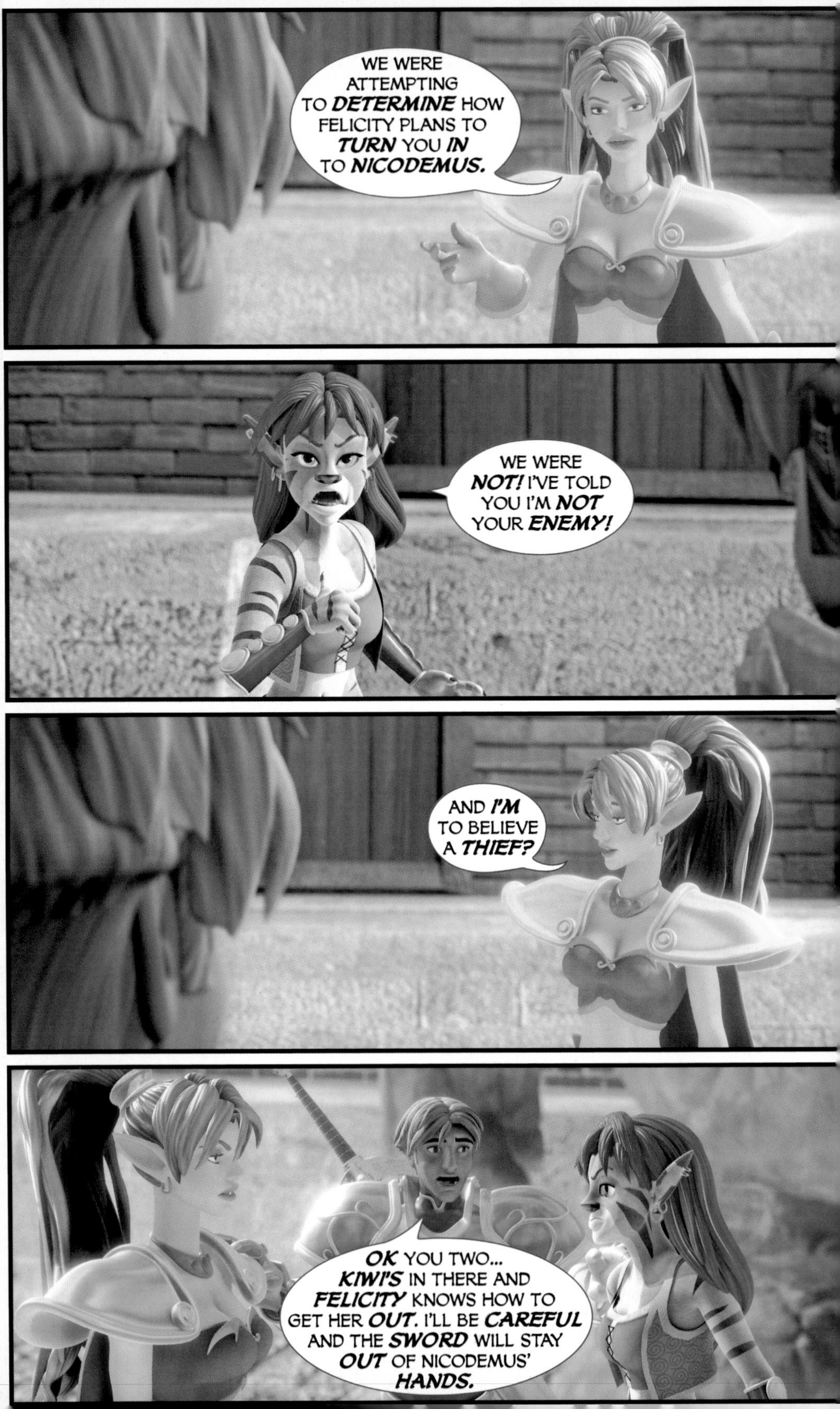
WE WERE ATTEMPTING TO DETERMINE HOW FELICITY PLANS TO TURN YOU IN TO NICODEMUS.
WE WERE NOT! I'VE TOLD YOU I'M NOT YOUR ENEMY!
AND I'M TO BELIEVE A THIEF?
OK YOU TWO... KIWI'S IN THERE AND FELICITY KNOWS HOW TO GET HER OUT. I'LL BE CAREFUL AND THE SWORD WILL STAY OUT OF NICODEMUS' HANDS.

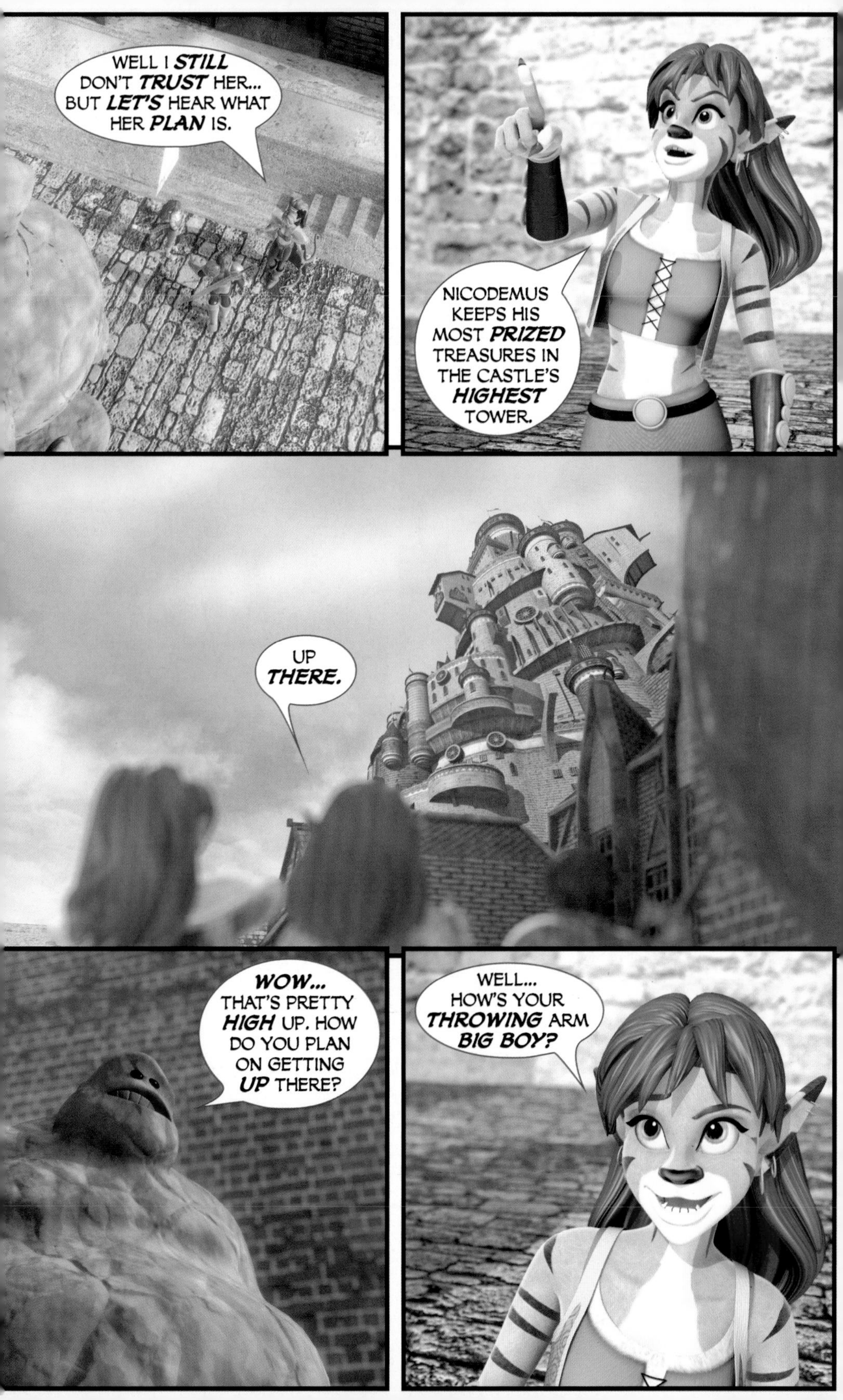
WELL I STILL DON'T TRUST HER... BUT LET'S HEAR WHAT HER PLAN IS.
NICODEMUS KEEPS HIS MOST PRIZED TREASURES IN THE CASTLE'S HIGHEST TOWER.
UP THERE.
WOW... THAT'S PRETTY HIGH UP. HOW DO YOU PLAN ON GETTING UP THERE?
WELL... HOW'S YOUR THROWING ARM BIG BOY?

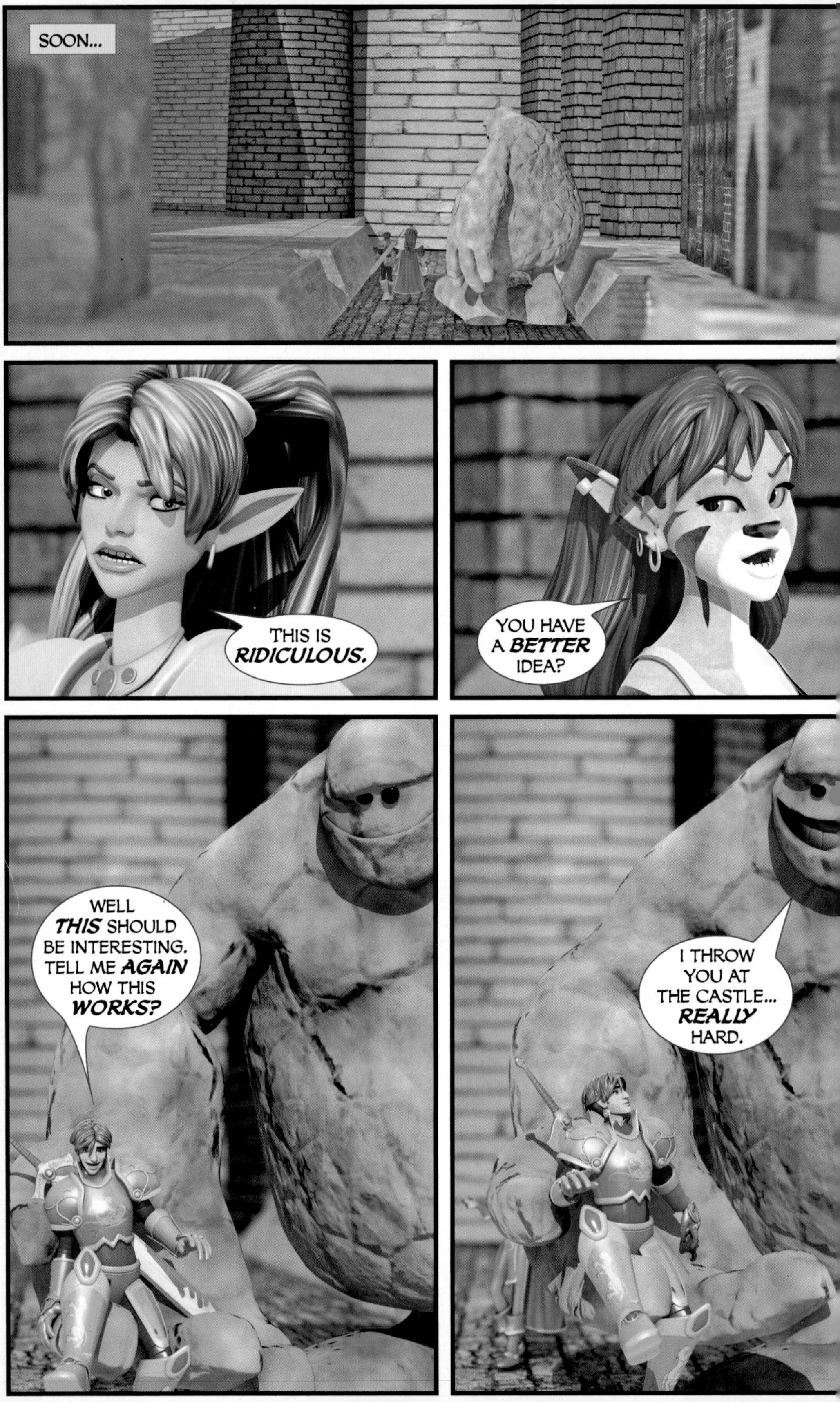
SOON...
THIS IS RIDICULOUS.
YOU HAVE A BETTER IDEA?
WELL THIS SHOULD BE INTERESTING. TELL ME AGAIN HOW THIS WORKS?
I THROW YOU AT THE CASTLE... REALLY HARD.

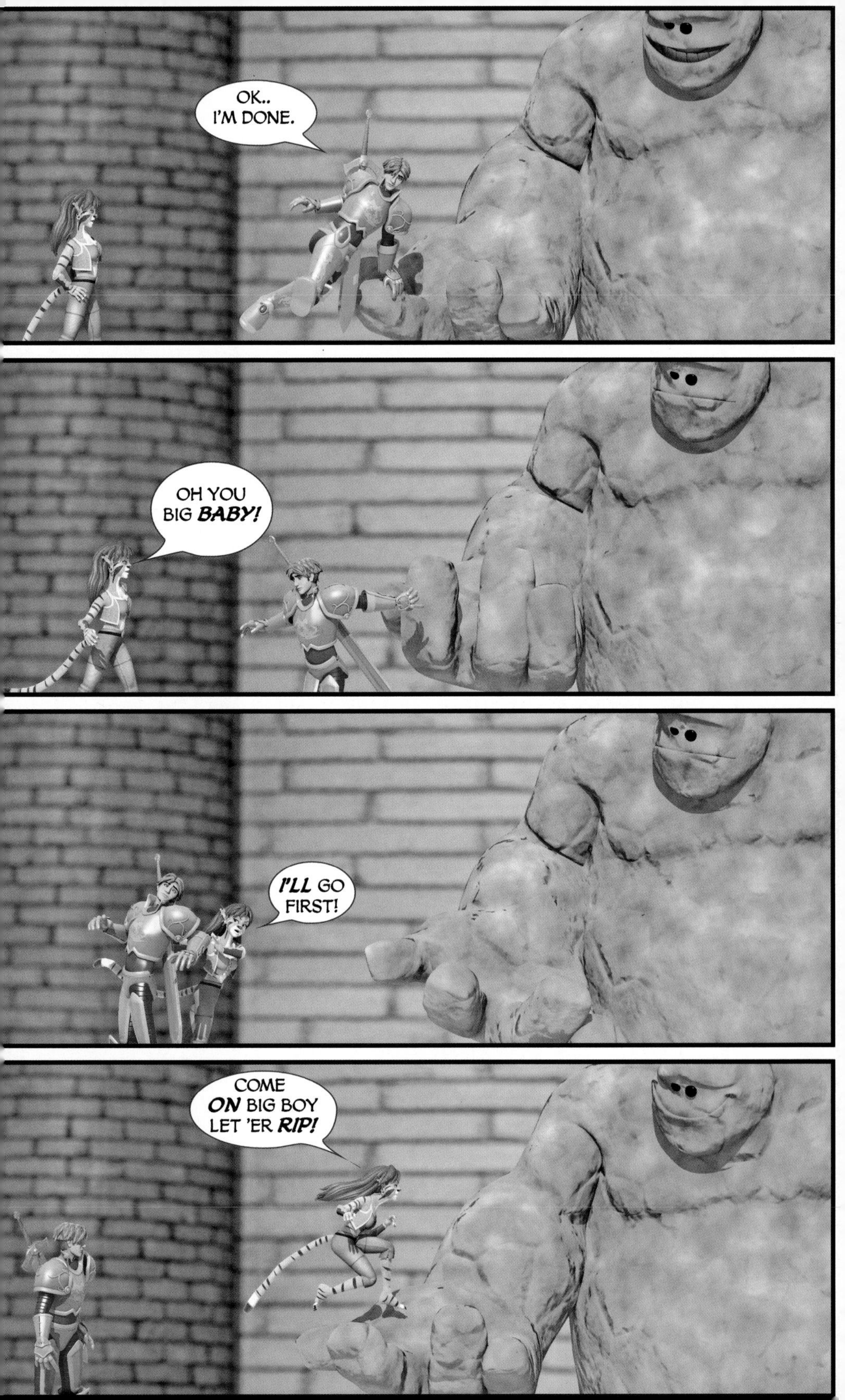
OK.. I'M DONE.
OH YOU BIG BABY!
I'LL GO FIRST!
COME ON BIG BOY LET 'ER RIP!

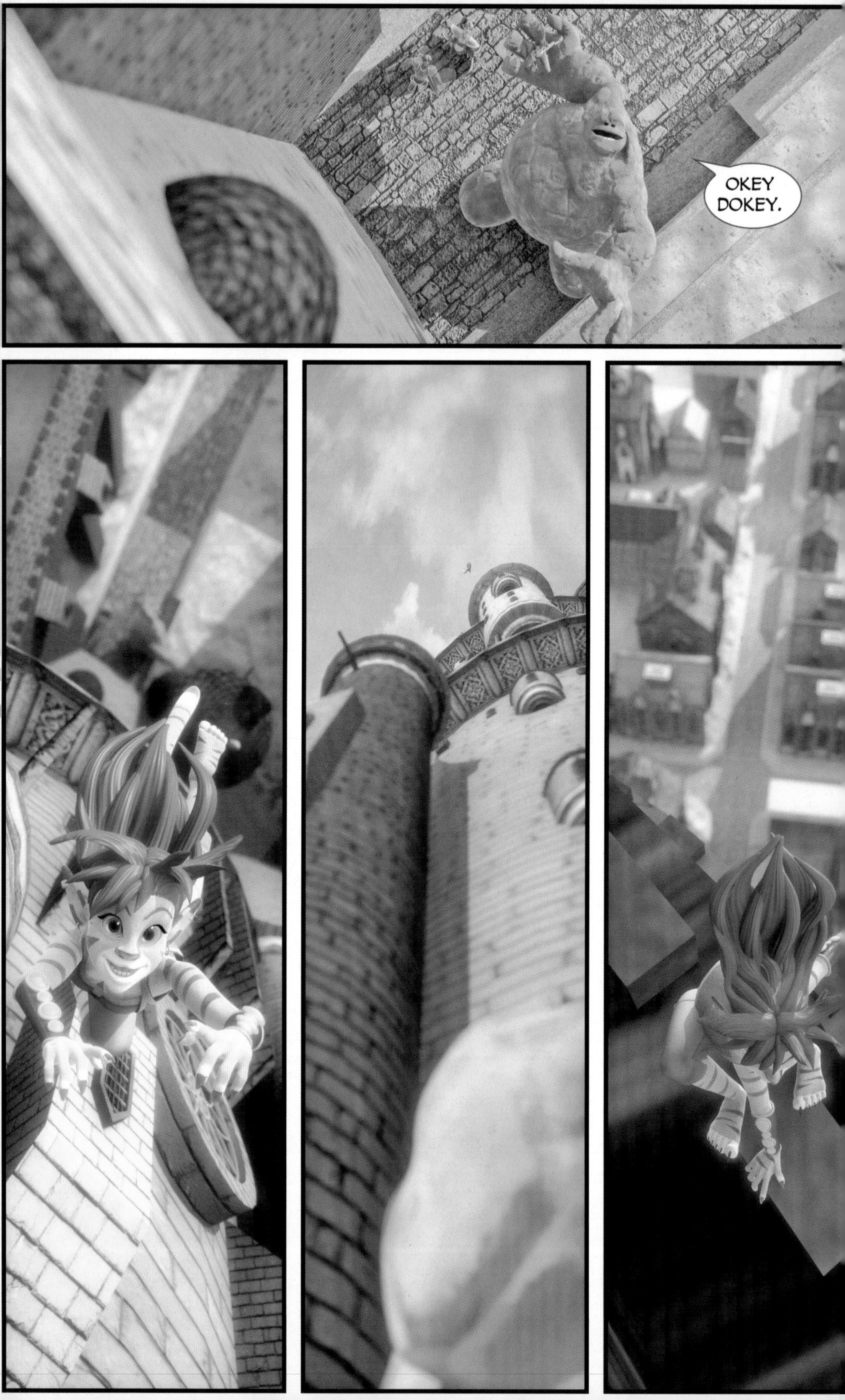
OKEY DOKEY.

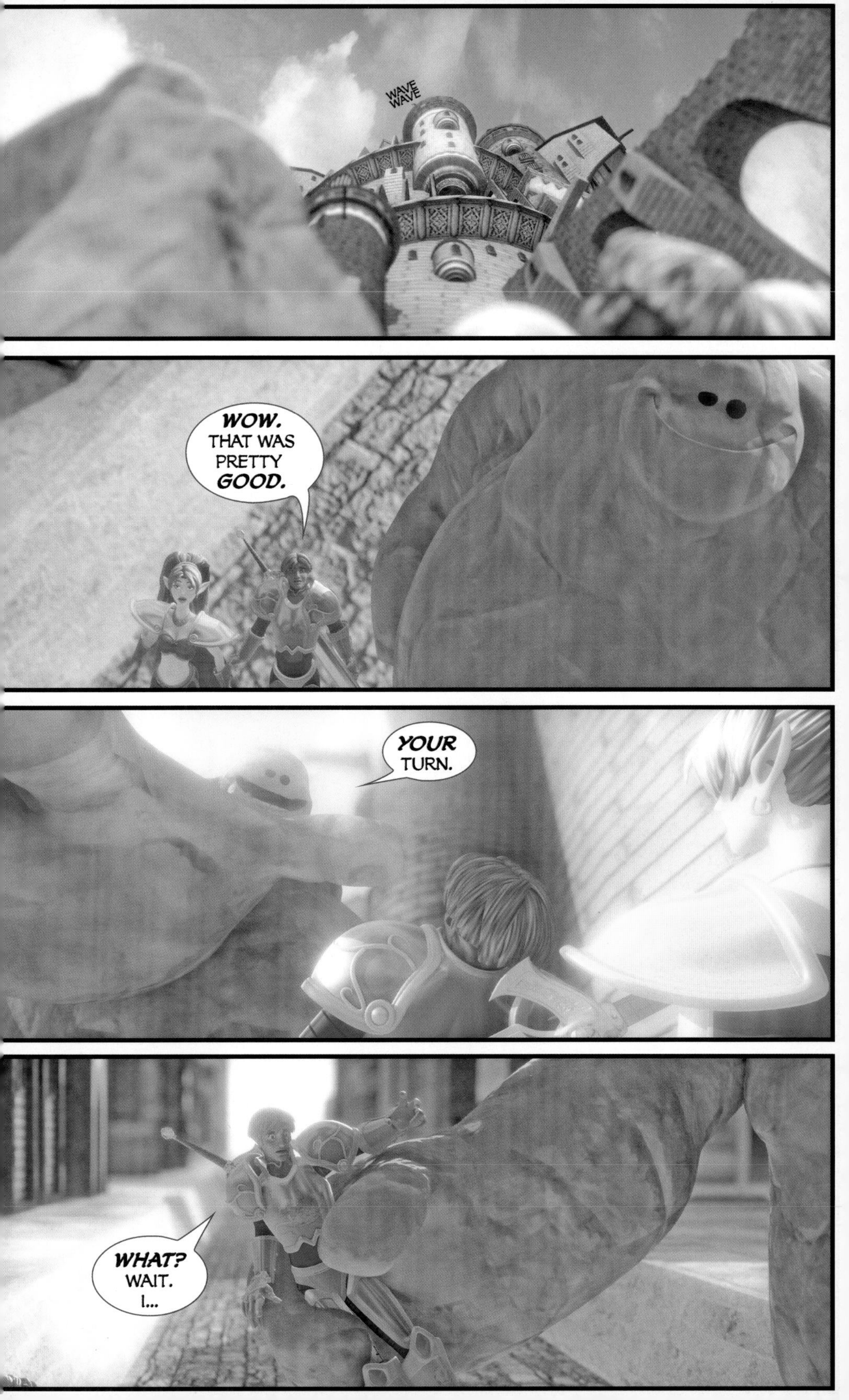
WAVE WAVE
WOW. THAT WAS PRETTY GOOD.
YOUR TURN.
WHAT? WAIT. I...

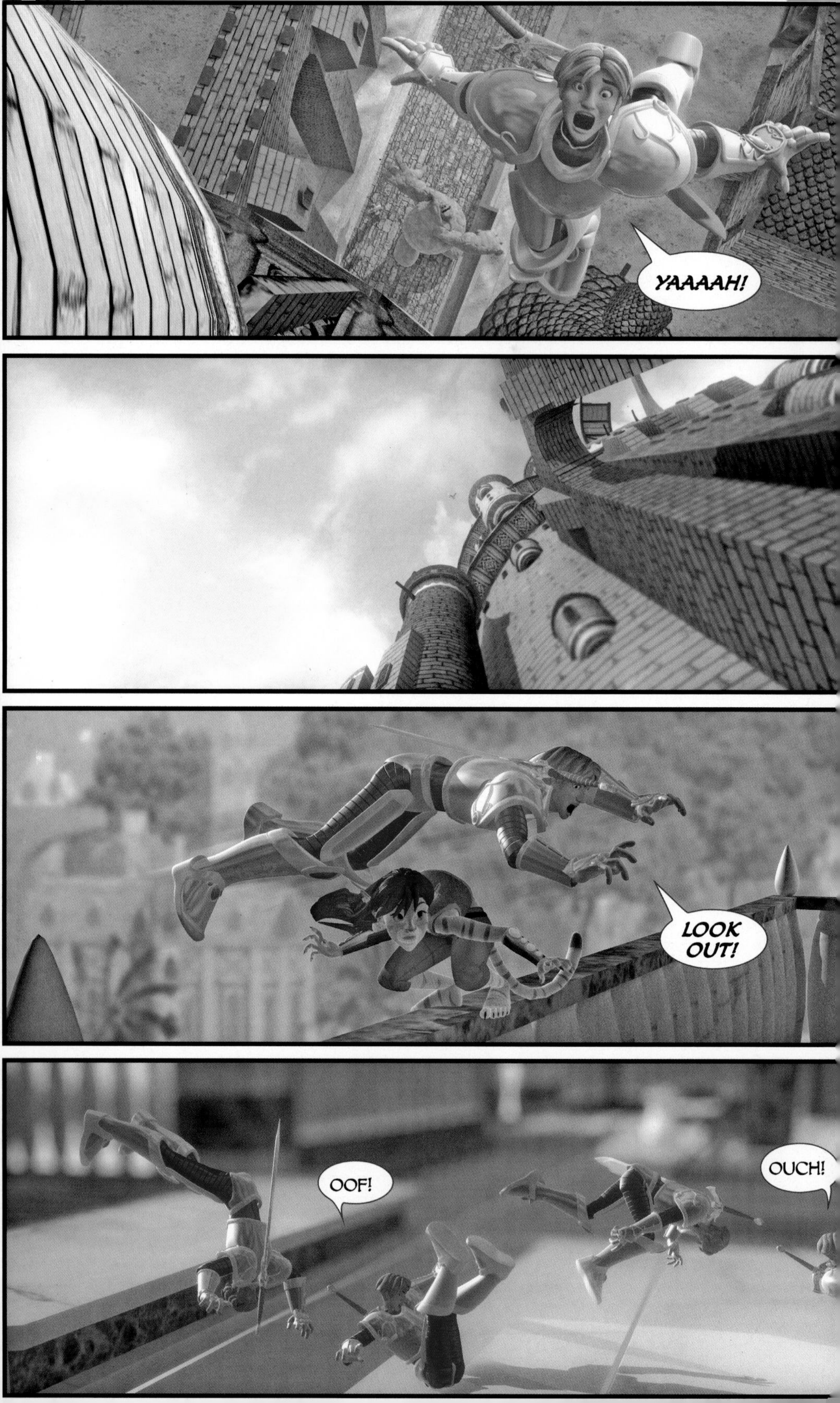
YAAAAH!
LOOK OUT!
OOF!
OUCH!

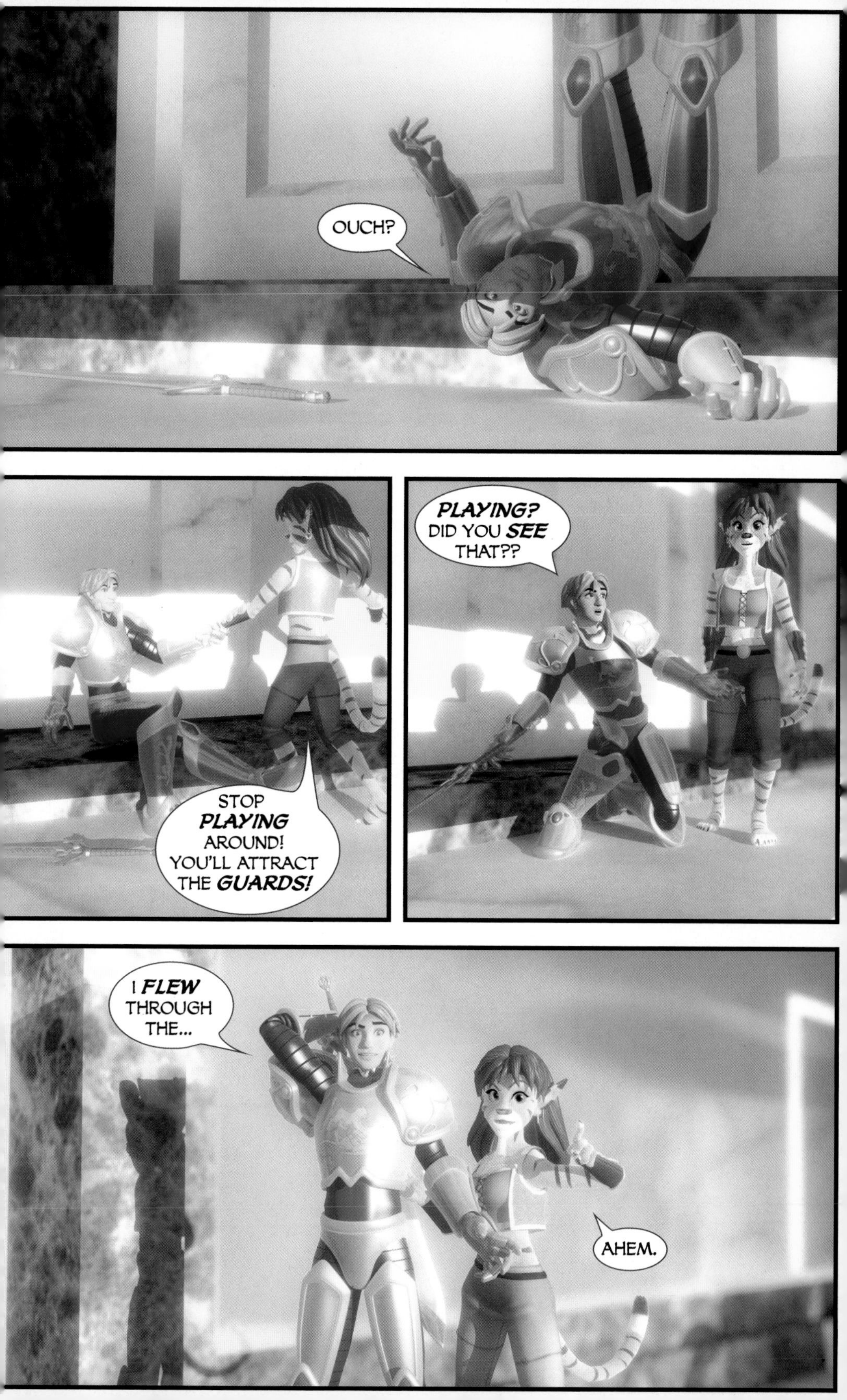
OUCH?
STOP PLAYING AROUND! YOU'LL ATTRACT THE GUARDS!
PLAYING? DID YOU SEE THAT??
I FLEW THROUGH THE...
AHEM.

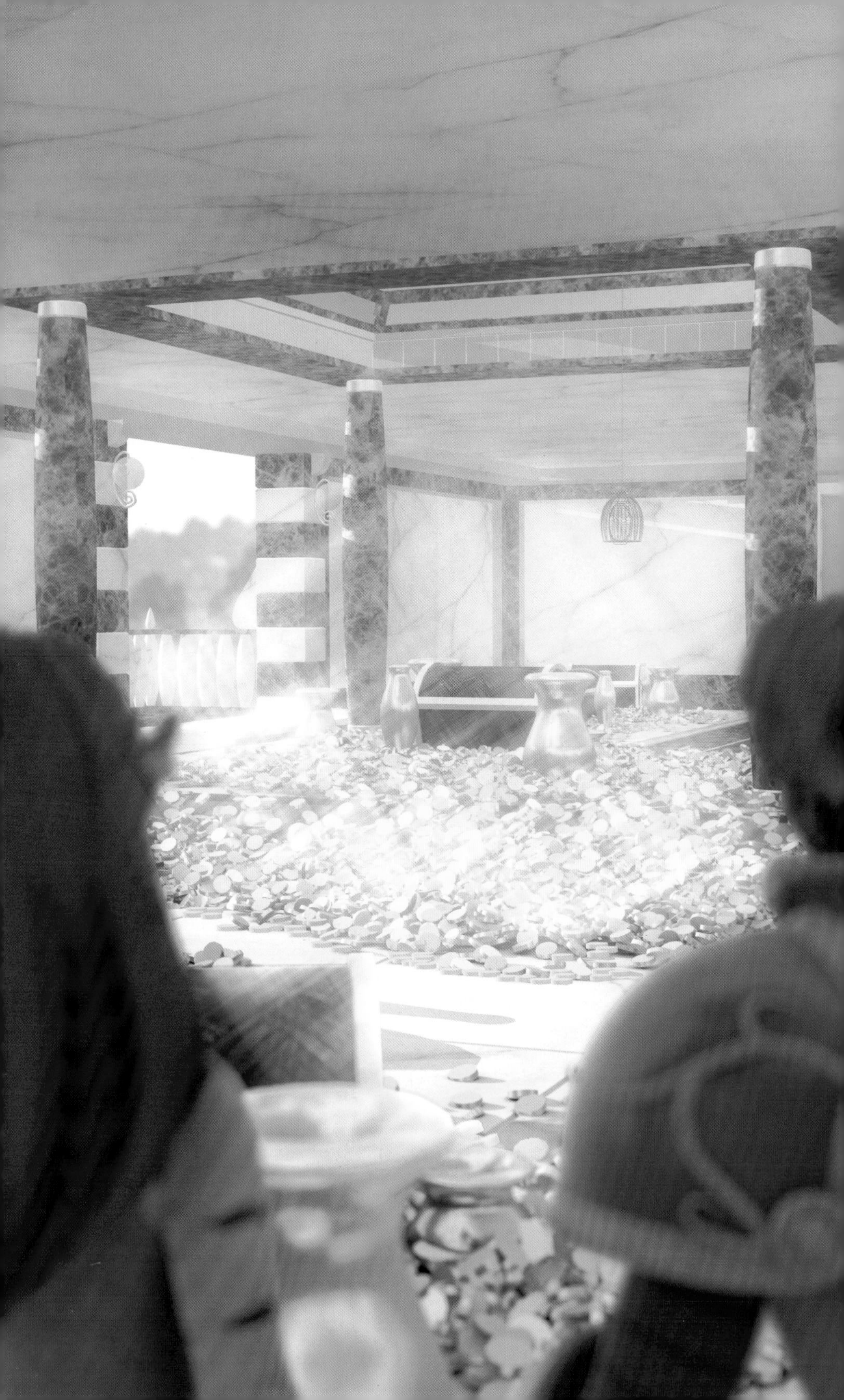

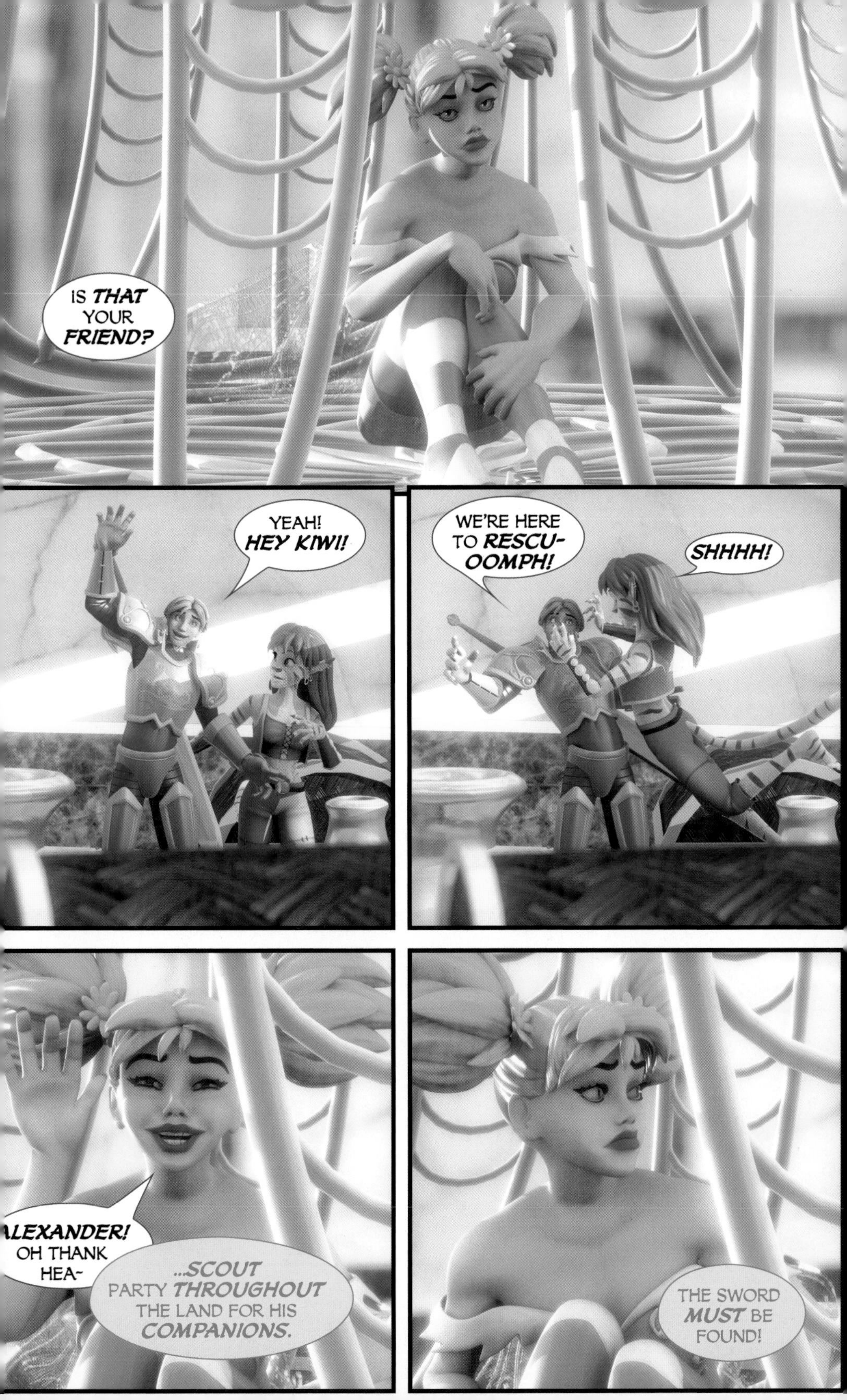
IS THAT YOUR FRIEND?
YEAH! HEY KIWI!
WE'RE HERE TO RESCU-OOMPH!
SHHHH!
ALEXANDER! OH THANK HEA-
...SCOUT PARTY THROUGHOUT THE LAND FOR HIS COMPANIONS.
THE SWORD MUST BE FOUND!

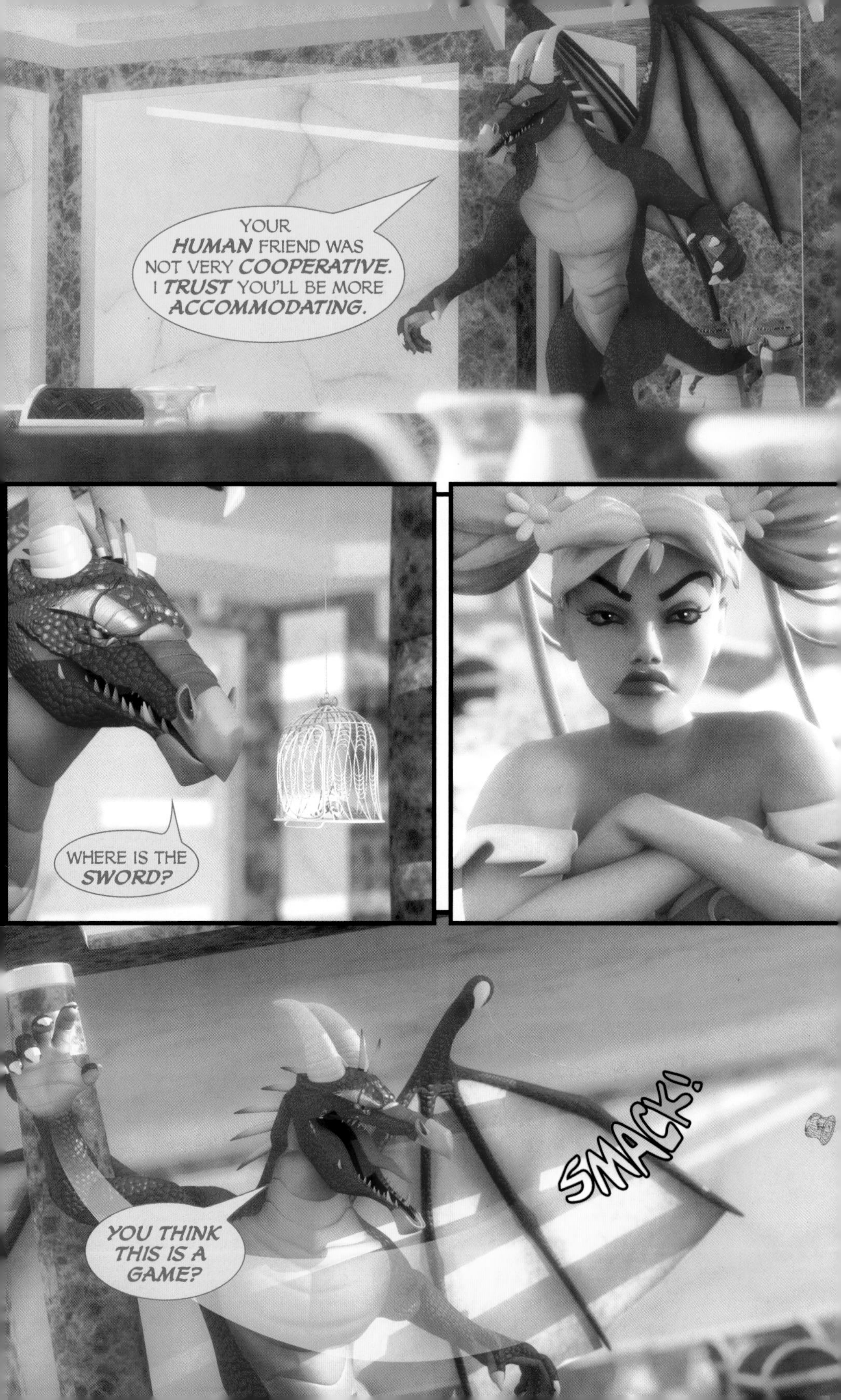
YOUR HUMAN FRIEND WAS NOT VERY COOPERATIVE. I TRUST YOU'LL BE MORE ACCOMMODATING.
WHERE IS THE SWORD?
SMACK!
YOU THINK THIS IS A GAME?

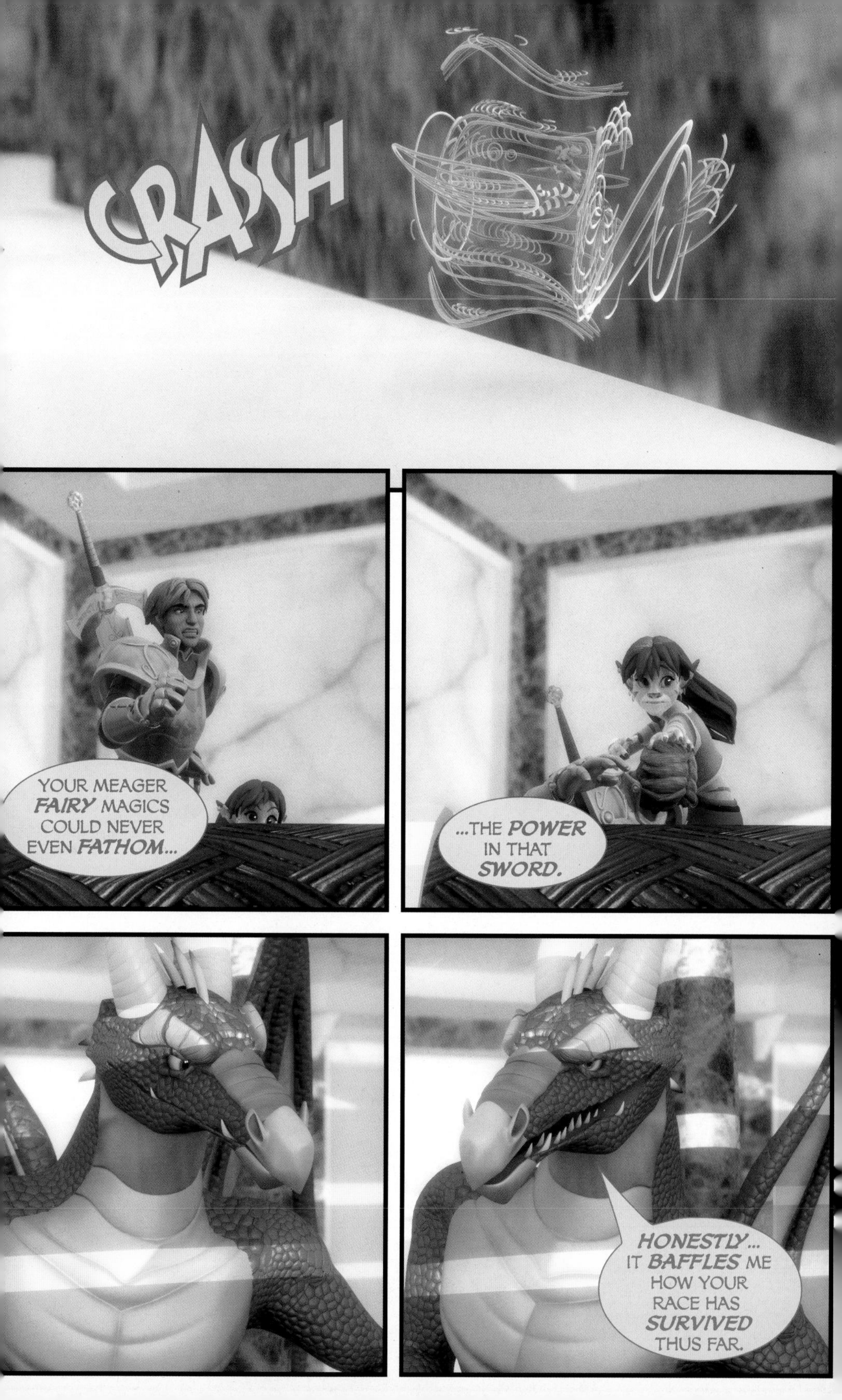
CRASH
YOUR MEAGER FAIRY MAGICS COULD NEVER EVEN FATHOM...
...THE POWER IN THAT SWORD.
HONESTLY... IT BAFFLES ME HOW YOUR RACE HAS SURVIVED THUS FAR.

SHE IS OF
NO USE T
ME.

DISPOSE
OF HER...

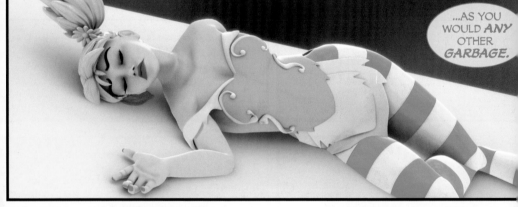

...AS YOU
WOULD *ANY*
OTHER
GARBAGE.

WITH *PLEASURE*
YOUR MAJESTY.

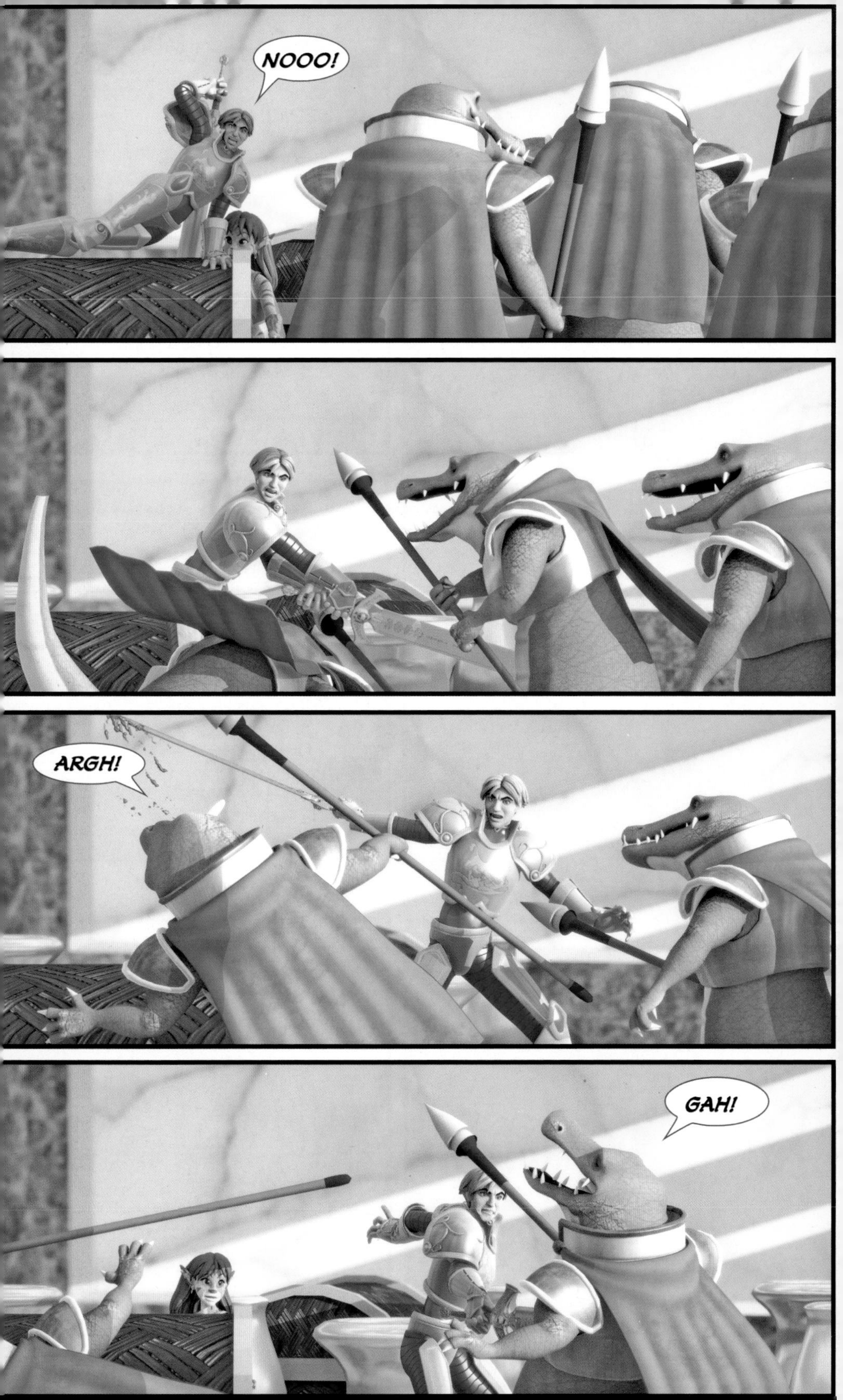
NOOO!
ARGH!
GAH!

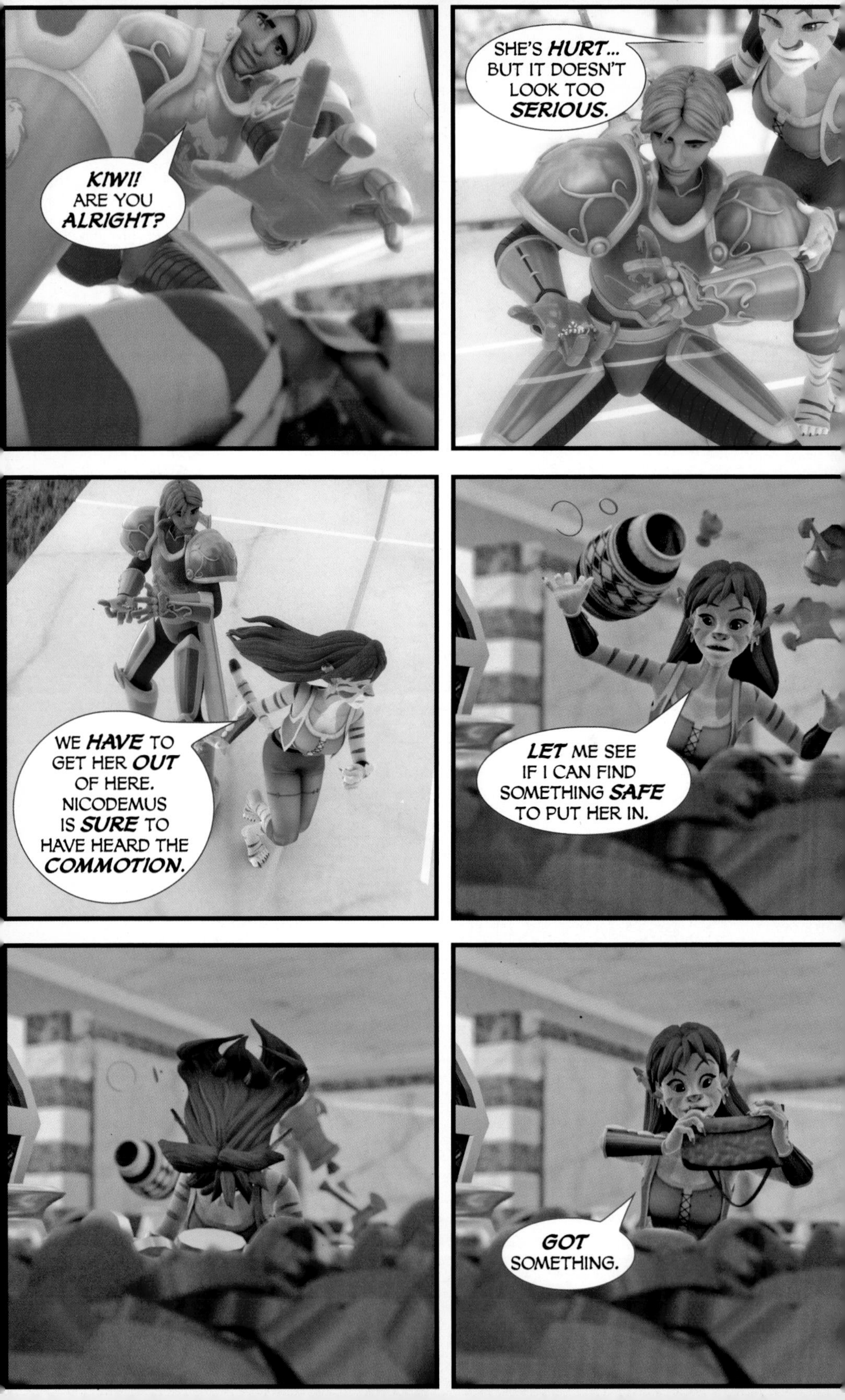
KIWI! ARE YOU ALRIGHT?
SHE'S HURT... BUT IT DOESN'T LOOK TOO SERIOUS.
WE HAVE TO GET HER OUT OF HERE. NICODEMUS IS SURE TO HAVE HEARD THE COMMOTION.
LET ME SEE IF I CAN FIND SOMETHING SAFE TO PUT HER IN.
GOT SOMETHING.

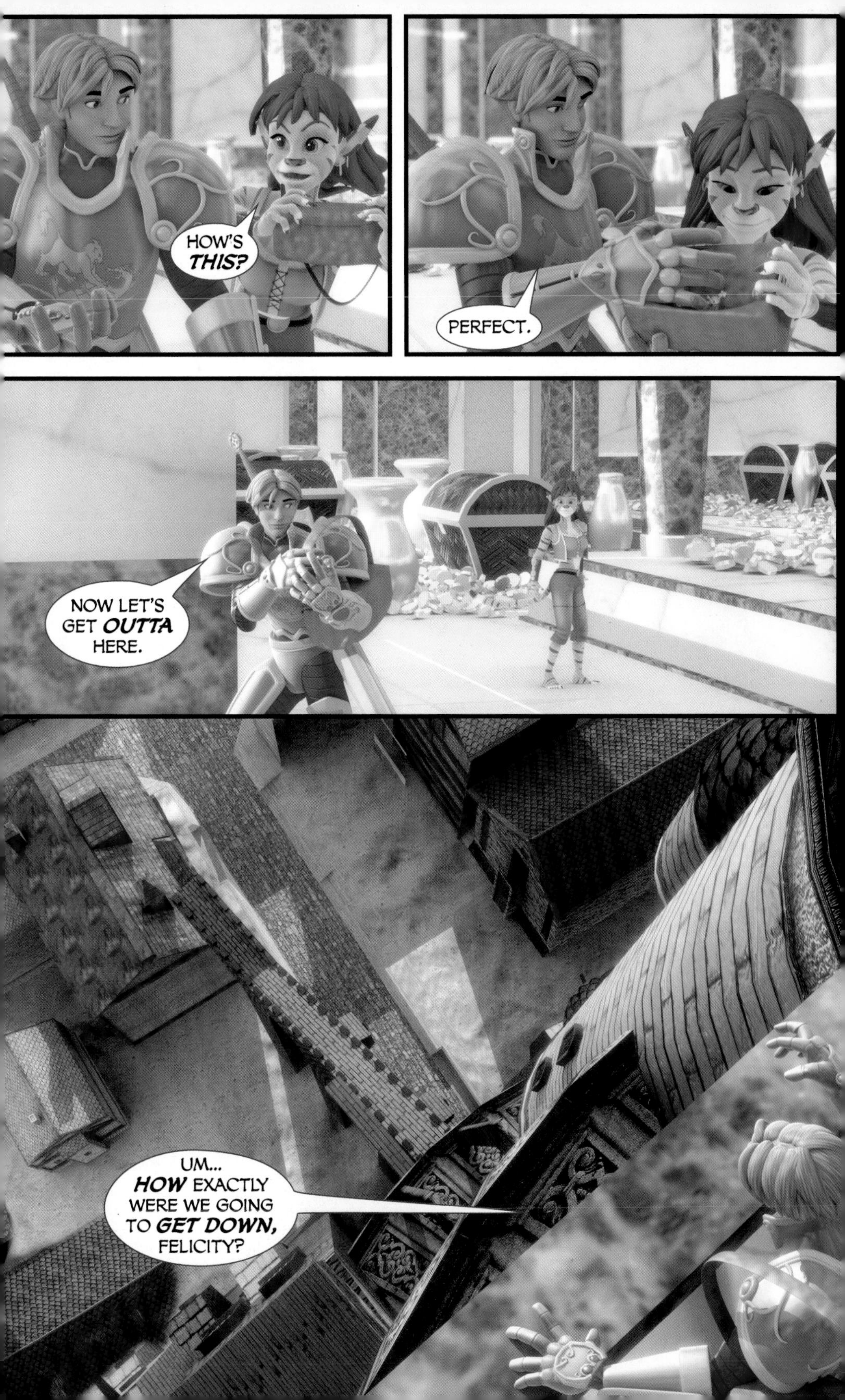
HOW'S *THIS?*
PERFECT.
NOW LET'S GET *OUTTA* HERE.
UM... *HOW* EXACTLY WERE WE GOING TO *GET DOWN,* FELICITY?

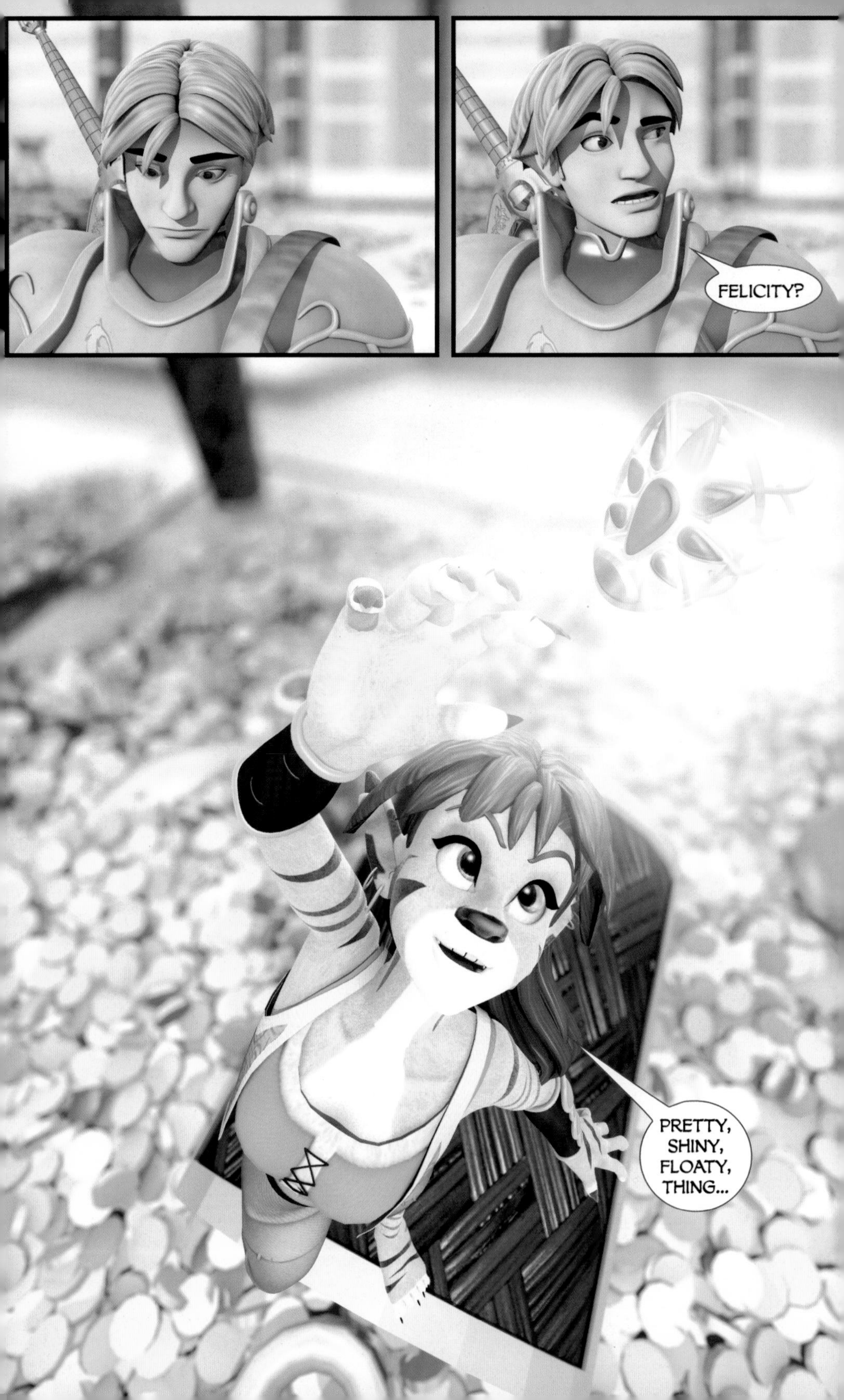
FELICITY?
PRETTY, SHINY, FLOATY, THING...

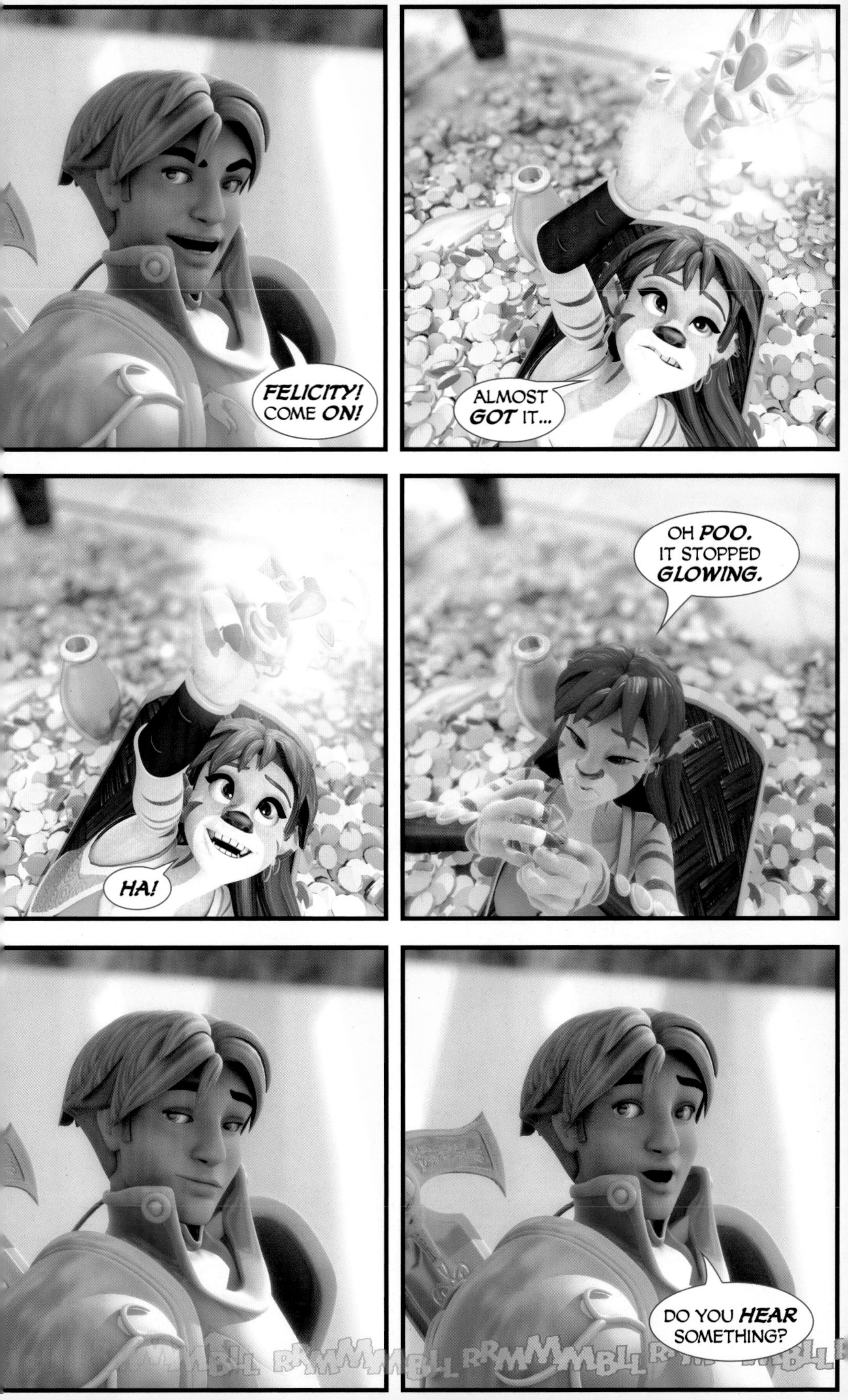
FELICITY! COME ON!
ALMOST GOT IT...
HA!
OH POO. IT STOPPED GLOWING.
DO YOU HEAR SOMETHING?
RRMMMMBLL RRMMMMBLL

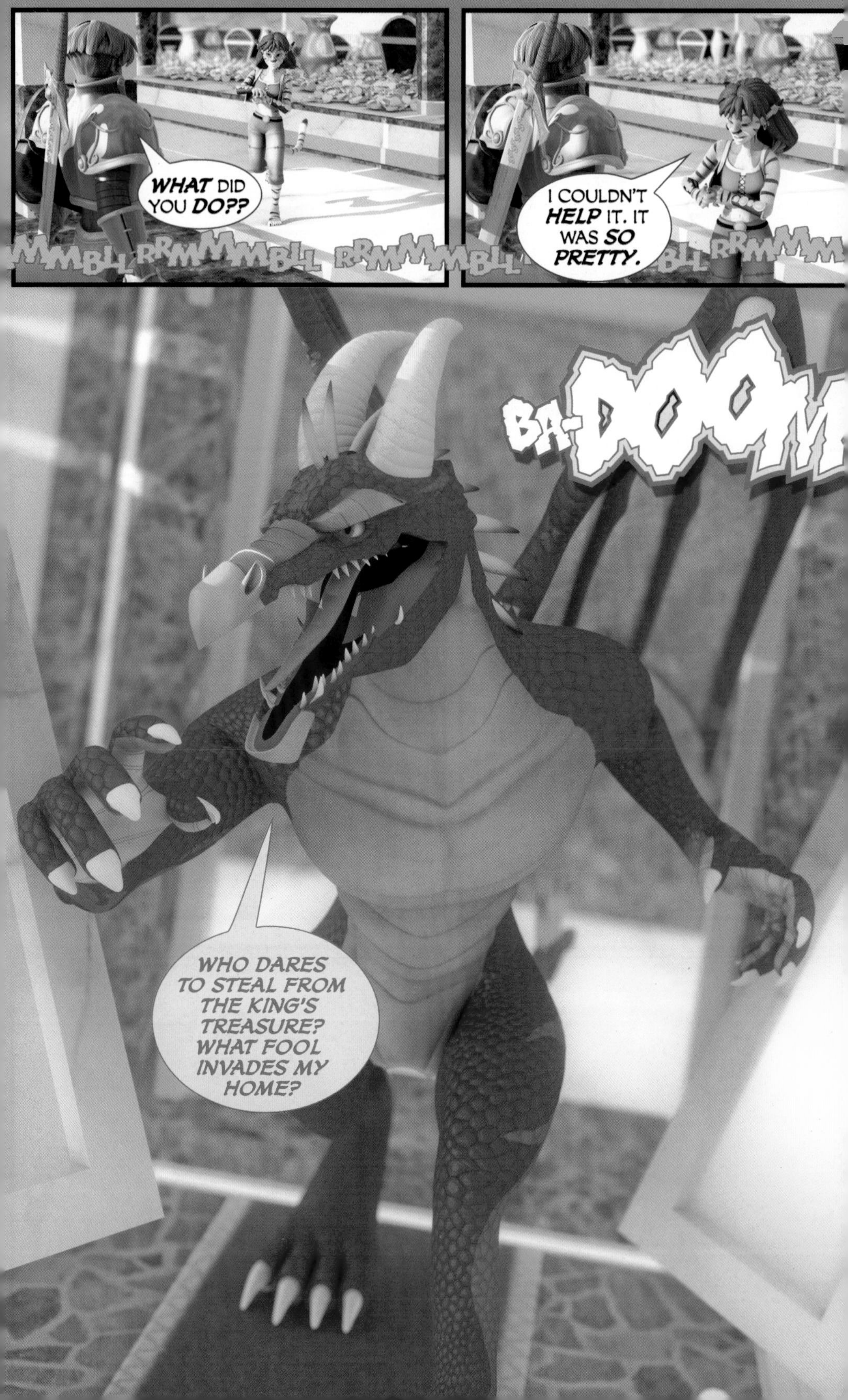
WHAT DID YOU DO??
I COULDN'T HELP IT. IT WAS SO PRETTY.
BA-DOOM
WHO DARES TO STEAL FROM THE KING'S TREASURE? WHAT FOOL INVADES MY HOME?

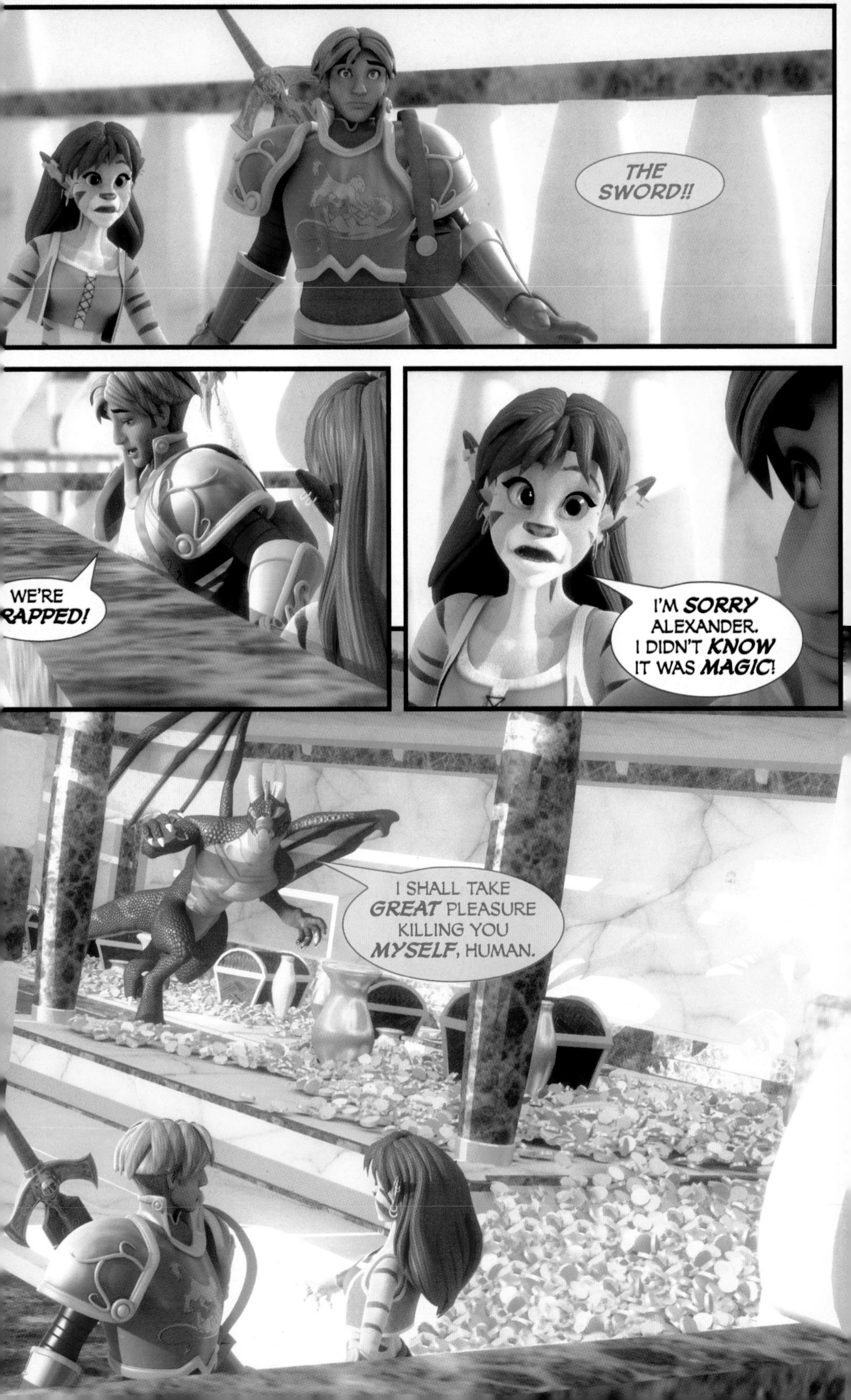
THE SWORD!!
WE'RE RAPPED!
I'M SORRY ALEXANDER. I DIDN'T KNOW IT WAS MAGIC!
I SHALL TAKE GREAT PLEASURE KILLING YOU MYSELF, HUMAN.

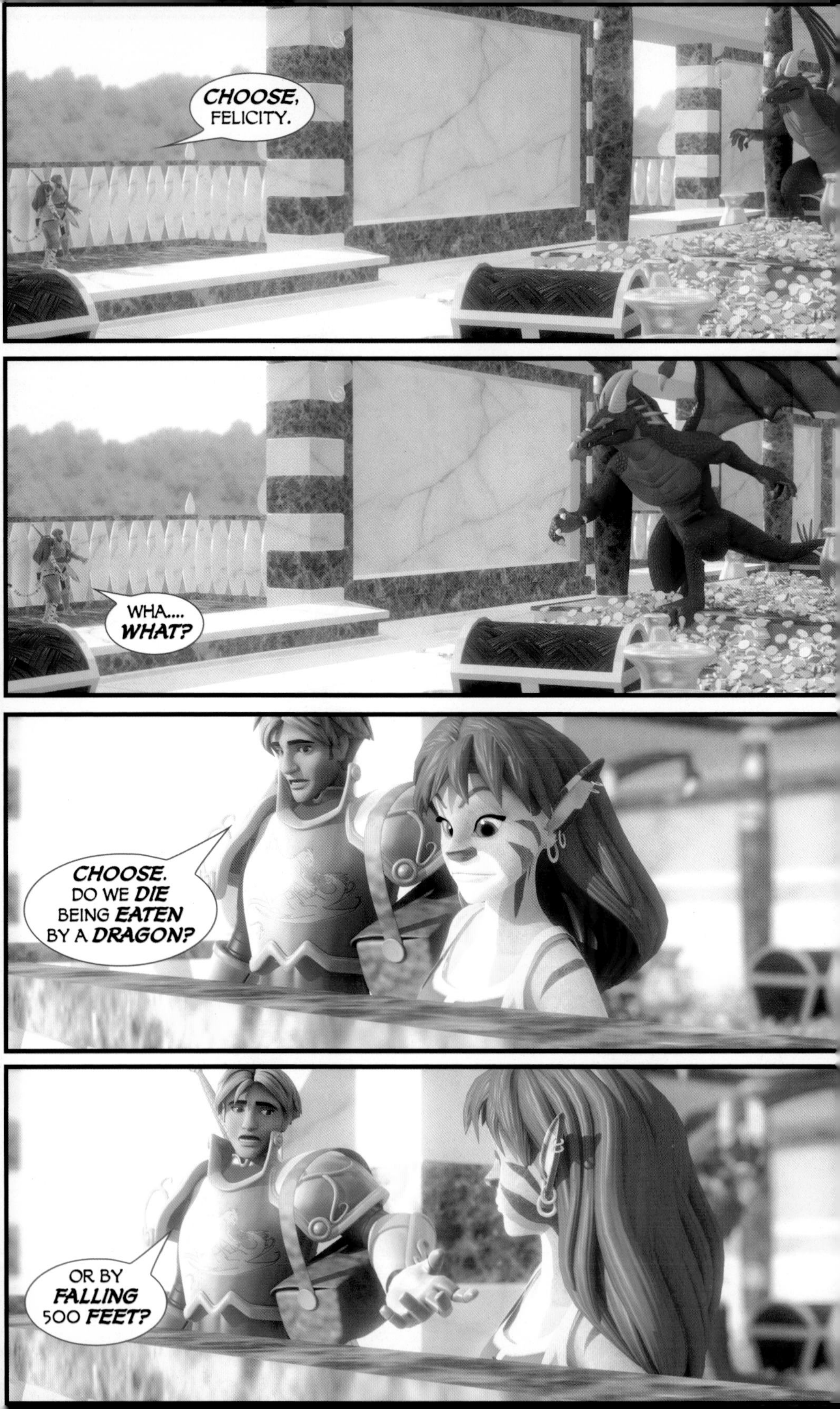
CHOOSE, FELICITY.
WHA.... WHAT?
CHOOSE. DO WE DIE BEING EATEN BY A DRAGON?
OR BY FALLING 500 FEET?

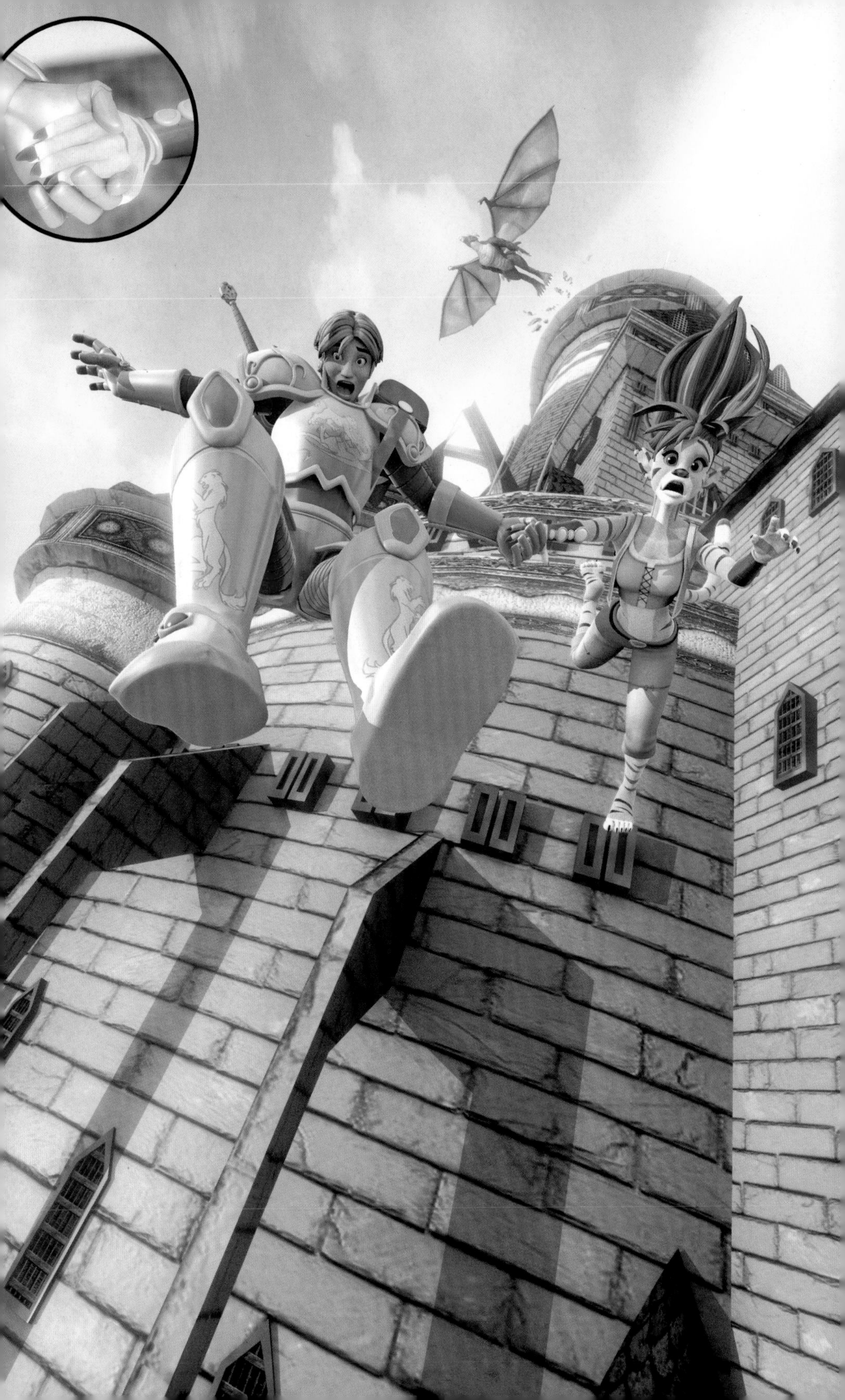

CHAPTER SIX

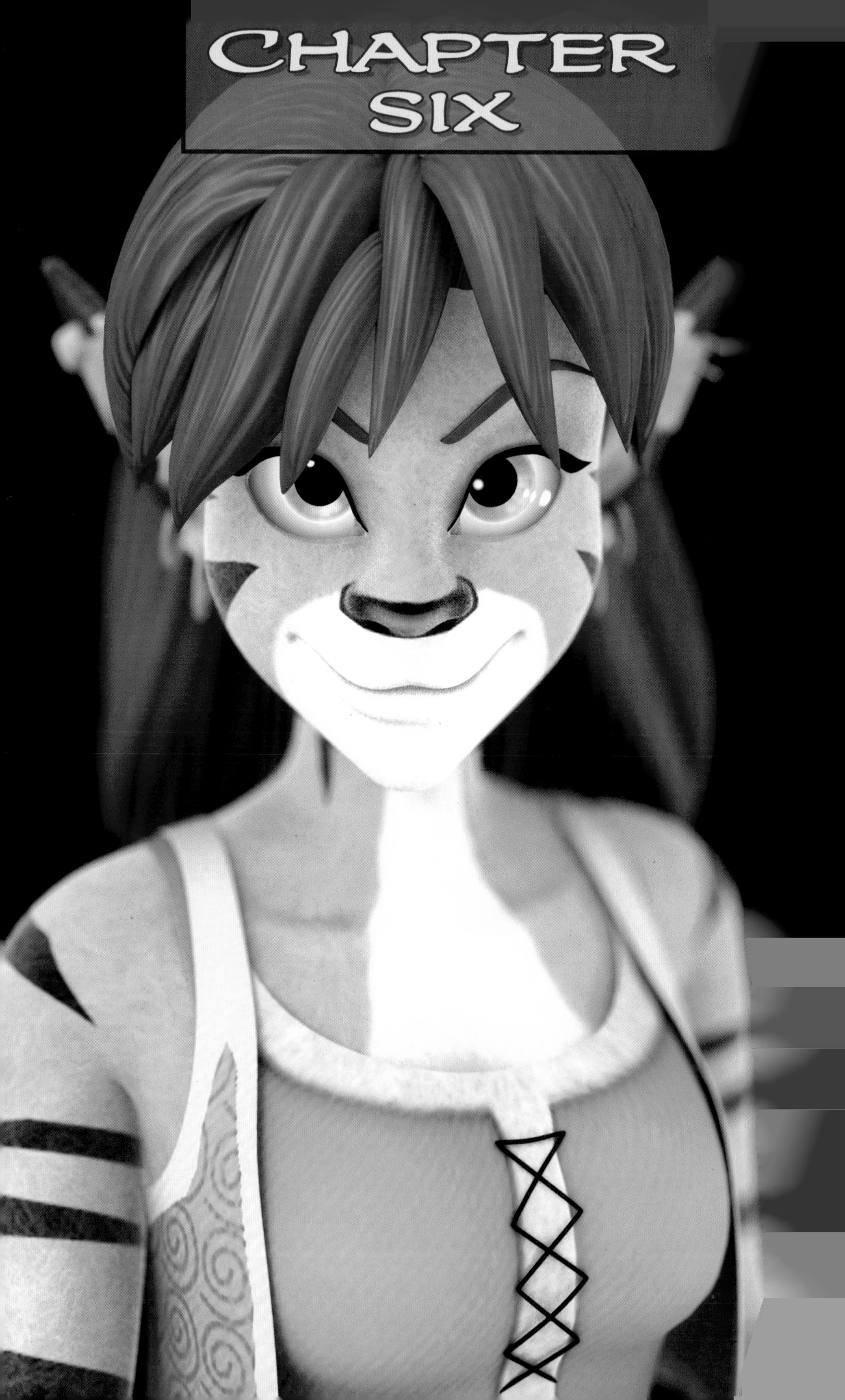

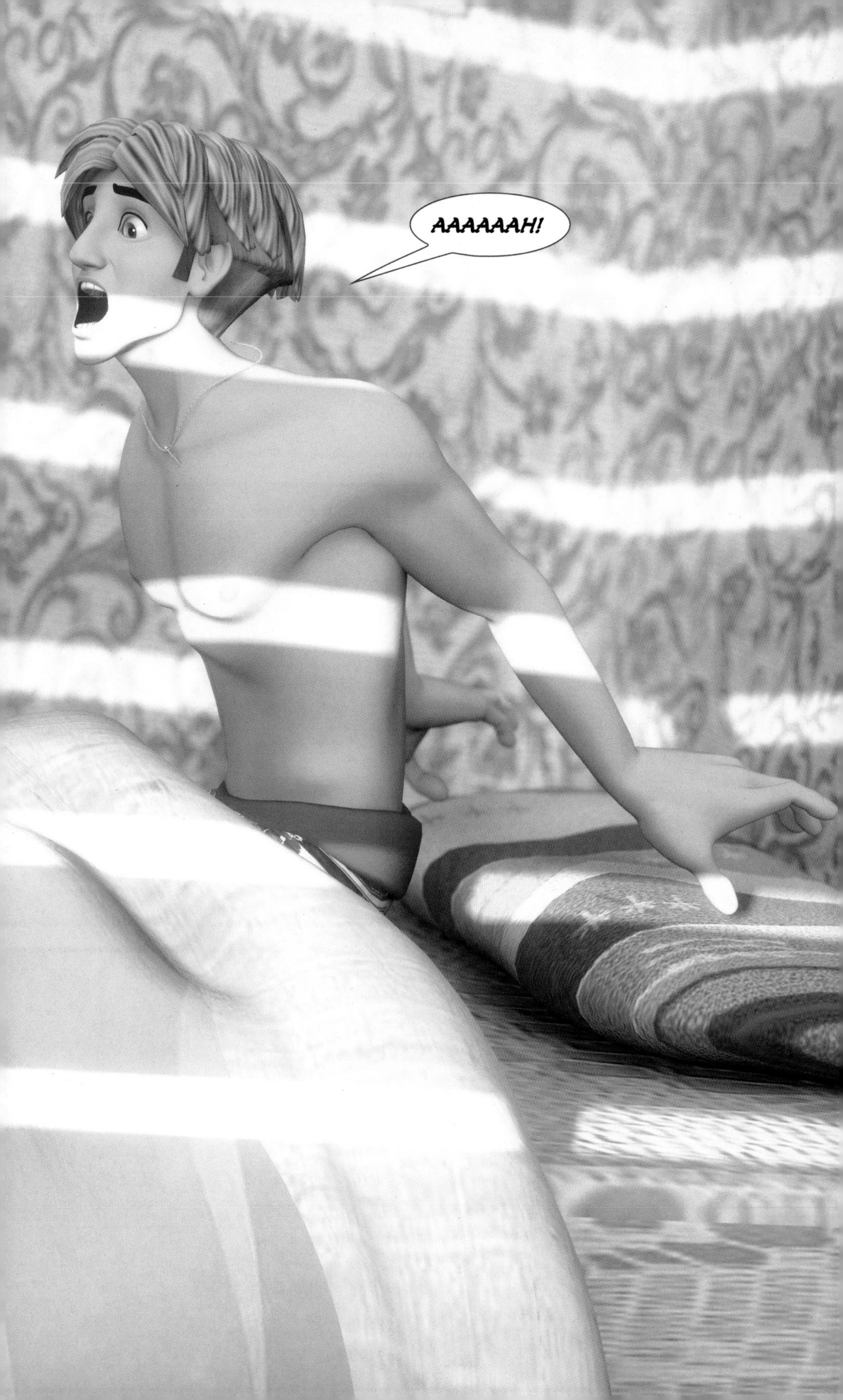
AAAAAAH!

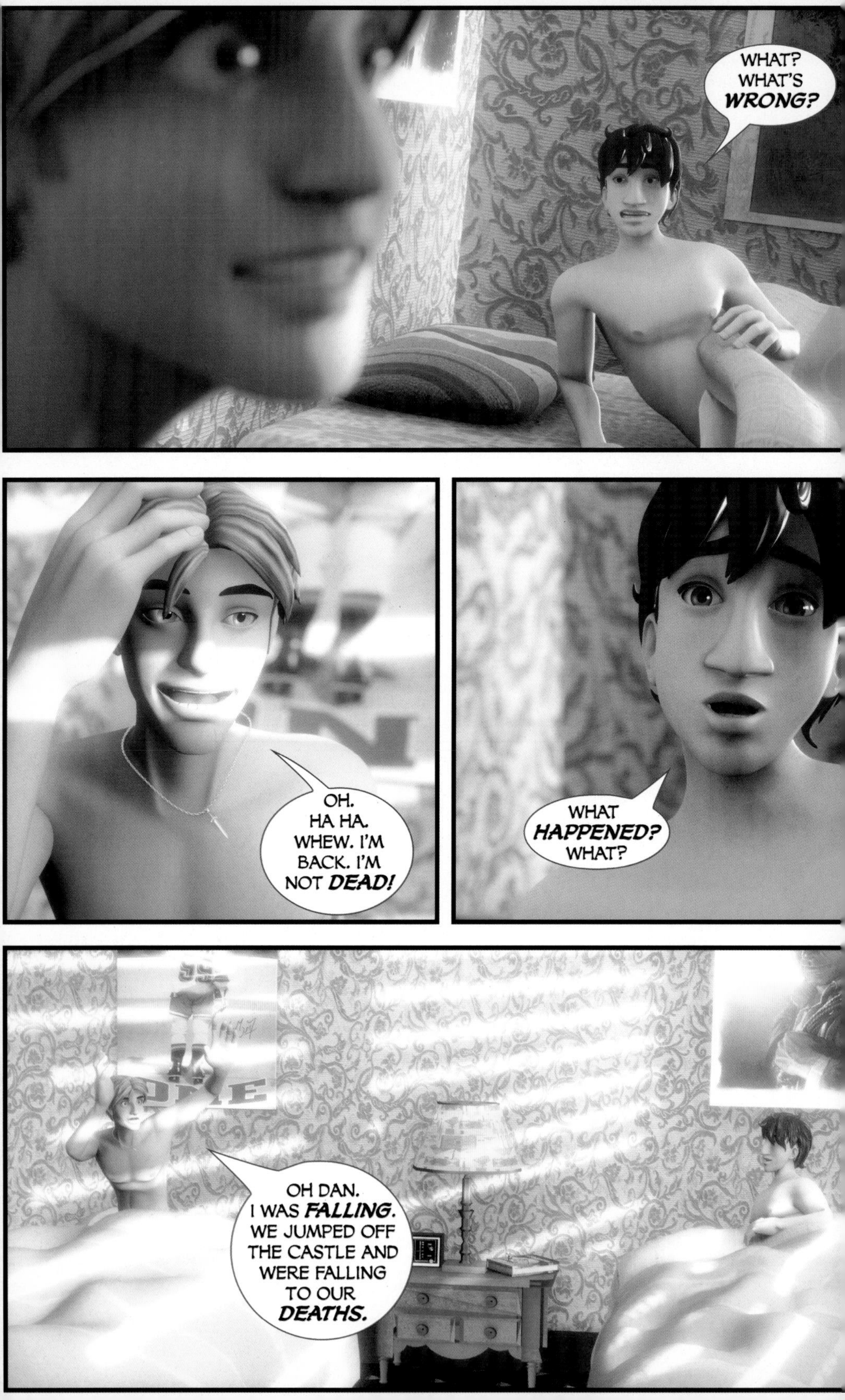
WHAT? WHAT'S WRONG?
OH. HA HA. WHEW. I'M BACK. I'M NOT DEAD!
WHAT HAPPENED? WHAT?
OH DAN. I WAS FALLING. WE JUMPED OFF THE CASTLE AND WERE FALLING TO OUR DEATHS.

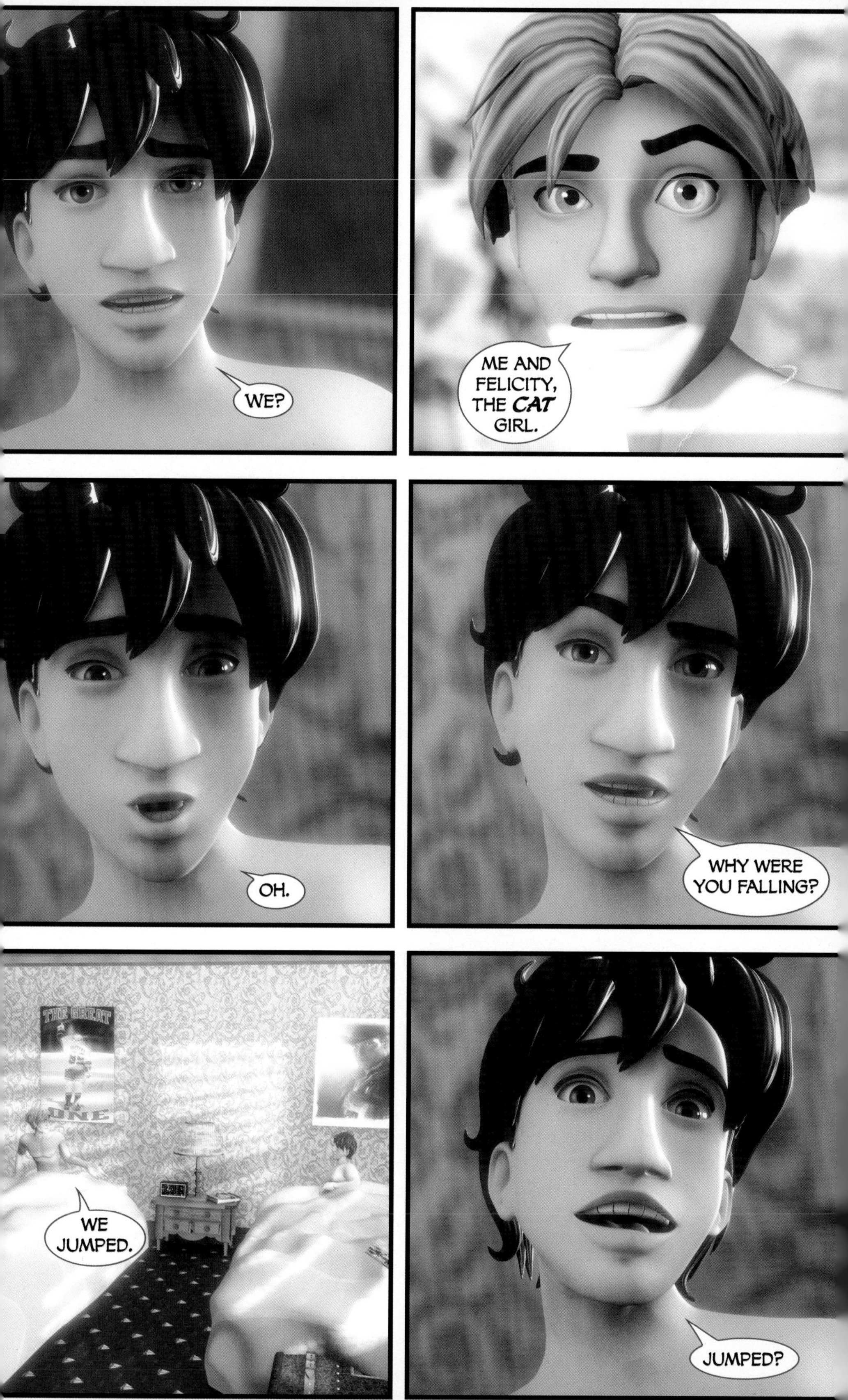
WE?
ME AND FELICITY, THE *CAT* GIRL.
OH.
WHY WERE YOU FALLING?
WE JUMPED.
JUMPED?

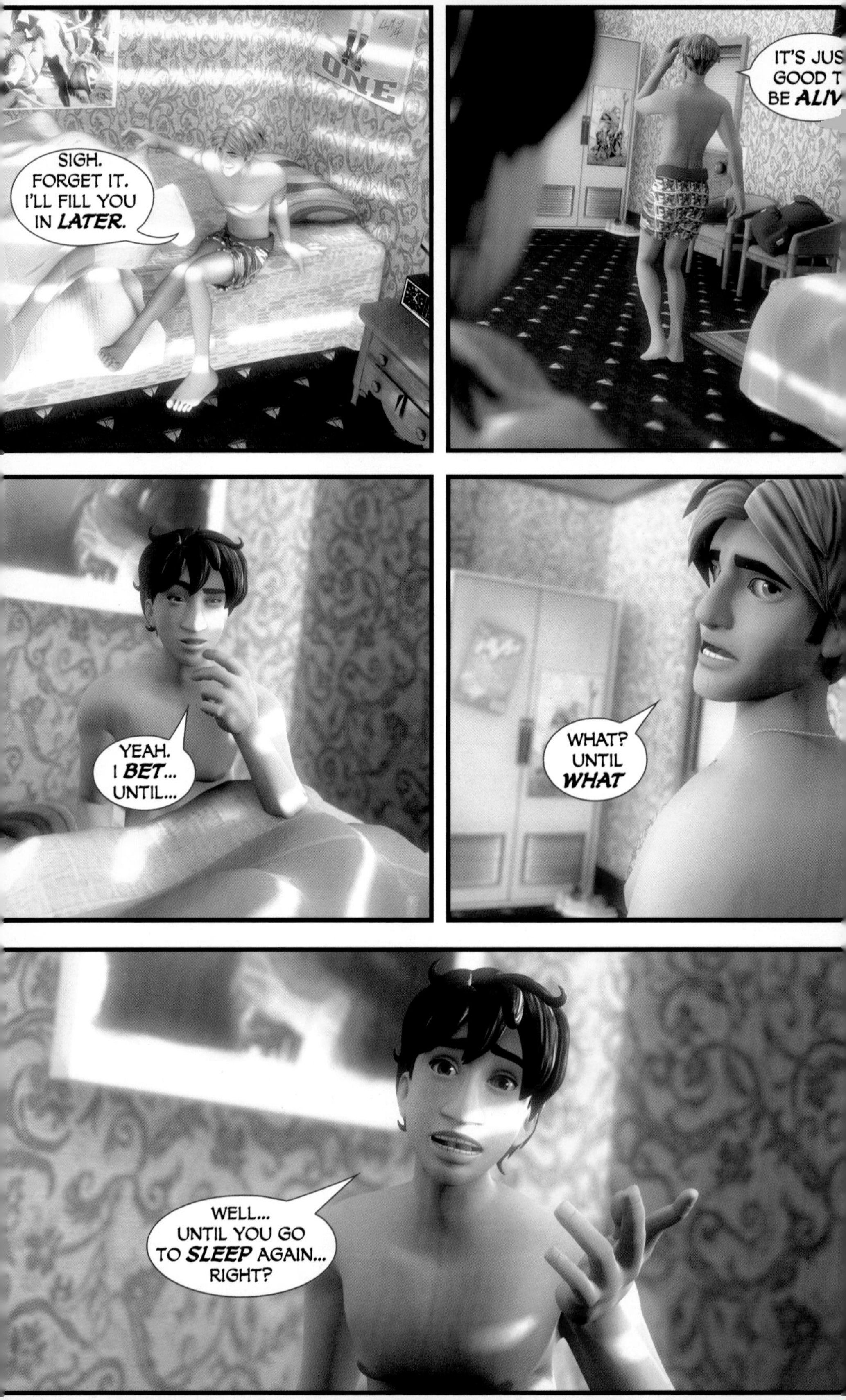
SIGH. FORGET IT. I'LL FILL YOU IN LATER.
IT'S JUS GOOD T BE ALIV
YEAH. I BET... UNTIL...
WHAT? UNTIL WHAT
WELL... UNTIL YOU GO TO SLEEP AGAIN... RIGHT?

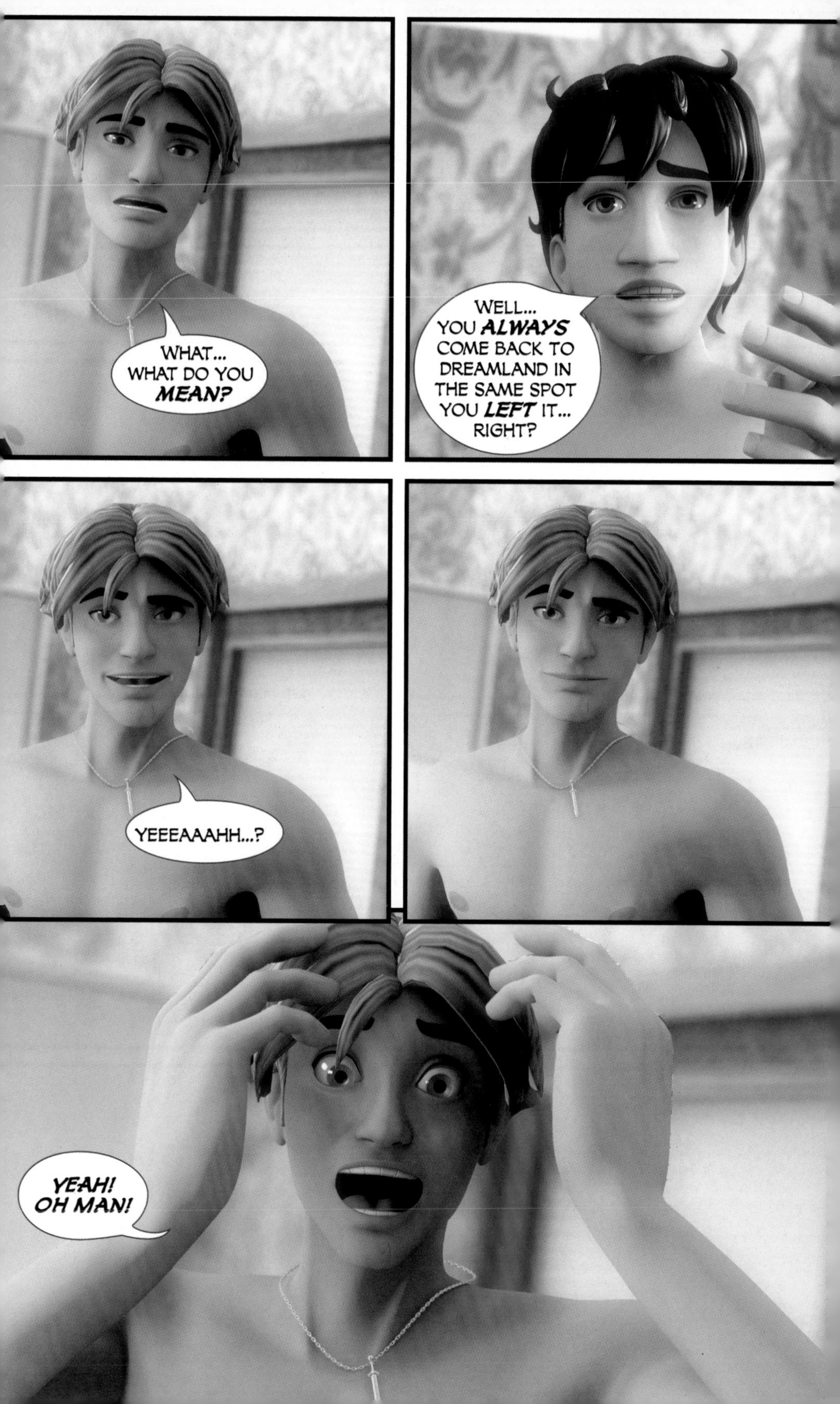
WHAT... WHAT DO YOU *MEAN?*
WELL... YOU *ALWAYS* COME BACK TO DREAMLAND IN THE SAME SPOT YOU *LEFT* IT... RIGHT?
YEEEAAAHH...?
YEAH! OH MAN!

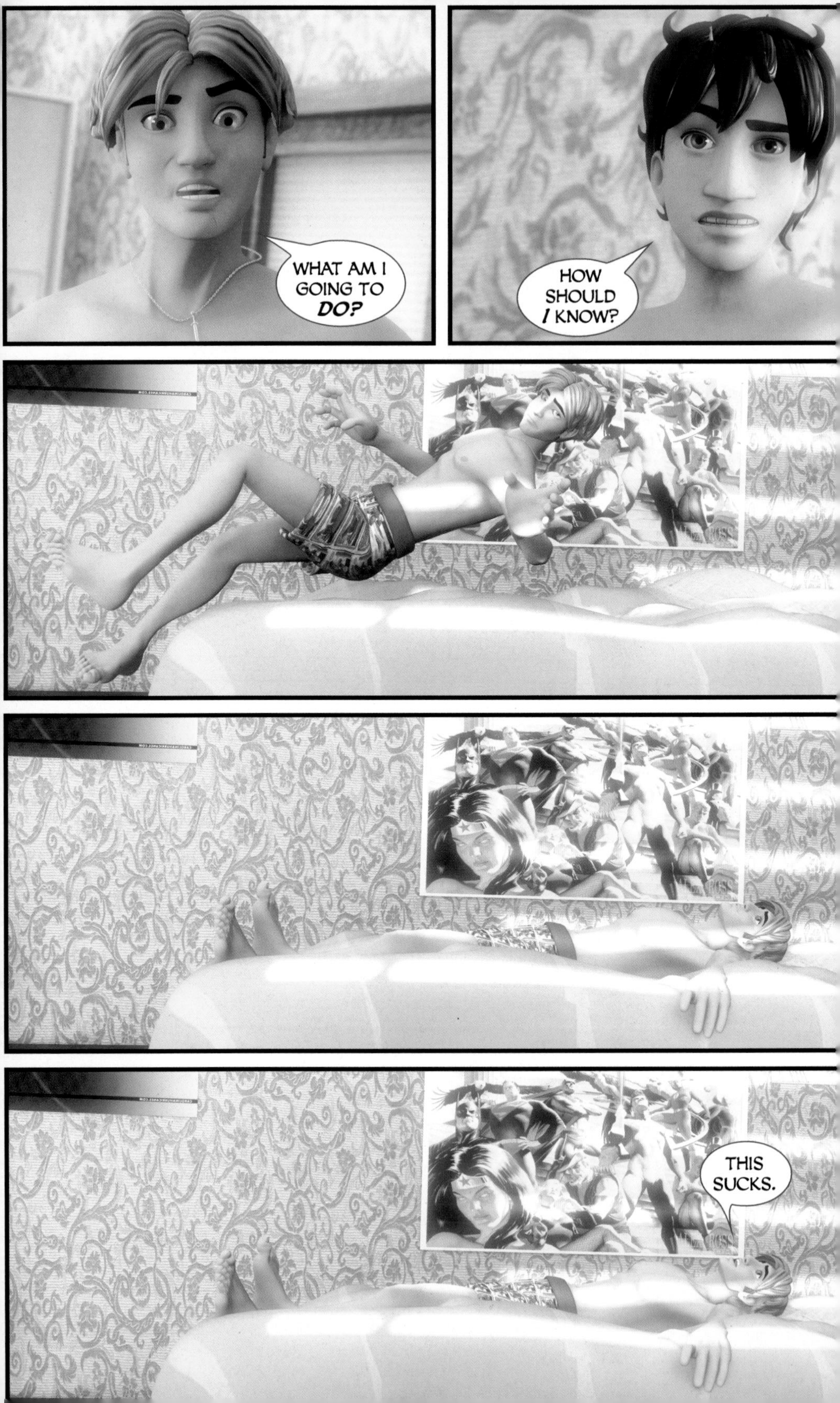
WHAT AM I GOING TO DO?
HOW SHOULD I KNOW?
THIS SUCKS.

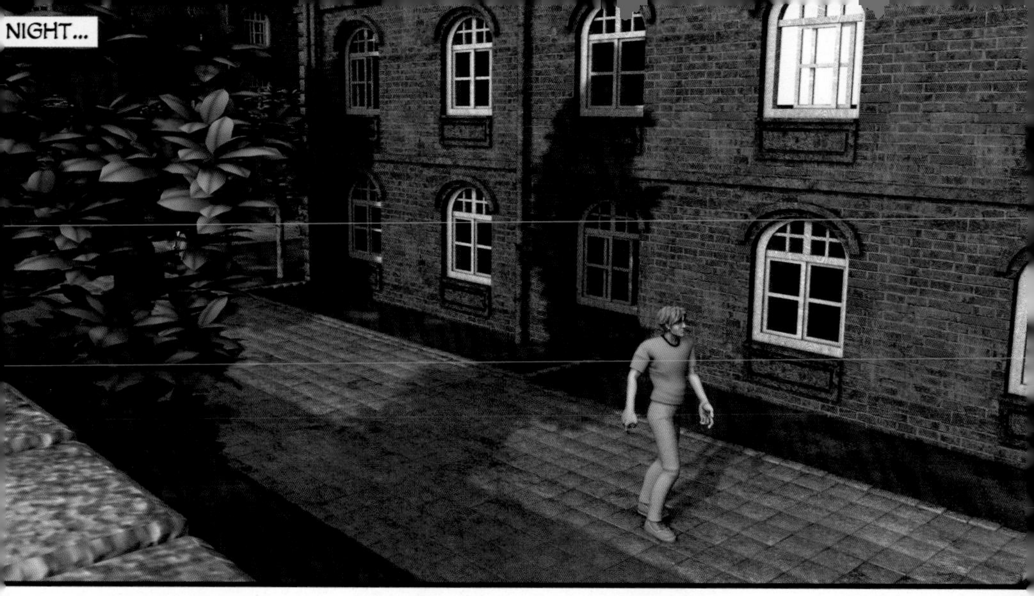
NIGHT...

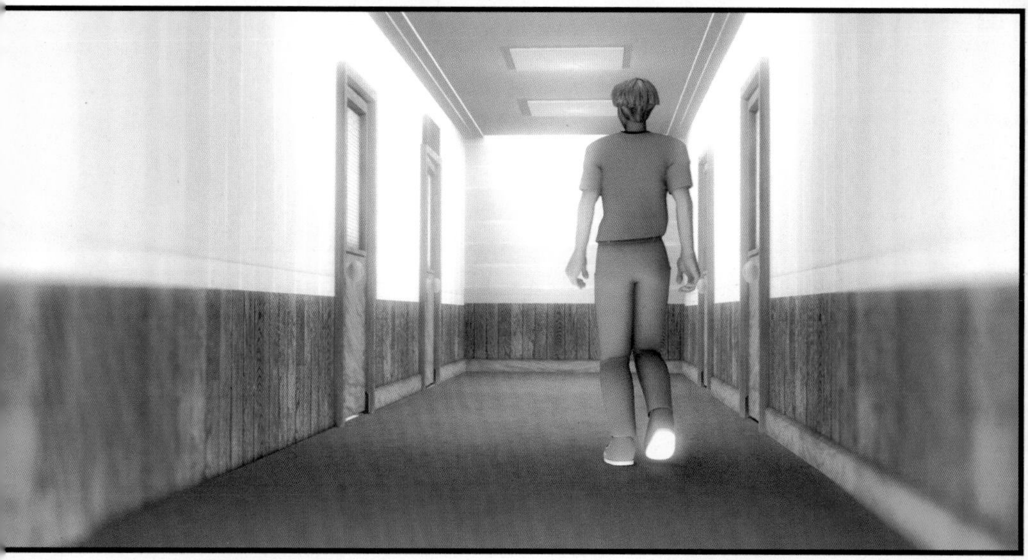

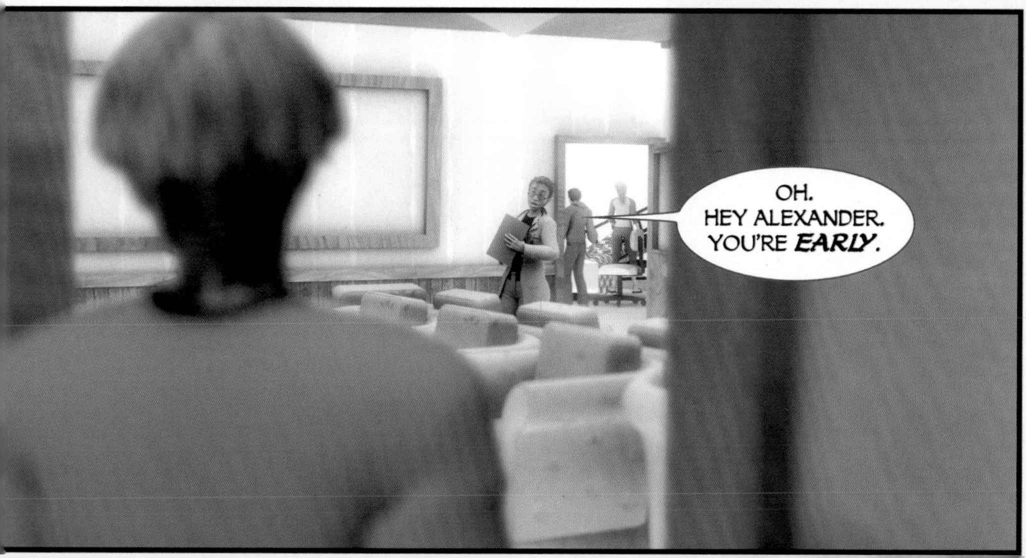
OH.
HEY ALEXANDER.
YOU'RE *EARLY*.

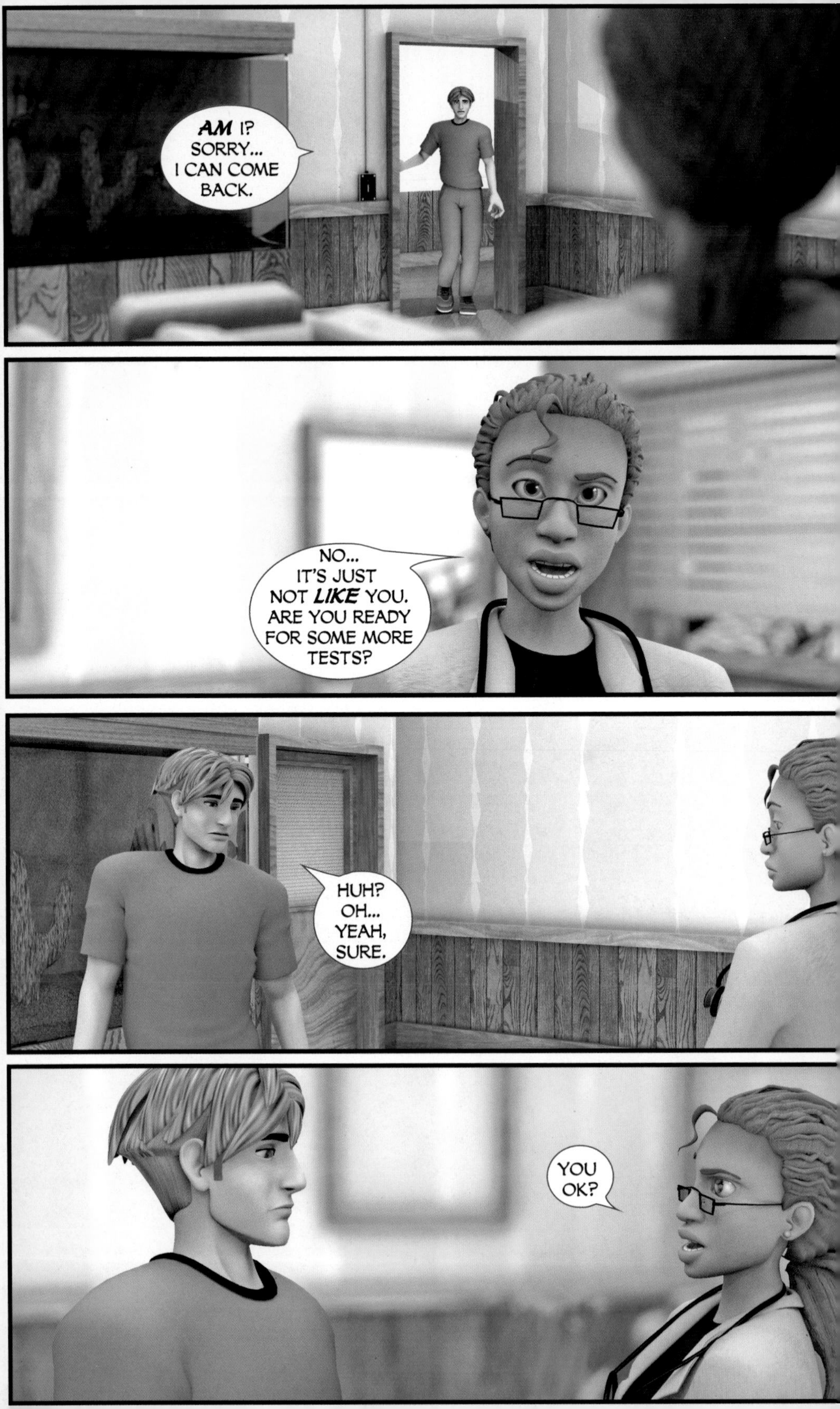
AM I? SORRY... I CAN COME BACK.
NO... IT'S JUST NOT LIKE YOU. ARE YOU READY FOR SOME MORE TESTS?
HUH? OH... YEAH, SURE.
YOU OK?

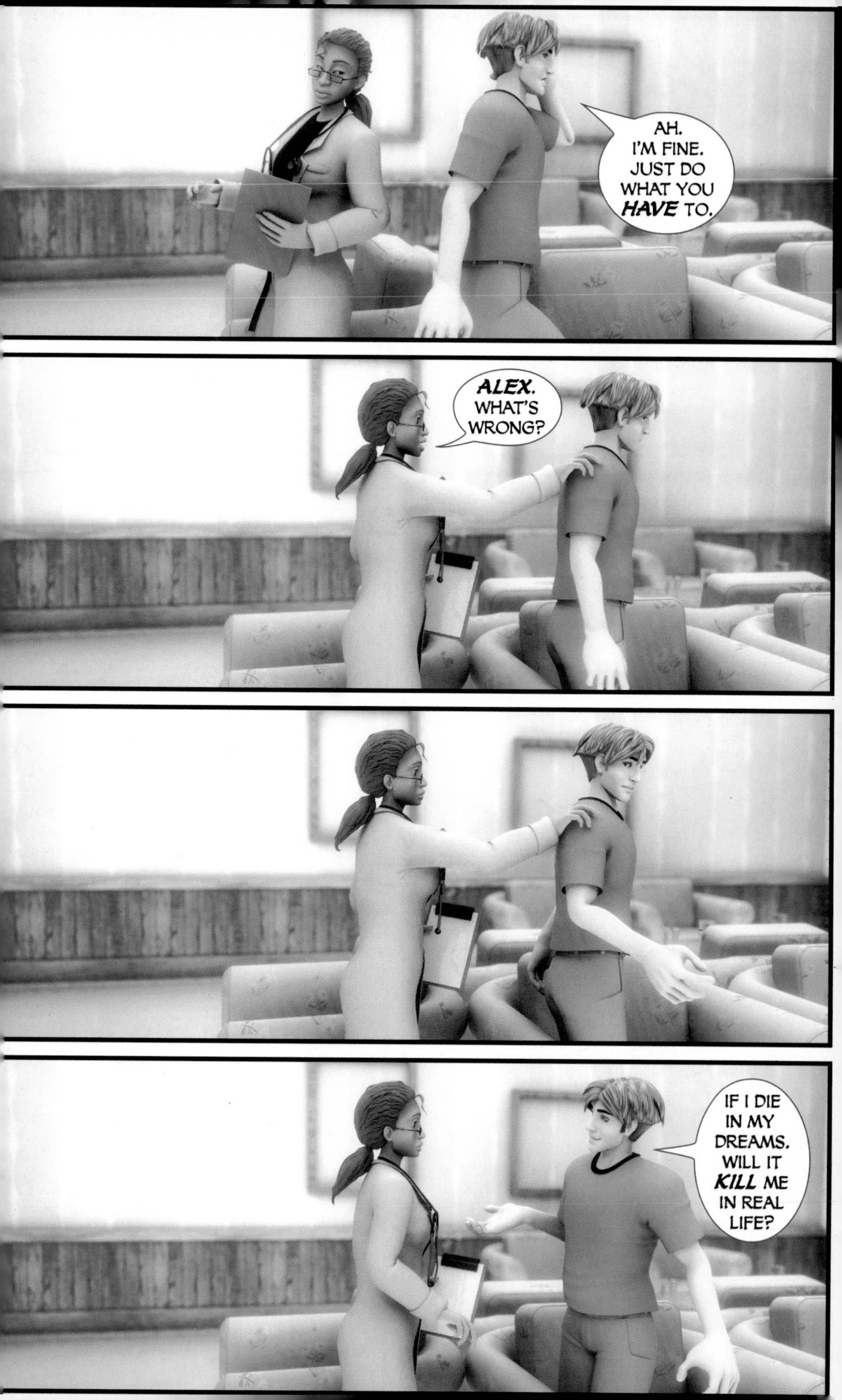
AH. I'M FINE. JUST DO WHAT YOU HAVE TO.
ALEX. WHAT'S WRONG?
IF I DIE IN MY DREAMS. WILL IT KILL ME IN REAL LIFE?

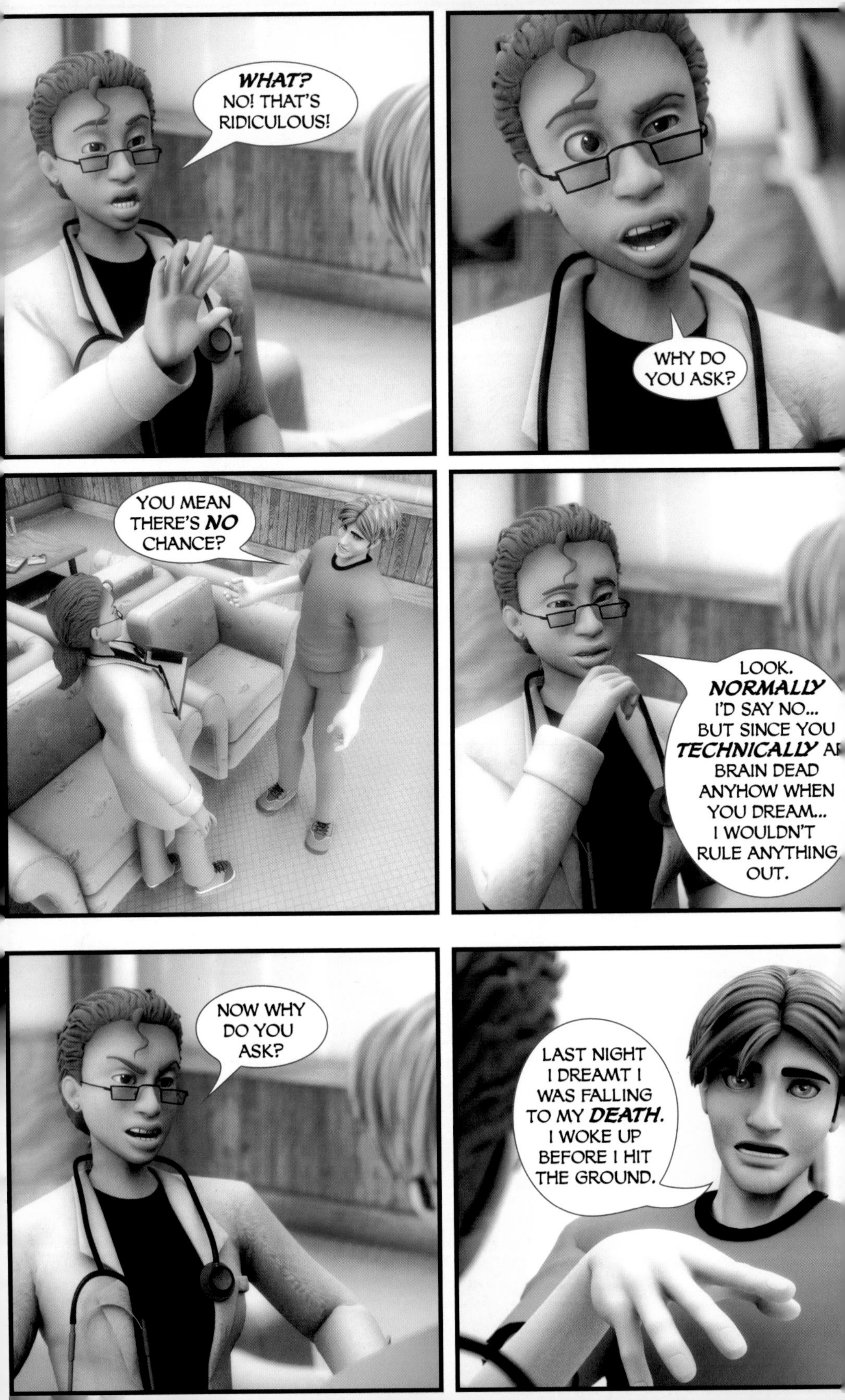
WHAT? NO! THAT'S RIDICULOUS!
WHY DO YOU ASK?
YOU MEAN THERE'S NO CHANCE?
LOOK. NORMALLY I'D SAY NO... BUT SINCE YOU TECHNICALLY A BRAIN DEAD ANYHOW WHEN YOU DREAM... I WOULDN'T RULE ANYTHING OUT.
NOW WHY DO YOU ASK?
LAST NIGHT I DREAMT I WAS FALLING TO MY DEATH. I WOKE UP BEFORE I HIT THE GROUND.

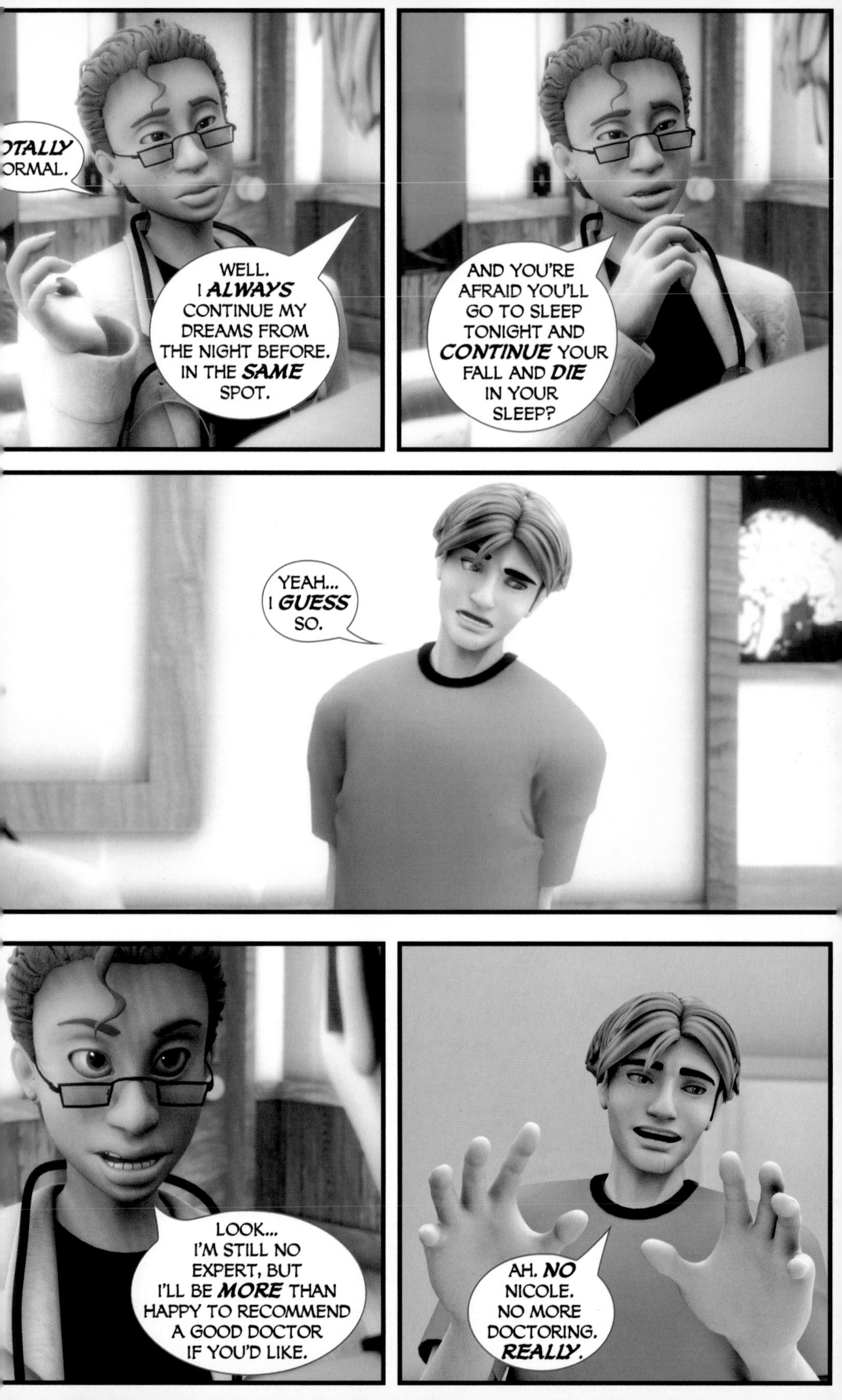

OTALLY ORMAL.
WELL. I ALWAYS CONTINUE MY DREAMS FROM THE NIGHT BEFORE. IN THE SAME SPOT.
AND YOU'RE AFRAID YOU'LL GO TO SLEEP TONIGHT AND CONTINUE YOUR FALL AND DIE IN YOUR SLEEP?
YEAH... I GUESS SO.
LOOK... I'M STILL NO EXPERT, BUT I'LL BE MORE THAN HAPPY TO RECOMMEND A GOOD DOCTOR IF YOU'D LIKE.
AH. NO NICOLE. NO MORE DOCTORING. REALLY.

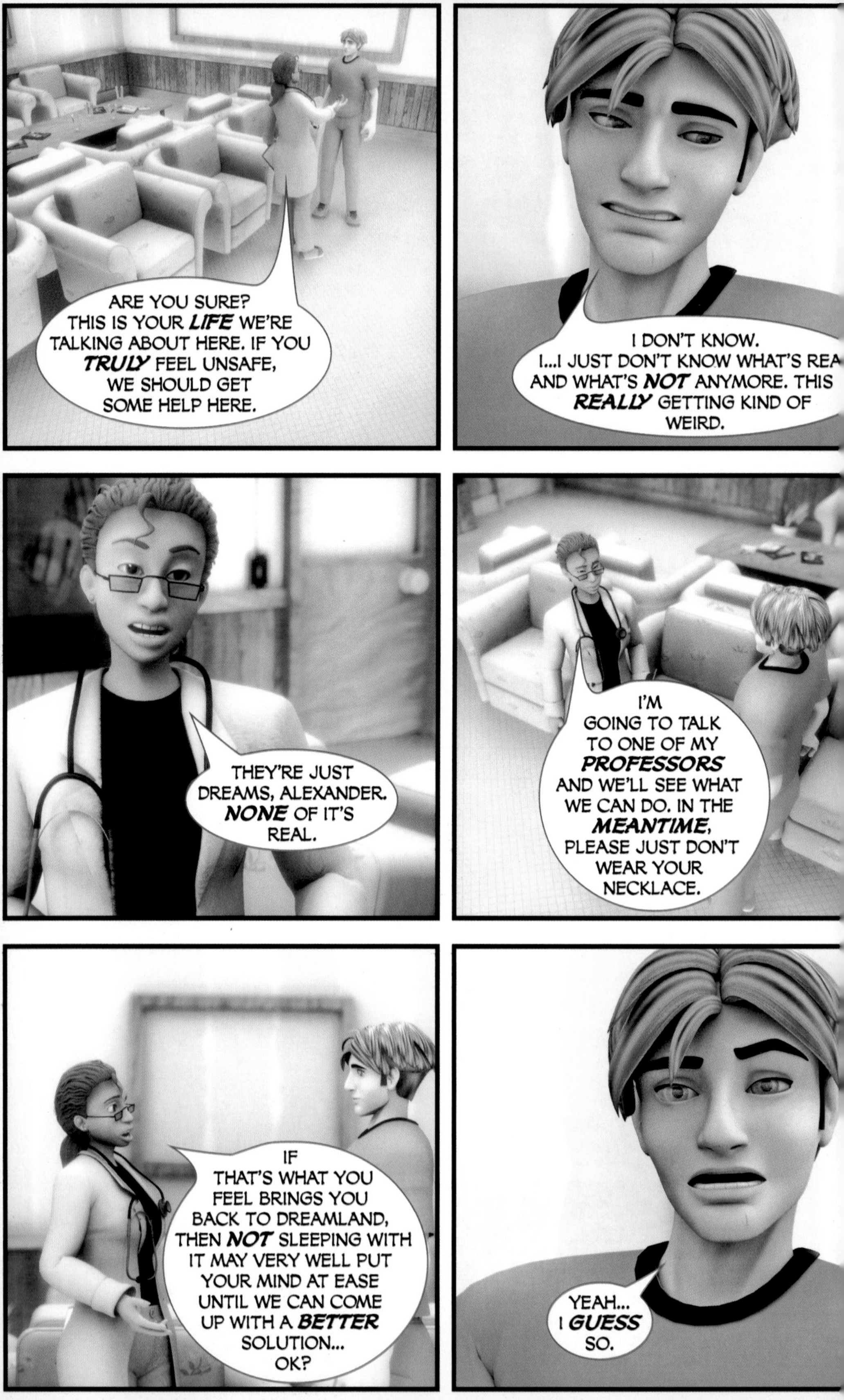
ARE YOU SURE? THIS IS YOUR LIFE WE'RE TALKING ABOUT HERE. IF YOU TRULY FEEL UNSAFE, WE SHOULD GET SOME HELP HERE.
I DON'T KNOW. I...I JUST DON'T KNOW WHAT'S REA AND WHAT'S NOT ANYMORE. THIS REALLY GETTING KIND OF WEIRD.
THEY'RE JUST DREAMS, ALEXANDER. NONE OF IT'S REAL.
I'M GOING TO TALK TO ONE OF MY PROFESSORS AND WE'LL SEE WHAT WE CAN DO. IN THE MEANTIME, PLEASE JUST DON'T WEAR YOUR NECKLACE.
IF THAT'S WHAT YOU FEEL BRINGS YOU BACK TO DREAMLAND, THEN NOT SLEEPING WITH IT MAY VERY WELL PUT YOUR MIND AT EASE UNTIL WE CAN COME UP WITH A BETTER SOLUTION... OK?
YEAH... I GUESS SO.

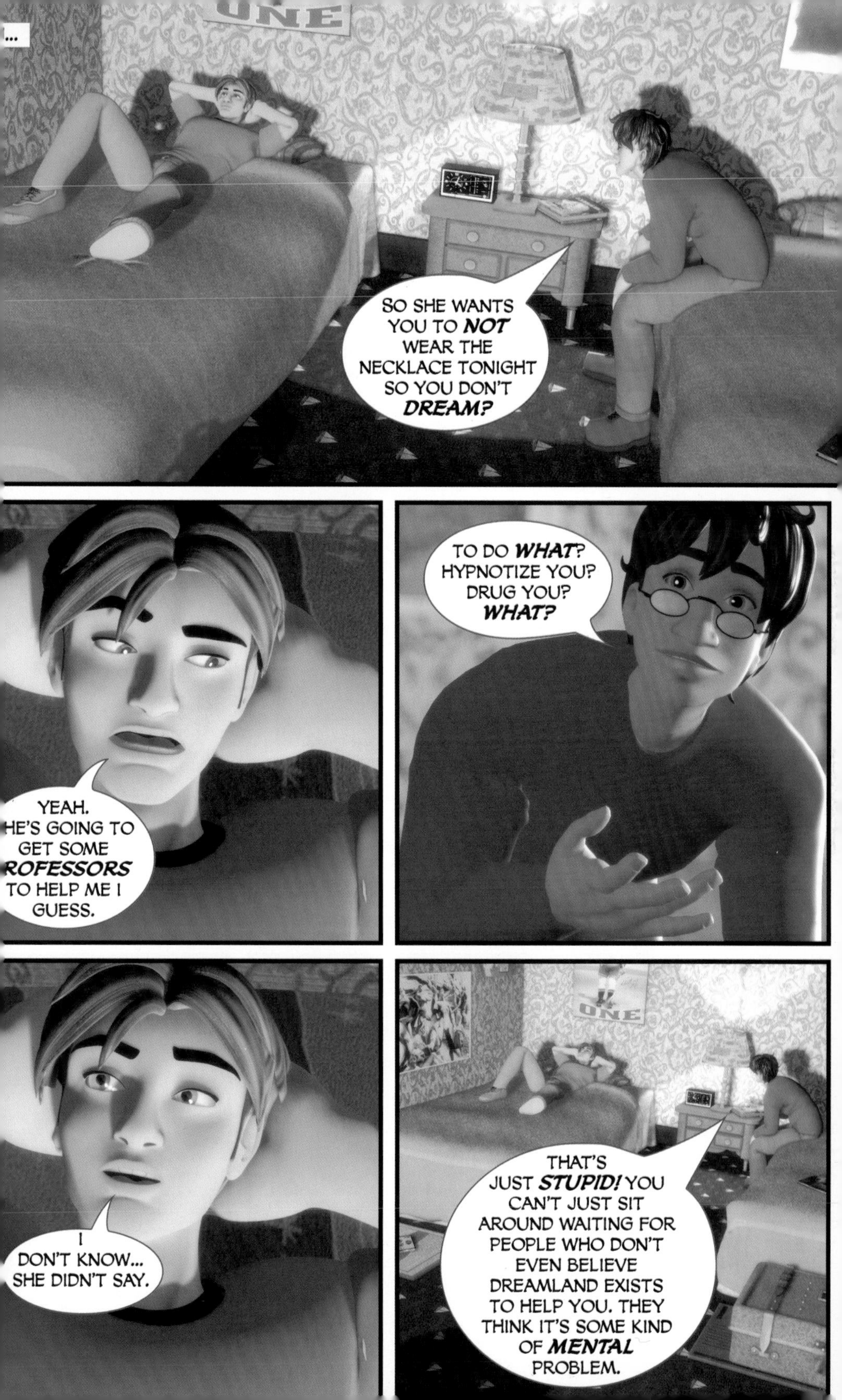
...
UNE
SO SHE WANTS YOU TO NOT WEAR THE NECKLACE TONIGHT SO YOU DON'T DREAM?
YEAH. HE'S GOING TO GET SOME ROFESSORS TO HELP ME I GUESS.
TO DO WHAT? HYPNOTIZE YOU? DRUG YOU? WHAT?
I DON'T KNOW... SHE DIDN'T SAY.
ONE
THAT'S JUST STUPID! YOU CAN'T JUST SIT AROUND WAITING FOR PEOPLE WHO DON'T EVEN BELIEVE DREAMLAND EXISTS TO HELP YOU. THEY THINK IT'S SOME KIND OF MENTAL PROBLEM.

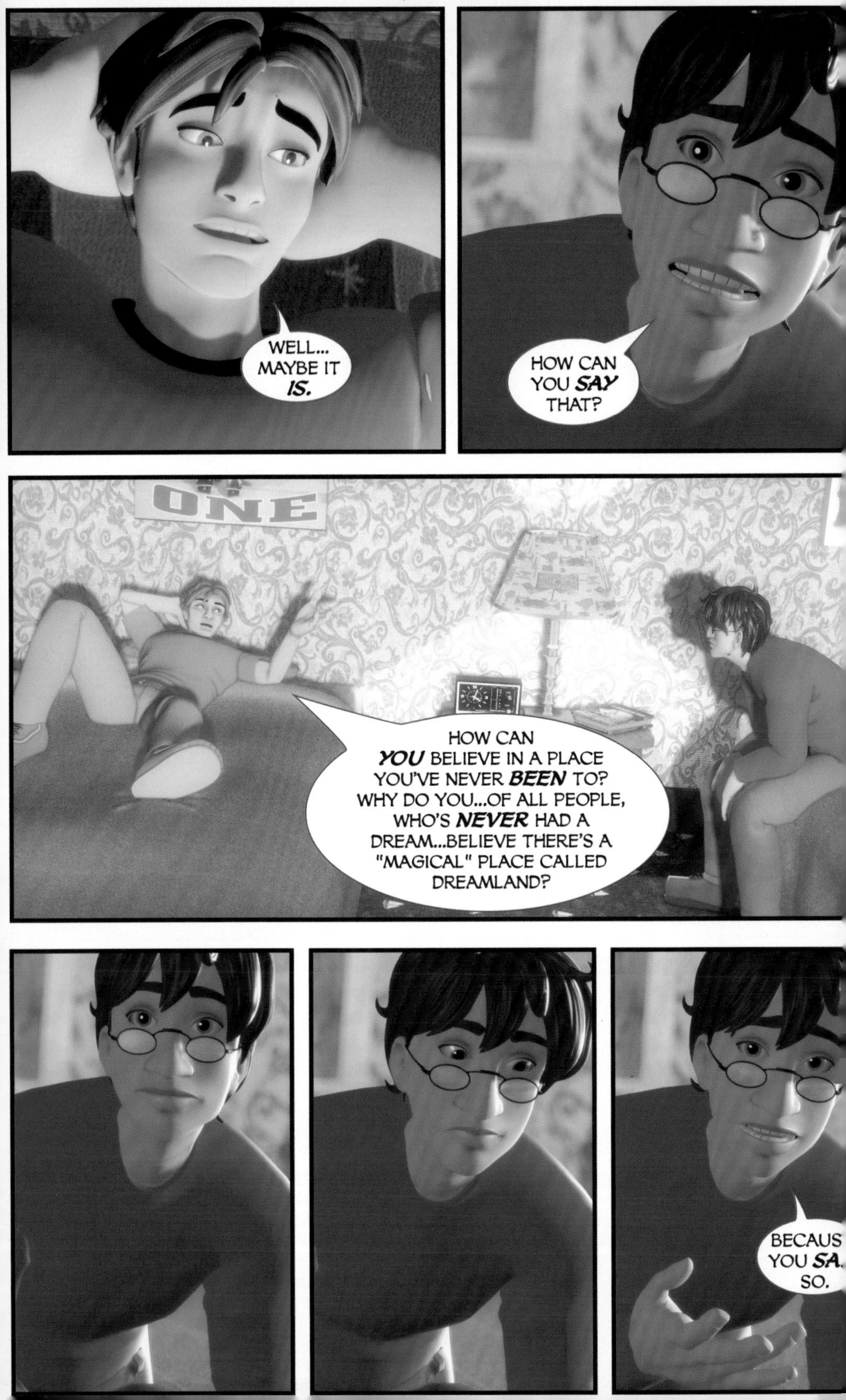
WELL... MAYBE IT *IS.*
HOW CAN YOU ***SAY*** THAT?
ONE
HOW CAN ***YOU*** BELIEVE IN A PLACE YOU'VE NEVER ***BEEN*** TO? WHY DO YOU...OF ALL PEOPLE, WHO'S ***NEVER*** HAD A DREAM...BELIEVE THERE'S A "MAGICAL" PLACE CALLED DREAMLAND?
BECAUS YOU ***SA*** SO.

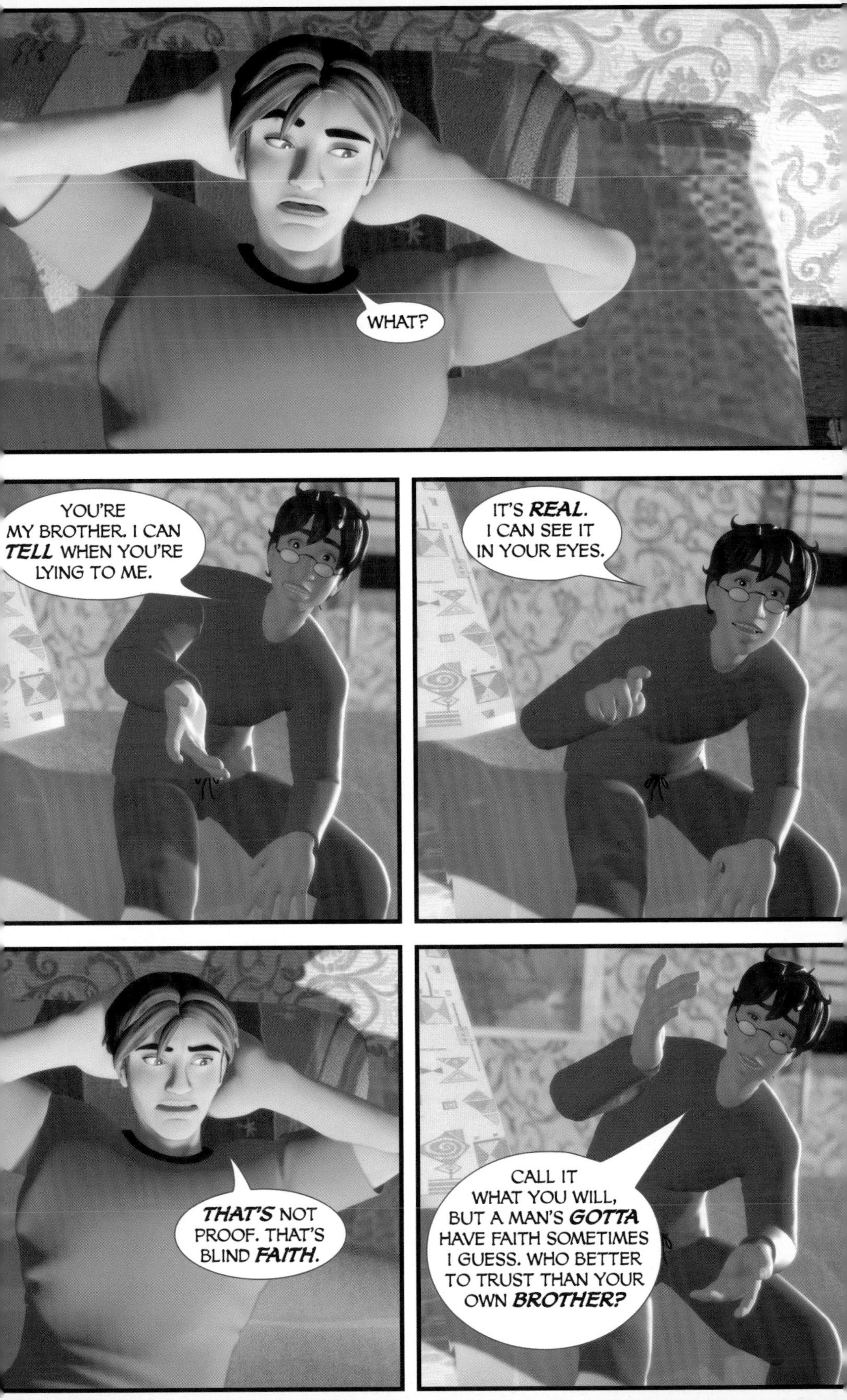
WHAT?
YOU'RE MY BROTHER. I CAN TELL WHEN YOU'RE LYING TO ME.
IT'S REAL. I CAN SEE IT IN YOUR EYES.
THAT'S NOT PROOF. THAT'S BLIND FAITH.
CALL IT WHAT YOU WILL, BUT A MAN'S GOTTA HAVE FAITH SOMETIMES I GUESS. WHO BETTER TO TRUST THAN YOUR OWN BROTHER?

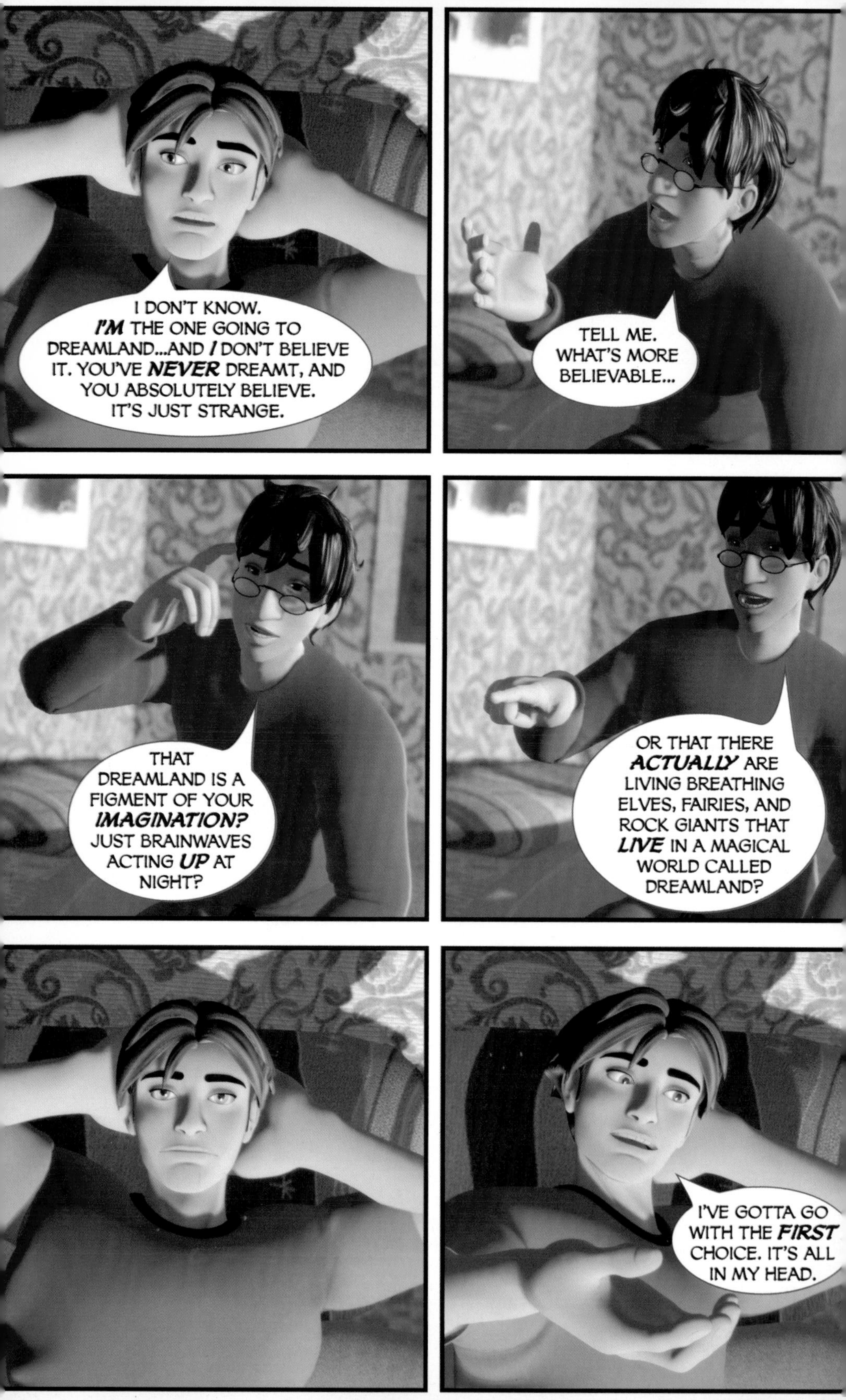
I DON'T KNOW. I'M THE ONE GOING TO DREAMLAND...AND I DON'T BELIEVE IT. YOU'VE NEVER DREAMT, AND YOU ABSOLUTELY BELIEVE. IT'S JUST STRANGE.
TELL ME. WHAT'S MORE BELIEVABLE...
THAT DREAMLAND IS A FIGMENT OF YOUR IMAGINATION? JUST BRAINWAVES ACTING UP AT NIGHT?
OR THAT THERE ACTUALLY ARE LIVING BREATHING ELVES, FAIRIES, AND ROCK GIANTS THAT LIVE IN A MAGICAL WORLD CALLED DREAMLAND?
I'VE GOTTA GO WITH THE FIRST CHOICE. IT'S ALL IN MY HEAD.

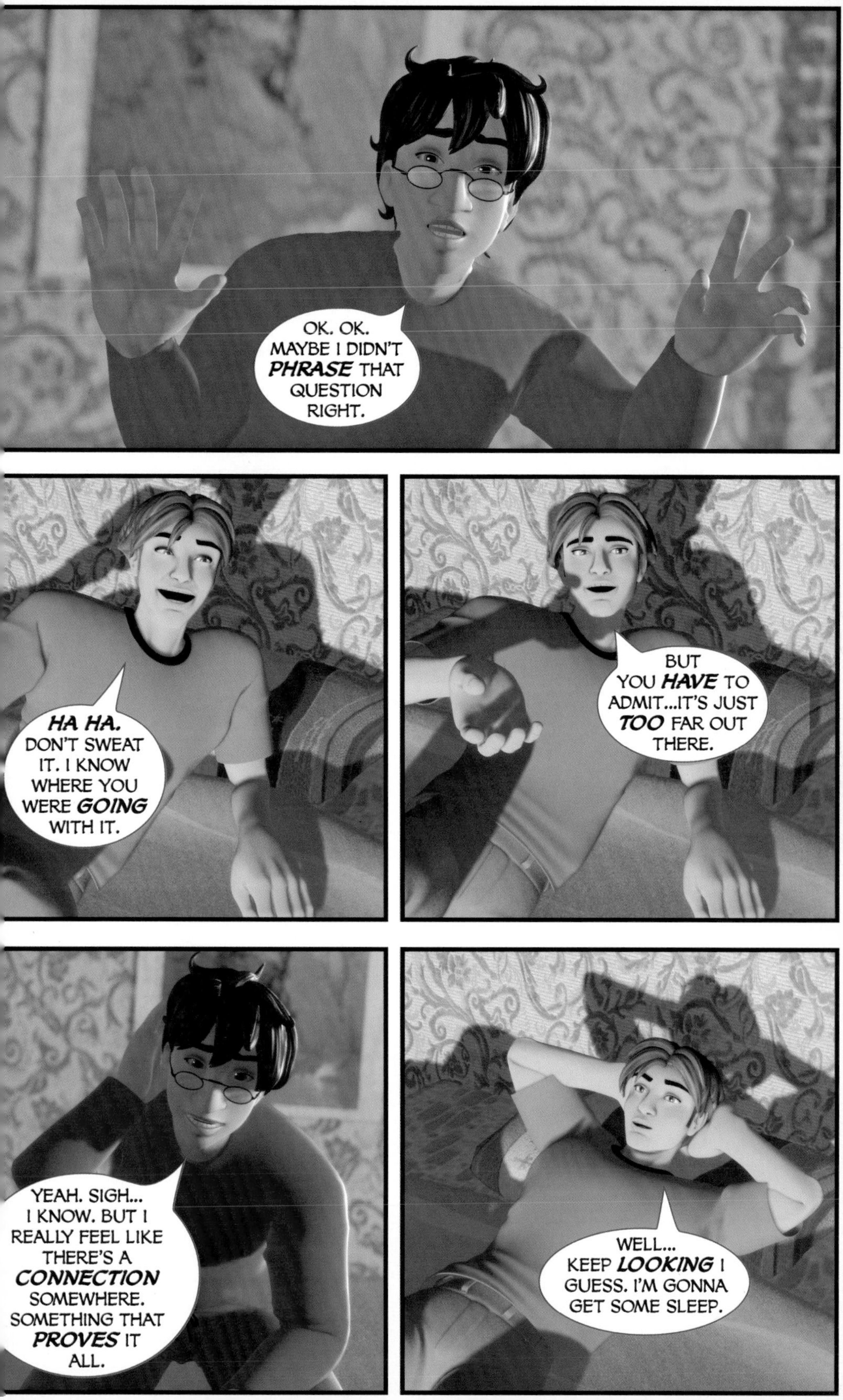

OK. OK. MAYBE I DIDN'T *PHRASE* THAT QUESTION RIGHT.
HA HA. DON'T SWEAT IT. I KNOW WHERE YOU WERE *GOING* WITH IT.
BUT YOU *HAVE* TO ADMIT...IT'S JUST *TOO* FAR OUT THERE.
YEAH. SIGH... I KNOW. BUT I REALLY FEEL LIKE THERE'S A *CONNECTION* SOMEWHERE. SOMETHING THAT *PROVES* IT ALL.
WELL... KEEP *LOOKING* I GUESS. I'M GONNA GET SOME SLEEP.

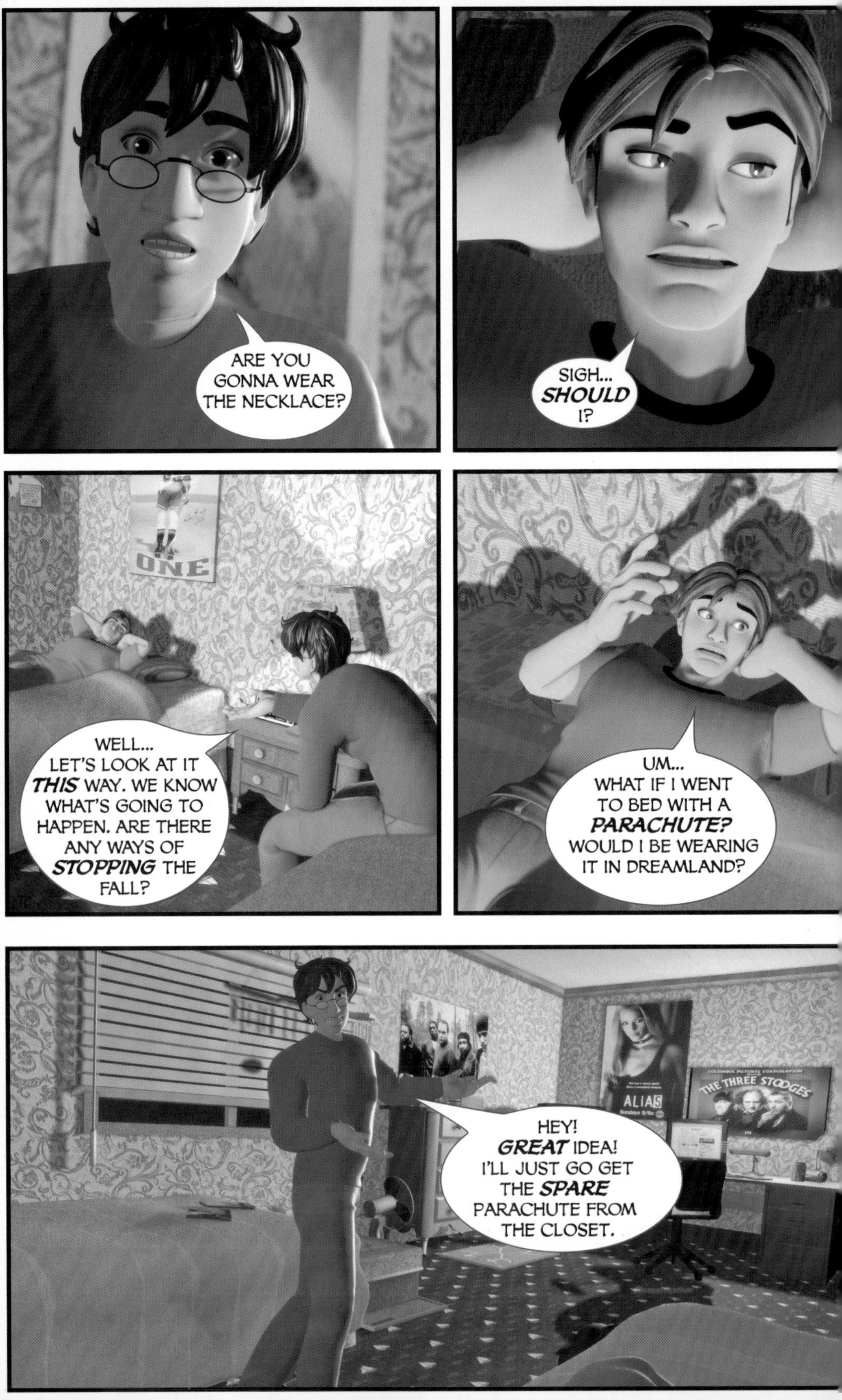
ARE YOU GONNA WEAR THE NECKLACE?
SIGH... *SHOULD* I?
ONE
WELL... LET'S LOOK AT IT *THIS* WAY. WE KNOW WHAT'S GOING TO HAPPEN. ARE THERE ANY WAYS OF *STOPPING* THE FALL?
UM... WHAT IF I WENT TO BED WITH A *PARACHUTE?* WOULD I BE WEARING IT IN DREAMLAND?
ALIAS
THE THREE STOOGES
HEY! *GREAT* IDEA! I'LL JUST GO GET THE *SPARE* PARACHUTE FROM THE CLOSET.

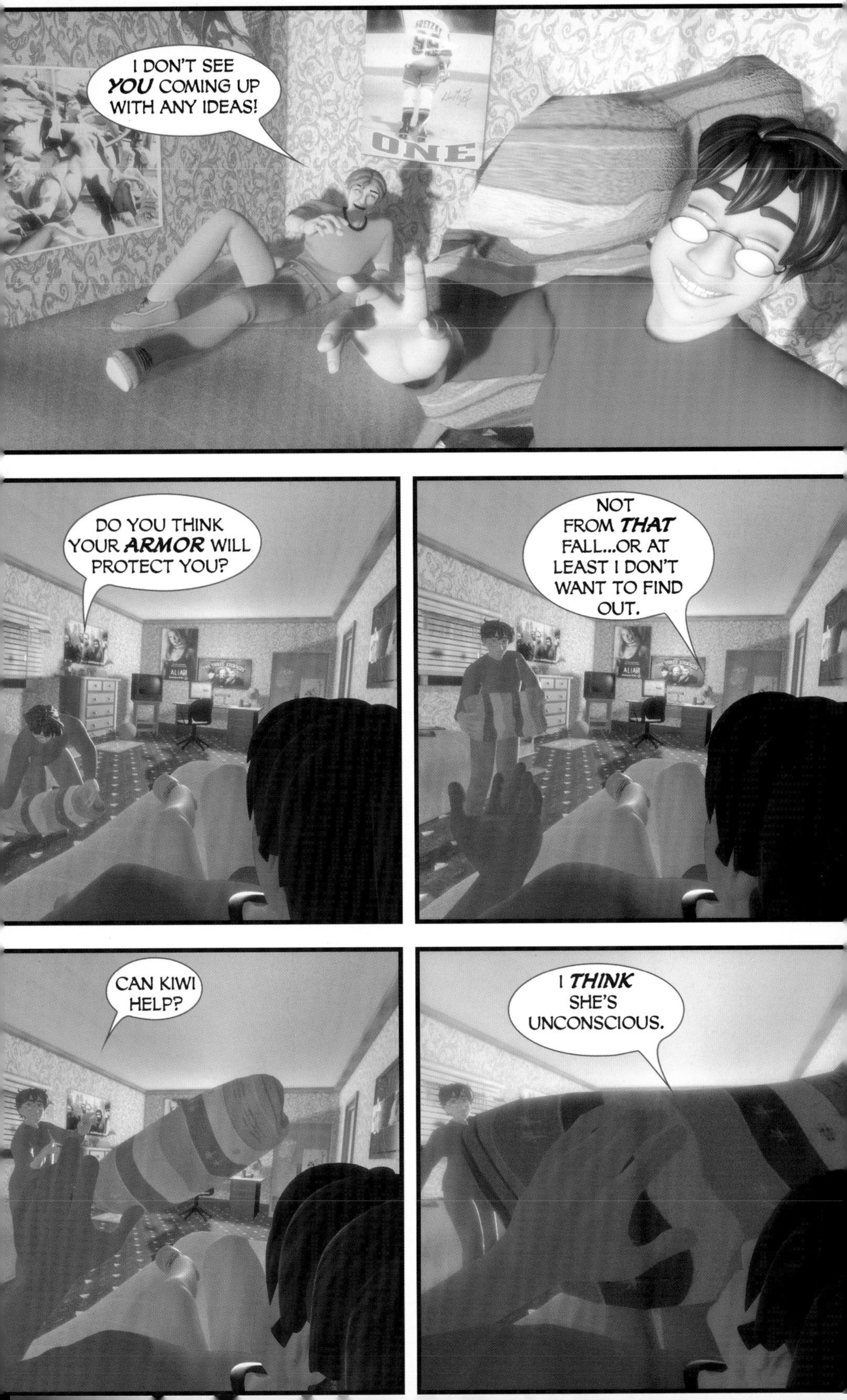

I DON'T SEE *YOU* COMING UP WITH ANY IDEAS!
DO YOU THINK YOUR *ARMOR* WILL PROTECT YOU?
NOT FROM *THAT* FALL...OR AT LEAST I DON'T WANT TO FIND OUT.
CAN KIWI HELP?
I *THINK* SHE'S UNCONSCIOUS.

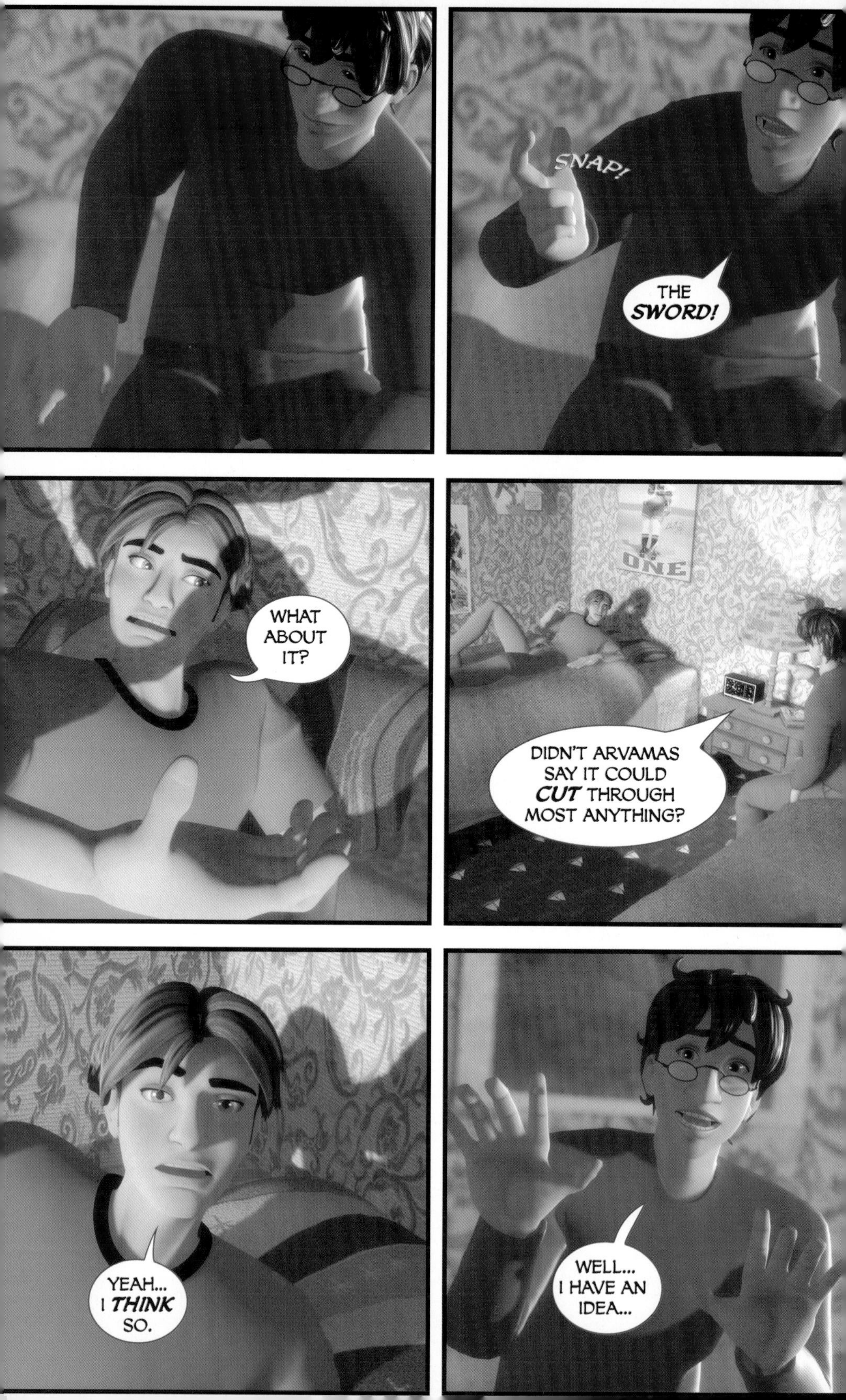
SNAP!
THE SWORD!
WHAT ABOUT IT?
DIDN'T ARVAMAS SAY IT COULD CUT THROUGH MOST ANYTHING?
YEAH... I THINK SO.
WELL... I HAVE AN IDEA...

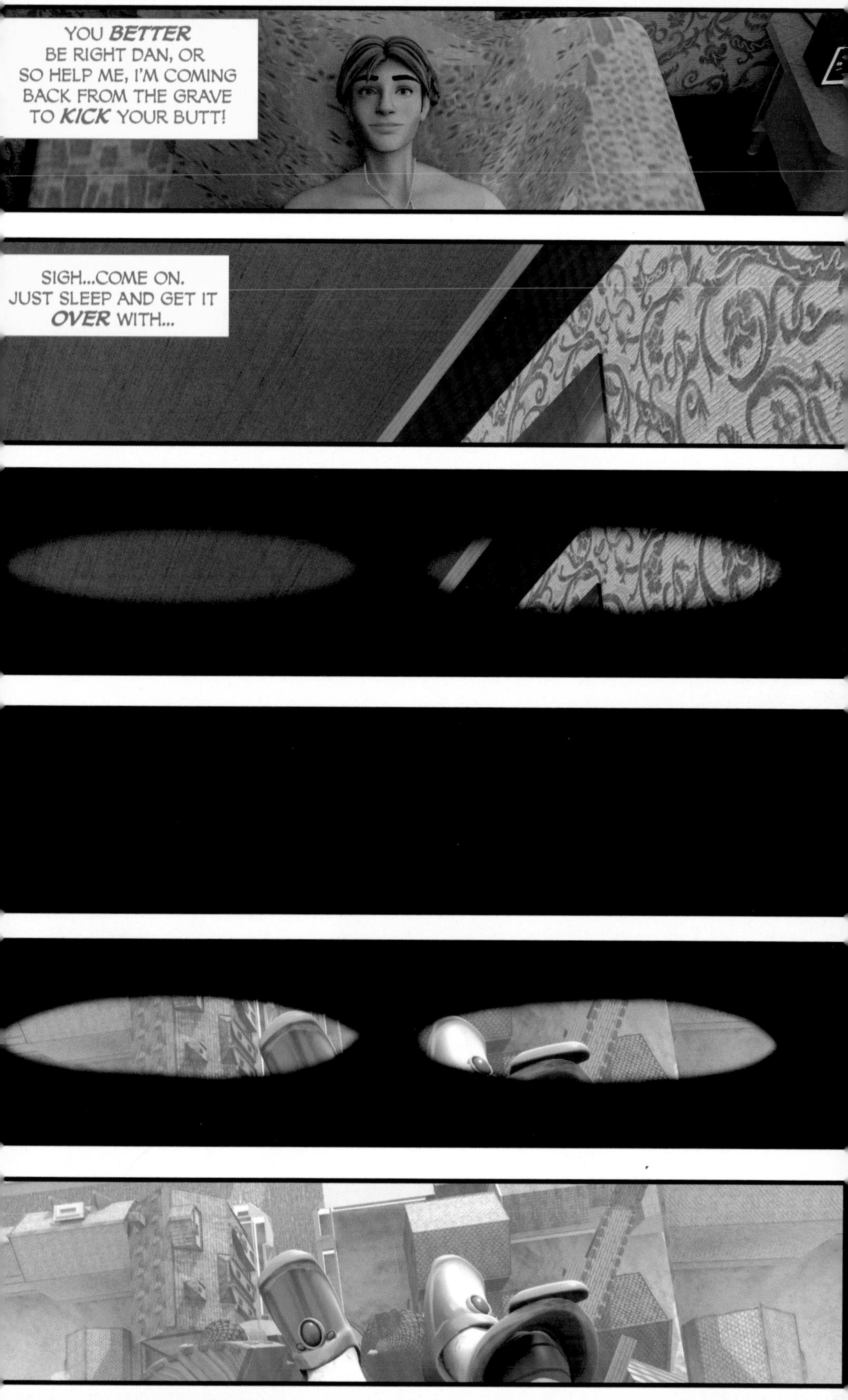
YOU **BETTER** BE RIGHT DAN, OR SO HELP ME, I'M COMING BACK FROM THE GRAVE TO **KICK** YOUR BUTT!
SIGH...COME ON. JUST SLEEP AND GET IT **OVER** WITH...

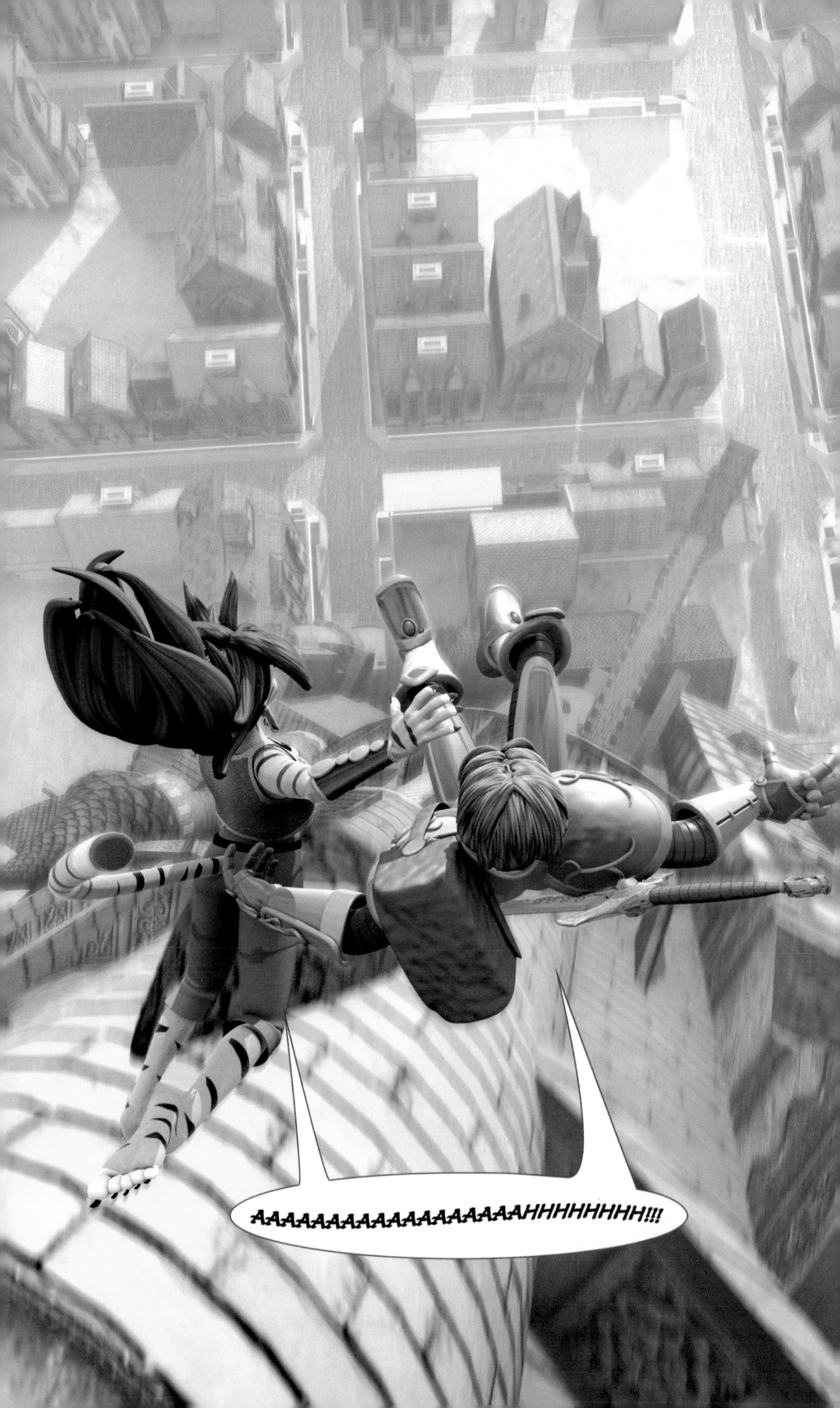
AAAAAAAAAAAAAAAAAAAAAHHHHHHHH!!!

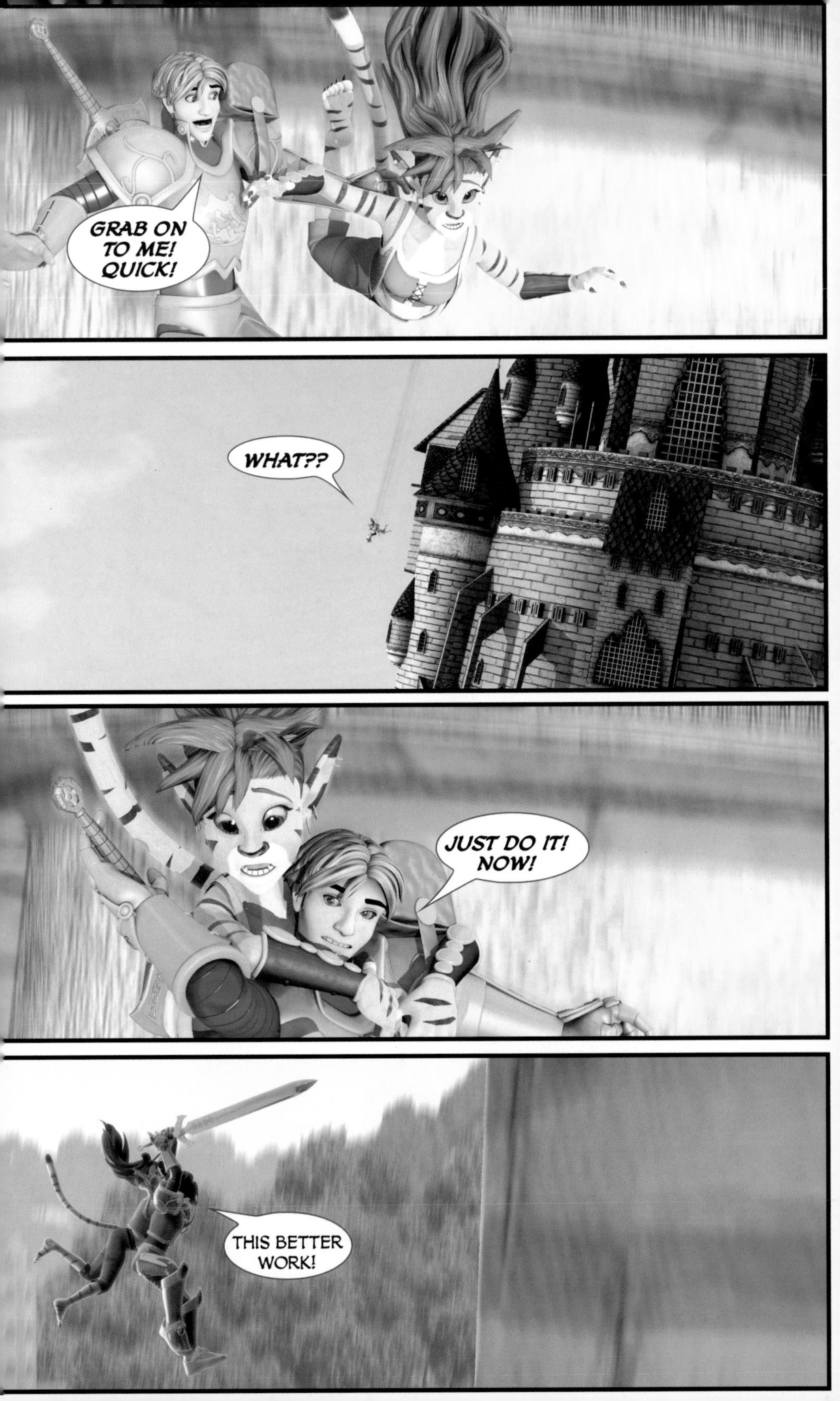
GRAB ON TO ME! QUICK!
WHAT??
JUST DO IT! NOW!
THIS BETTER WORK!

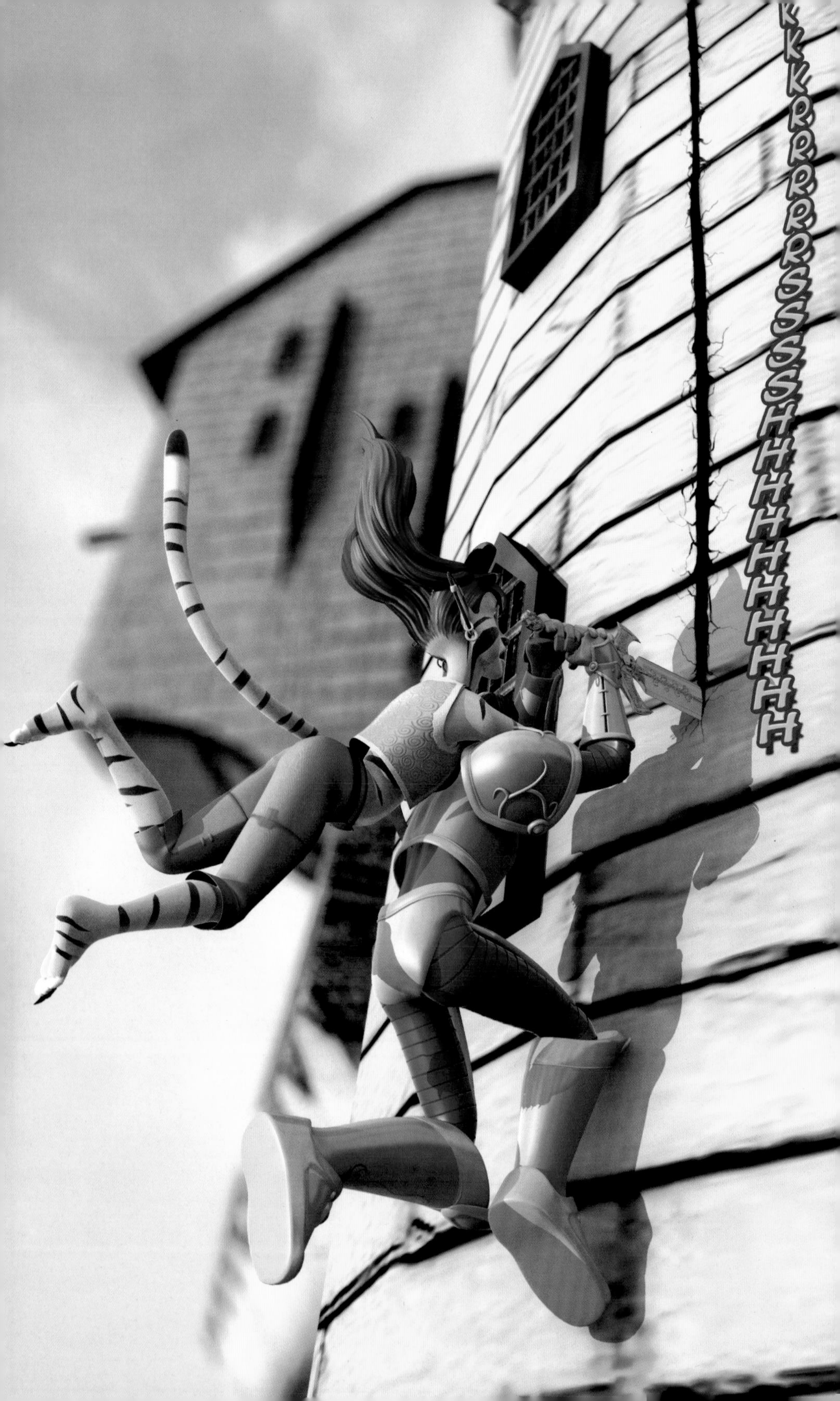
KKKRRRRRSSSSHHHHHHHHHHH

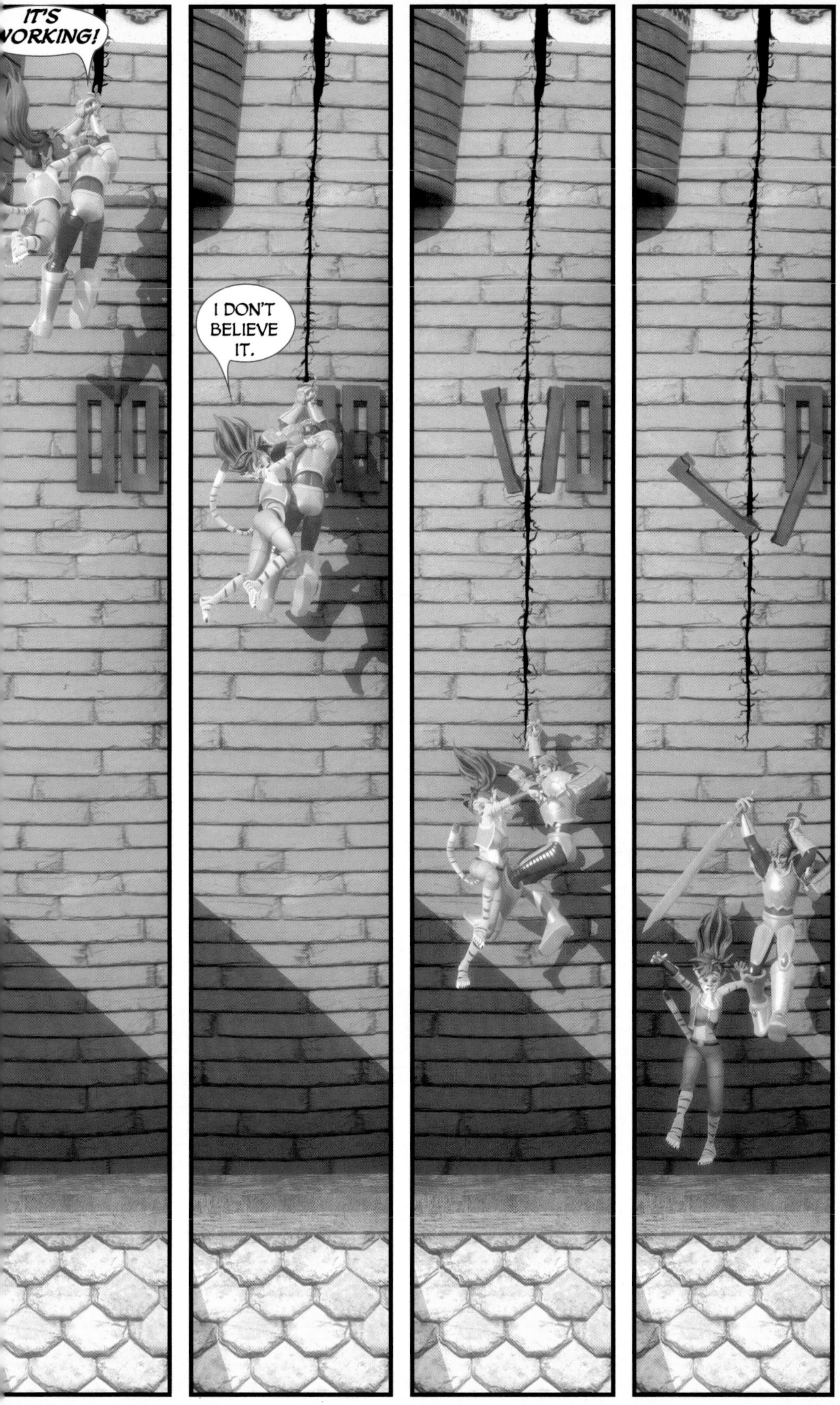
IT'S WORKING!
I DON'T BELIEVE IT.

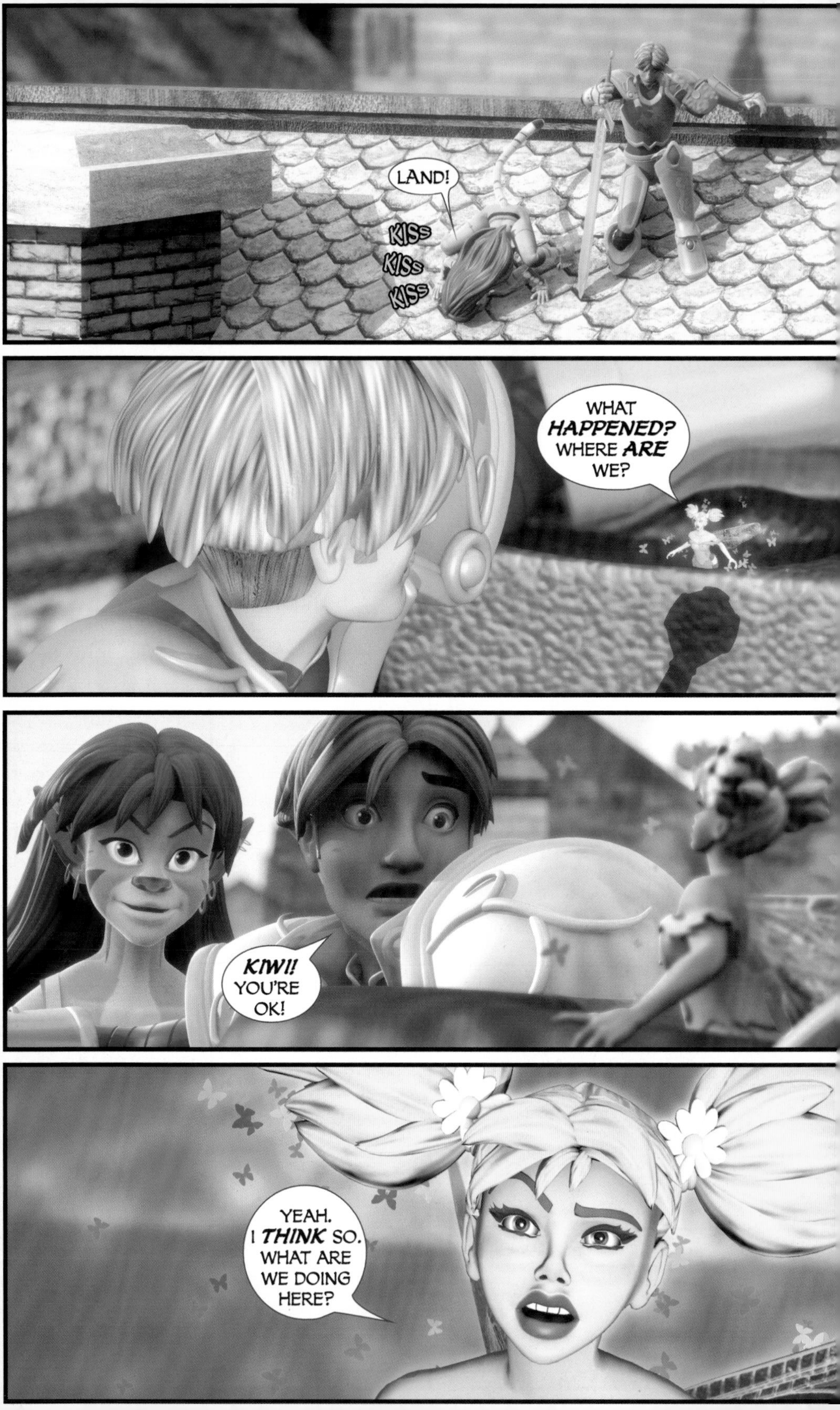
LAND!
KISS
KISS
KISS
WHAT *HAPPENED?* WHERE *ARE* WE?
KIWI! YOU'RE OK!
YEAH. I *THINK* SO. WHAT ARE WE DOING HERE?

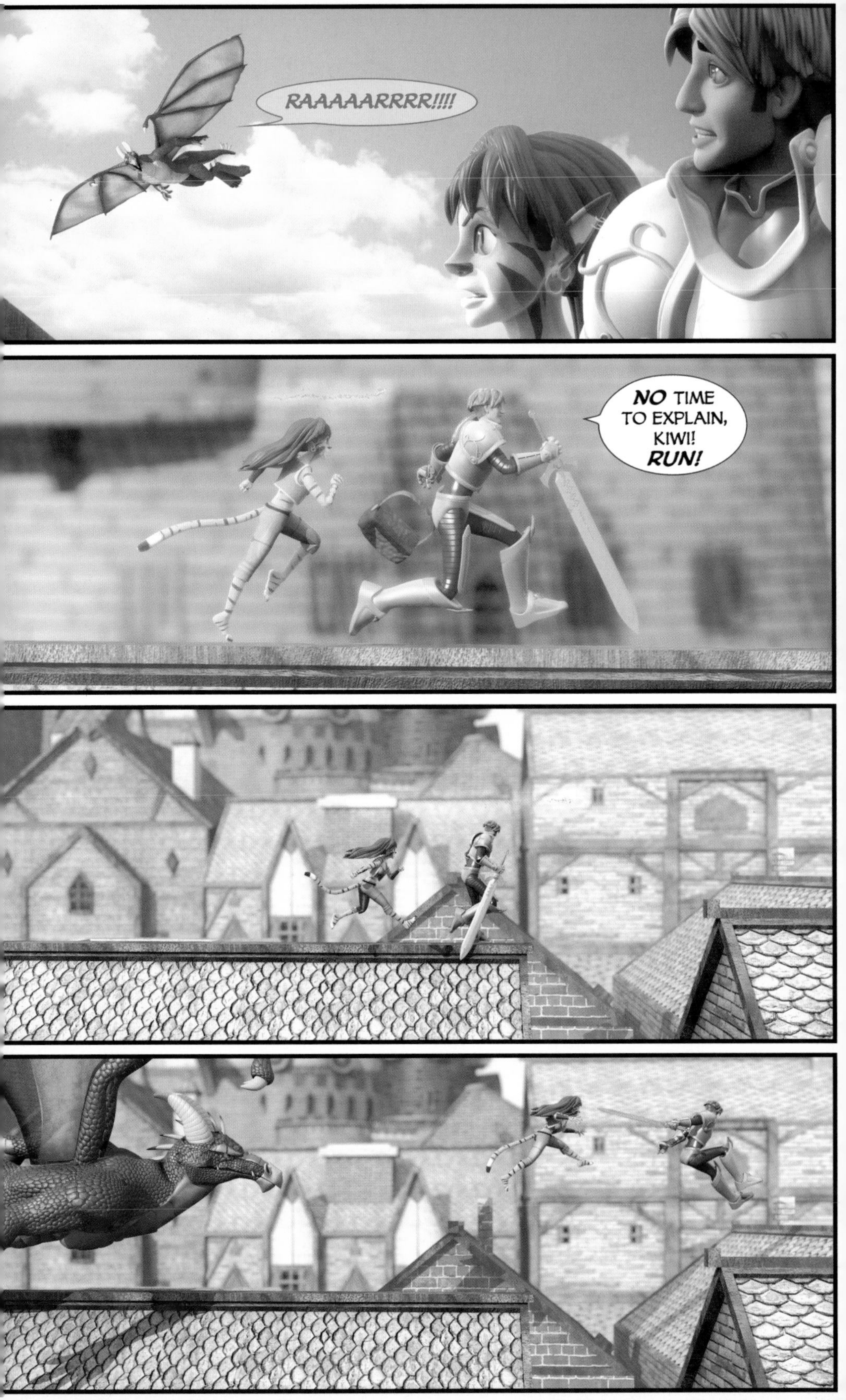
RAAAAARRRR!!!!
NO TIME TO EXPLAIN, KIWI! RUN!

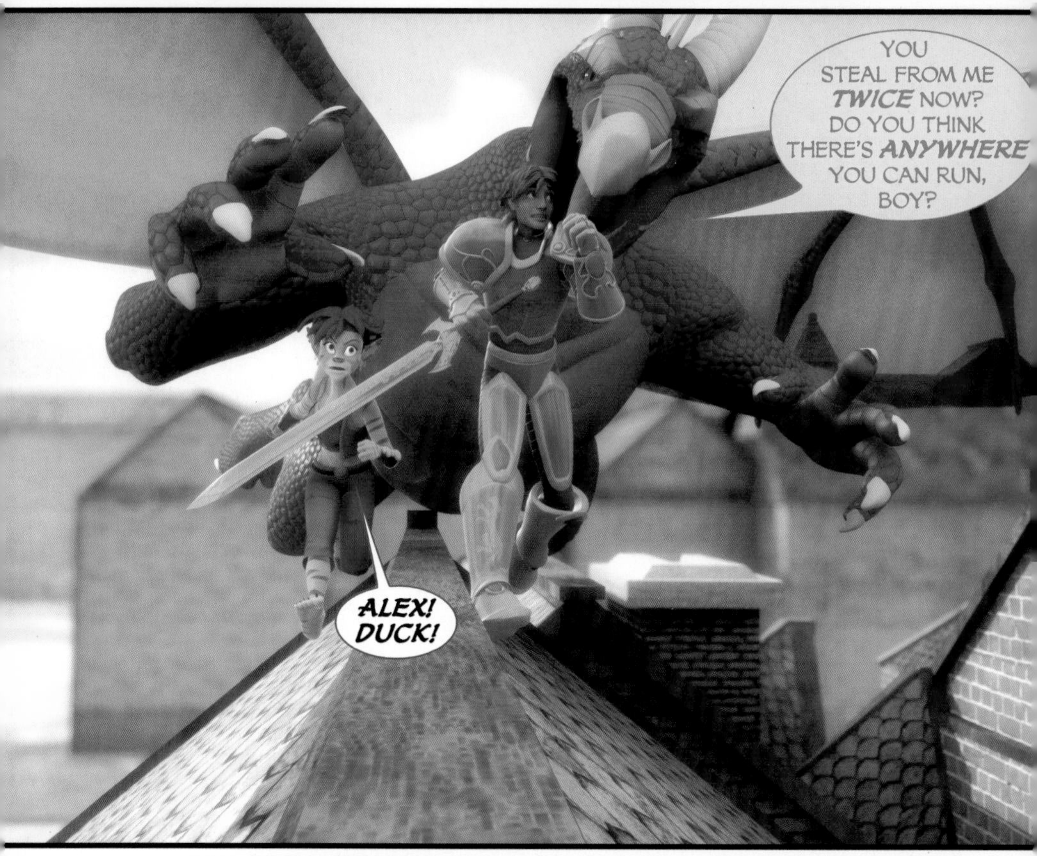
YOU STEAL FROM ME TWICE NOW? DO YOU THINK THERE'S ANYWHERE YOU CAN RUN, BOY?
ALEX! DUCK!

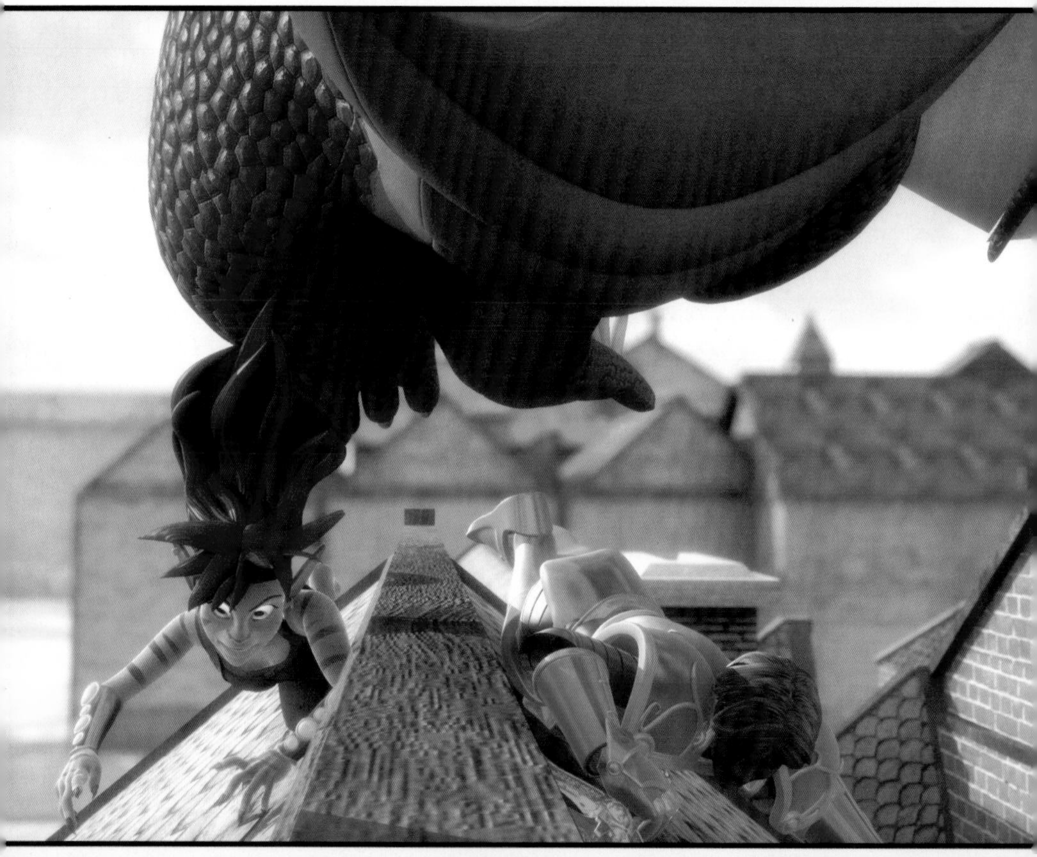

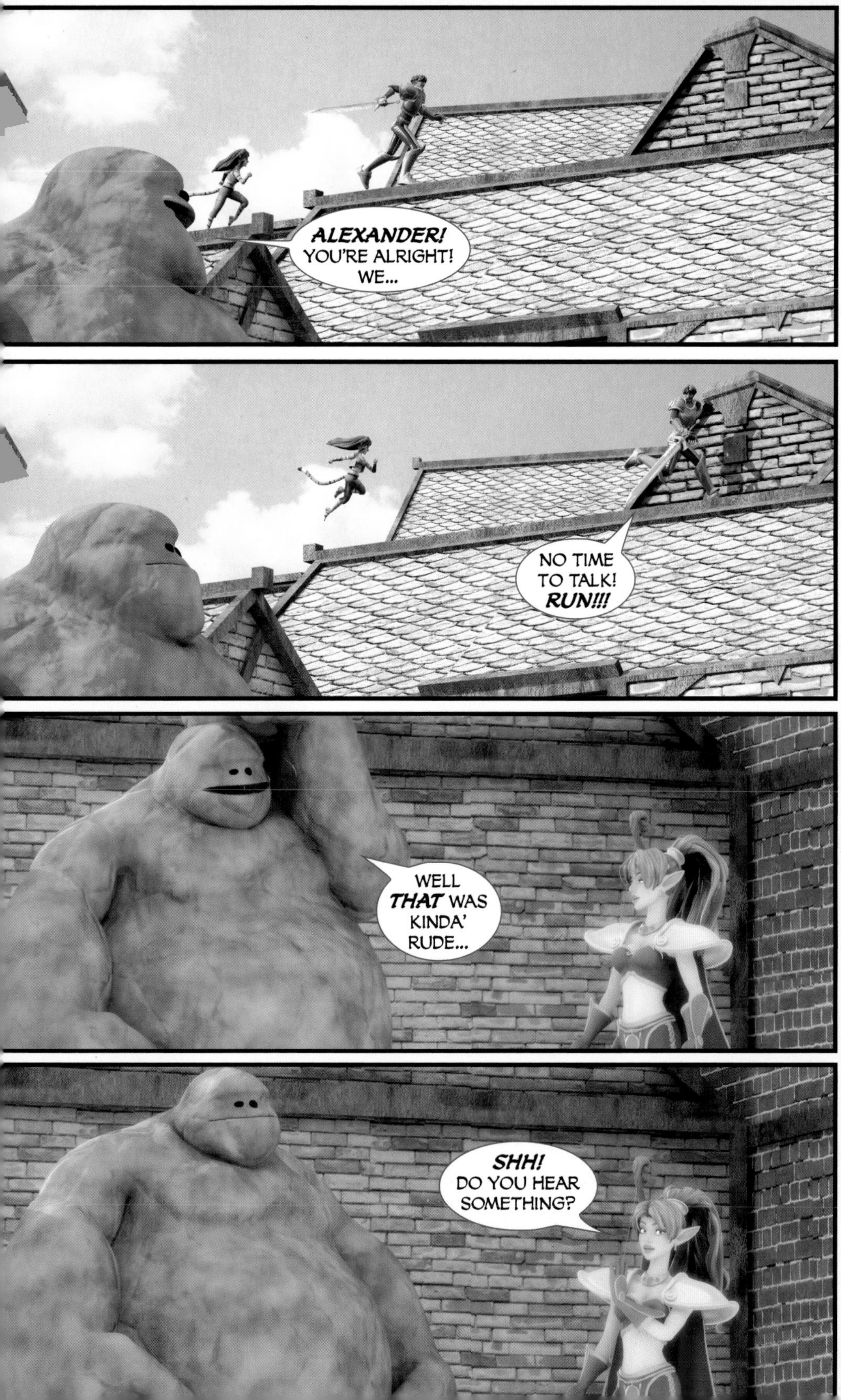
ALEXANDER! YOU'RE ALRIGHT! WE...
NO TIME TO TALK! RUN!!!
WELL THAT WAS KINDA' RUDE...
SHH! DO YOU HEAR SOMETHING?

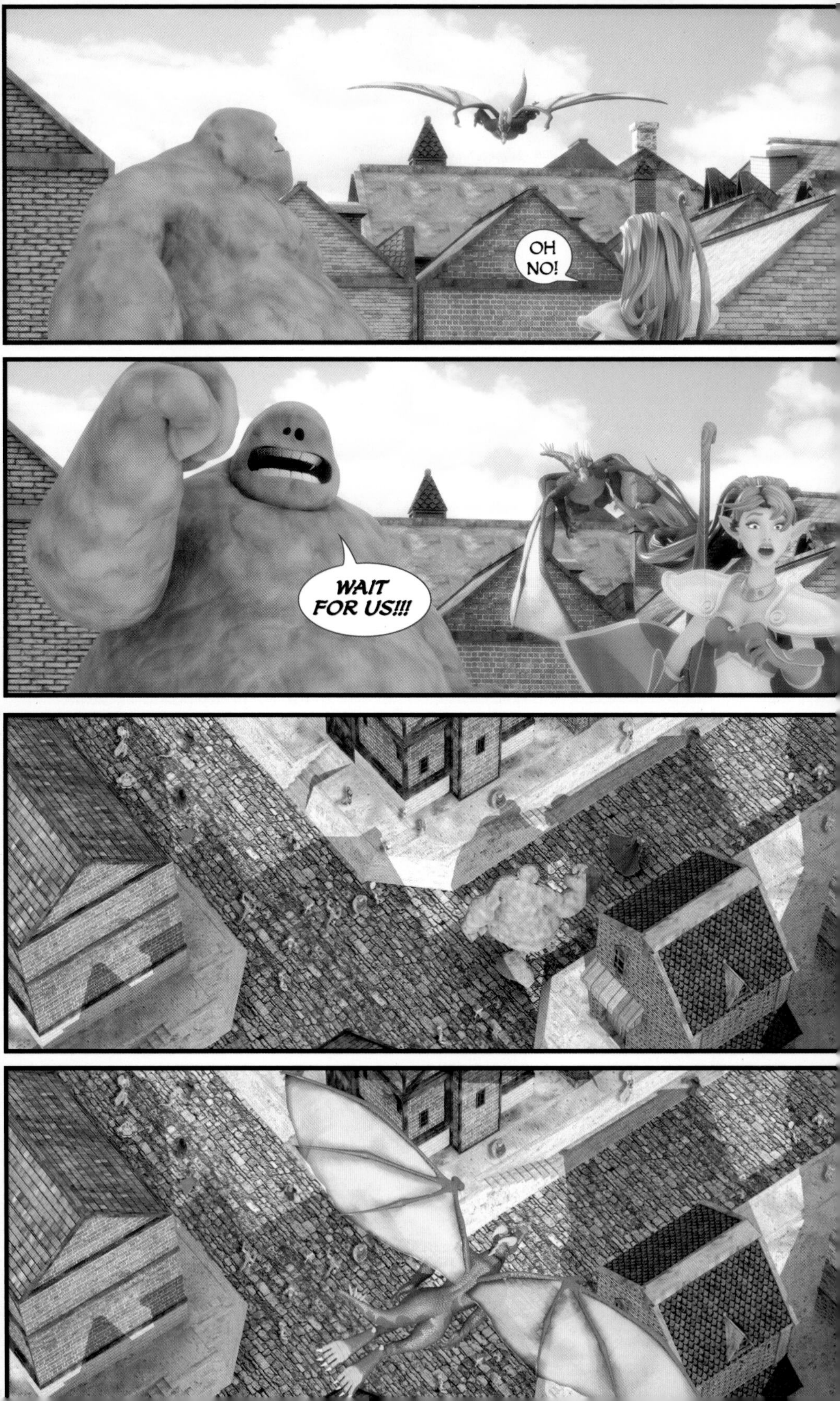
OH NO!
WAIT FOR US!!!

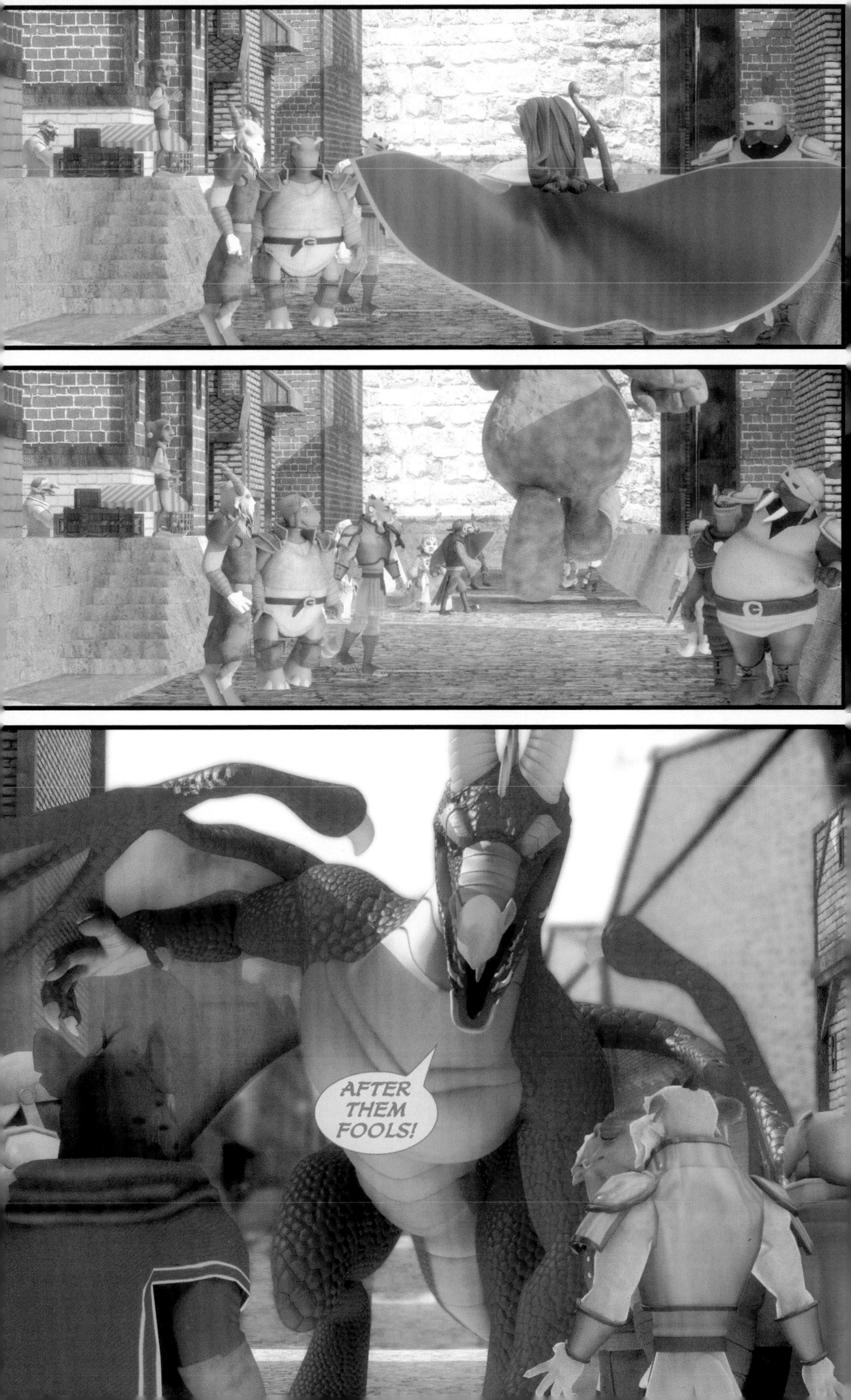
AFTER THEM FOOLS!

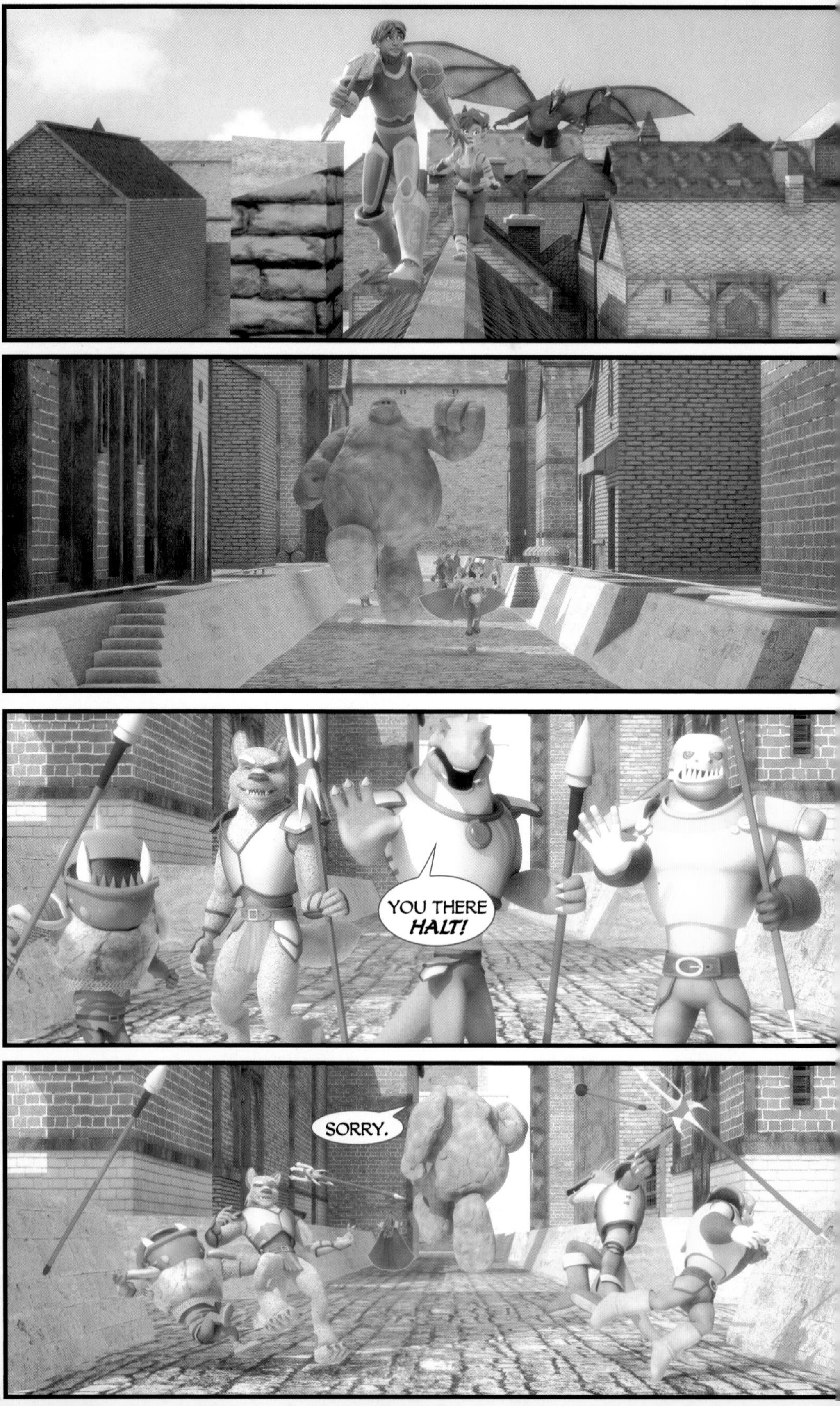
YOU THERE
HALT!
SORRY.

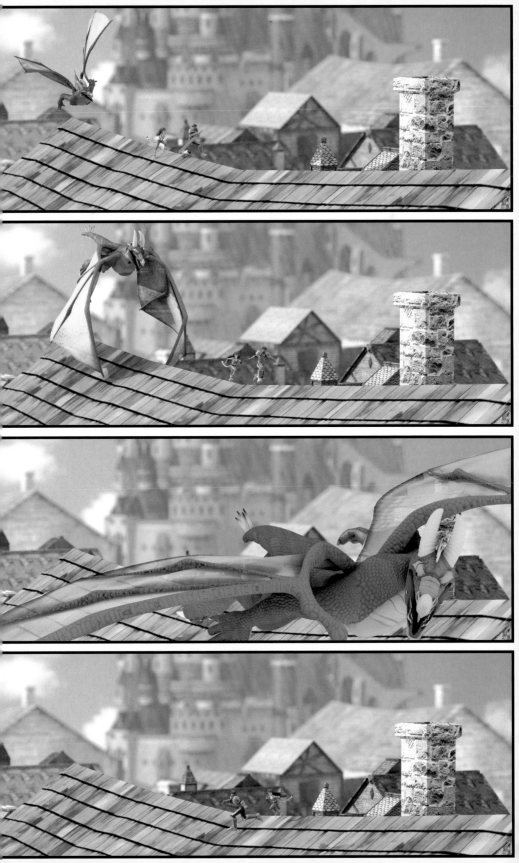

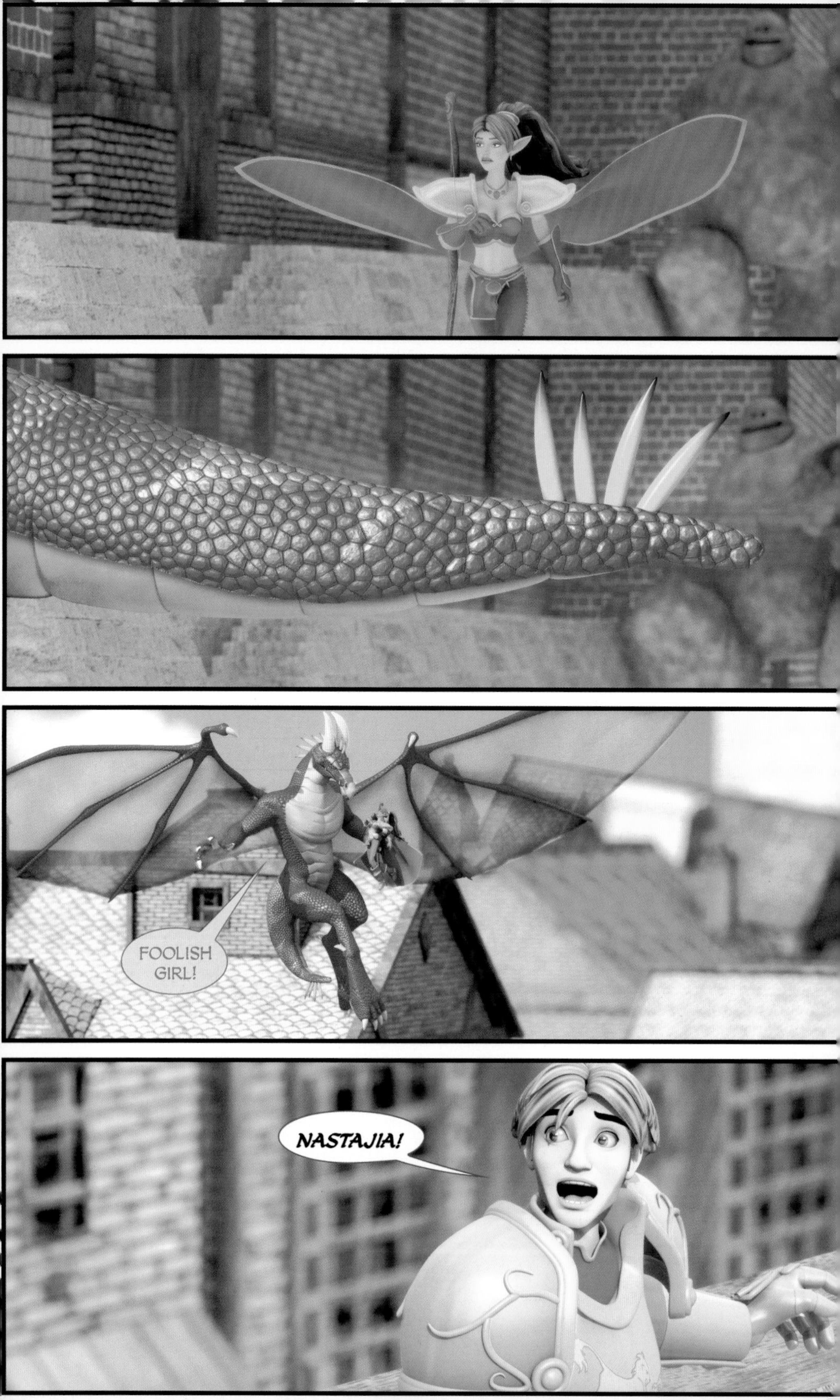
FOOLISH GIRL!
NASTAJIA!

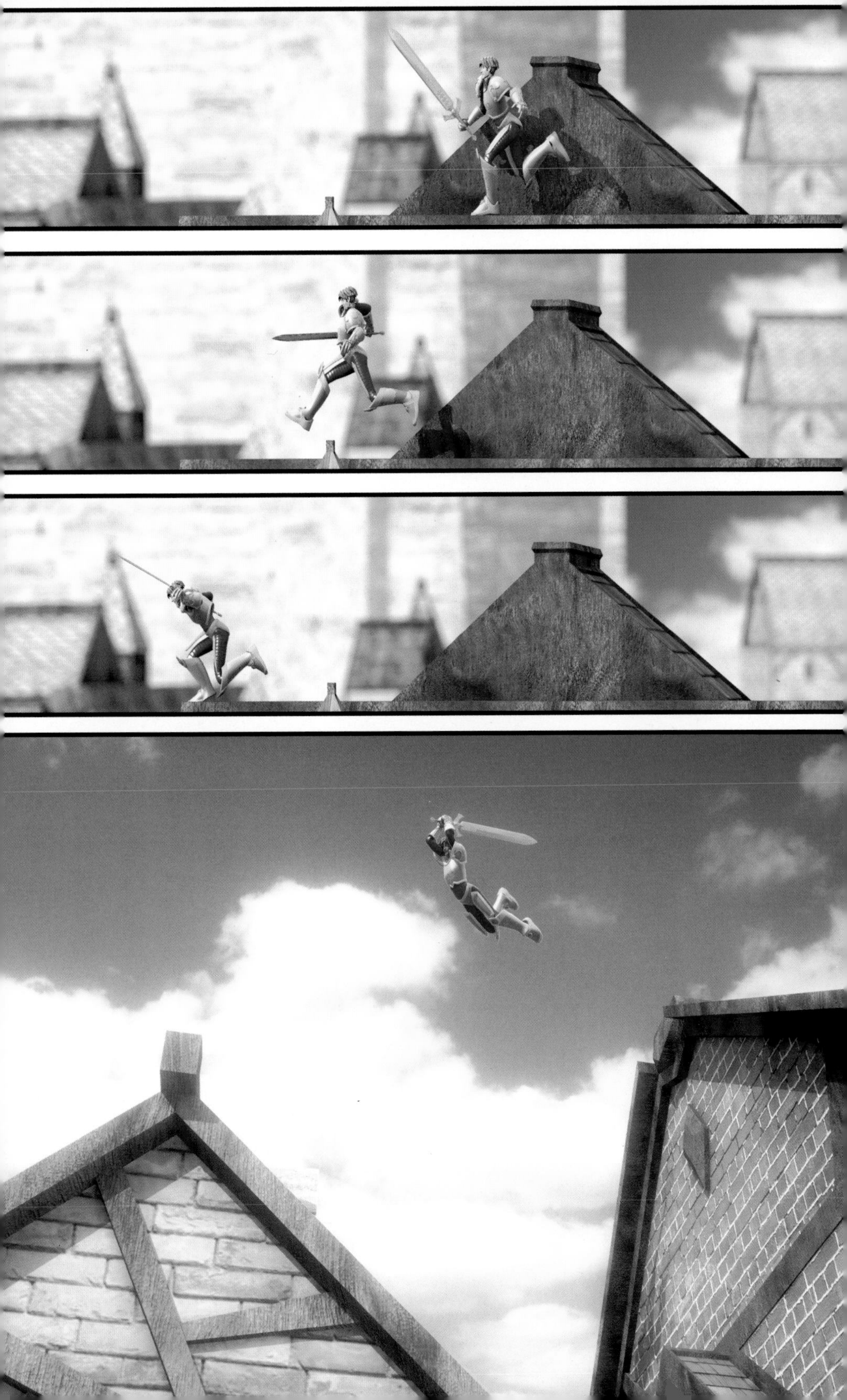

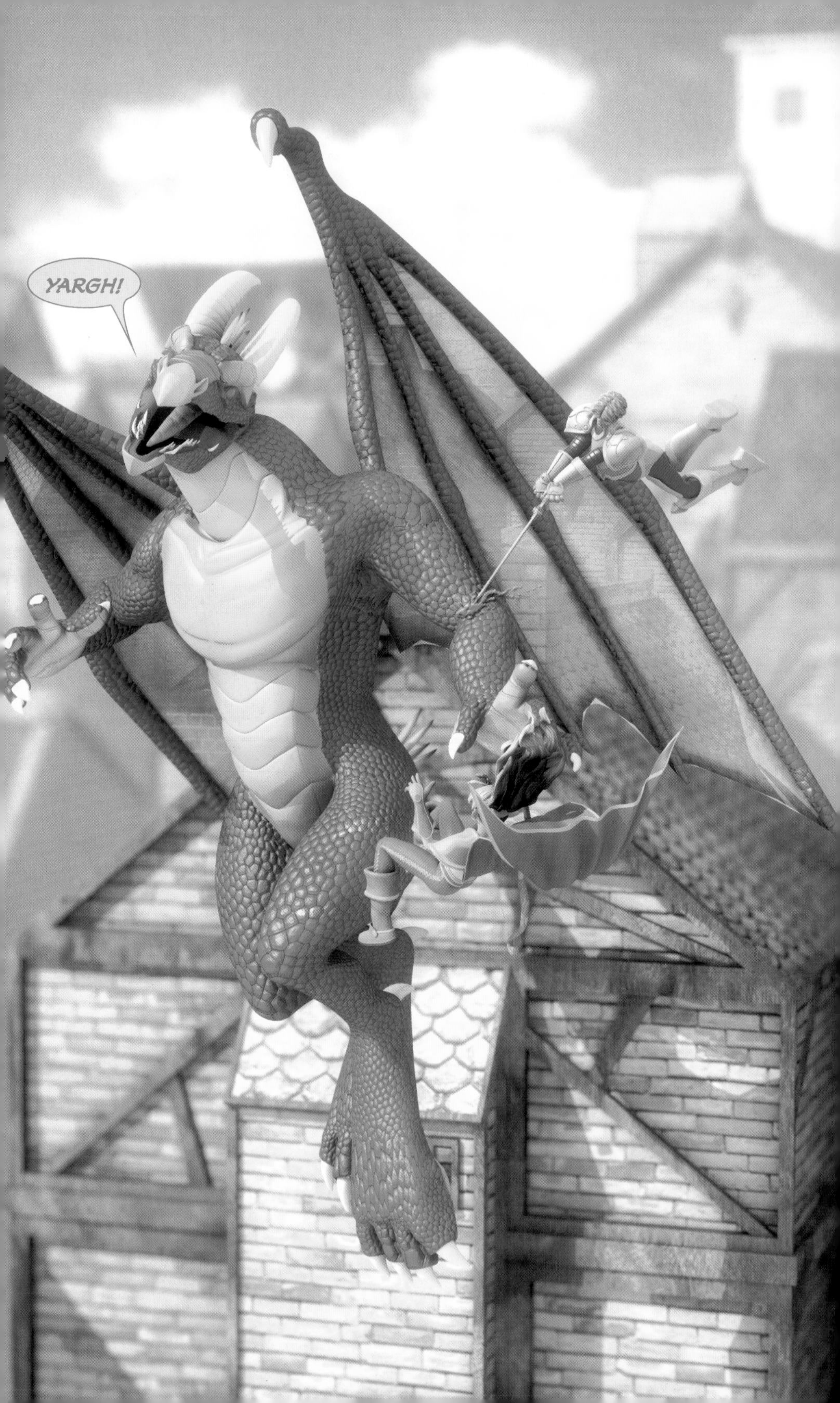
YARGH!

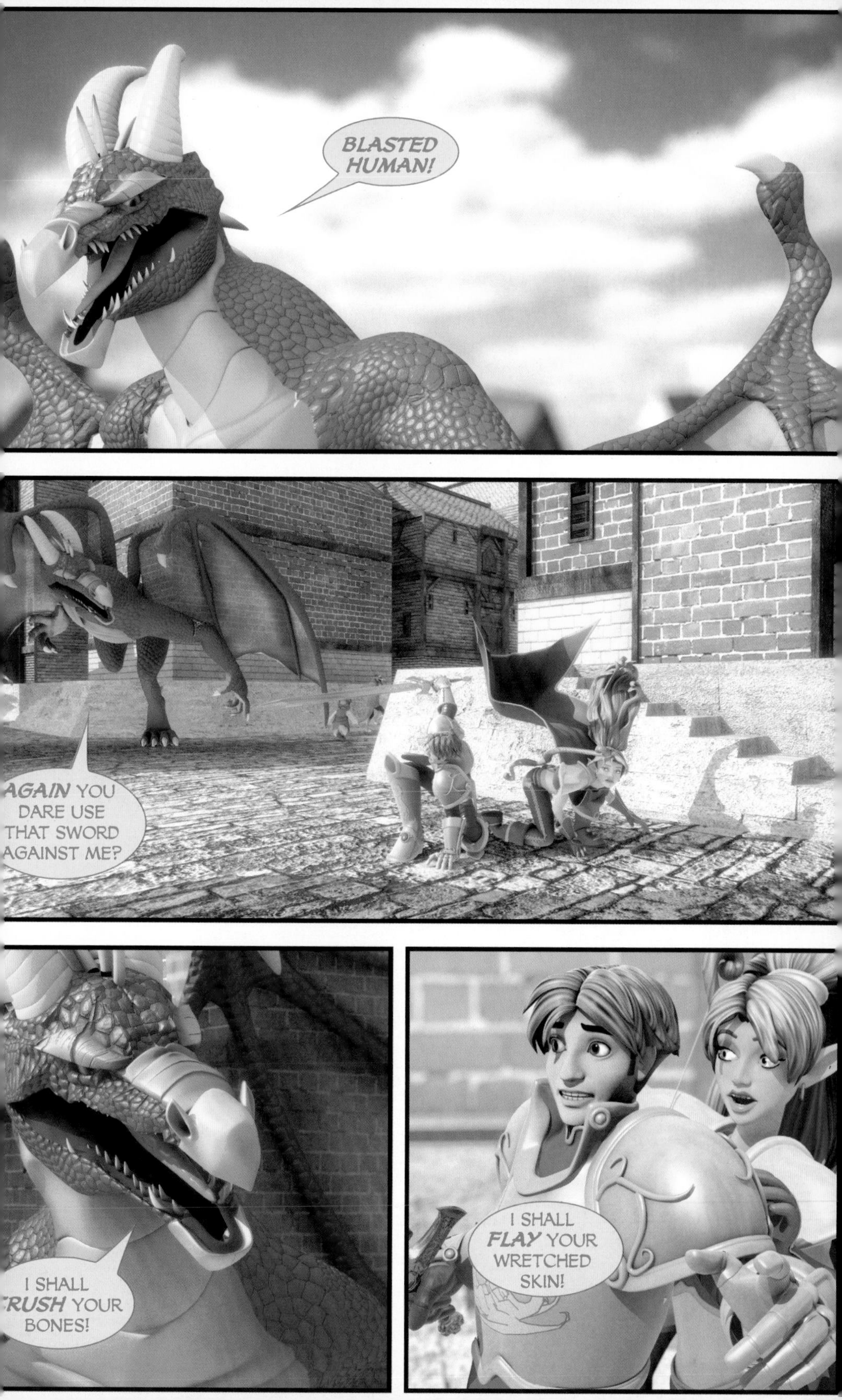
BLASTED HUMAN!
AGAIN YOU DARE USE THAT SWORD AGAINST ME?
I SHALL CRUSH YOUR BONES!
I SHALL FLAY YOUR WRETCHED SKIN!

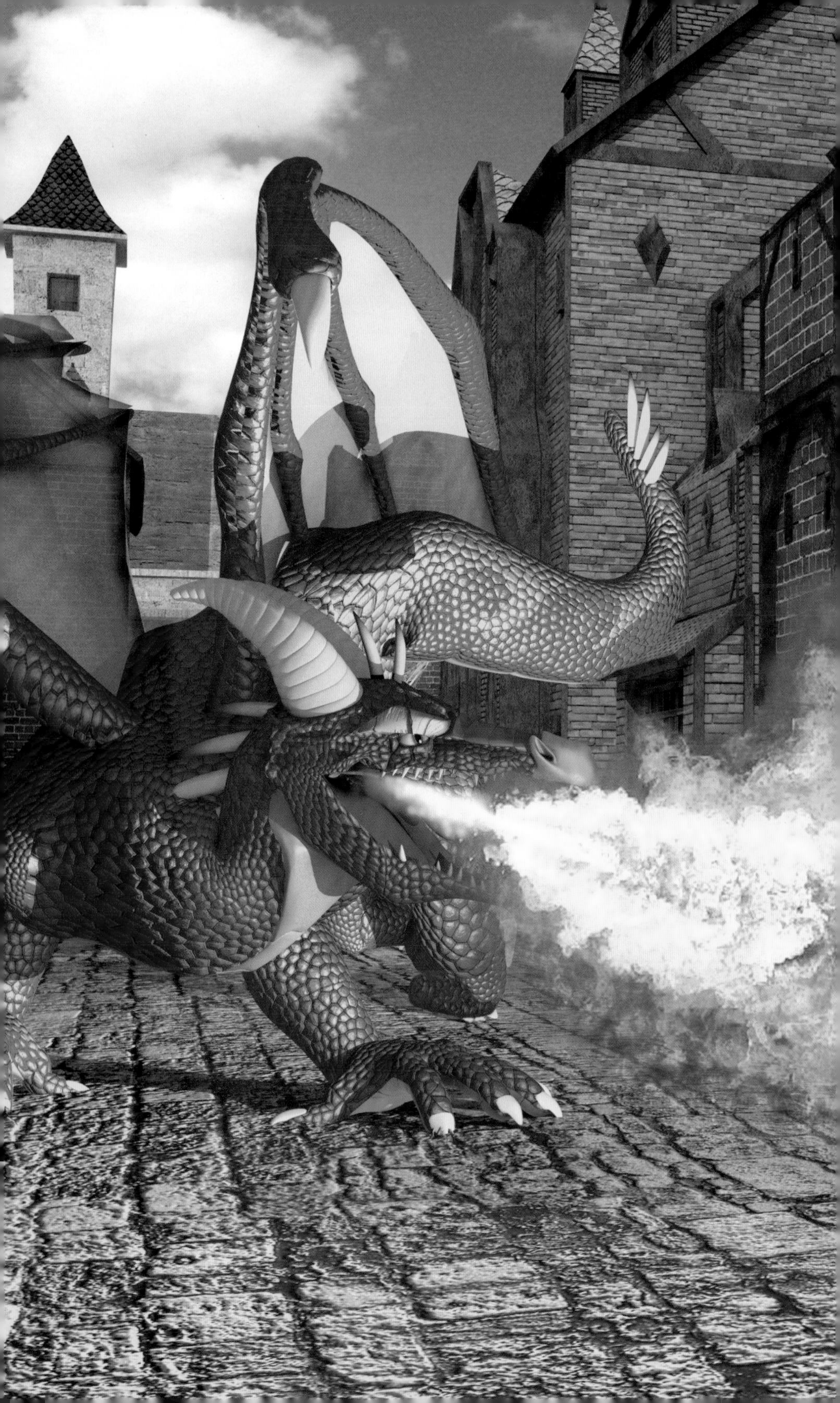

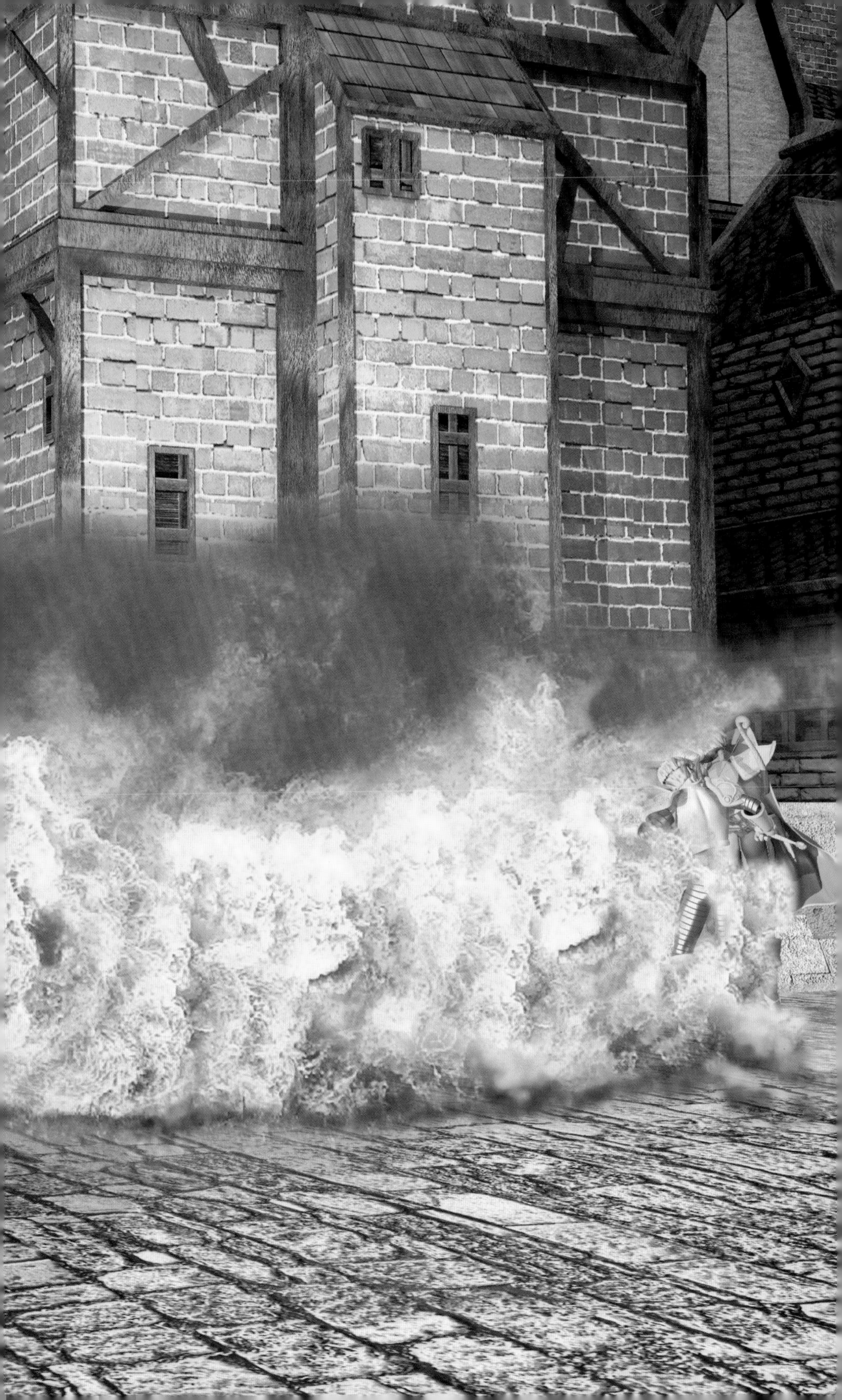

HOW... HOW DID YOU...??

I DON'T KNOW!

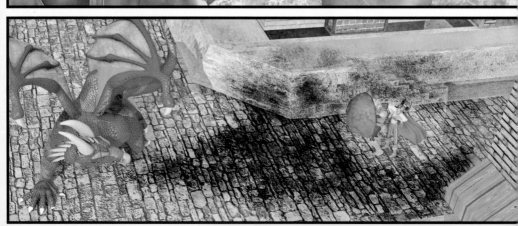

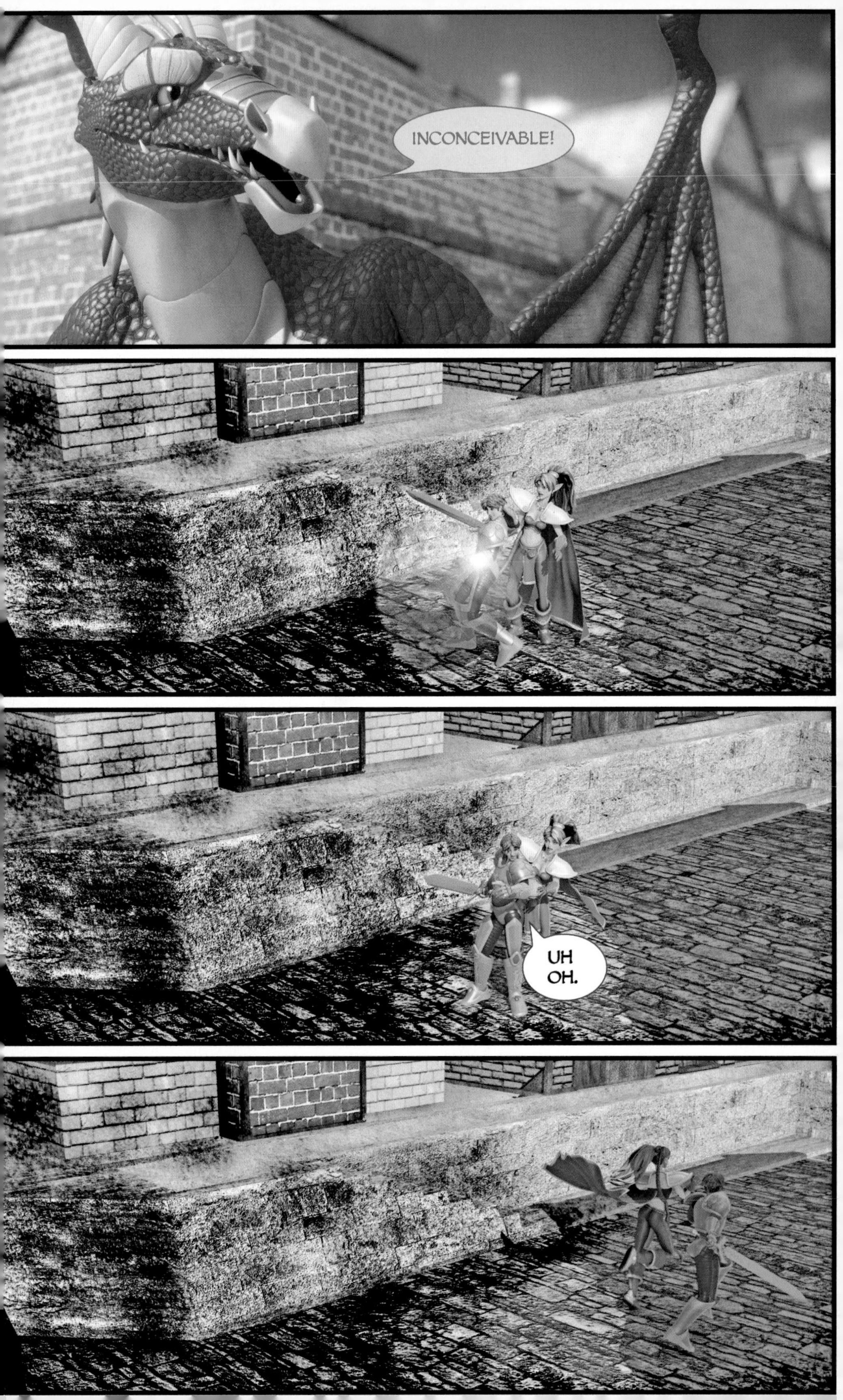
INCONCEIVABLE!
UH OH.

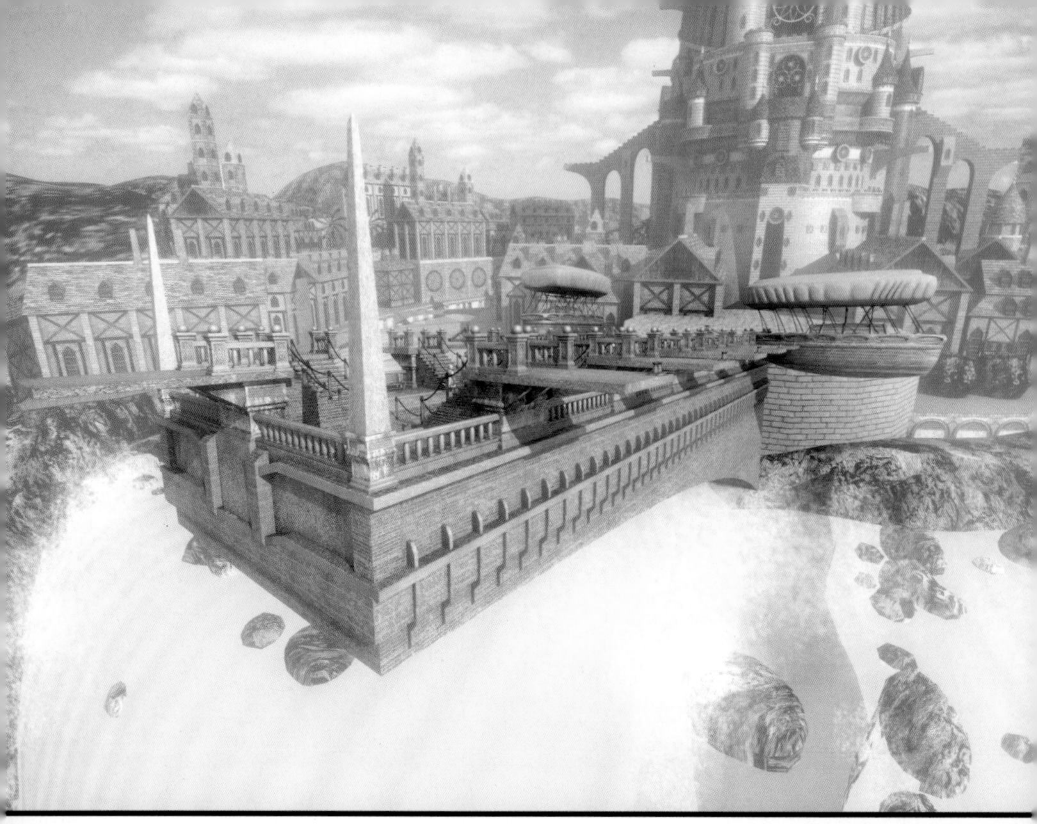

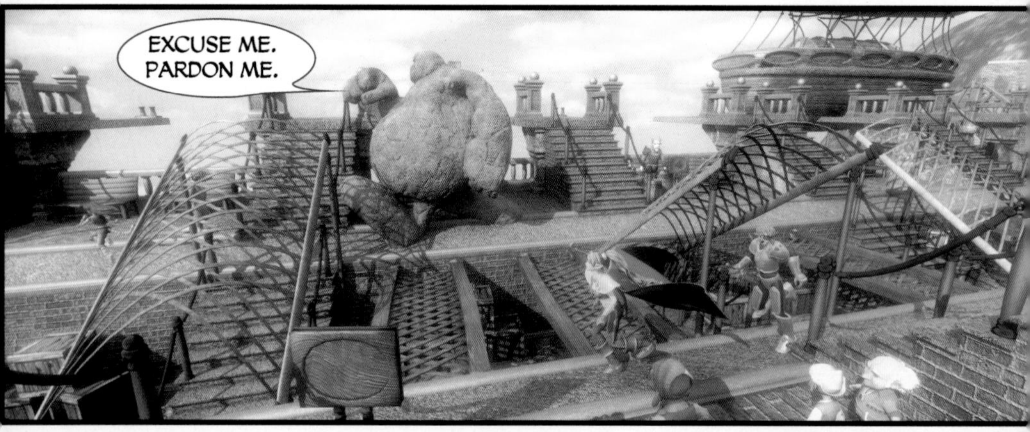
EXCUSE ME.
PARDON ME.

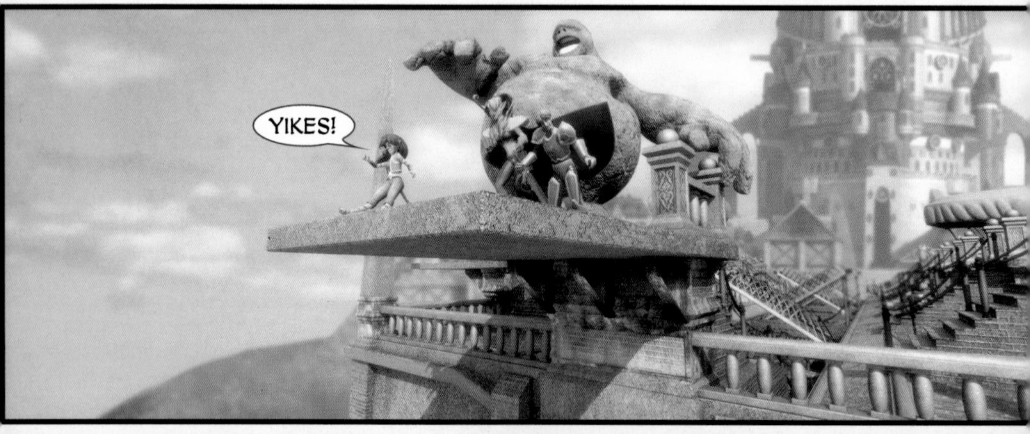
YIKES!

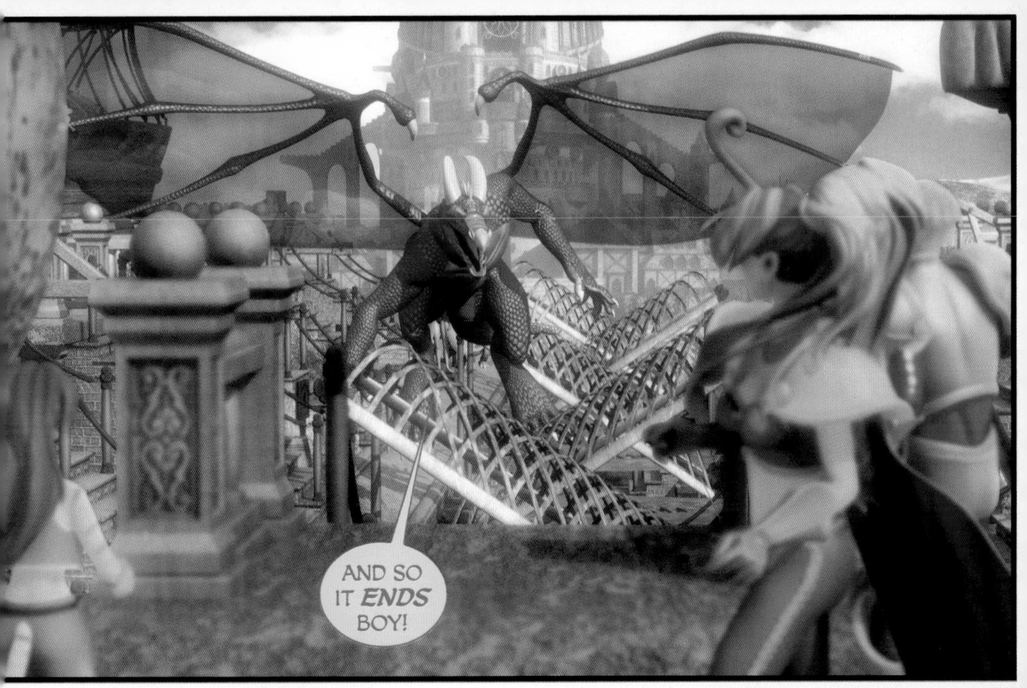
AND SO IT *ENDS* BOY!

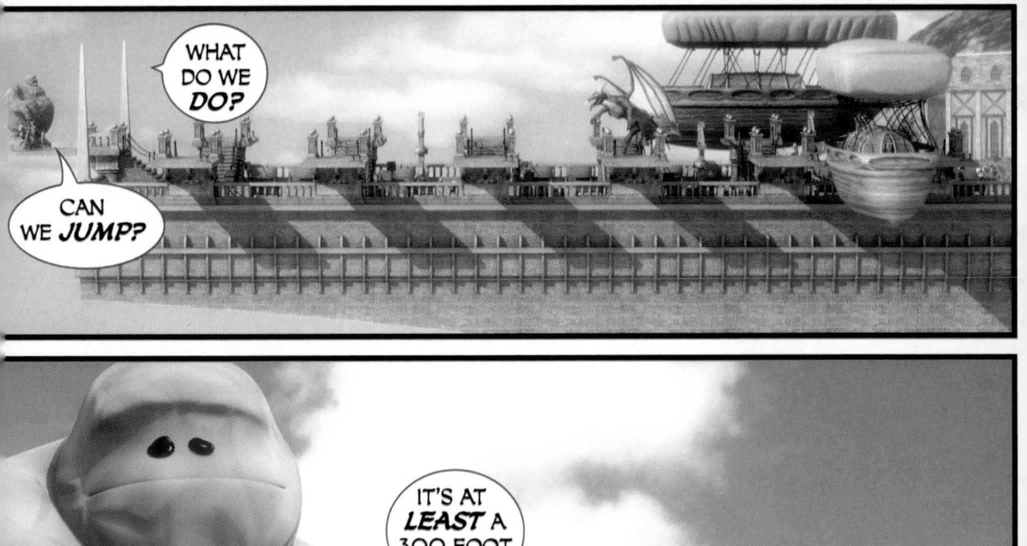
WHAT DO WE *DO?*
CAN WE *JUMP?*

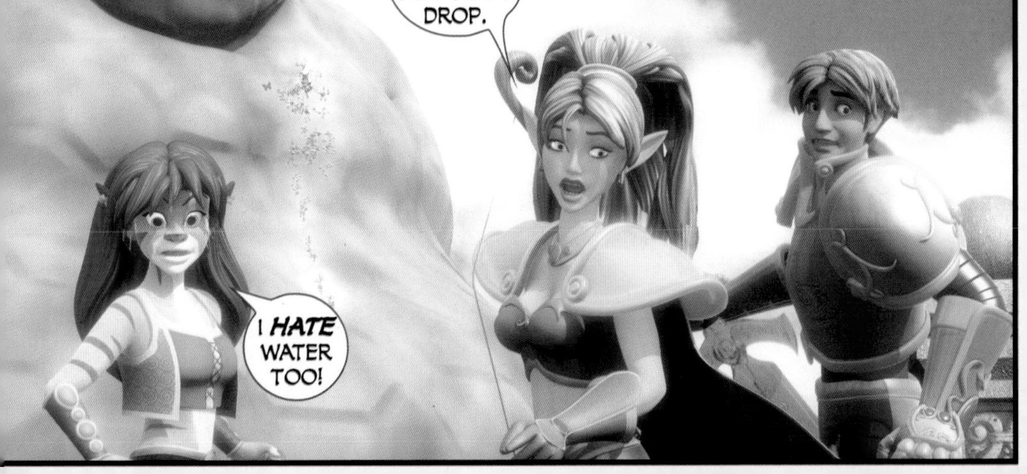
IT'S AT *LEAST* A 300 FOOT DROP.
I *HATE* WATER TOO!

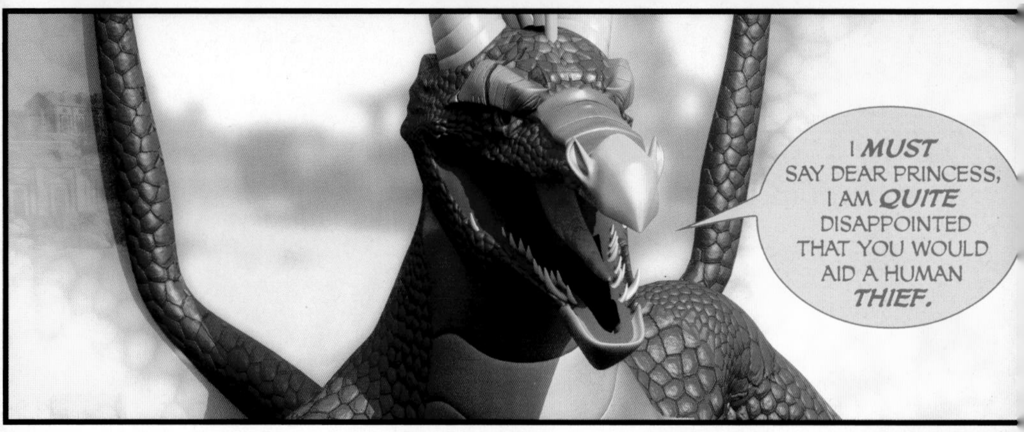
I MUST SAY DEAR PRINCESS, I AM QUITE DISAPPOINTED THAT YOU WOULD AID A HUMAN THIEF.

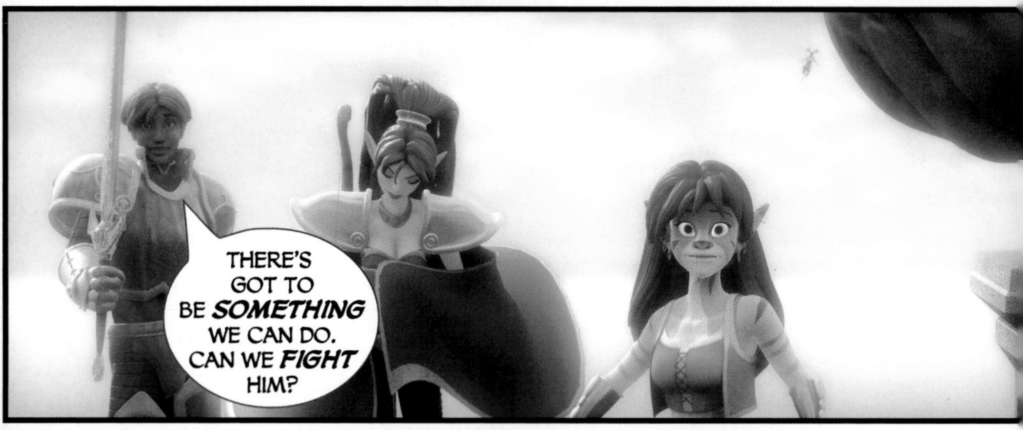
THERE'S GOT TO BE SOMETHING WE CAN DO. CAN WE FIGHT HIM?

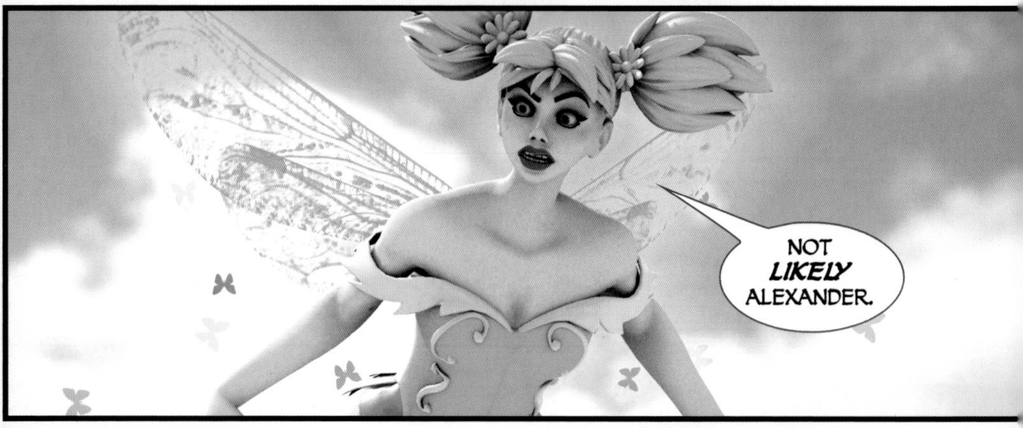
NOT LIKELY ALEXANDER.

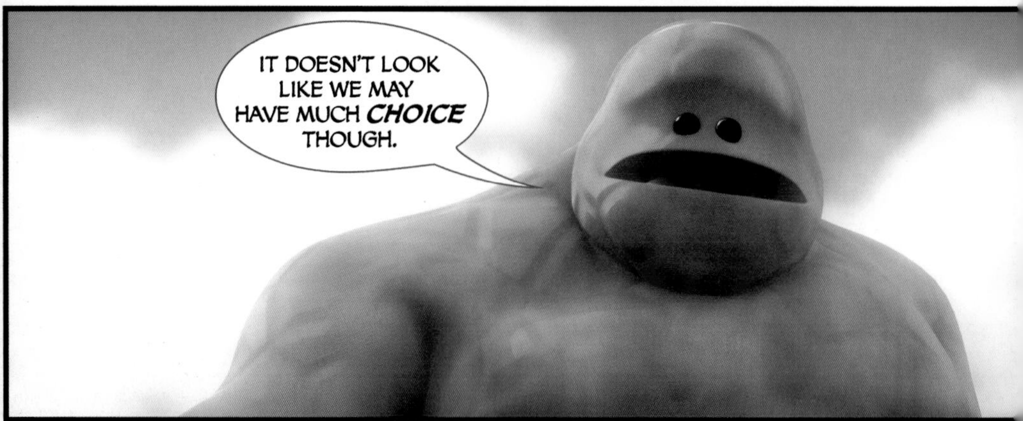
IT DOESN'T LOOK LIKE WE MAY HAVE MUCH CHOICE THOUGH.

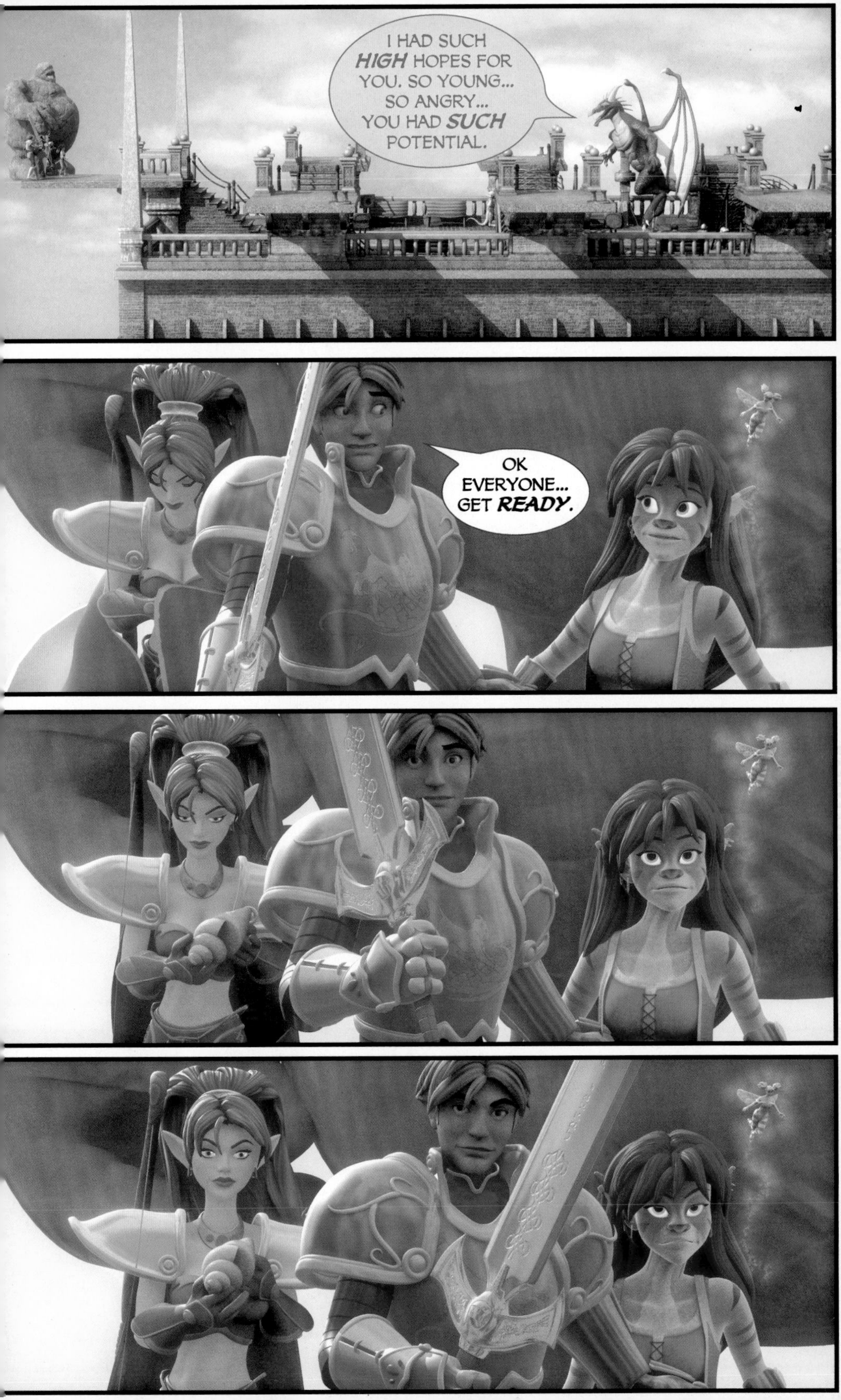
I HAD SUCH *HIGH* HOPES FOR YOU. SO YOUNG... SO ANGRY... YOU HAD *SUCH* POTENTIAL.
OK EVERYONE... GET *READY*.

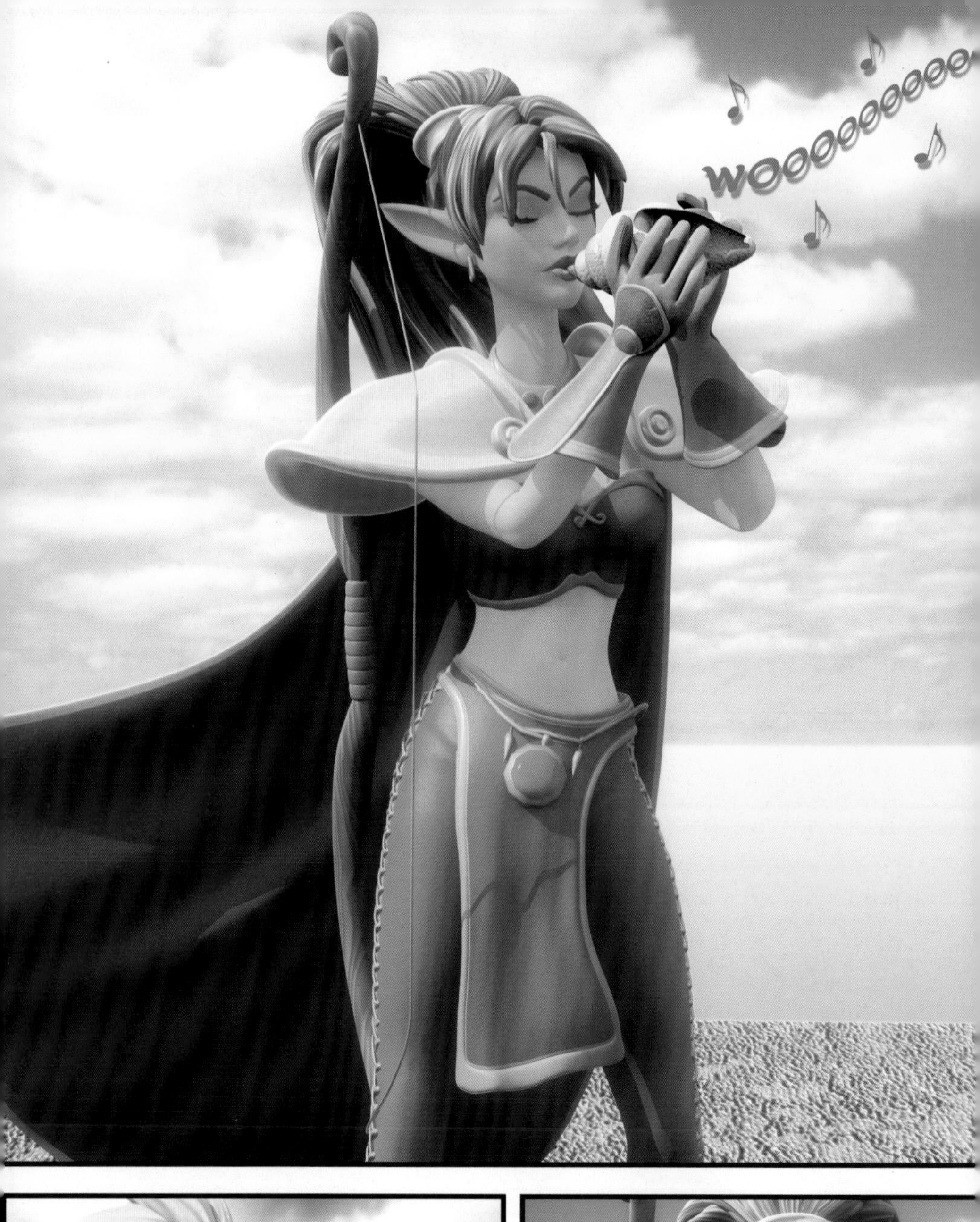
WOOOOOOOOO

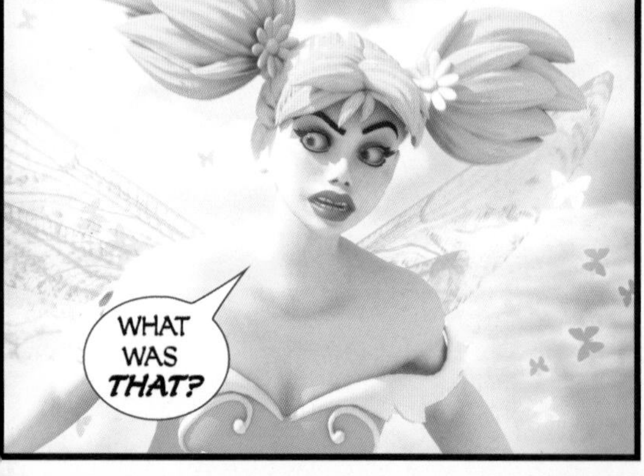
WHAT WAS THAT?

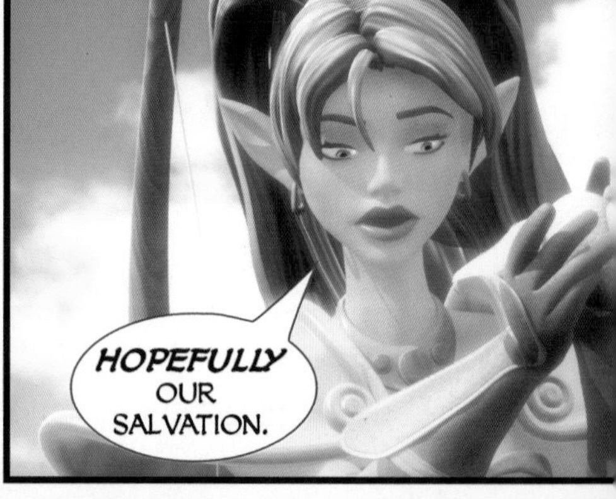
HOPEFULLY OUR SALVATION.

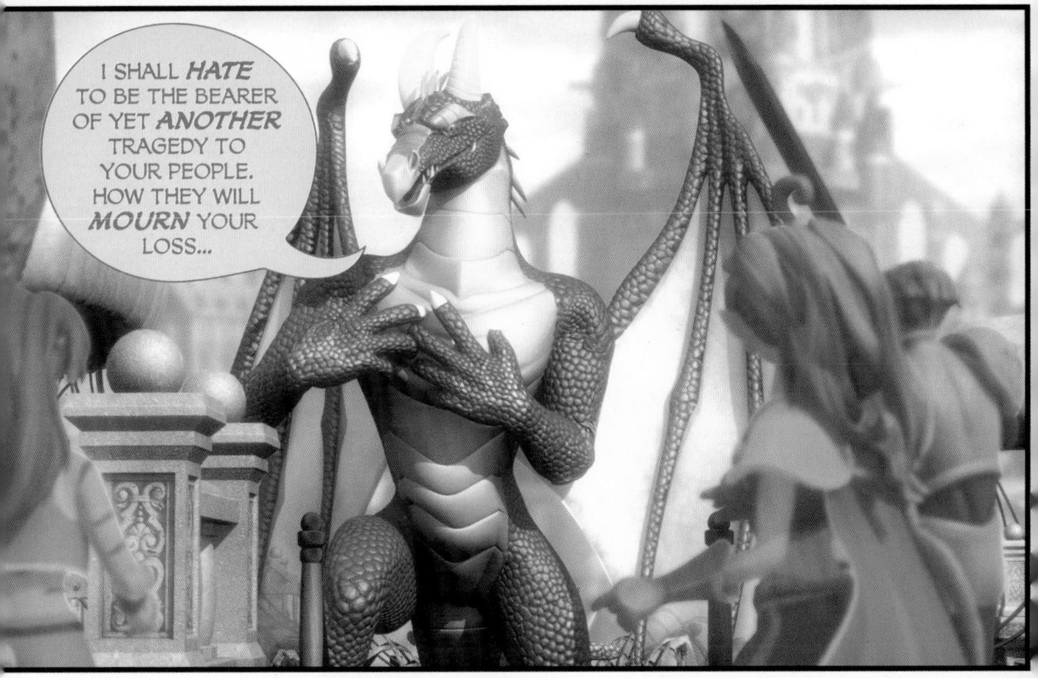
I SHALL HATE TO BE THE BEARER OF YET ANOTHER TRAGEDY TO YOUR PEOPLE. HOW THEY WILL MOURN YOUR LOSS...

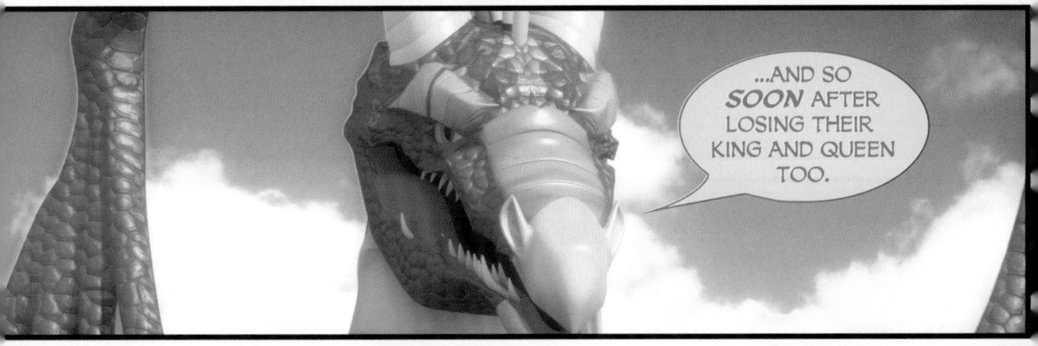
...AND SO SOON AFTER LOSING THEIR KING AND QUEEN TOO.

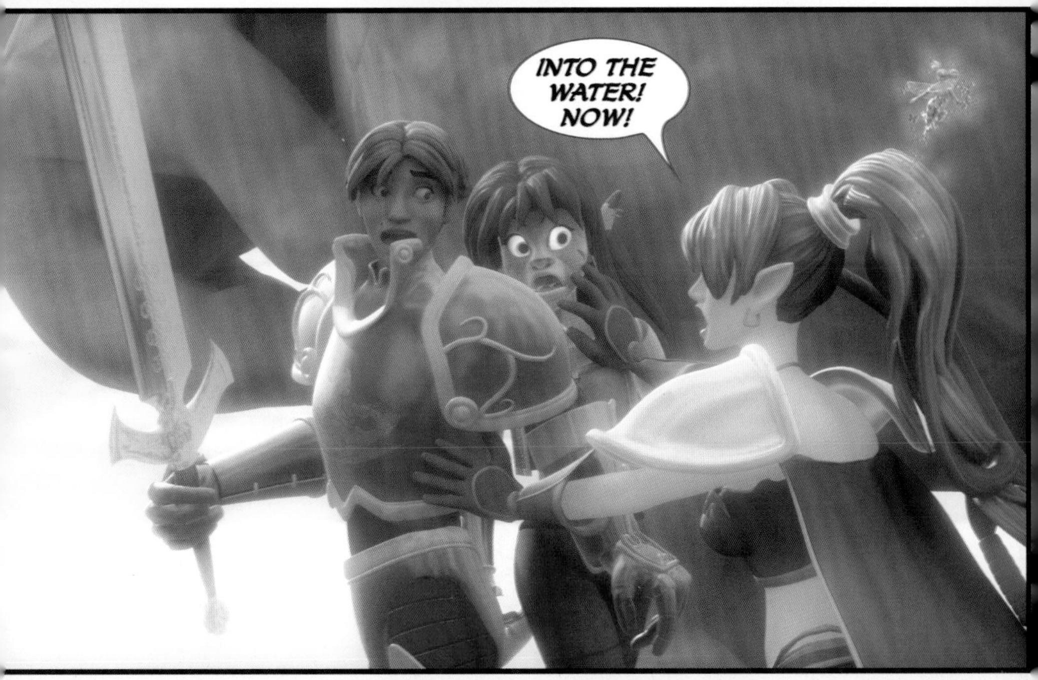
INTO THE WATER! NOW!

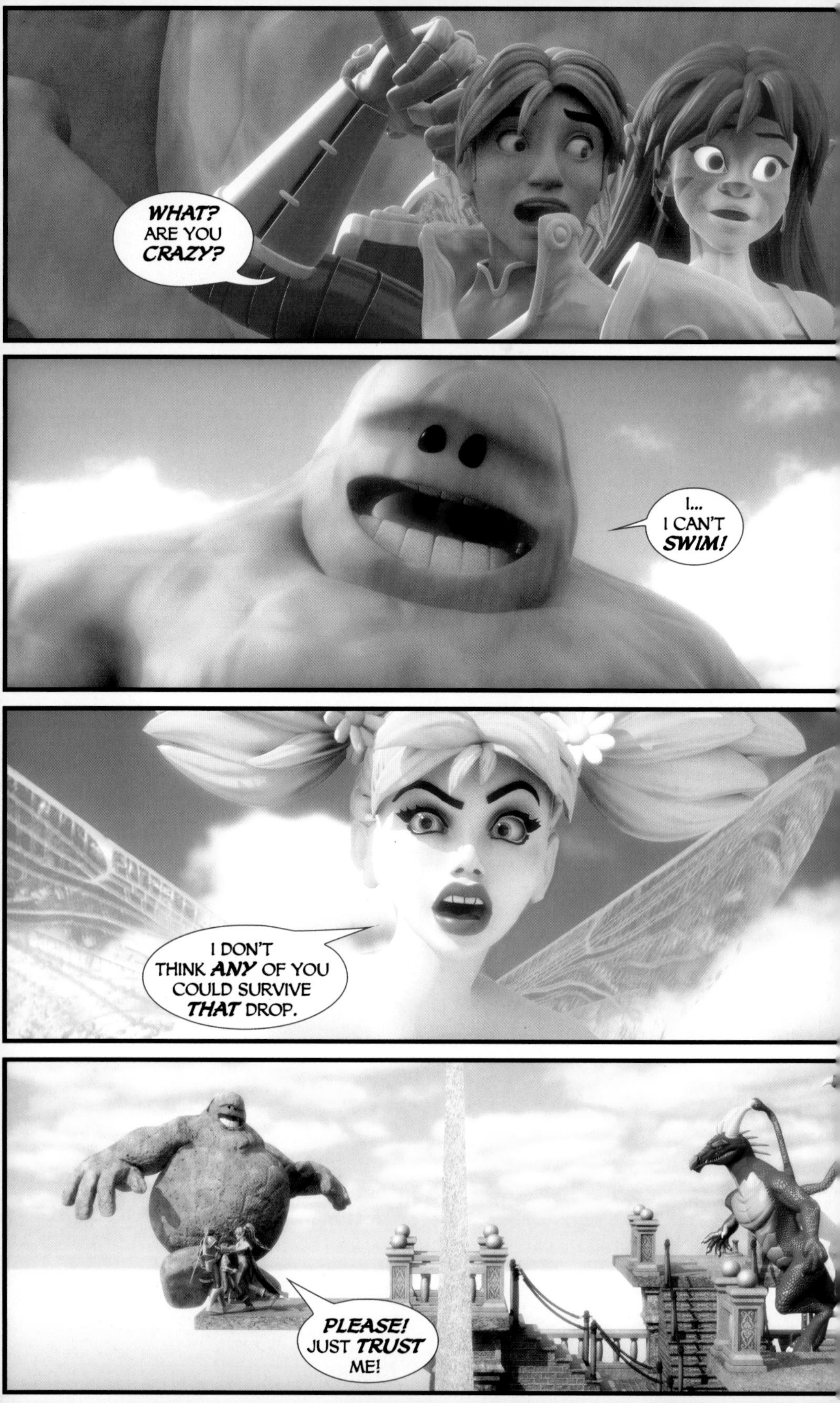
WHAT? ARE YOU CRAZY?
I... I CAN'T SWIM!
I DON'T THINK ANY OF YOU COULD SURVIVE THAT DROP.
PLEASE! JUST TRUST ME!

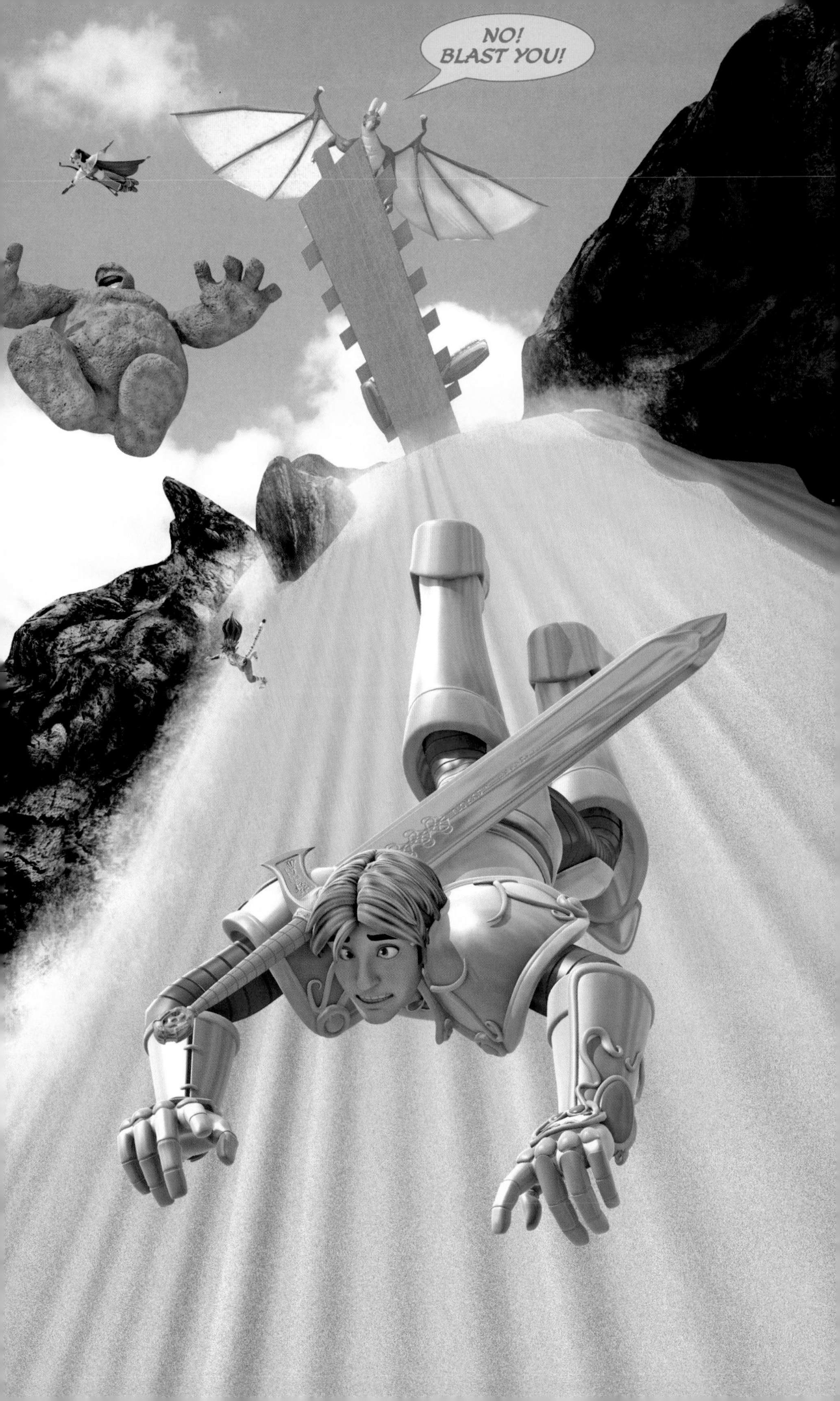
NO! BLAST YOU!

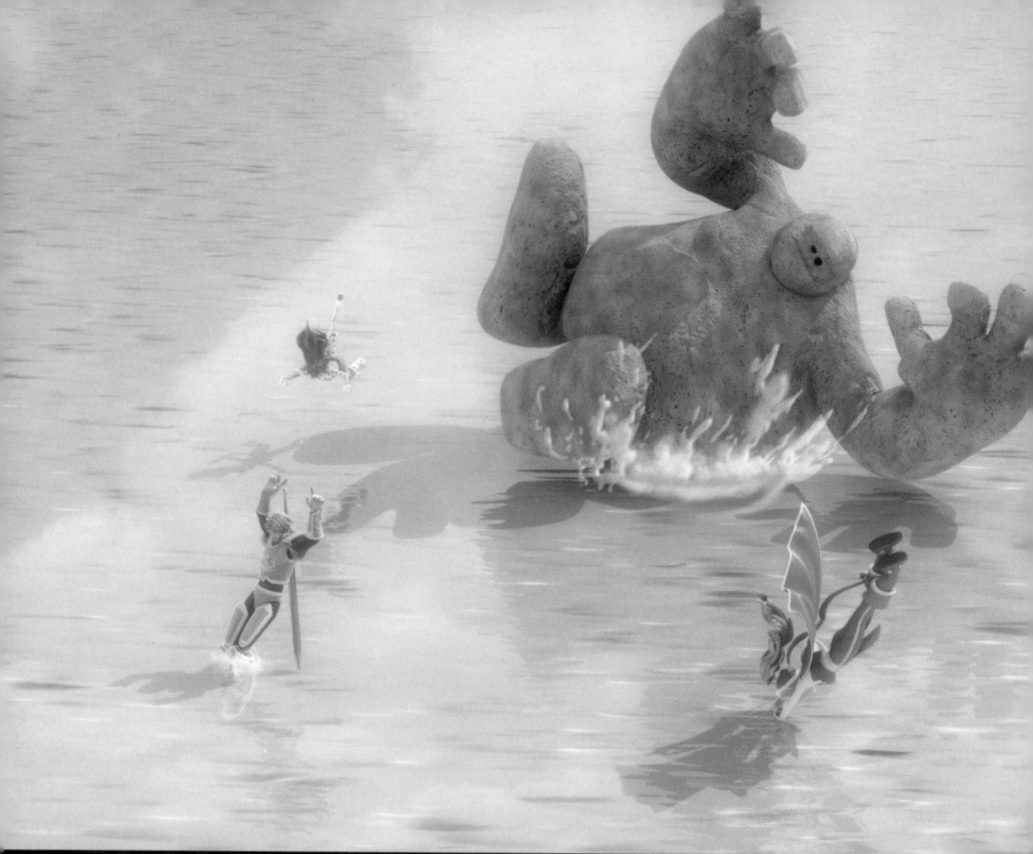
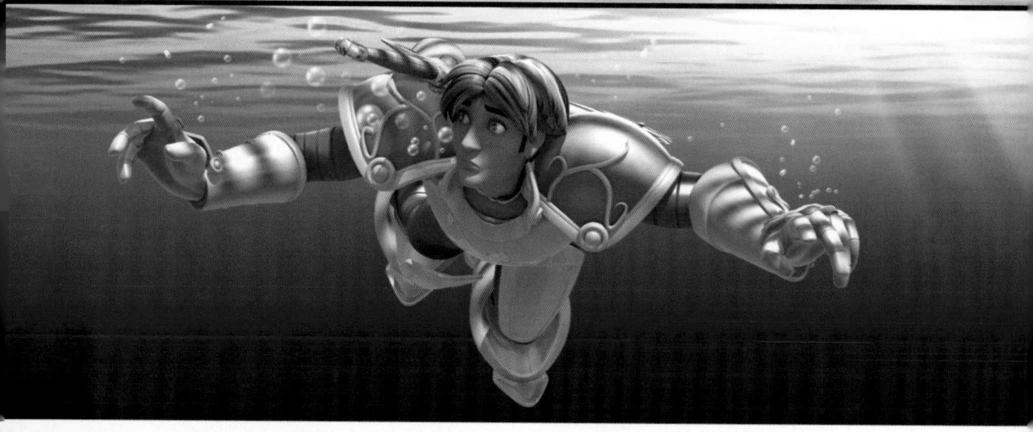
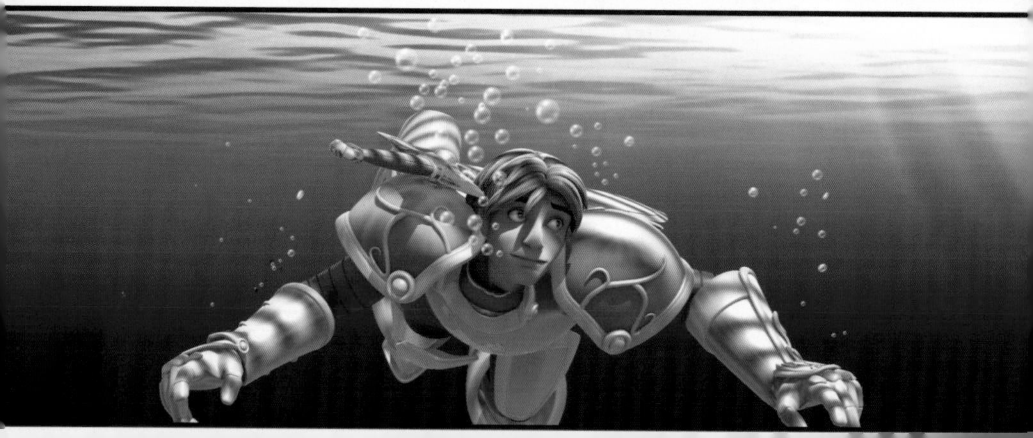

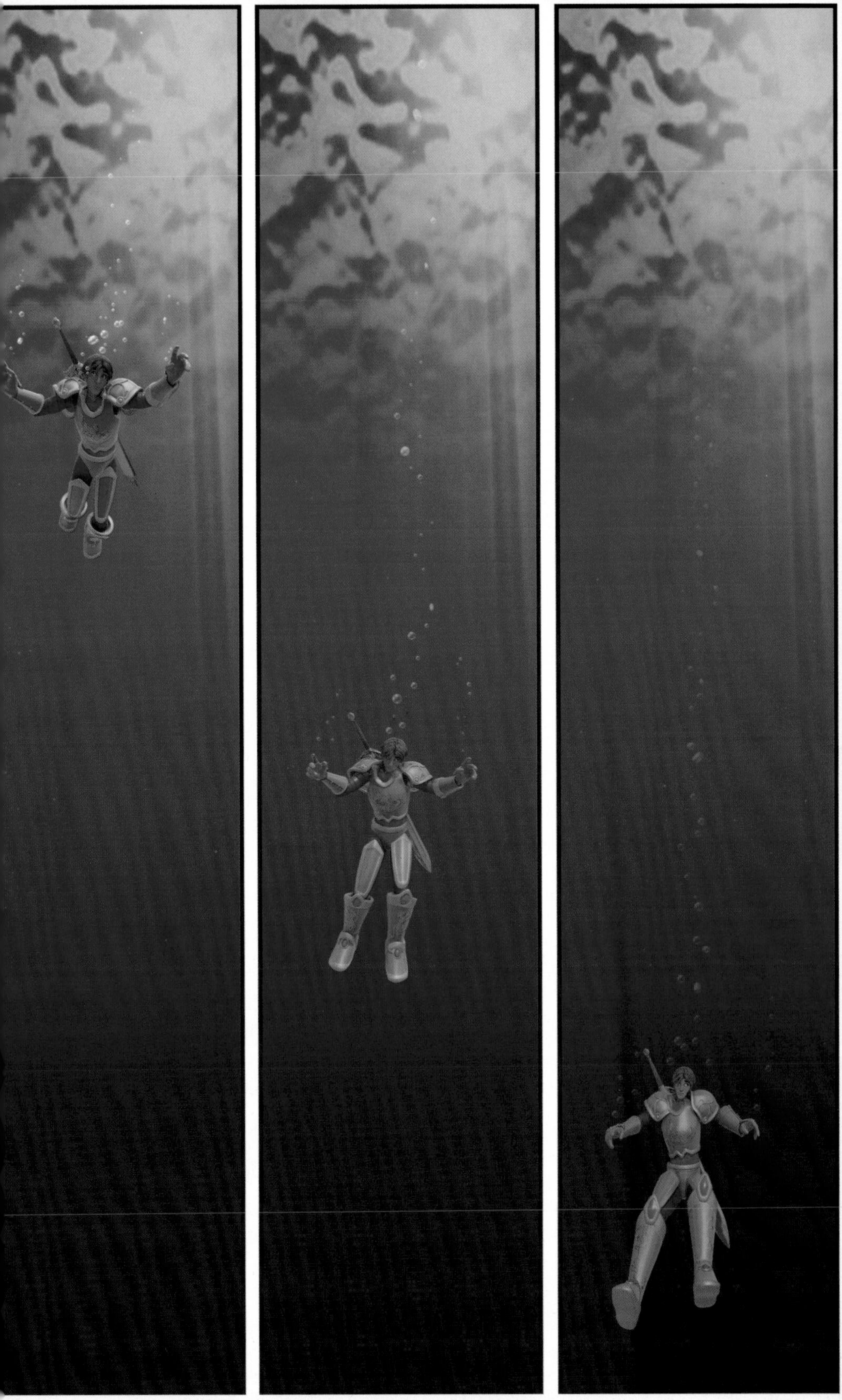

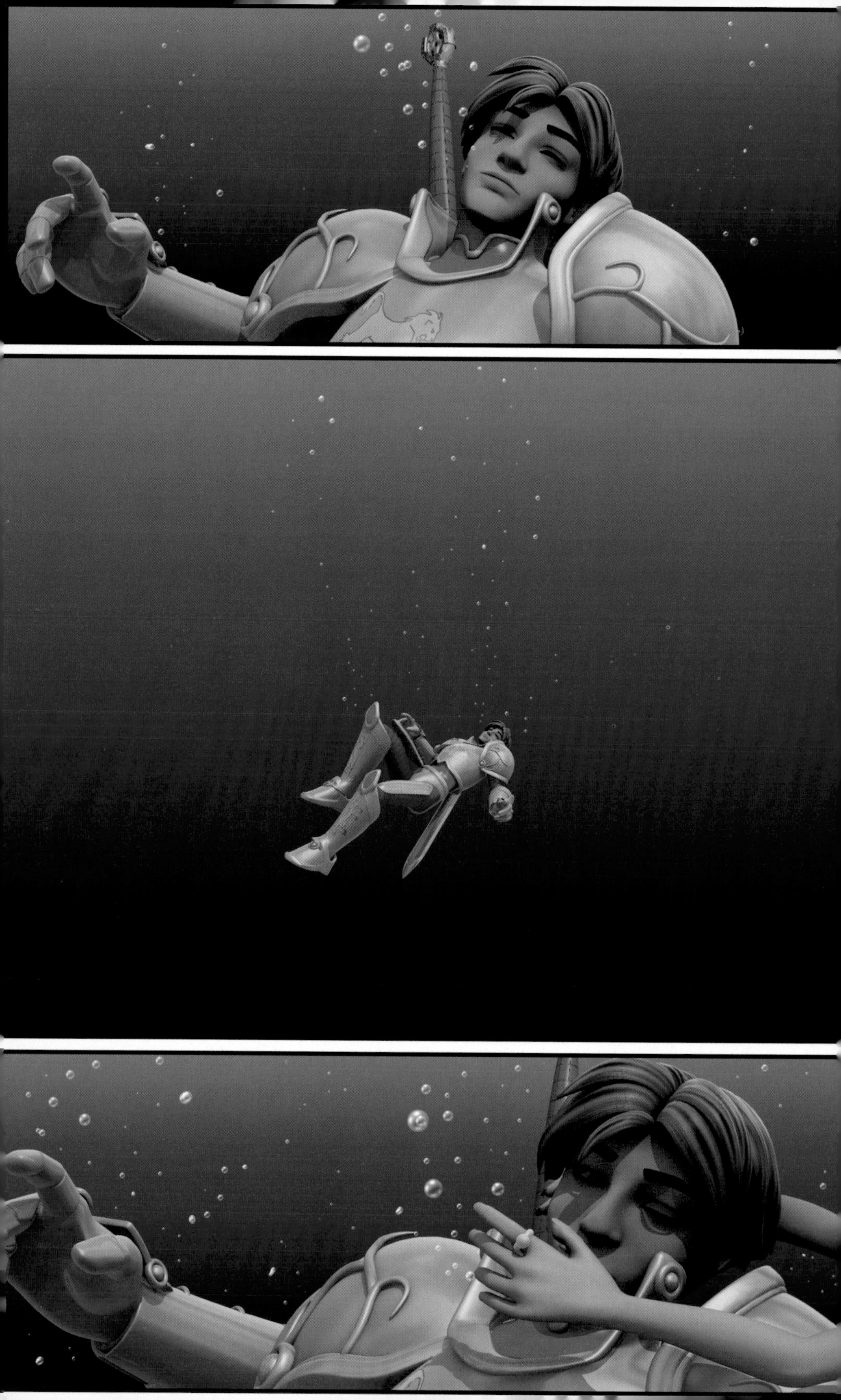

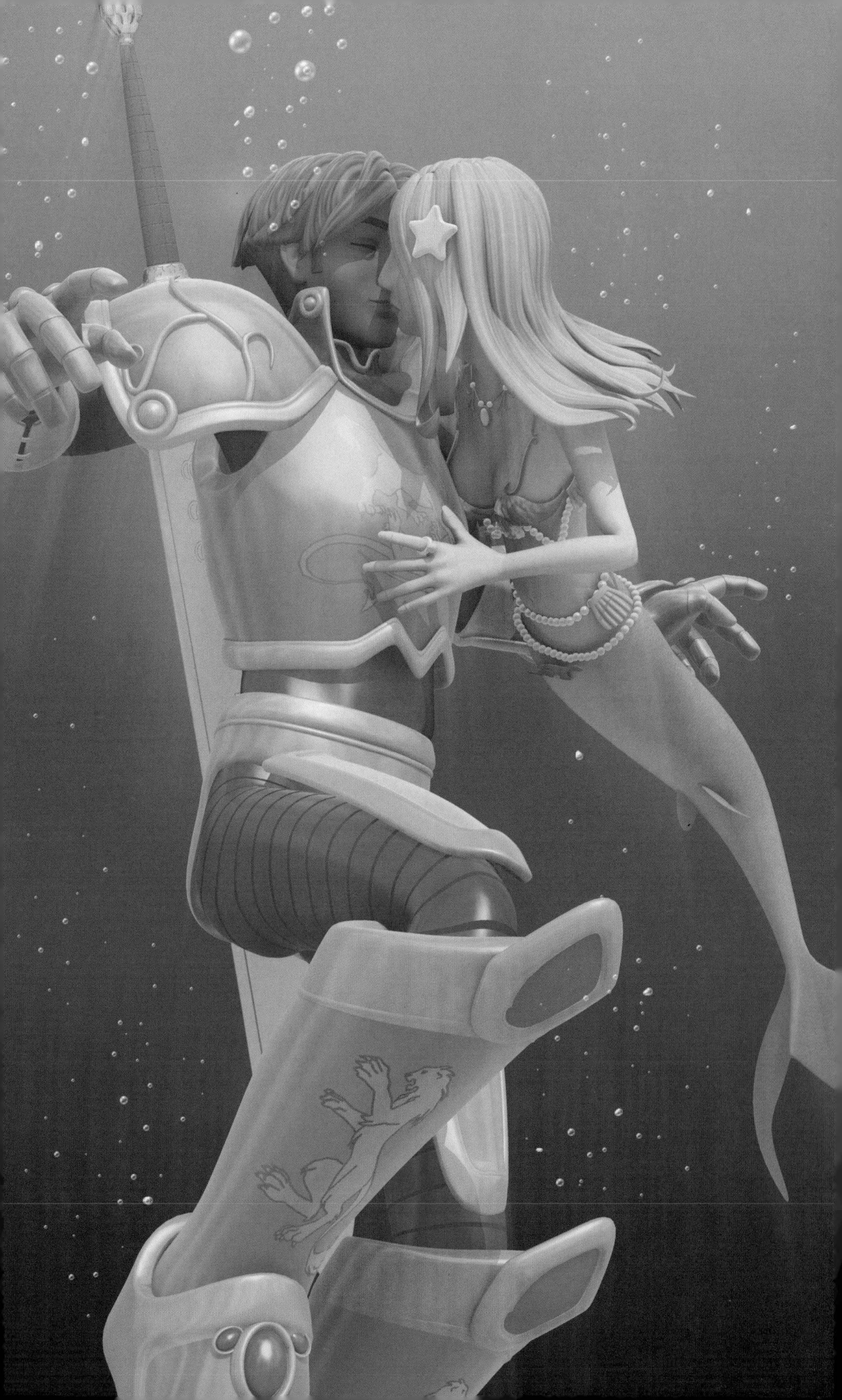

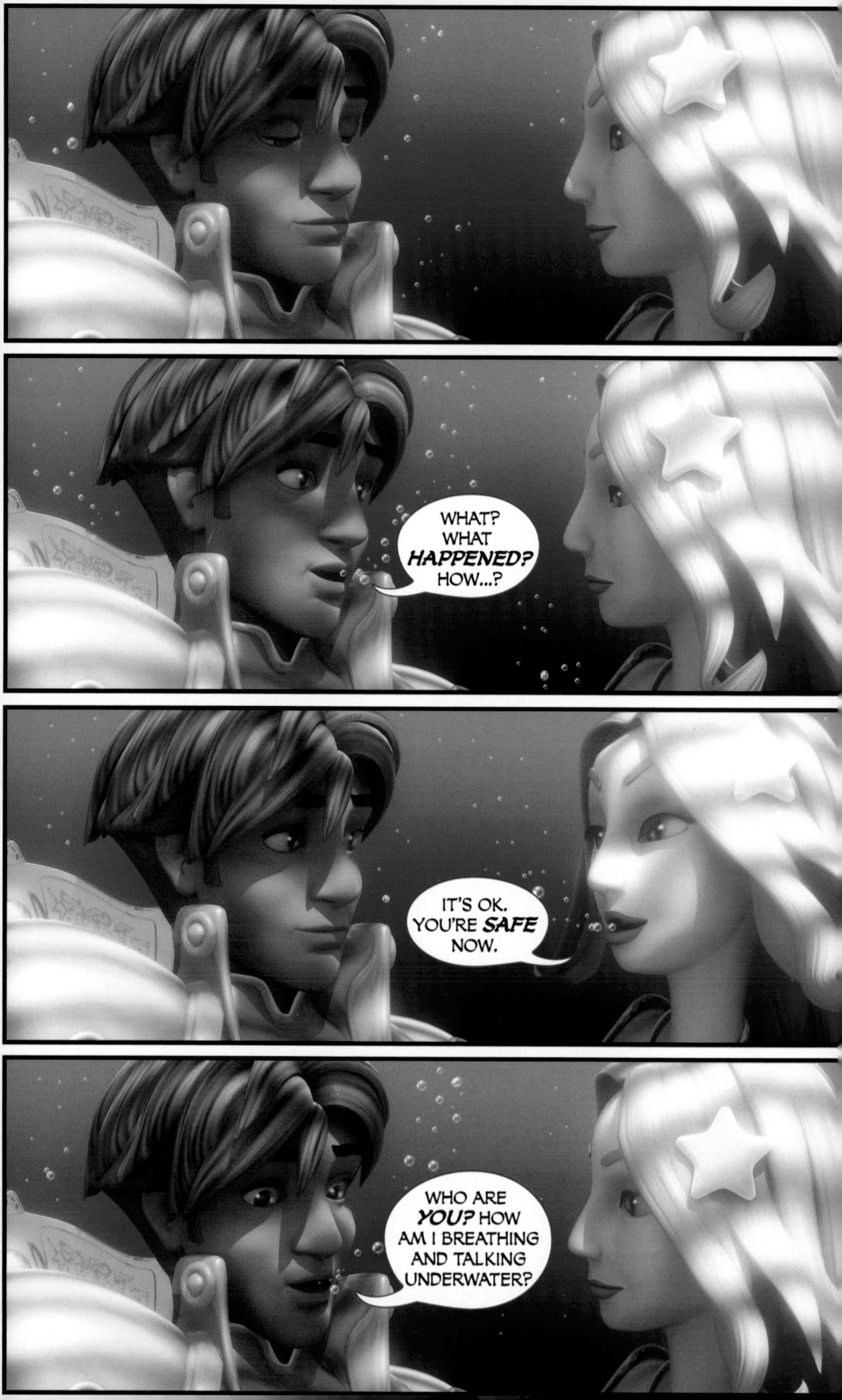
WHAT? WHAT HAPPENED? HOW...?
IT'S OK. YOU'RE SAFE NOW.
WHO ARE YOU? HOW AM I BREATHING AND TALKING UNDERWATER?

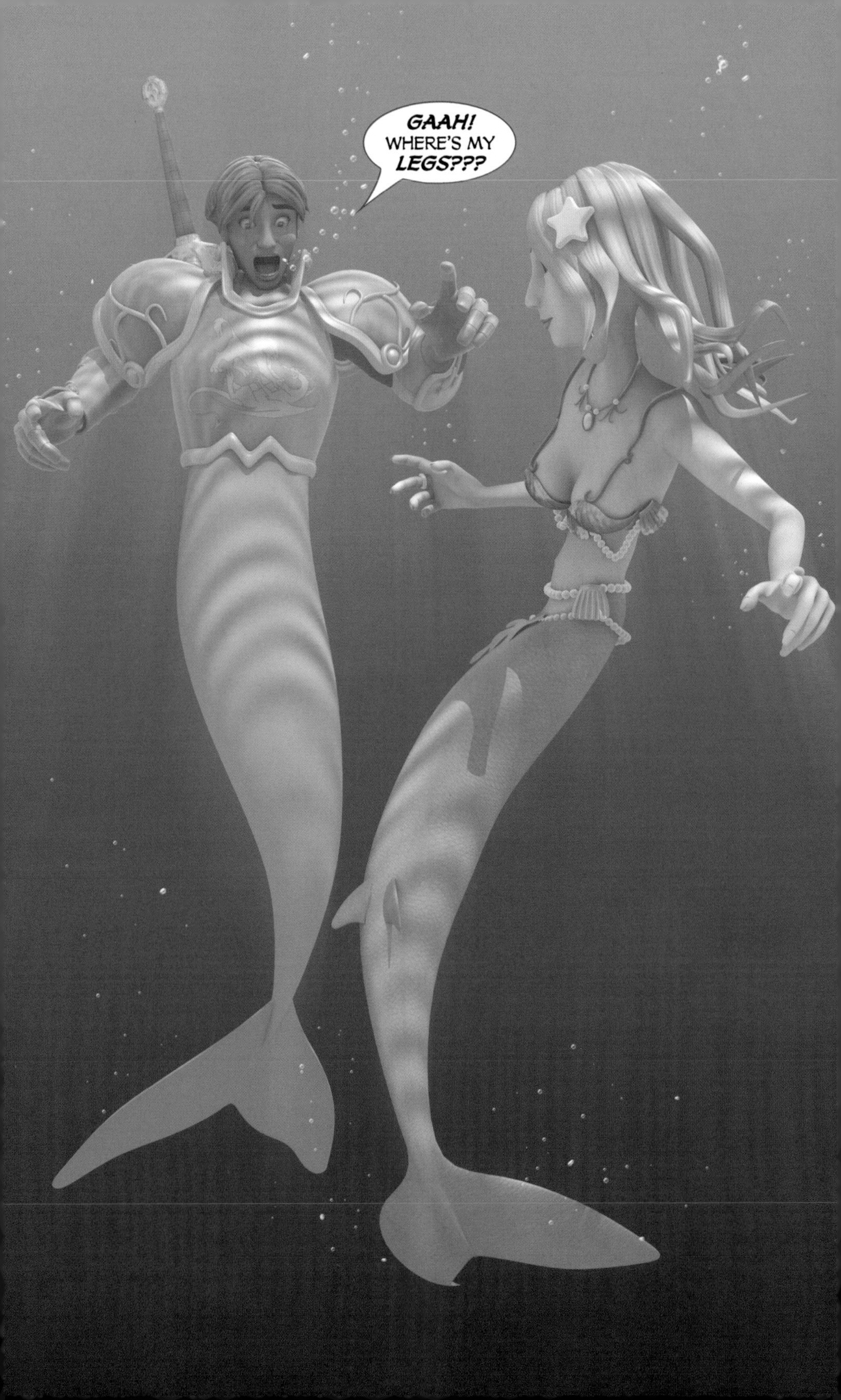
GAAH! WHERE'S MY LEGS???

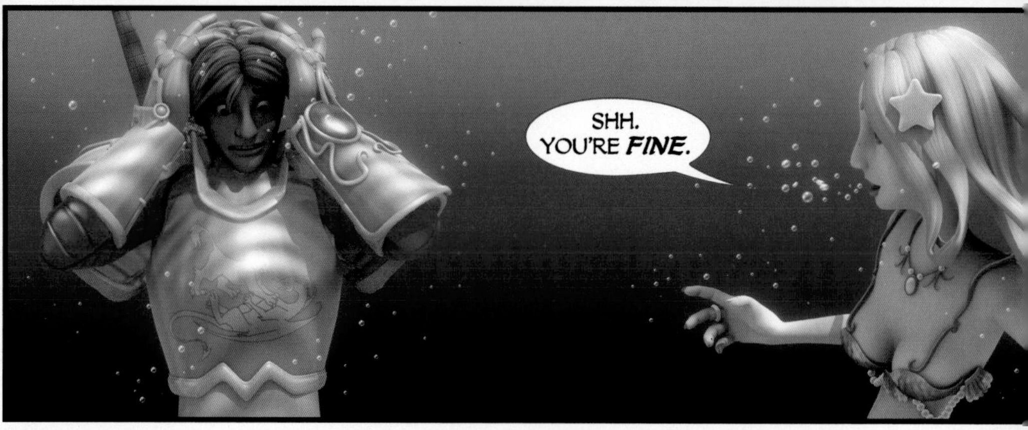
SHH.
YOU'RE *FINE*.

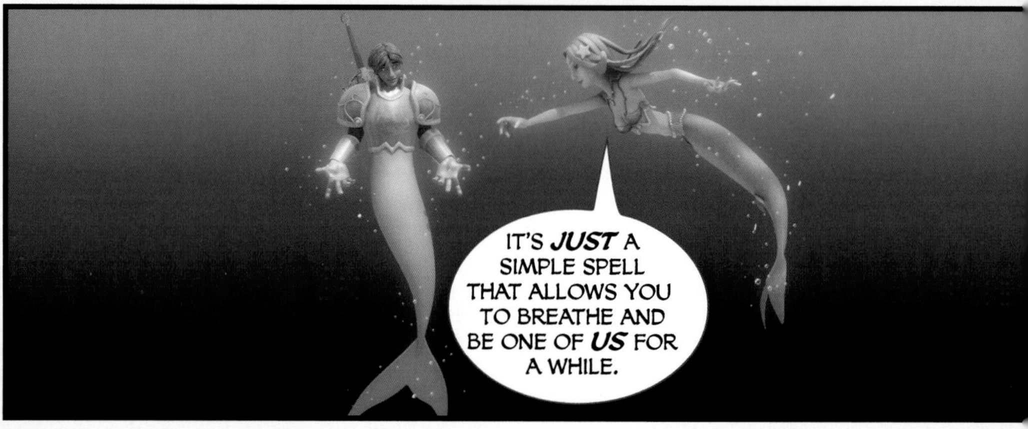
IT'S *JUST* A SIMPLE SPELL THAT ALLOWS YOU TO BREATHE AND BE ONE OF *US* FOR A WHILE.

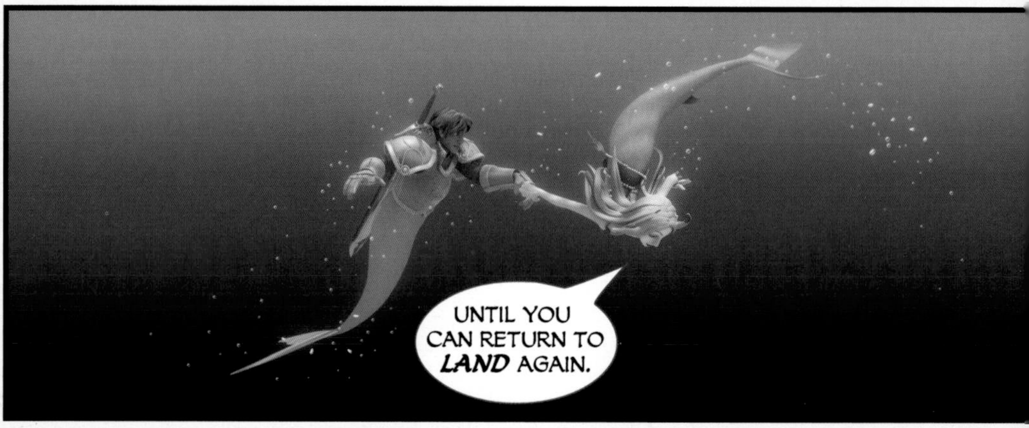
UNTIL YOU CAN RETURN TO *LAND* AGAIN.

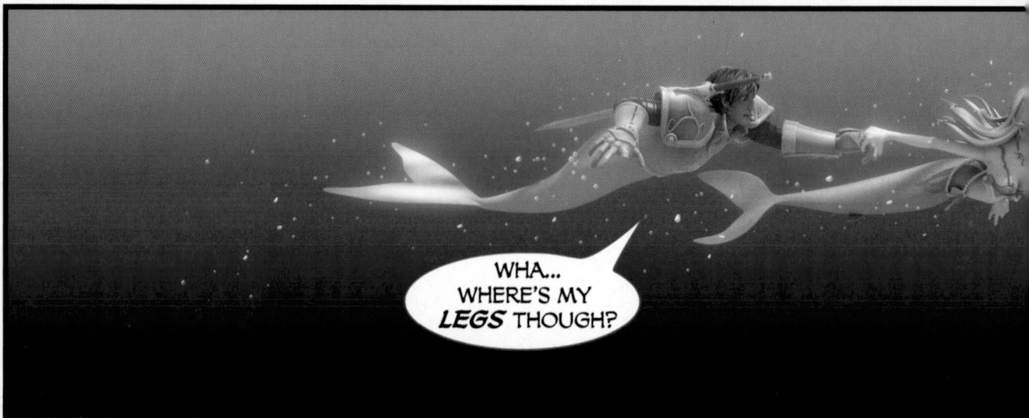
WHA...
WHERE'S MY *LEGS* THOUGH?

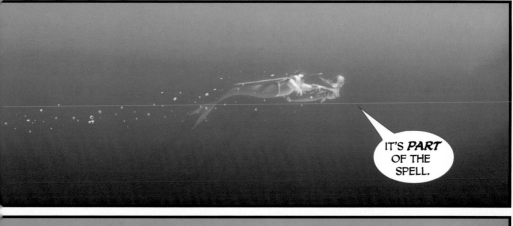

IT'S *PART* OF THE SPELL.

THEY WILL *RETURN* ONCE YOU'VE BREATHED *AIR* AGAIN ON LAND.

YOUR ARMOR AND ALL WILL BE *RESTORED*... I PROMISE.

COME... YOUR FRIENDS ARE WAITING.

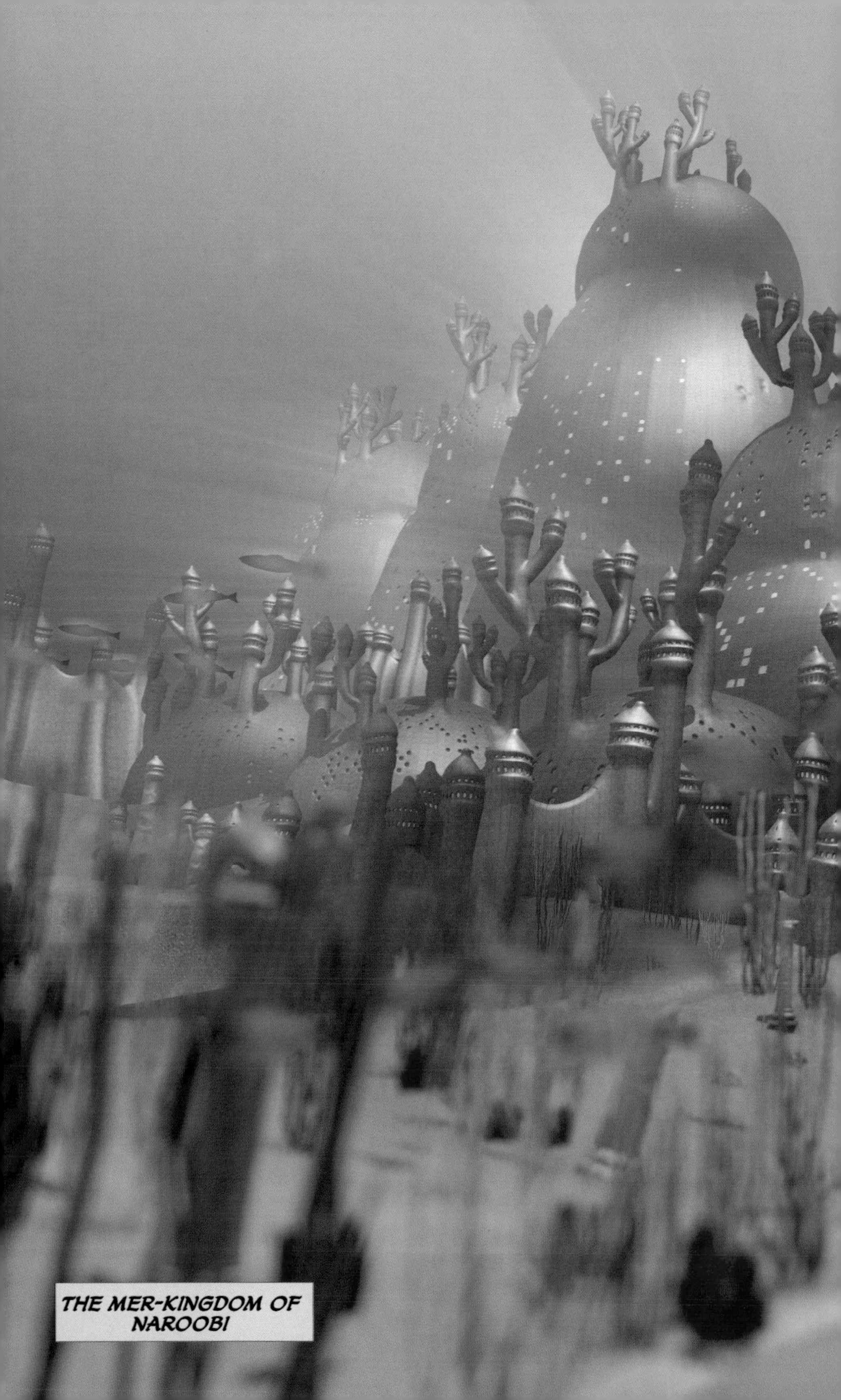
THE MER-KINGDOM OF NAROOBI

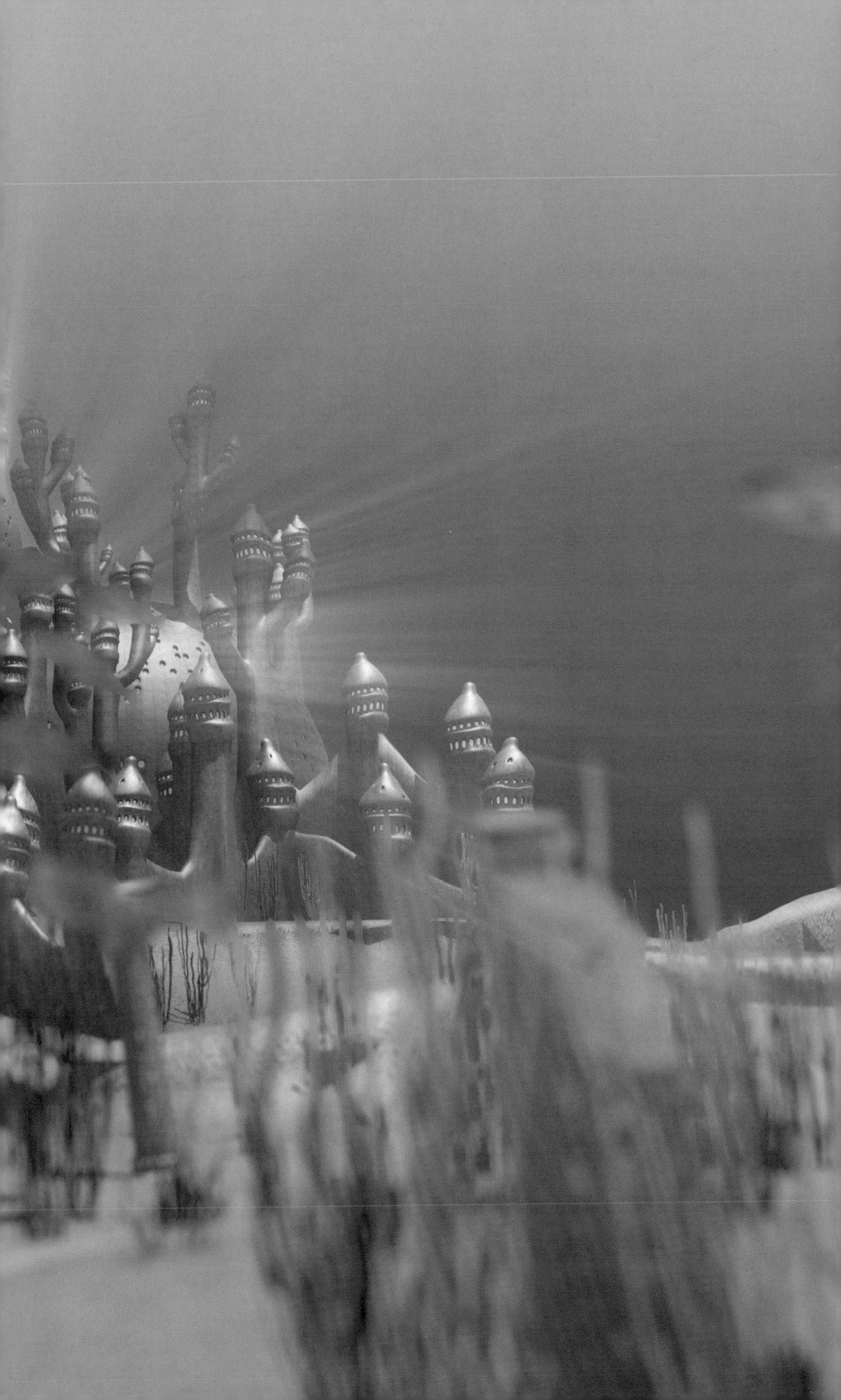

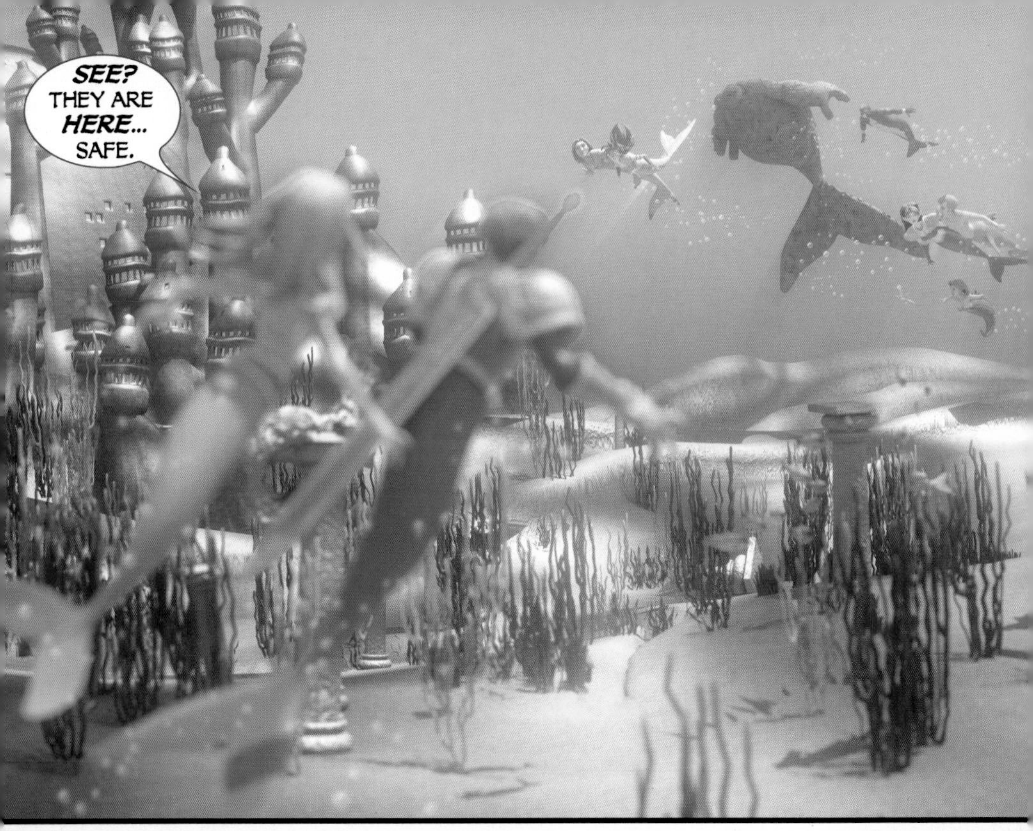
SEE? THEY ARE HERE... SAFE.

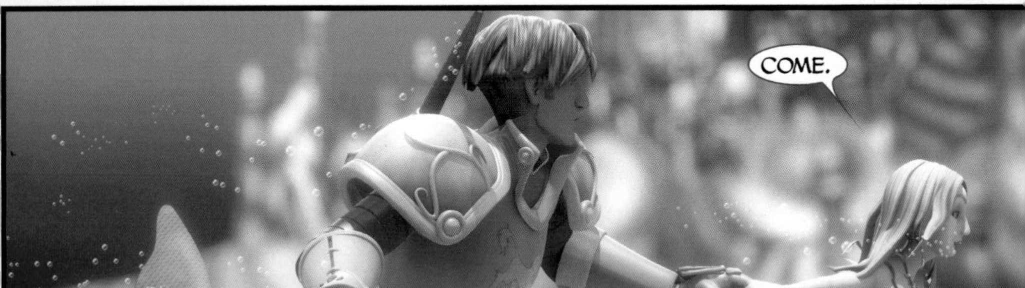
COME.

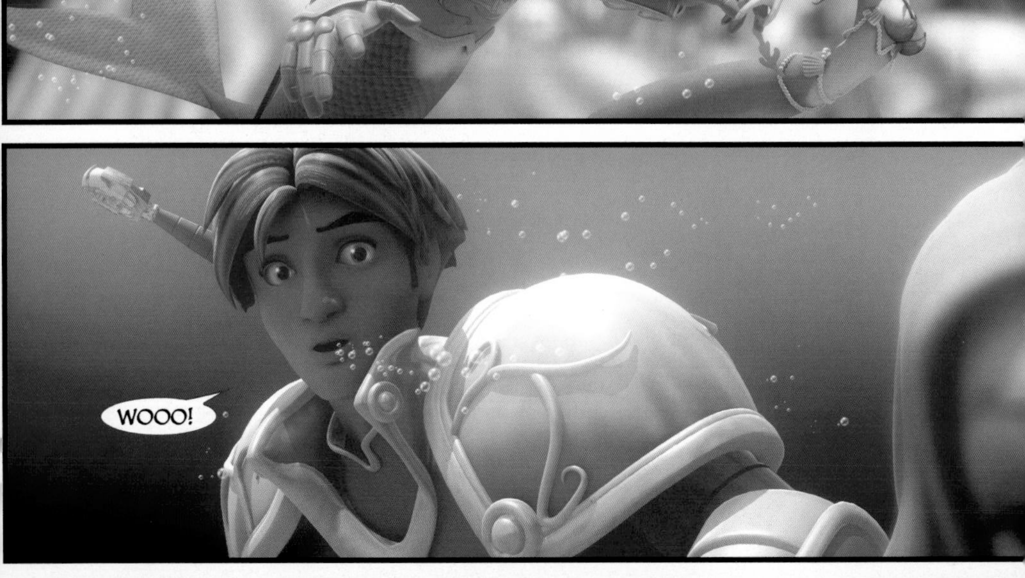
WOOO!

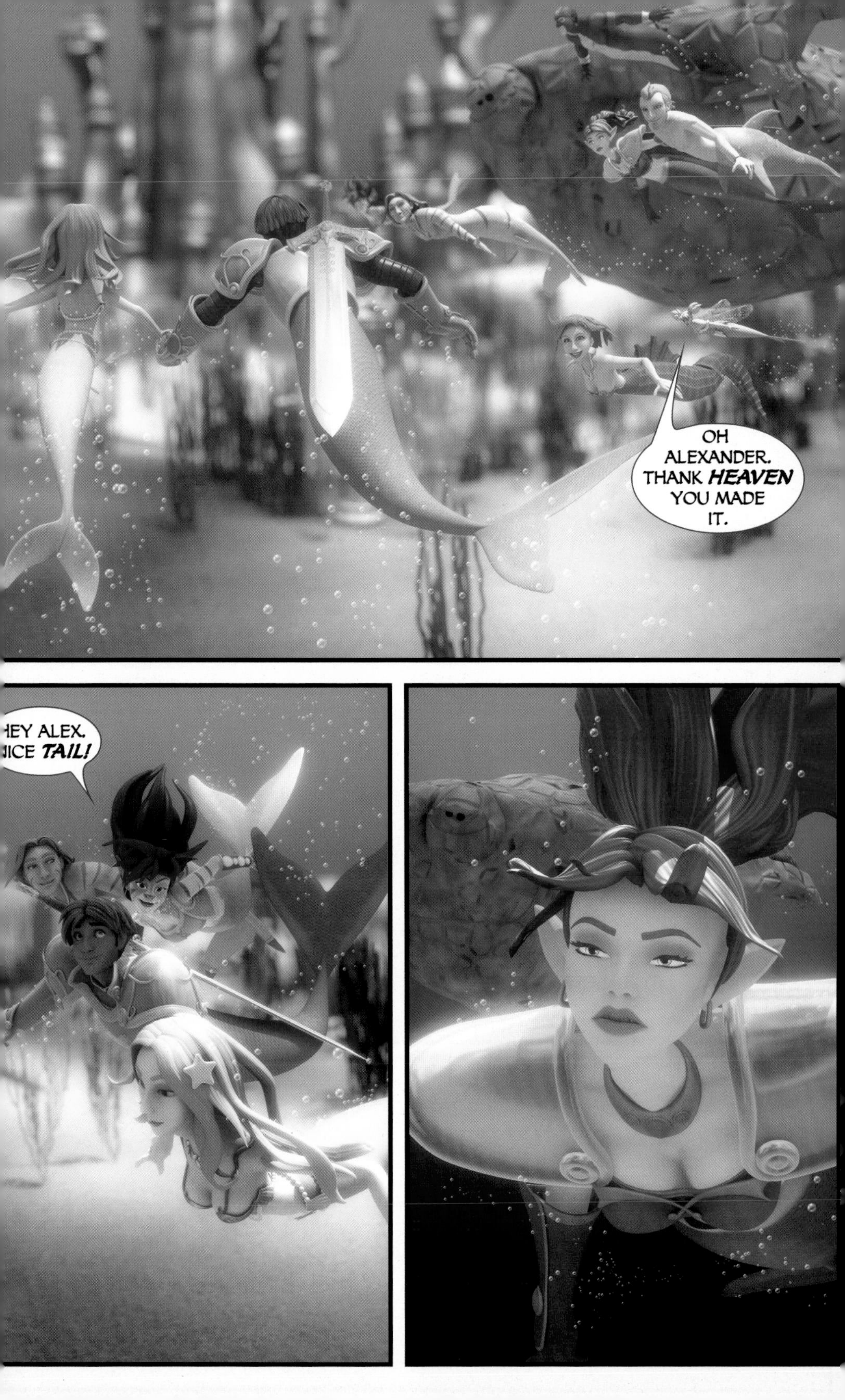
OH ALEXANDER. THANK *HEAVEN* YOU MADE IT.
HEY ALEX. NICE *TAIL!*

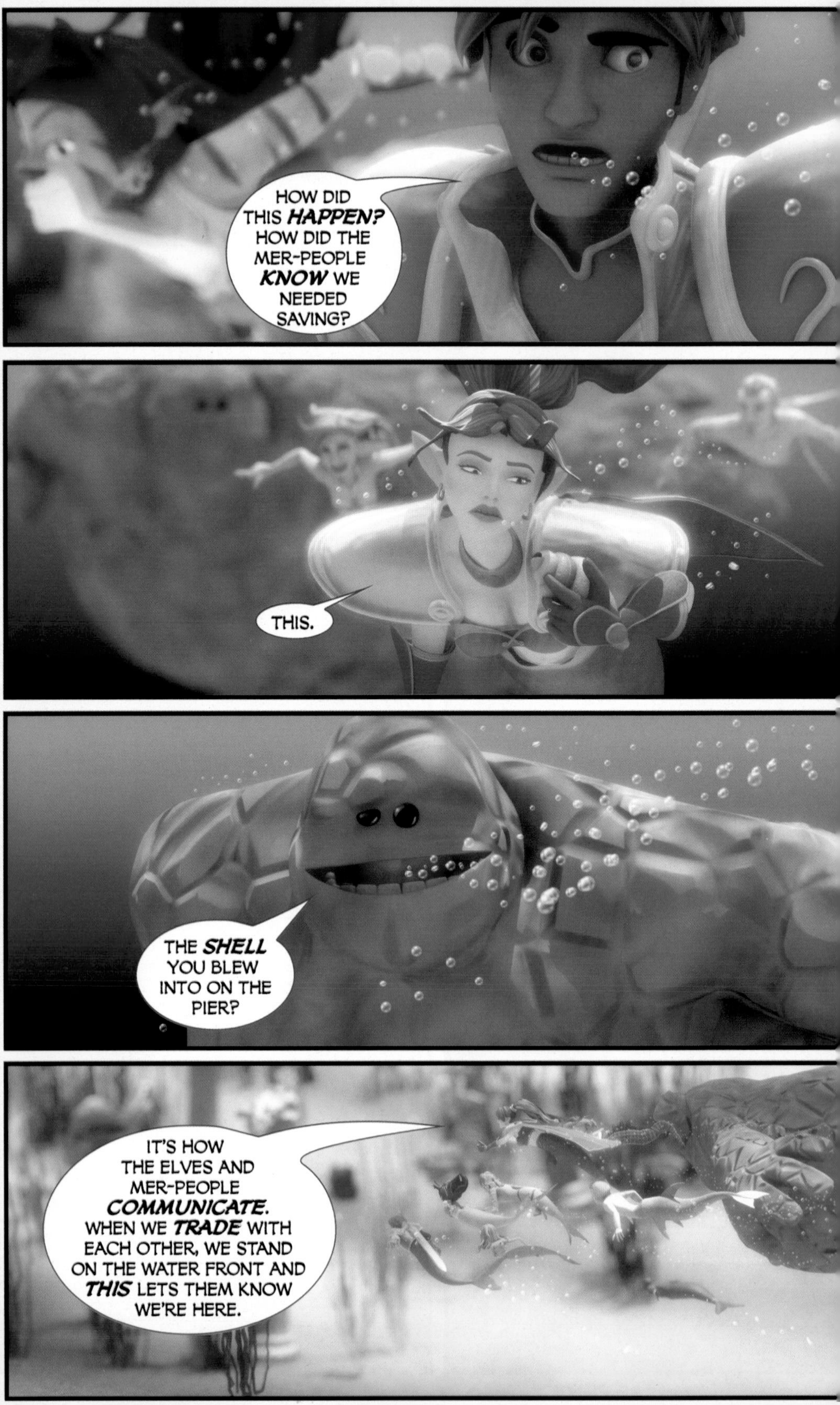
HOW DID THIS HAPPEN? HOW DID THE MER-PEOPLE KNOW WE NEEDED SAVING?
THIS.
THE SHELL YOU BLEW INTO ON THE PIER?
IT'S HOW THE ELVES AND MER-PEOPLE COMMUNICATE. WHEN WE TRADE WITH EACH OTHER, WE STAND ON THE WATER FRONT AND THIS LETS THEM KNOW WE'RE HERE.

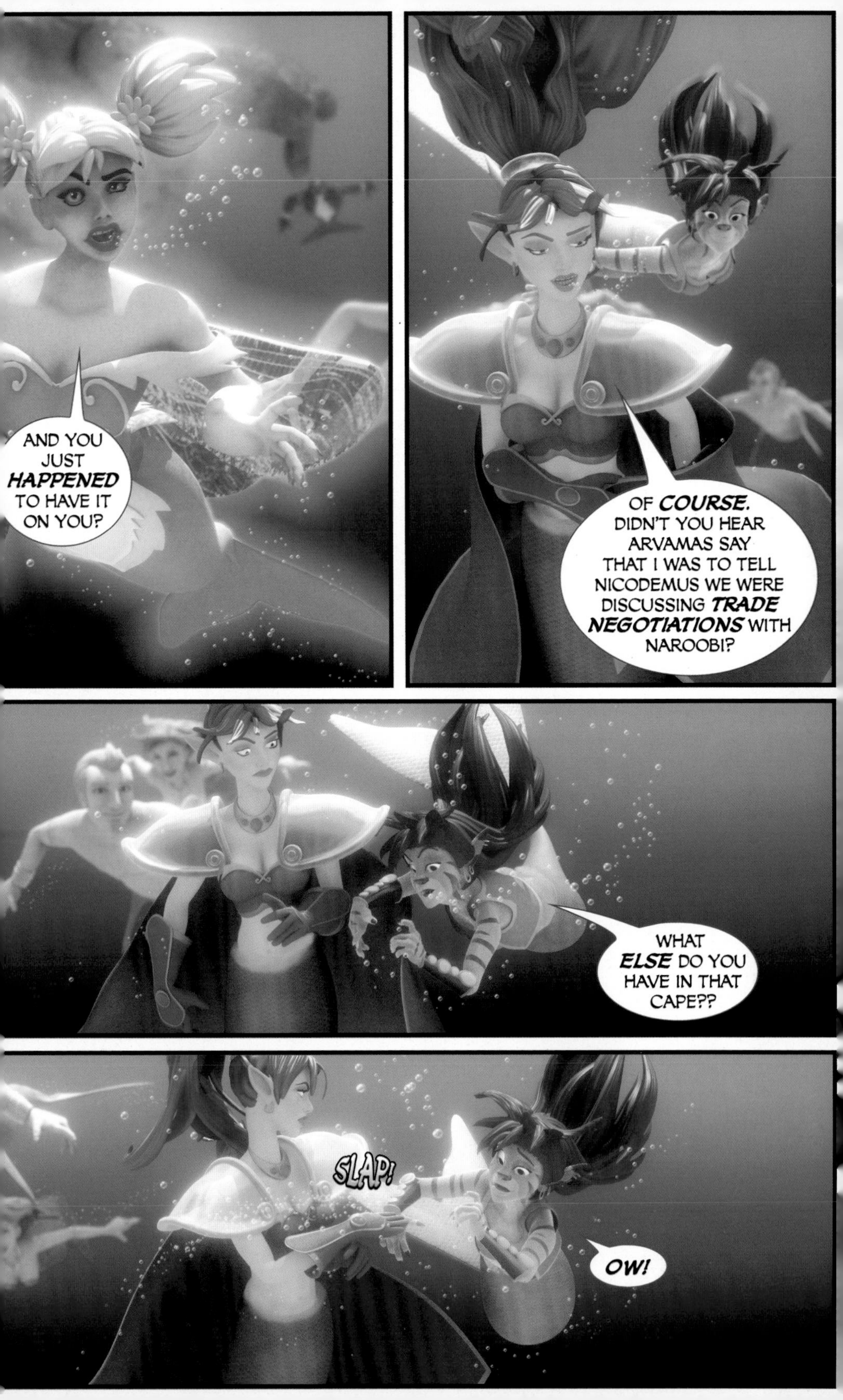
AND YOU JUST HAPPENED TO HAVE IT ON YOU?
OF COURSE. DIDN'T YOU HEAR ARVAMAS SAY THAT I WAS TO TELL NICODEMUS WE WERE DISCUSSING TRADE NEGOTIATIONS WITH NAROOBI?
WHAT ELSE DO YOU HAVE IN THAT CAPE??
SLAP!
OW!

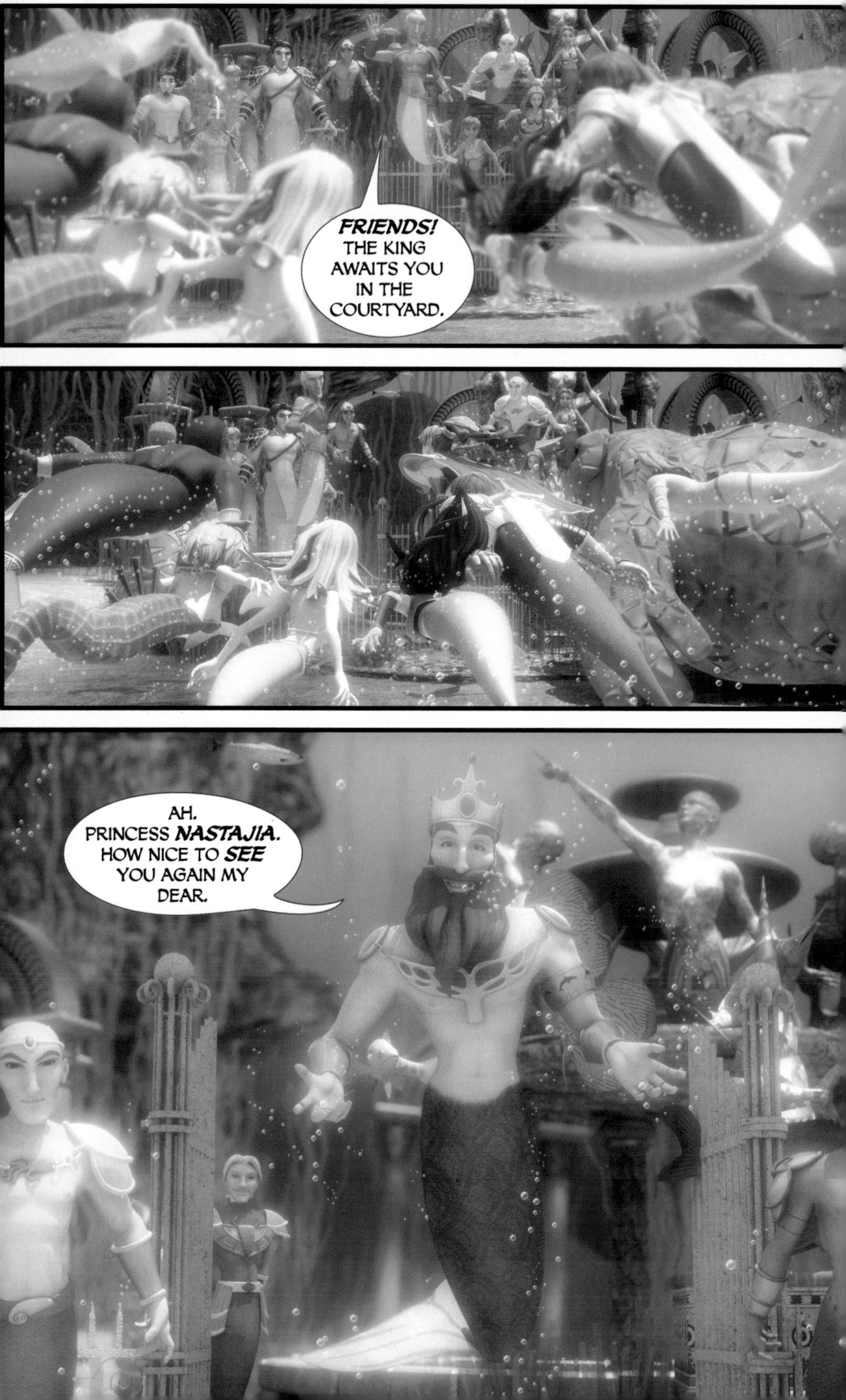
FRIENDS! THE KING AWAITS YOU IN THE COURTYARD.
AH. PRINCESS NASTAJIA. HOW NICE TO SEE YOU AGAIN MY DEAR.

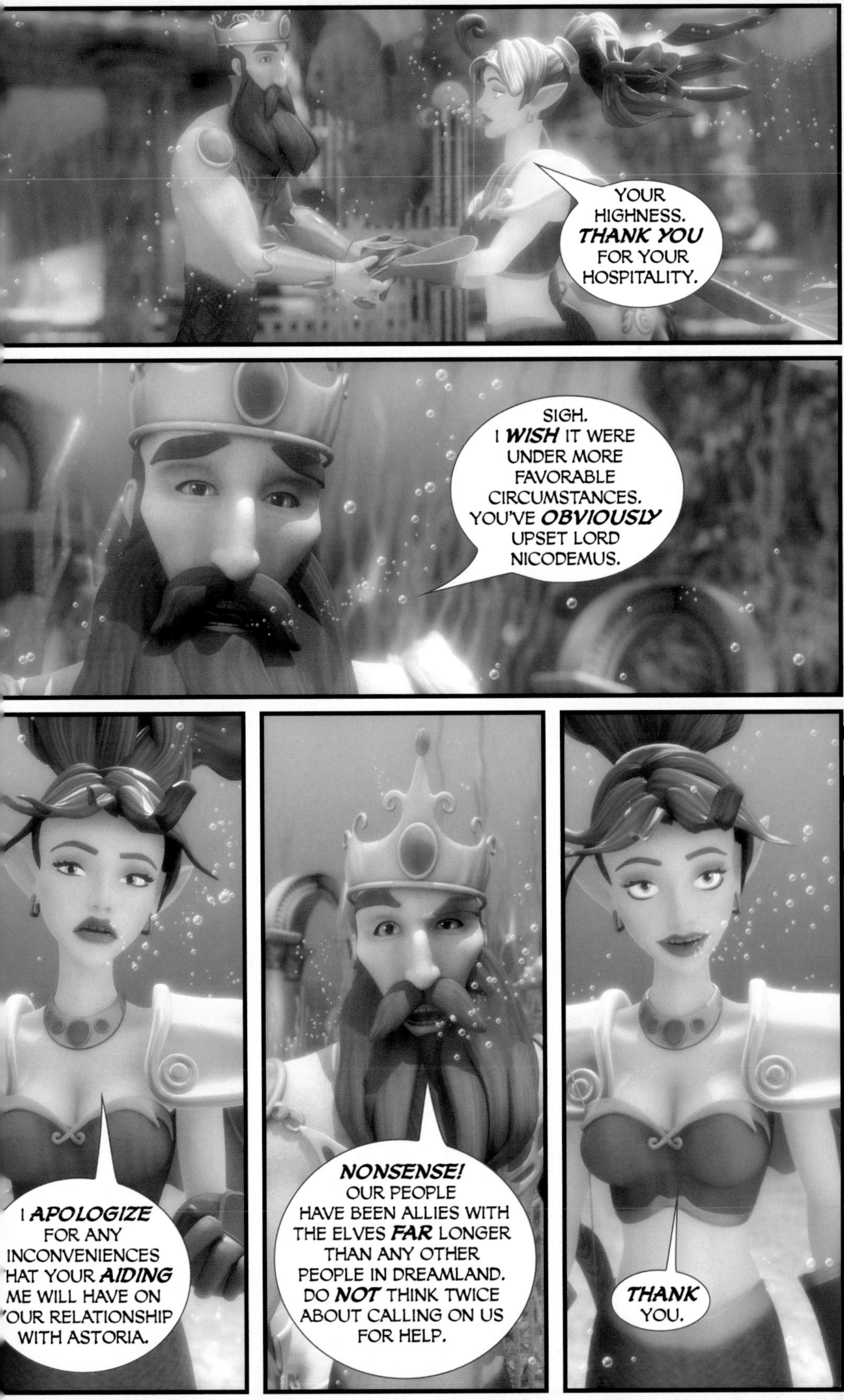
YOUR HIGHNESS. THANK YOU FOR YOUR HOSPITALITY.
SIGH. I WISH IT WERE UNDER MORE FAVORABLE CIRCUMSTANCES. YOU'VE OBVIOUSLY UPSET LORD NICODEMUS.
I APOLOGIZE FOR ANY INCONVENIENCES HAT YOUR AIDING ME WILL HAVE ON 'OUR RELATIONSHIP WITH ASTORIA.
NONSENSE! OUR PEOPLE HAVE BEEN ALLIES WITH THE ELVES FAR LONGER THAN ANY OTHER PEOPLE IN DREAMLAND. DO NOT THINK TWICE ABOUT CALLING ON US FOR HELP.
THANK YOU.

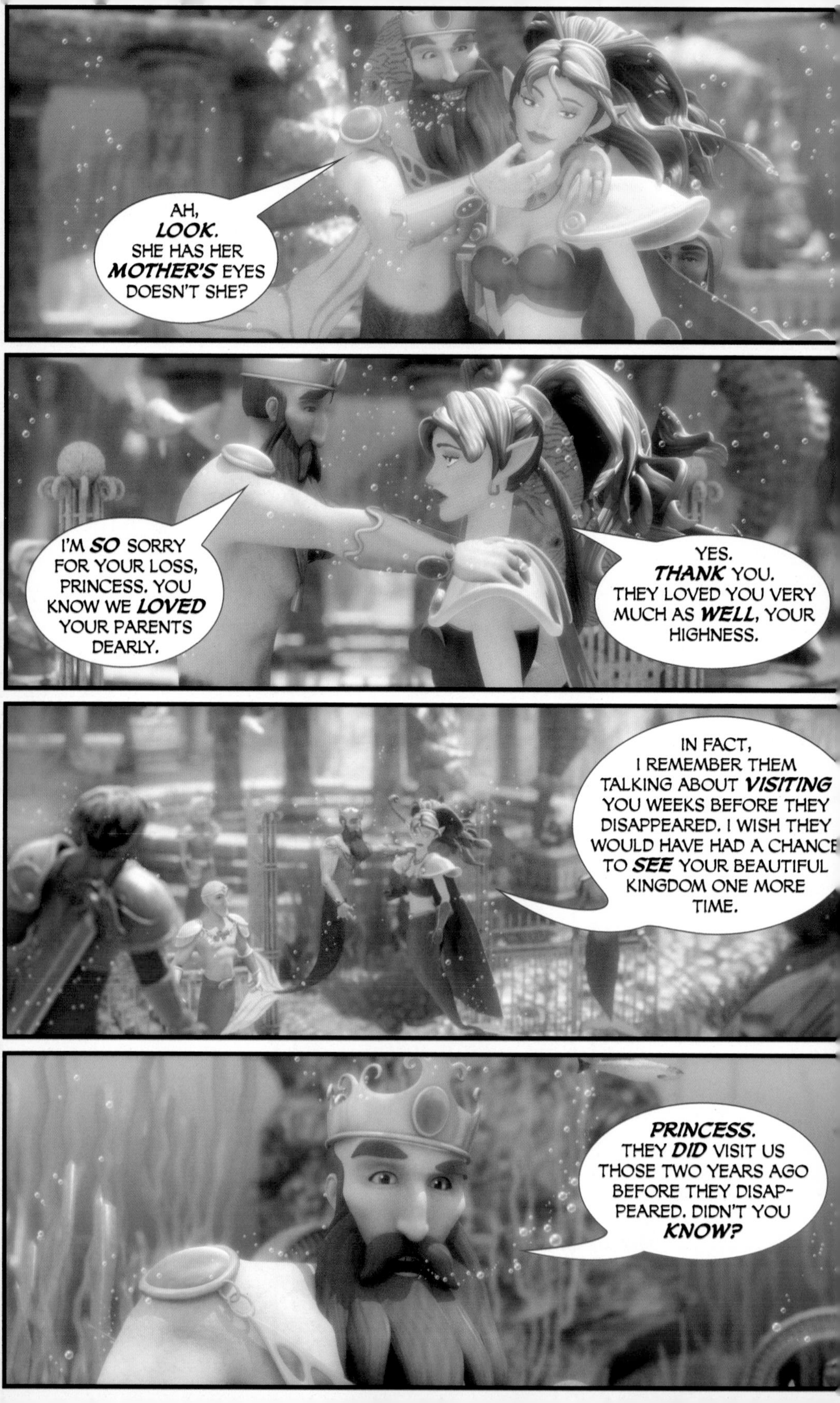
AH, LOOK. SHE HAS HER MOTHER'S EYES DOESN'T SHE?
I'M SO SORRY FOR YOUR LOSS, PRINCESS. YOU KNOW WE LOVED YOUR PARENTS DEARLY.
YES. THANK YOU. THEY LOVED YOU VERY MUCH AS WELL, YOUR HIGHNESS.
IN FACT, I REMEMBER THEM TALKING ABOUT VISITING YOU WEEKS BEFORE THEY DISAPPEARED. I WISH THEY WOULD HAVE HAD A CHANCE TO SEE YOUR BEAUTIFUL KINGDOM ONE MORE TIME.
PRINCESS. THEY DID VISIT US THOSE TWO YEARS AGO BEFORE THEY DISAP-PEARED. DIDN'T YOU KNOW?

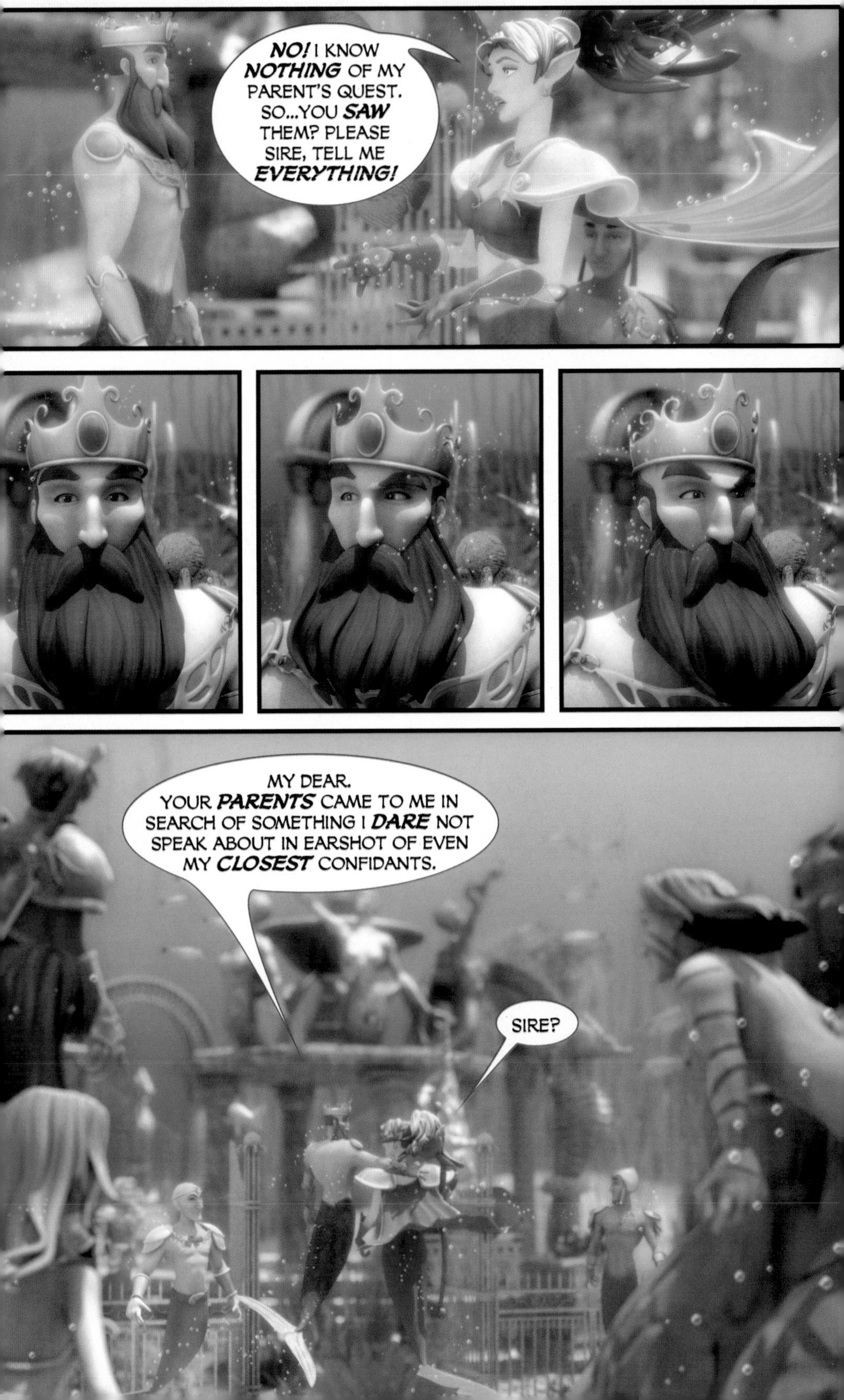
NO! I KNOW NOTHING OF MY PARENT'S QUEST. SO...YOU SAW THEM? PLEASE SIRE, TELL ME EVERYTHING!
MY DEAR. YOUR PARENTS CAME TO ME IN SEARCH OF SOMETHING I DARE NOT SPEAK ABOUT IN EARSHOT OF EVEN MY CLOSEST CONFIDANTS.
SIRE?

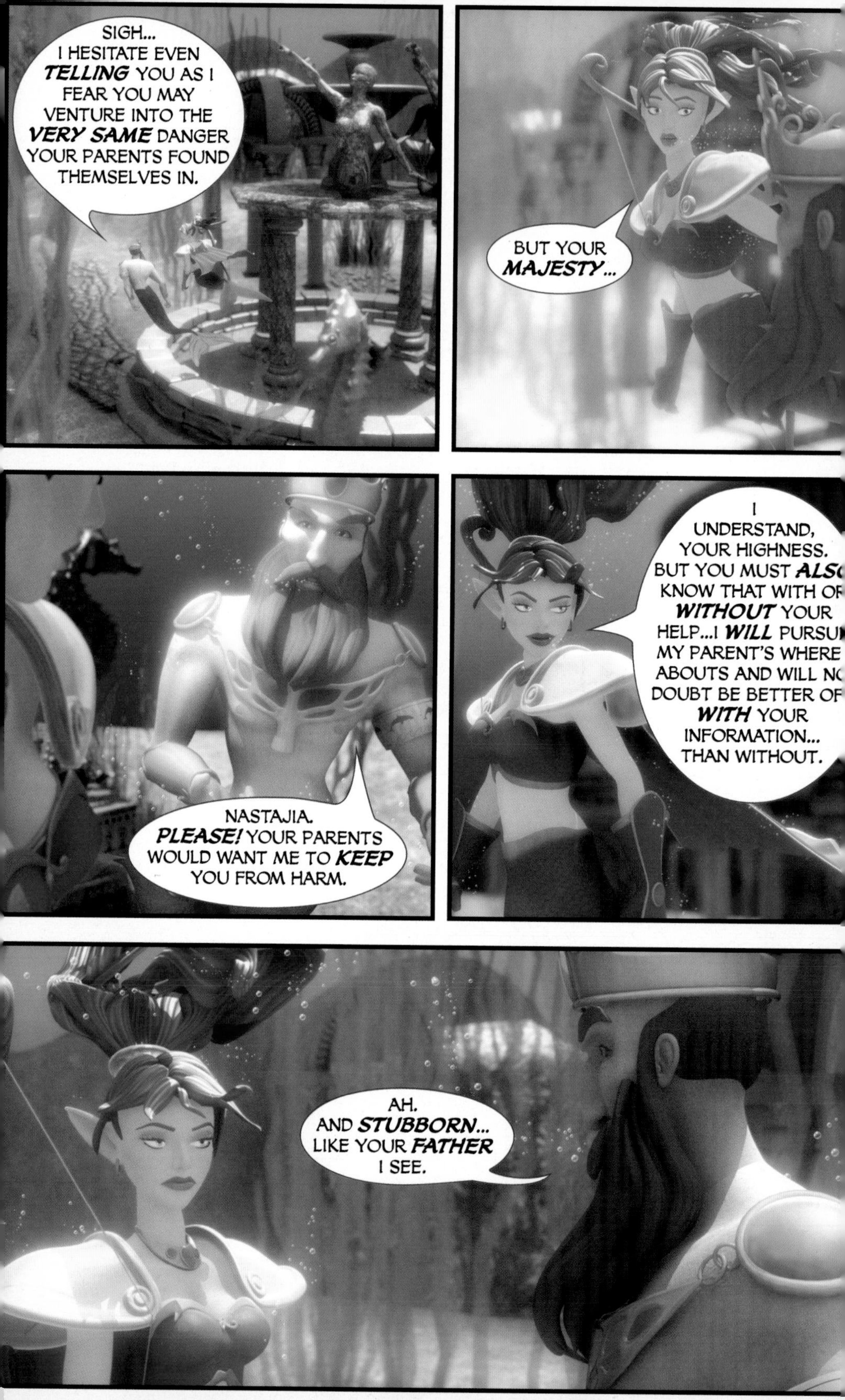
SIGH... I HESITATE EVEN TELLING YOU AS I FEAR YOU MAY VENTURE INTO THE VERY SAME DANGER YOUR PARENTS FOUND THEMSELVES IN.
BUT YOUR MAJESTY...
NASTAJIA. PLEASE! YOUR PARENTS WOULD WANT ME TO KEEP YOU FROM HARM.
I UNDERSTAND, YOUR HIGHNESS. BUT YOU MUST ALSO KNOW THAT WITH OR WITHOUT YOUR HELP...I WILL PURSUE MY PARENT'S WHEREABOUTS AND WILL NO DOUBT BE BETTER OFF WITH YOUR INFORMATION... THAN WITHOUT.
AH. AND STUBBORN... LIKE YOUR FATHER I SEE.

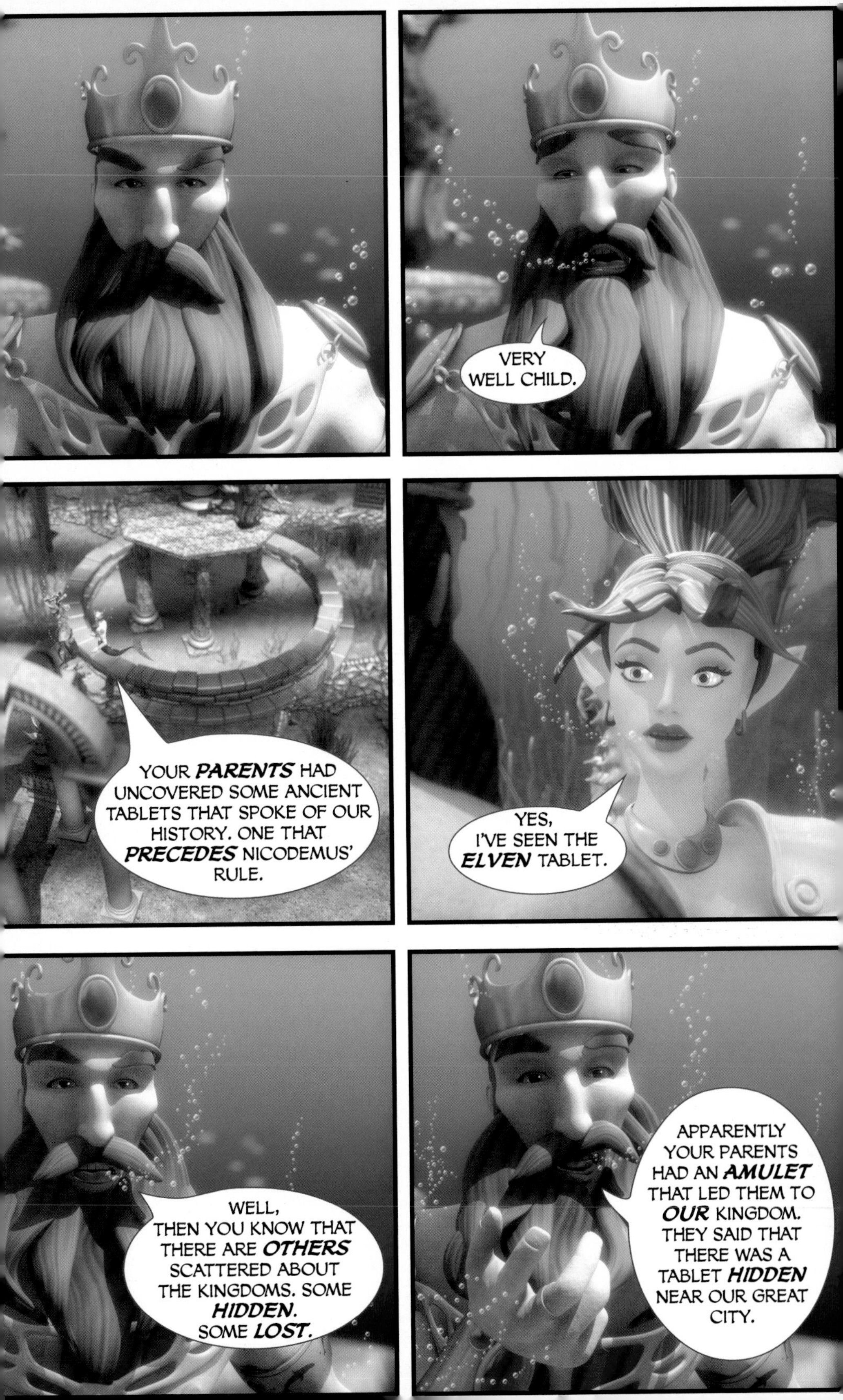
VERY WELL CHILD.
YOUR PARENTS HAD UNCOVERED SOME ANCIENT TABLETS THAT SPOKE OF OUR HISTORY. ONE THAT PRECEDES NICODEMUS' RULE.
YES, I'VE SEEN THE ELVEN TABLET.
WELL, THEN YOU KNOW THAT THERE ARE OTHERS SCATTERED ABOUT THE KINGDOMS. SOME HIDDEN. SOME LOST.
APPARENTLY YOUR PARENTS HAD AN AMULET THAT LED THEM TO OUR KINGDOM. THEY SAID THAT THERE WAS A TABLET HIDDEN NEAR OUR GREAT CITY.

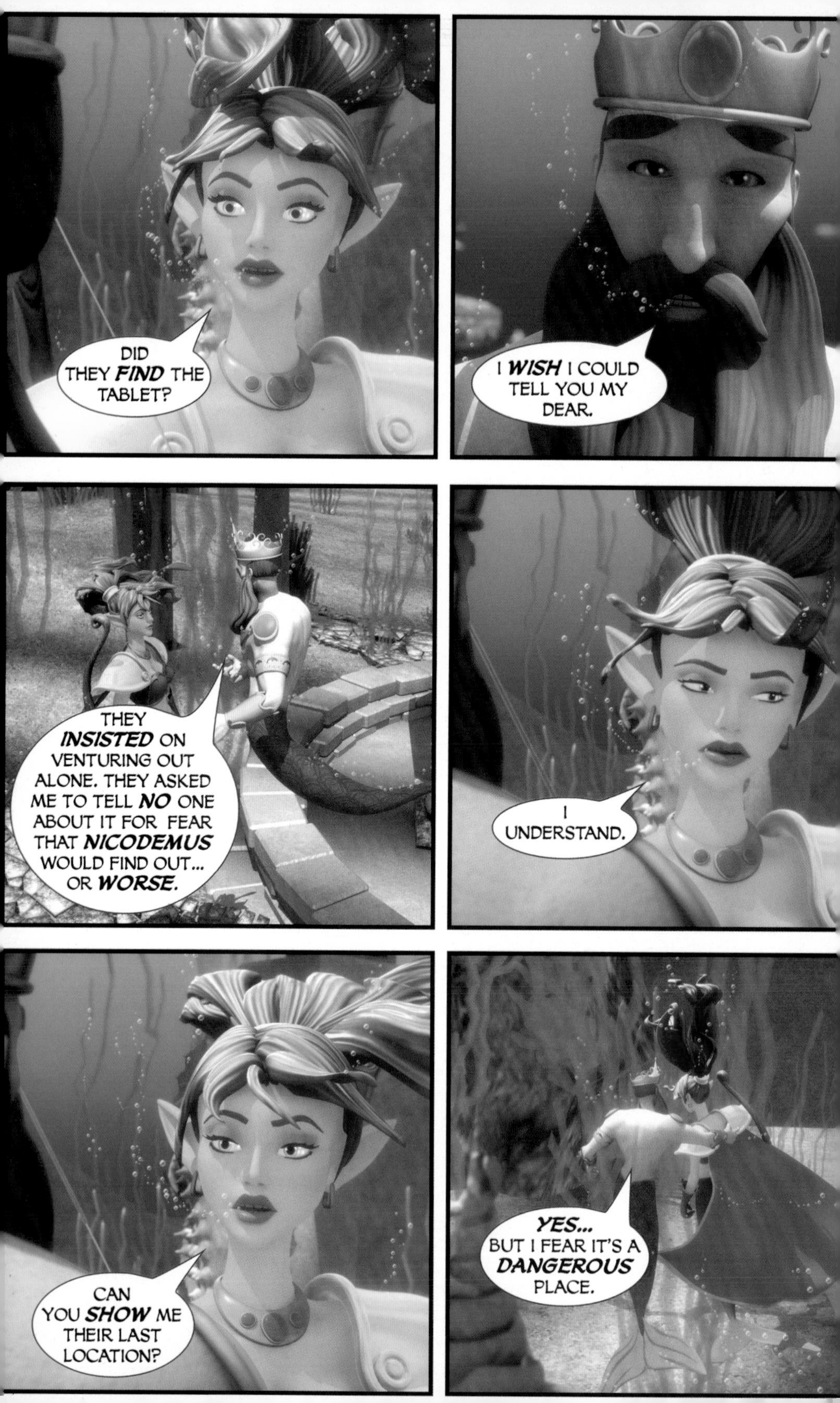
DID THEY FIND THE TABLET?
I WISH I COULD TELL YOU MY DEAR.
THEY INSISTED ON VENTURING OUT ALONE. THEY ASKED ME TO TELL NO ONE ABOUT IT FOR FEAR THAT NICODEMUS WOULD FIND OUT... OR WORSE.
I UNDERSTAND.
CAN YOU SHOW ME THEIR LAST LOCATION?
YES... BUT I FEAR IT'S A DANGEROUS PLACE.

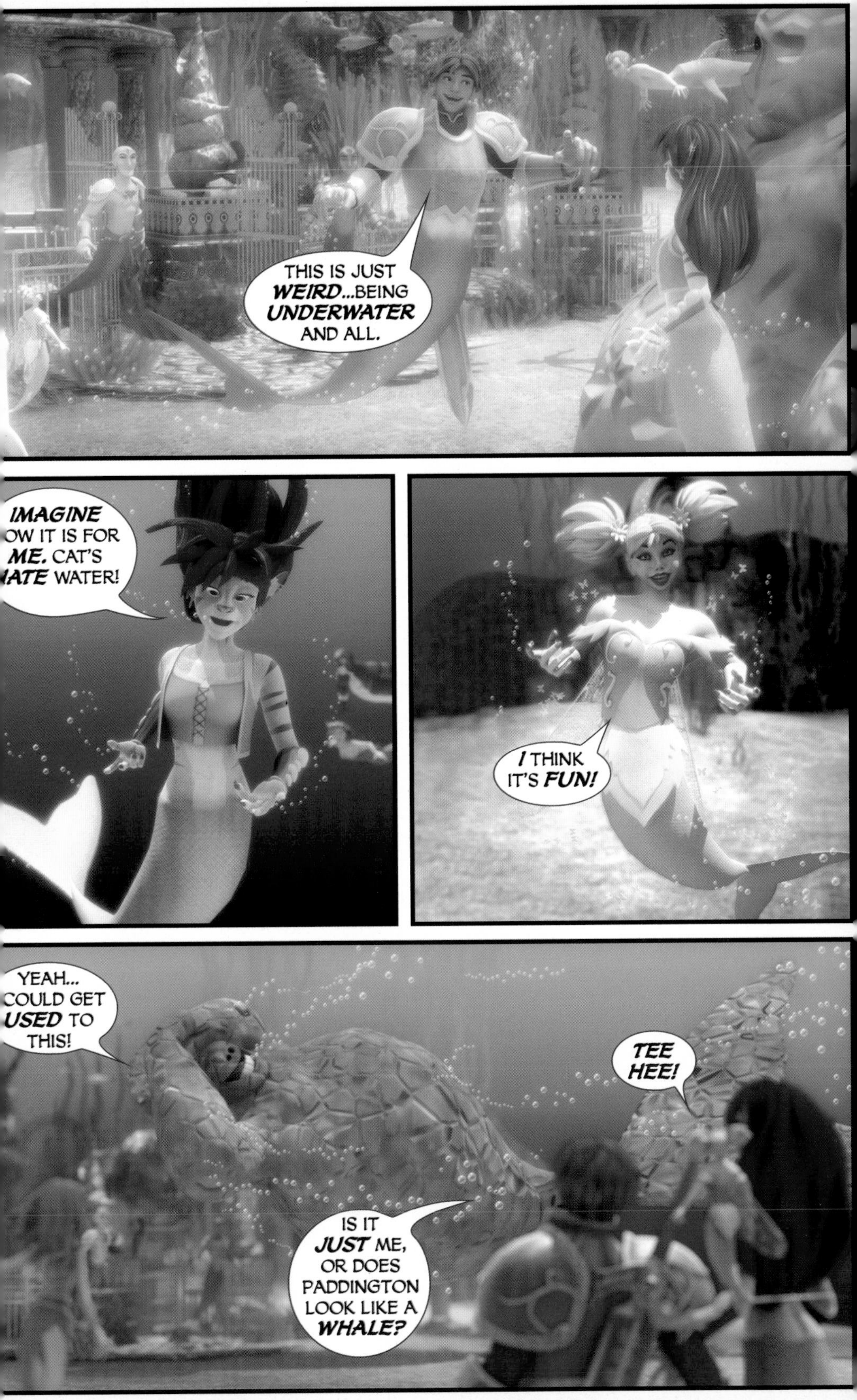

THIS IS JUST WEIRD...BEING UNDERWATER AND ALL.
IMAGINE OW IT IS FOR ME. CAT'S ATE WATER!
I THINK IT'S FUN!
YEAH... COULD GET USED TO THIS!
TEE HEE!
IS IT JUST ME, OR DOES PADDINGTON LOOK LIKE A WHALE?

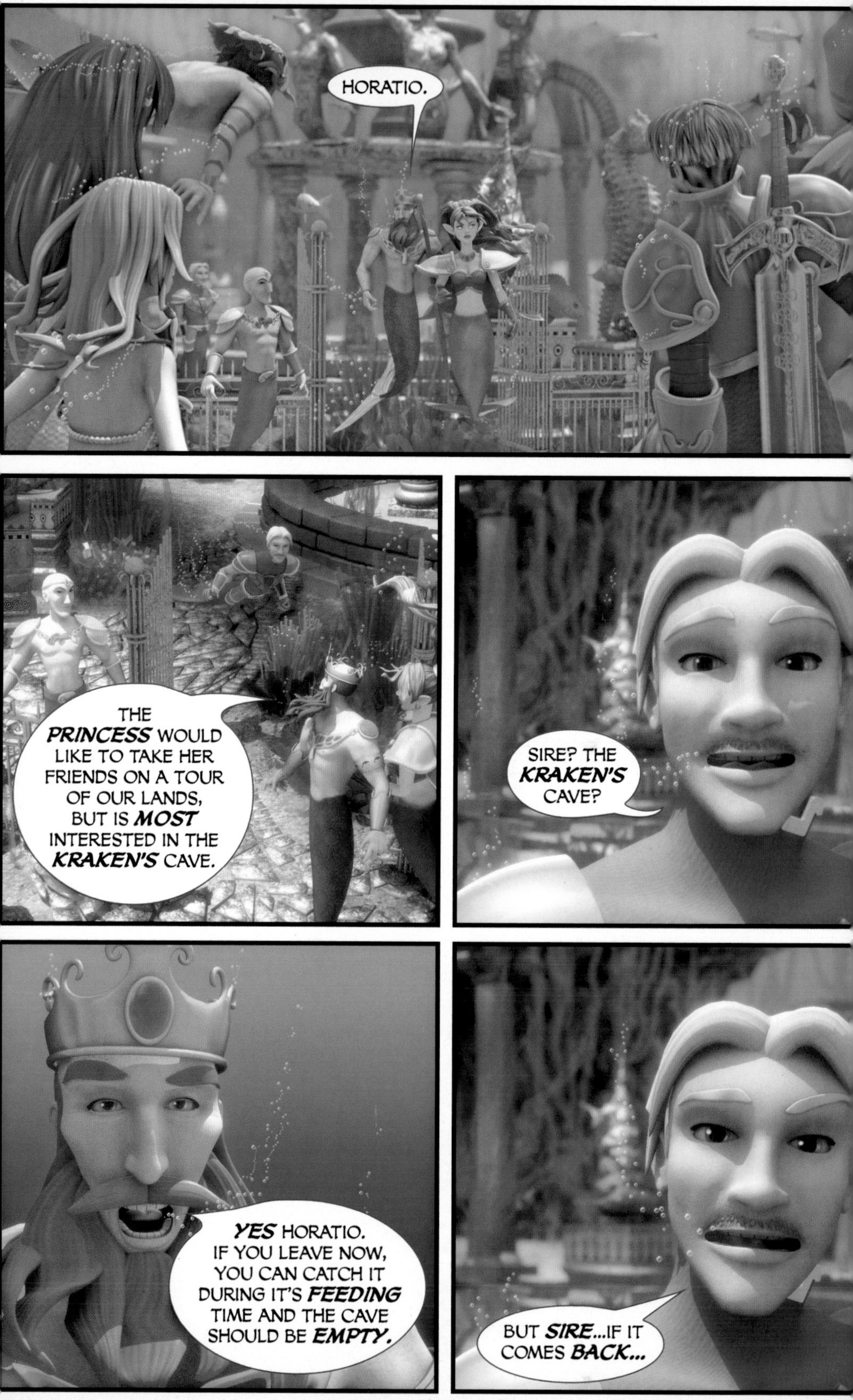
HORATIO.
THE PRINCESS WOULD LIKE TO TAKE HER FRIENDS ON A TOUR OF OUR LANDS, BUT IS MOST INTERESTED IN THE KRAKEN'S CAVE.
SIRE? THE KRAKEN'S CAVE?
YES HORATIO. IF YOU LEAVE NOW, YOU CAN CATCH IT DURING IT'S FEEDING TIME AND THE CAVE SHOULD BE EMPTY.
BUT SIRE...IF IT COMES BACK...

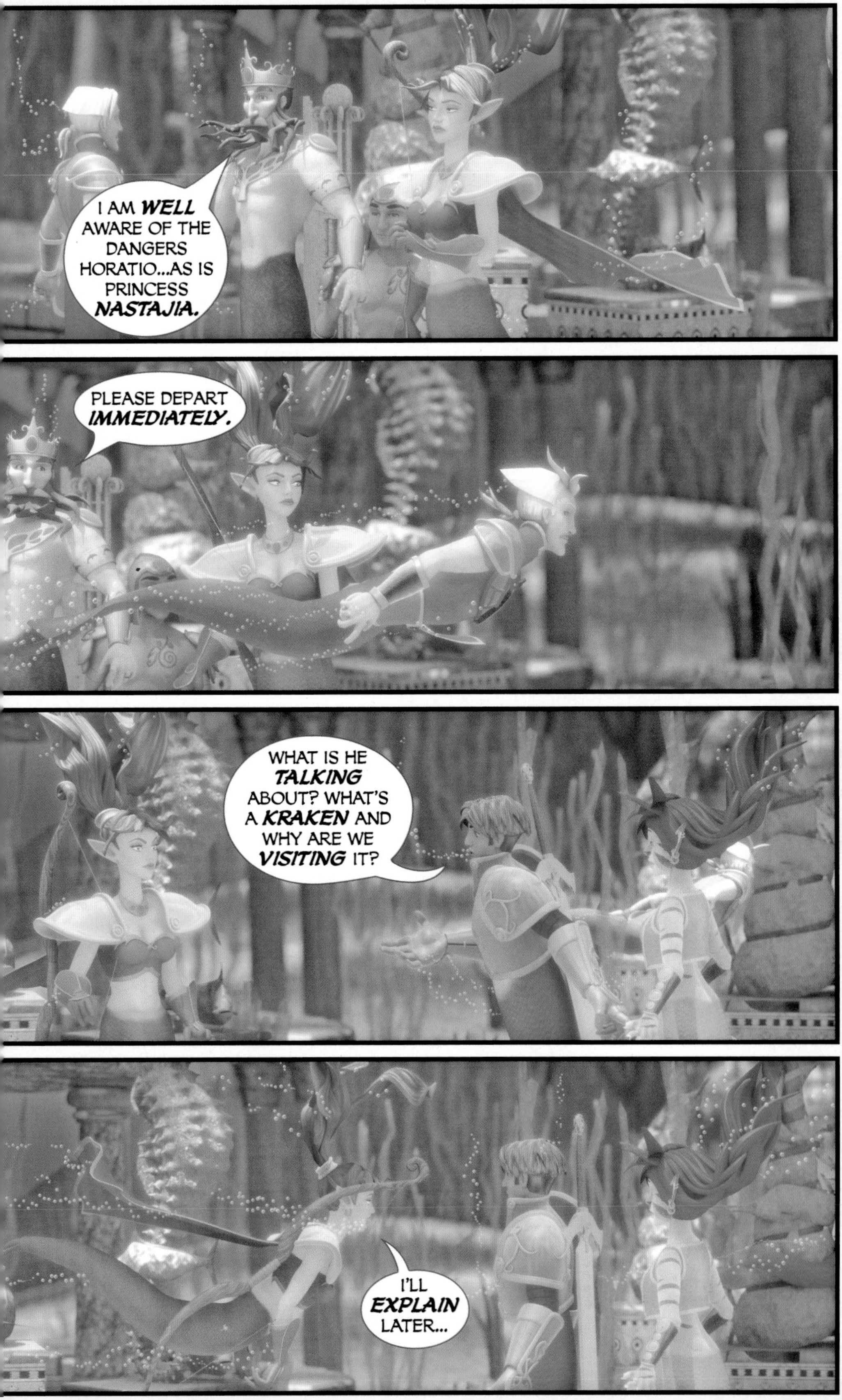
I AM WELL AWARE OF THE DANGERS HORATIO...AS IS PRINCESS NASTAJIA.
PLEASE DEPART IMMEDIATELY.
WHAT IS HE TALKING ABOUT? WHAT'S A KRAKEN AND WHY ARE WE VISITING IT?
I'LL EXPLAIN LATER...

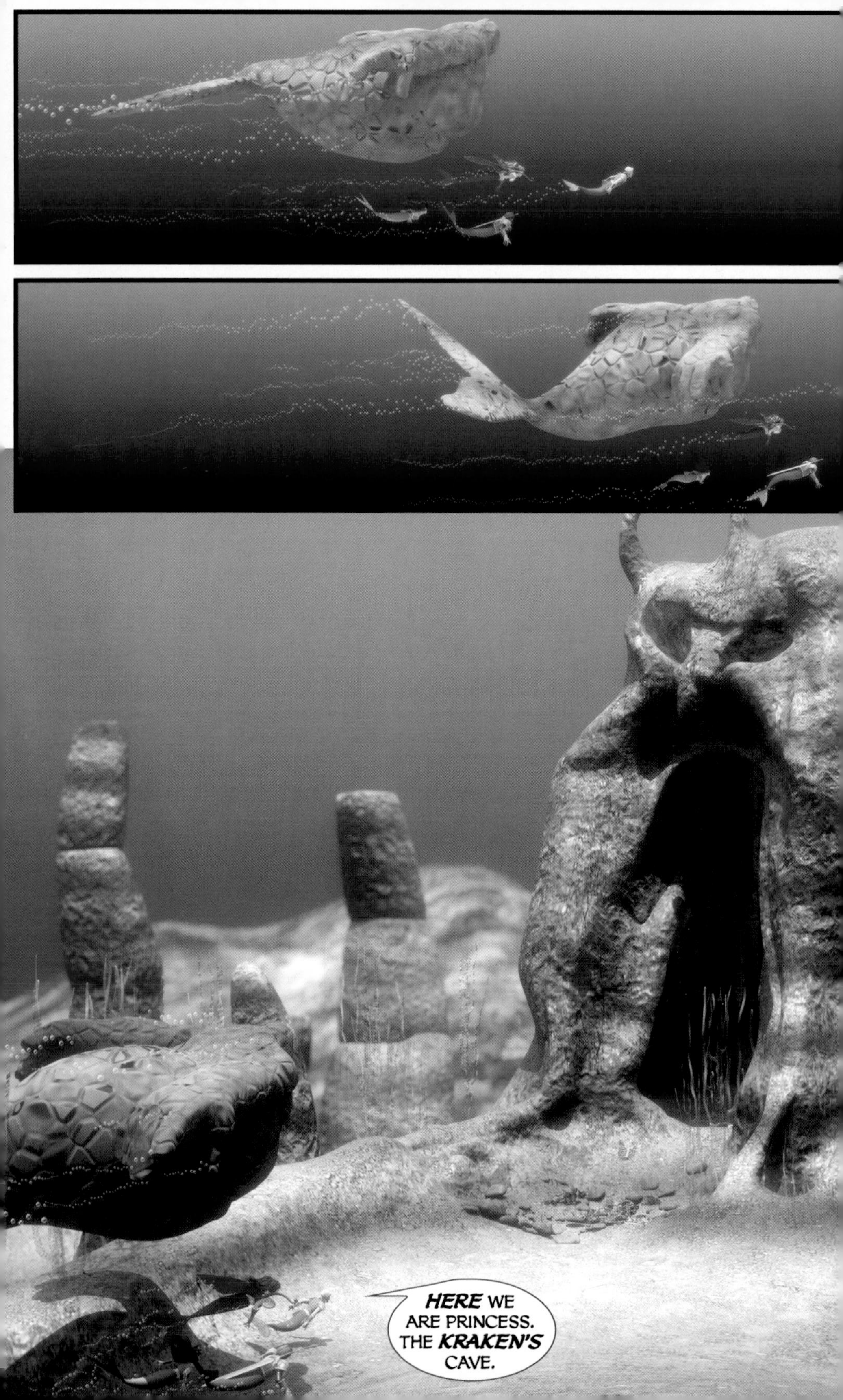
HERE WE ARE PRINCESS. THE KRAKEN'S CAVE.

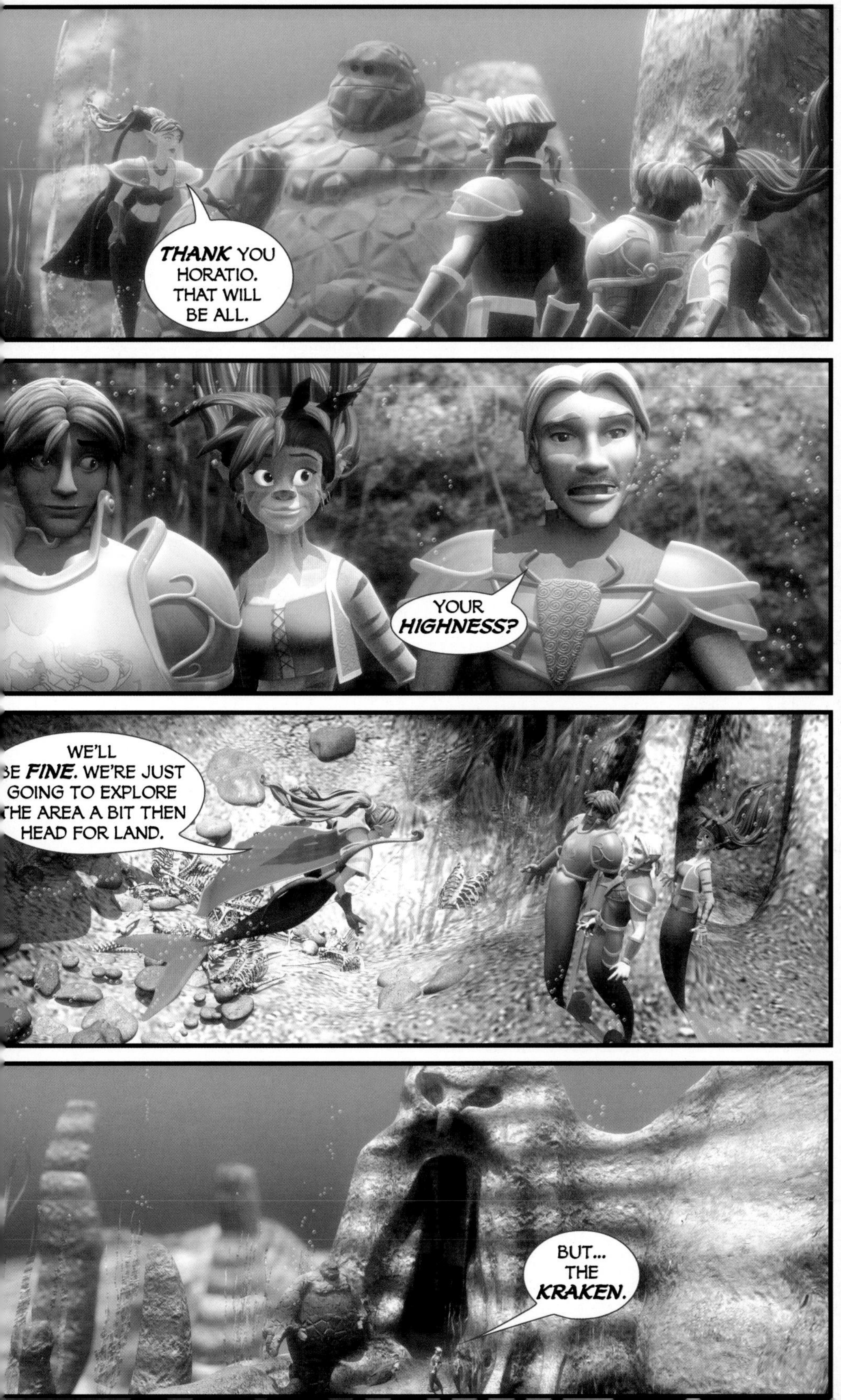
THANK YOU HORATIO. THAT WILL BE ALL.
YOUR HIGHNESS?
WE'LL BE FINE. WE'RE JUST GOING TO EXPLORE THE AREA A BIT THEN HEAD FOR LAND.
BUT... THE KRAKEN.

OH *PLEASE* HORATIO! DO YOU BELIEVE WE'RE *FOOLISH* ENOUGH TO ACTUALLY *BE* HERE WHEN THE MONSTER RETURNS?

NO NO, YOUR HIGHNESS. OF *COURSE* NOT. BU[T] THE KING ASKED M[E] TO STAY WITH YO[U] AS HE FELT YOU MAY NEED MY *SERVICES* AT SOME POINT.

I SEE...

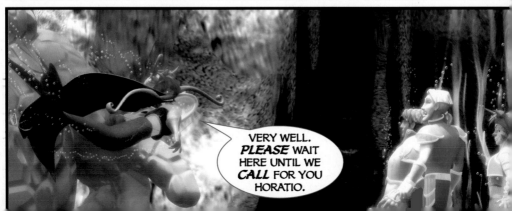

VERY WELL. *PLEASE* WAIT HERE UNTIL WE *CALL* FOR YOU HORATIO.

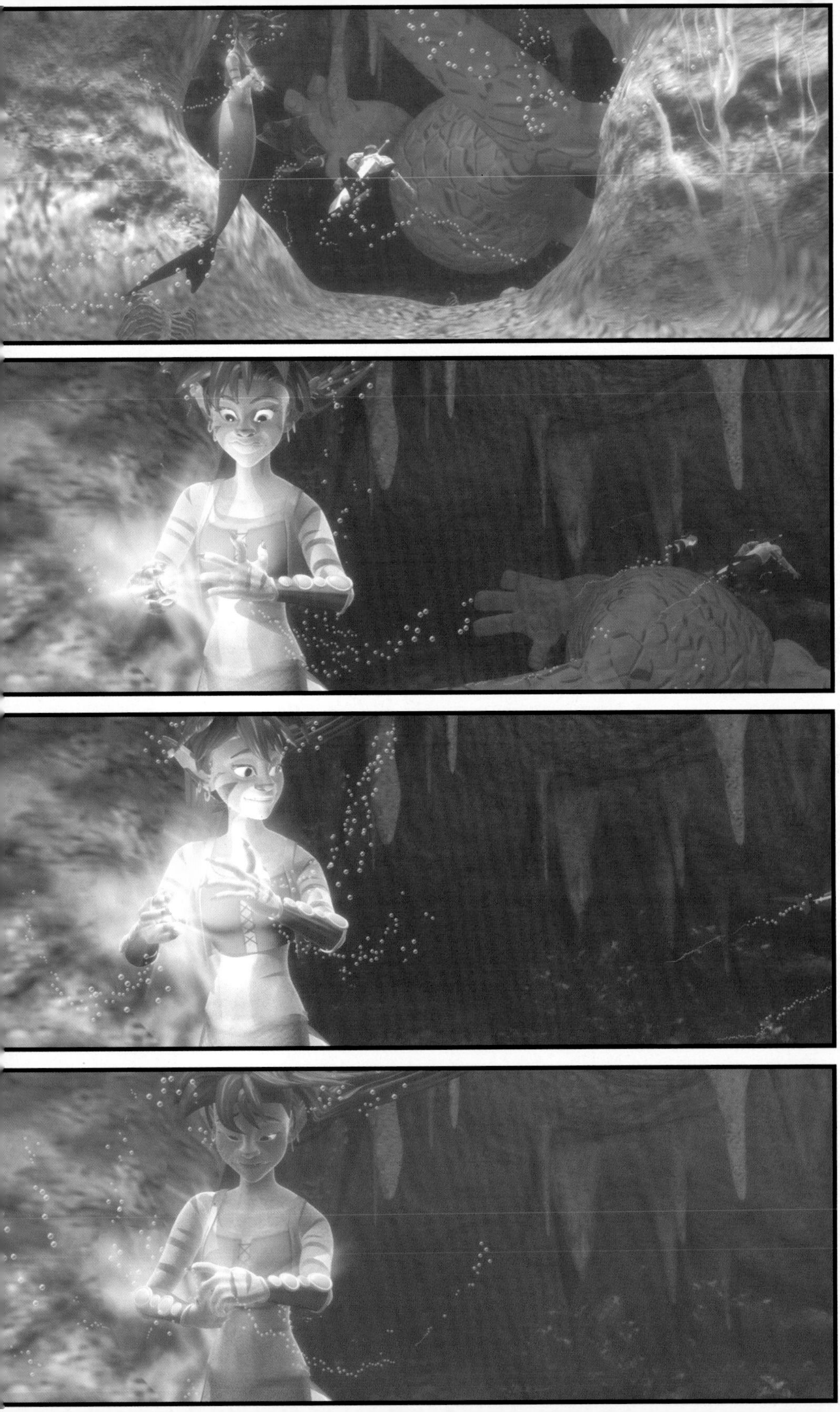

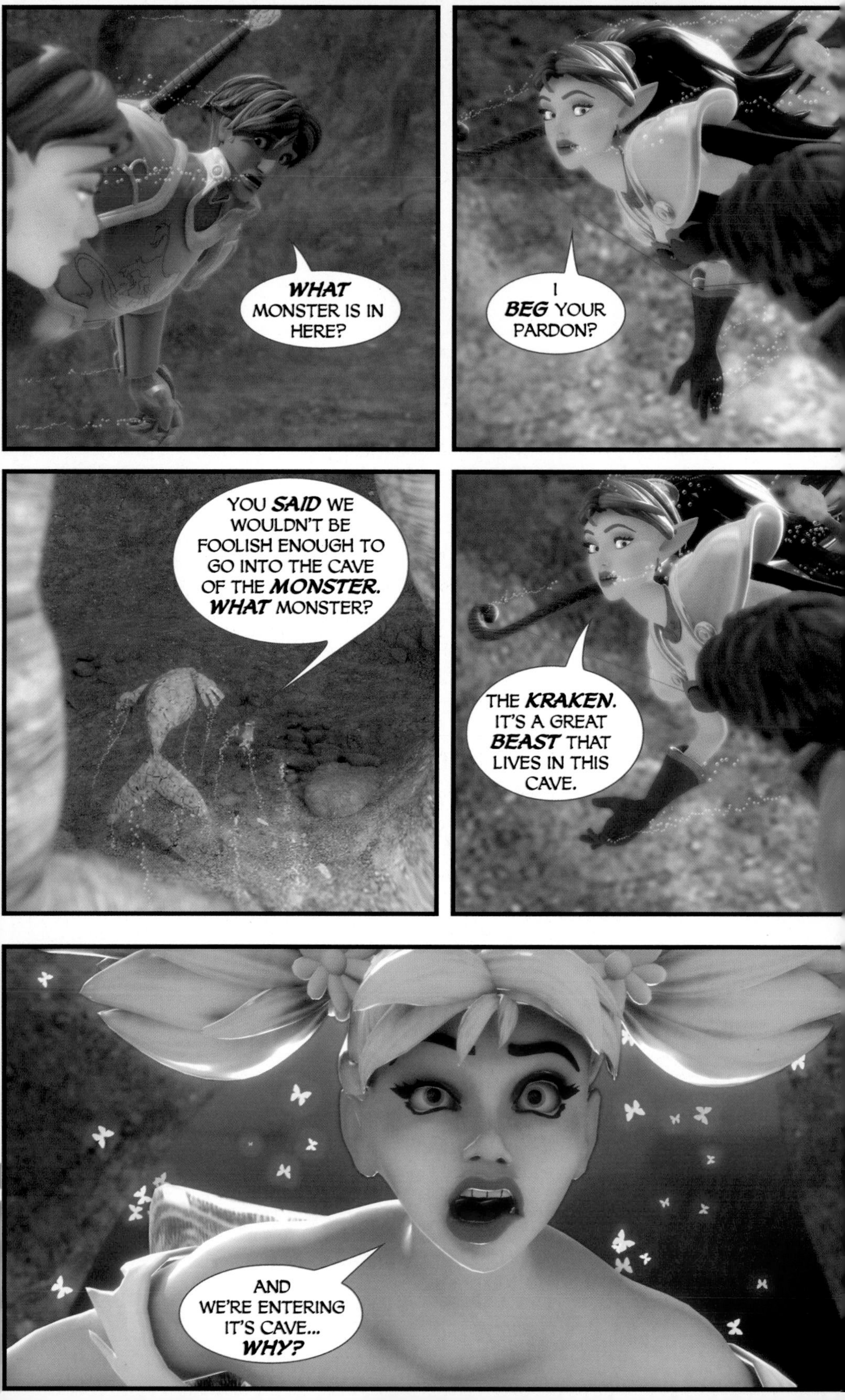
WHAT MONSTER IS IN HERE?
I BEG YOUR PARDON?
YOU SAID WE WOULDN'T BE FOOLISH ENOUGH TO GO INTO THE CAVE OF THE MONSTER. WHAT MONSTER?
THE KRAKEN. IT'S A GREAT BEAST THAT LIVES IN THIS CAVE.
AND WE'RE ENTERING IT'S CAVE... WHY?

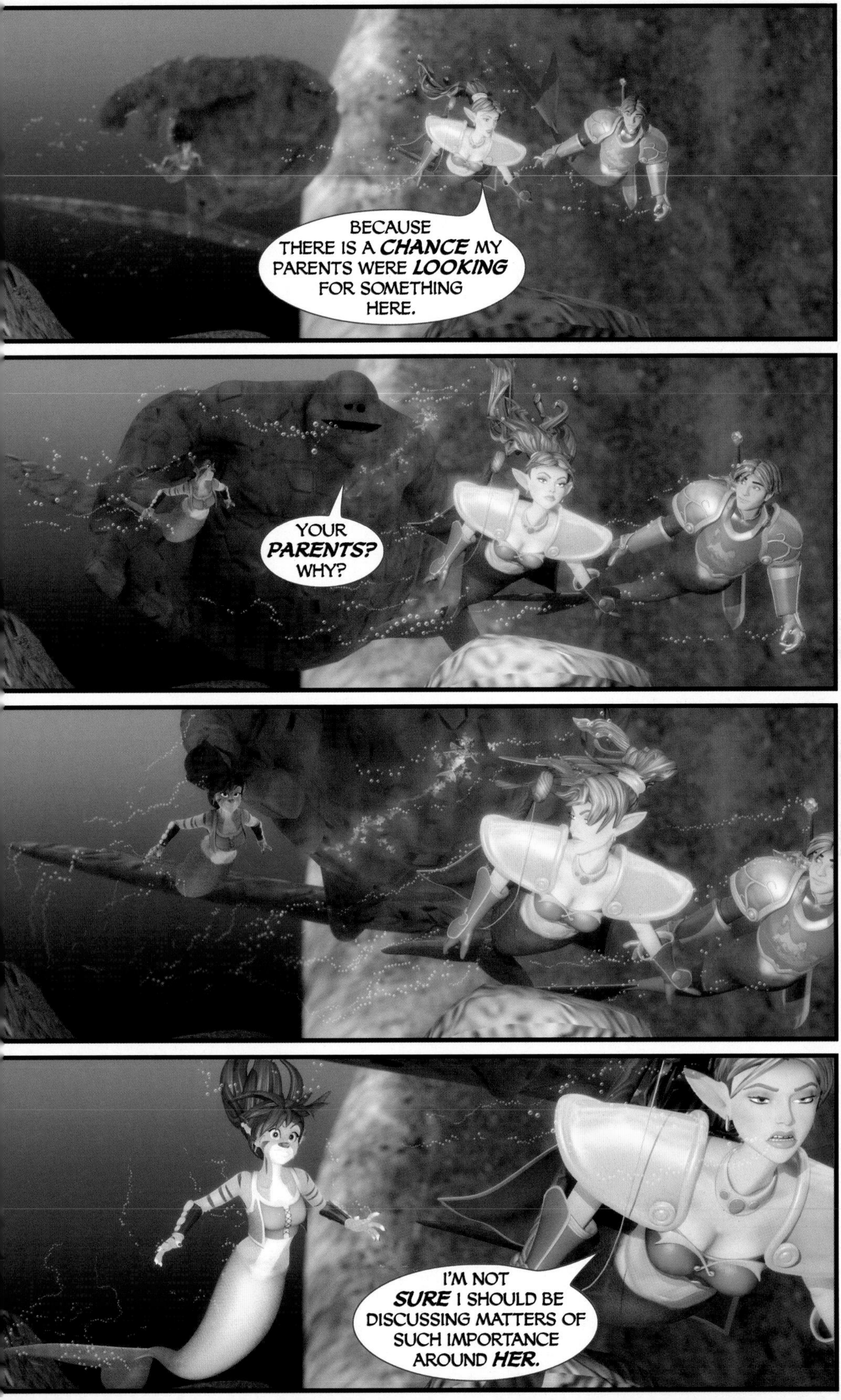
BECAUSE THERE IS A *CHANCE* MY PARENTS WERE *LOOKING* FOR SOMETHING HERE.
YOUR *PARENTS?* WHY?
I'M NOT *SURE* I SHOULD BE DISCUSSING MATTERS OF SUCH IMPORTANCE AROUND *HER.*

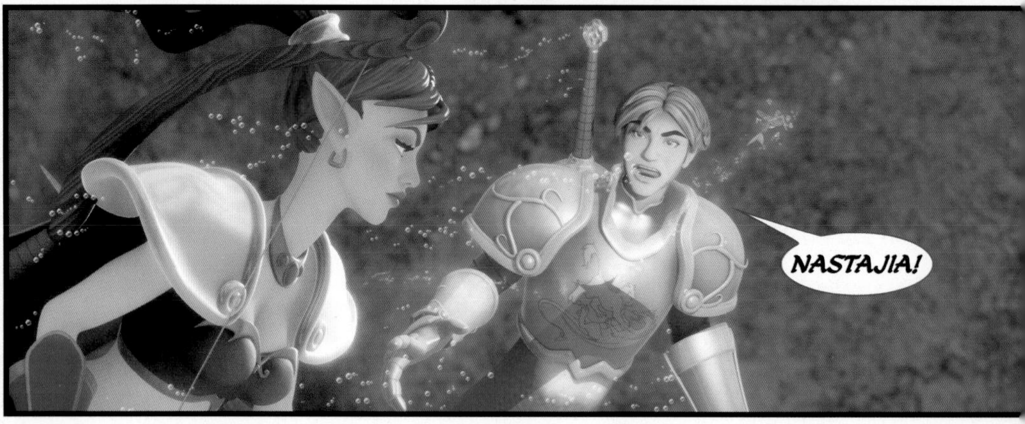
NASTAJIA!

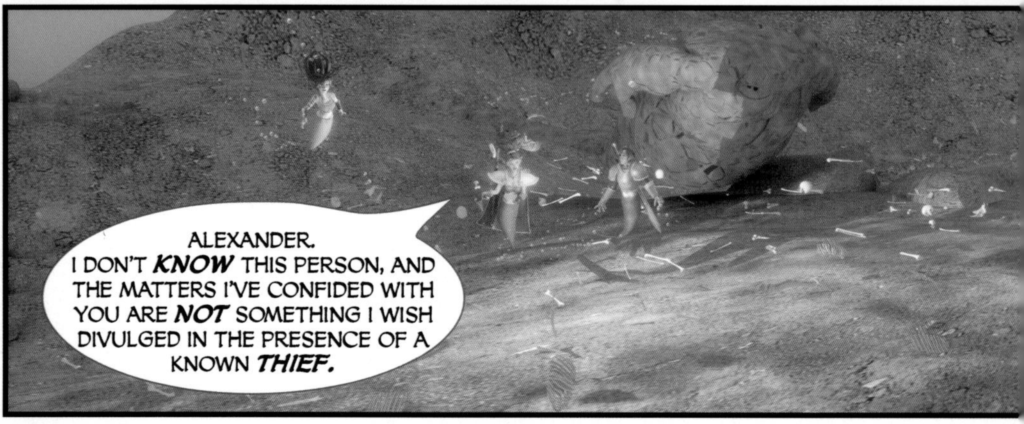
ALEXANDER. I DON'T KNOW THIS PERSON, AND THE MATTERS I'VE CONFIDED WITH YOU ARE NOT SOMETHING I WISH DIVULGED IN THE PRESENCE OF A KNOWN THIEF.

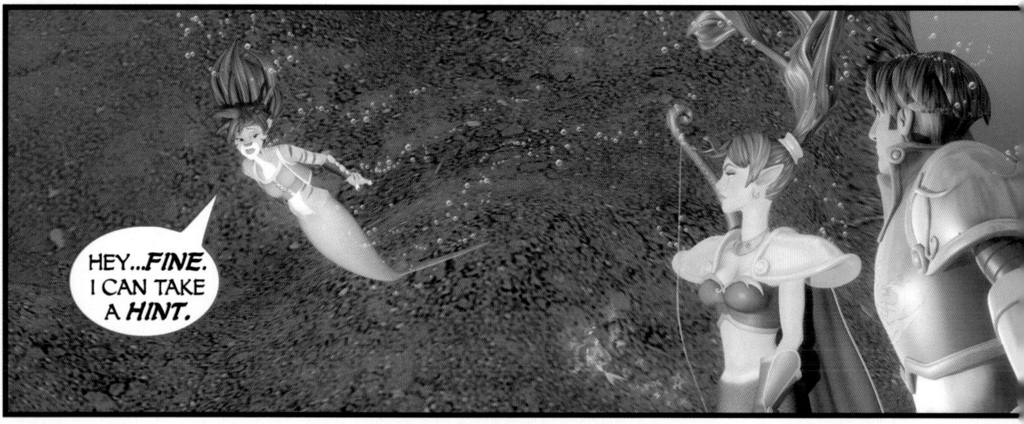
HEY...FINE. I CAN TAKE A HINT.

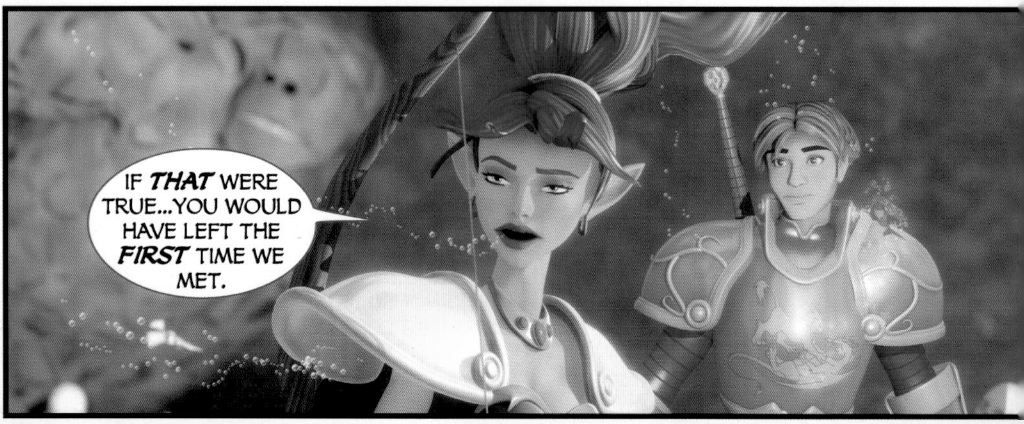
IF THAT WERE TRUE...YOU WOULD HAVE LEFT THE FIRST TIME WE MET.

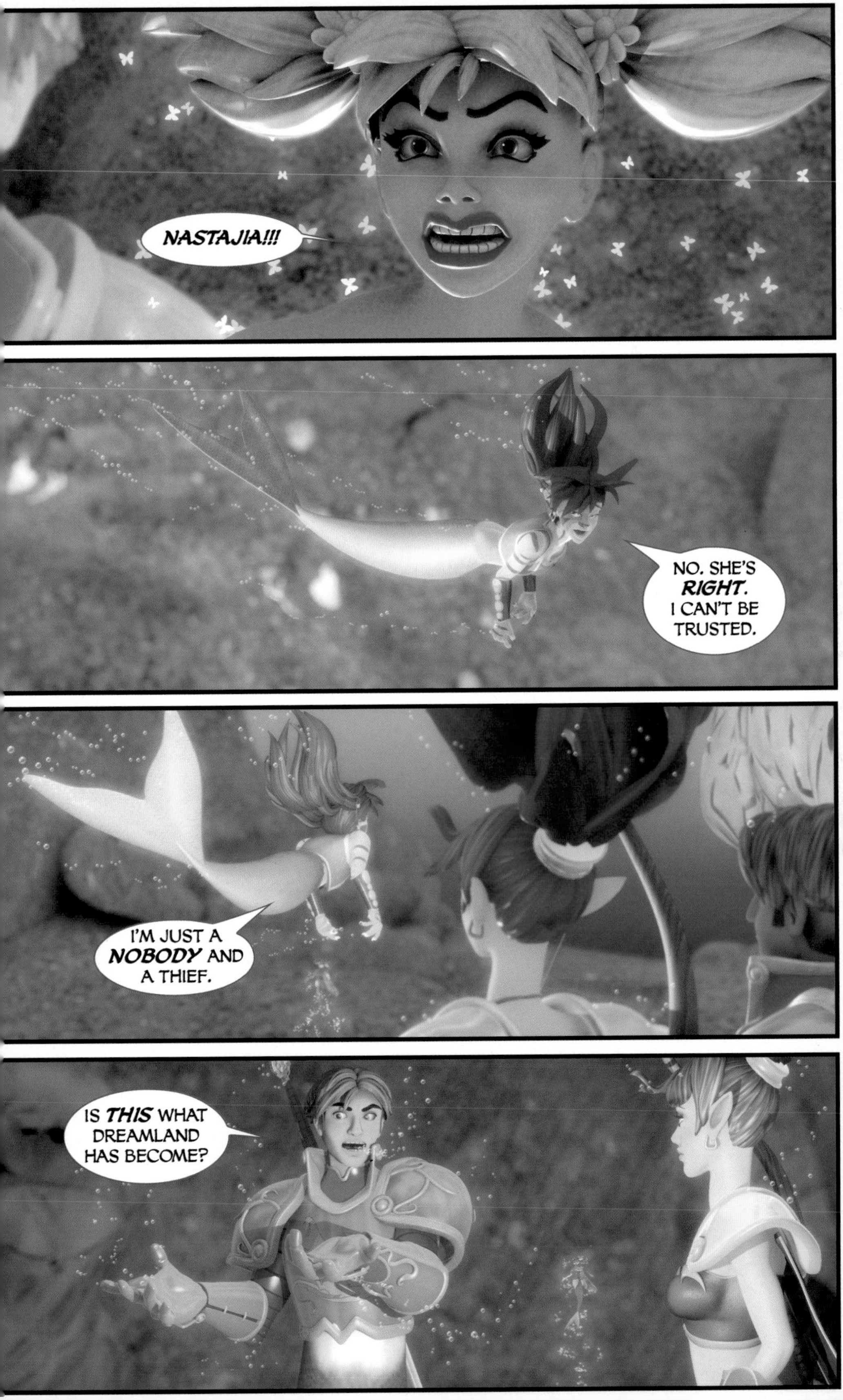
NASTAJIA!!!
NO. SHE'S RIGHT. I CAN'T BE TRUSTED.
I'M JUST A NOBODY AND A THIEF.
IS THIS WHAT DREAMLAND HAS BECOME?

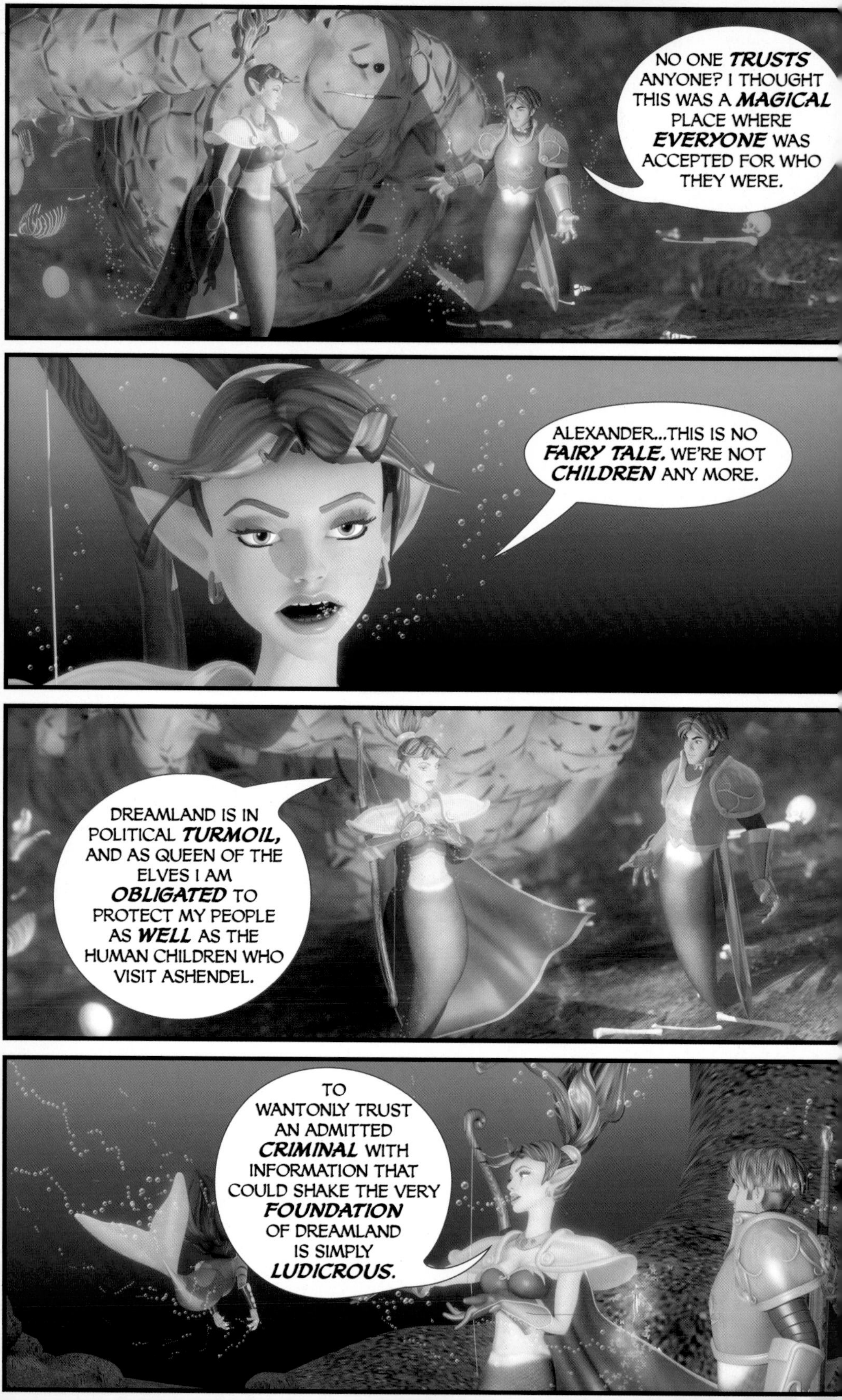
NO ONE TRUSTS ANYONE? I THOUGHT THIS WAS A MAGICAL PLACE WHERE EVERYONE WAS ACCEPTED FOR WHO THEY WERE.
ALEXANDER...THIS IS NO FAIRY TALE. WE'RE NOT CHILDREN ANY MORE.
DREAMLAND IS IN POLITICAL TURMOIL, AND AS QUEEN OF THE ELVES I AM OBLIGATED TO PROTECT MY PEOPLE AS WELL AS THE HUMAN CHILDREN WHO VISIT ASHENDEL.
TO WANTONLY TRUST AN ADMITTED CRIMINAL WITH INFORMATION THAT COULD SHAKE THE VERY FOUNDATION OF DREAMLAND IS SIMPLY LUDICROUS.

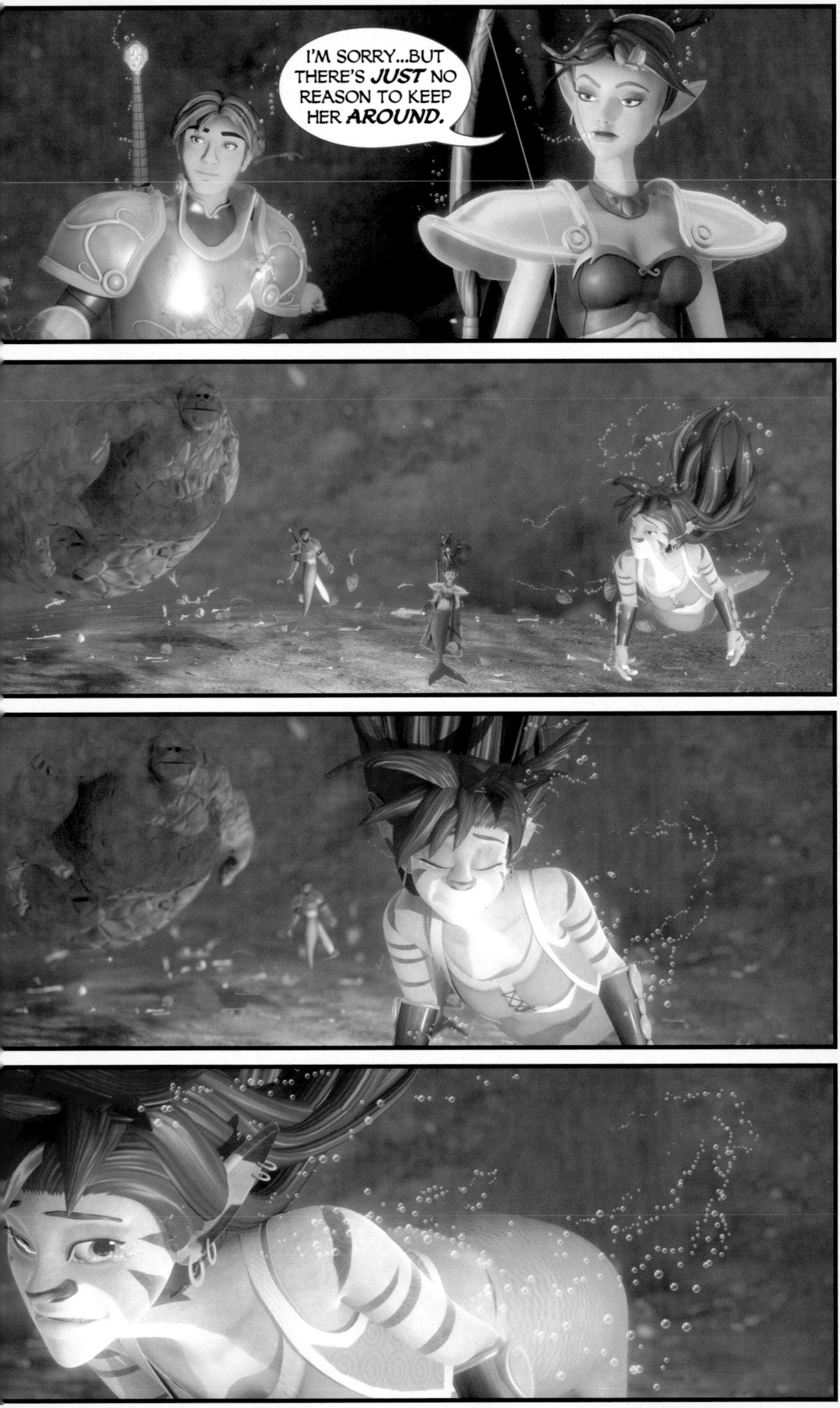
I'M SORRY...BUT THERE'S *JUST* NO REASON TO KEEP HER *AROUND.*

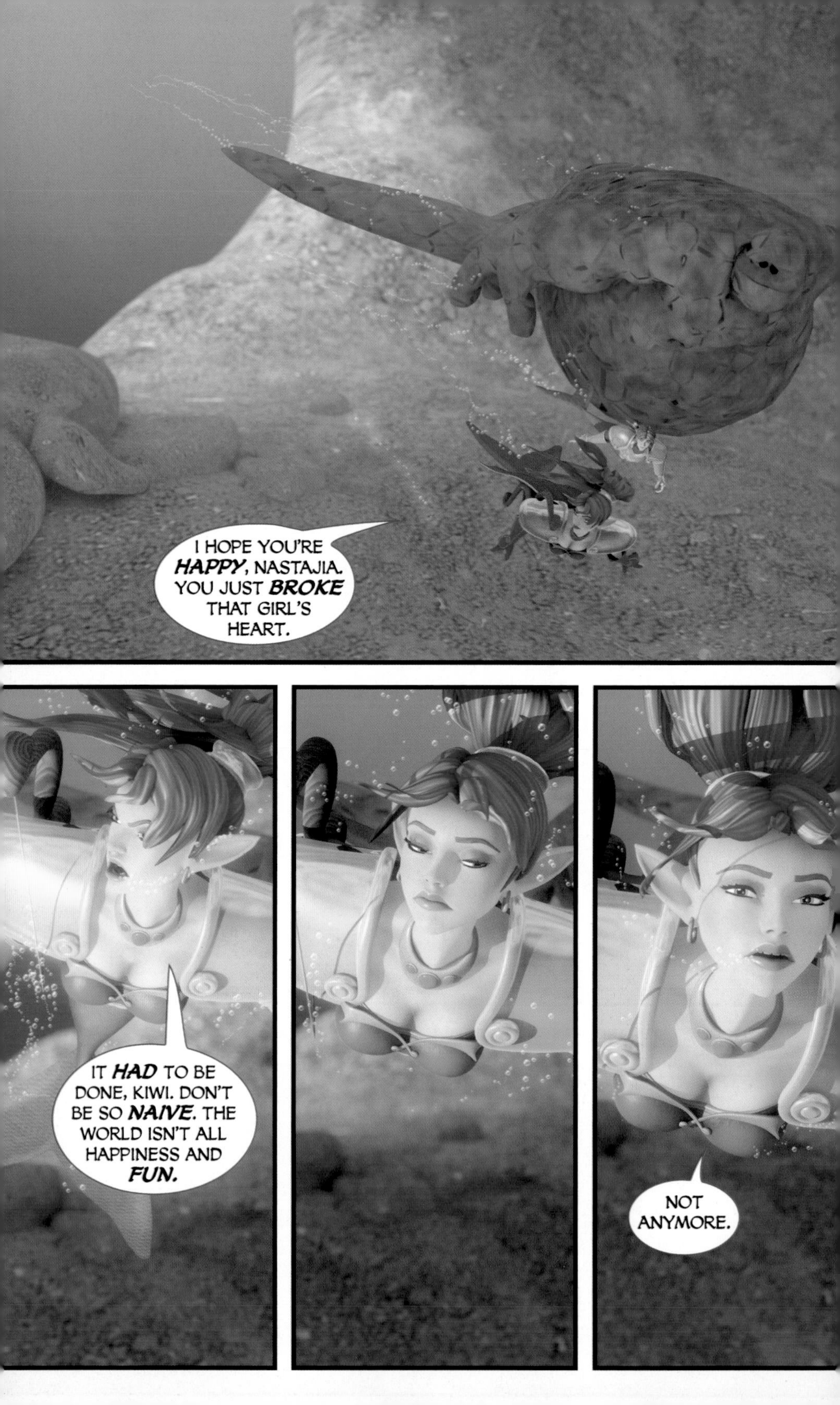
I HOPE YOU'RE HAPPY, NASTAJIA. YOU JUST BROKE THAT GIRL'S HEART.
IT HAD TO BE DONE, KIWI. DON'T BE SO NAIVE. THE WORLD ISN'T ALL HAPPINESS AND FUN.
NOT ANYMORE.

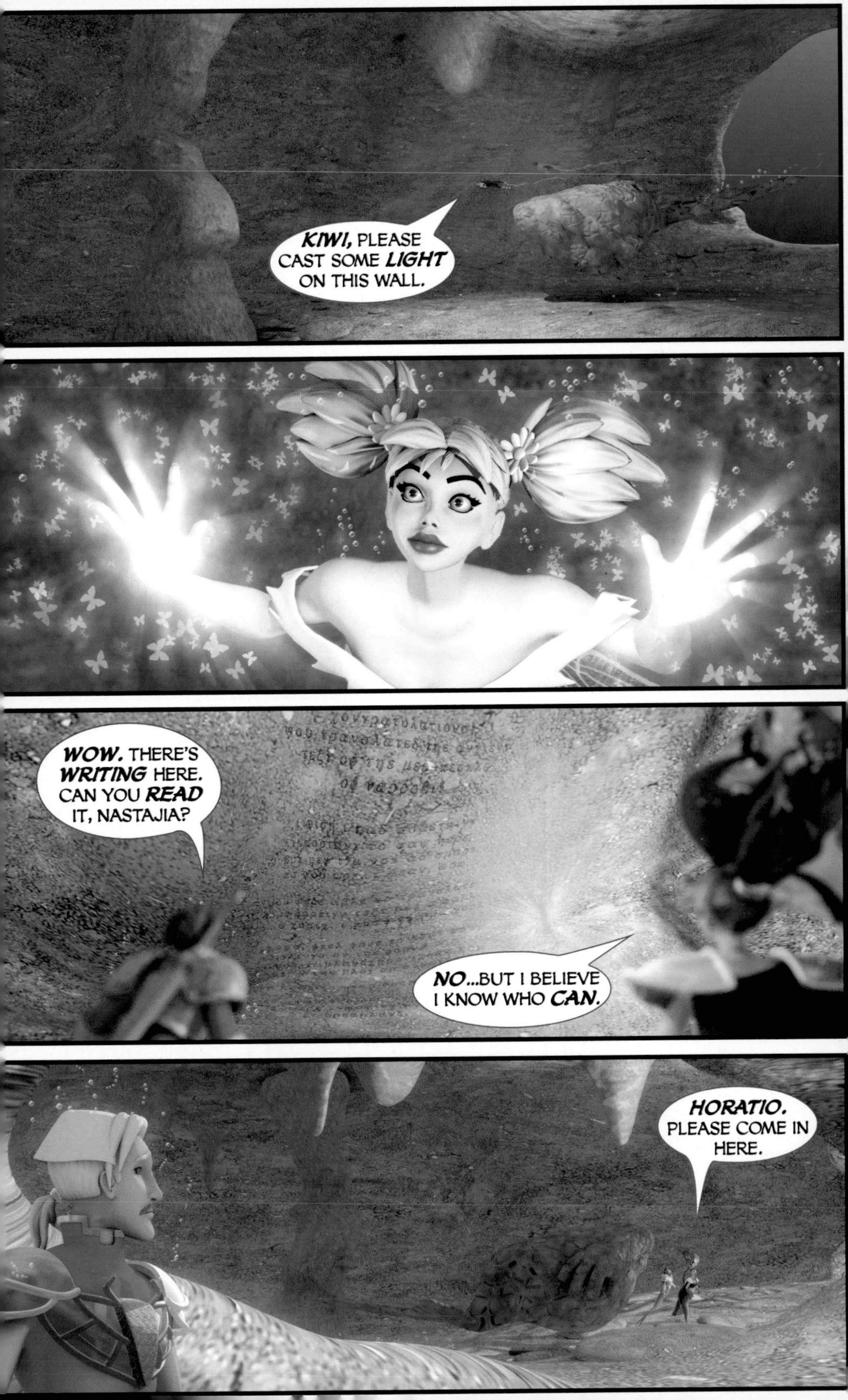
KIWI, PLEASE CAST SOME LIGHT ON THIS WALL.
WOW. THERE'S WRITING HERE. CAN YOU READ IT, NASTAJIA?
NO...BUT I BELIEVE I KNOW WHO CAN.
HORATIO. PLEASE COME IN HERE.

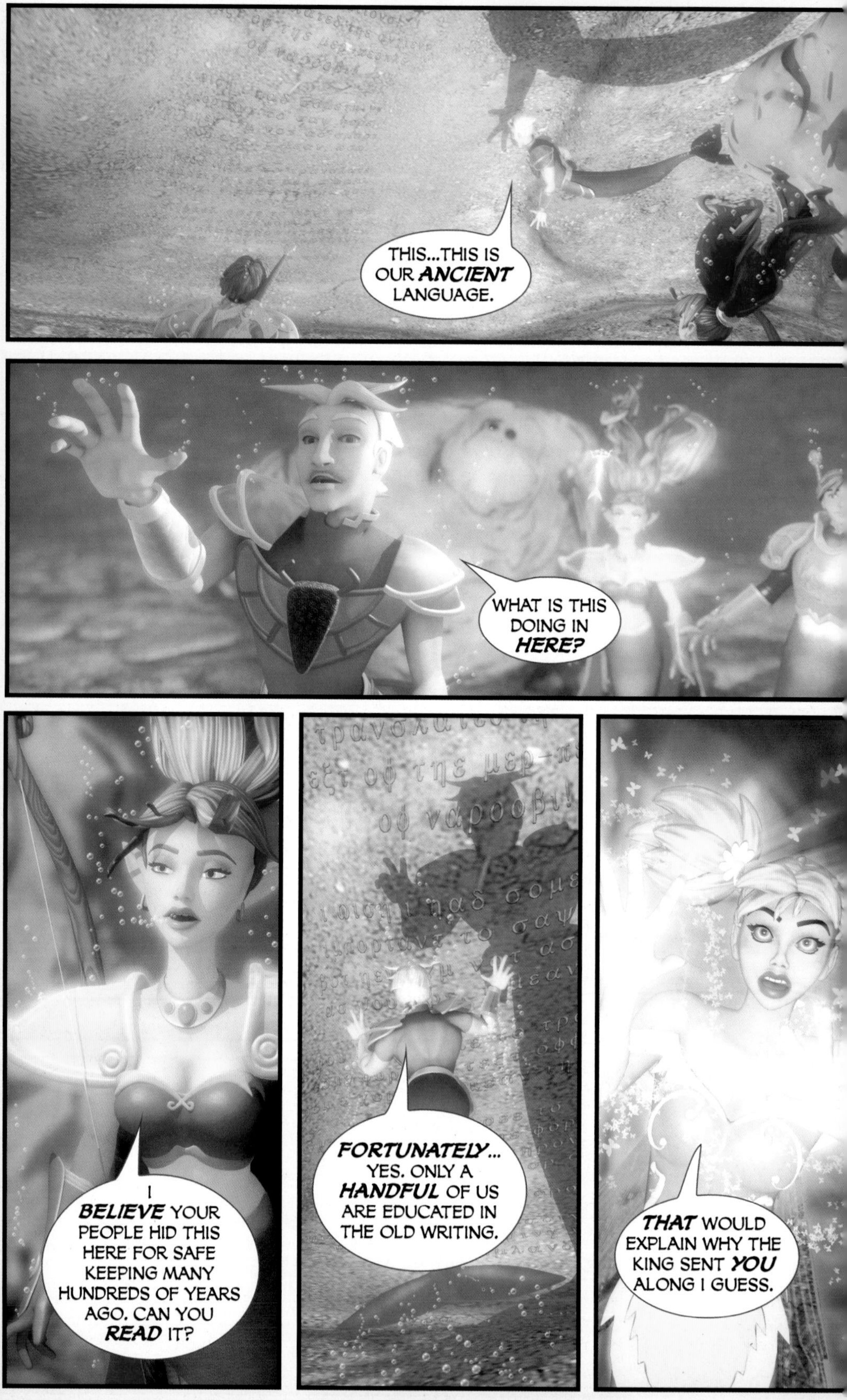
THIS...THIS IS OUR *ANCIENT* LANGUAGE.
WHAT IS THIS DOING IN *HERE?*
I *BELIEVE* YOUR PEOPLE HID THIS HERE FOR SAFE KEEPING MANY HUNDREDS OF YEARS AGO. CAN YOU *READ* IT?
FORTUNATELY... YES. ONLY A *HANDFUL* OF US ARE EDUCATED IN THE OLD WRITING.
THAT WOULD EXPLAIN WHY THE KING SENT *YOU* ALONG I GUESS.

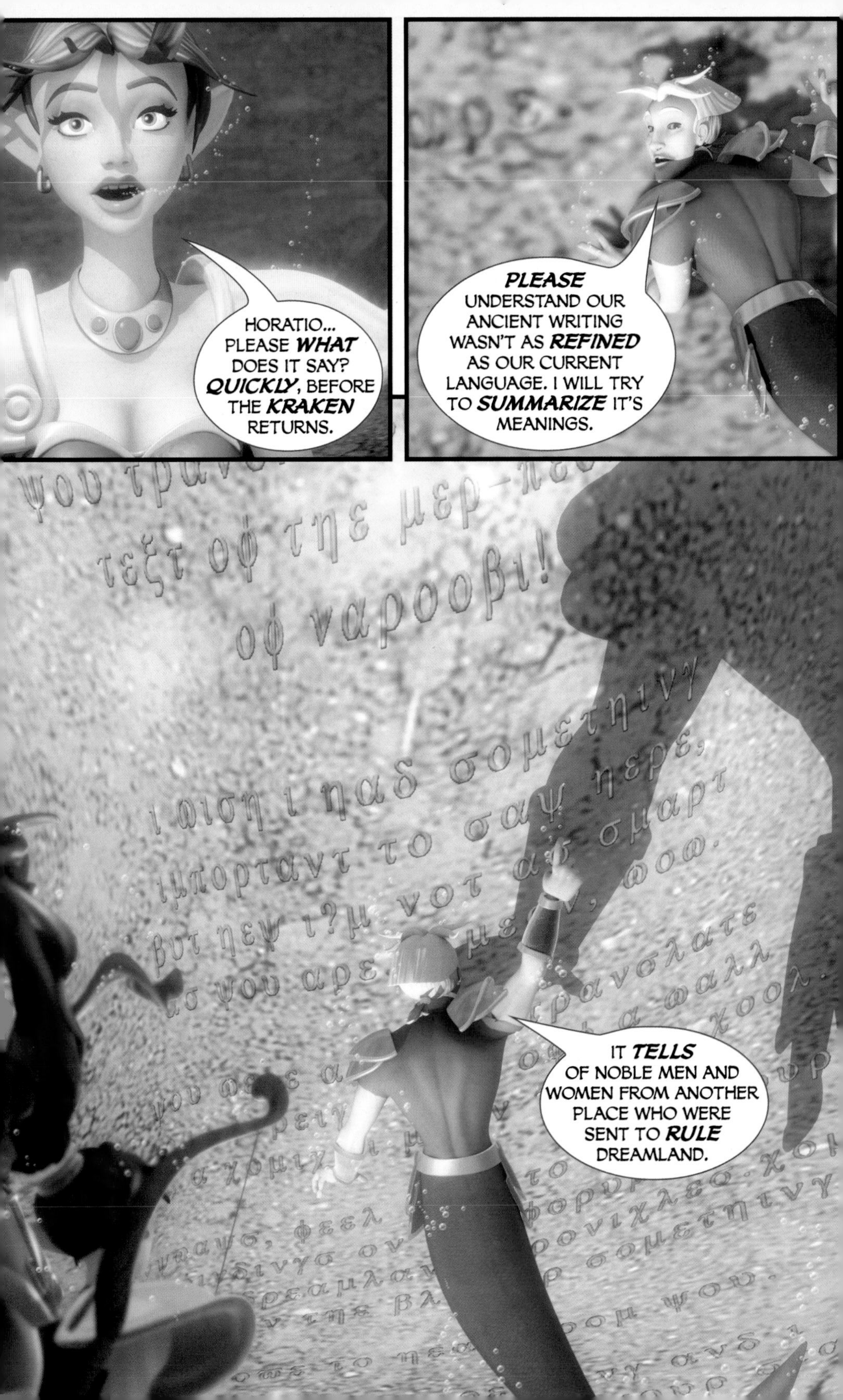
HORATIO... PLEASE WHAT DOES IT SAY? QUICKLY, BEFORE THE KRAKEN RETURNS.
PLEASE UNDERSTAND OUR ANCIENT WRITING WASN'T AS REFINED AS OUR CURRENT LANGUAGE. I WILL TRY TO SUMMARIZE IT'S MEANINGS.
IT TELLS OF NOBLE MEN AND WOMEN FROM ANOTHER PLACE WHO WERE SENT TO RULE DREAMLAND.

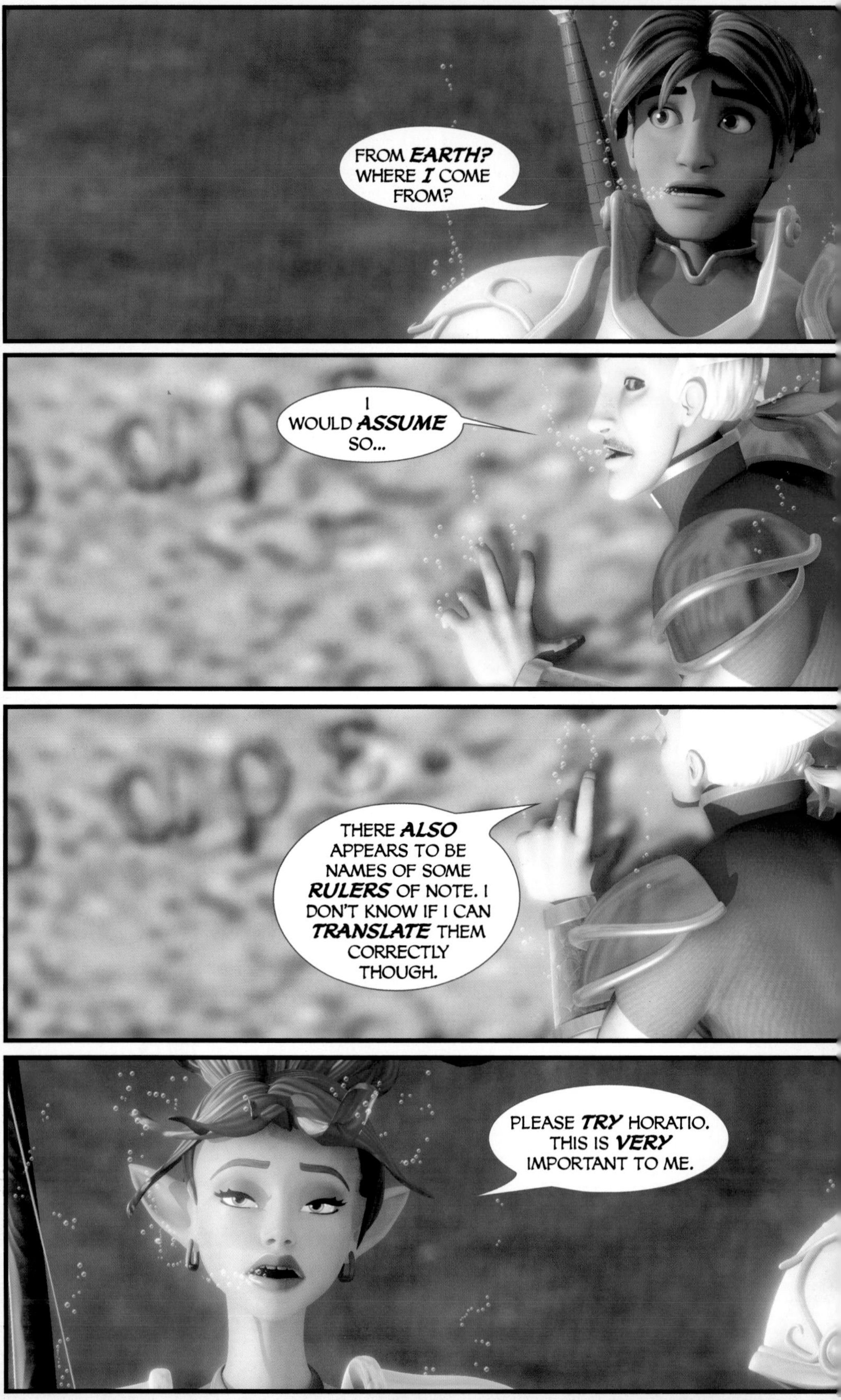
FROM EARTH? WHERE I COME FROM?
I WOULD ASSUME SO...
THERE ALSO APPEARS TO BE NAMES OF SOME RULERS OF NOTE. I DON'T KNOW IF I CAN TRANSLATE THEM CORRECTLY THOUGH.
PLEASE TRY HORATIO. THIS IS VERY IMPORTANT TO ME.

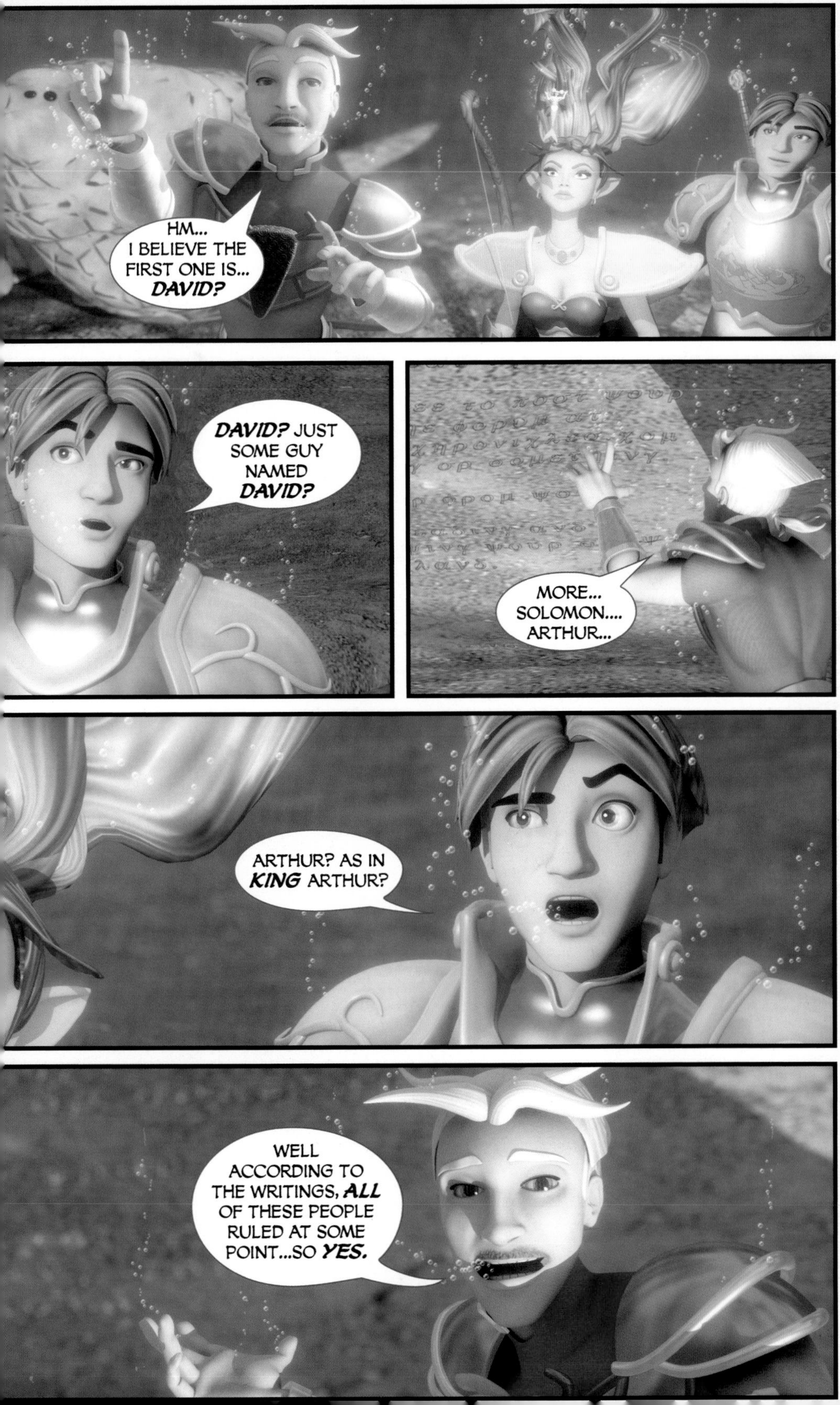
HM... I BELIEVE THE FIRST ONE IS... *DAVID?*
DAVID? JUST SOME GUY NAMED *DAVID?*
MORE... SOLOMON.... ARTHUR...
ARTHUR? AS IN *KING* ARTHUR?
WELL ACCORDING TO THE WRITINGS, *ALL* OF THESE PEOPLE RULED AT SOME POINT...SO *YES.*

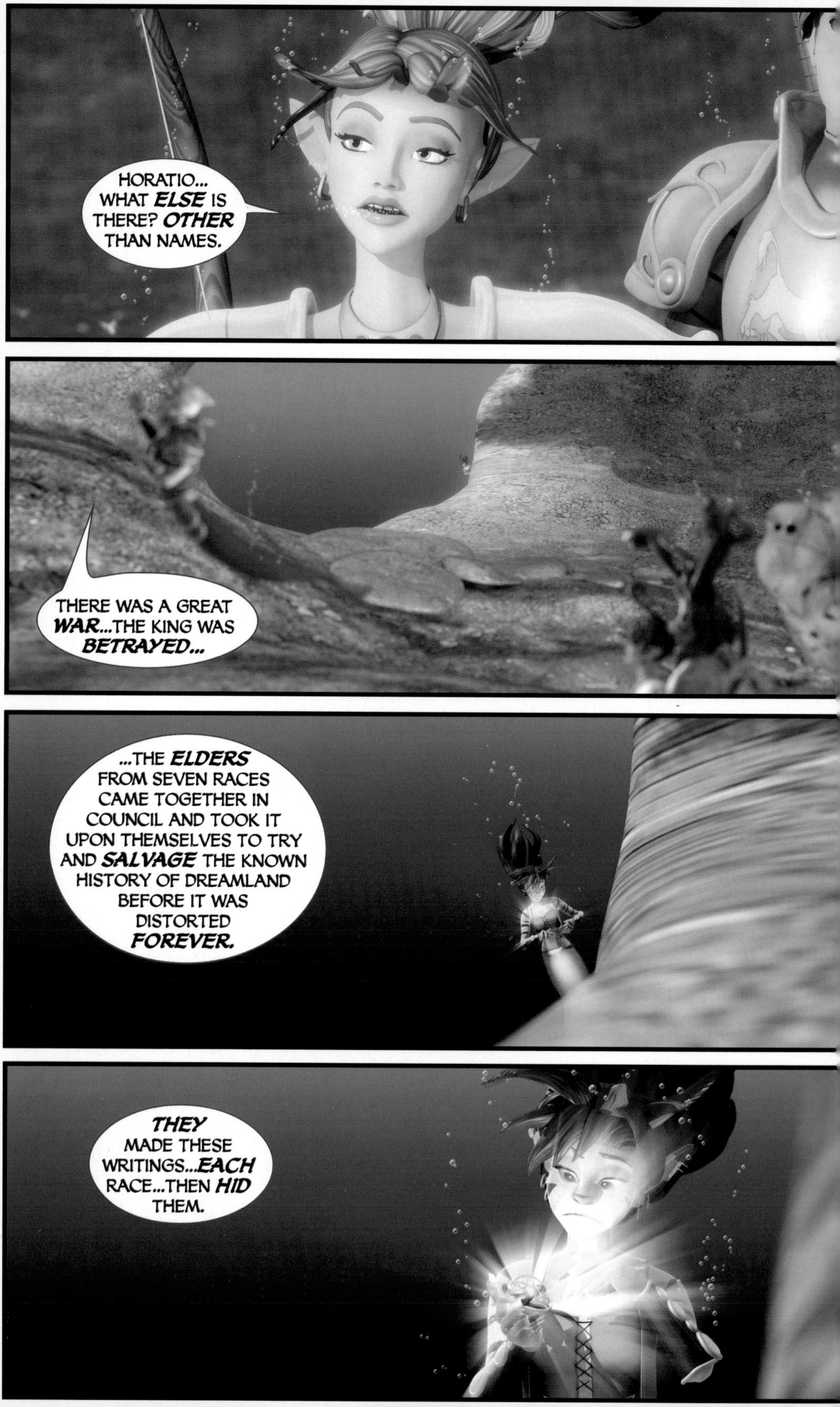
HORATIO... WHAT ELSE IS THERE? OTHER THAN NAMES.
THERE WAS A GREAT WAR...THE KING WAS BETRAYED...
...THE ELDERS FROM SEVEN RACES CAME TOGETHER IN COUNCIL AND TOOK IT UPON THEMSELVES TO TRY AND SALVAGE THE KNOWN HISTORY OF DREAMLAND BEFORE IT WAS DISTORTED FOREVER.
THEY MADE THESE WRITINGS...EACH RACE...THEN HID THEM.

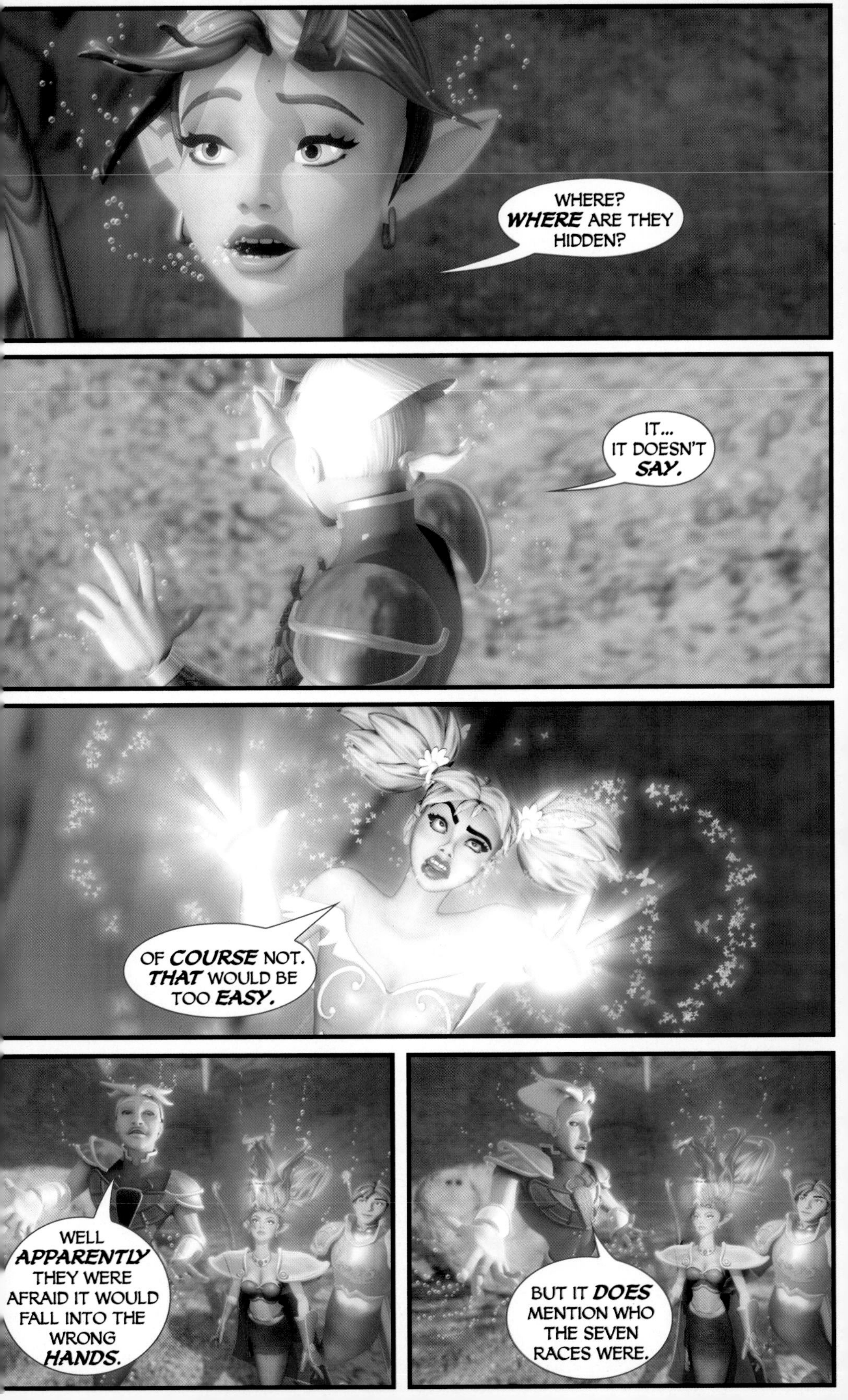
WHERE? WHERE ARE THEY HIDDEN?
IT... IT DOESN'T SAY.
OF COURSE NOT. THAT WOULD BE TOO EASY.
WELL APPARENTLY THEY WERE AFRAID IT WOULD FALL INTO THE WRONG HANDS.
BUT IT DOES MENTION WHO THE SEVEN RACES WERE.

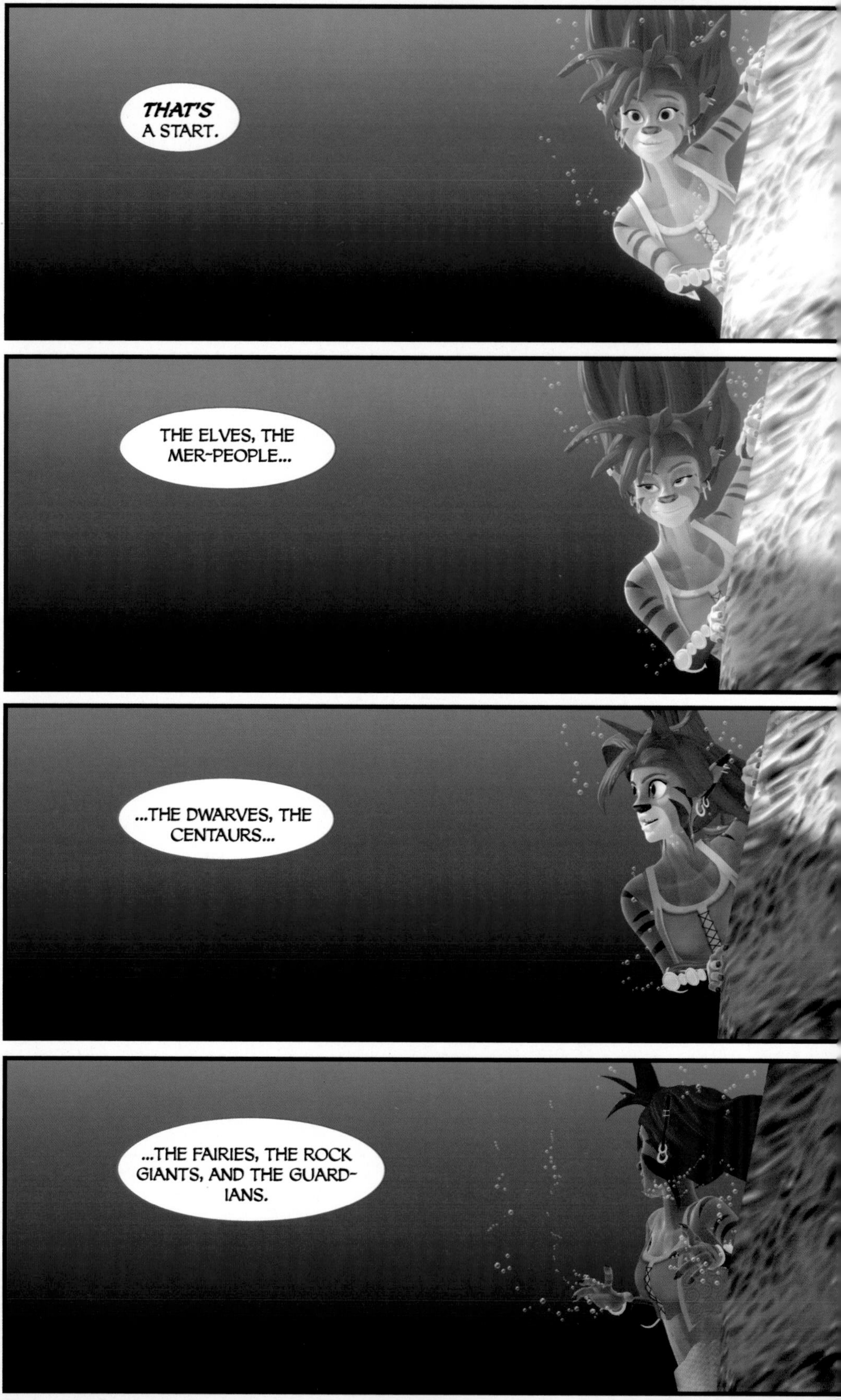
THAT'S A START.
THE ELVES, THE MER-PEOPLE...
...THE DWARVES, THE CENTAURS...
...THE FAIRIES, THE ROCK GIANTS, AND THE GUARD- IANS.

THE *WHO?*
I DON'T *RECOGNIZE* THE NAME...
...BUT THE *TRANSLATION* FROM THE OLD LANGUAGE IS *EQUAL* TO...
...THE *GUARDIANS.*

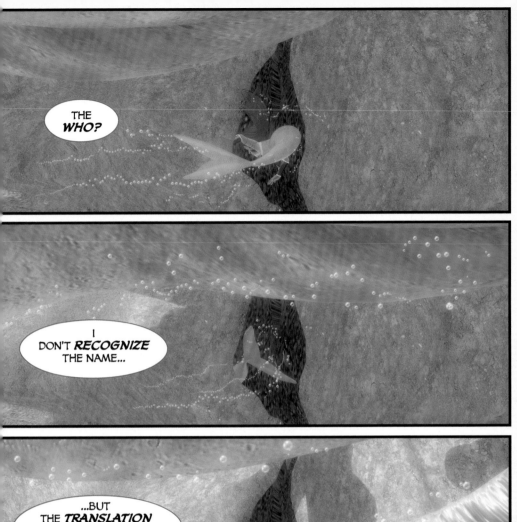

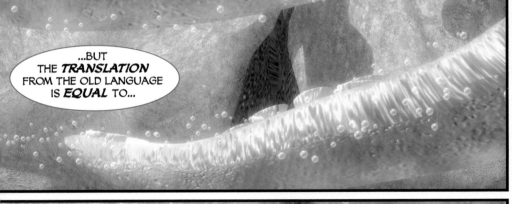

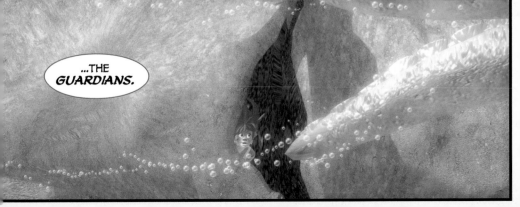

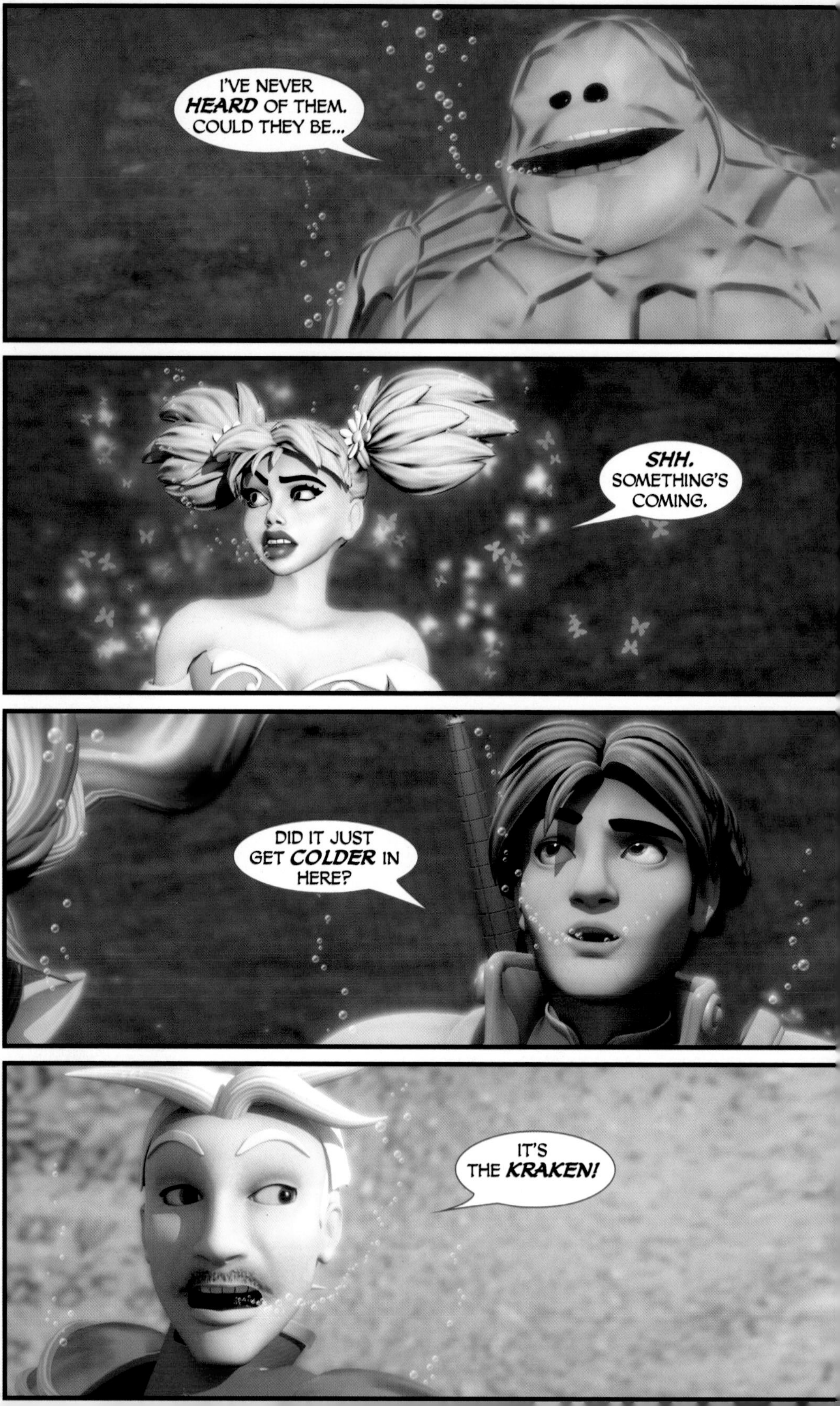
I'VE NEVER HEARD OF THEM. COULD THEY BE...
SHH. SOMETHING'S COMING.
DID IT JUST GET COLDER IN HERE?
IT'S THE KRAKEN!

CHAPTER SEVEN

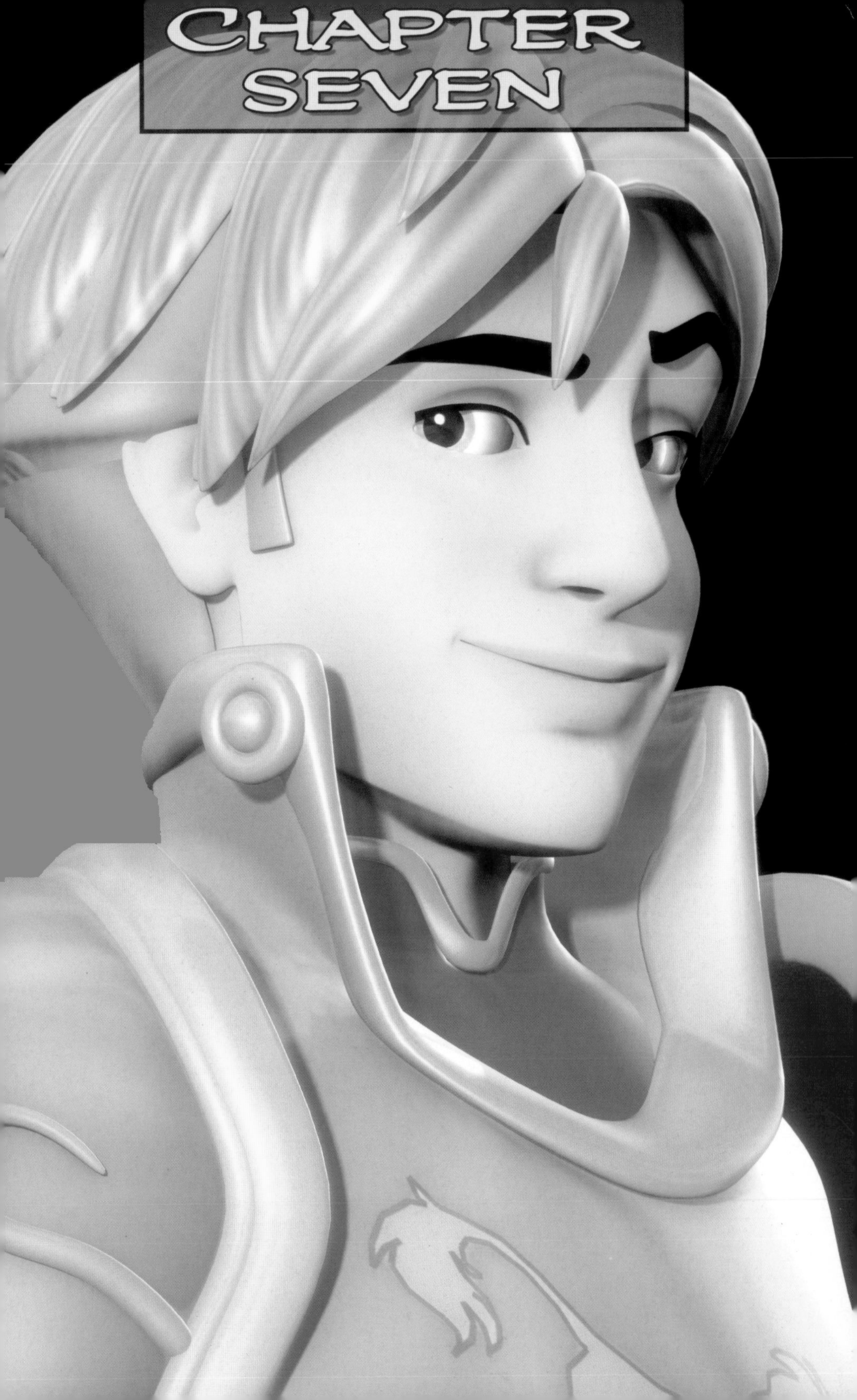

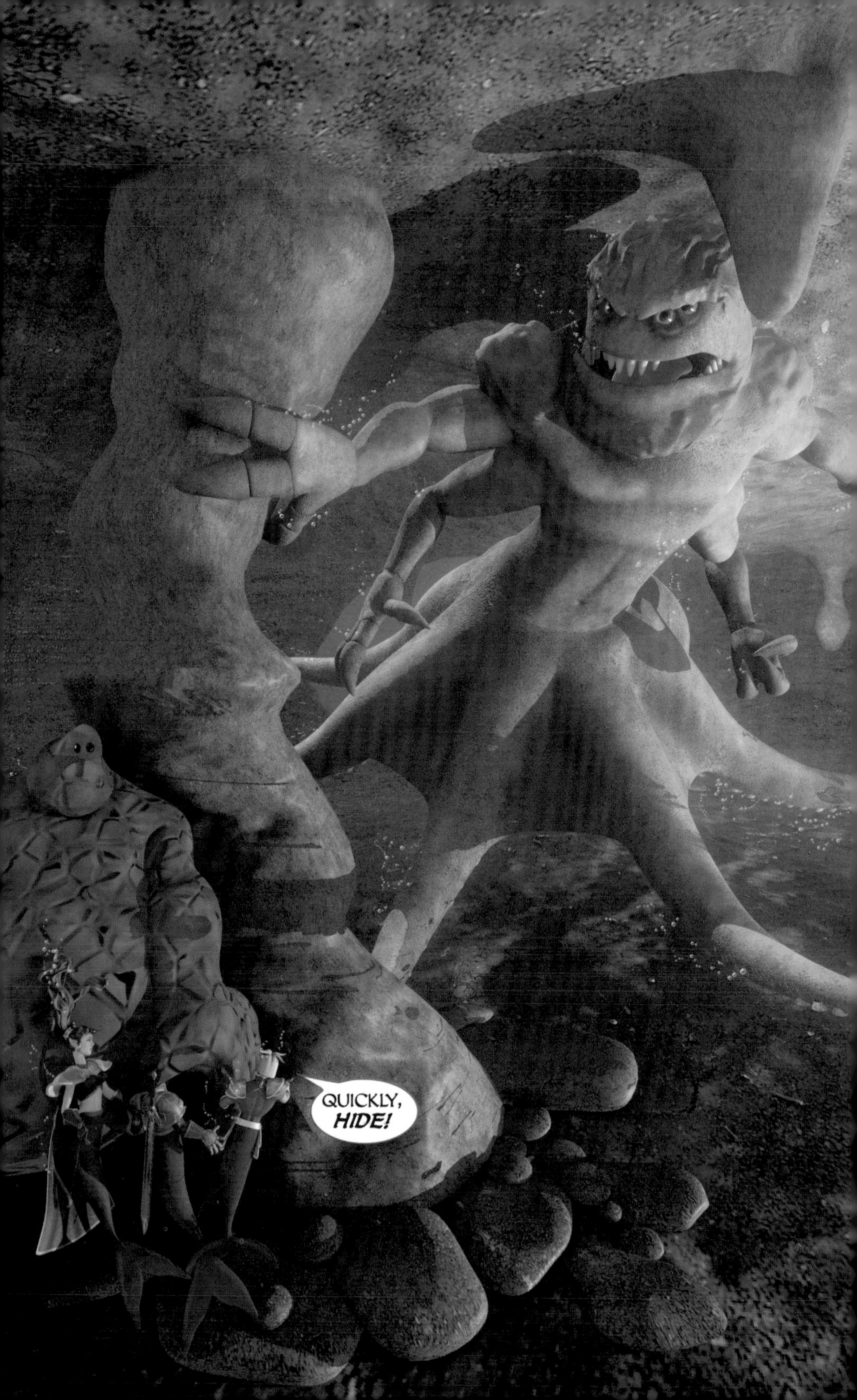
QUICKLY, HIDE!

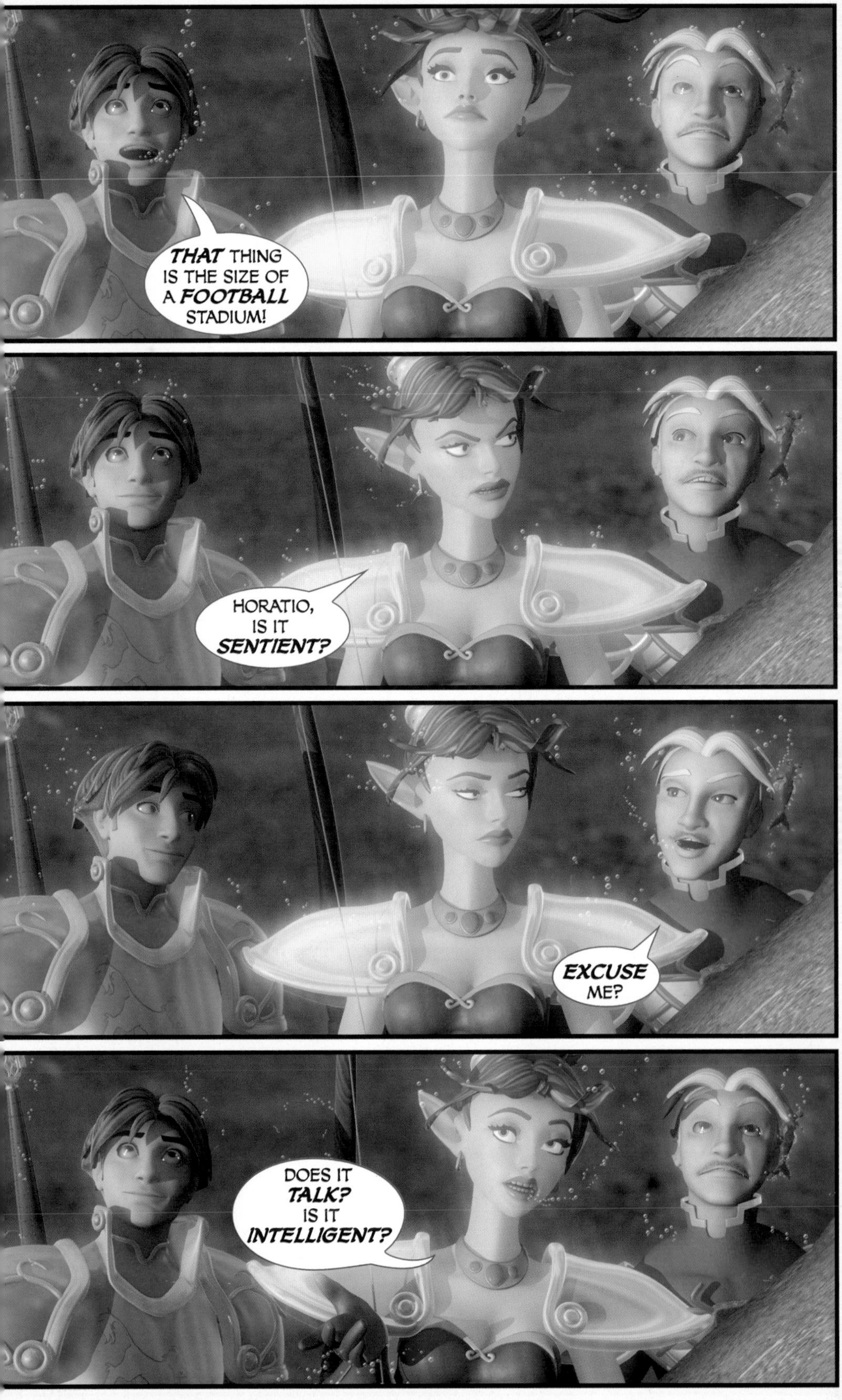
THAT THING IS THE SIZE OF A FOOTBALL STADIUM!
HORATIO, IS IT SENTIENT?
EXCUSE ME?
DOES IT TALK? IS IT INTELLIGENT?

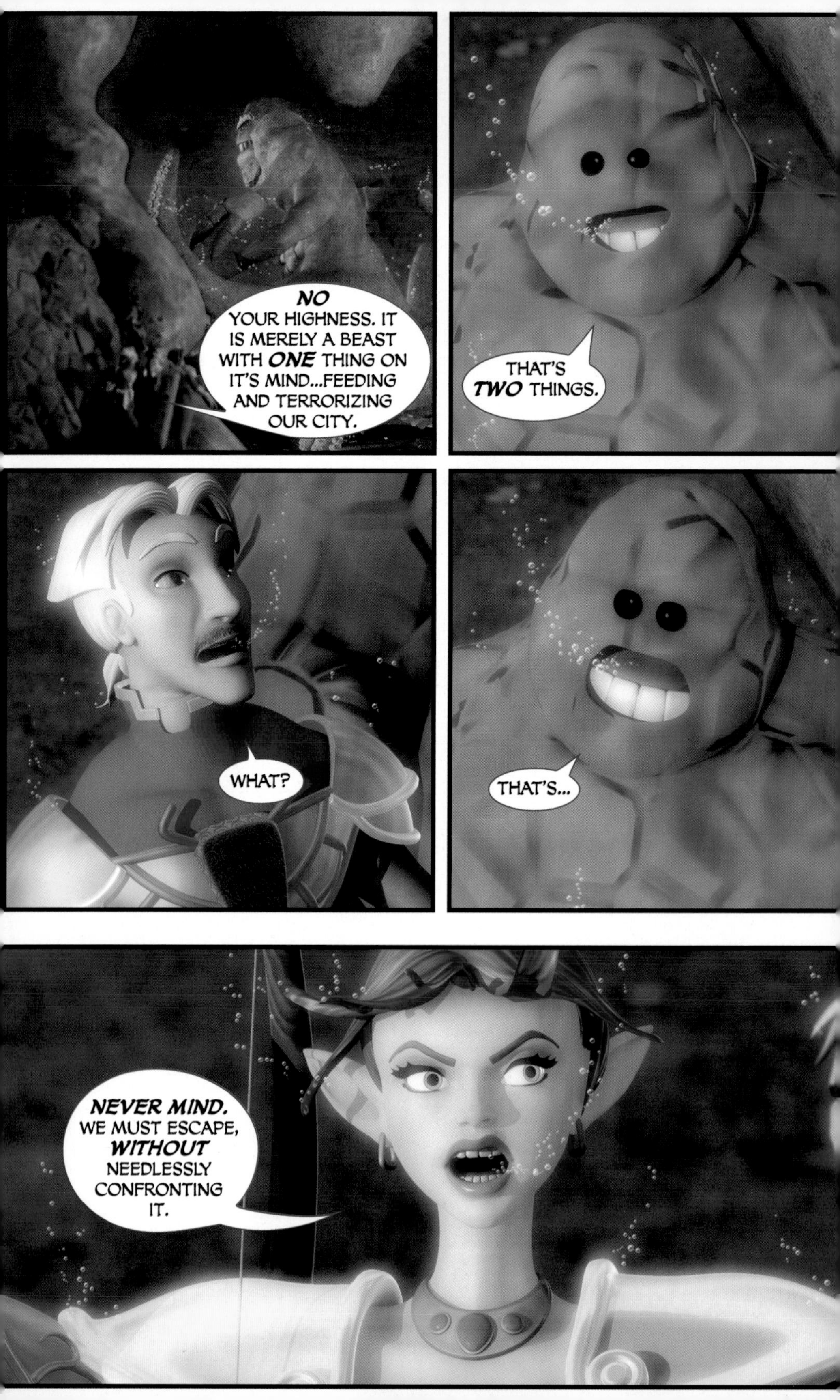
NO YOUR HIGHNESS. IT IS MERELY A BEAST WITH ONE THING ON IT'S MIND...FEEDING AND TERRORIZING OUR CITY.
THAT'S TWO THINGS.
WHAT?
THAT'S...
NEVER MIND. WE MUST ESCAPE, WITHOUT NEEDLESSLY CONFRONTING IT.

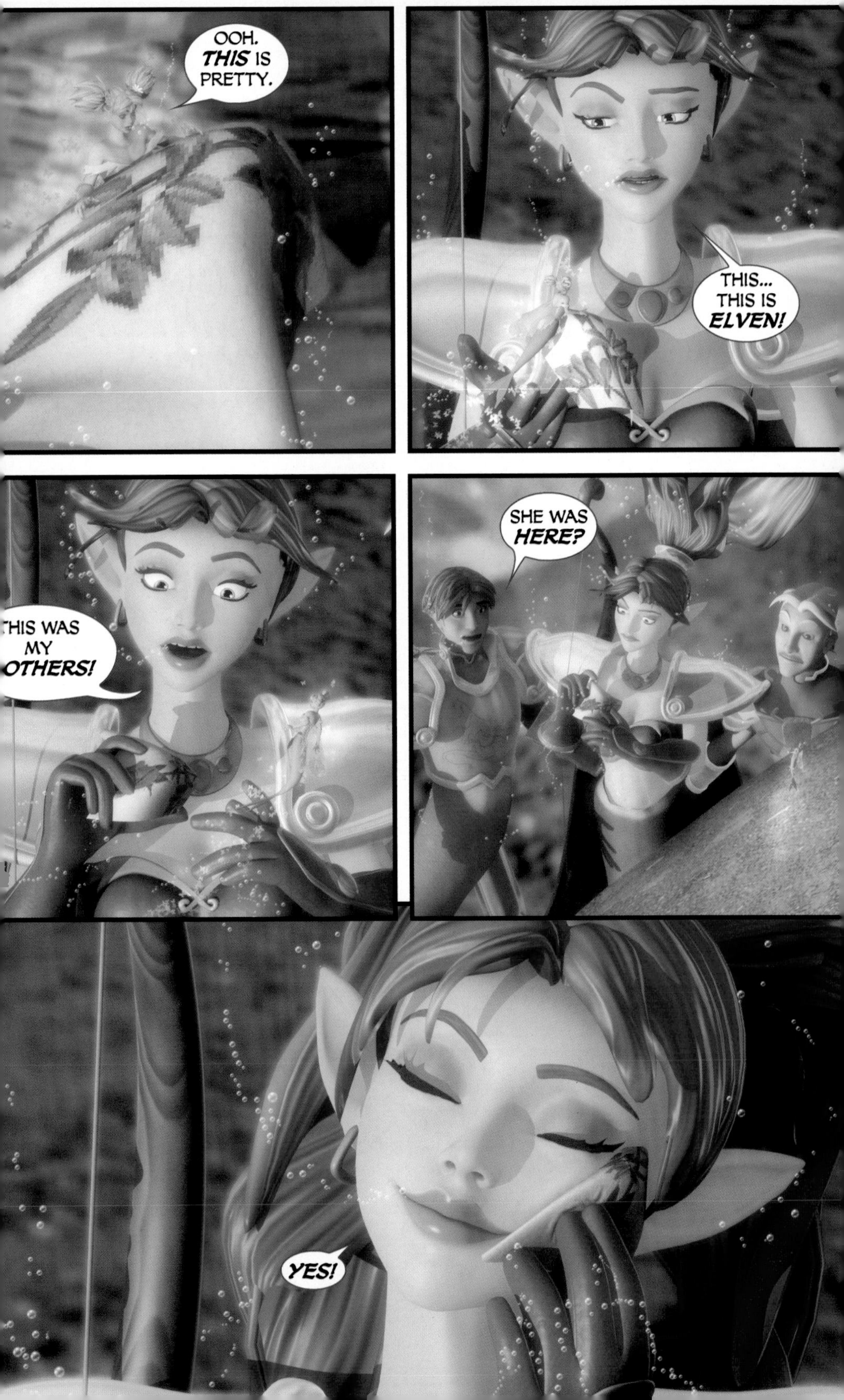
OOH. THIS IS PRETTY.
THIS... THIS IS ELVEN!
THIS WAS MY OTHERS!
SHE WAS HERE?
YES!

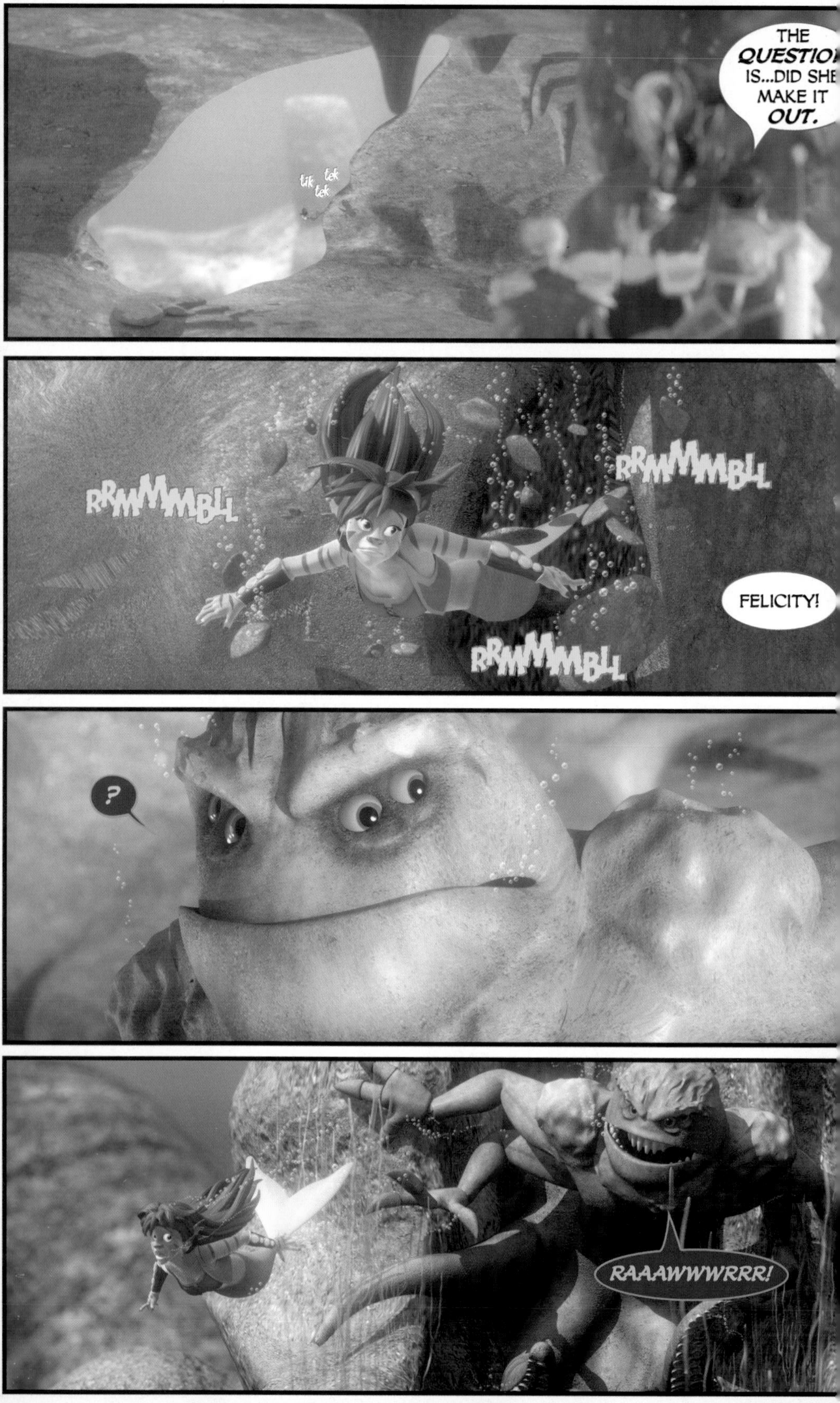
THE QUESTIO IS...DID SHE MAKE IT OUT.
tik tek tek
RRMMMMBLL
RRMMMMBLL
FELICITY!
RRMMMMBLL
?
RAAAWWWRRR!

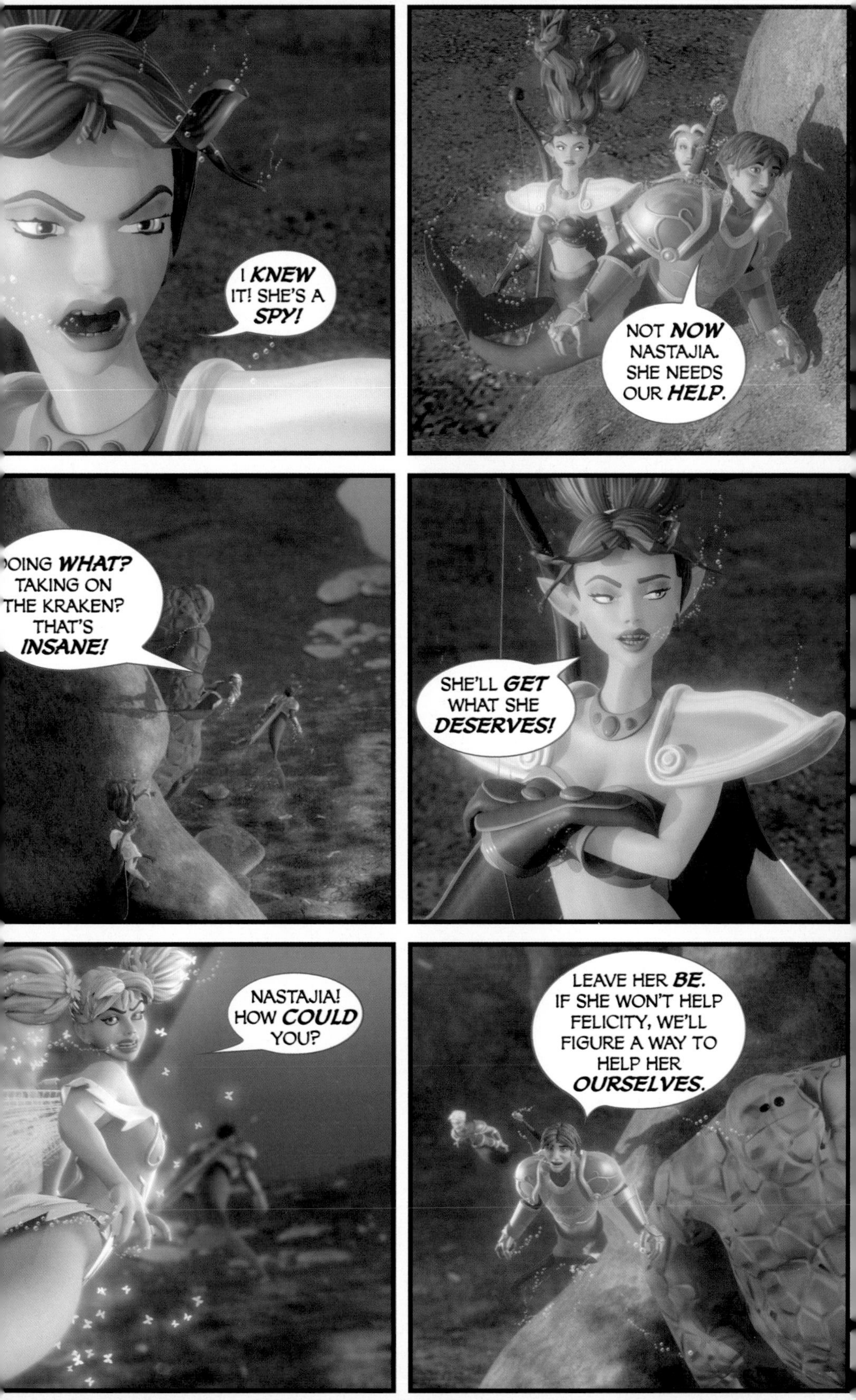
I KNEW IT! SHE'S A SPY!
NOT NOW NASTAJIA. SHE NEEDS OUR HELP.
DOING WHAT? TAKING ON THE KRAKEN? THAT'S INSANE!
SHE'LL GET WHAT SHE DESERVES!
NASTAJIA! HOW COULD YOU?
LEAVE HER BE. IF SHE WON'T HELP FELICITY, WE'LL FIGURE A WAY TO HELP HER OURSELVES.

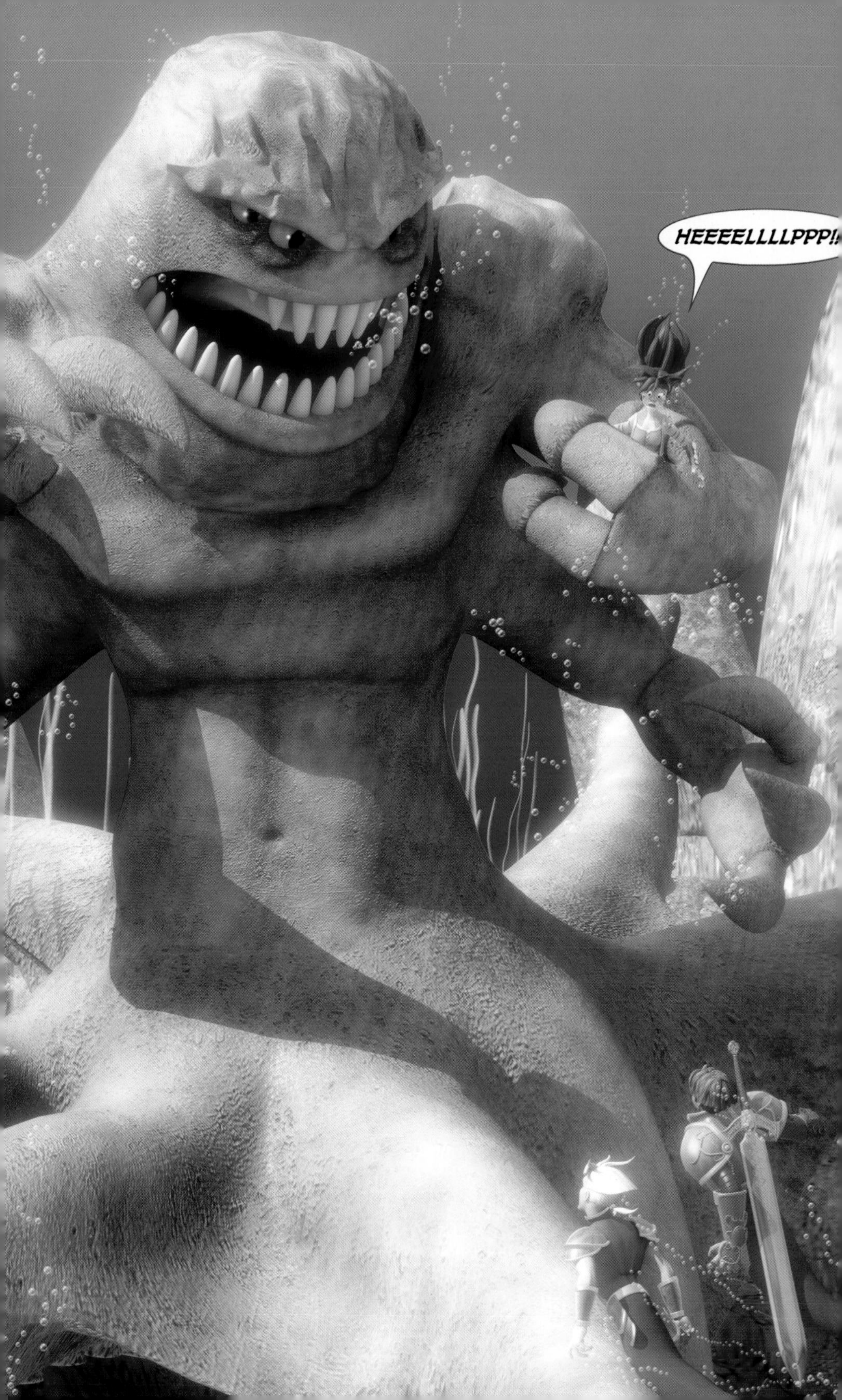
HEEEELLLLLPPP!!

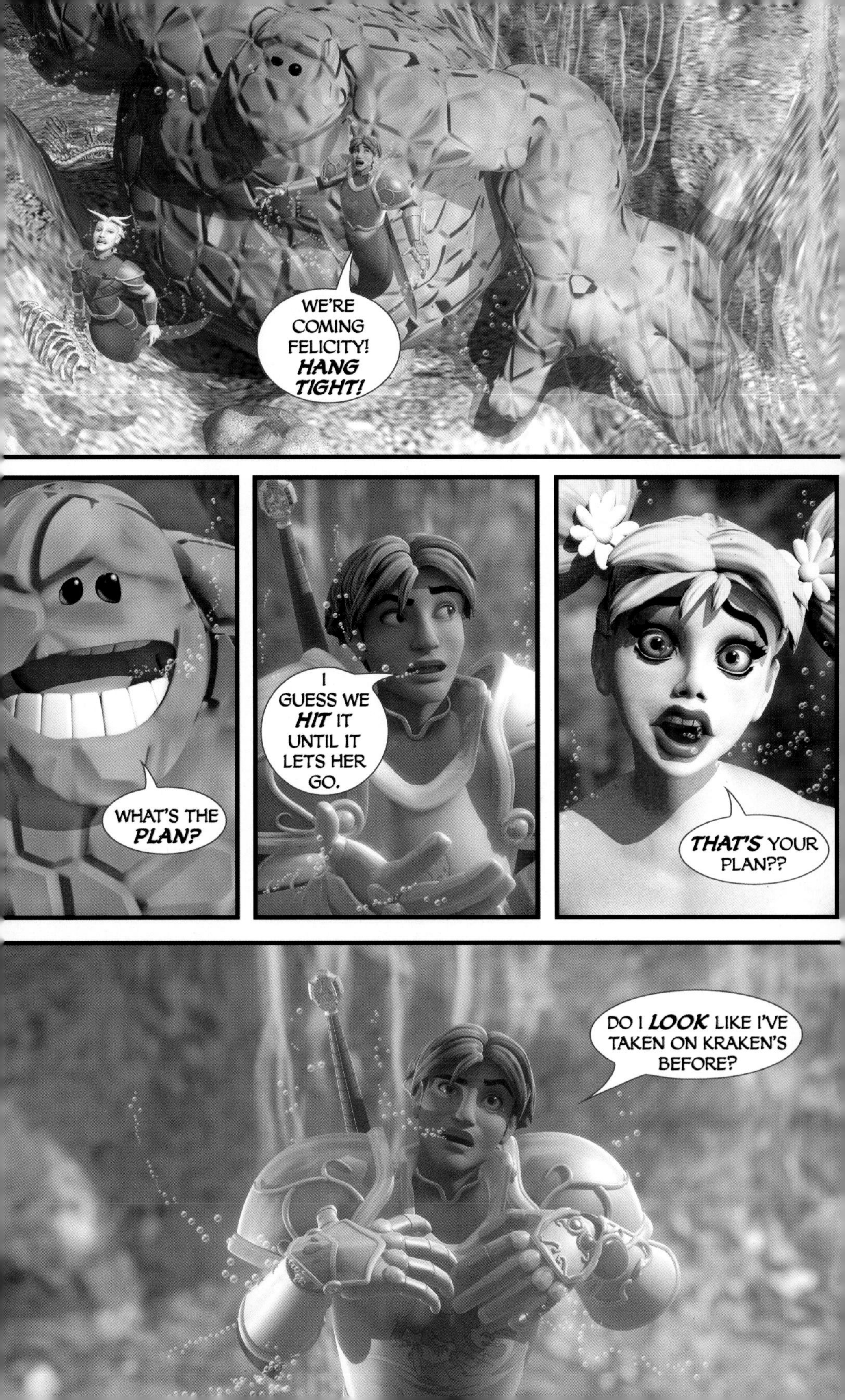
WE'RE COMING FELICITY! HANG TIGHT!
WHAT'S THE PLAN?
I GUESS WE HIT IT UNTIL IT LETS HER GO.
THAT'S YOUR PLAN??
DO I LOOK LIKE I'VE TAKEN ON KRAKEN'S BEFORE?

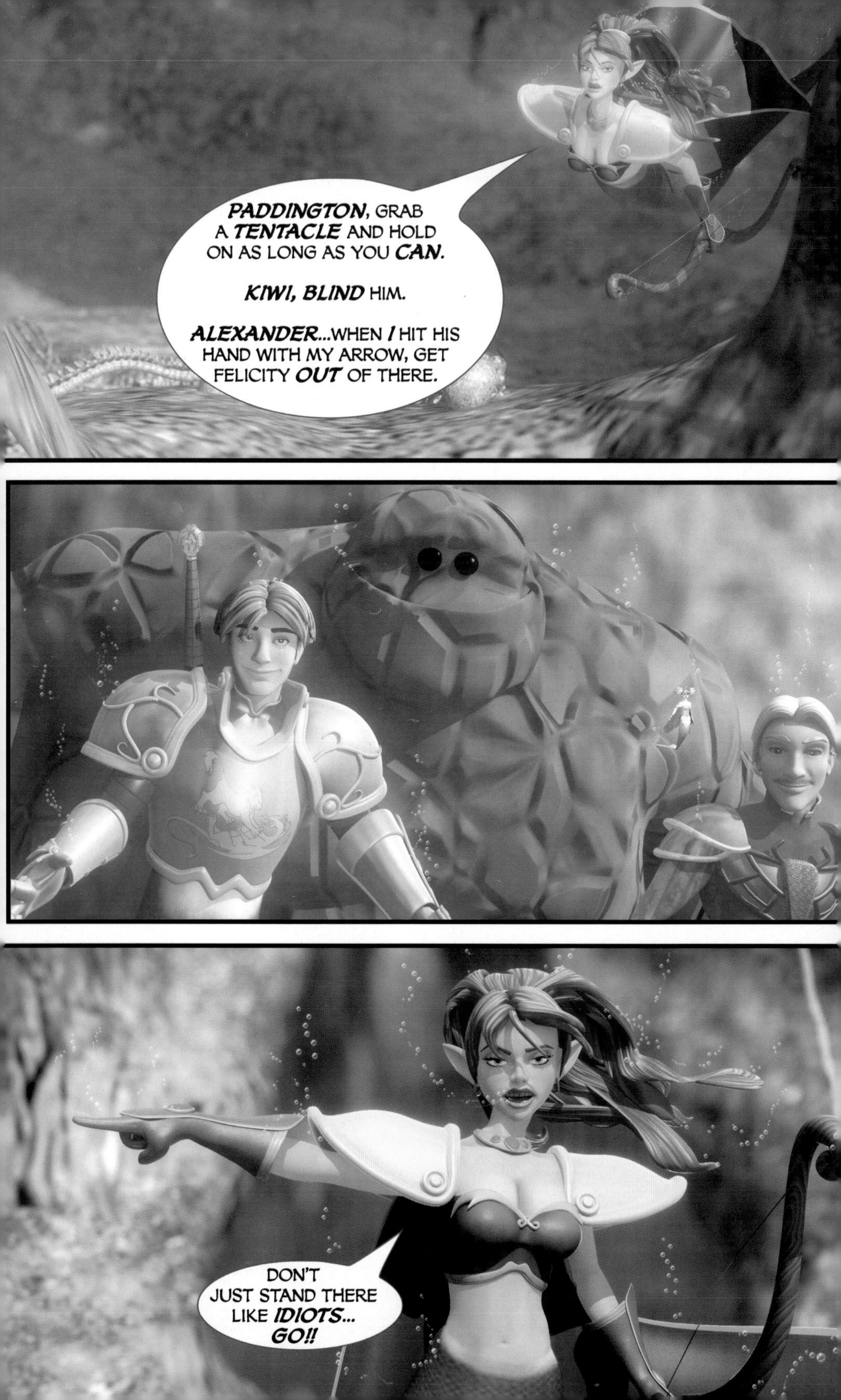
PADDINGTON, GRAB A TENTACLE AND HOLD ON AS LONG AS YOU CAN.
KIWI, BLIND HIM.
ALEXANDER...WHEN I HIT HIS HAND WITH MY ARROW, GET FELICITY OUT OF THERE.
DON'T JUST STAND THERE LIKE IDIOTS... GO!!

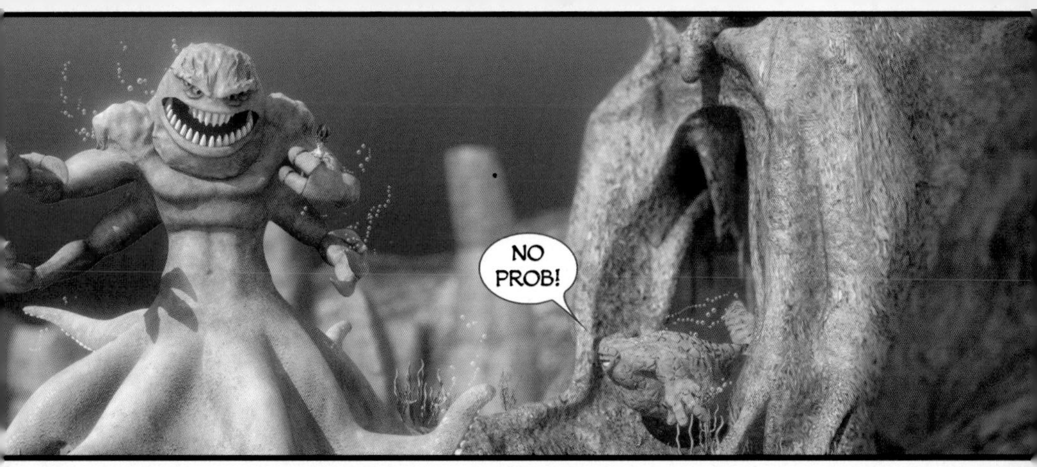
NO PROB!

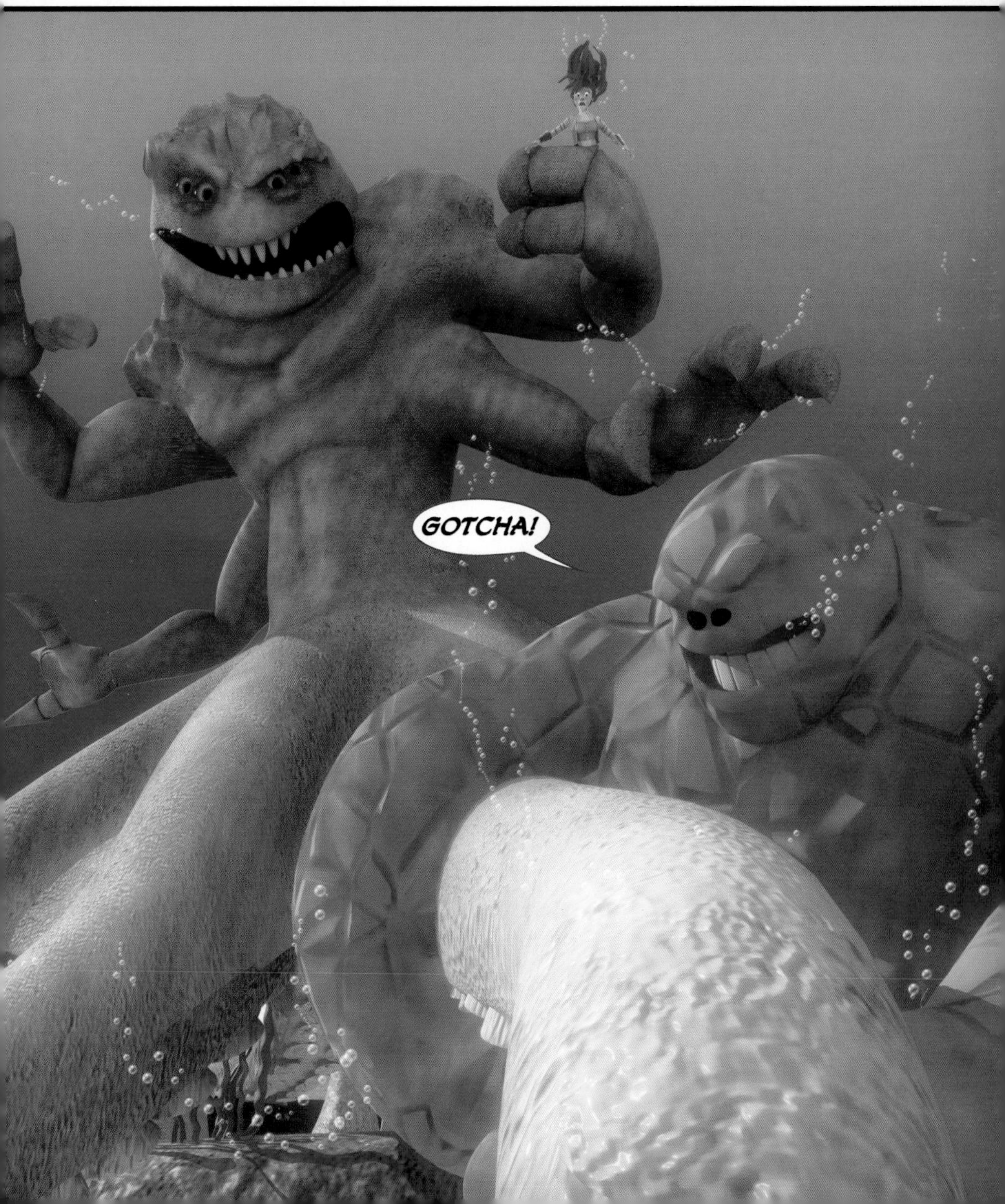
GOTCHA!

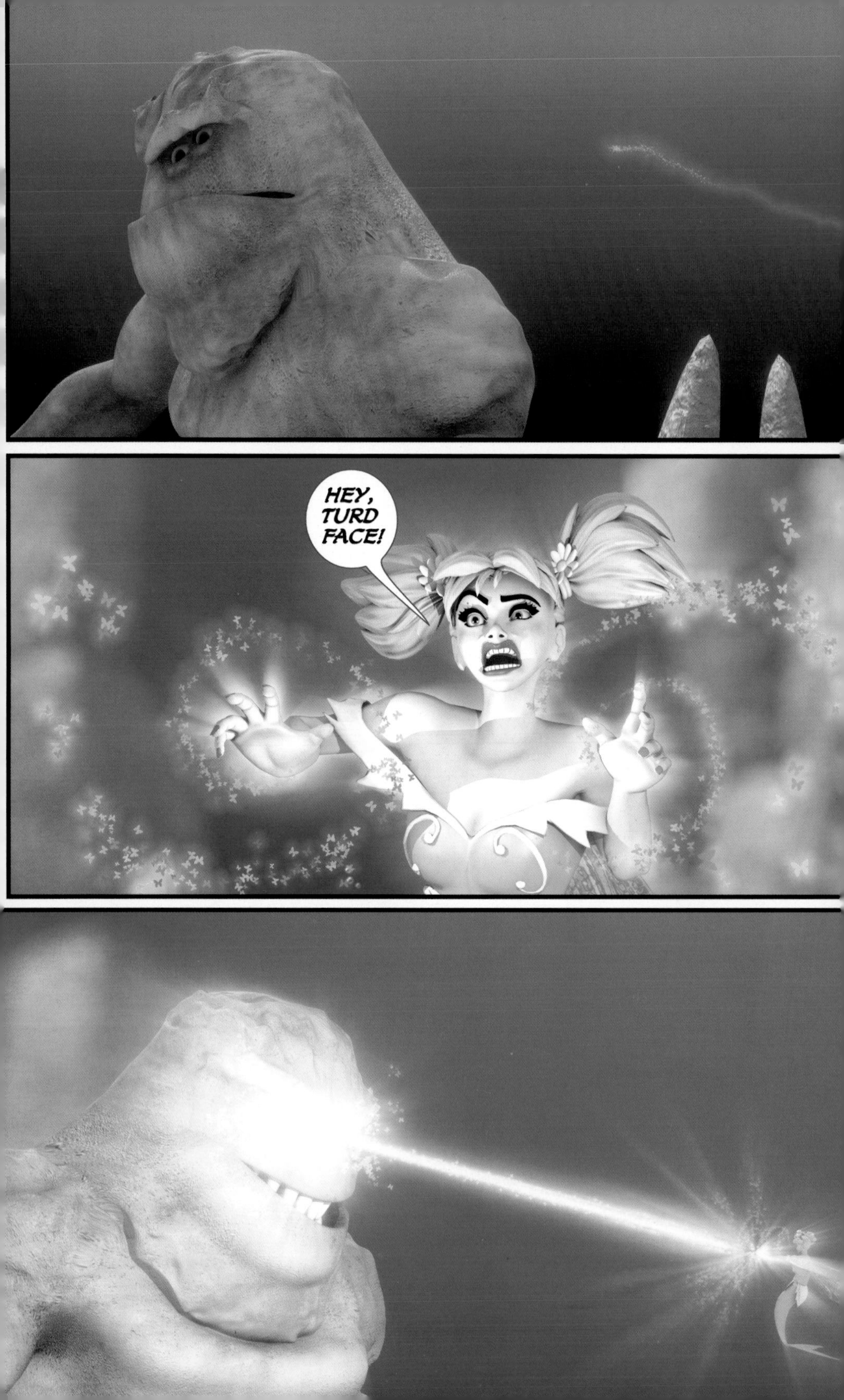
HEY, TURD FACE!

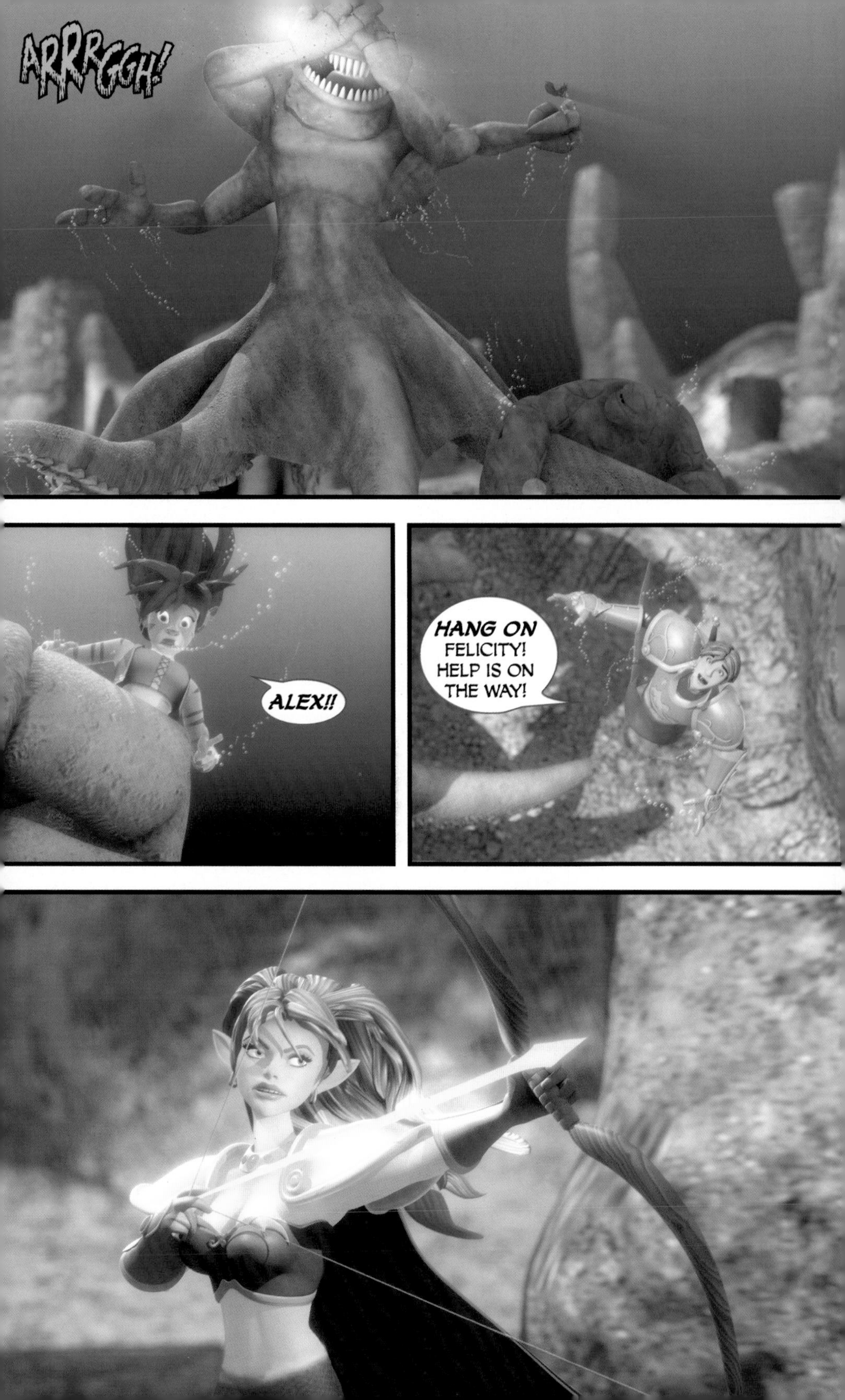
ARRRGGH!
ALEX!!
HANG ON FELICITY! HELP IS ON THE WAY!

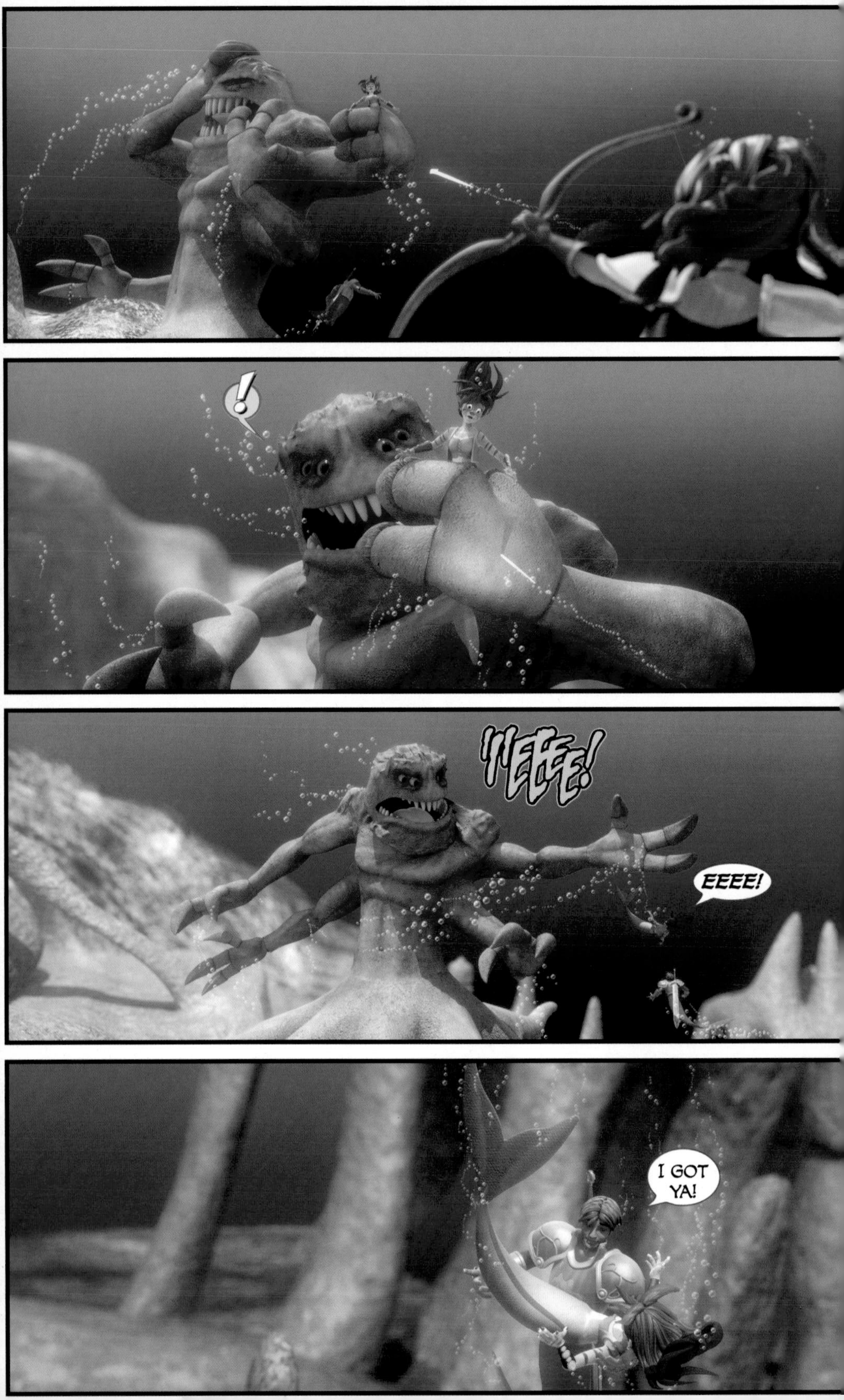
!
'EEEE!
EEEE!
I GOT YA!

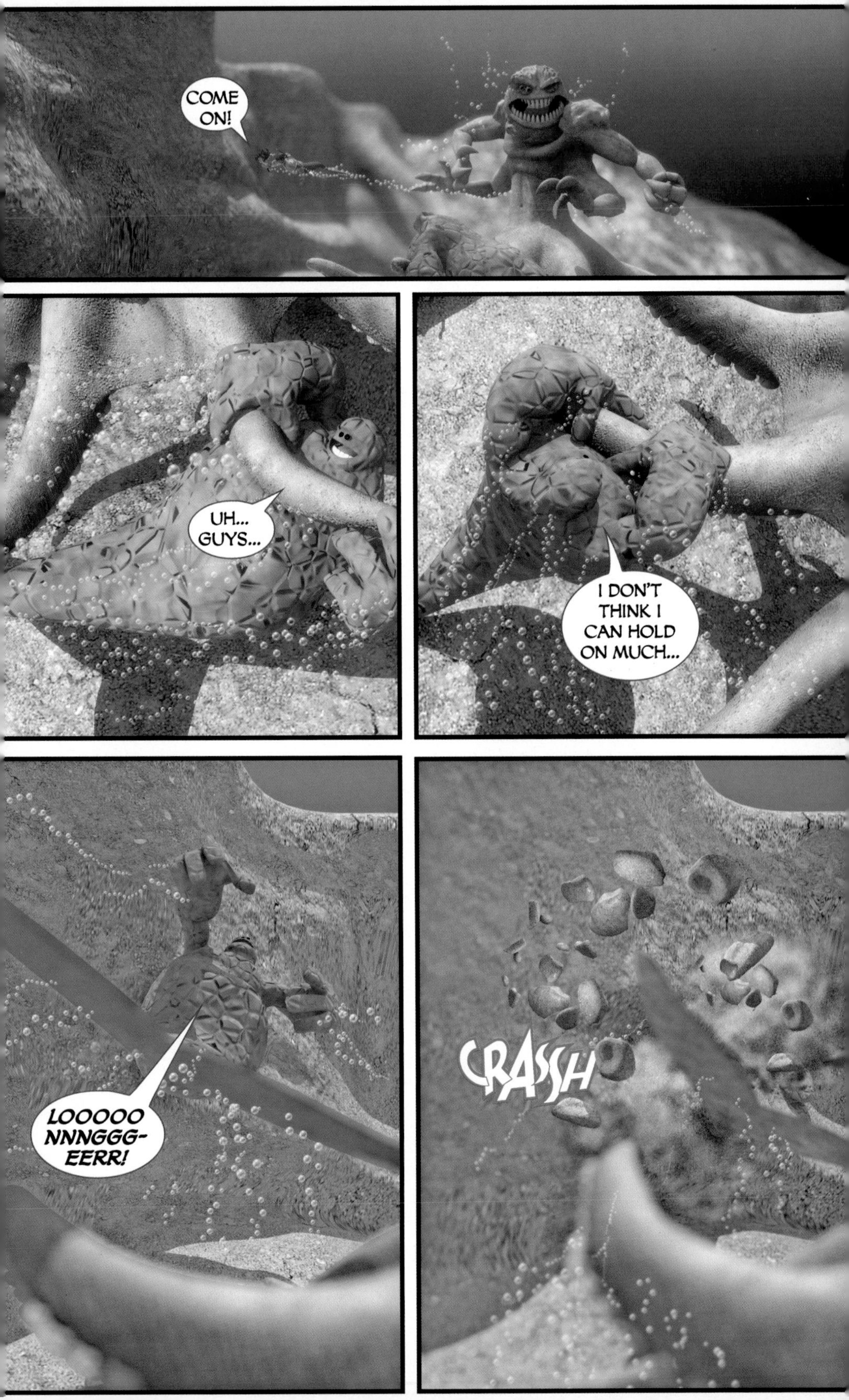
COME ON!
UH... GUYS...
I DON'T THINK I CAN HOLD ON MUCH...
LOOOOO NNNGGG- EERR!
CRASSH

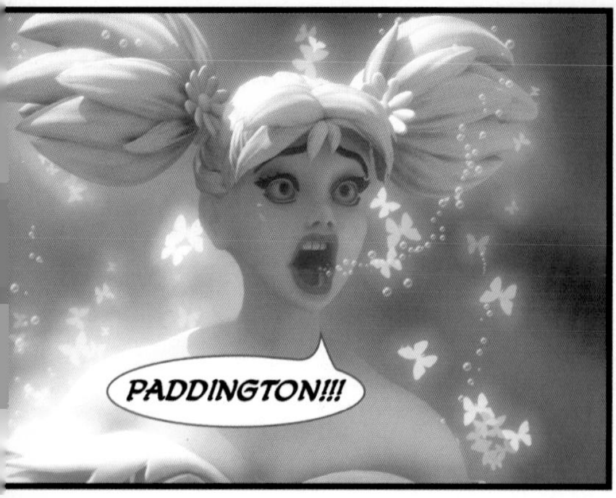
PADDINGTON!!!

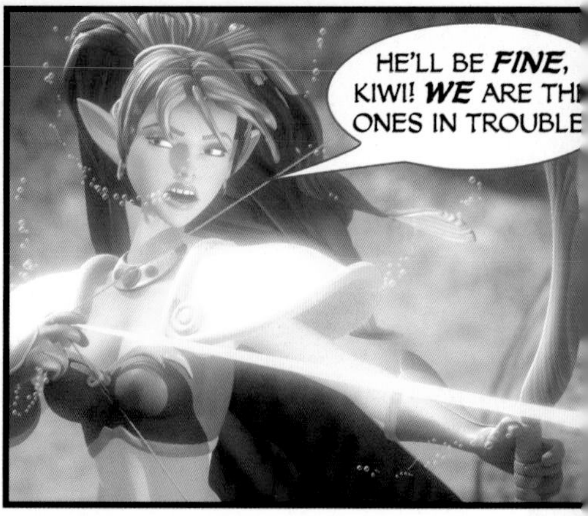
HE'LL BE *FINE*,
KIWI! *WE* ARE TH
ONES IN TROUBLE

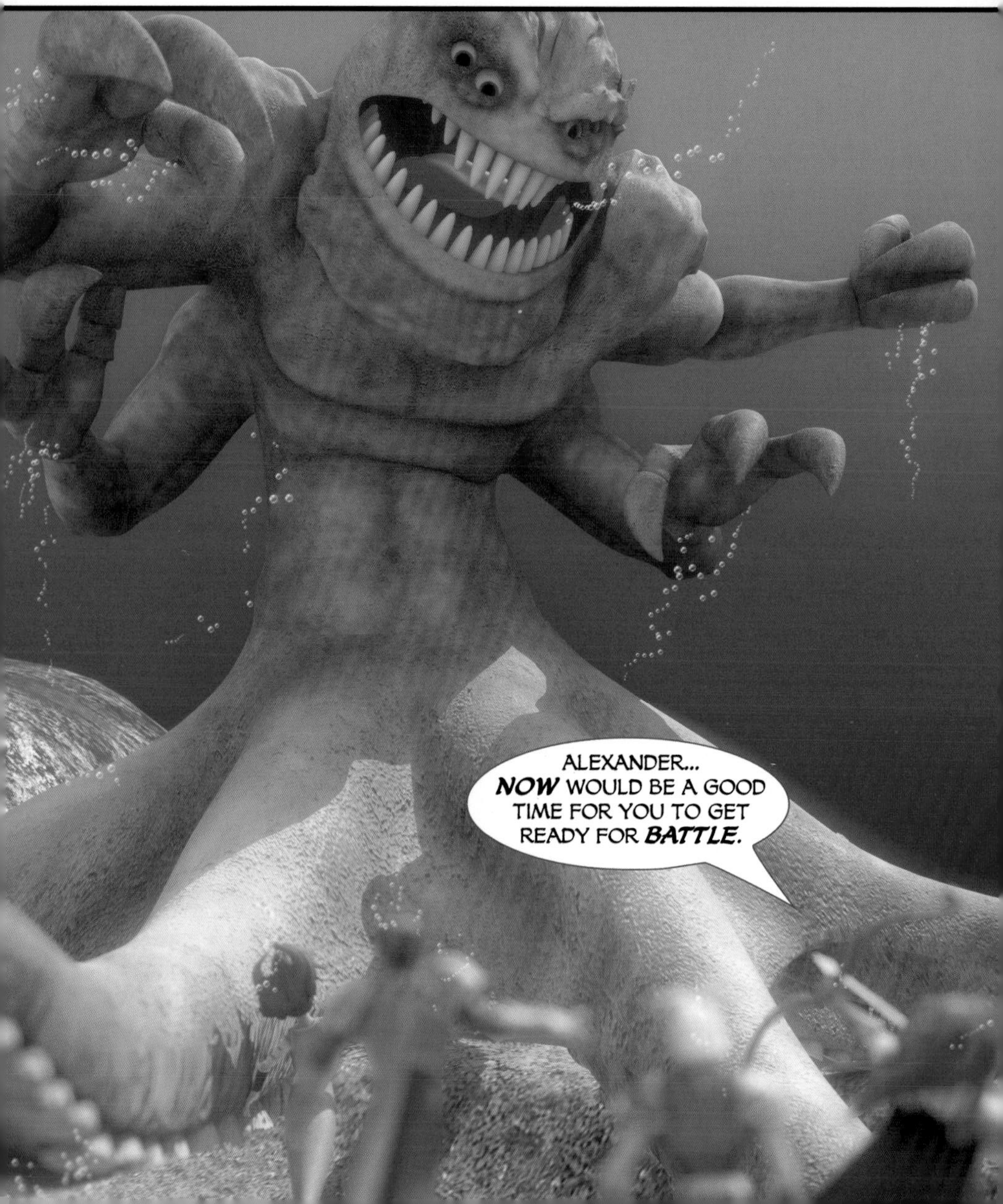
ALEXANDER... *NOW* WOULD BE A GOOD TIME FOR YOU TO GET READY FOR *BATTLE*.

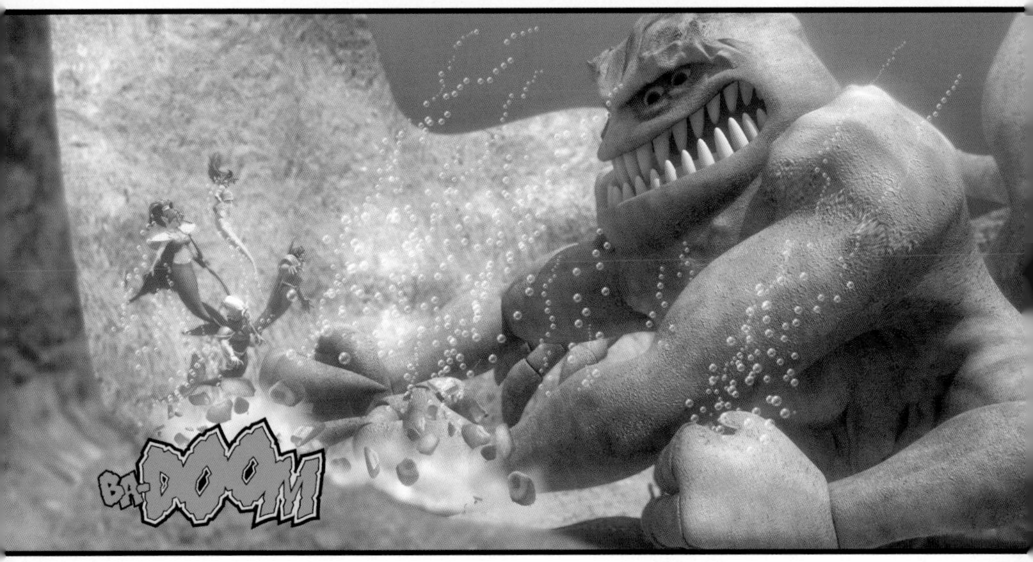
BA-DOOM
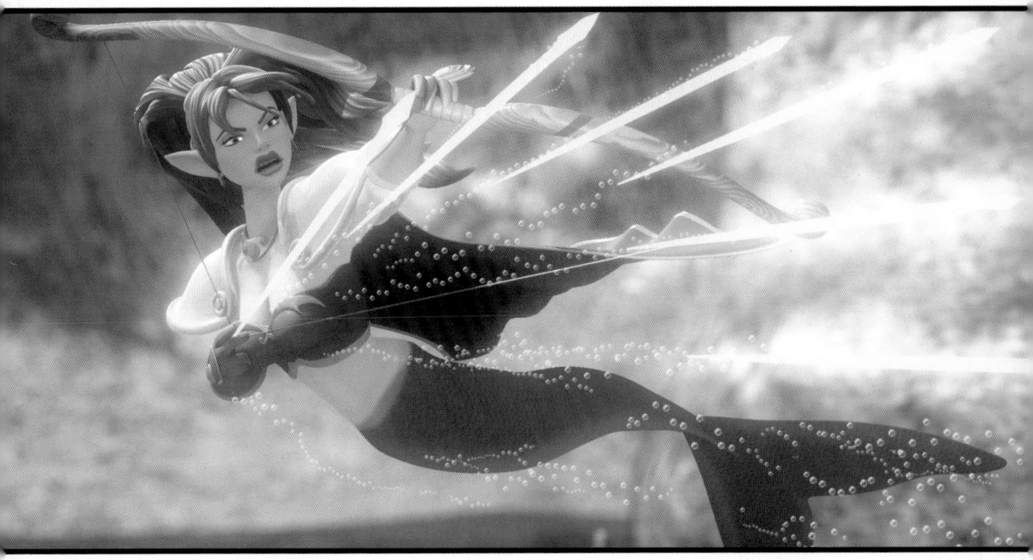
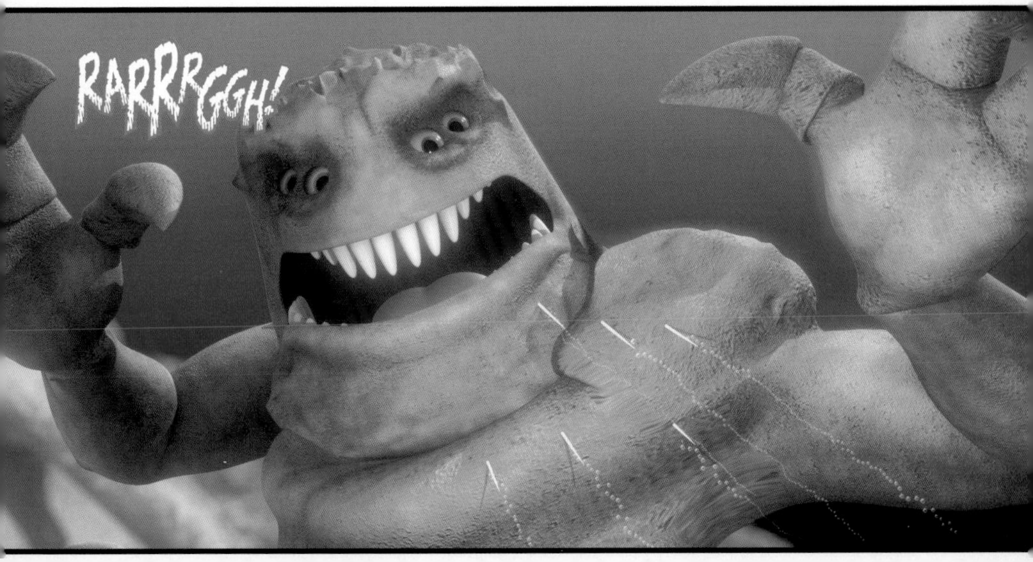
RARRRGGH!

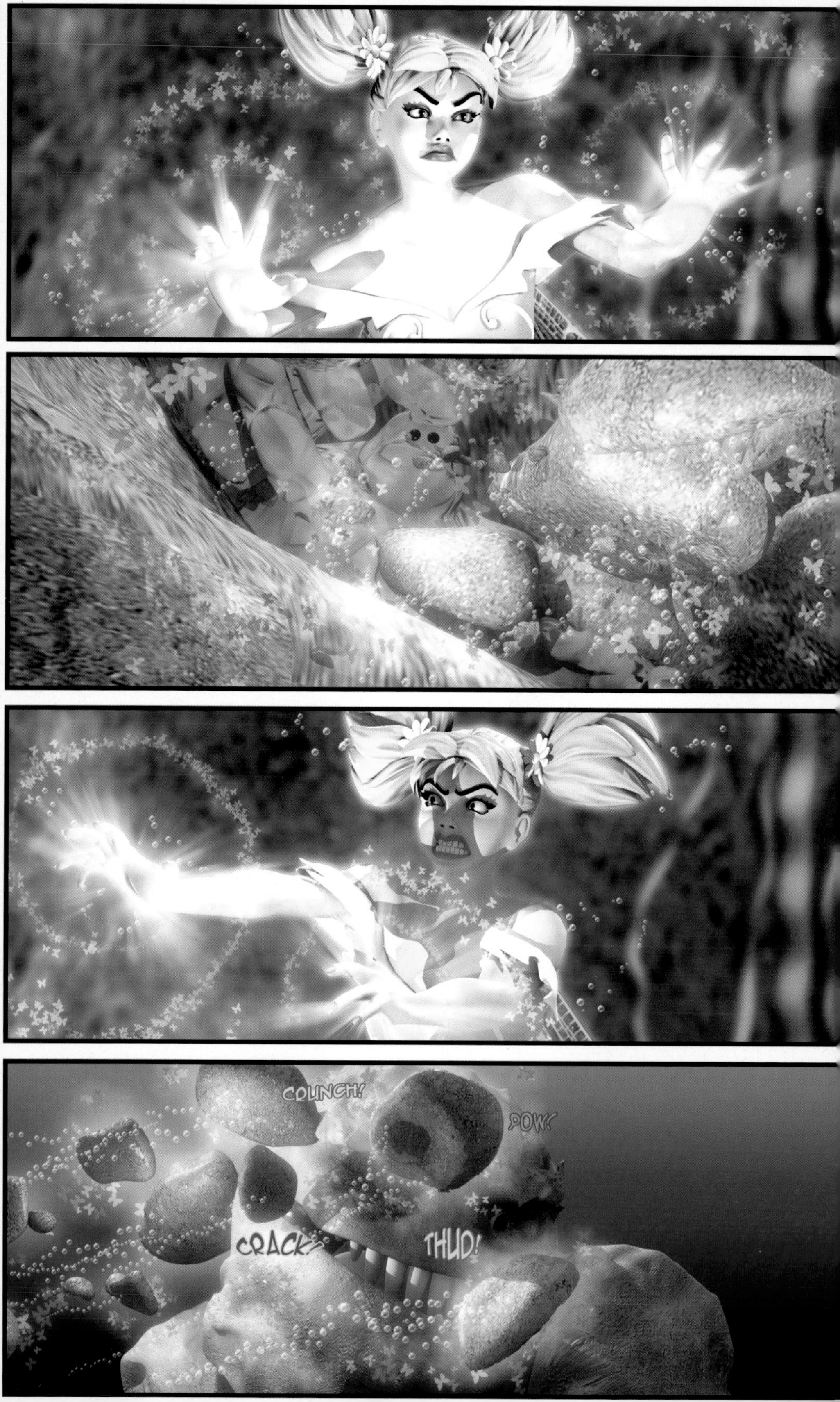
CRUNCH!
POW!
CRACK!
THUD!

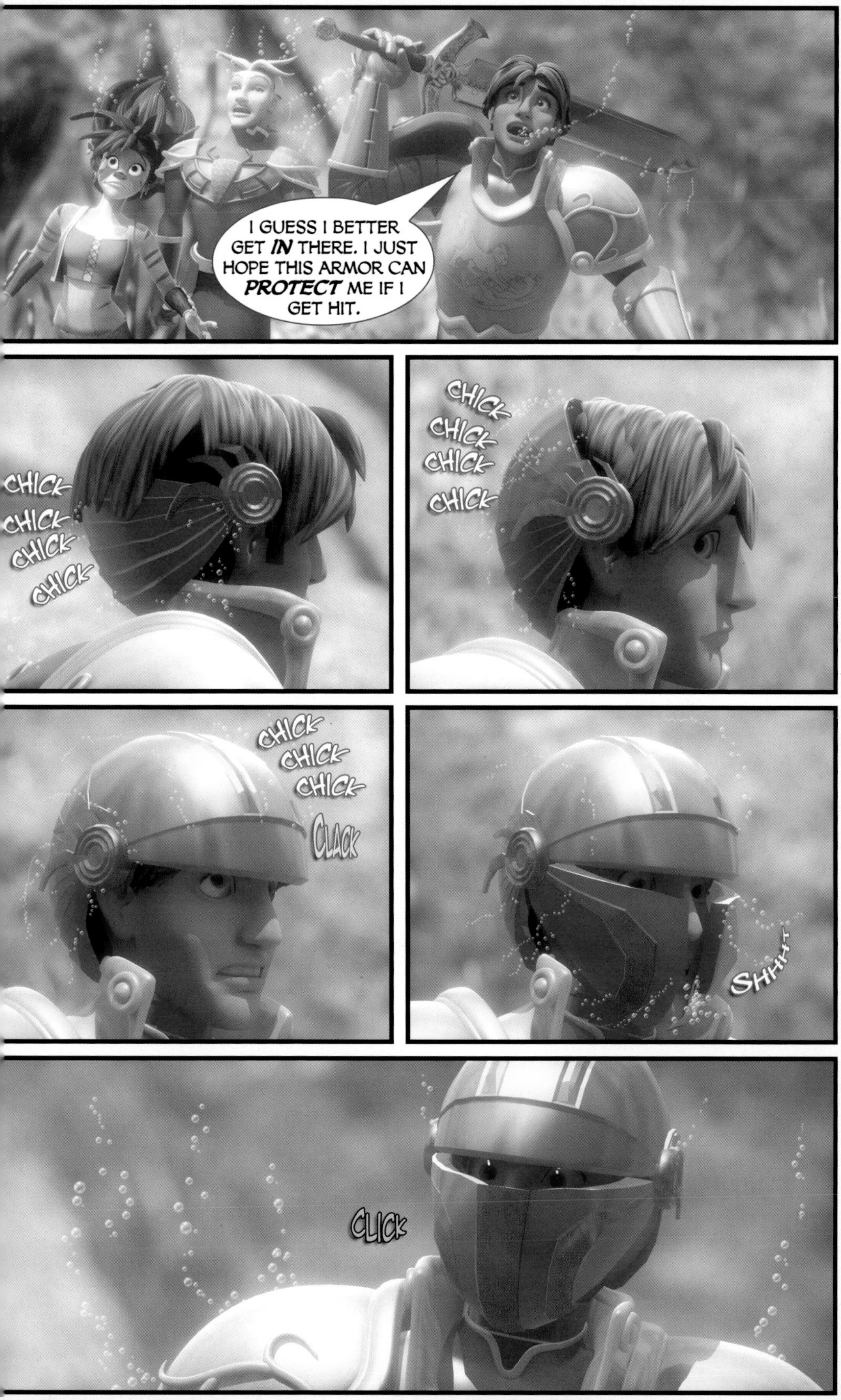
I GUESS I BETTER GET *IN* THERE. I JUST HOPE THIS ARMOR CAN *PROTECT* ME IF I GET HIT.
CHICK CHICK CHICK CHICK
CHICK CHICK CHICK CHICK
CHICK CHICK CHICK
CLACK
SHHH
CLICK

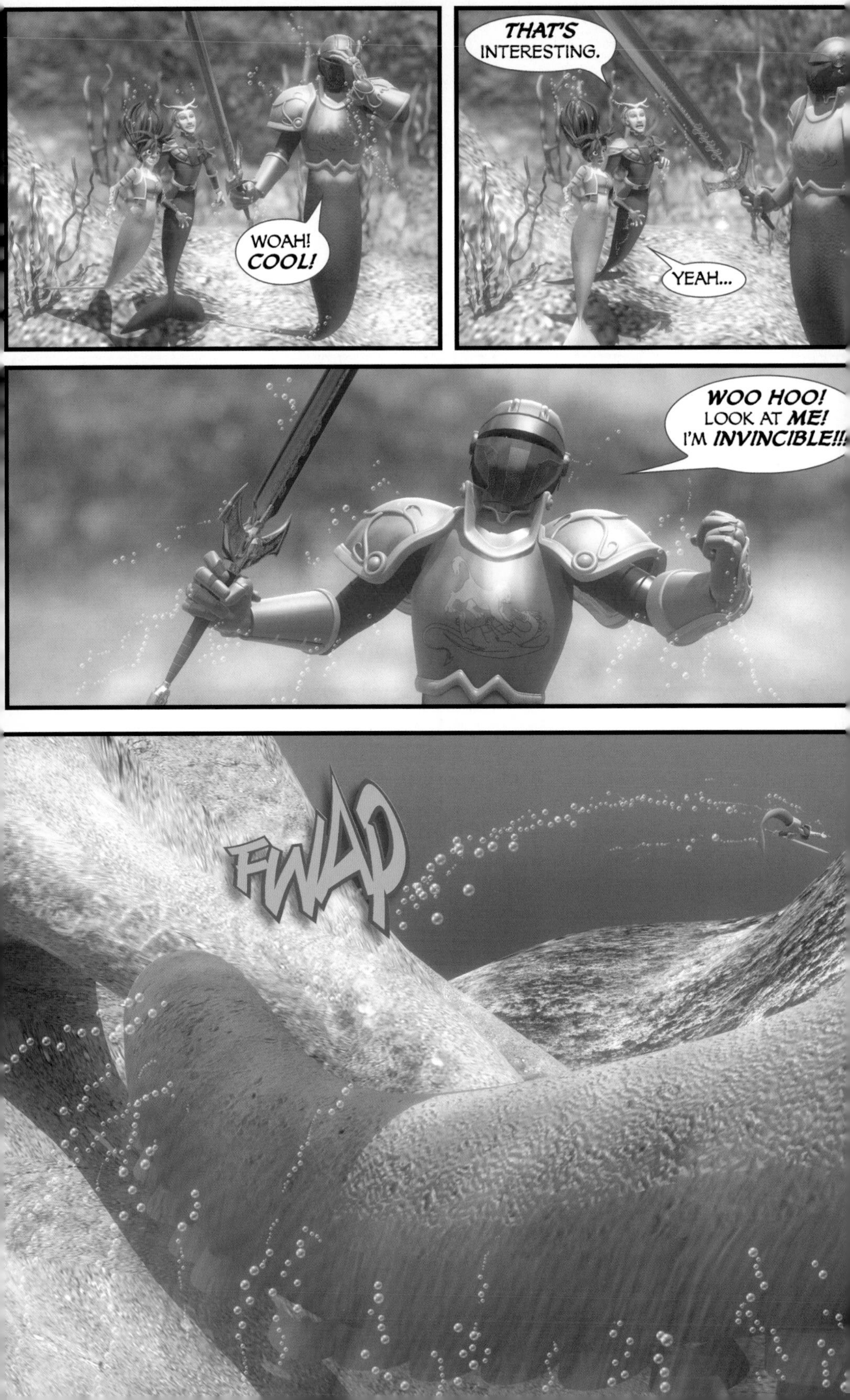

WOAH! COOL!
THAT'S INTERESTING.
YEAH...
WOO HOO! LOOK AT ME! I'M INVINCIBLE!!!
FWAP

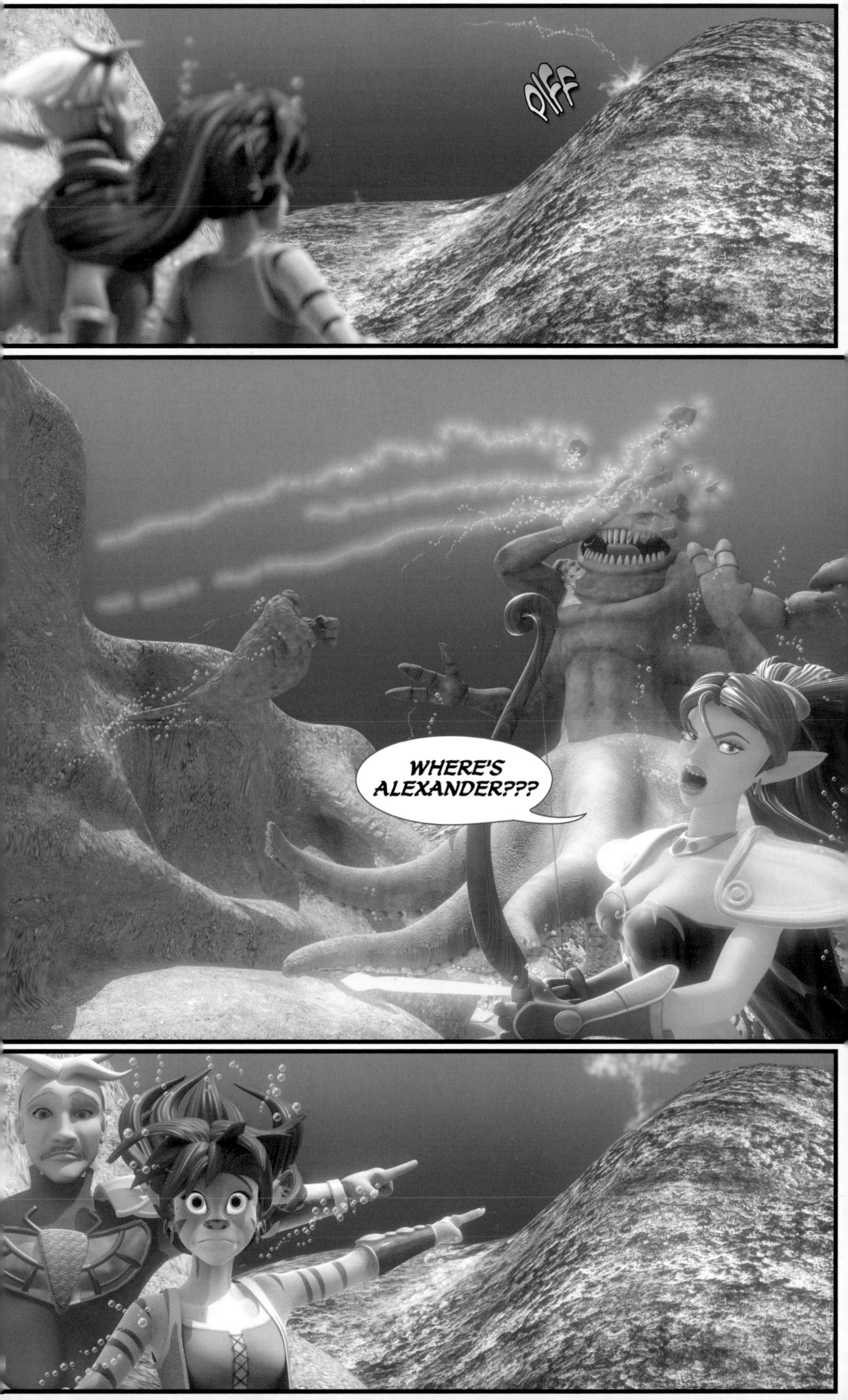
PIFF
WHERE'S ALEXANDER???

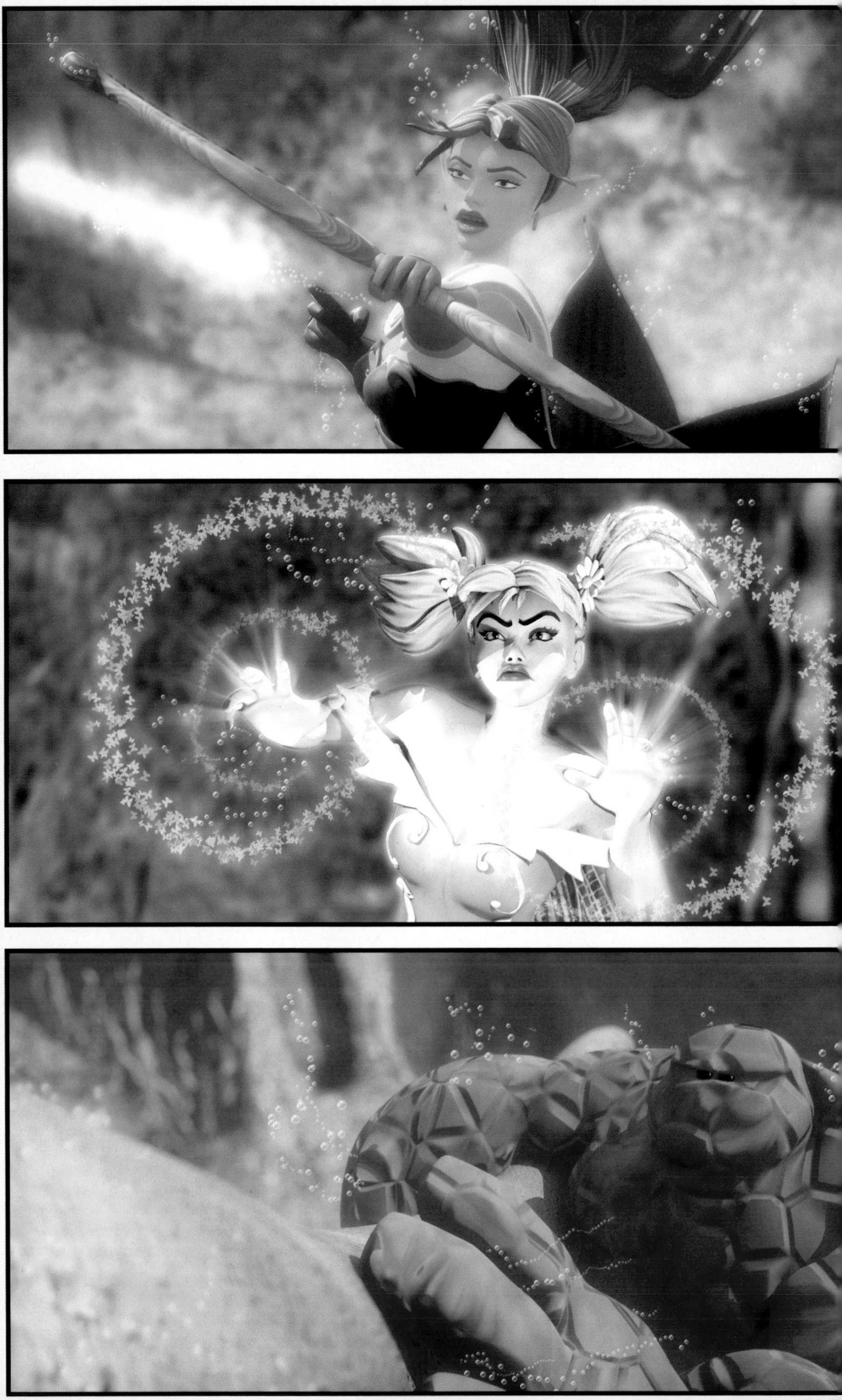

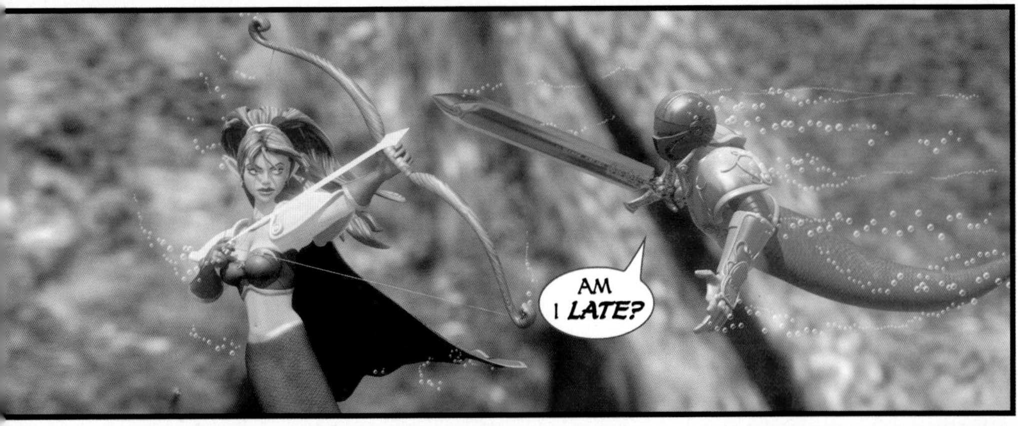
AM
I LATE?

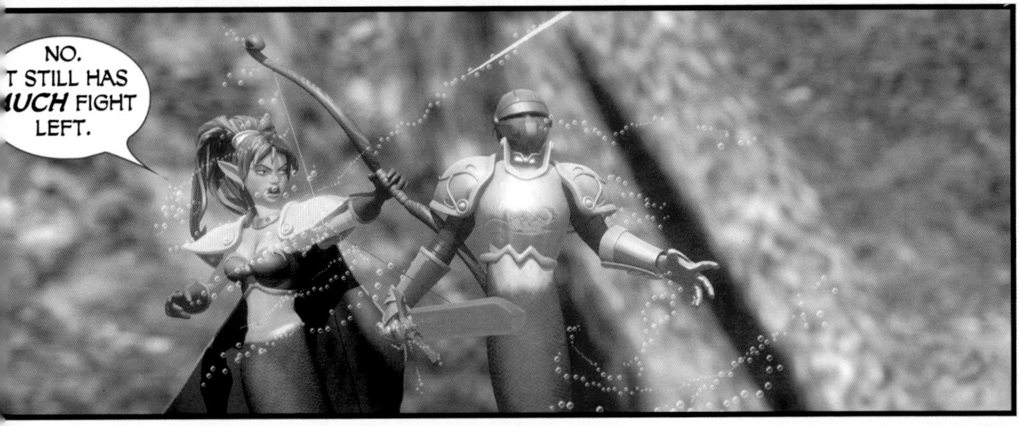
NO.
T STILL HAS
UCH FIGHT
LEFT.

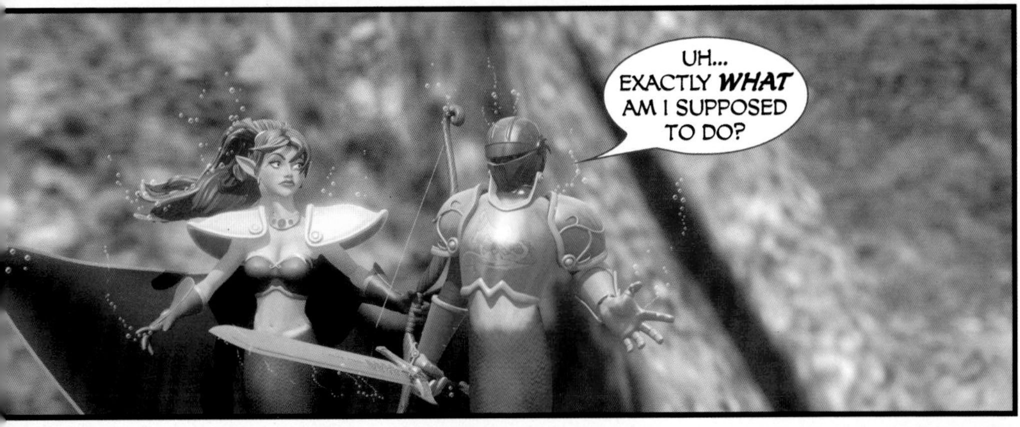
UH...
EXACTLY WHAT
AM I SUPPOSED
TO DO?

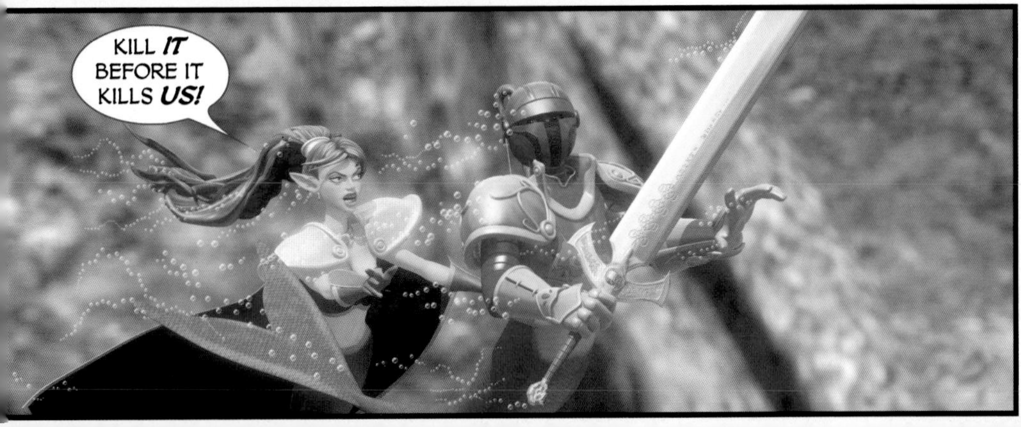
KILL IT
BEFORE IT
KILLS US!

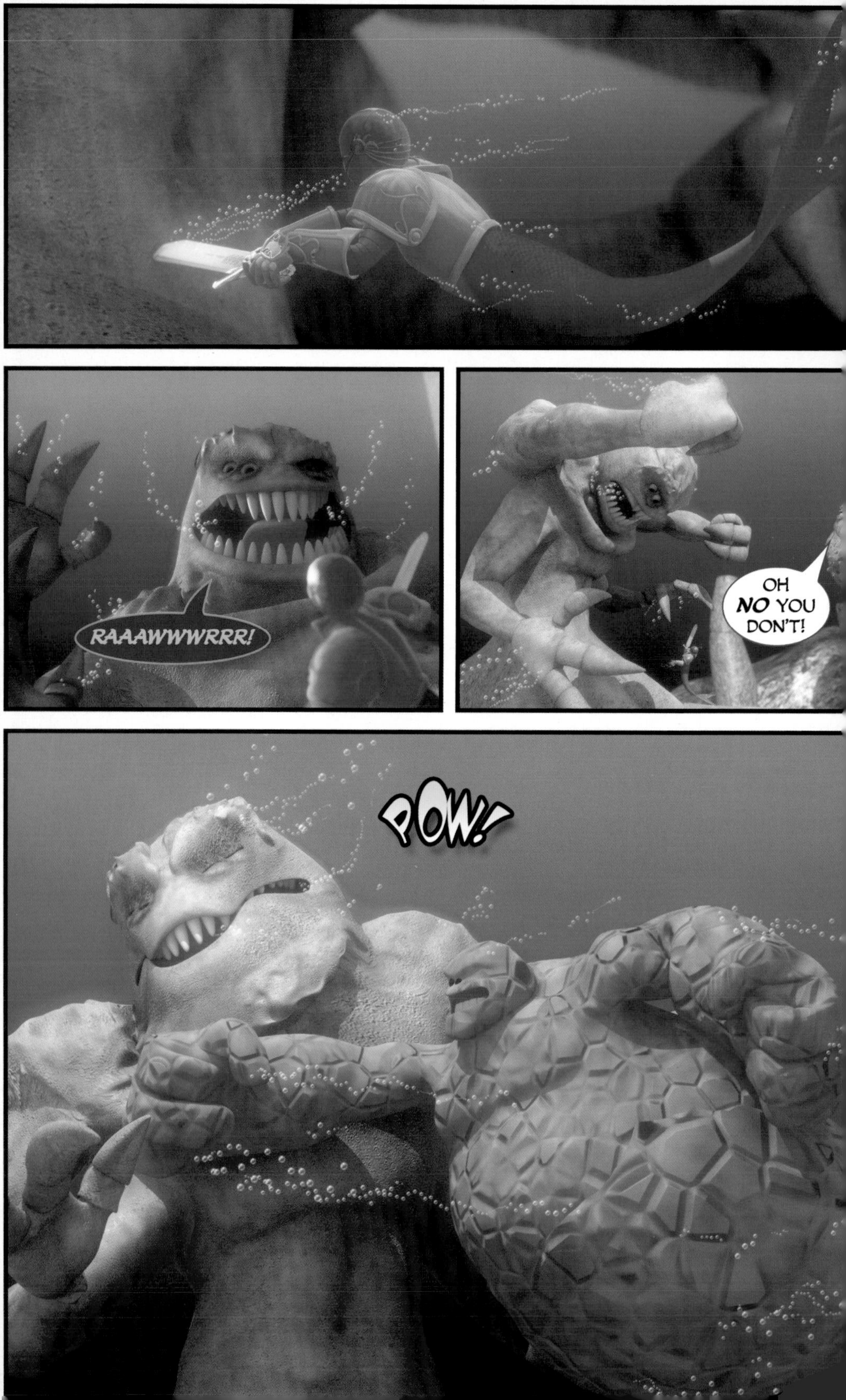
RAAAWWWRRR!
OH NO YOU DON'T!
POW!

NOW! WHILE HE'S *STUNNED,* LEXANDER! USE THE *SWORD!*

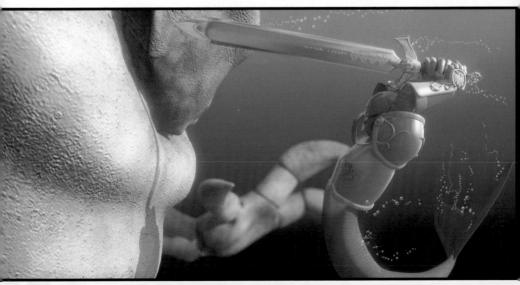

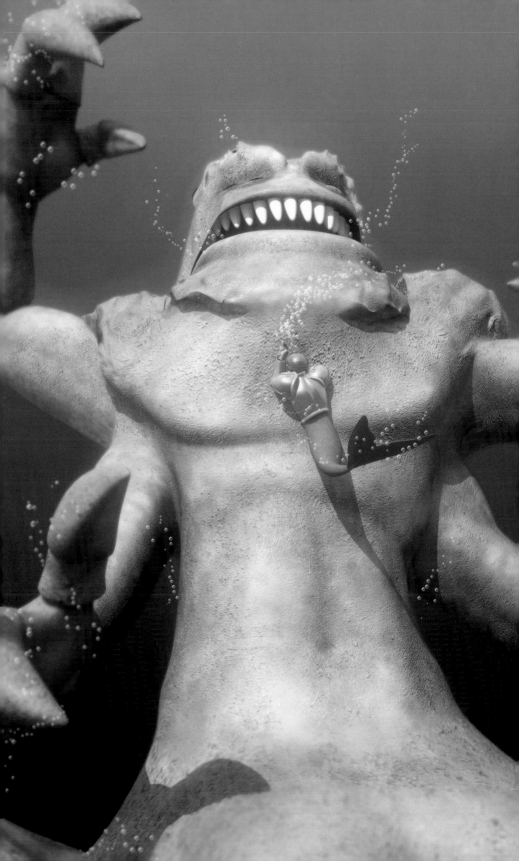

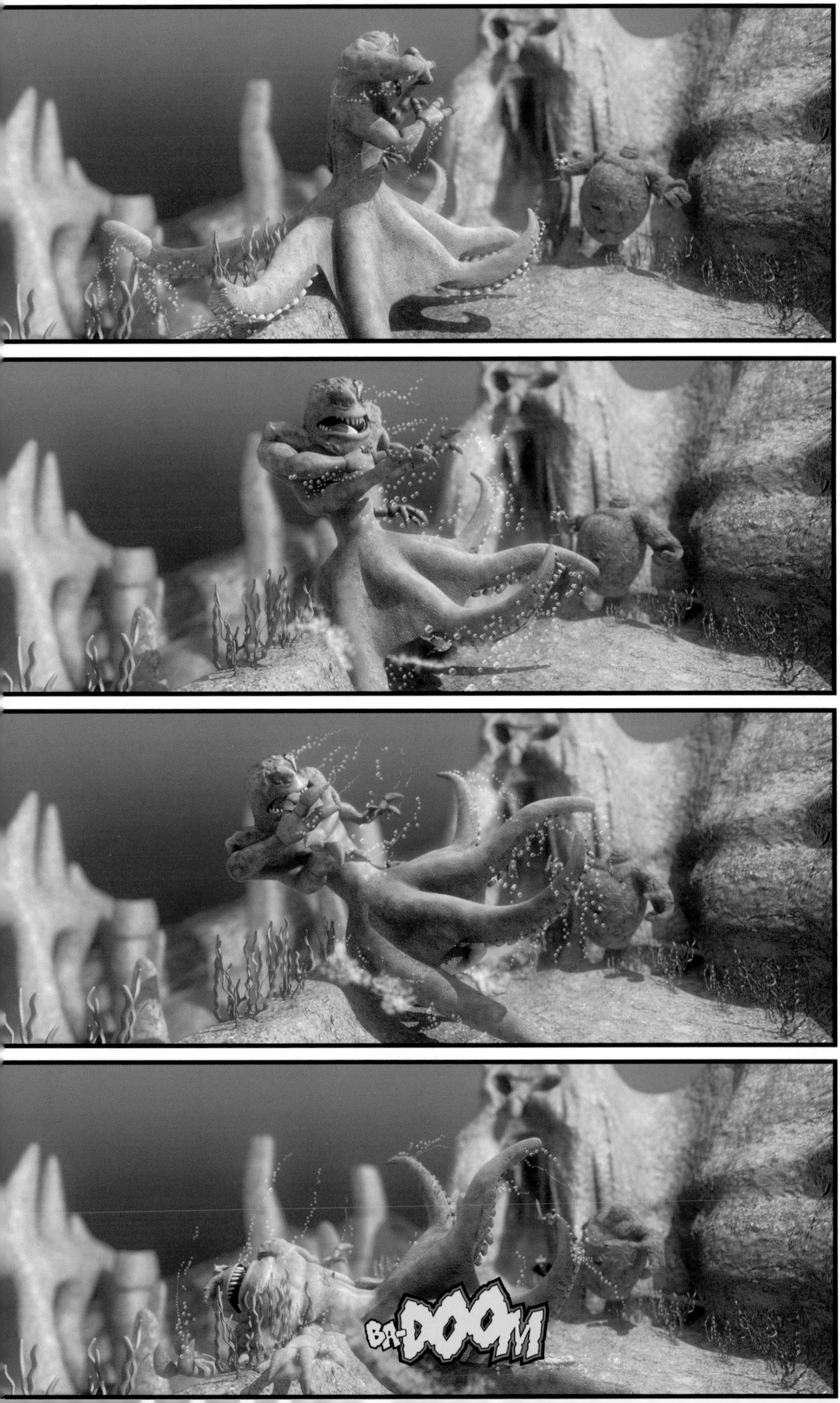
BA-DOOM

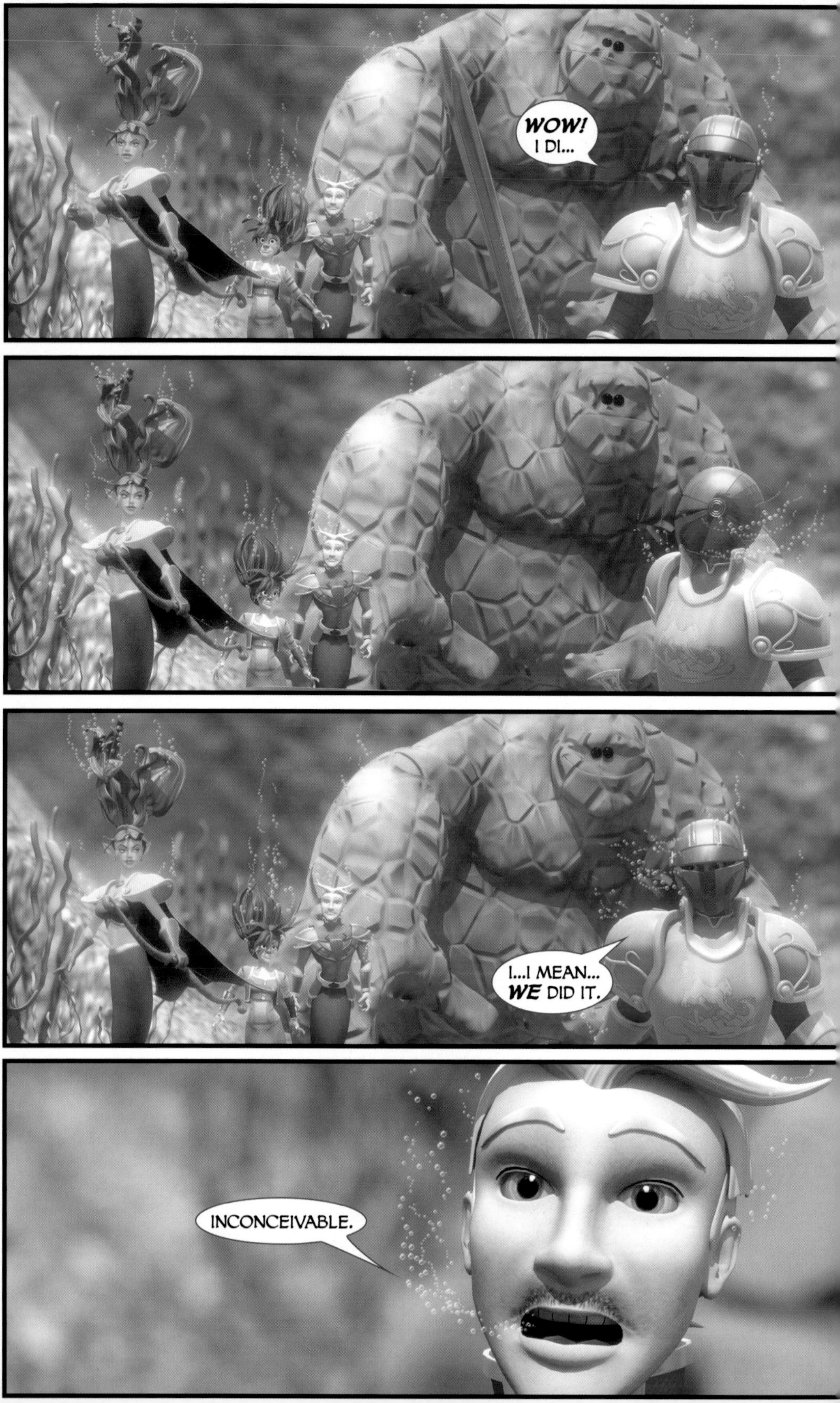
WOW!
I DI...
I...I MEAN... WE DID IT.
INCONCEIVABLE.

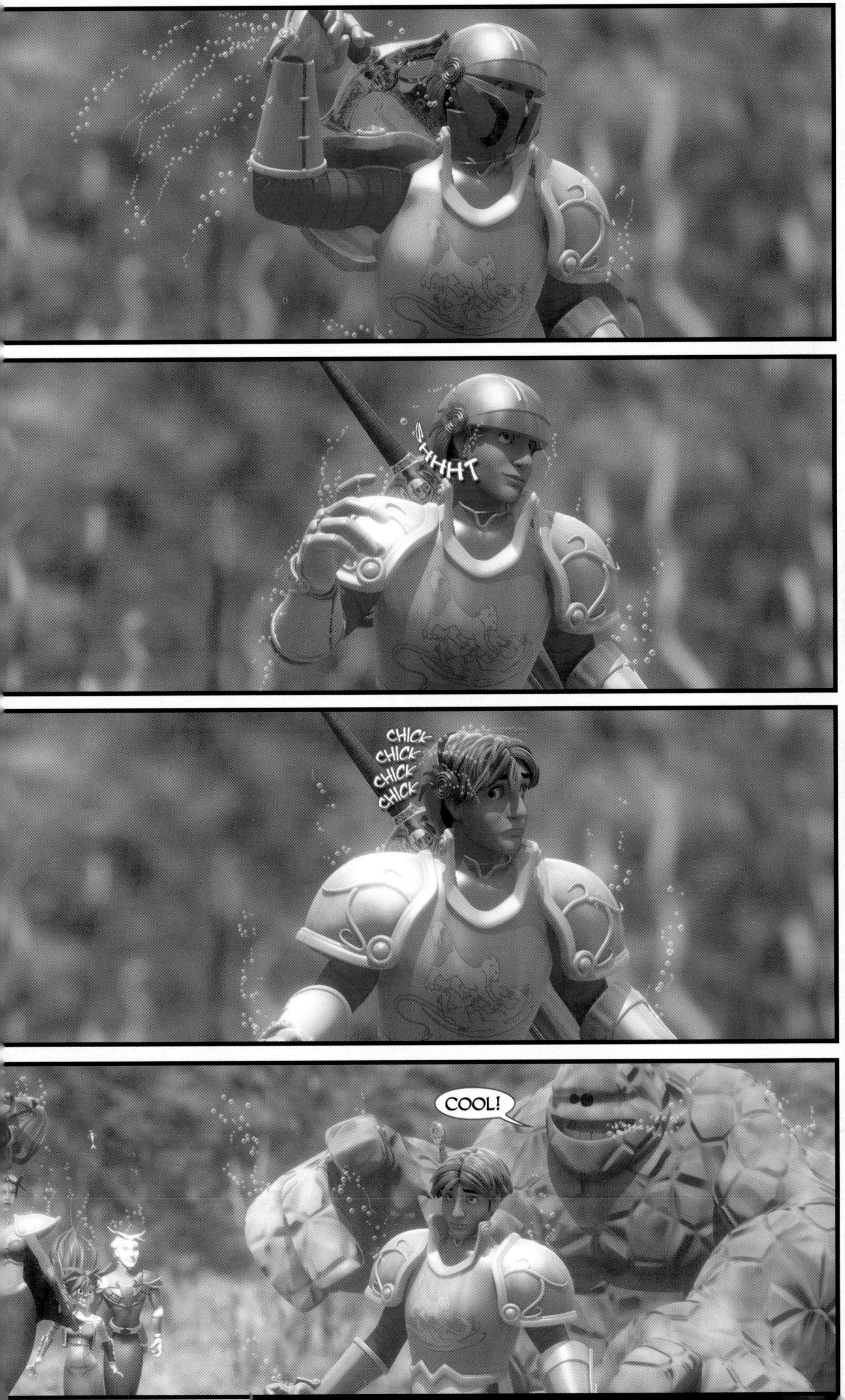
SHHHT
CHICK CHICK CHICK CHICK
COOL!

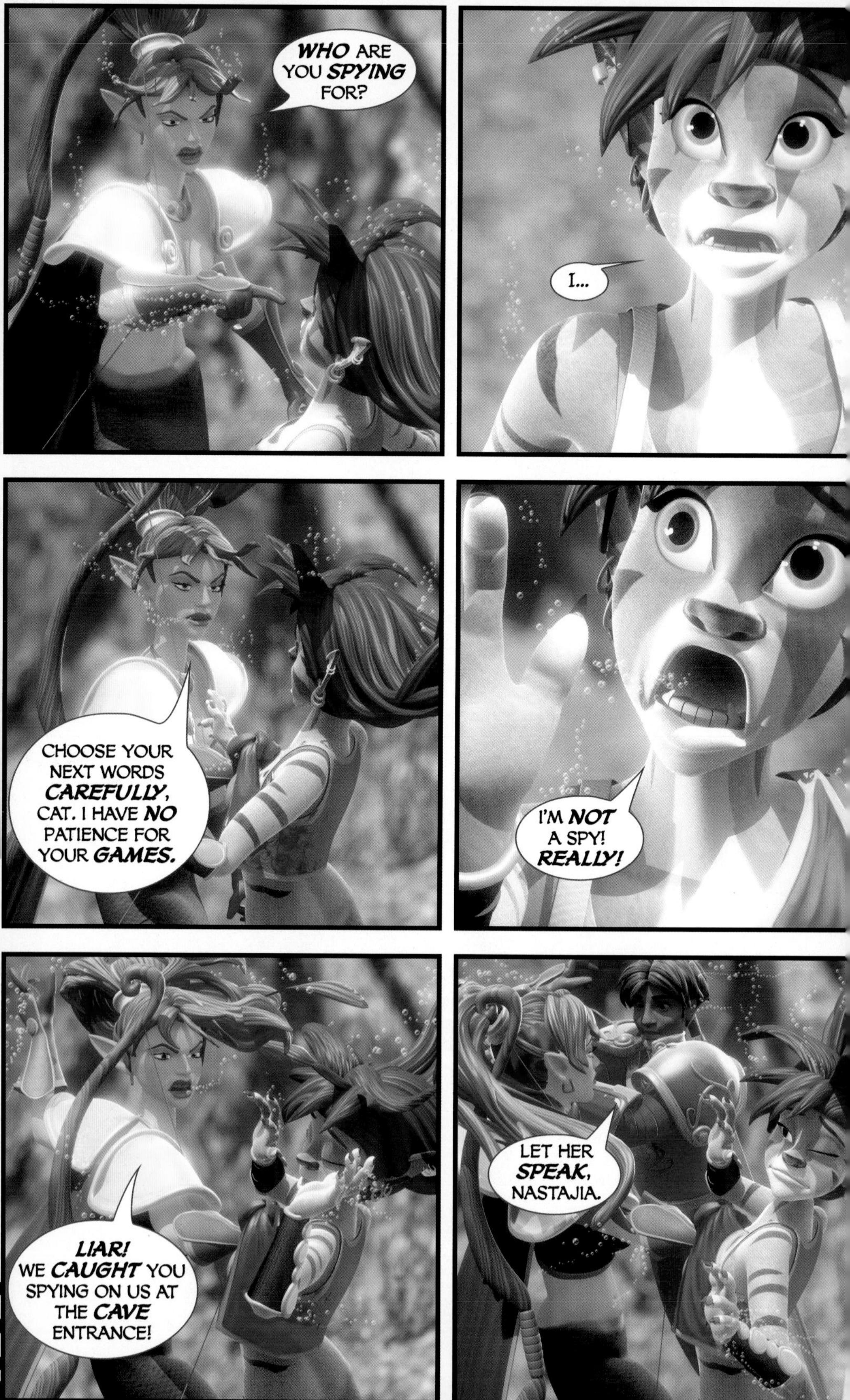
WHO ARE YOU SPYING FOR?
I...
CHOOSE YOUR NEXT WORDS CAREFULLY, CAT. I HAVE NO PATIENCE FOR YOUR GAMES.
I'M NOT A SPY! REALLY!
LIAR! WE CAUGHT YOU SPYING ON US AT THE CAVE ENTRANCE!
LET HER SPEAK, NASTAJIA.

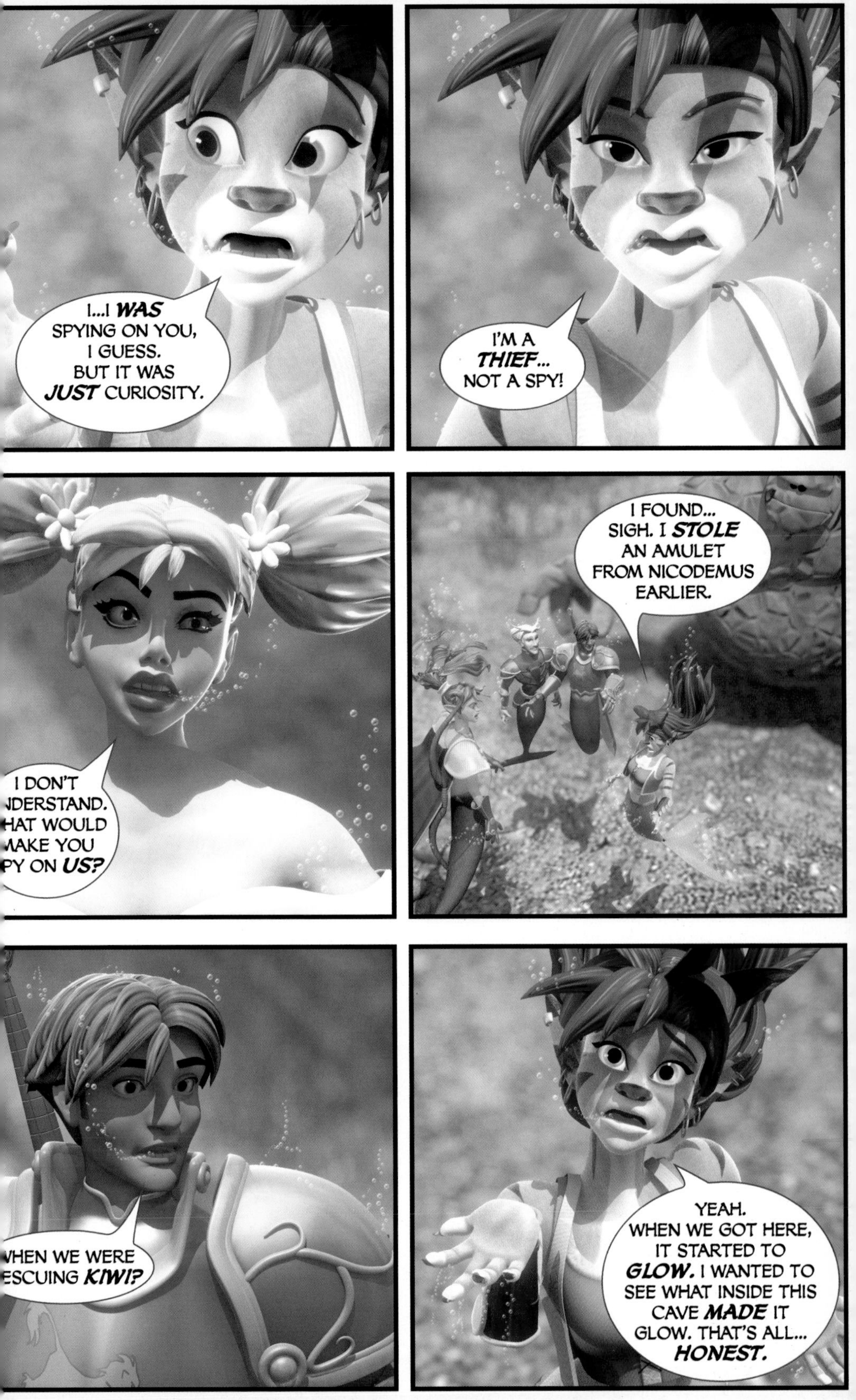
I...I WAS SPYING ON YOU, I GUESS. BUT IT WAS JUST CURIOSITY.
I'M A THIEF... NOT A SPY!
I DON'T NDERSTAND. HAT WOULD MAKE YOU PY ON US?
I FOUND... SIGH. I STOLE AN AMULET FROM NICODEMUS EARLIER.
HEN WE WERE ESCUING KIWI?
YEAH. WHEN WE GOT HERE, IT STARTED TO GLOW. I WANTED TO SEE WHAT INSIDE THIS CAVE MADE IT GLOW. THAT'S ALL... HONEST.

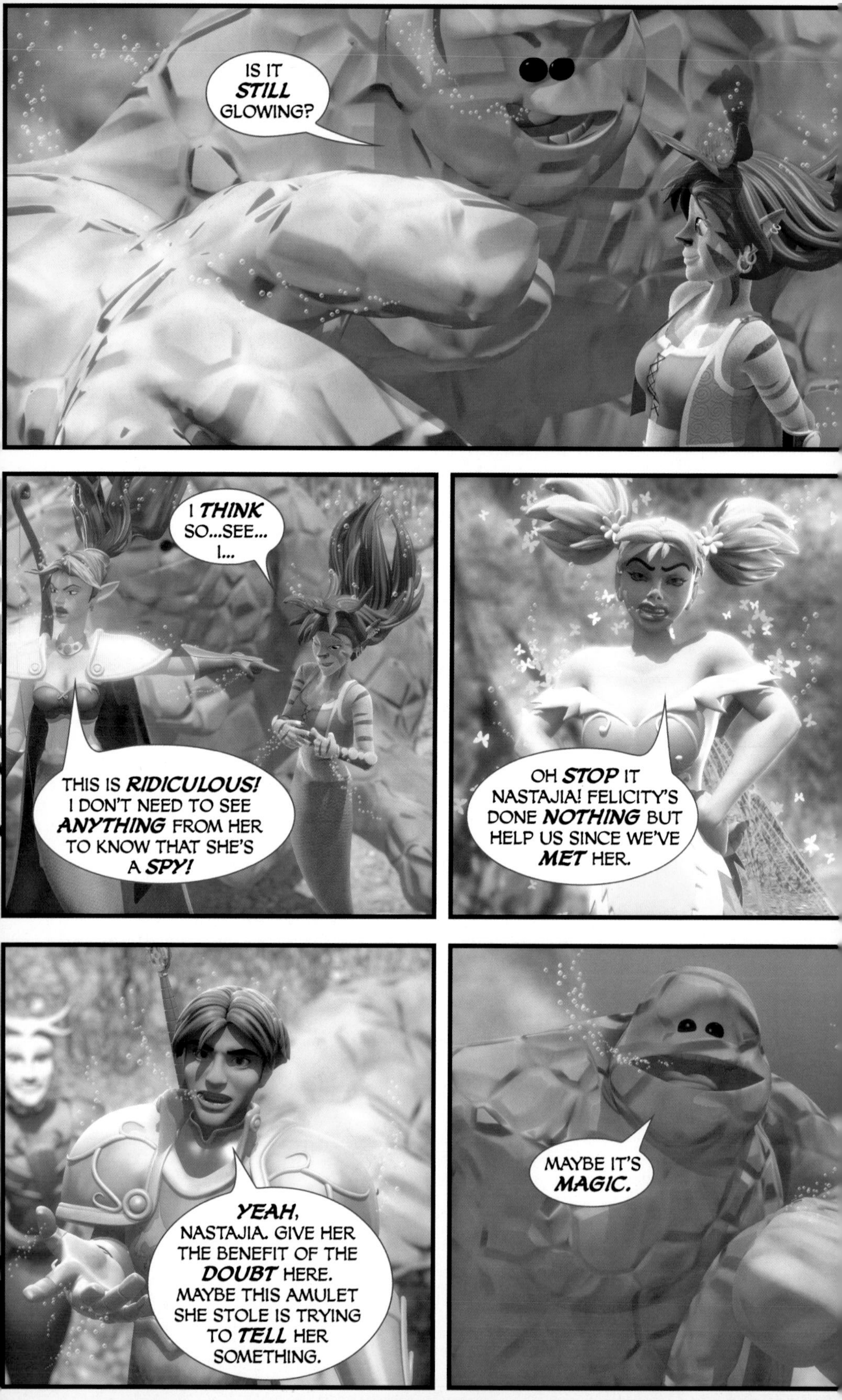

IS IT STILL GLOWING?
I THINK SO...SEE... I...
THIS IS RIDICULOUS! I DON'T NEED TO SEE ANYTHING FROM HER TO KNOW THAT SHE'S A SPY!
OH STOP IT NASTAJIA! FELICITY'S DONE NOTHING BUT HELP US SINCE WE'VE MET HER.
YEAH, NASTAJIA. GIVE HER THE BENEFIT OF THE DOUBT HERE. MAYBE THIS AMULET SHE STOLE IS TRYING TO TELL HER SOMETHING.
MAYBE IT'S MAGIC.

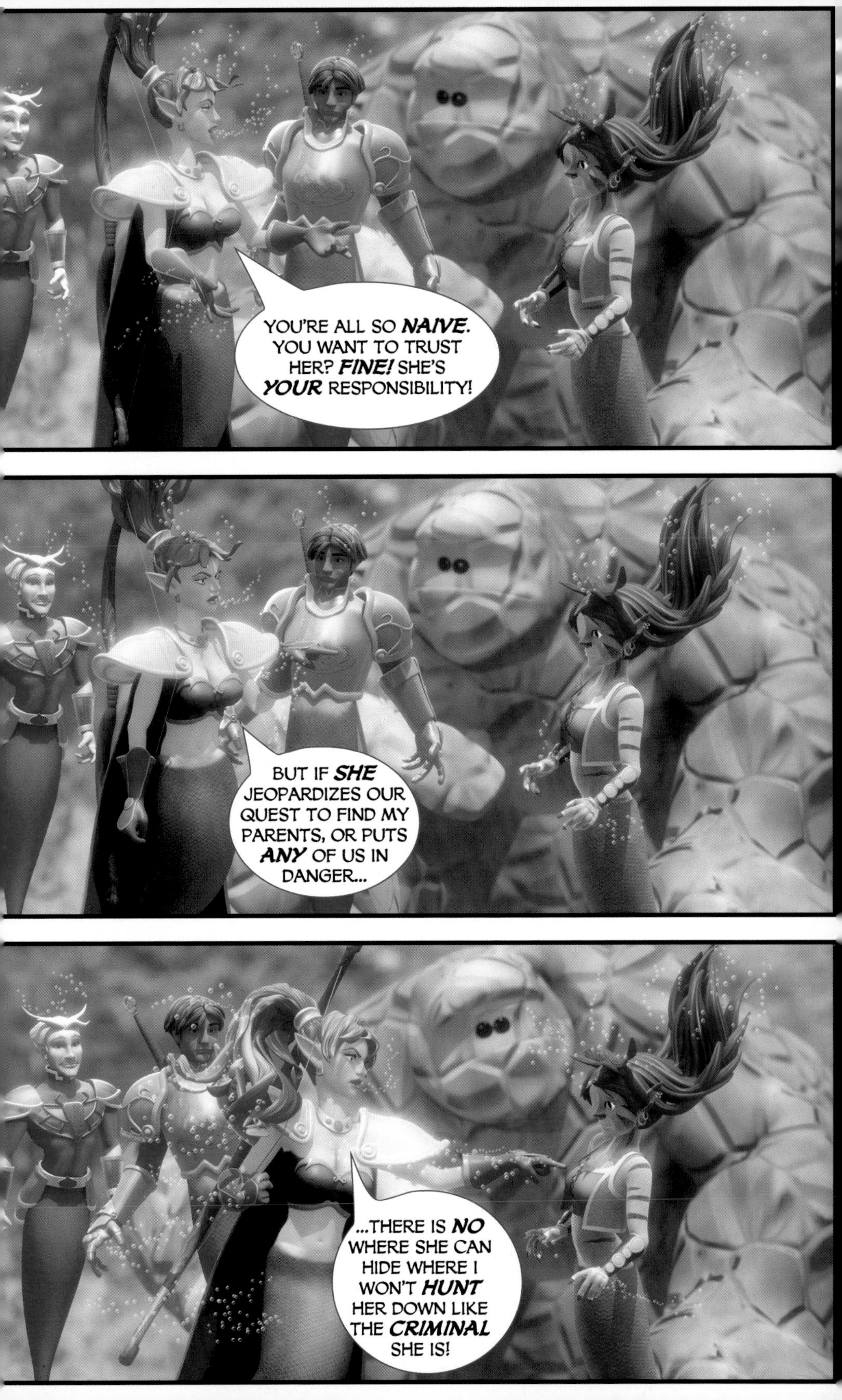
YOU'RE ALL SO NAIVE. YOU WANT TO TRUST HER? FINE! SHE'S YOUR RESPONSIBILITY!
BUT IF SHE JEOPARDIZES OUR QUEST TO FIND MY PARENTS, OR PUTS ANY OF US IN DANGER...
...THERE IS NO WHERE SHE CAN HIDE WHERE I WON'T HUNT HER DOWN LIKE THE CRIMINAL SHE IS!

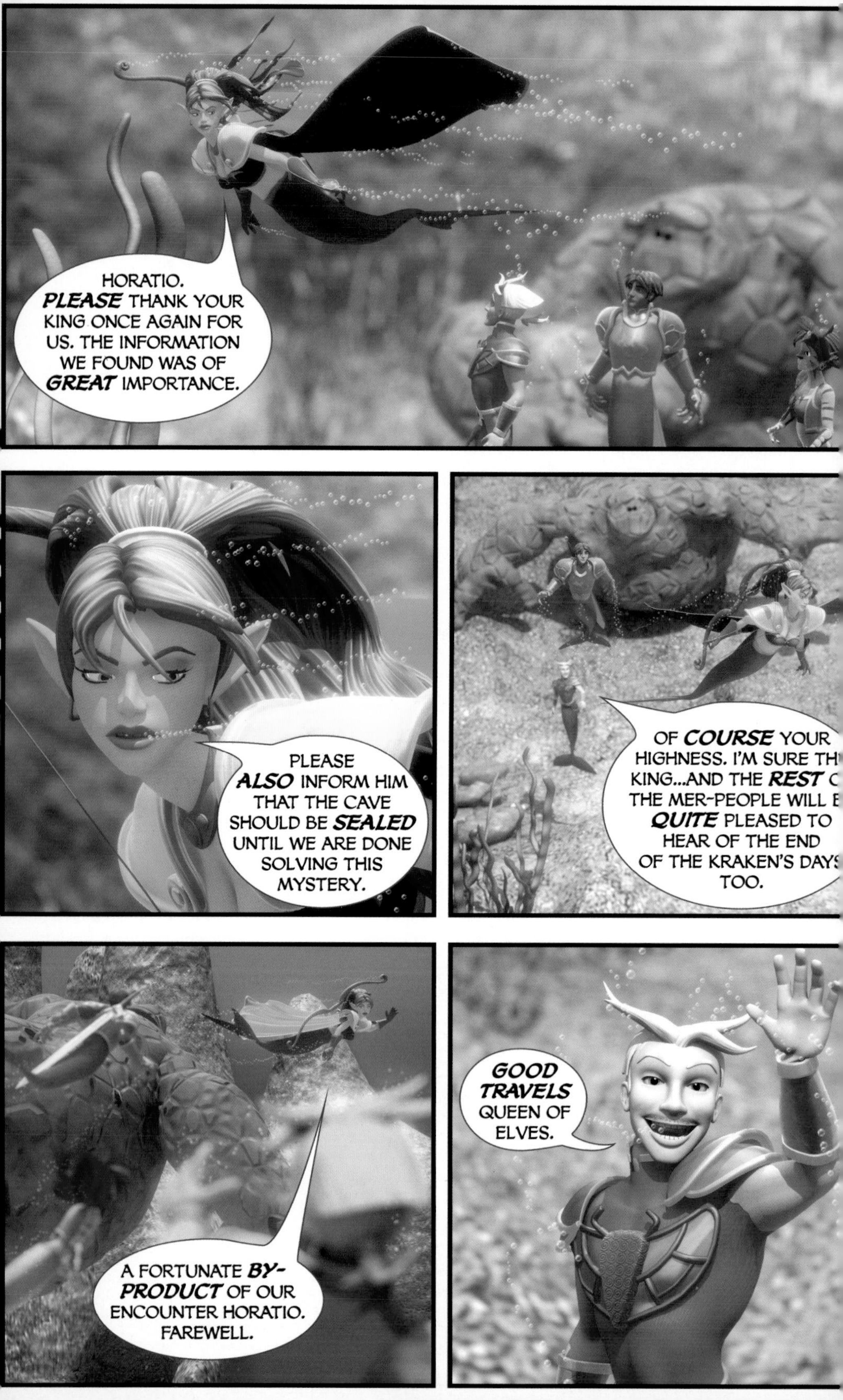
HORATIO. PLEASE THANK YOUR KING ONCE AGAIN FOR US. THE INFORMATION WE FOUND WAS OF GREAT IMPORTANCE.
PLEASE ALSO INFORM HIM THAT THE CAVE SHOULD BE SEALED UNTIL WE ARE DONE SOLVING THIS MYSTERY.
OF COURSE YOUR HIGHNESS. I'M SURE TH KING...AND THE REST C THE MER-PEOPLE WILL E QUITE PLEASED TO HEAR OF THE END OF THE KRAKEN'S DAYS TOO.
A FORTUNATE BY-PRODUCT OF OUR ENCOUNTER HORATIO. FAREWELL.
GOOD TRAVELS QUEEN OF ELVES.

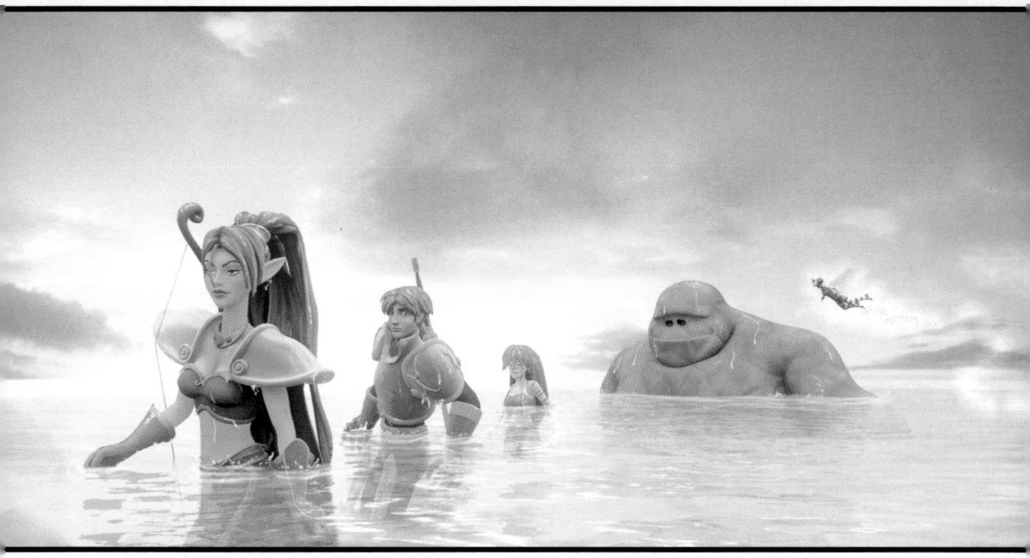

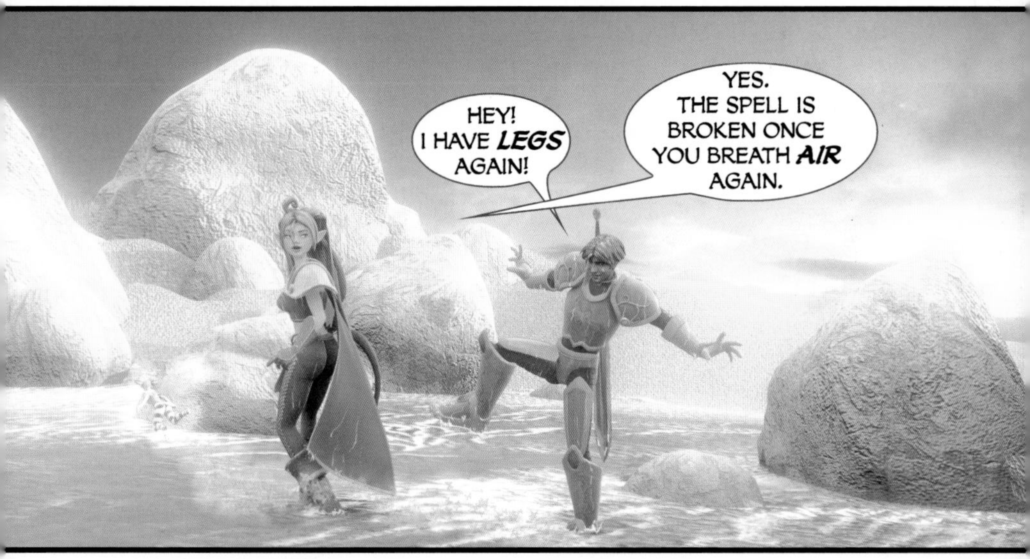
HEY! I HAVE LEGS AGAIN!
YES. THE SPELL IS BROKEN ONCE YOU BREATH AIR AGAIN.

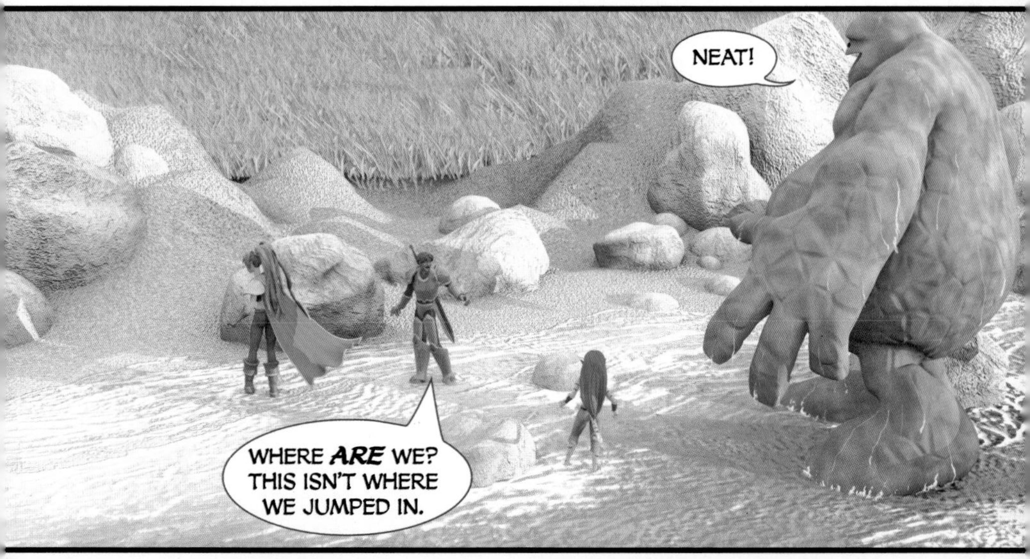
NEAT!
WHERE ARE WE? THIS ISN'T WHERE WE JUMPED IN.

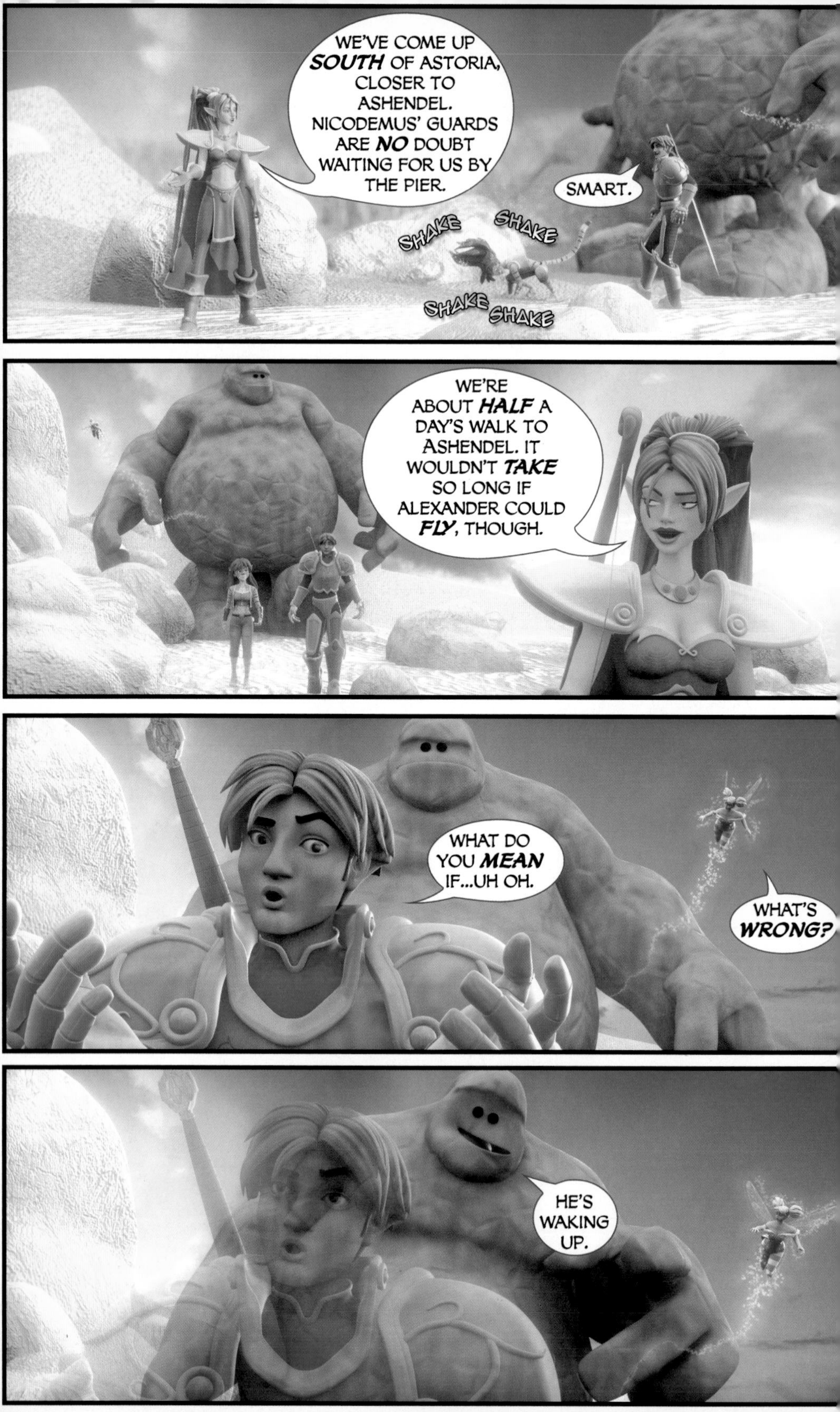
WE'VE COME UP SOUTH OF ASTORIA, CLOSER TO ASHENDEL. NICODEMUS' GUARDS ARE NO DOUBT WAITING FOR US BY THE PIER.
SMART.
SHAKE SHAKE
SHAKE SHAKE
WE'RE ABOUT HALF A DAY'S WALK TO ASHENDEL. IT WOULDN'T TAKE SO LONG IF ALEXANDER COULD FLY, THOUGH.
WHAT DO YOU MEAN IF...UH OH.
WHAT'S WRONG?
HE'S WAKING UP.

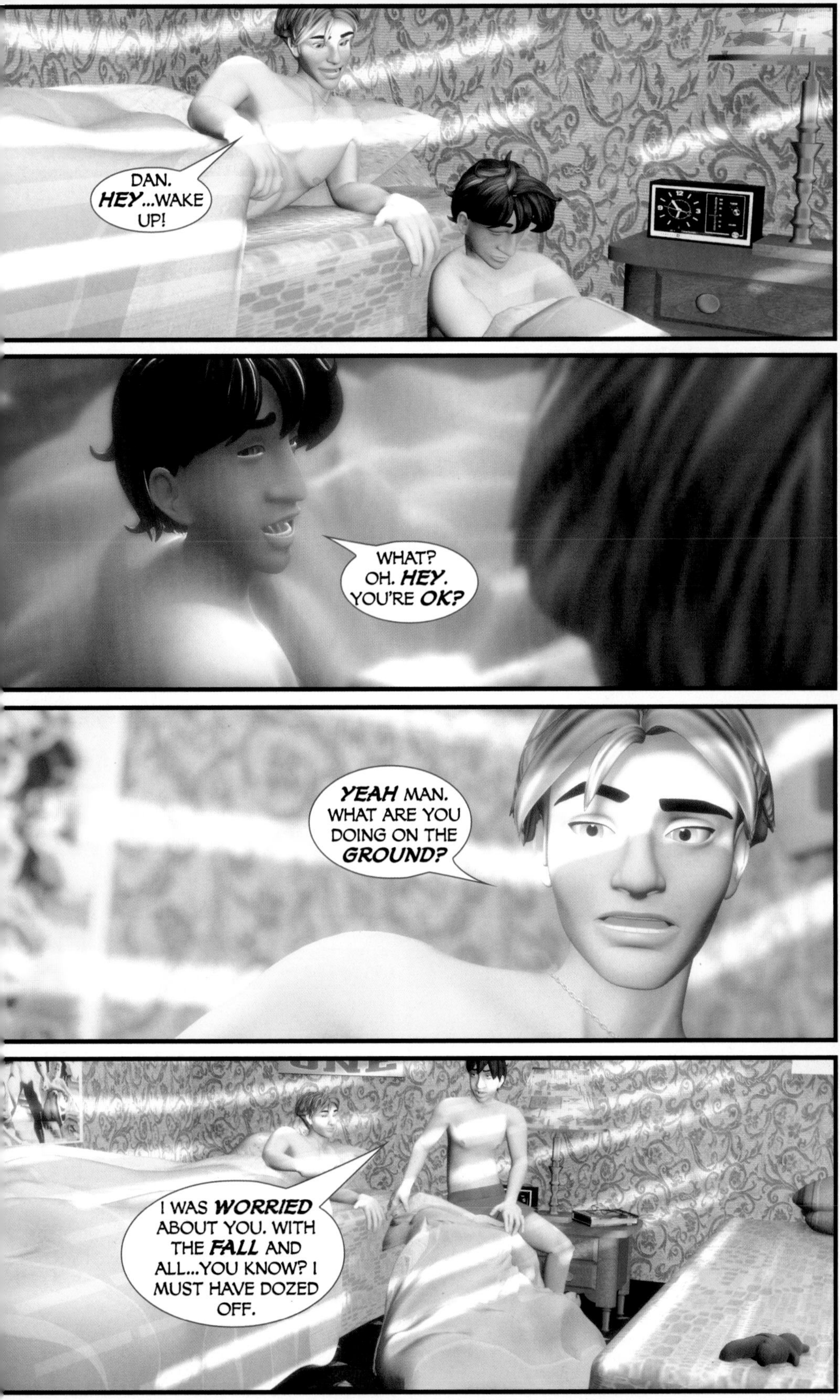
DAN. HEY...WAKE UP!
WHAT? OH. HEY. YOU'RE OK?
YEAH MAN. WHAT ARE YOU DOING ON THE GROUND?
I WAS WORRIED ABOUT YOU. WITH THE FALL AND ALL...YOU KNOW? I MUST HAVE DOZED OFF.

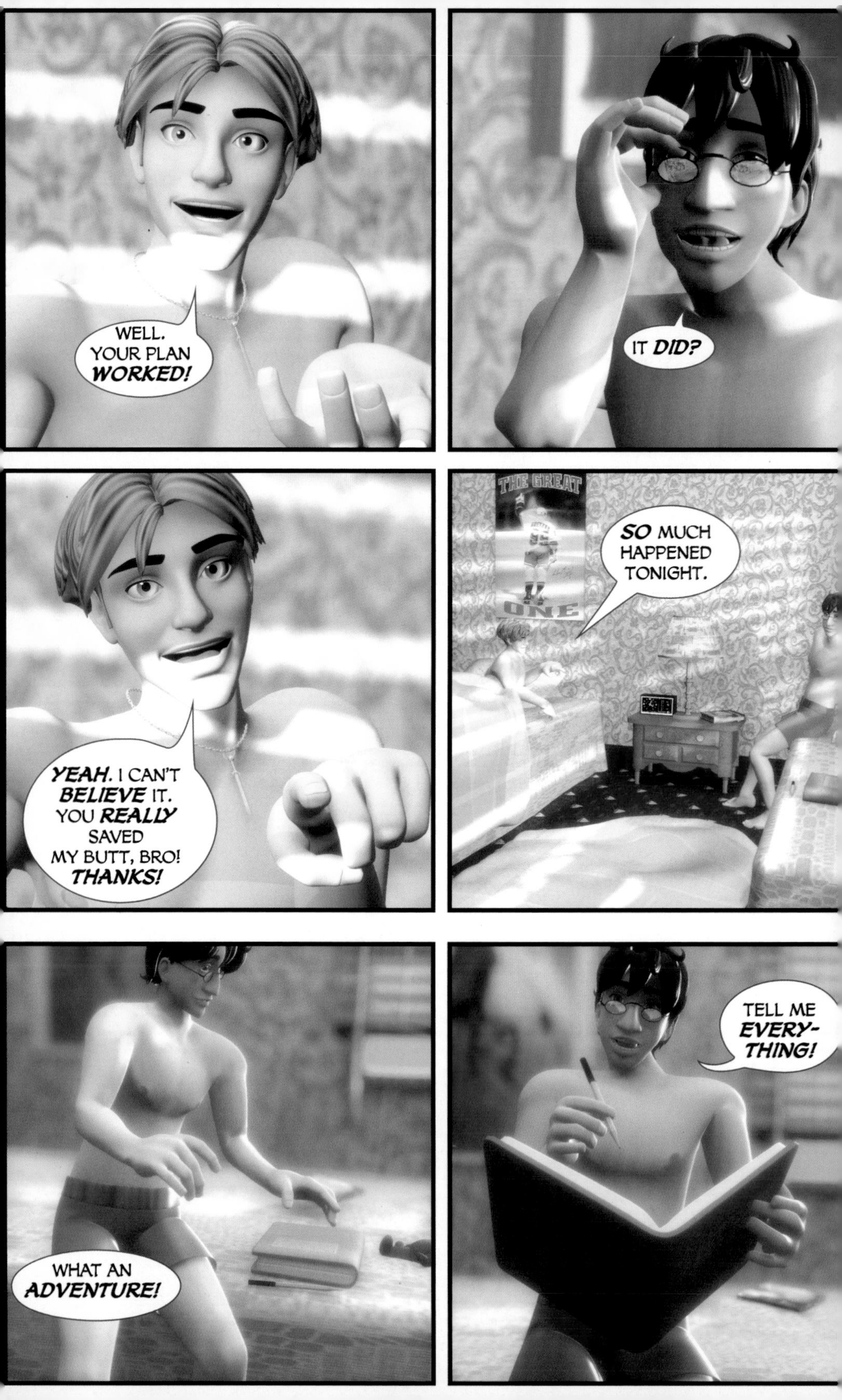
WELL. YOUR PLAN WORKED!
IT DID?
YEAH. I CAN'T BELIEVE IT. YOU REALLY SAVED MY BUTT, BRO! THANKS!
THE GREAT ONE
SO MUCH HAPPENED TONIGHT.
WHAT AN ADVENTURE!
TELL ME EVERY-THING!

CHAPTER EIGHT

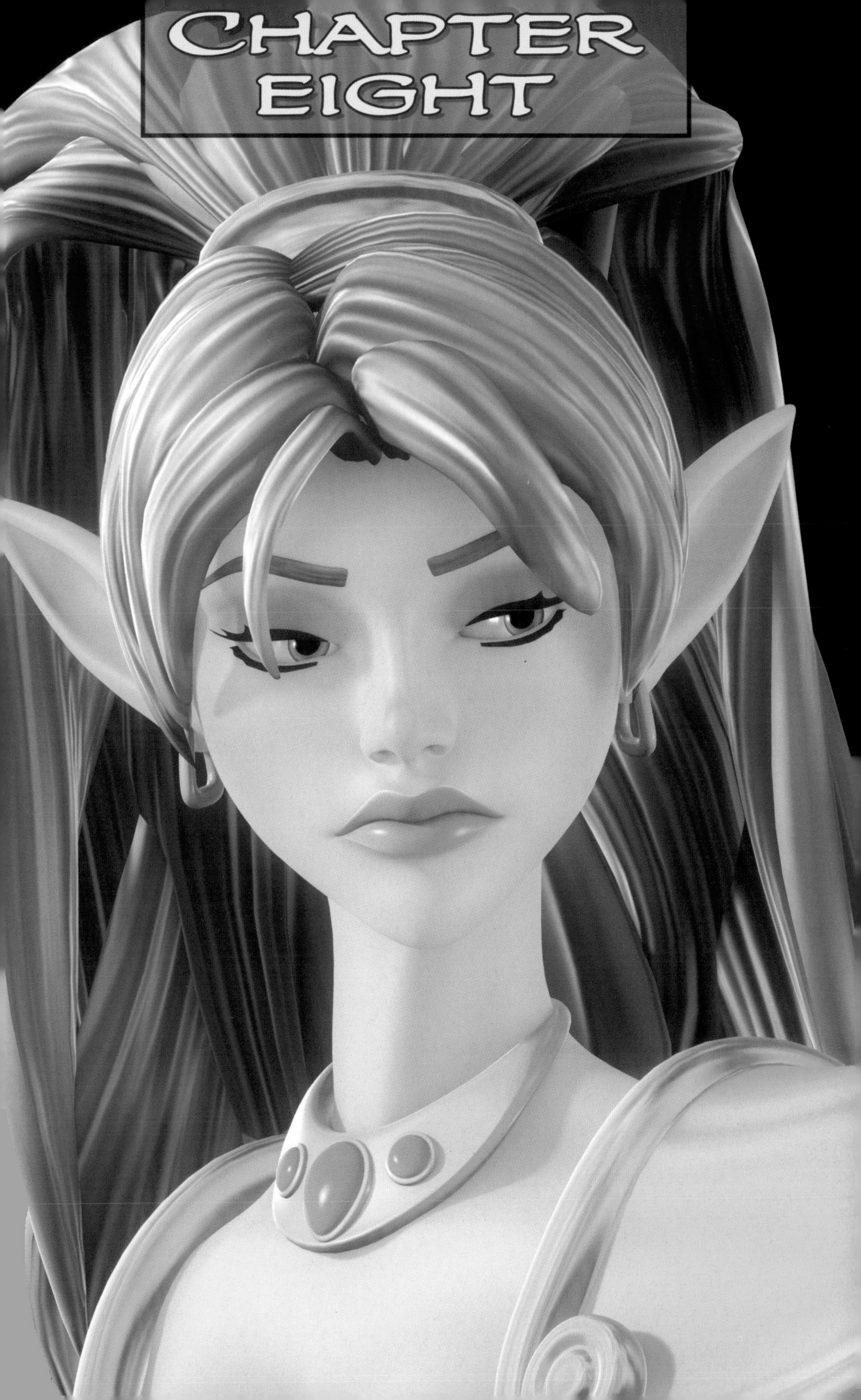

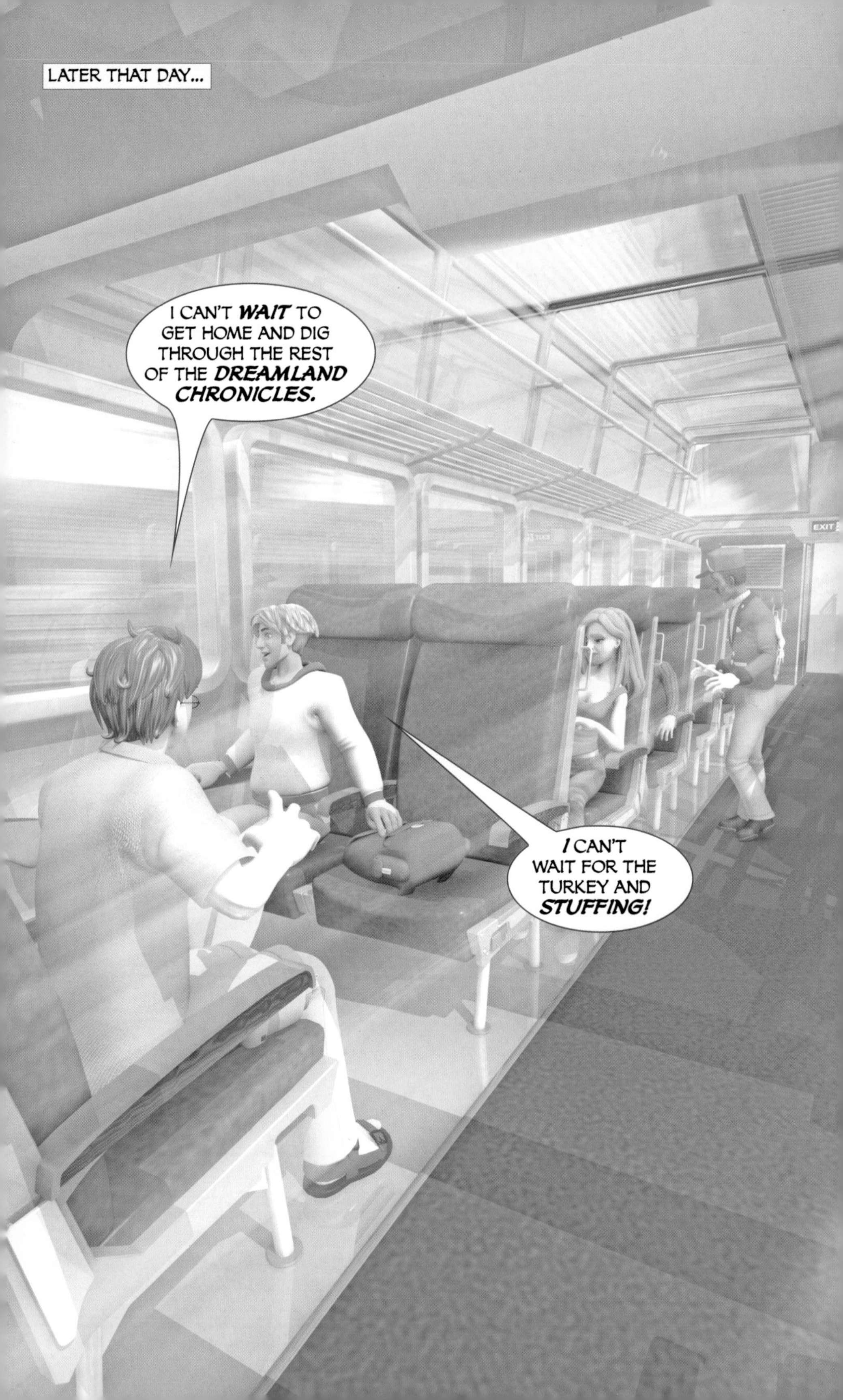
LATER THAT DAY...
I CAN'T *WAIT* TO GET HOME AND DIG THROUGH THE REST OF THE *DREAMLAND CHRONICLES.*
I CAN'T WAIT FOR THE TURKEY AND *STUFFING!*
EXIT

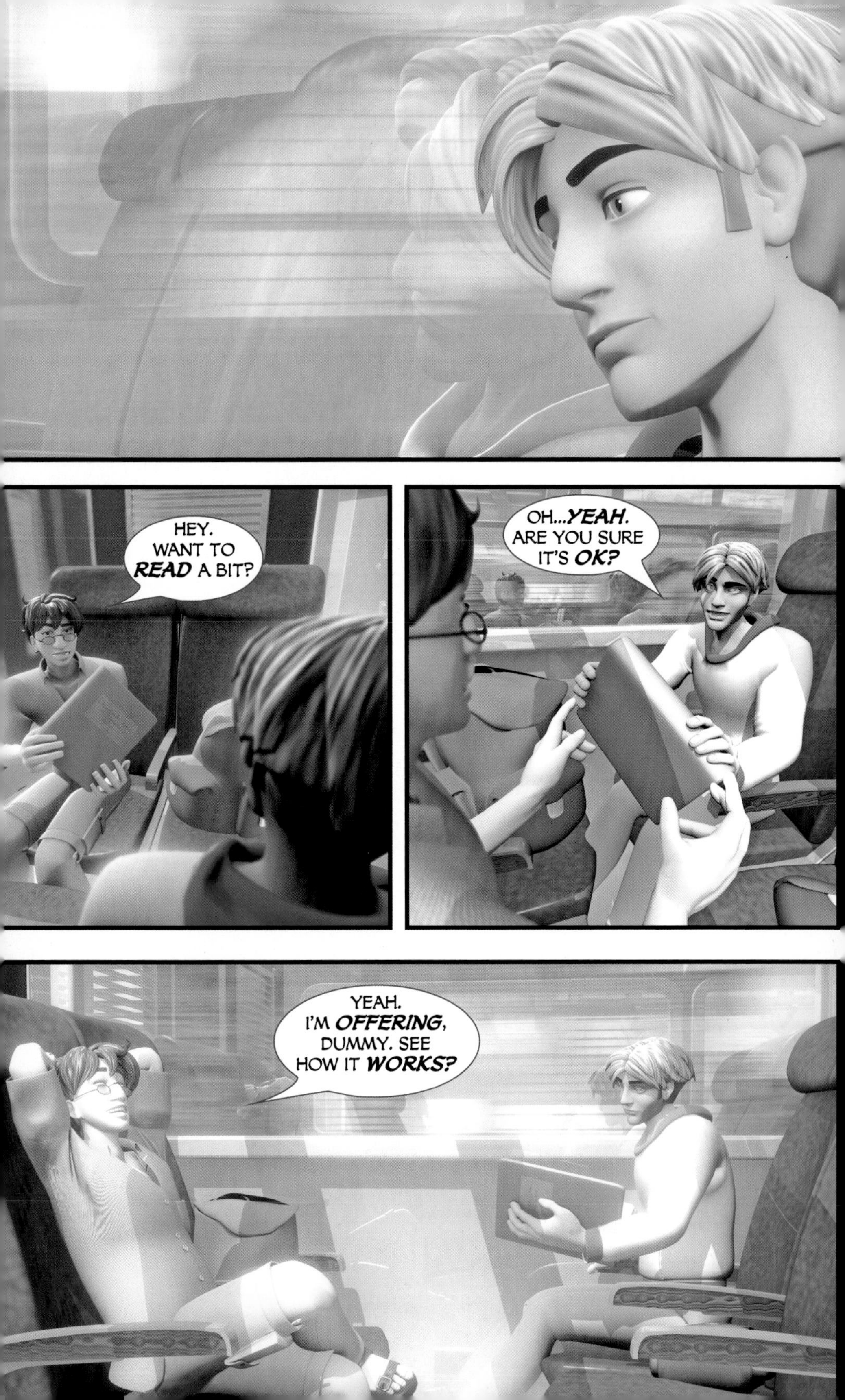
HEY. WANT TO READ A BIT?
OH...YEAH. ARE YOU SURE IT'S OK?
YEAH. I'M OFFERING, DUMMY. SEE HOW IT WORKS?

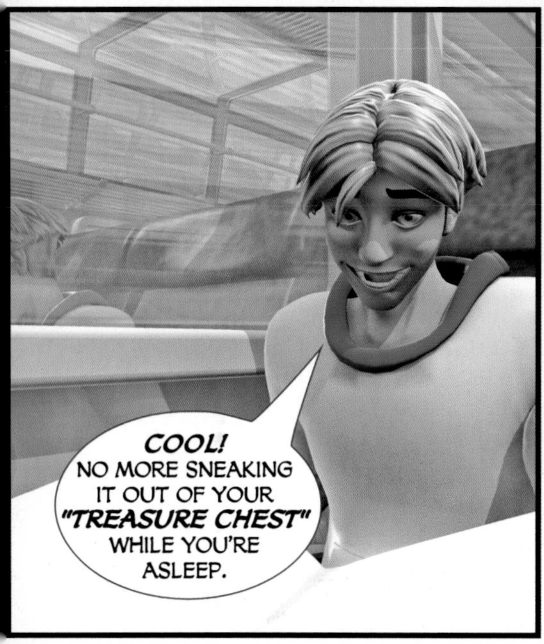
COOL! NO MORE SNEAKING IT OUT OF YOUR "TREASURE CHEST" WHILE YOU'RE ASLEEP.

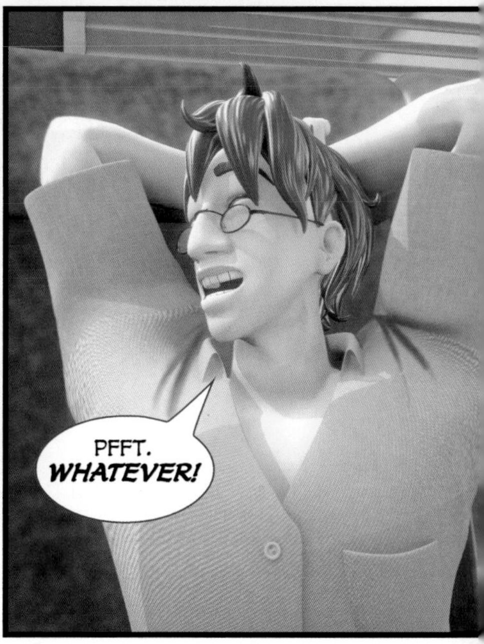
PFFT. WHATEVER!

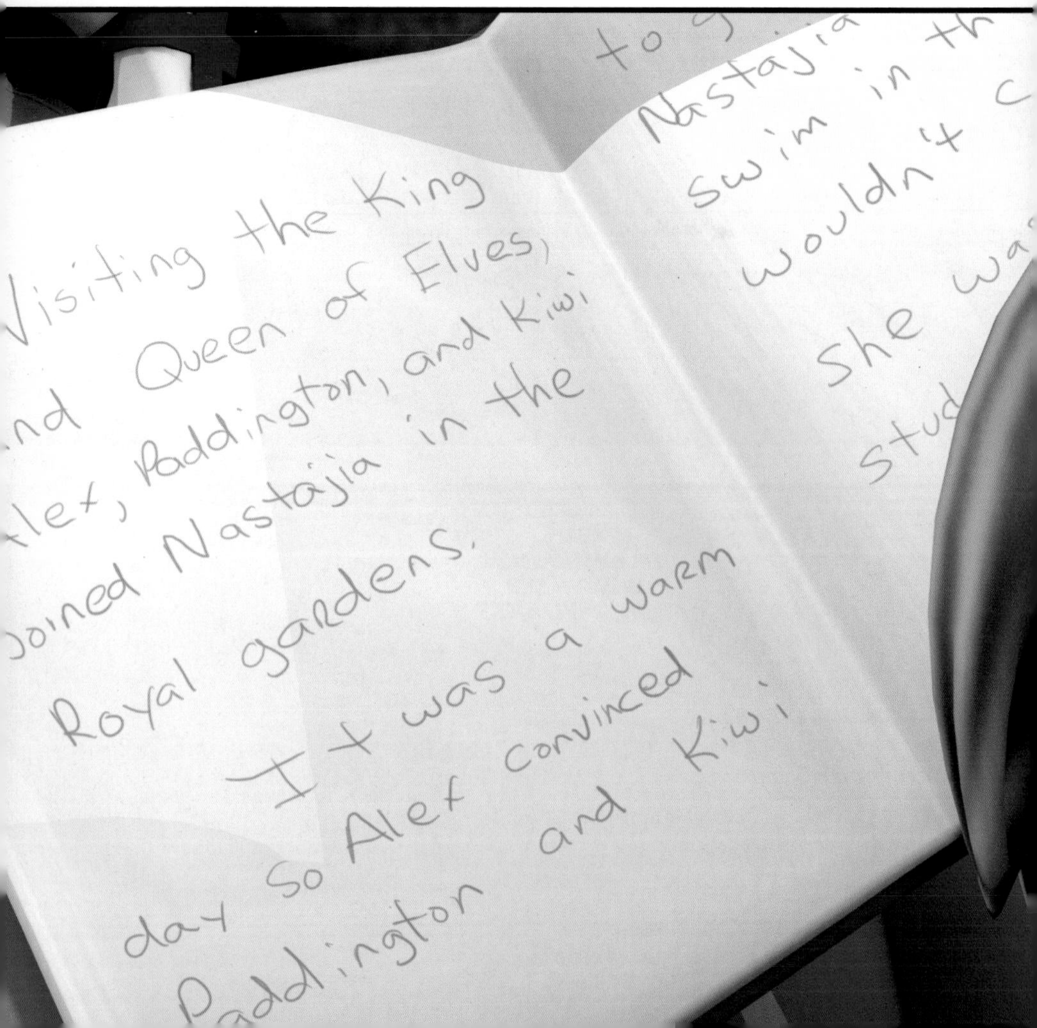
Visiting the King
nd Queen of Elves,
lex, Paddington, and Kiwi
Joined Nastajia in the
Royal gardens.
It was a warm
day so Alex convinced
Paddington and Kiwi
to
Nastajia
swim in th
wouldn't
She wa
stud

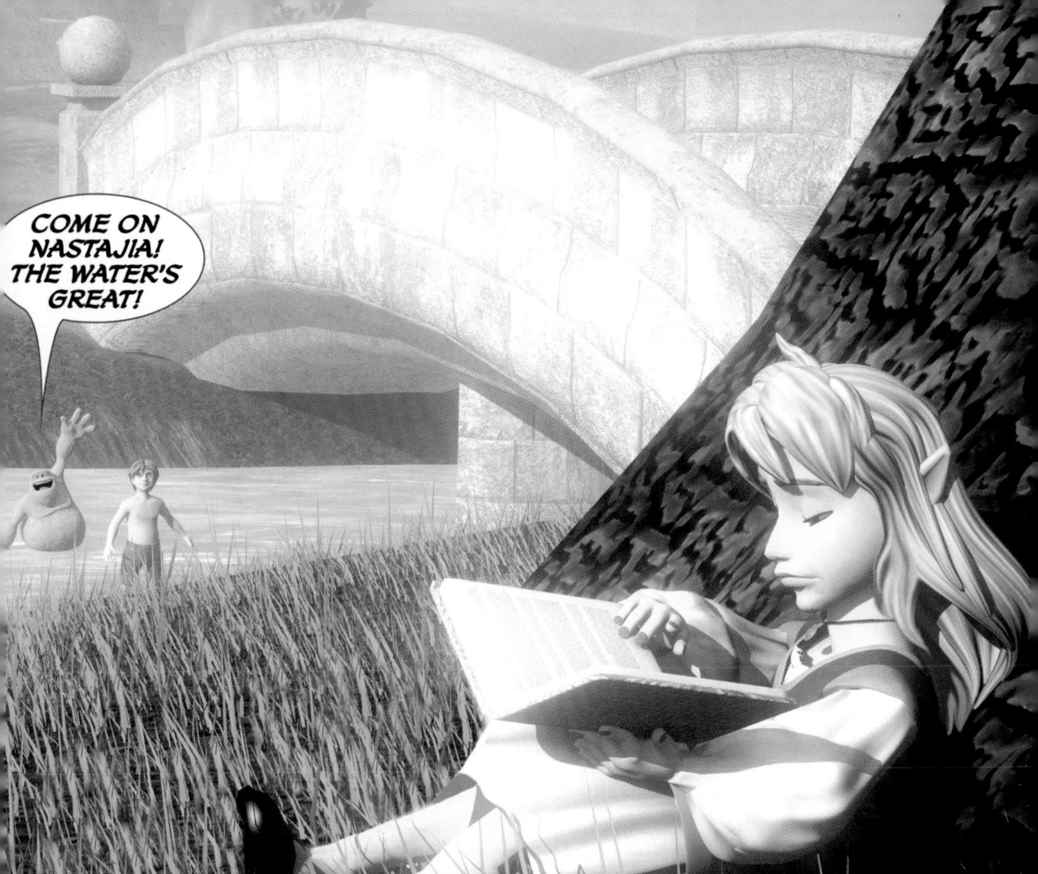
COME ON NASTAJIA! THE WATER'S GREAT!

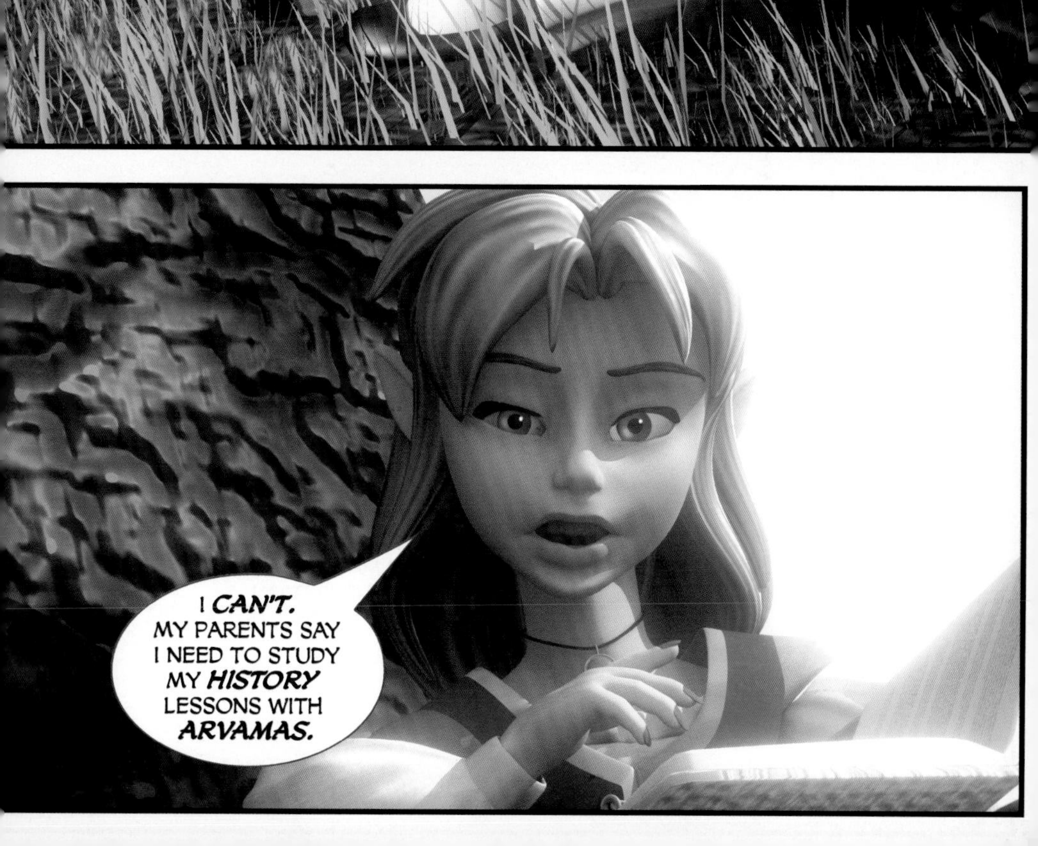
I CAN'T. MY PARENTS SAY I NEED TO STUDY MY HISTORY LESSONS WITH ARVAMAS.

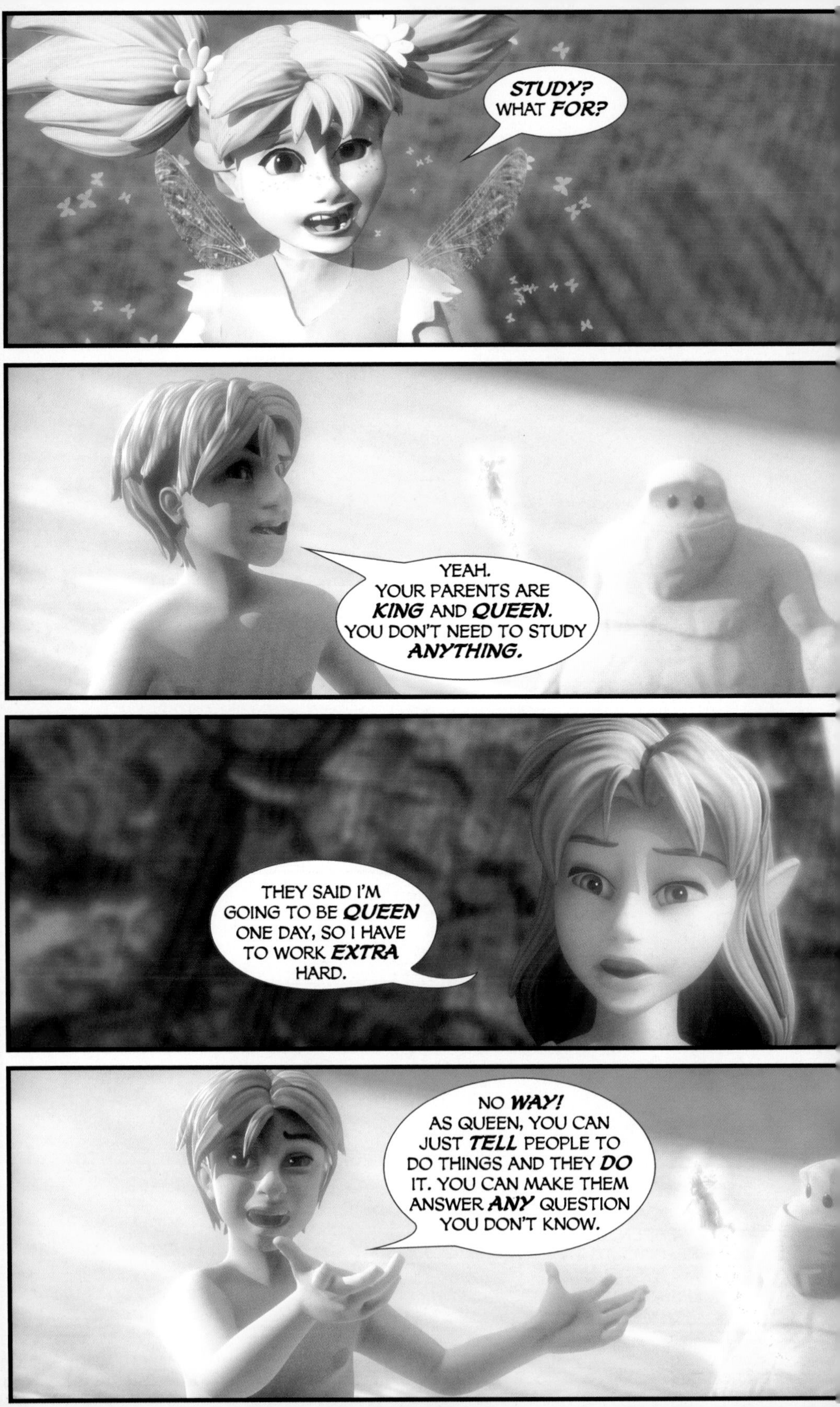
STUDY? WHAT FOR?
YEAH. YOUR PARENTS ARE KING AND QUEEN. YOU DON'T NEED TO STUDY ANYTHING.
THEY SAID I'M GOING TO BE QUEEN ONE DAY, SO I HAVE TO WORK EXTRA HARD.
NO WAY! AS QUEEN, YOU CAN JUST TELL PEOPLE TO DO THINGS AND THEY DO IT. YOU CAN MAKE THEM ANSWER ANY QUESTION YOU DON'T KNOW.

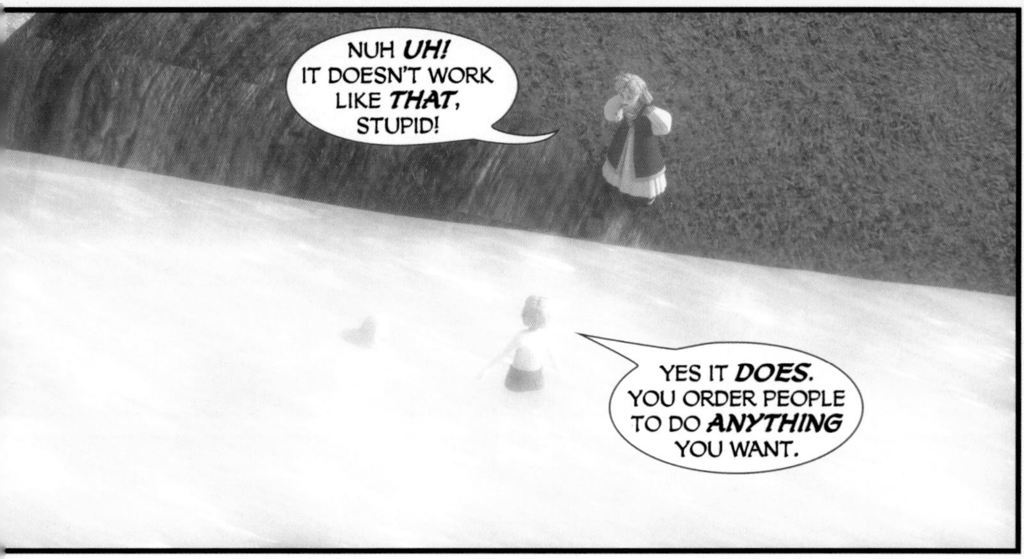
NUH UH! IT DOESN'T WORK LIKE THAT, STUPID!
YES IT DOES. YOU ORDER PEOPLE TO DO ANYTHING YOU WANT.

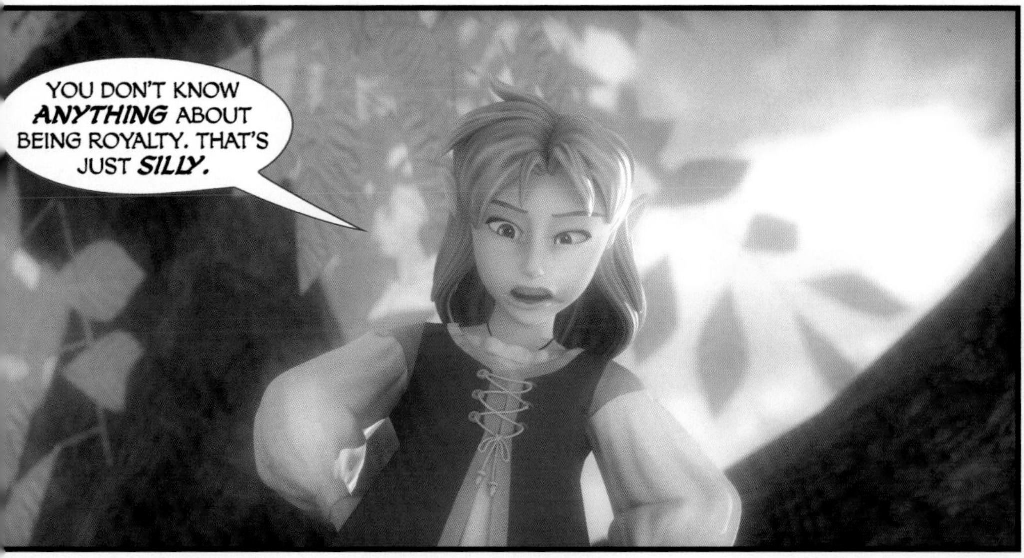
YOU DON'T KNOW ANYTHING ABOUT BEING ROYALTY. THAT'S JUST SILLY.

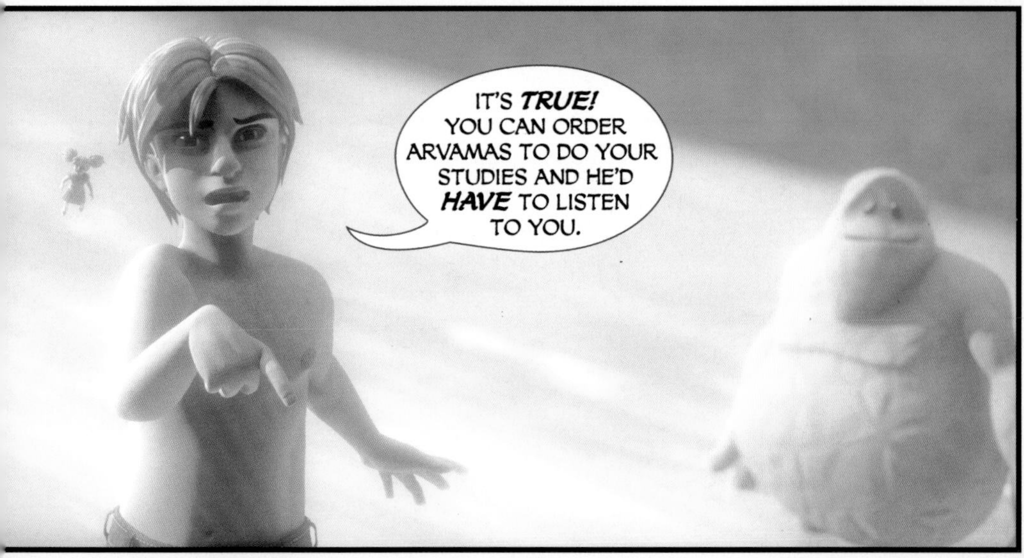
IT'S TRUE! YOU CAN ORDER ARVAMAS TO DO YOUR STUDIES AND HE'D HAVE TO LISTEN TO YOU.

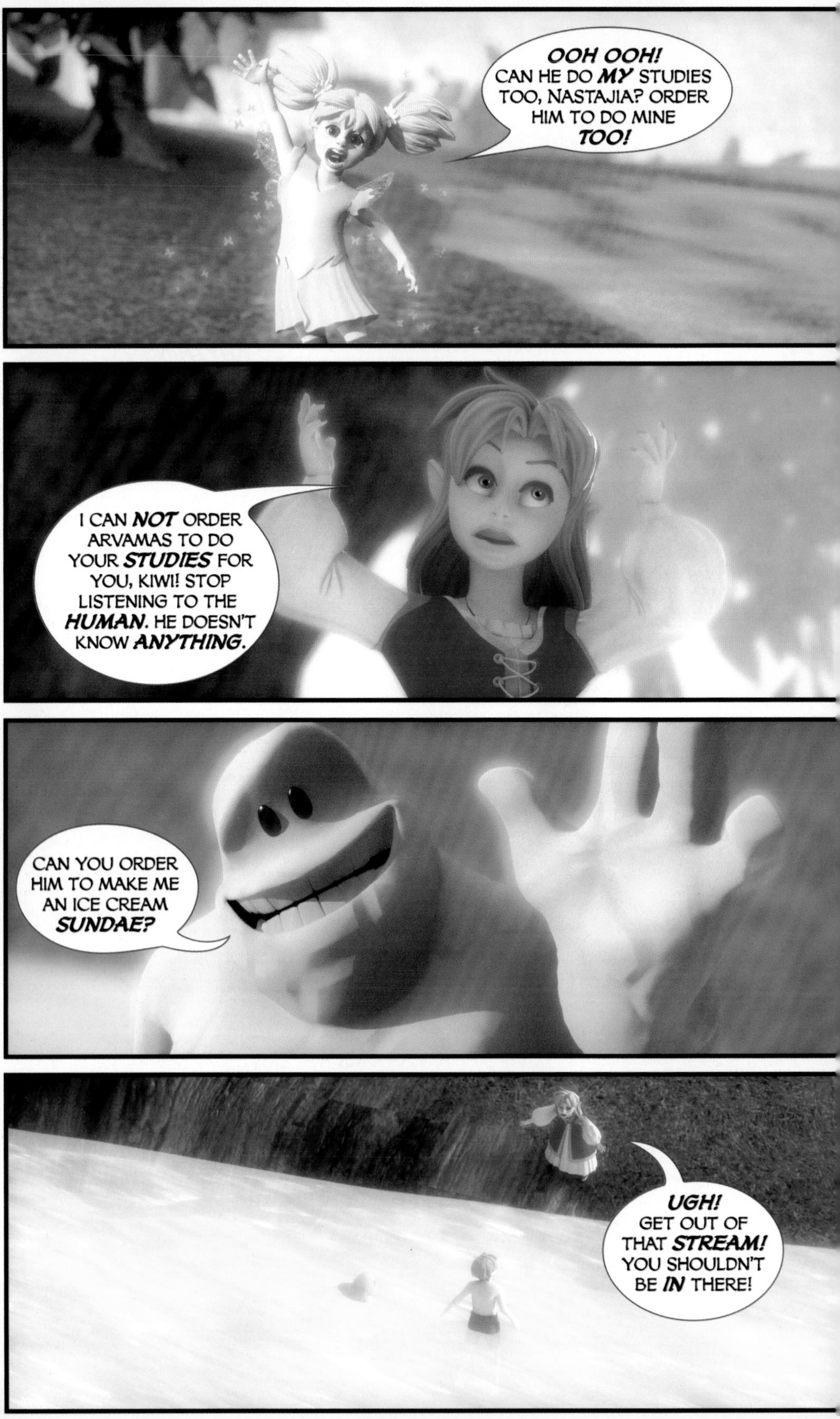
OOH OOH! CAN HE DO MY STUDIES TOO, NASTAJIA? ORDER HIM TO DO MINE TOO!
I CAN NOT ORDER ARVAMAS TO DO YOUR STUDIES FOR YOU, KIWI! STOP LISTENING TO THE HUMAN. HE DOESN'T KNOW ANYTHING.
CAN YOU ORDER HIM TO MAKE ME AN ICE CREAM SUNDAE?
UGH! GET OUT OF THAT STREAM! YOU SHOULDN'T BE IN THERE!

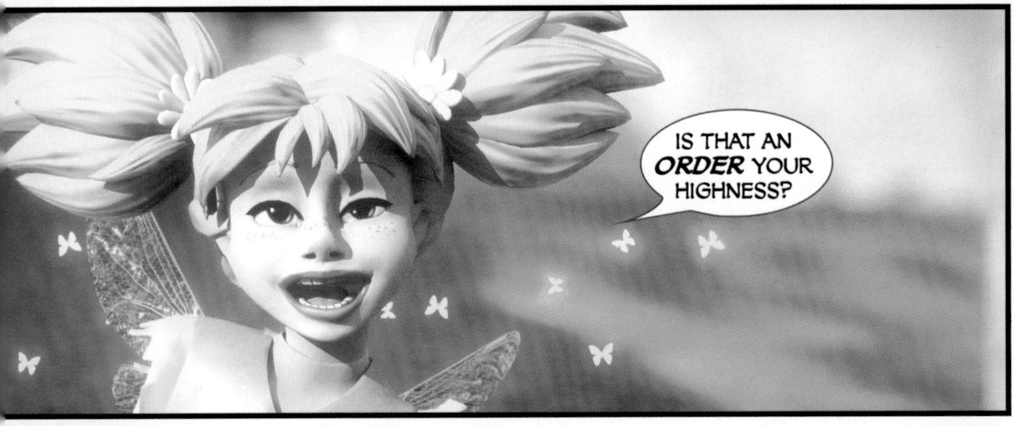
IS THAT AN ORDER YOUR HIGHNESS?

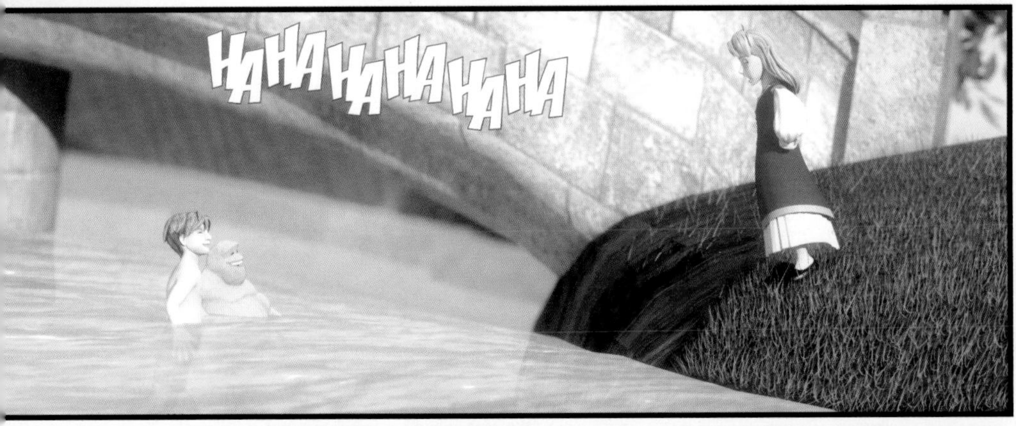
HAHAHAHAHAHA

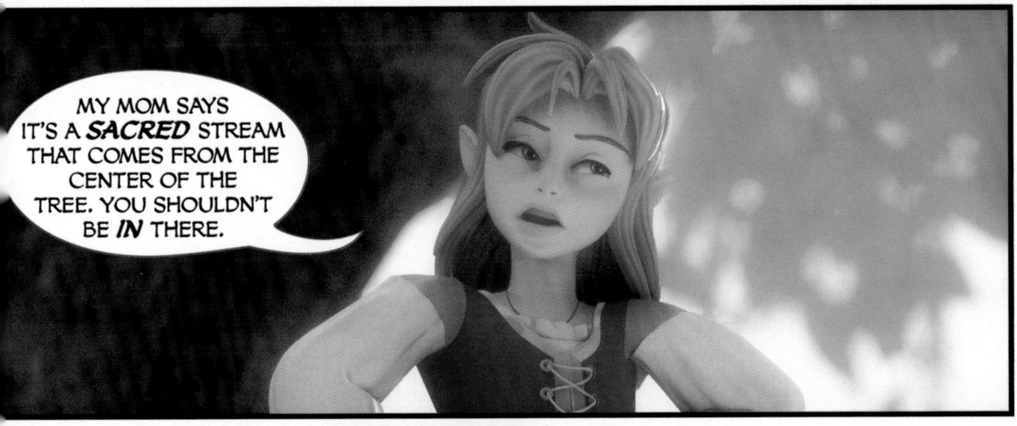
MY MOM SAYS IT'S A SACRED STREAM THAT COMES FROM THE CENTER OF THE TREE. YOU SHOULDN'T BE IN THERE.

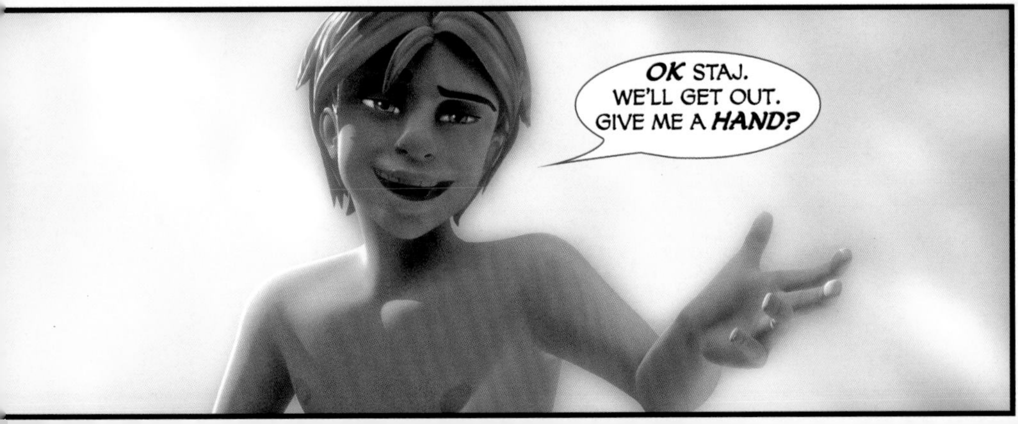
OK STAJ. WE'LL GET OUT. GIVE ME A HAND?

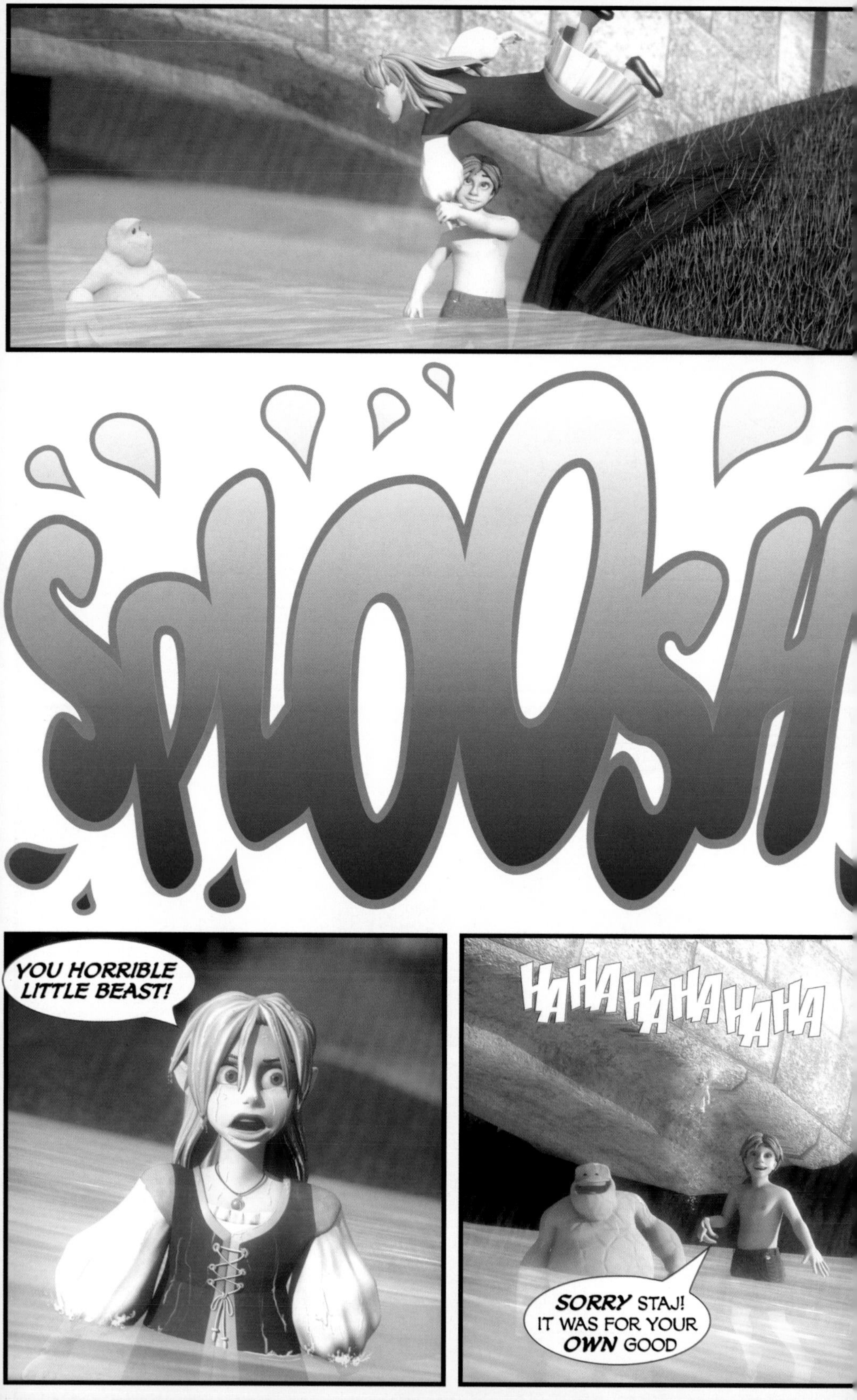

SPLOOSH
YOU HORRIBLE LITTLE BEAST!
HAHA HAHA HAHA
SORRY STAJ! IT WAS FOR YOUR OWN GOOD

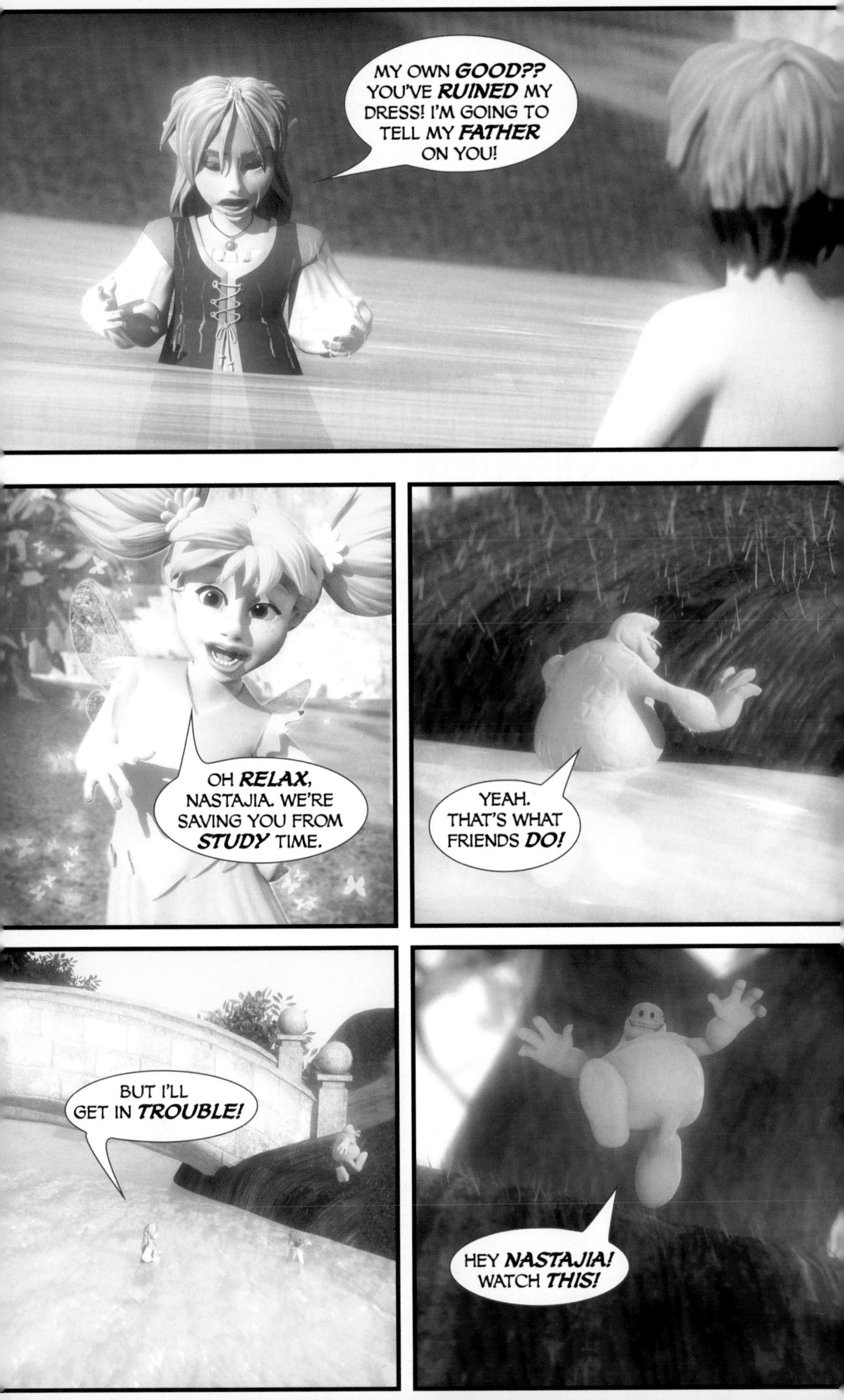
MY OWN GOOD?? YOU'VE RUINED MY DRESS! I'M GOING TO TELL MY FATHER ON YOU!
OH RELAX, NASTAJIA. WE'RE SAVING YOU FROM STUDY TIME.
YEAH. THAT'S WHAT FRIENDS DO!
BUT I'LL GET IN TROUBLE!
HEY NASTAJIA! WATCH THIS!

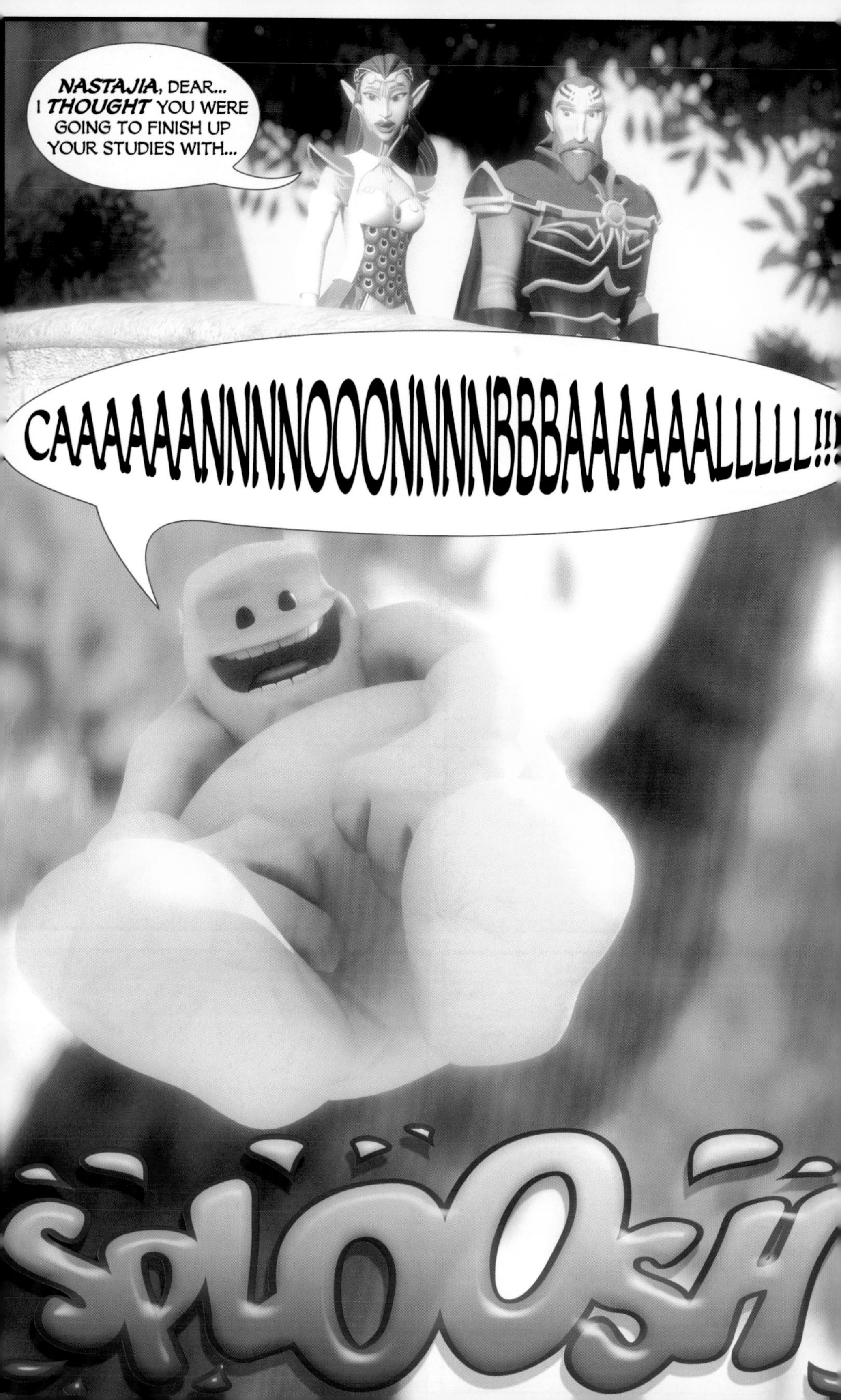

NASTAJIA, DEAR... I *THOUGHT* YOU WERE GOING TO FINISH UP YOUR STUDIES WITH...
CAAAAAANNNNOOONNNNBBBAAAAAALLLLL!!!
SPLOOSH

HAHAHAHAHAHAHAHAHAHAHAHAHAHAHAHAHAHAHAHAHAHA

EH...HEH HEH HEH...

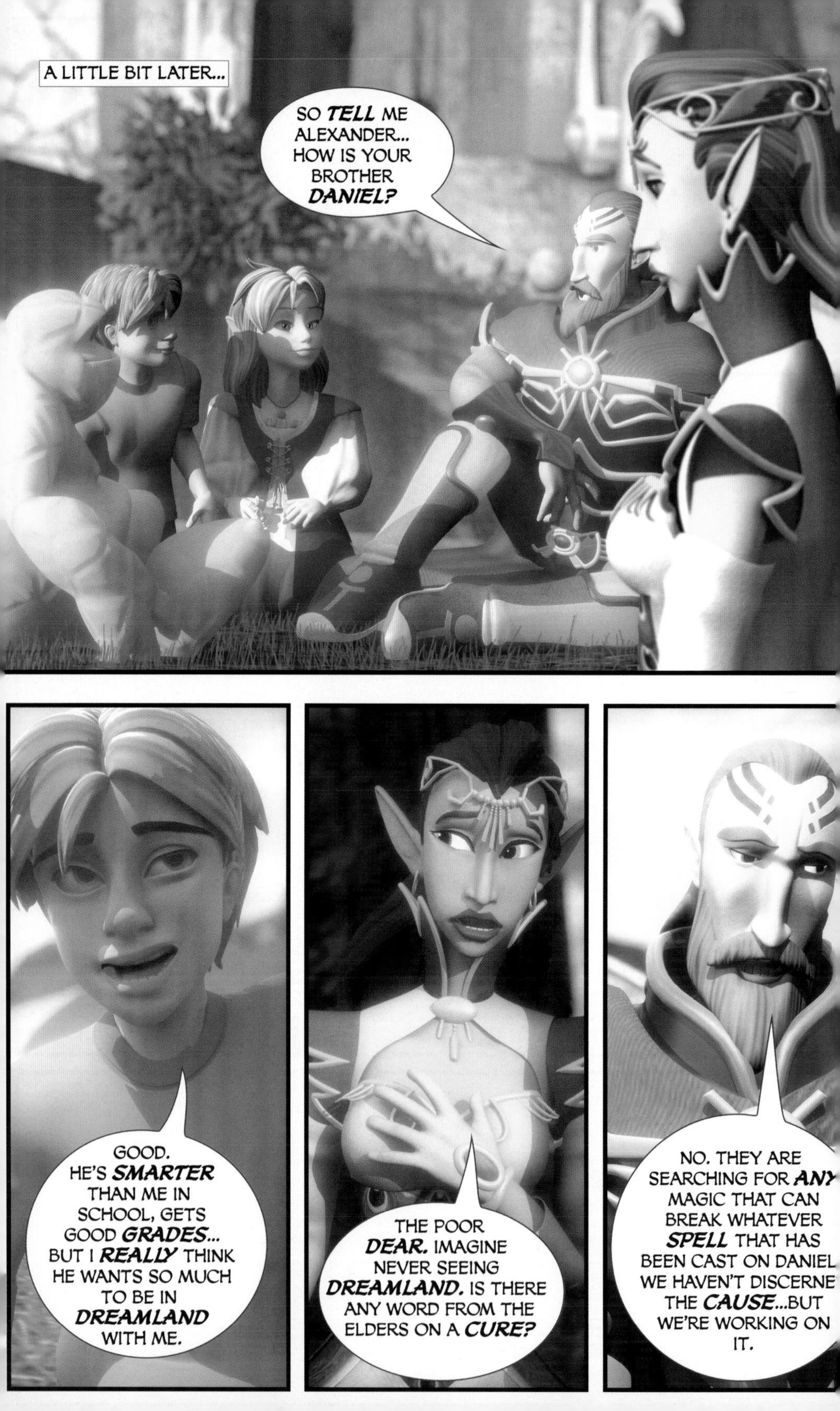
A LITTLE BIT LATER...
SO TELL ME ALEXANDER... HOW IS YOUR BROTHER DANIEL?
GOOD. HE'S SMARTER THAN ME IN SCHOOL, GETS GOOD GRADES... BUT I REALLY THINK HE WANTS SO MUCH TO BE IN DREAMLAND WITH ME.
THE POOR DEAR. IMAGINE NEVER SEEING DREAMLAND. IS THERE ANY WORD FROM THE ELDERS ON A CURE?
NO. THEY ARE SEARCHING FOR ANY MAGIC THAT CAN BREAK WHATEVER SPELL THAT HAS BEEN CAST ON DANIEL WE HAVEN'T DISCERNE THE CAUSE...BUT WE'RE WORKING ON IT.

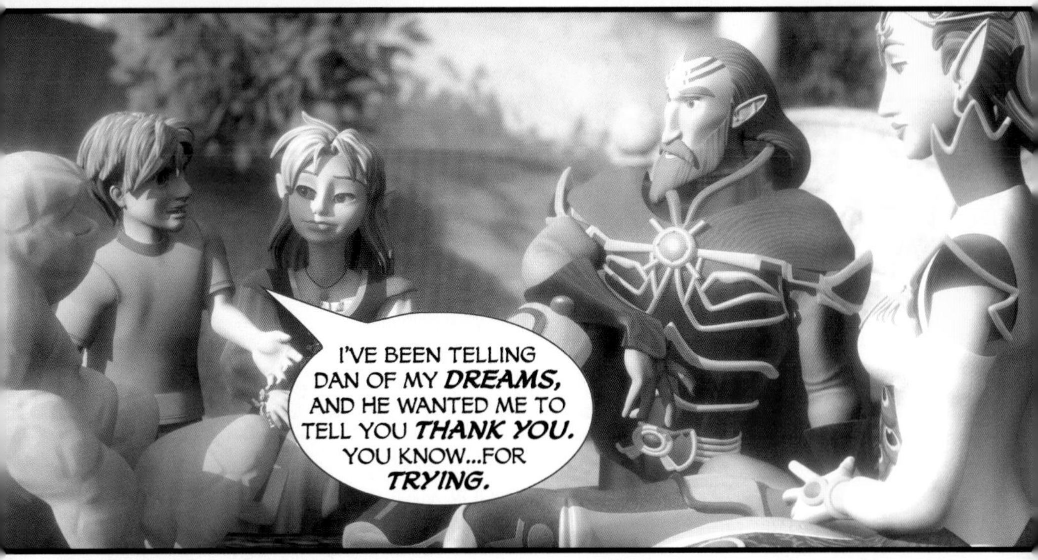
I'VE BEEN TELLING DAN OF MY DREAMS, AND HE WANTED ME TO TELL YOU THANK YOU. YOU KNOW...FOR TRYING.

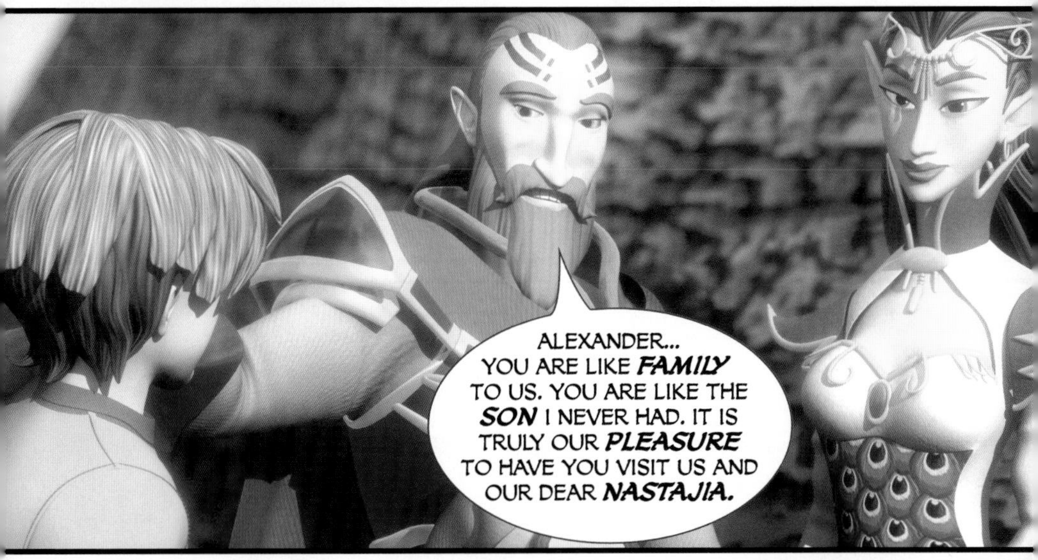
ALEXANDER... YOU ARE LIKE FAMILY TO US. YOU ARE LIKE THE SON I NEVER HAD. IT IS TRULY OUR PLEASURE TO HAVE YOU VISIT US AND OUR DEAR NASTAJIA.

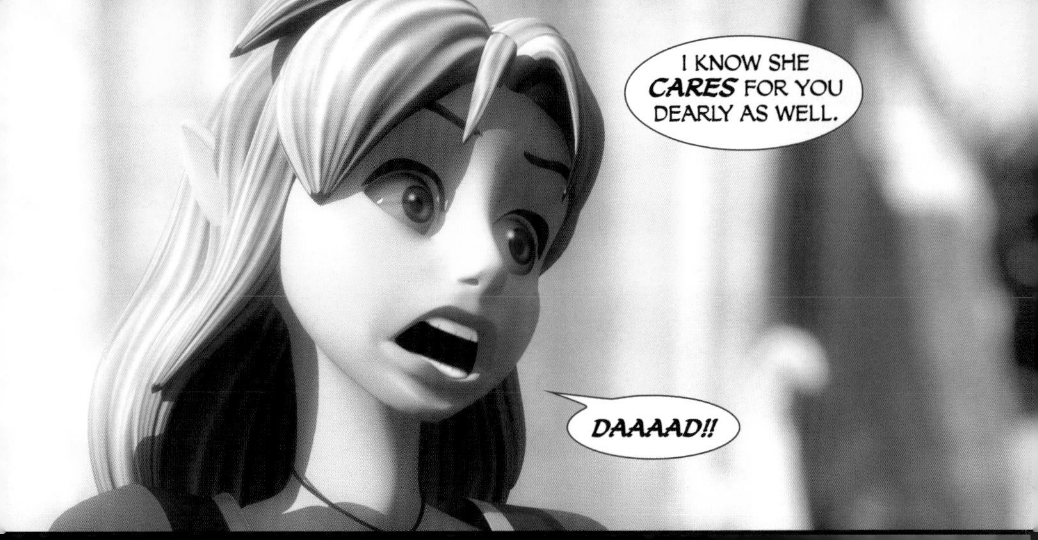
I KNOW SHE CARES FOR YOU DEARLY AS WELL.
DAAAAD!!

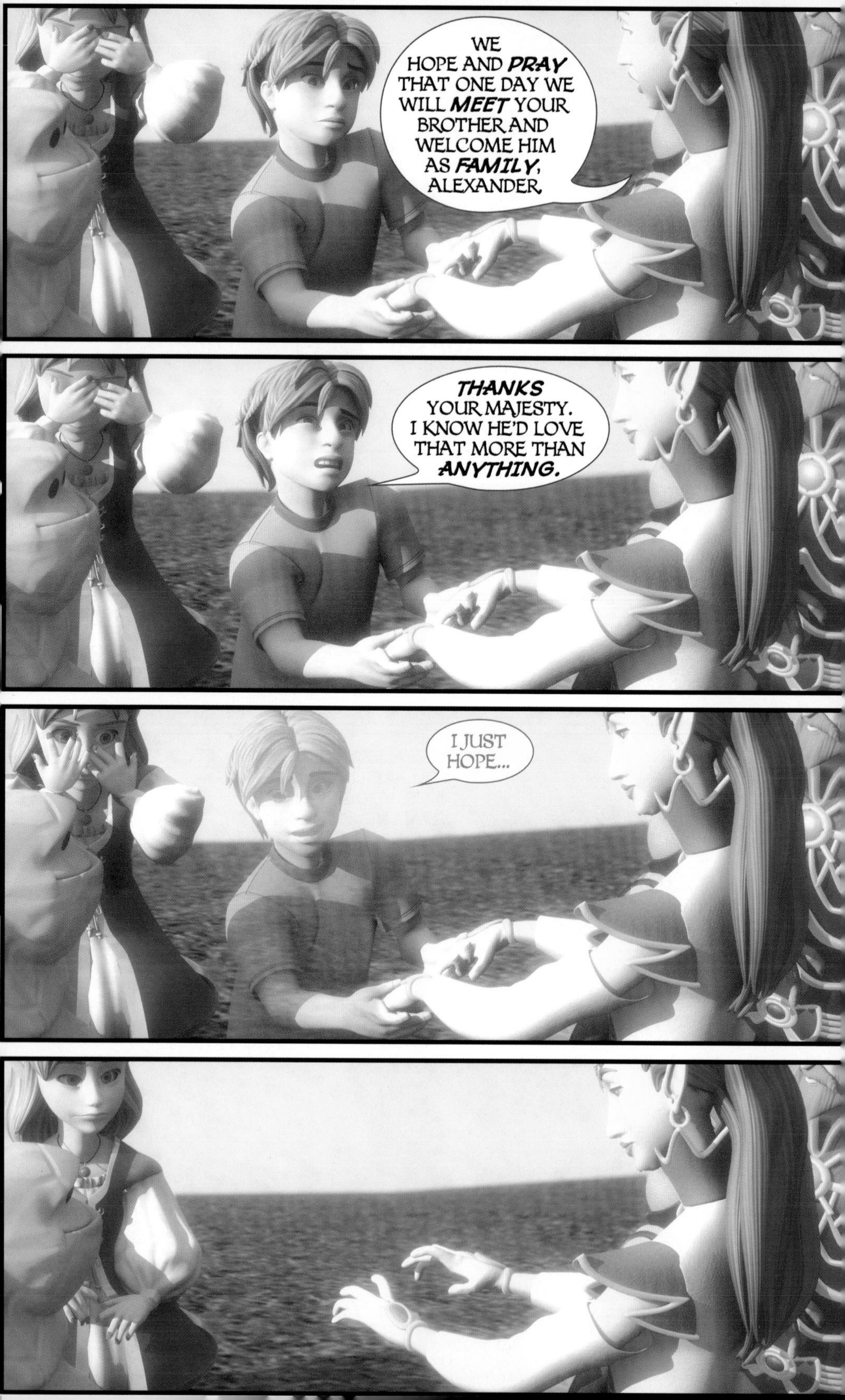
WE HOPE AND PRAY THAT ONE DAY WE WILL MEET YOUR BROTHER AND WELCOME HIM AS FAMILY, ALEXANDER.
THANKS YOUR MAJESTY. I KNOW HE'D LOVE THAT MORE THAN ANYTHING.
I JUST HOPE...

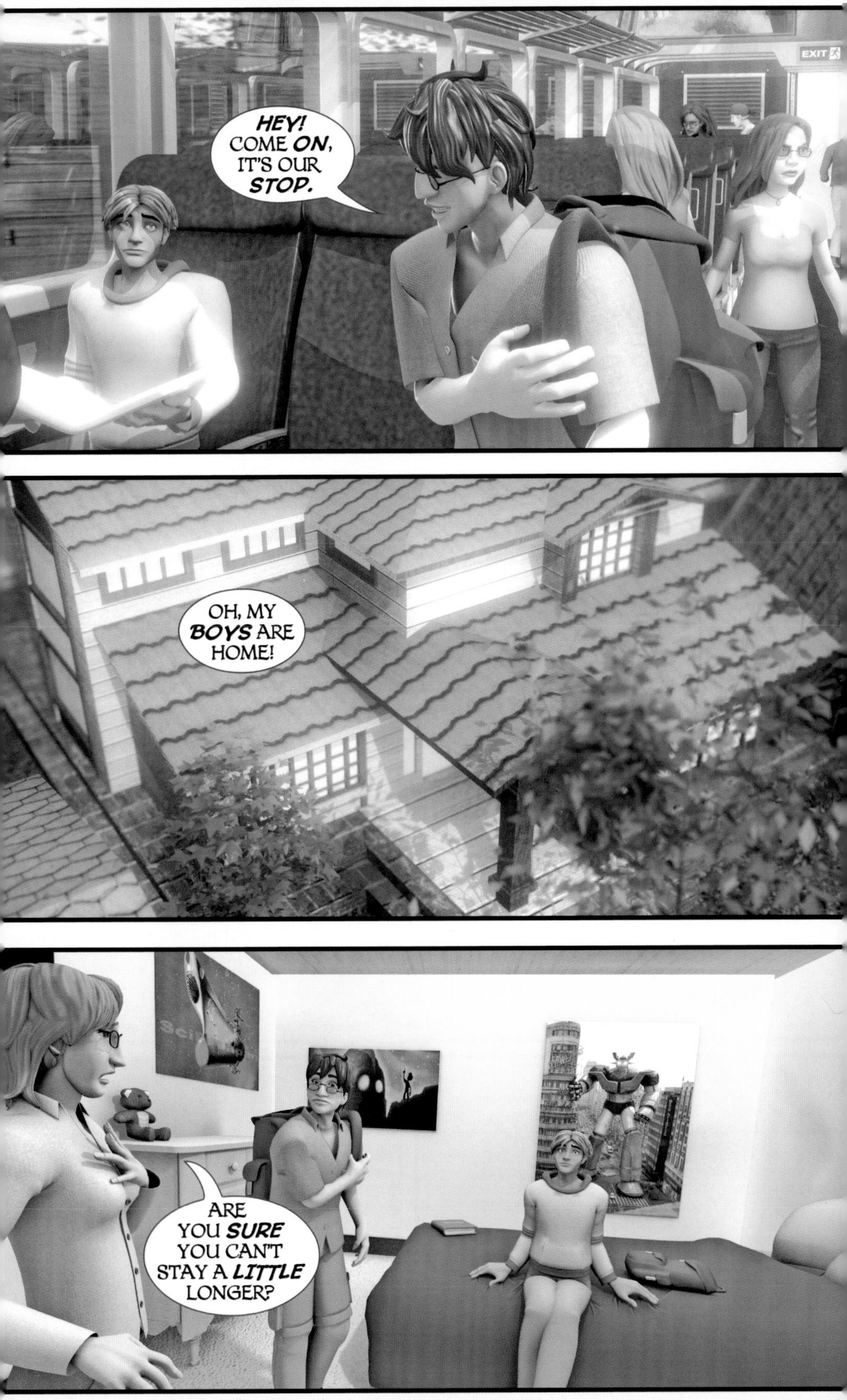
EXIT
HEY! COME ON, IT'S OUR STOP.
OH, MY BOYS ARE HOME!
ARE YOU SURE YOU CAN'T STAY A LITTLE LONGER?

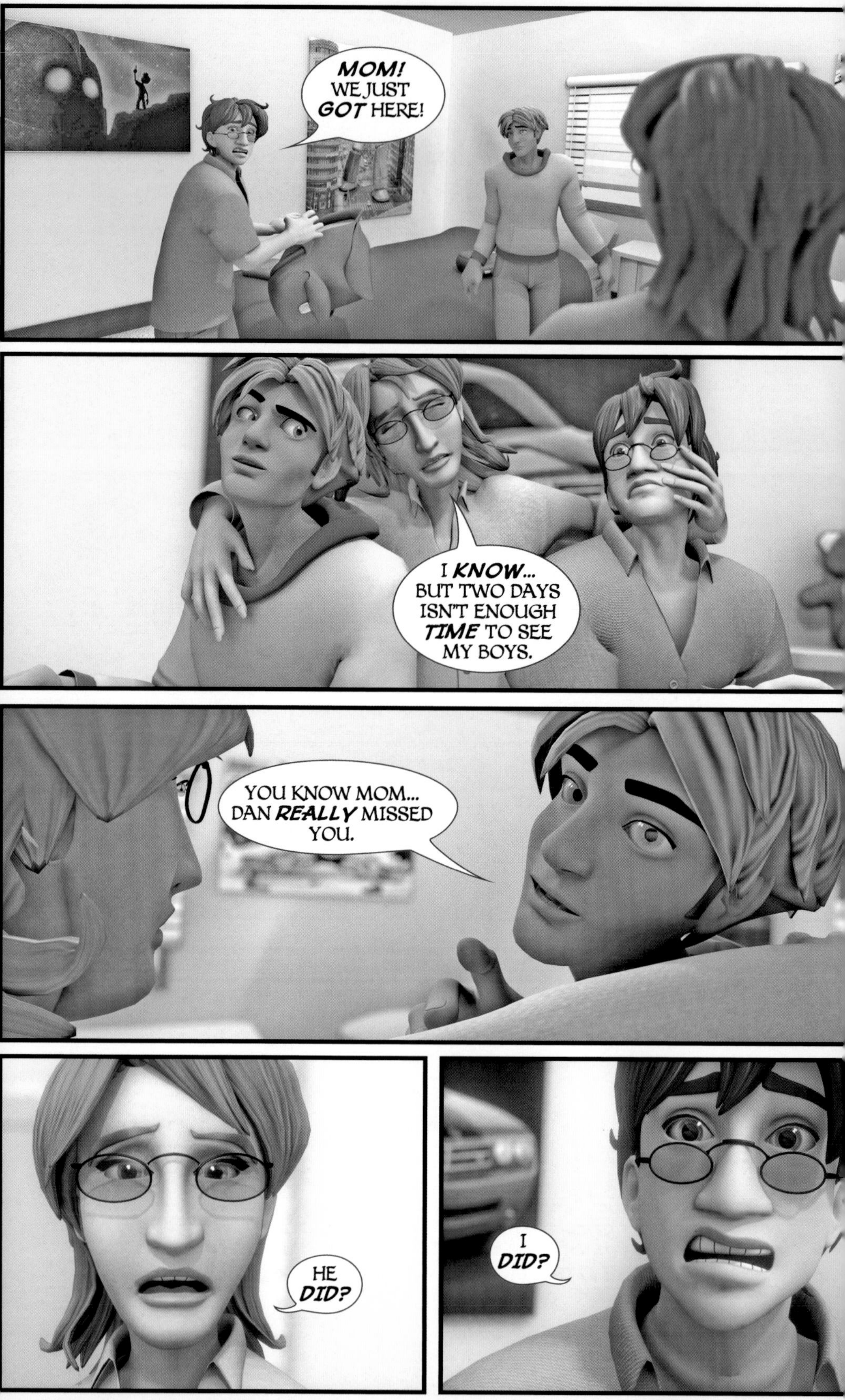
MOM!
WE JUST
GOT HERE!
I KNOW...
BUT TWO DAYS
ISN'T ENOUGH
TIME TO SEE
MY BOYS.
YOU KNOW MOM...
DAN REALLY MISSED
YOU.
HE
DID?
I
DID?

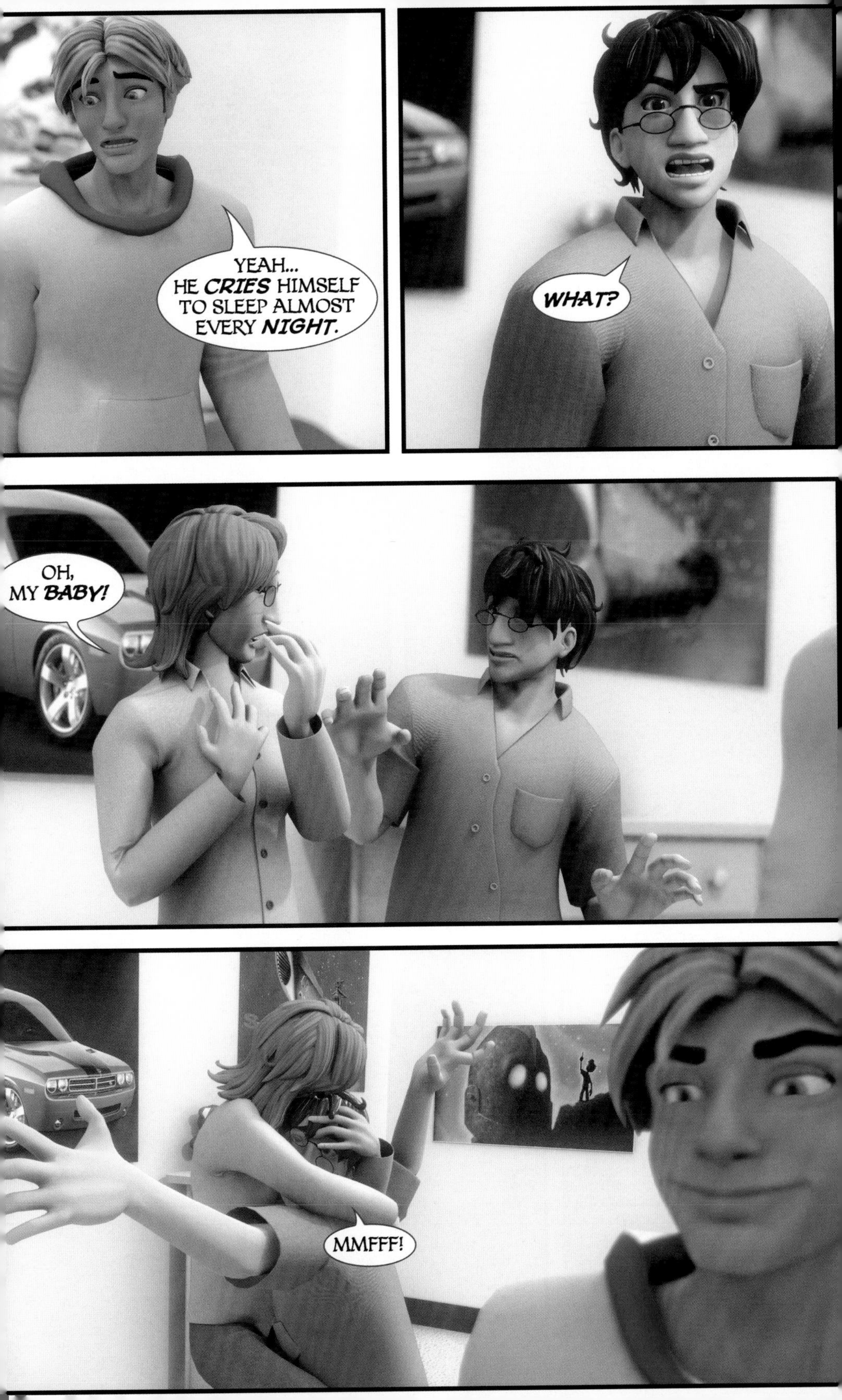
YEAH... HE CRIES HIMSELF TO SLEEP ALMOST EVERY NIGHT.
WHAT?
OH, MY BABY!
MMFFF!

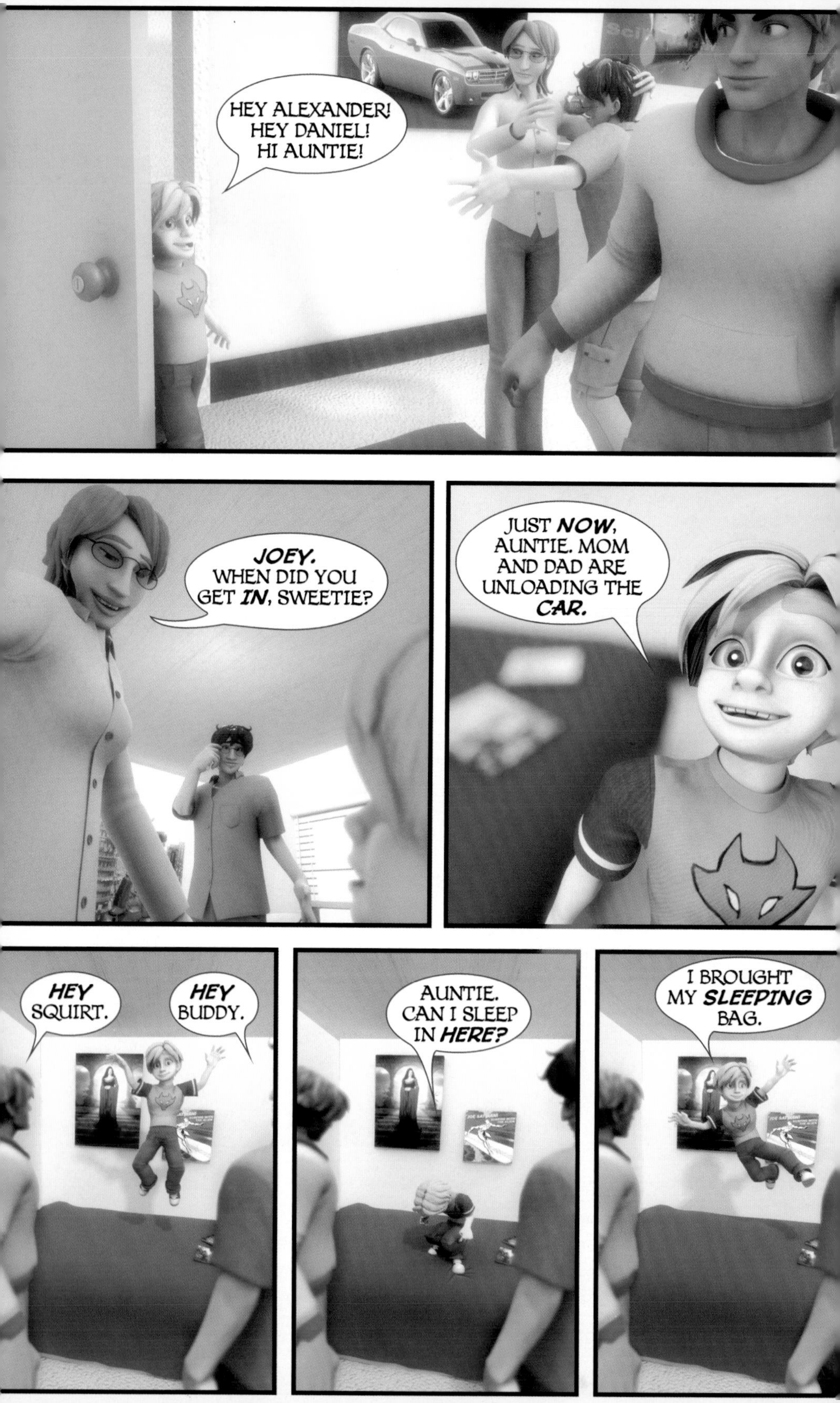
HEY ALEXANDER! HEY DANIEL! HI AUNTIE!
JOEY. WHEN DID YOU GET IN, SWEETIE?
JUST NOW, AUNTIE. MOM AND DAD ARE UNLOADING THE CAR.
HEY SQUIRT.
HEY BUDDY.
AUNTIE. CAN I SLEEP IN HERE?
I BROUGHT MY SLEEPING BAG.

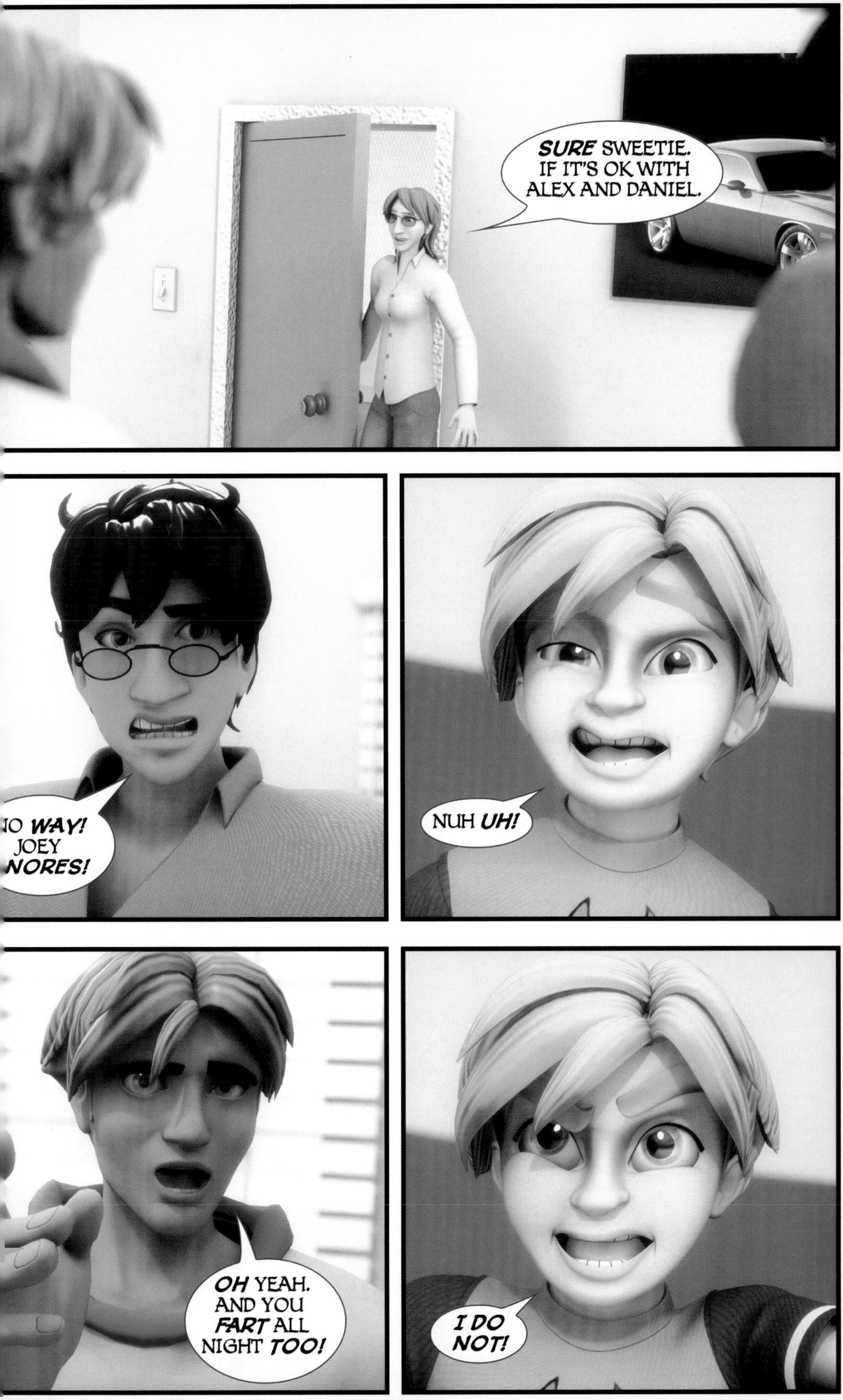
SURE SWEETIE. IF IT'S OK WITH ALEX AND DANIEL.
O WAY! JOEY NORES!
NUH UH!
OH YEAH. AND YOU FART ALL NIGHT TOO!
I DO NOT!

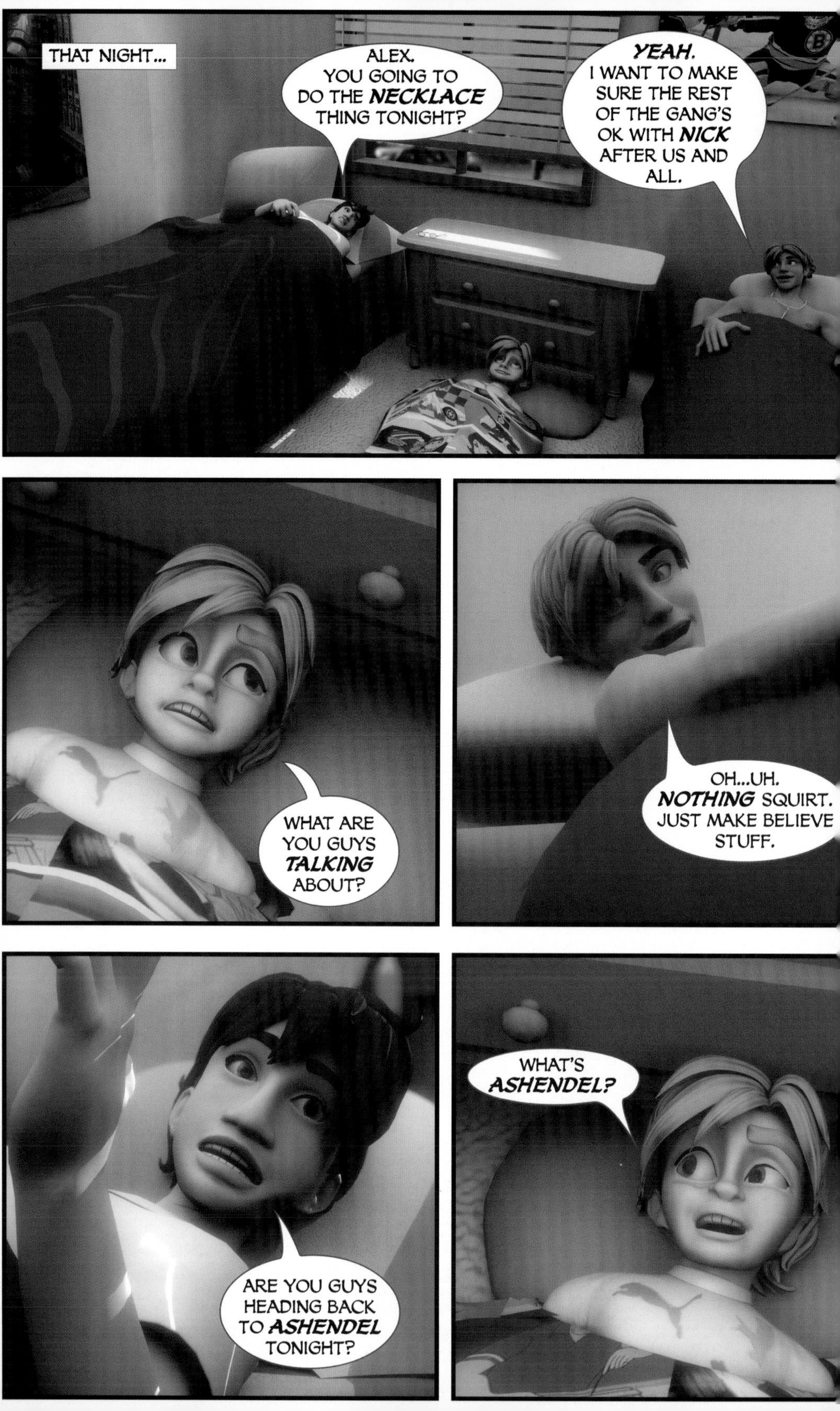

THAT NIGHT...
ALEX. YOU GOING TO DO THE **NECKLACE** THING TONIGHT?
YEAH. I WANT TO MAKE SURE THE REST OF THE GANG'S OK WITH **NICK** AFTER US AND ALL.
WHAT ARE YOU GUYS **TALKING** ABOUT?
OH...UH. **NOTHING** SQUIRT. JUST MAKE BELIEVE STUFF.
ARE YOU GUYS HEADING BACK TO **ASHENDEL** TONIGHT?
WHAT'S **ASHENDEL?**

WE'RE JUST TALKING ABOUT A...UM... BOOK WE'RE WRITING. GO TO SLEEP.
I LIKE STORIES. I CAN HELP.
I BET YOU COULD, SHORT STUFF. MAYBE YOU COULD HELP IN THE MORNING.
I LIKE FAIRIES. THEY CAN FLY, YOU KNOW. DOES YOUR BOOK HAVE FAIRIES?
AS A MATTER OF FACT IT DOES. AND DRAGONS AND ONE EYED GIANTS AND SEA MONSTERS. IF WE TELL YOU MORE, YOU'LL HAVE NIGHTMARES.
OK, THEN. I'LL JUST GO HANG OUT WITH MY FRIENDS IN THE FAIRY VILLAGE WITH THE MUSHROOM HOUSES. GOOD NIGHT.

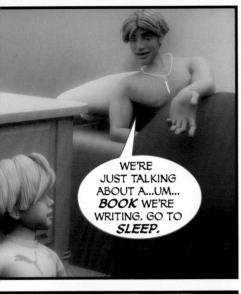

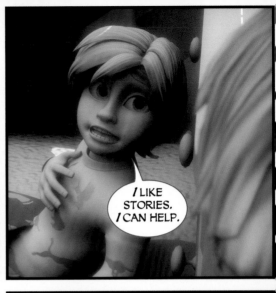

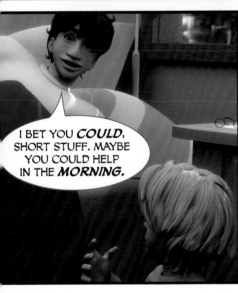

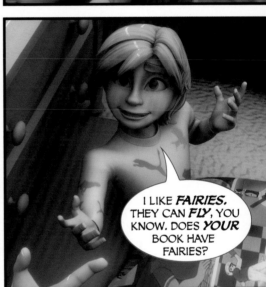

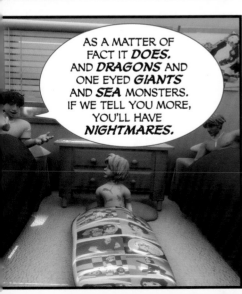

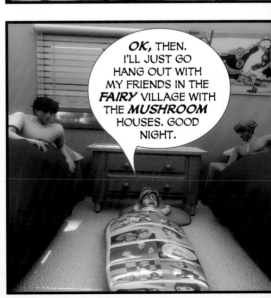

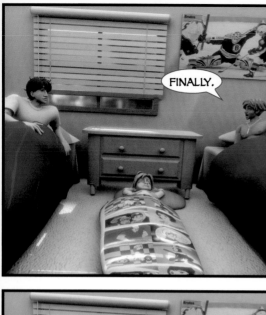

FINALLY.

SO...WHAT ARE YOU GOING TO DO WITH *FELICITY?* IS SHE...

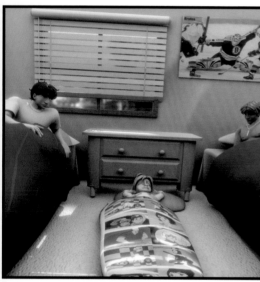

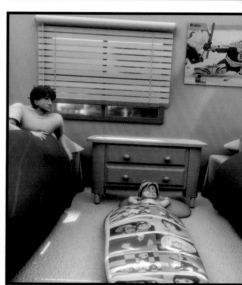

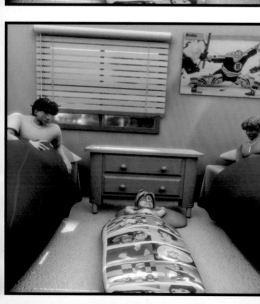

DID YOU SAY *FAIRY VILLAGE WITH MUSHROOM HOUSES??*

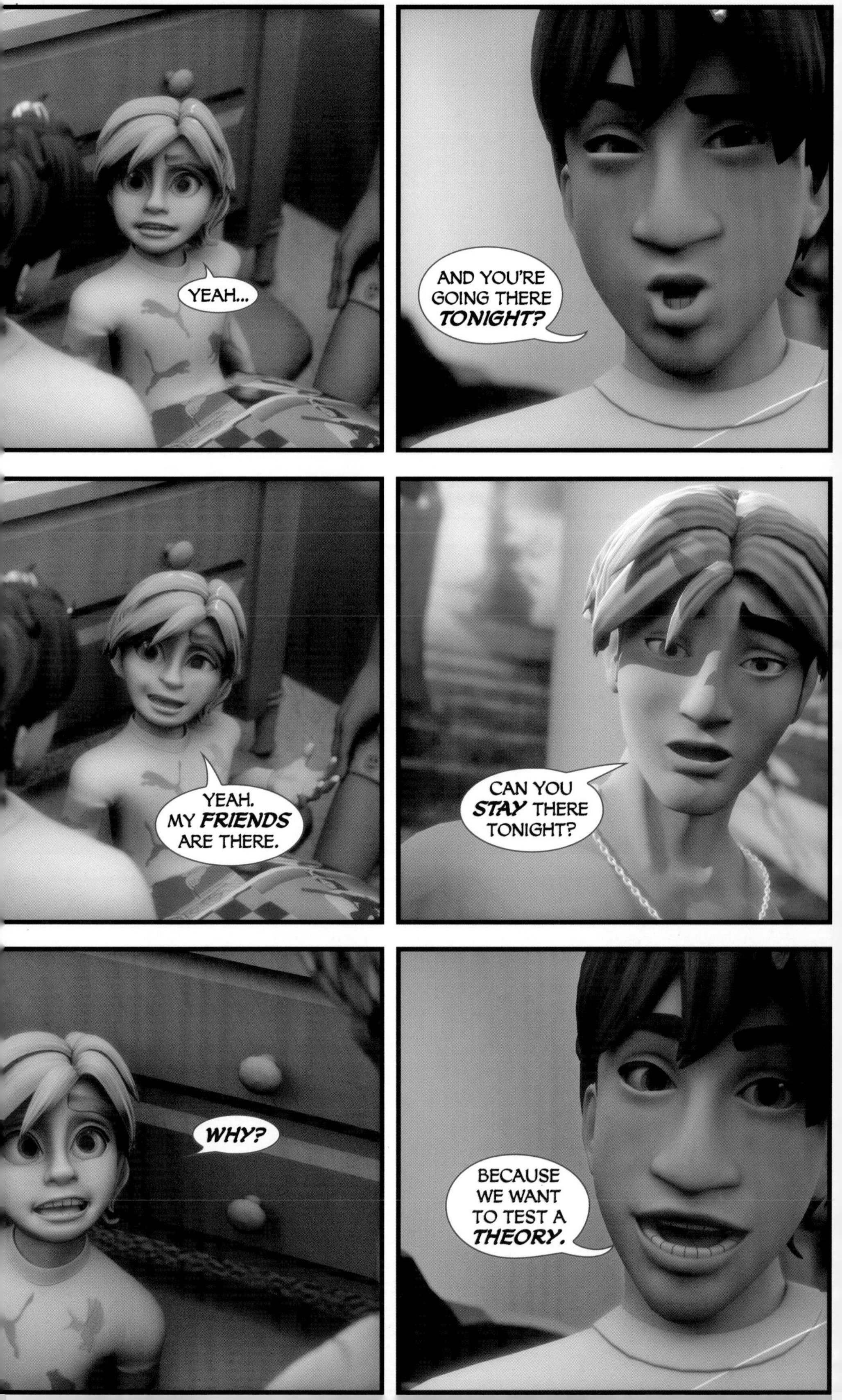
YEAH...
AND YOU'RE GOING THERE *TONIGHT?*
YEAH. MY *FRIENDS* ARE THERE.
CAN YOU *STAY* THERE TONIGHT?
WHY?
BECAUSE WE WANT TO TEST A *THEORY.*

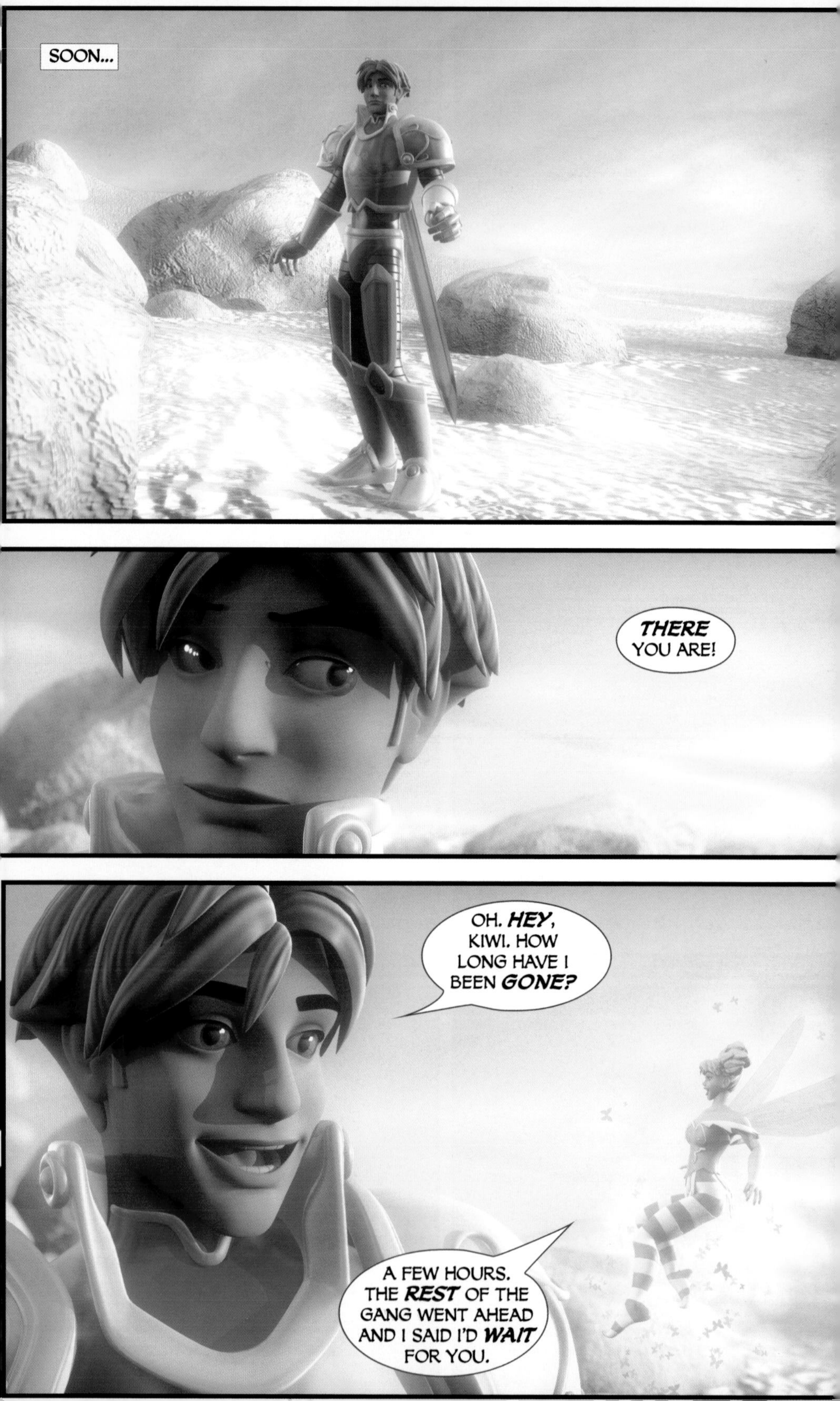
SOON...
THERE YOU ARE!
OH. HEY, KIWI. HOW LONG HAVE I BEEN GONE?
A FEW HOURS. THE REST OF THE GANG WENT AHEAD AND I SAID I'D WAIT FOR YOU.

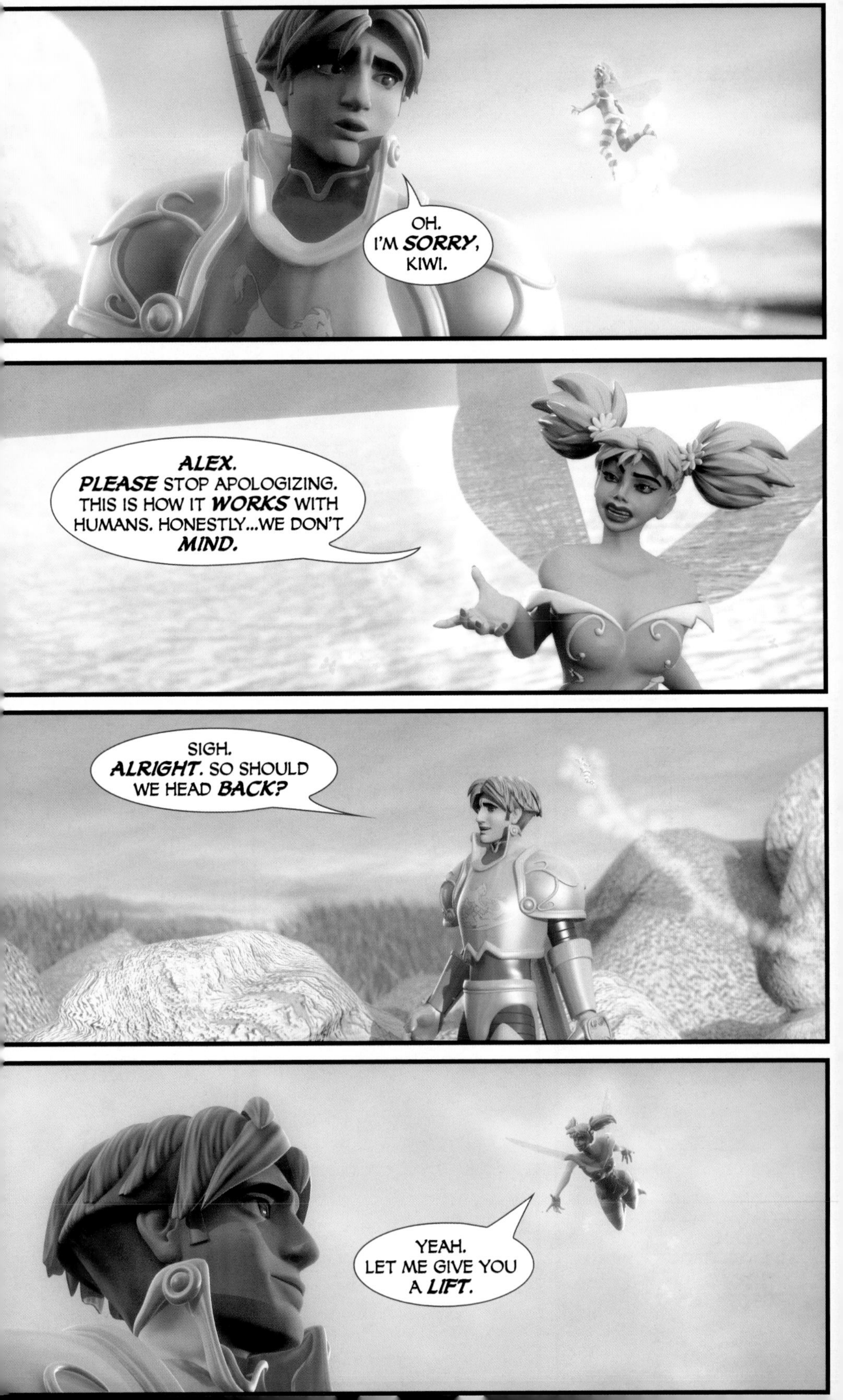
OH. I'M **SORRY**, KIWI.
ALEX. **PLEASE** STOP APOLOGIZING. THIS IS HOW IT **WORKS** WITH HUMANS. HONESTLY...WE DON'T **MIND.**
SIGH. **ALRIGHT.** SO SHOULD WE HEAD **BACK?**
YEAH. LET ME GIVE YOU A **LIFT.**

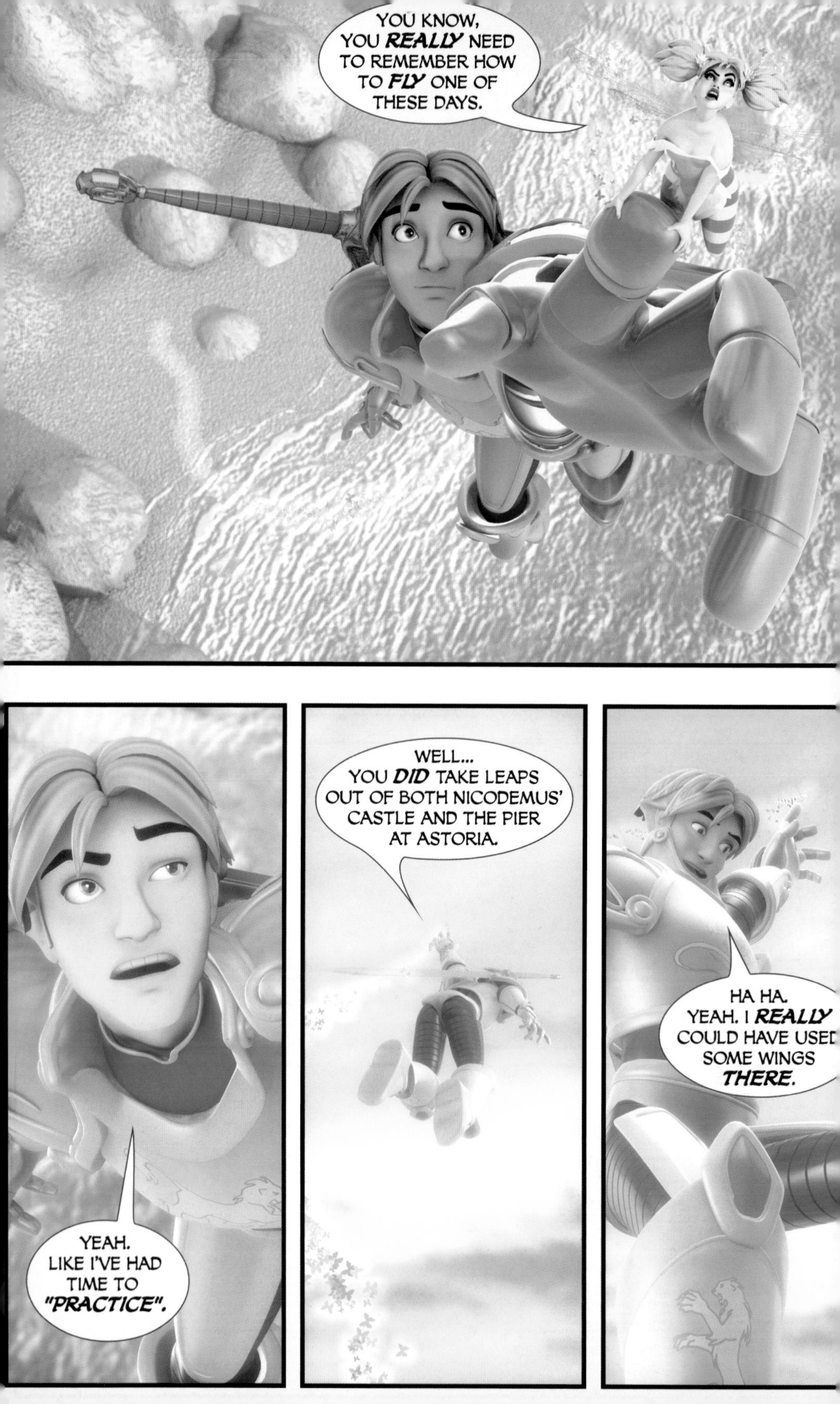
YOU KNOW, YOU *REALLY* NEED TO REMEMBER HOW TO *FLY* ONE OF THESE DAYS.
YEAH. LIKE I'VE HAD TIME TO *"PRACTICE"*.
WELL... YOU *DID* TAKE LEAPS OUT OF BOTH NICODEMUS' CASTLE AND THE PIER AT ASTORIA.
HA HA. YEAH. I *REALLY* COULD HAVE USE
SOME WINGS *THERE*.

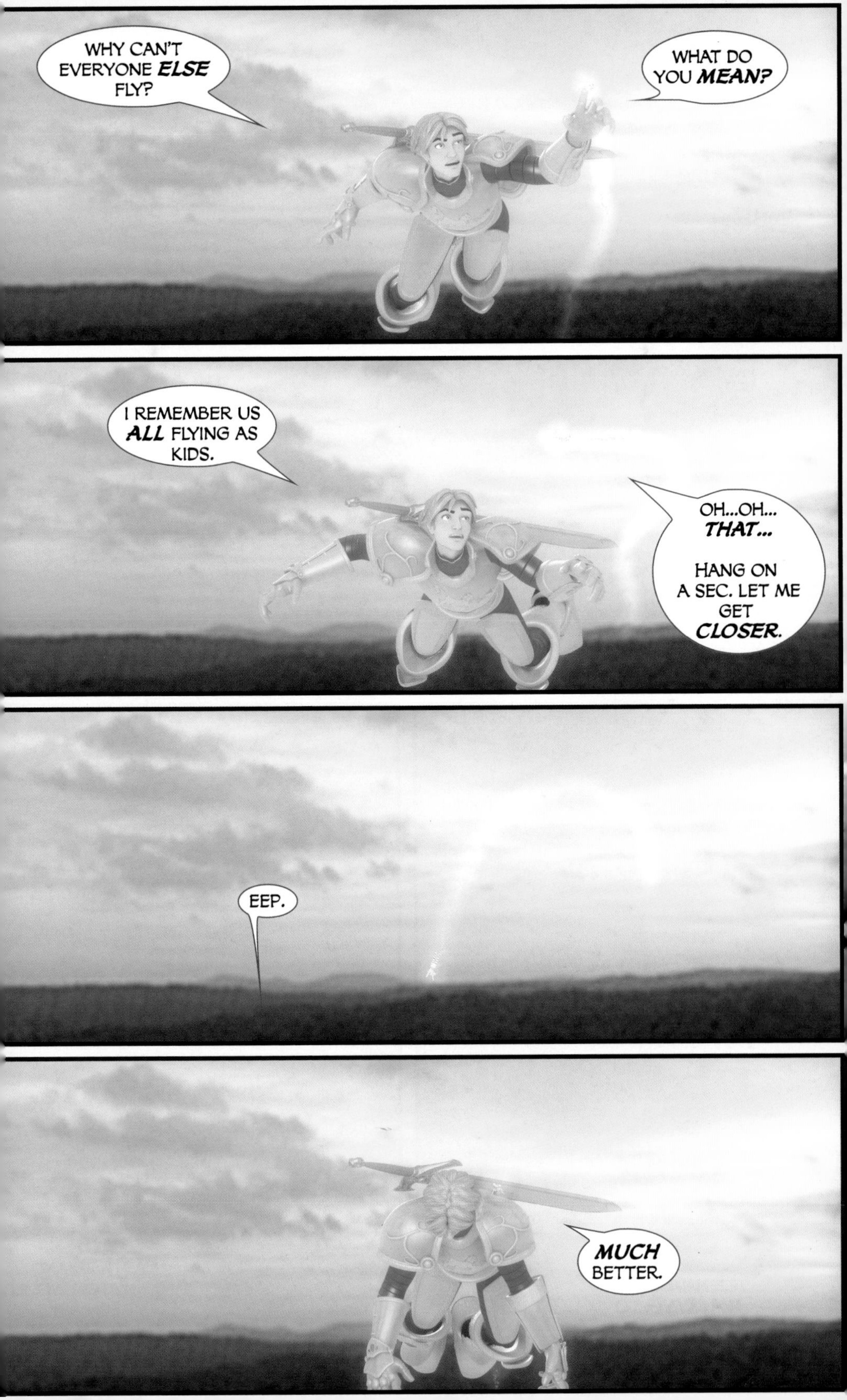
WHY CAN'T EVERYONE ELSE FLY?
WHAT DO YOU MEAN?
I REMEMBER US ALL FLYING AS KIDS.
OH...OH... THAT...
HANG ON A SEC. LET ME GET CLOSER.
EEP.
MUCH BETTER.

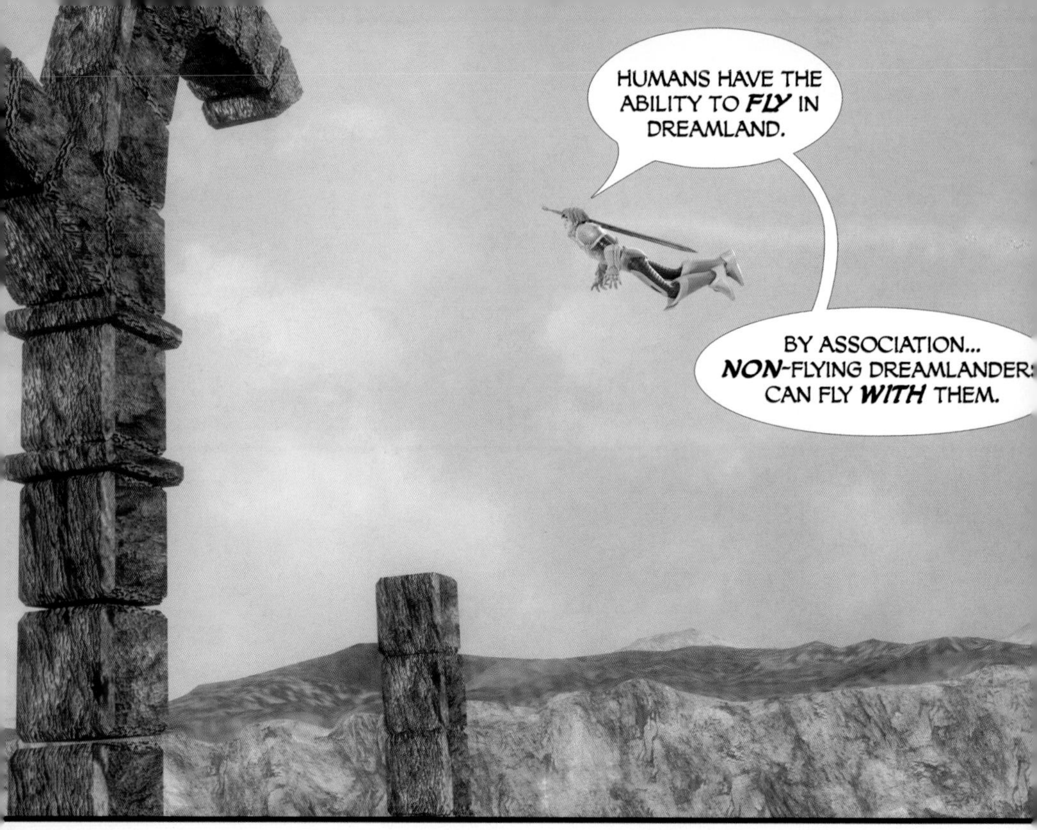
HUMANS HAVE THE ABILITY TO *FLY* IN DREAMLAND.
BY ASSOCIATION... *NON*-FLYING DREAMLANDERS CAN FLY *WITH* THEM.

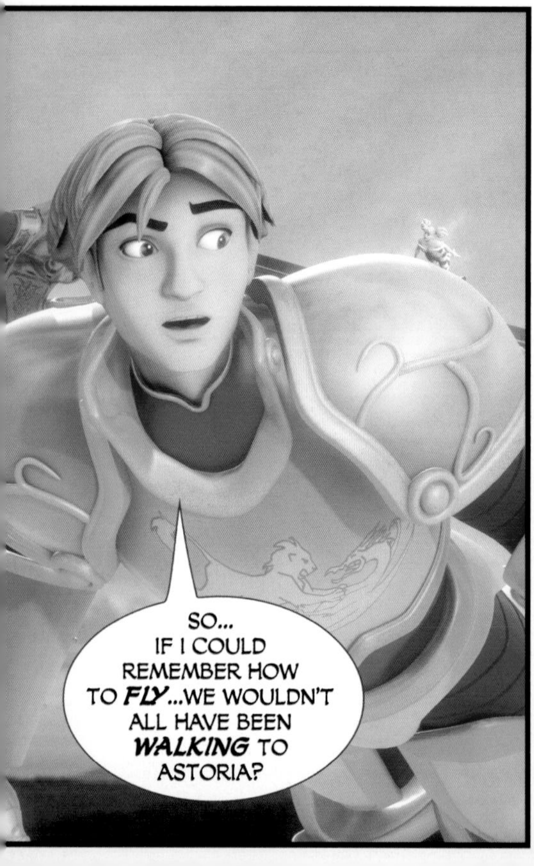
SO... IF I COULD REMEMBER HOW TO *FLY*...WE WOULDN'T ALL HAVE BEEN *WALKING* TO ASTORIA?

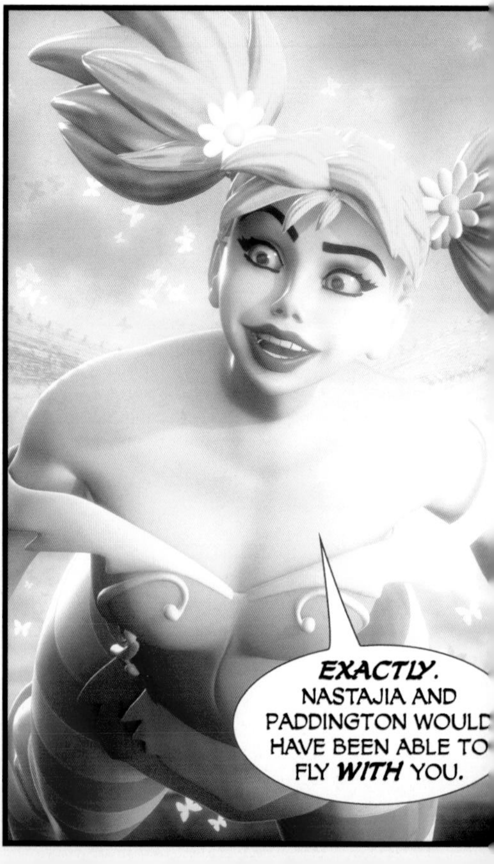
EXACTLY. NASTAJIA AND PADDINGTON WOULD HAVE BEEN ABLE TO FLY *WITH* YOU.

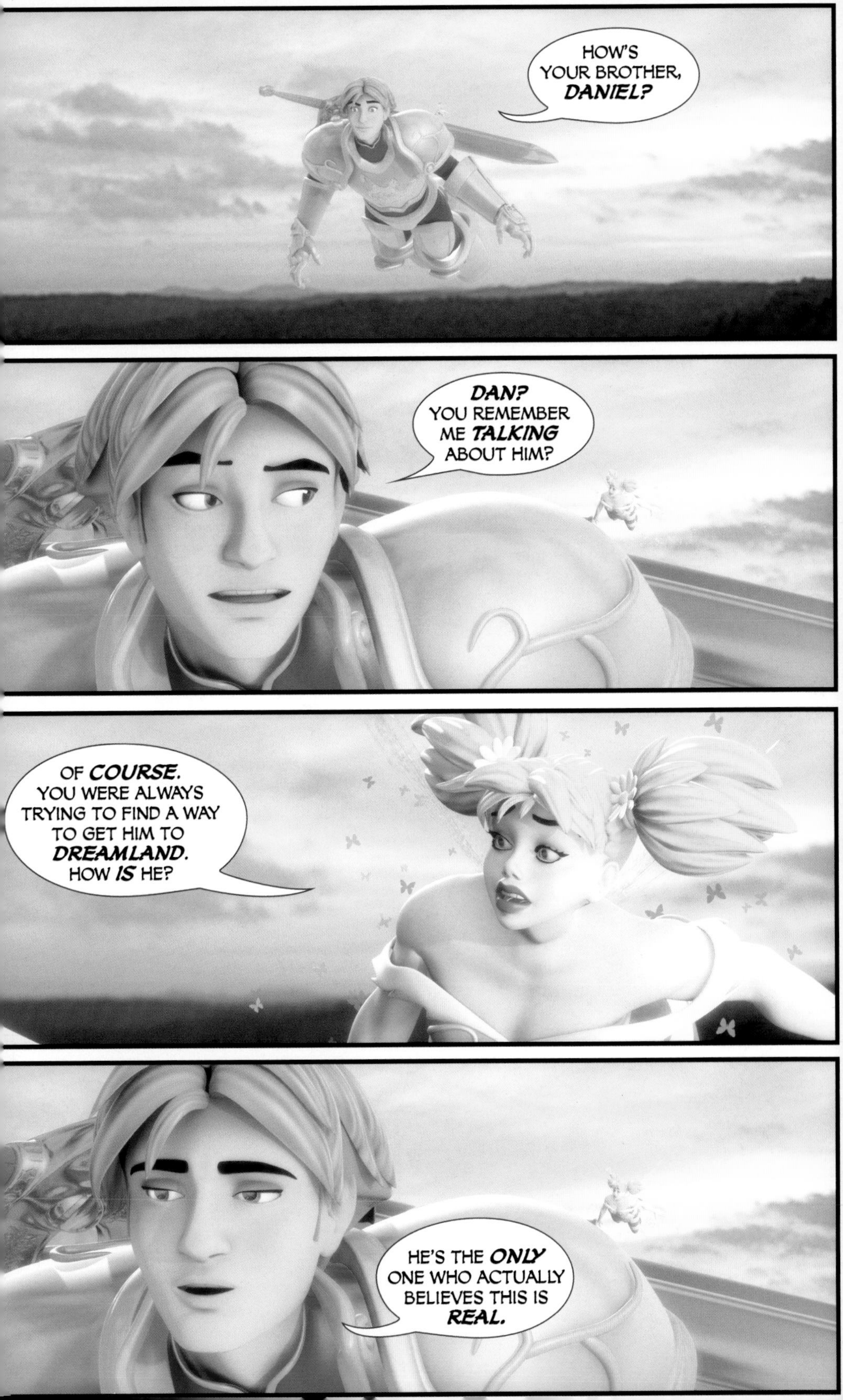
HOW'S YOUR BROTHER, *DANIEL?*
DAN? YOU REMEMBER ME *TALKING* ABOUT HIM?
OF *COURSE.* YOU WERE ALWAYS TRYING TO FIND A WAY TO GET HIM TO *DREAMLAND.* HOW *IS* HE?
HE'S THE *ONLY* ONE WHO ACTUALLY BELIEVES THIS IS *REAL.*

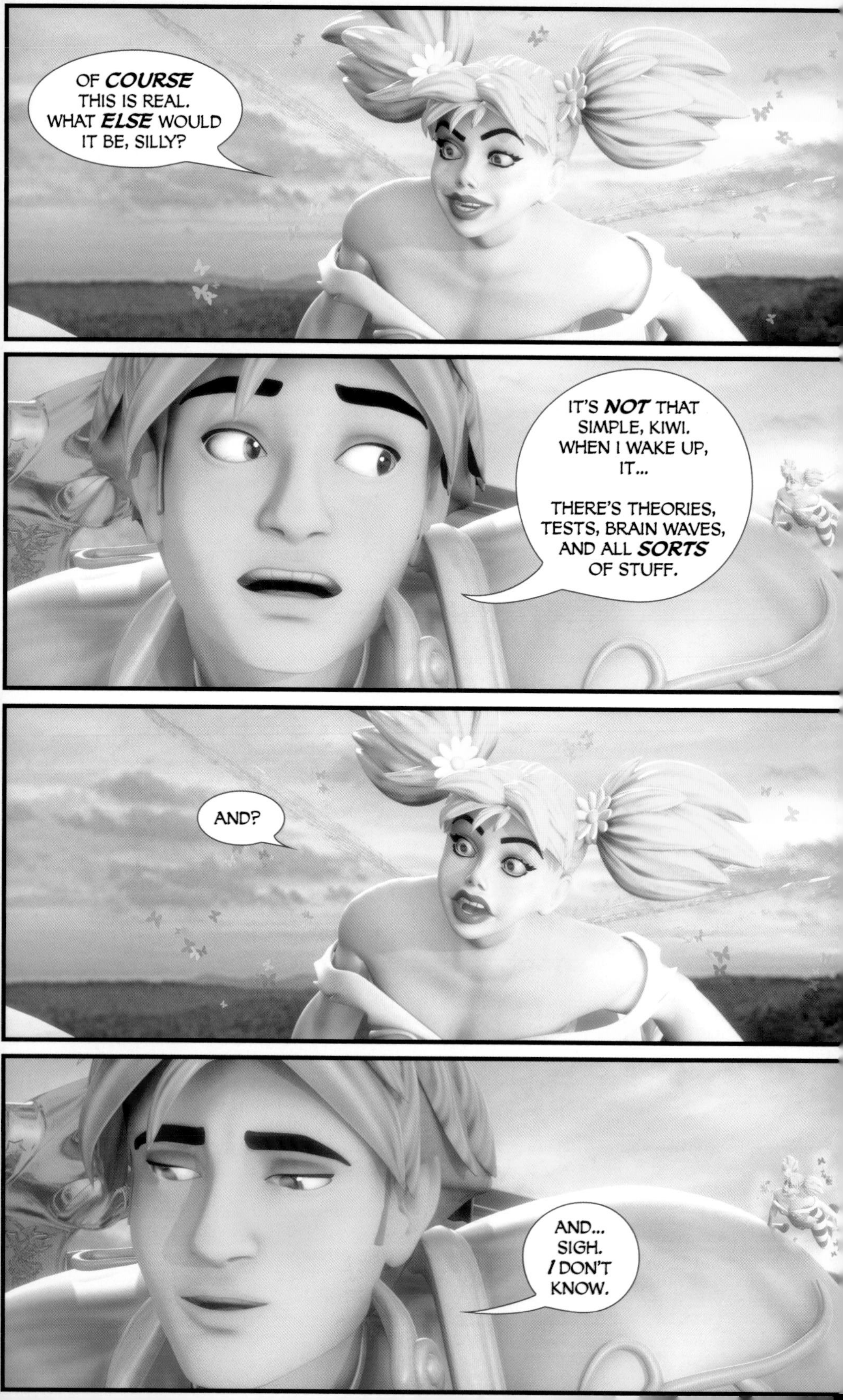
OF COURSE THIS IS REAL. WHAT ELSE WOULD IT BE, SILLY?
IT'S NOT THAT SIMPLE, KIWI. WHEN I WAKE UP, IT...
THERE'S THEORIES, TESTS, BRAIN WAVES, AND ALL SORTS OF STUFF.
AND?
AND... SIGH. I DON'T KNOW.

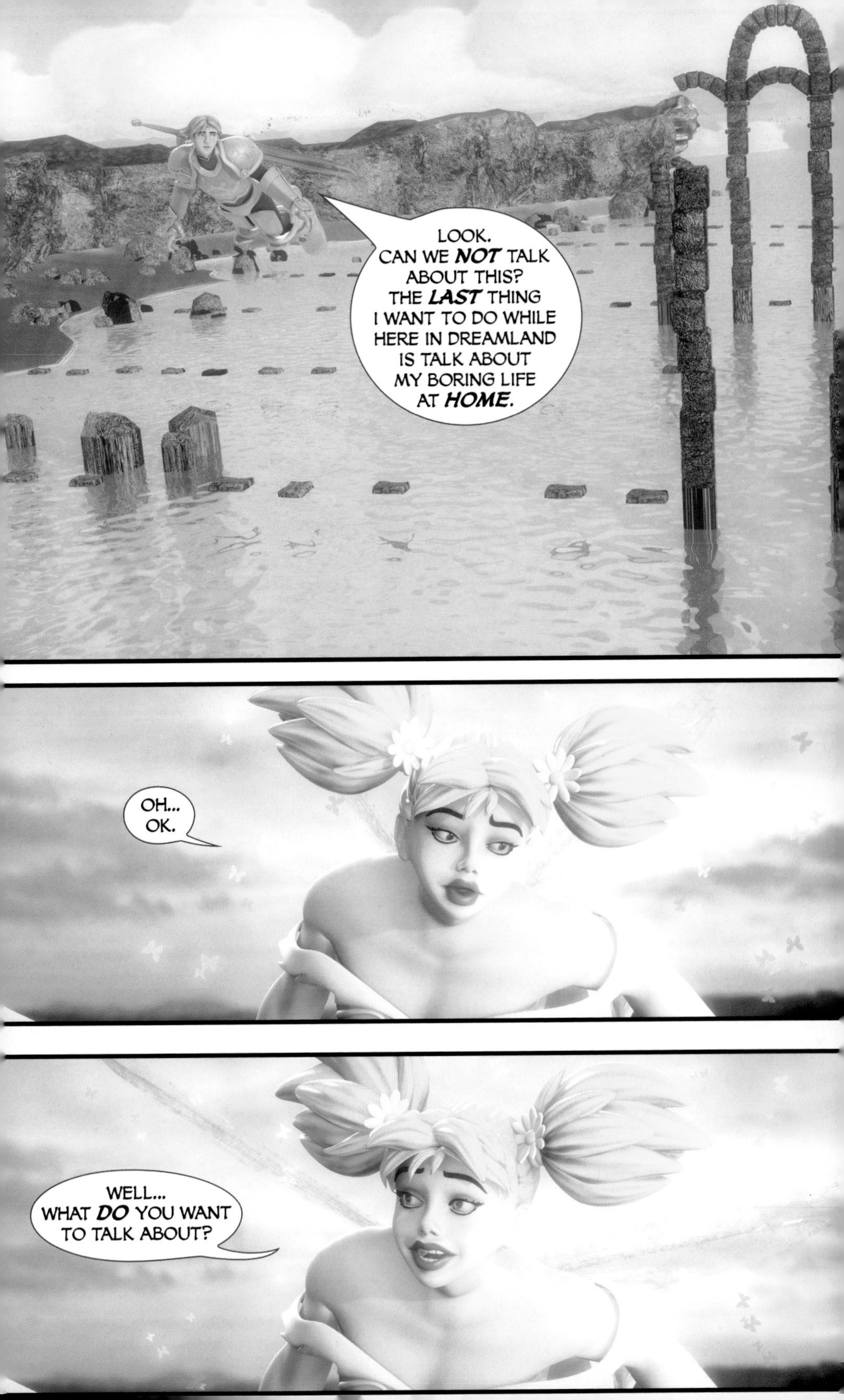
LOOK. CAN WE NOT TALK ABOUT THIS? THE LAST THING I WANT TO DO WHILE HERE IN DREAMLAND IS TALK ABOUT MY BORING LIFE AT HOME.
OH... OK.
WELL... WHAT DO YOU WANT TO TALK ABOUT?

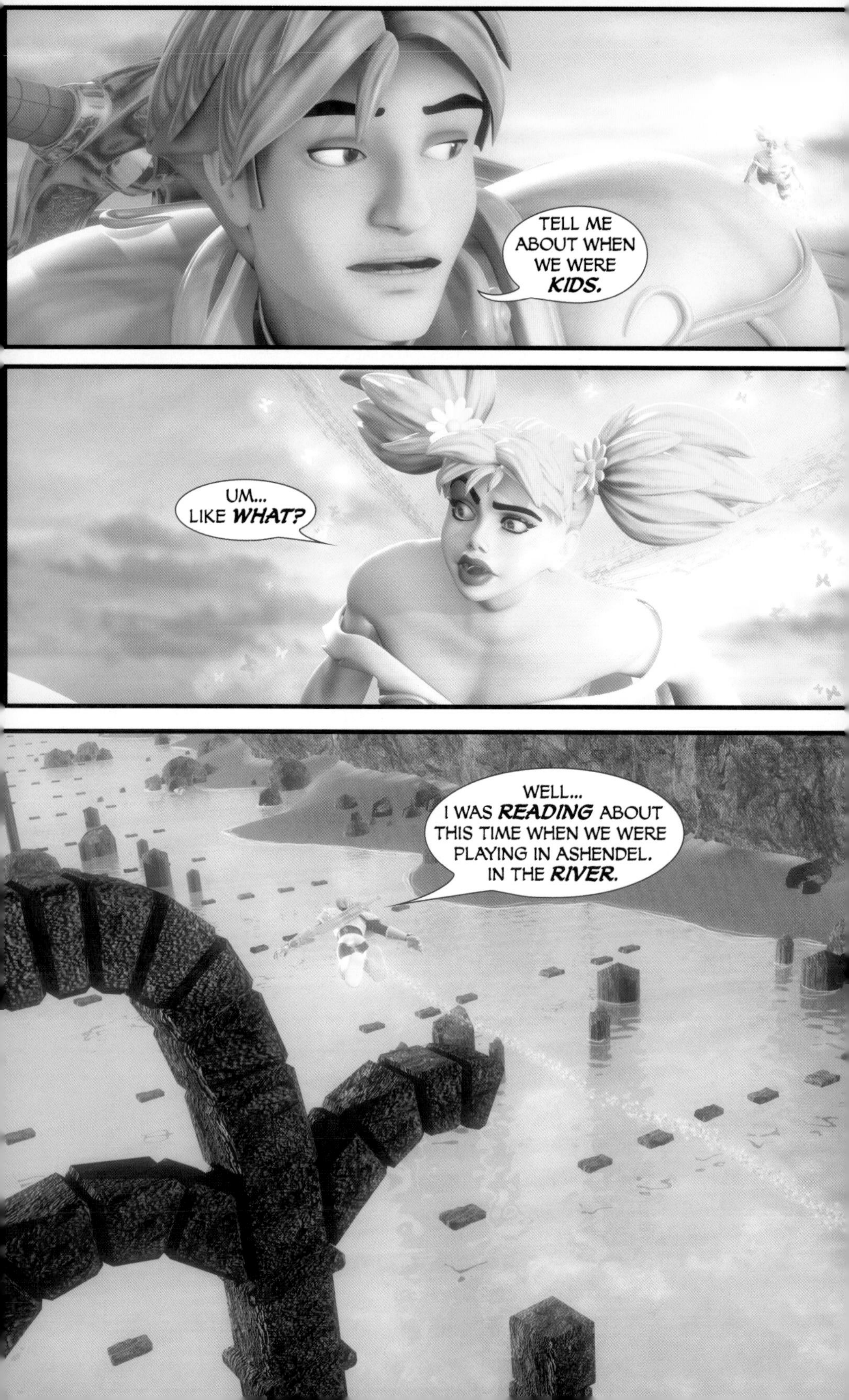
TELL ME ABOUT WHEN WE WERE *KIDS.*
UM... LIKE *WHAT?*
WELL... I WAS *READING* ABOUT THIS TIME WHEN WE WERE PLAYING IN ASHENDEL. IN THE *RIVER*.

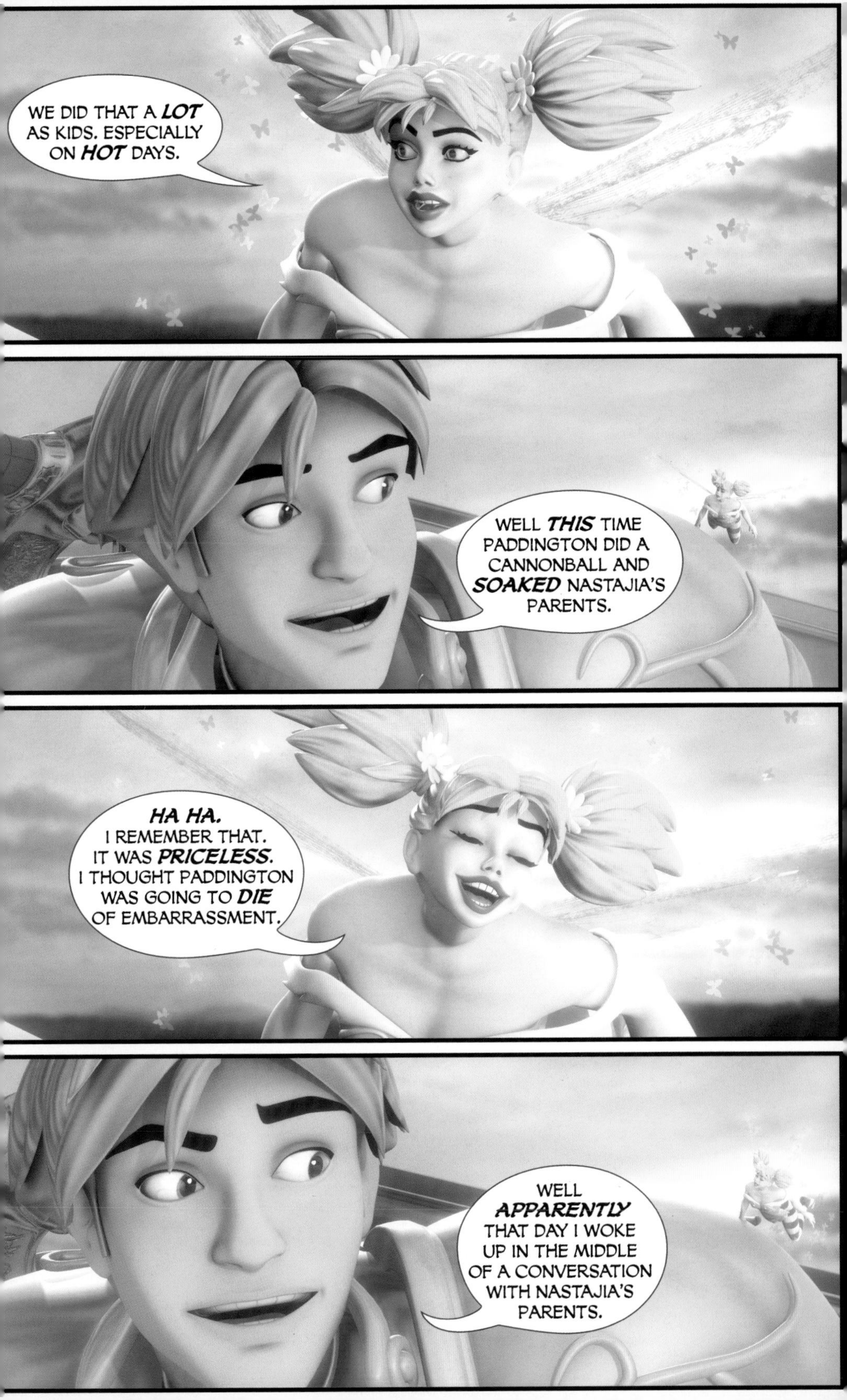
WE DID THAT A LOT AS KIDS. ESPECIALLY ON HOT DAYS.
WELL THIS TIME PADDINGTON DID A CANNONBALL AND SOAKED NASTAJIA'S PARENTS.
HA HA. I REMEMBER THAT. IT WAS PRICELESS. I THOUGHT PADDINGTON WAS GOING TO DIE OF EMBARRASSMENT.
WELL APPARENTLY THAT DAY I WOKE UP IN THE MIDDLE OF A CONVERSATION WITH NASTAJIA'S PARENTS.

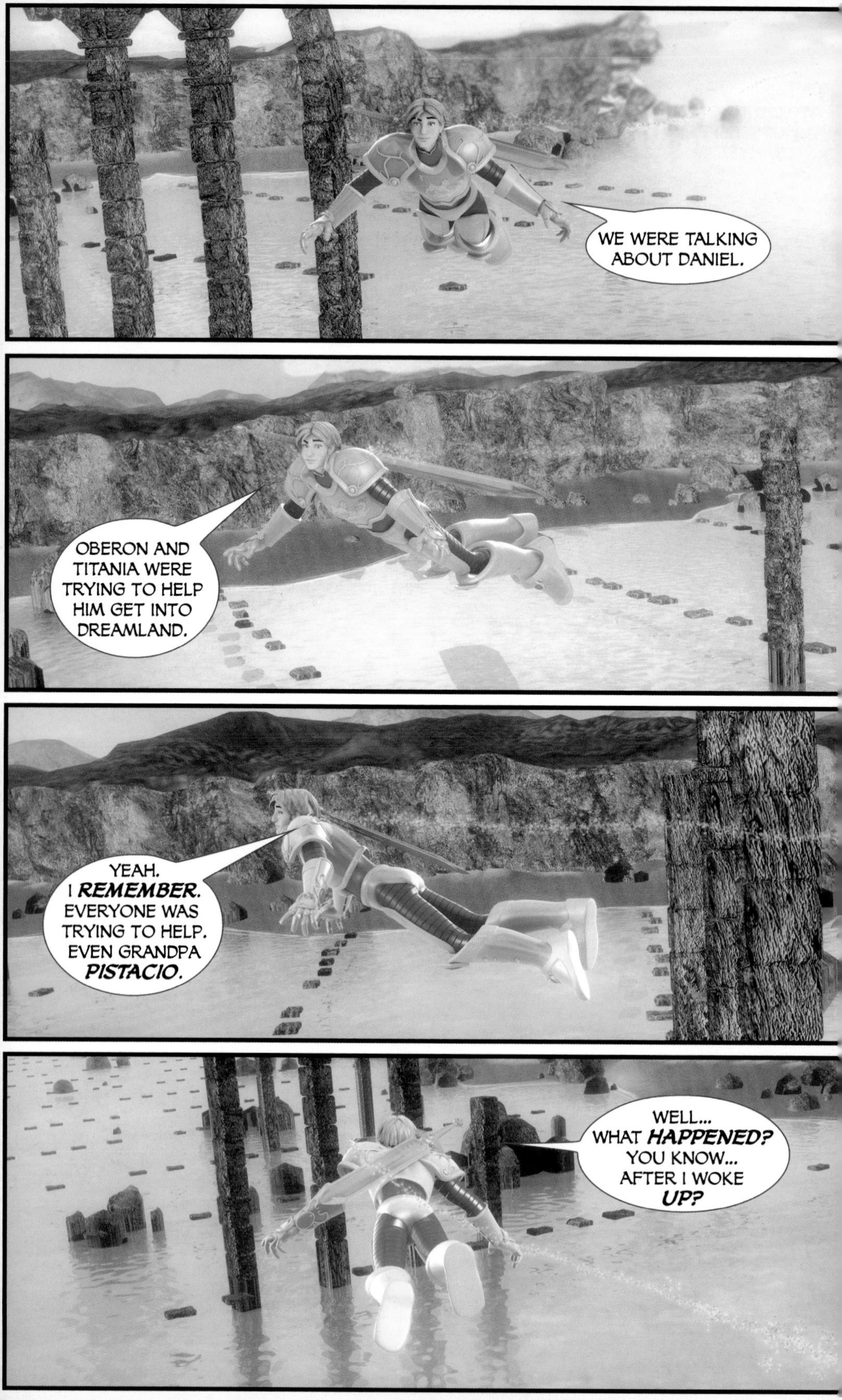
WE WERE TALKING ABOUT DANIEL.
OBERON AND TITANIA WERE TRYING TO HELP HIM GET INTO DREAMLAND.
YEAH. I **REMEMBER**. EVERYONE WAS TRYING TO HELP. EVEN GRANDPA **PISTACIO**.
WELL... WHAT **HAPPENED?** YOU KNOW... AFTER I WOKE **UP?**

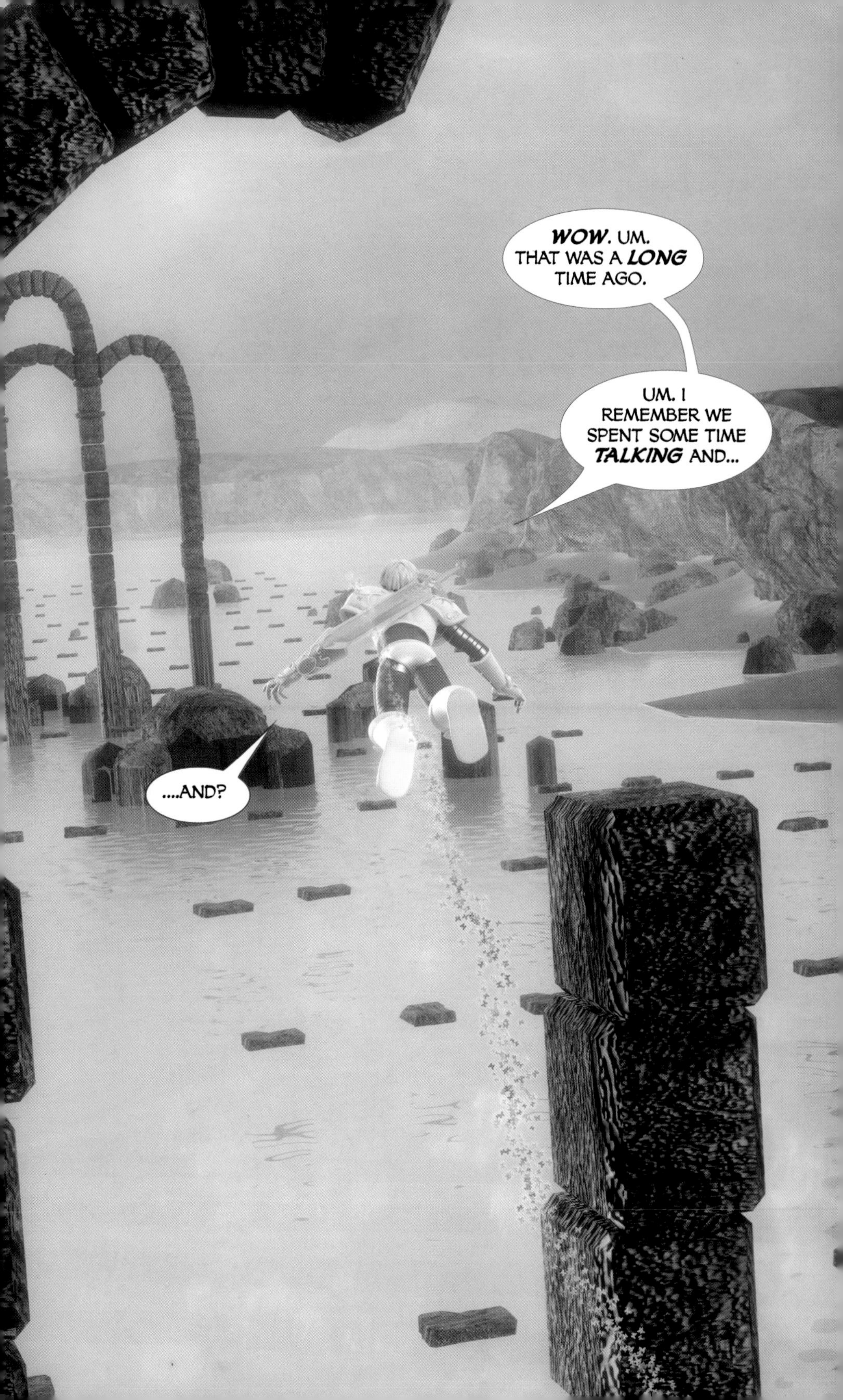
WOW. UM. THAT WAS A ***LONG*** TIME AGO.
UM. I REMEMBER WE SPENT SOME TIME ***TALKING*** AND...
....AND?

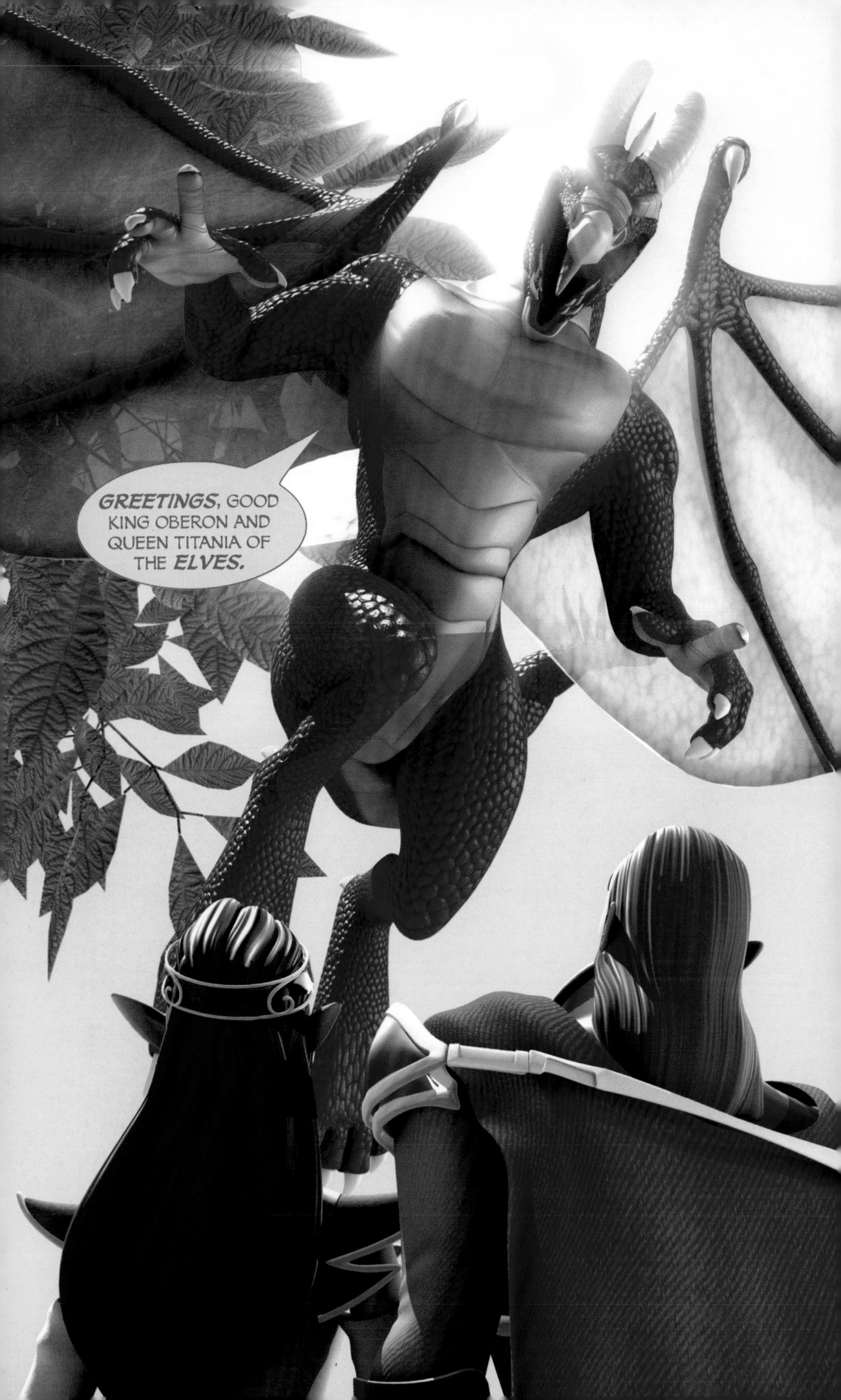
GREETINGS, GOOD KING OBERON AND QUEEN TITANIA OF THE ELVES.

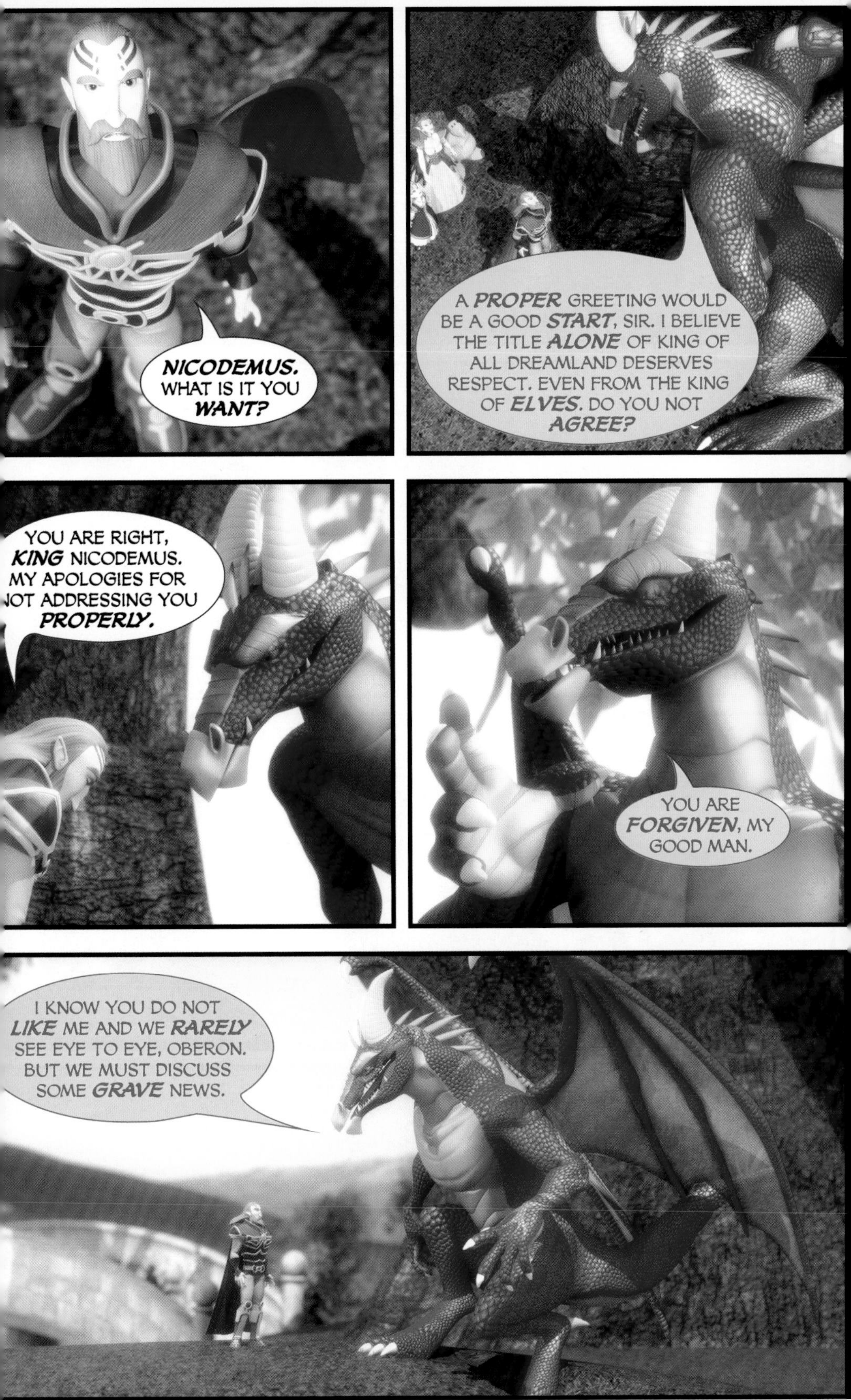
NICODEMUS. WHAT IS IT YOU WANT?
A PROPER GREETING WOULD BE A GOOD START, SIR. I BELIEVE THE TITLE ALONE OF KING OF ALL DREAMLAND DESERVES RESPECT. EVEN FROM THE KING OF ELVES. DO YOU NOT AGREE?
YOU ARE RIGHT, KING NICODEMUS. MY APOLOGIES FOR NOT ADDRESSING YOU PROPERLY.
YOU ARE FORGIVEN, MY GOOD MAN.
I KNOW YOU DO NOT LIKE ME AND WE RARELY SEE EYE TO EYE, OBERON. BUT WE MUST DISCUSS SOME GRAVE NEWS.

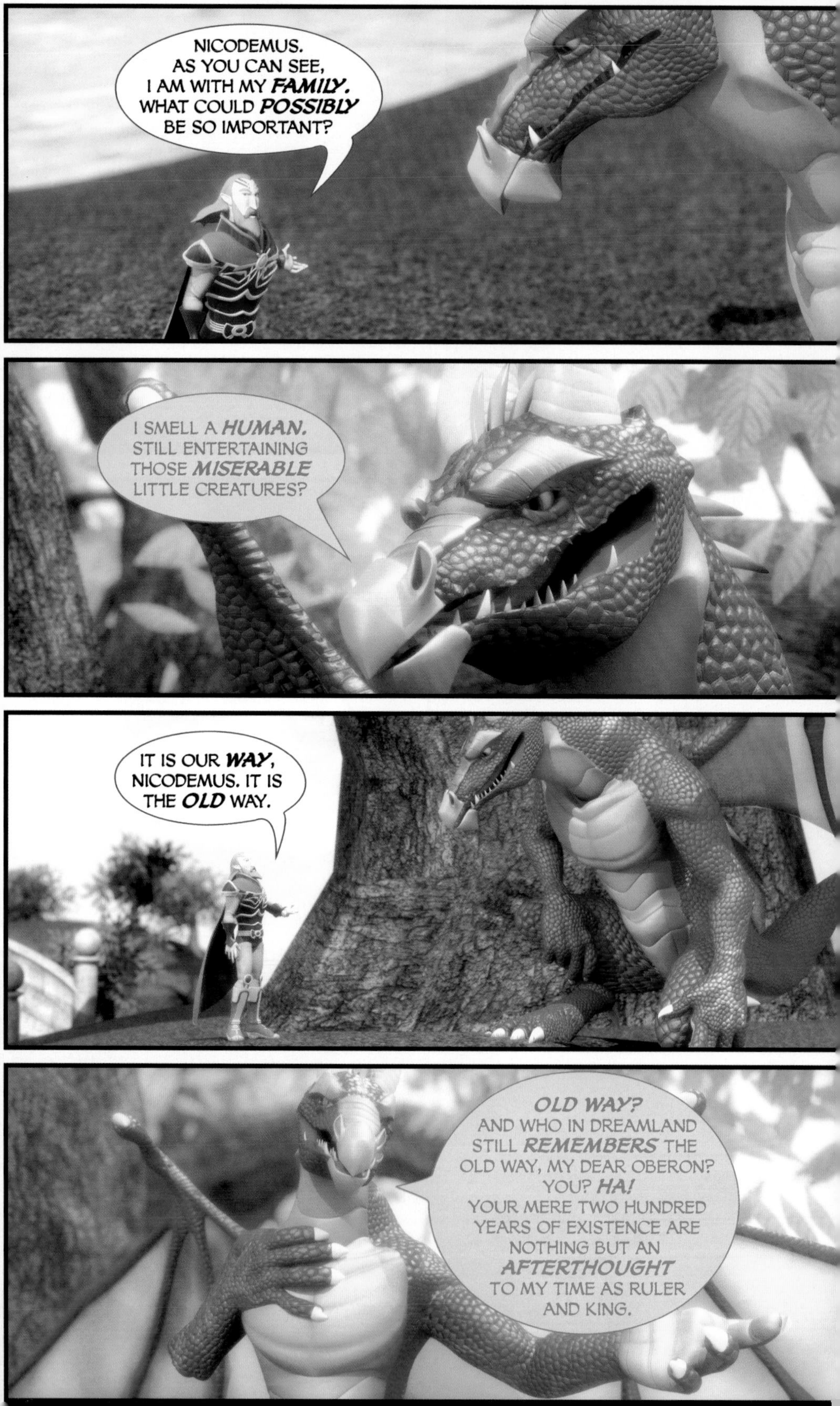
NICODEMUS. AS YOU CAN SEE, I AM WITH MY FAMILY. WHAT COULD POSSIBLY BE SO IMPORTANT?
I SMELL A HUMAN. STILL ENTERTAINING THOSE MISERABLE LITTLE CREATURES?
IT IS OUR WAY, NICODEMUS. IT IS THE OLD WAY.
OLD WAY? AND WHO IN DREAMLAND STILL REMEMBERS THE OLD WAY, MY DEAR OBERON? YOU? HA! YOUR MERE TWO HUNDRED YEARS OF EXISTENCE ARE NOTHING BUT AN AFTERTHOUGHT TO MY TIME AS RULER AND KING.

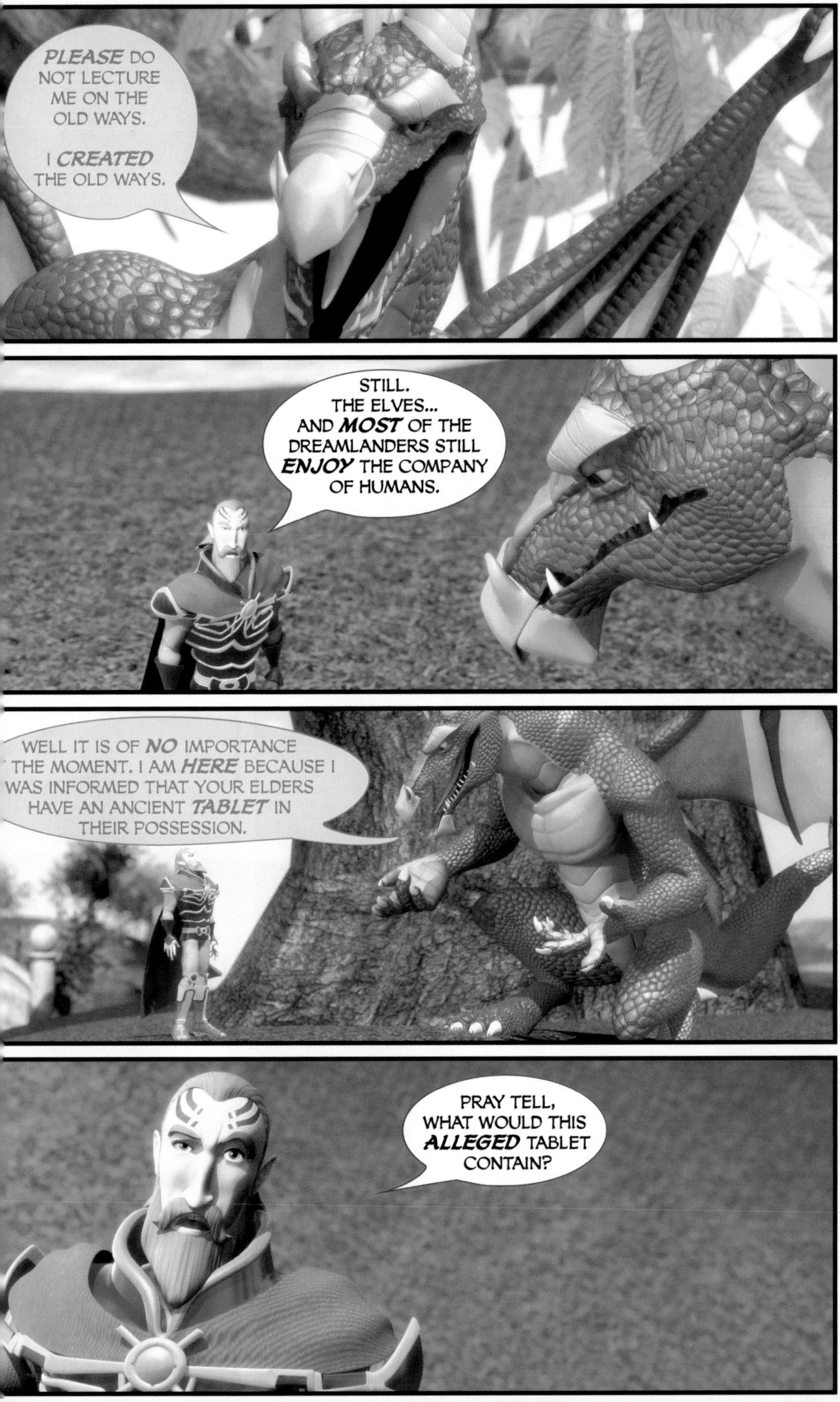

PLEASE DO NOT LECTURE ME ON THE OLD WAYS.
I CREATED THE OLD WAYS.
STILL. THE ELVES... AND MOST OF THE DREAMLANDERS STILL ENJOY THE COMPANY OF HUMANS.
WELL IT IS OF NO IMPORTANCE THE MOMENT. I AM HERE BECAUSE I WAS INFORMED THAT YOUR ELDERS HAVE AN ANCIENT TABLET IN THEIR POSSESSION.
PRAY TELL, WHAT WOULD THIS ALLEGED TABLET CONTAIN?

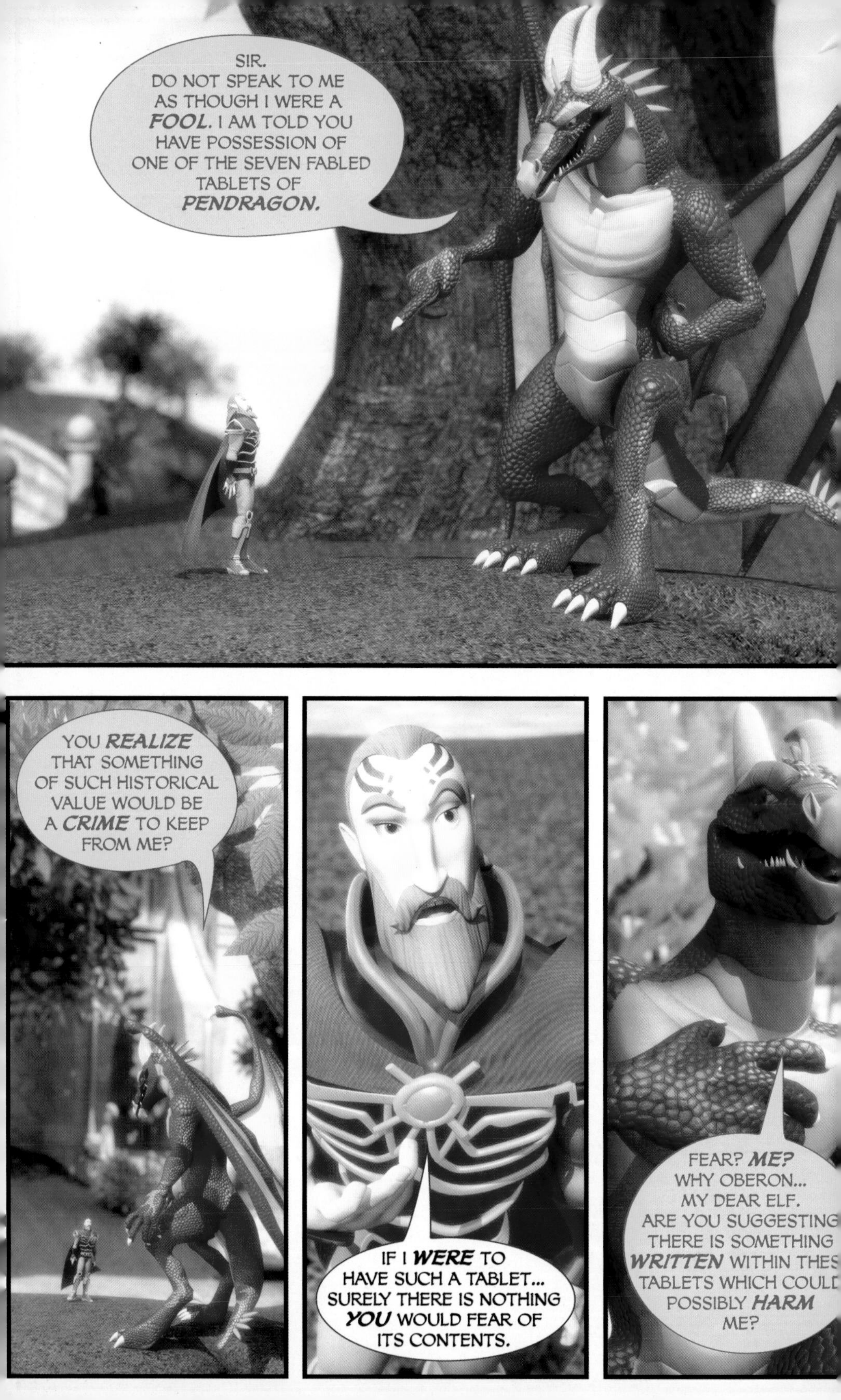
SIR. DO NOT SPEAK TO ME AS THOUGH I WERE A ***FOOL***. I AM TOLD YOU HAVE POSSESSION OF ONE OF THE SEVEN FABLED TABLETS OF ***PENDRAGON***.
YOU ***REALIZE*** THAT SOMETHING OF SUCH HISTORICAL VALUE WOULD BE A ***CRIME*** TO KEEP FROM ME?
IF I ***WERE*** TO HAVE SUCH A TABLET... SURELY THERE IS NOTHING ***YOU*** WOULD FEAR OF ITS CONTENTS.
FEAR? ***ME?*** WHY OBERON... MY DEAR ELF. ARE YOU SUGGESTING THERE IS SOMETHING ***WRITTEN*** WITHIN THES TABLETS WHICH COUL POSSIBLY ***HARM*** ME?

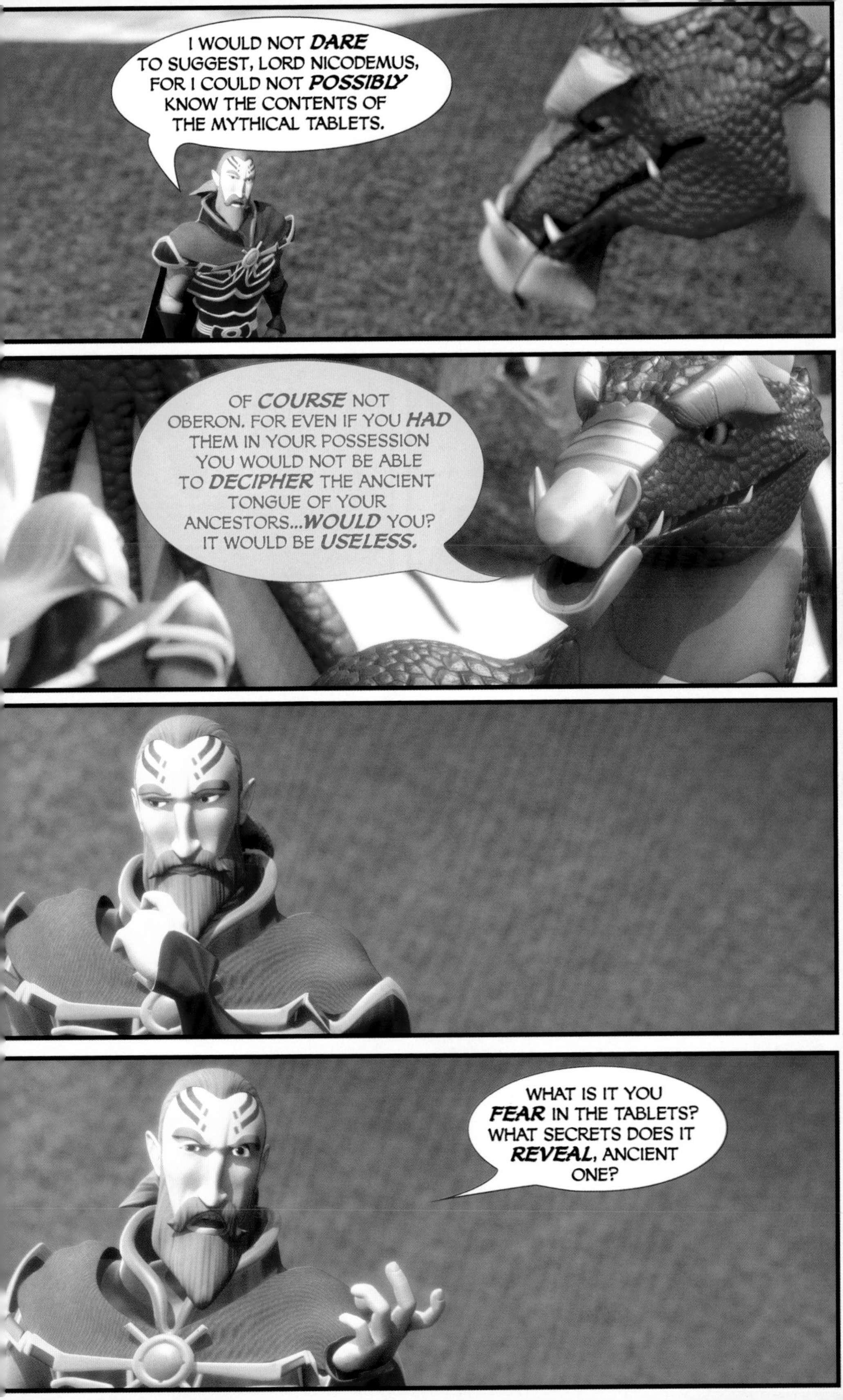
I WOULD NOT DARE TO SUGGEST, LORD NICODEMUS, FOR I COULD NOT POSSIBLY KNOW THE CONTENTS OF THE MYTHICAL TABLETS.
OF COURSE NOT OBERON. FOR EVEN IF YOU HAD THEM IN YOUR POSSESSION YOU WOULD NOT BE ABLE TO DECIPHER THE ANCIENT TONGUE OF YOUR ANCESTORS...WOULD YOU? IT WOULD BE USELESS.
WHAT IS IT YOU FEAR IN THE TABLETS? WHAT SECRETS DOES IT REVEAL, ANCIENT ONE?

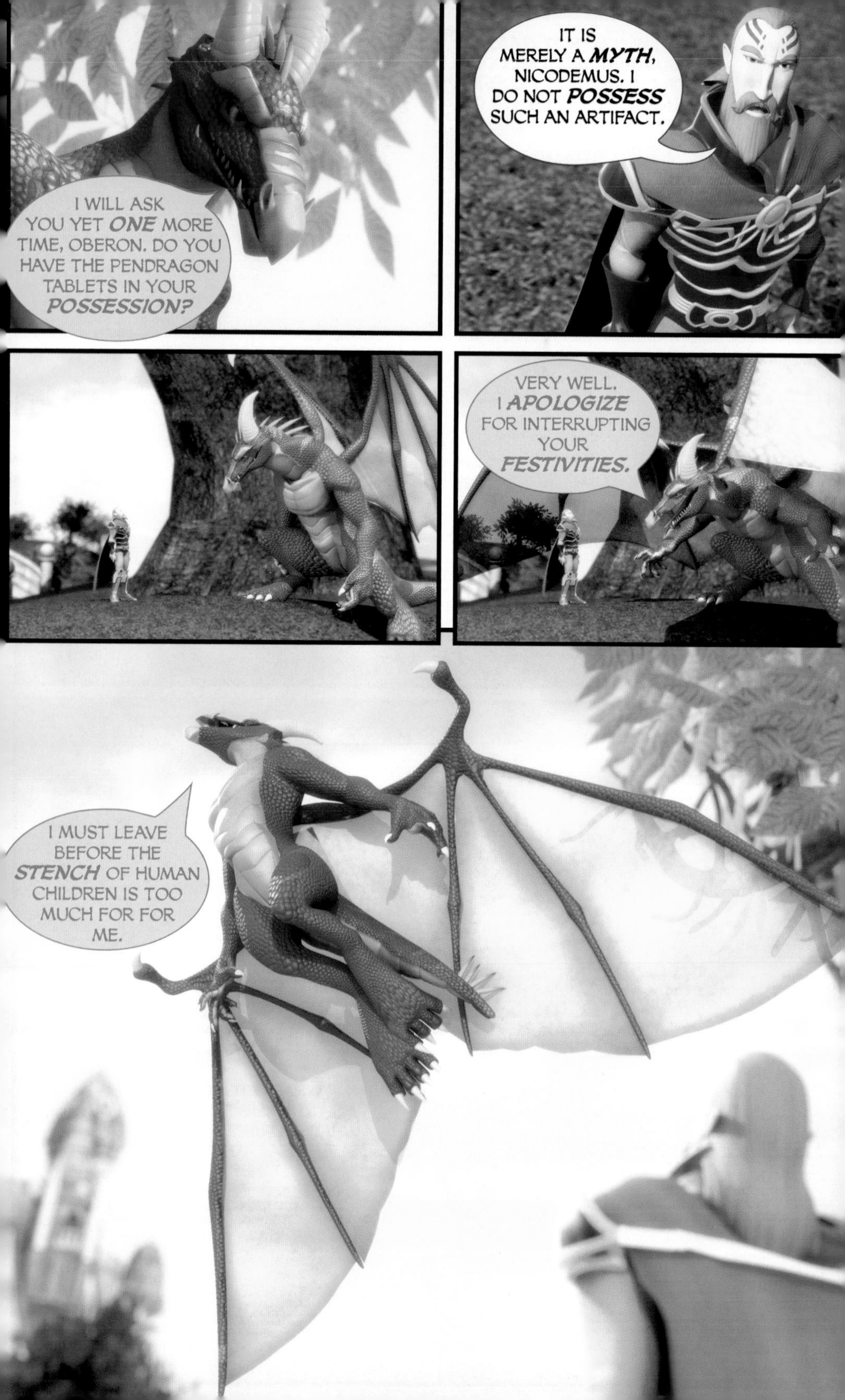
I WILL ASK YOU YET ONE MORE TIME, OBERON. DO YOU HAVE THE PENDRAGON TABLETS IN YOUR POSSESSION?
IT IS MERELY A MYTH, NICODEMUS. I DO NOT POSSESS SUCH AN ARTIFACT.
VERY WELL. I APOLOGIZE FOR INTERRUPTING YOUR FESTIVITIES.
I MUST LEAVE BEFORE THE STENCH OF HUMAN CHILDREN IS TOO MUCH FOR FOR ME.

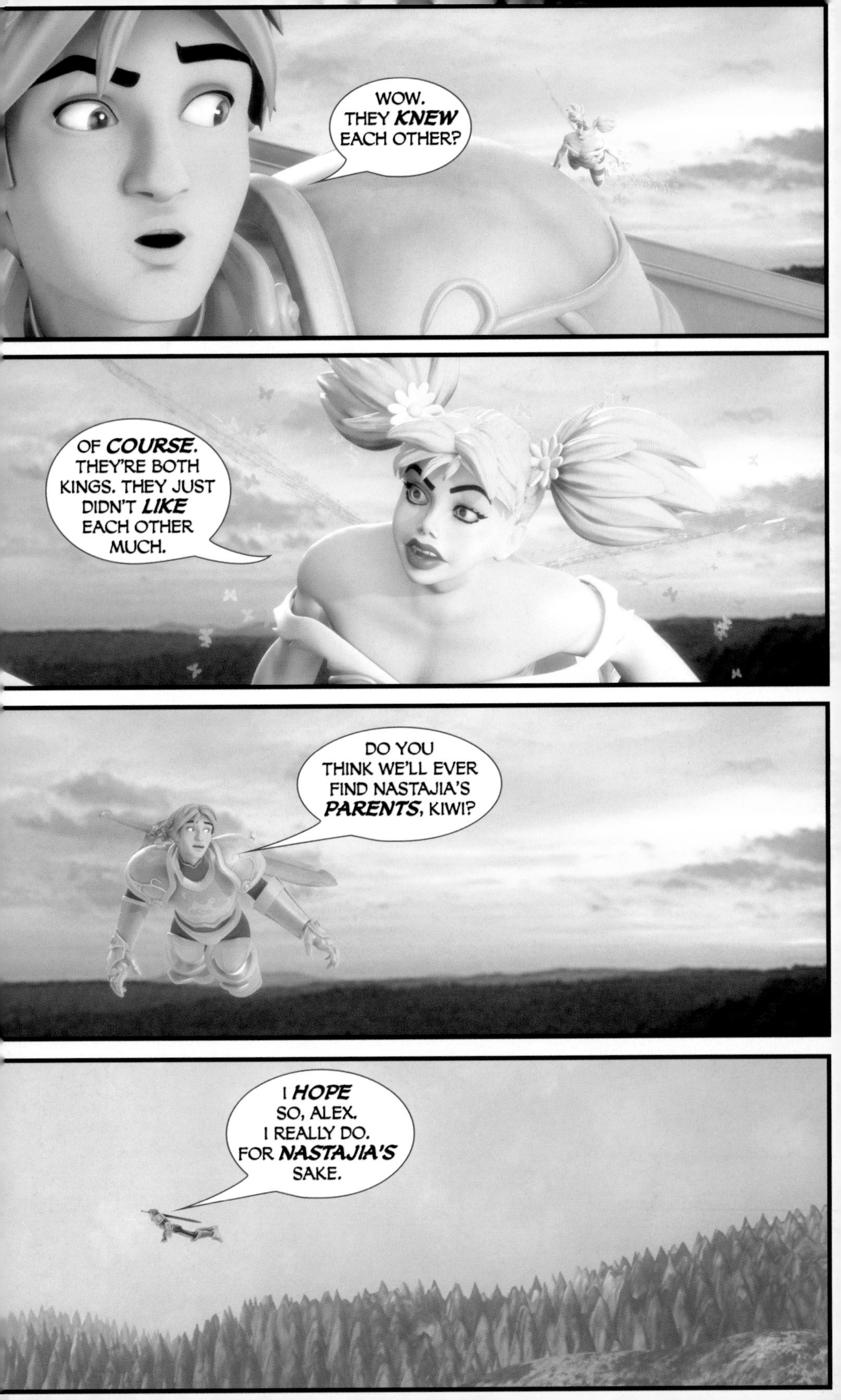
WOW. THEY **KNEW** EACH OTHER?
OF **COURSE**. THEY'RE BOTH KINGS. THEY JUST DIDN'T **LIKE** EACH OTHER MUCH.
DO YOU THINK WE'LL EVER FIND NASTAJIA'S **PARENTS**, KIWI?
I **HOPE** SO, ALEX. I REALLY DO. FOR **NASTAJIA'S** SAKE.

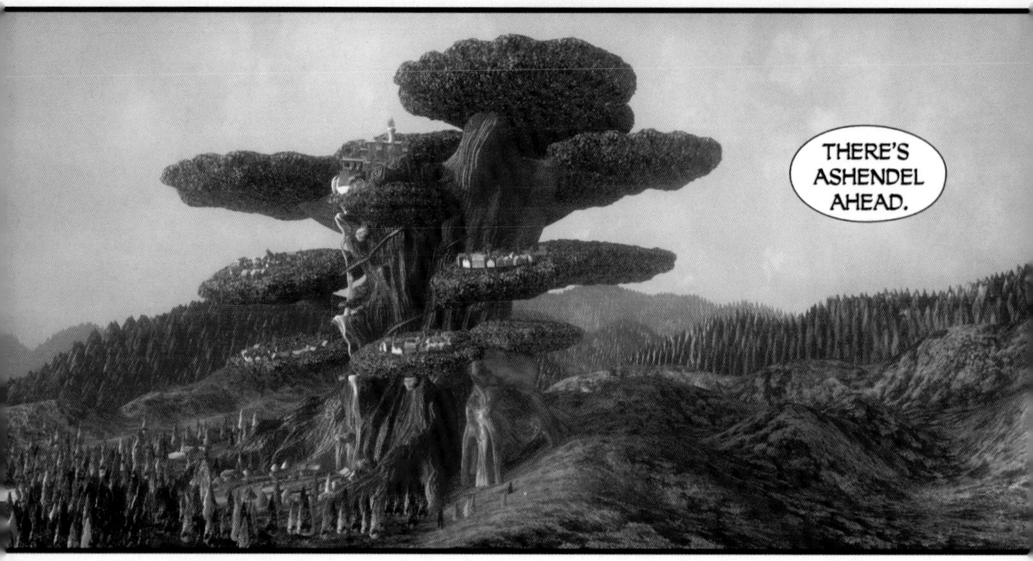
THERE'S ASHENDEL AHEAD.

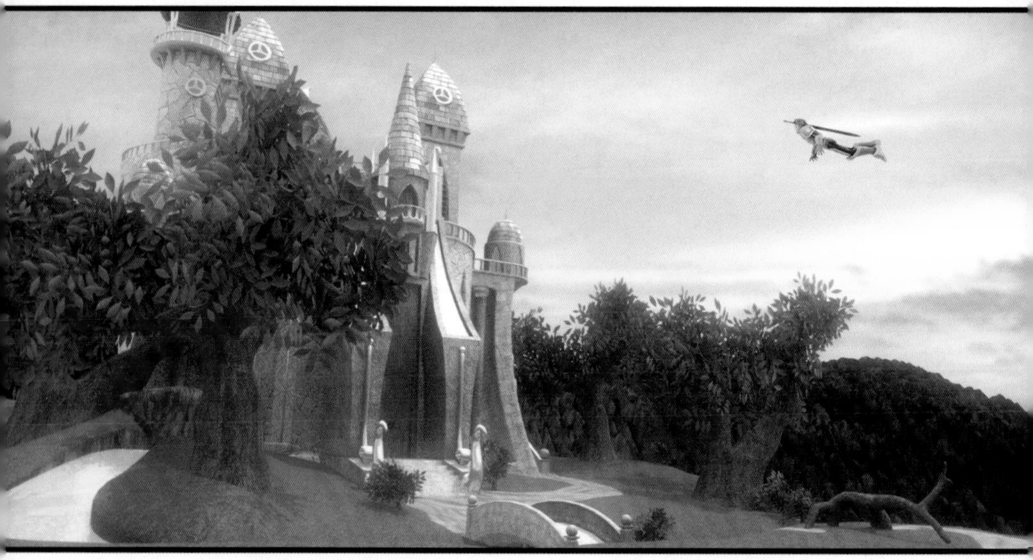

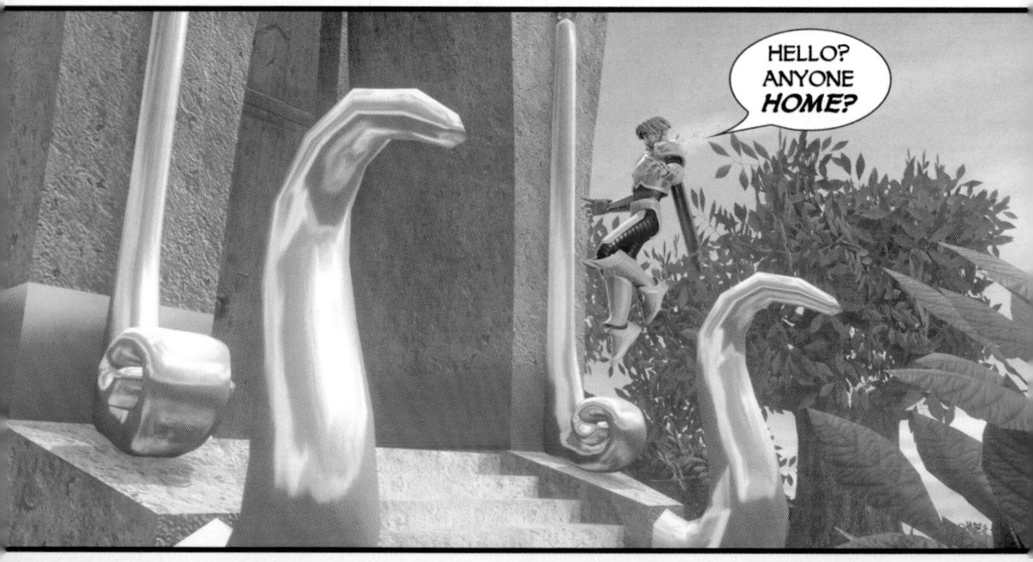
HELLO? ANYONE ***HOME?***

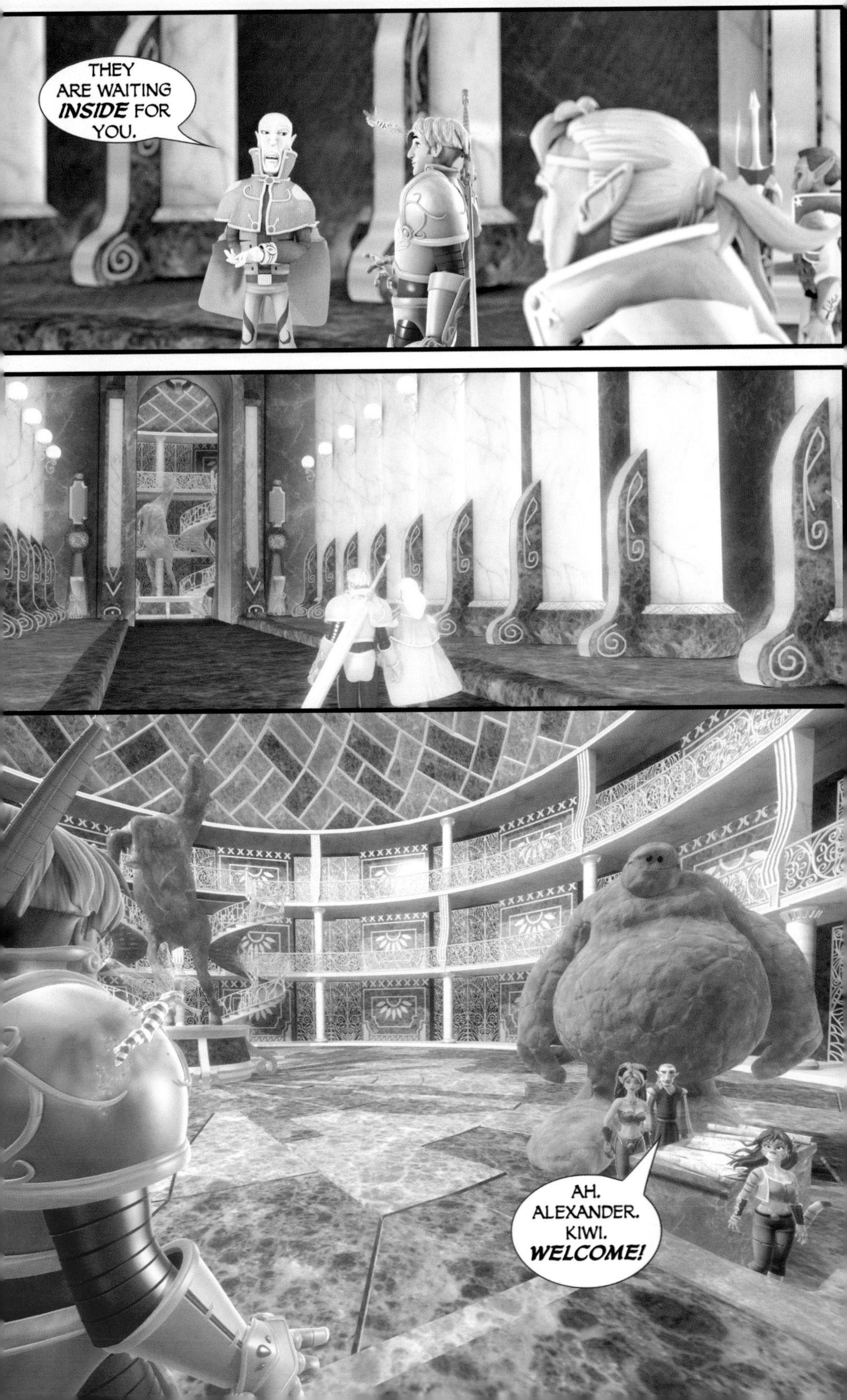
THEY ARE WAITING *INSIDE* FOR YOU.
AH. ALEXANDER. KIWI. *WELCOME!*

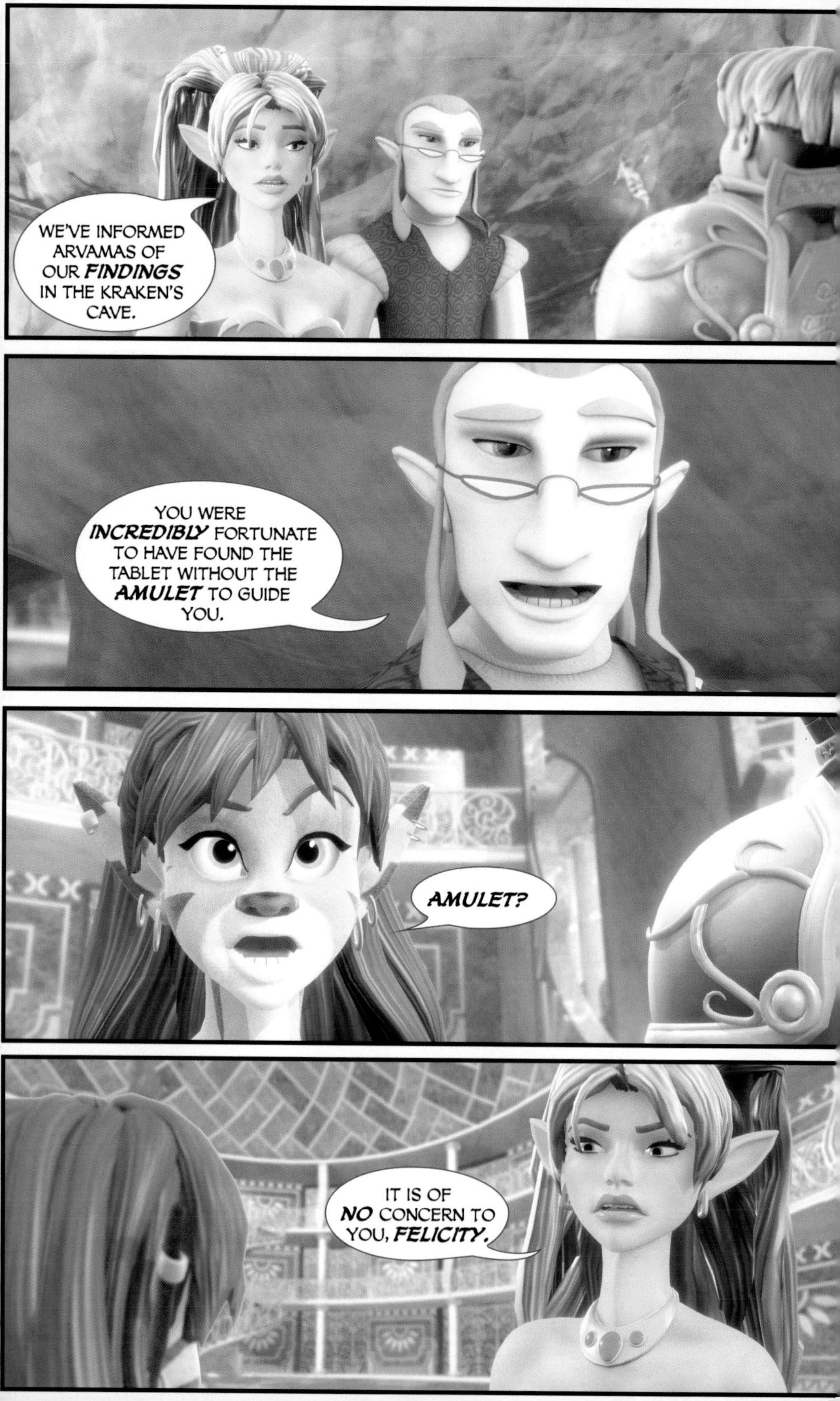
WE'VE INFORMED ARVAMAS OF OUR *FINDINGS* IN THE KRAKEN'S CAVE.
YOU WERE *INCREDIBLY* FORTUNATE TO HAVE FOUND THE TABLET WITHOUT THE *AMULET* TO GUIDE YOU.
AMULET?
IT IS OF *NO* CONCERN TO YOU, *FELICITY.*

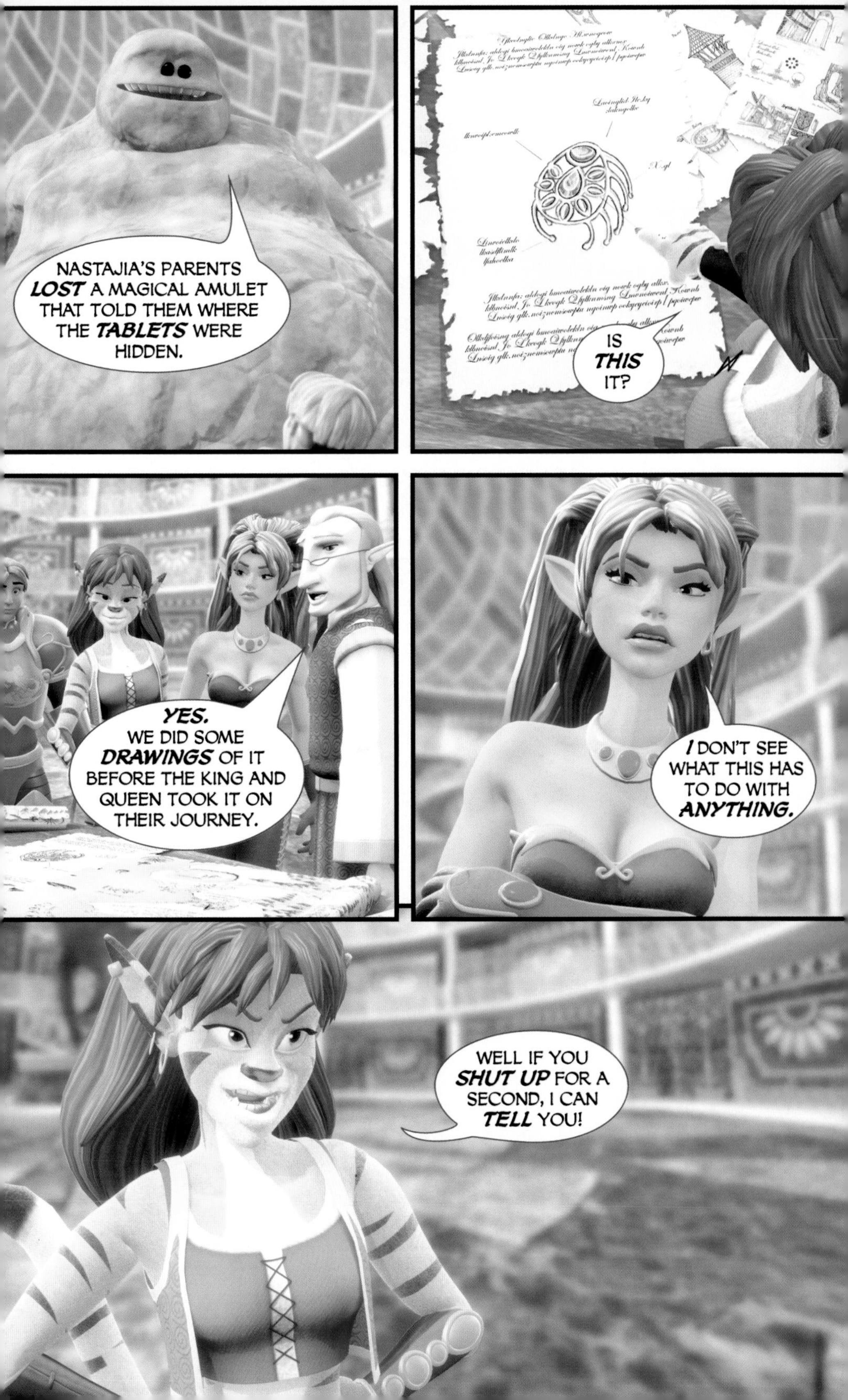
NASTAJIA'S PARENTS LOST A MAGICAL AMULET THAT TOLD THEM WHERE THE TABLETS WERE HIDDEN.
IS THIS IT?
YES. WE DID SOME DRAWINGS OF IT BEFORE THE KING AND QUEEN TOOK IT ON THEIR JOURNEY.
I DON'T SEE WHAT THIS HAS TO DO WITH ANYTHING.
WELL IF YOU SHUT UP FOR A SECOND, I CAN TELL YOU!

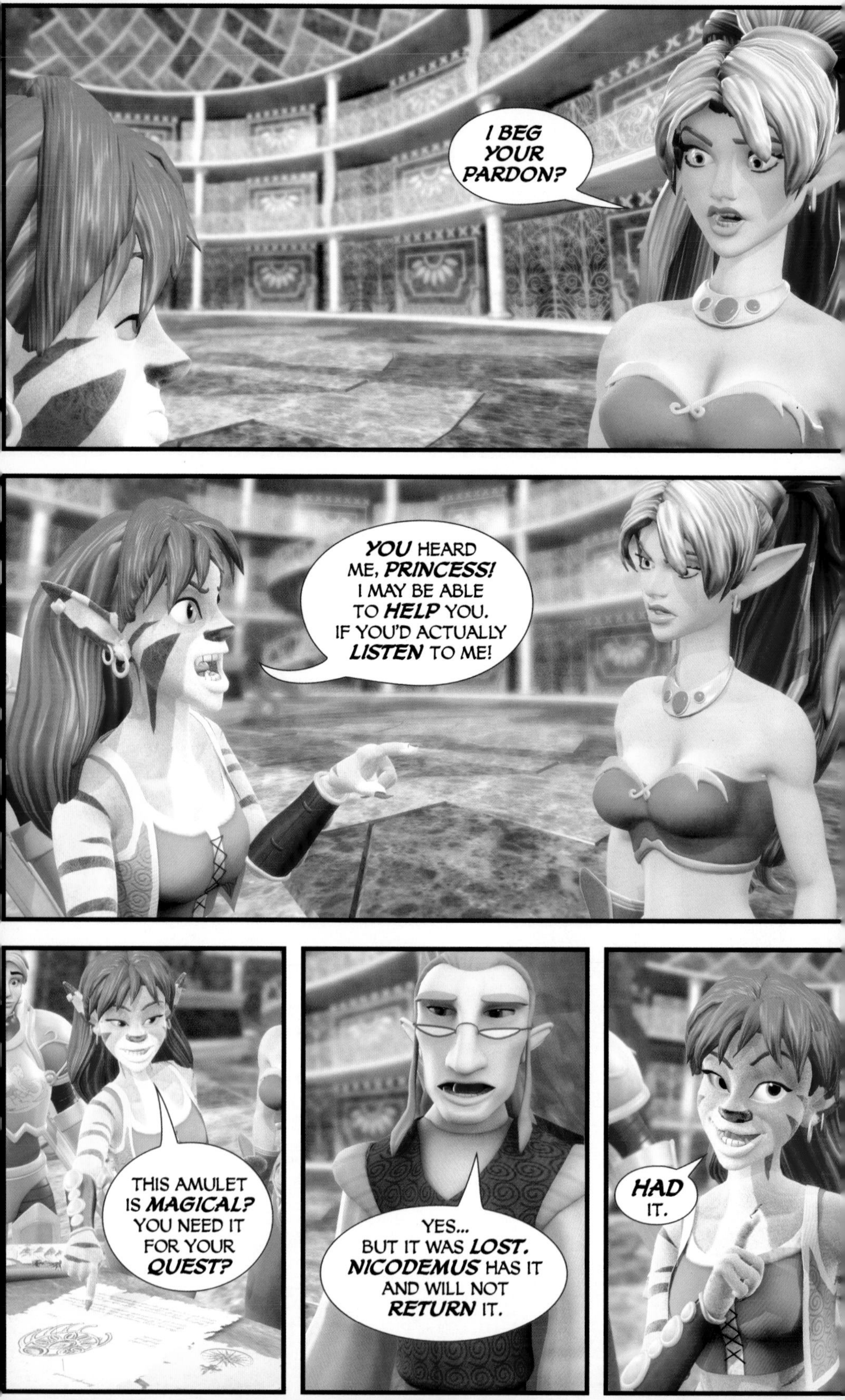

I BEG YOUR PARDON?
YOU HEARD ME, PRINCESS! I MAY BE ABLE TO HELP YOU. IF YOU'D ACTUALLY LISTEN TO ME!
THIS AMULET IS MAGICAL? YOU NEED IT FOR YOUR QUEST?
YES... BUT IT WAS LOST. NICODEMUS HAS IT AND WILL NOT RETURN IT.
HAD IT.

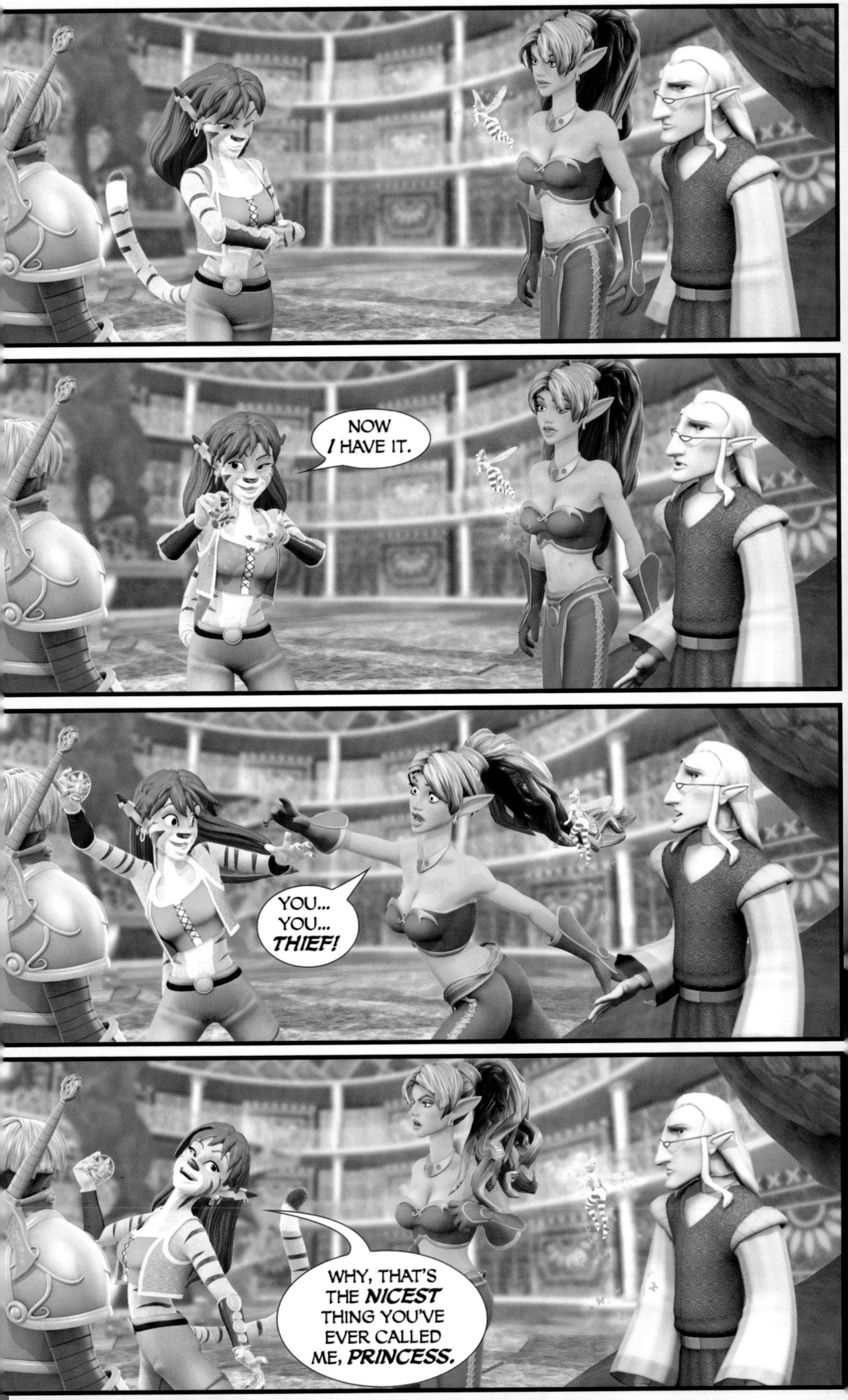
NOW
I HAVE IT.
YOU...
YOU...
THIEF!
WHY, THAT'S
THE ***NICEST***
THING YOU'VE
EVER CALLED
ME, ***PRINCESS.***

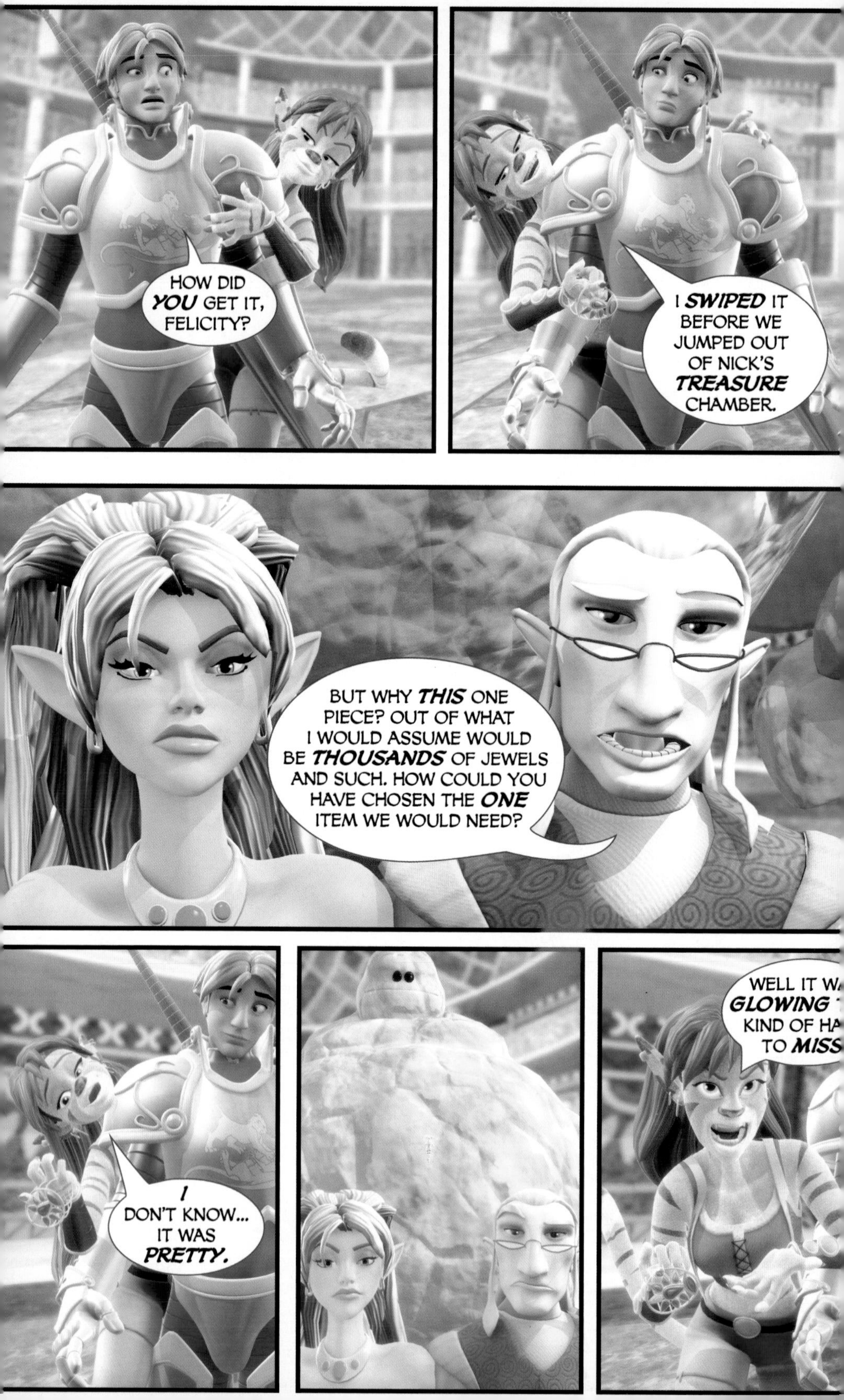
HOW DID YOU GET IT, FELICITY?
I SWIPED IT BEFORE WE JUMPED OUT OF NICK'S TREASURE CHAMBER.
BUT WHY THIS ONE PIECE? OUT OF WHAT I WOULD ASSUME WOULD BE THOUSANDS OF JEWELS AND SUCH. HOW COULD YOU HAVE CHOSEN THE ONE ITEM WE WOULD NEED?
I DON'T KNOW... IT WAS PRETTY.
WELL IT WA
GLOWING
KIND OF HA
TO MISS

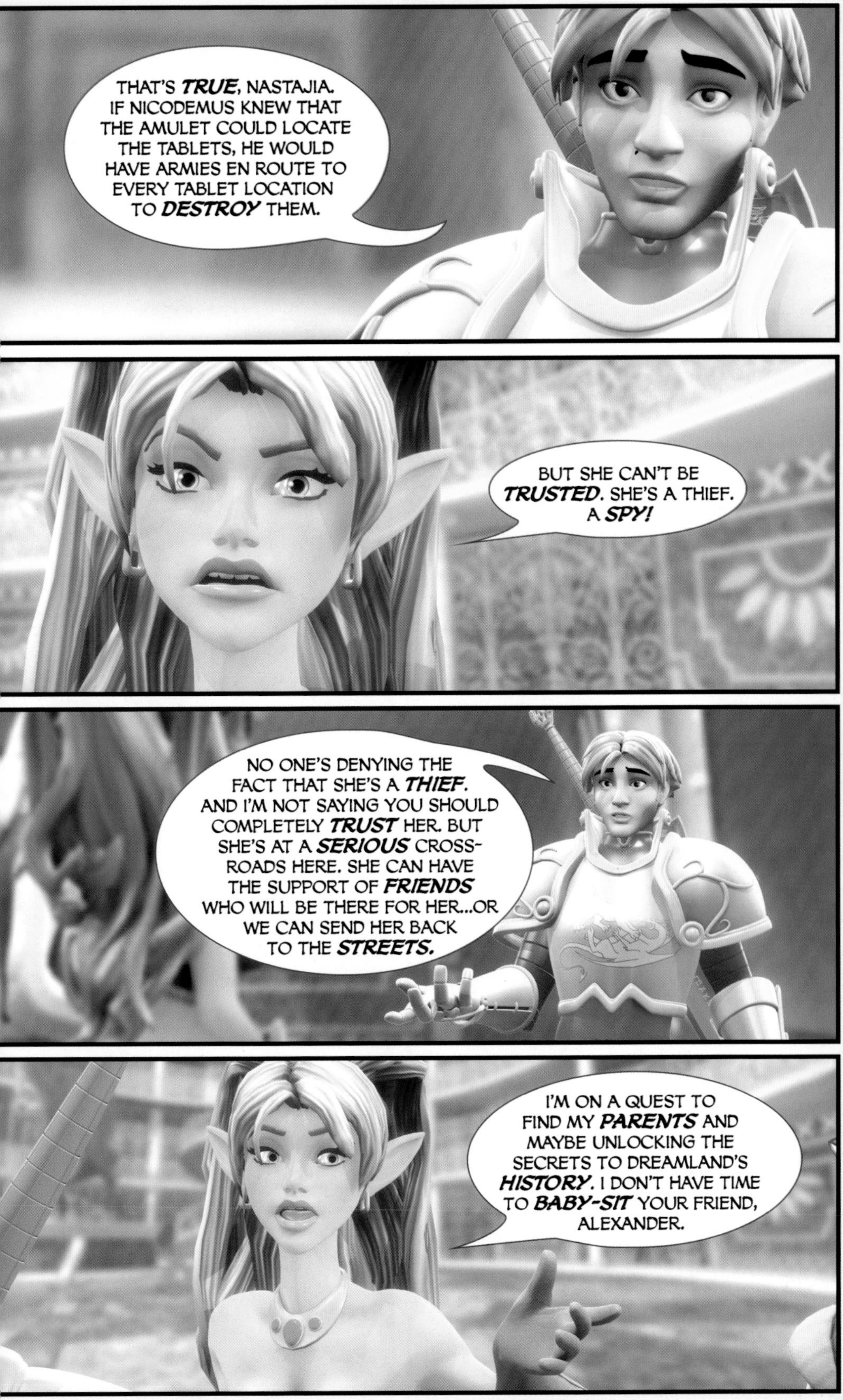
THAT'S TRUE, NASTAJIA. IF NICODEMUS KNEW THAT THE AMULET COULD LOCATE THE TABLETS, HE WOULD HAVE ARMIES EN ROUTE TO EVERY TABLET LOCATION TO DESTROY THEM.
BUT SHE CAN'T BE TRUSTED. SHE'S A THIEF. A SPY!
NO ONE'S DENYING THE FACT THAT SHE'S A THIEF. AND I'M NOT SAYING YOU SHOULD COMPLETELY TRUST HER. BUT SHE'S AT A SERIOUS CROSS-ROADS HERE. SHE CAN HAVE THE SUPPORT OF FRIENDS WHO WILL BE THERE FOR HER...OR WE CAN SEND HER BACK TO THE STREETS.
I'M ON A QUEST TO FIND MY PARENTS AND MAYBE UNLOCKING THE SECRETS TO DREAMLAND'S HISTORY. I DON'T HAVE TIME TO BABY-SIT YOUR FRIEND, ALEXANDER.

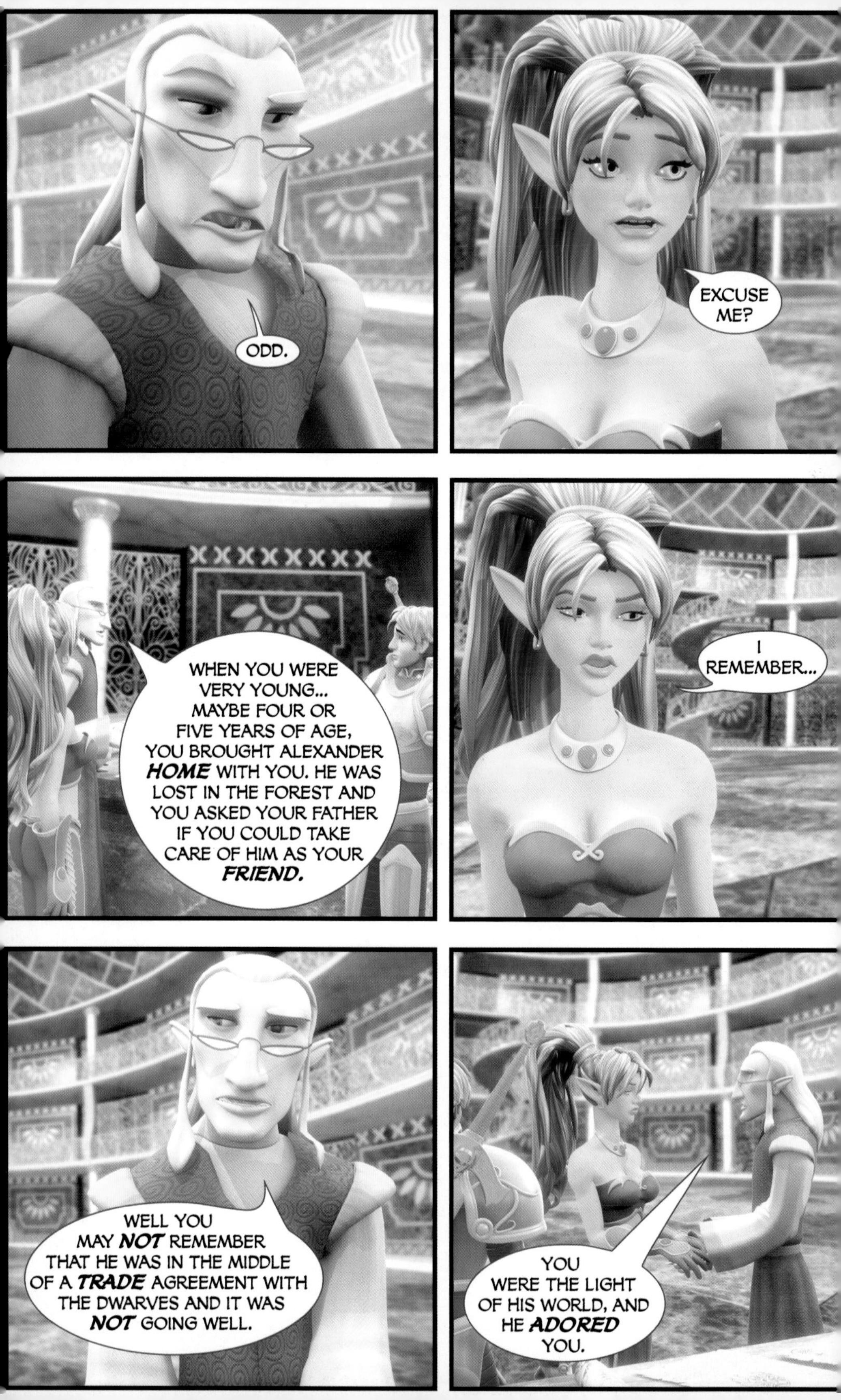
ODD.
EXCUSE ME?
WHEN YOU WERE VERY YOUNG... MAYBE FOUR OR FIVE YEARS OF AGE, YOU BROUGHT ALEXANDER HOME WITH YOU. HE WAS LOST IN THE FOREST AND YOU ASKED YOUR FATHER IF YOU COULD TAKE CARE OF HIM AS YOUR FRIEND.
I REMEMBER...
WELL YOU MAY NOT REMEMBER THAT HE WAS IN THE MIDDLE OF A TRADE AGREEMENT WITH THE DWARVES AND IT WAS NOT GOING WELL.
YOU WERE THE LIGHT OF HIS WORLD, AND HE ADORED YOU.

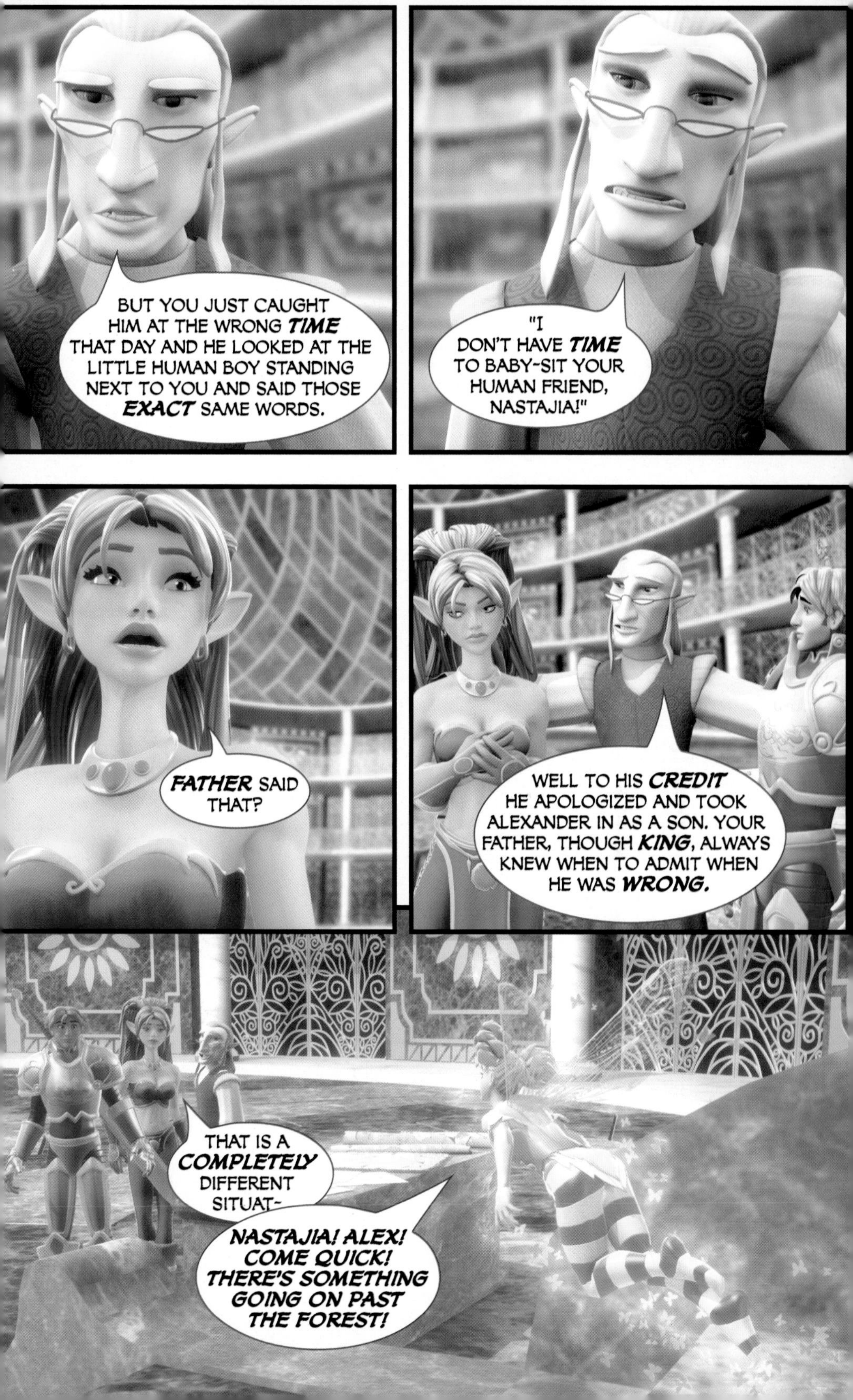
BUT YOU JUST CAUGHT HIM AT THE WRONG *TIME* THAT DAY AND HE LOOKED AT THE LITTLE HUMAN BOY STANDING NEXT TO YOU AND SAID THOSE *EXACT* SAME WORDS.
"I DON'T HAVE *TIME* TO BABY-SIT YOUR HUMAN FRIEND, NASTAJIA!"
FATHER SAID THAT?
WELL TO HIS *CREDIT* HE APOLOGIZED AND TOOK ALEXANDER IN AS A SON. YOUR FATHER, THOUGH *KING*, ALWAYS KNEW WHEN TO ADMIT WHEN HE WAS *WRONG.*
THAT IS A *COMPLETELY* DIFFERENT SITUAT-
NASTAJIA! ALEX! COME QUICK! THERE'S SOMETHING GOING ON PAST THE FOREST!

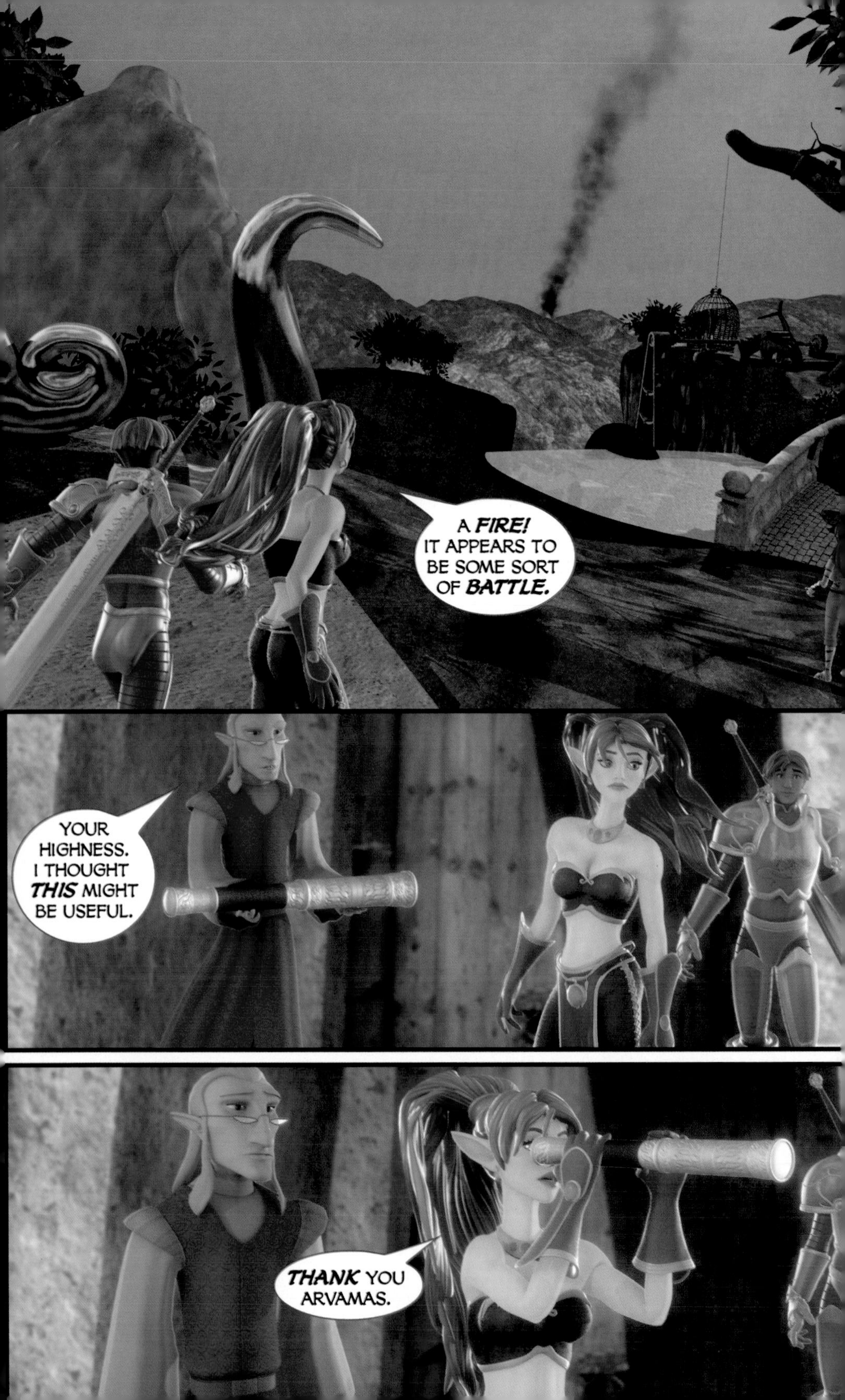
A FIRE! IT APPEARS TO BE SOME SORT OF BATTLE.
YOUR HIGHNESS. I THOUGHT THIS MIGHT BE USEFUL.
THANK YOU ARVAMAS.

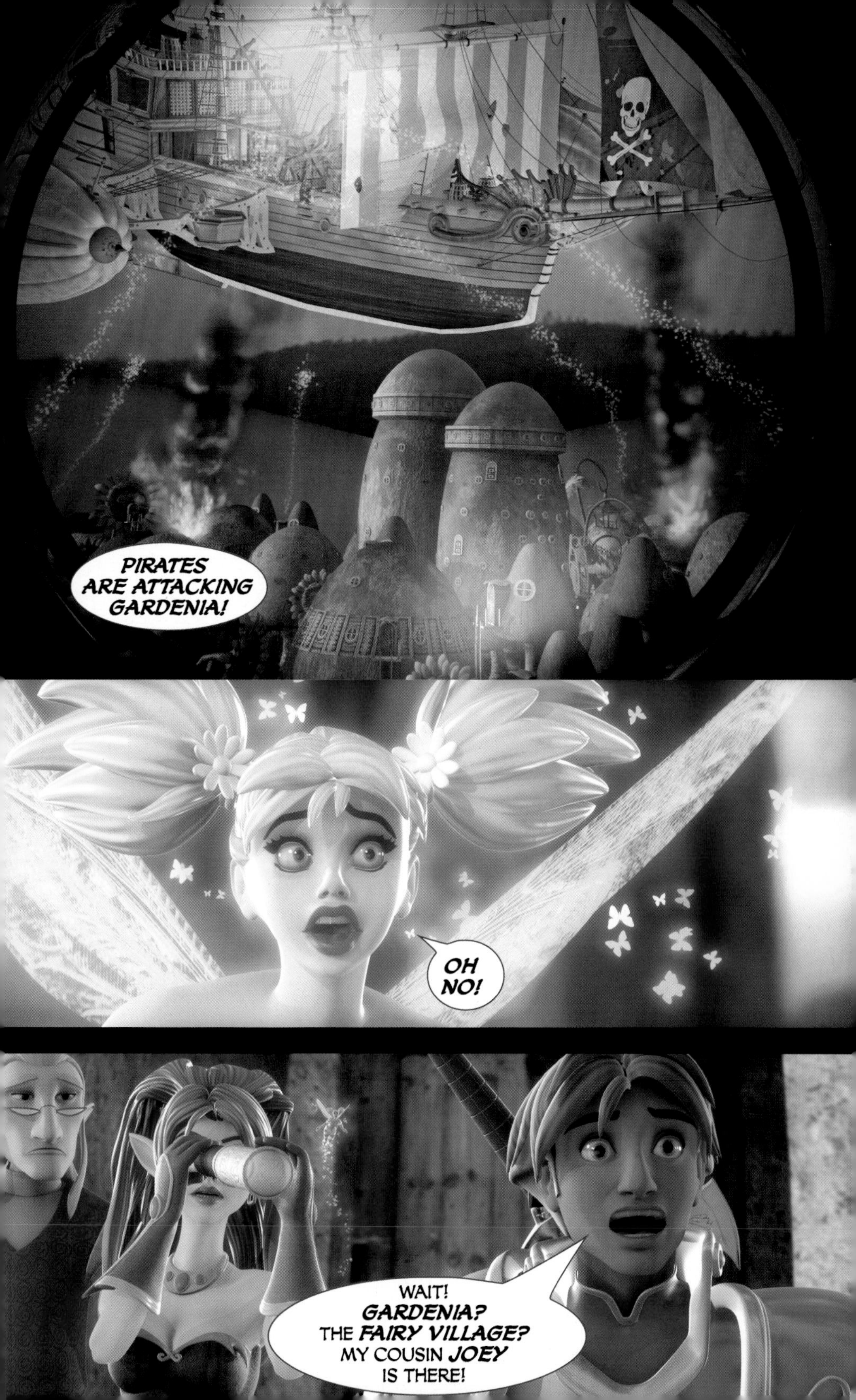
PIRATES ARE ATTACKING GARDENIA!
OH NO!
WAIT! GARDENIA? THE FAIRY VILLAGE? MY COUSIN JOEY IS THERE!

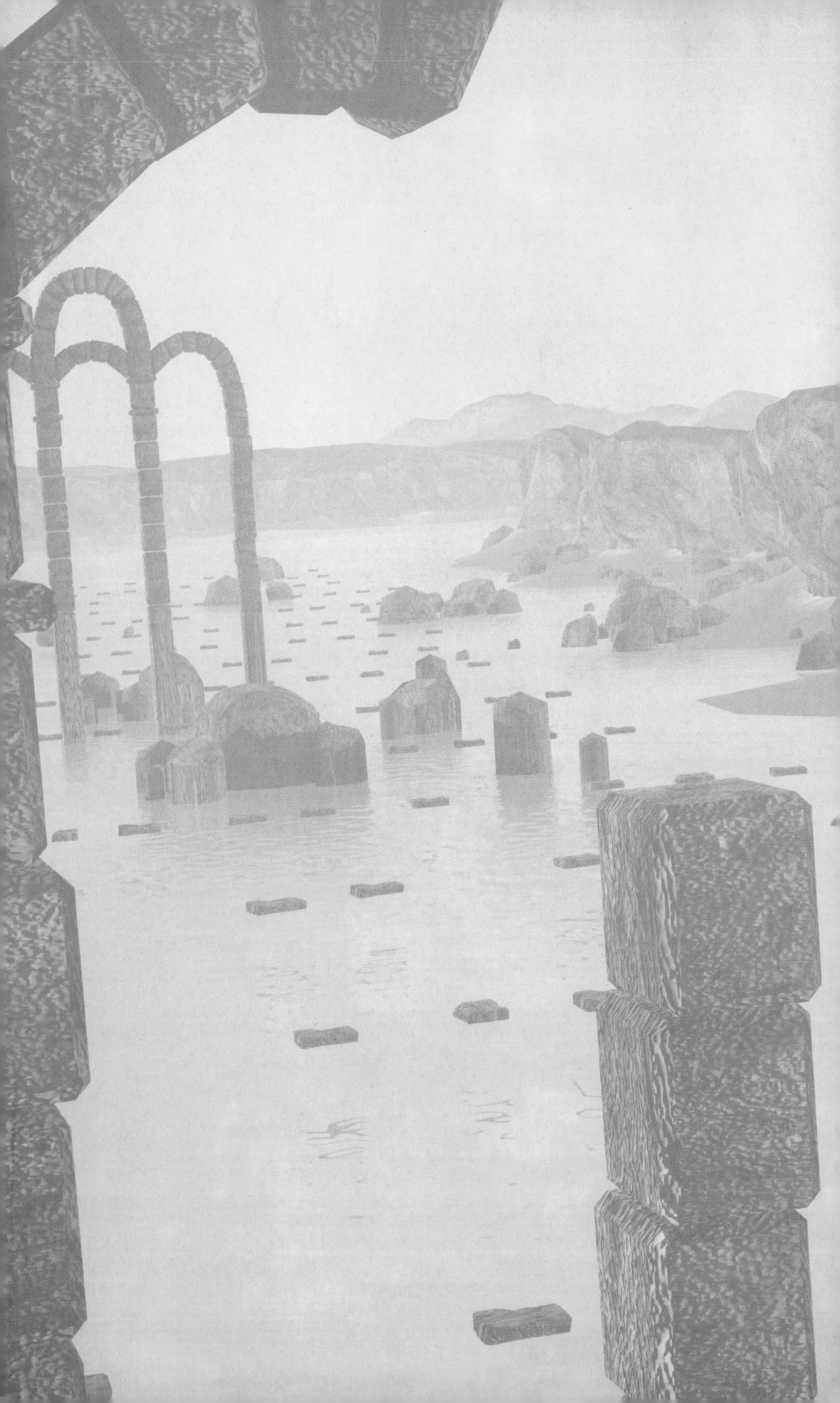

Bringing Dreamland To Life

THANK YOU FOR READING BOOK TWO OF THE DREAMLAND CHRONICLES.

AS IN THE FIRST BOOK... I'D LIKE TO SHOW YOU A BIT OF WHAT GOES INTO THIS EPIC FANTASY STORY.

THE FOLLOWING PAGES ARE SOME MORE BEHIND THE SCENES DESIGNS AND MODELS AND SUCH THAT WERE MADE TO BRING DREAMLAND TO LIFE.

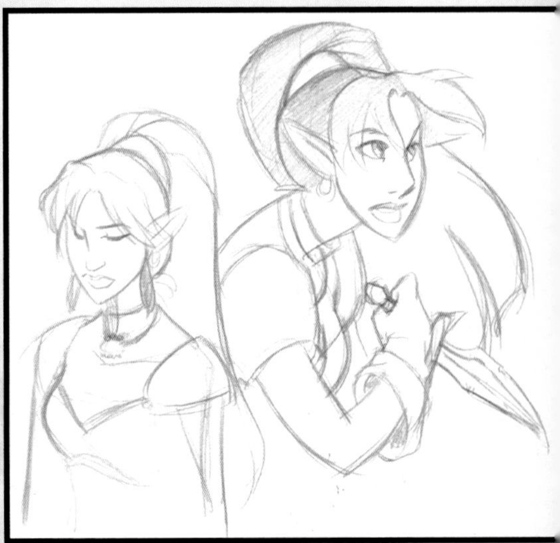

I THOUGHT WE'D START OFF WITH SOME MORE OF KAREN KRAJENBRINK'S WONDERFUL CHARACTER AND ENVIRONMENT DESIGNS.

ENJOY.

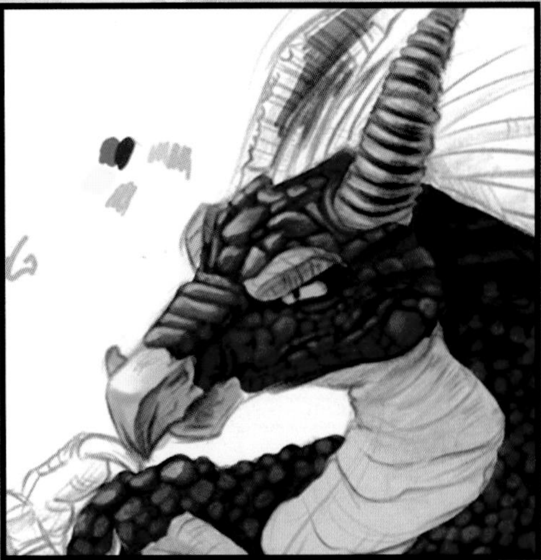

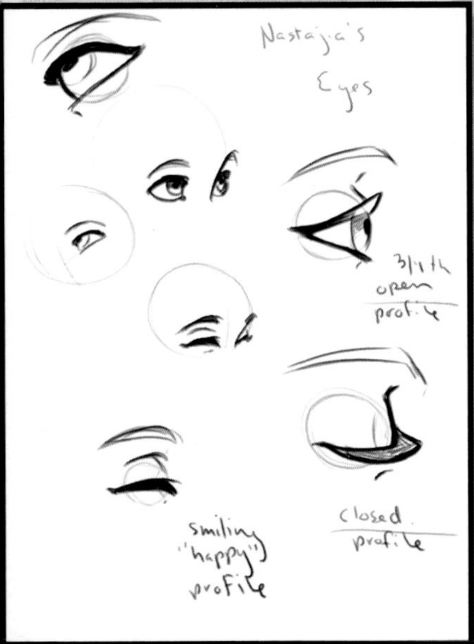
Nastajia's Eyes
3/4th open profile
smiling "happy" profile
closed profile

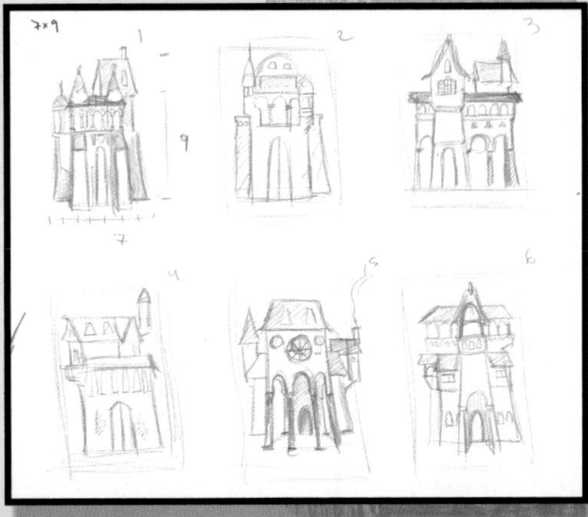

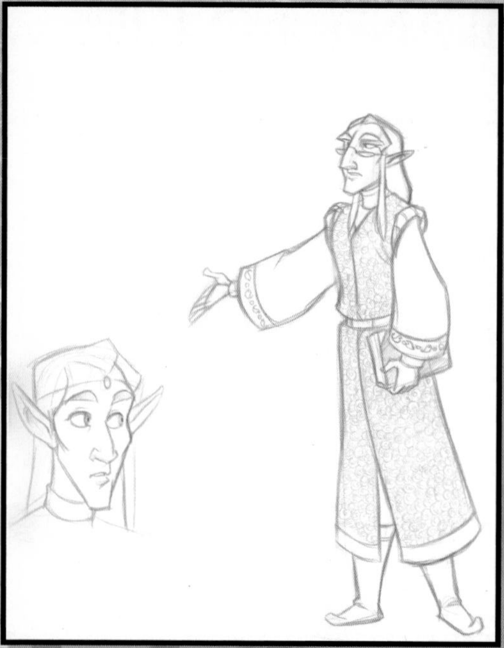

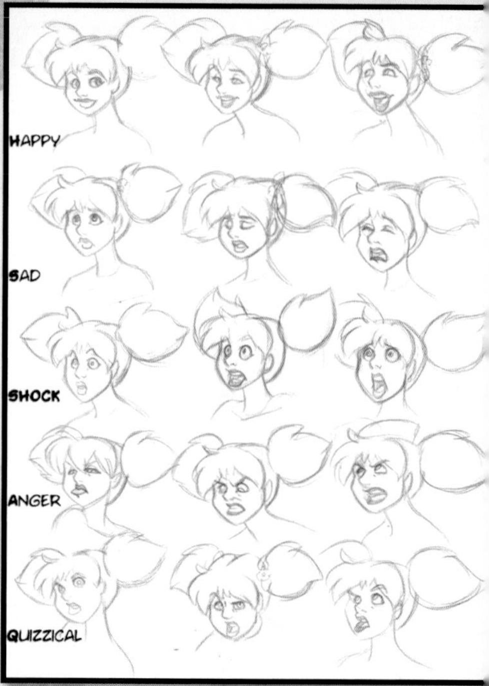
HAPPY
SAD
SHOCK
ANGER
QUIZZICAL

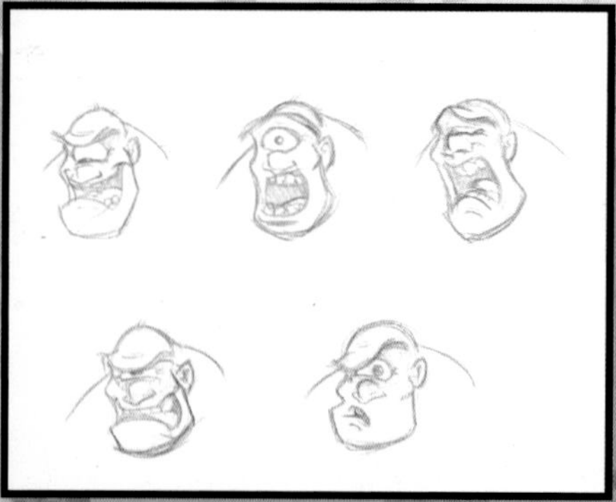

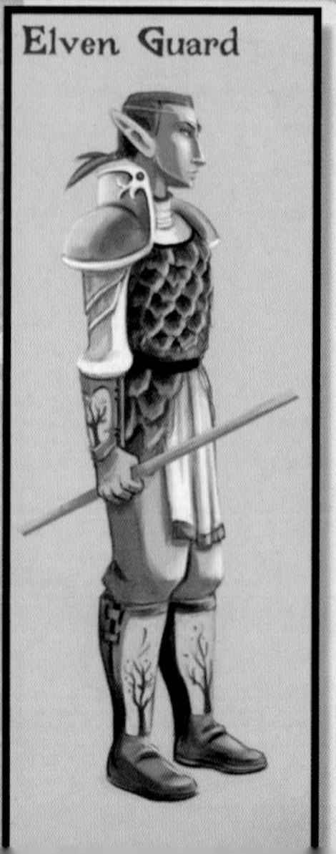
Elven Guard

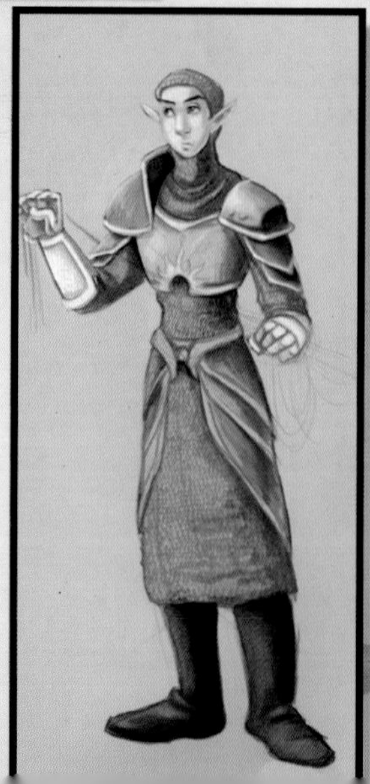

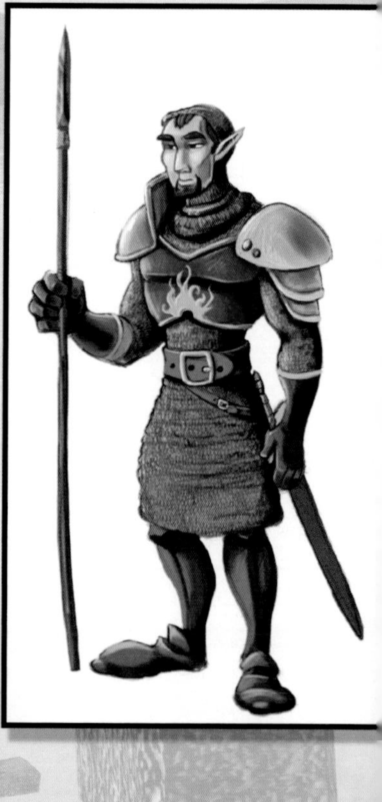

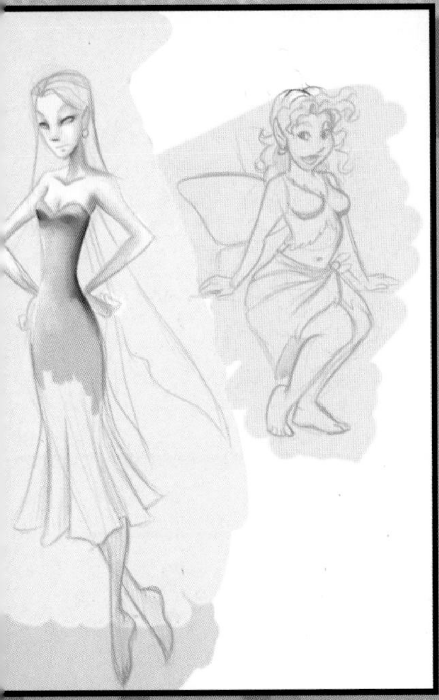

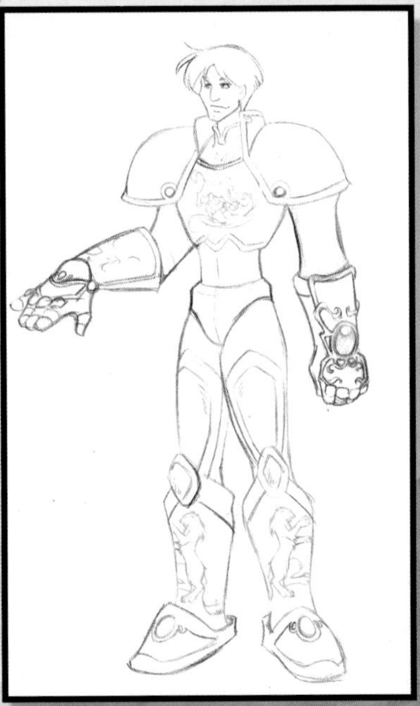

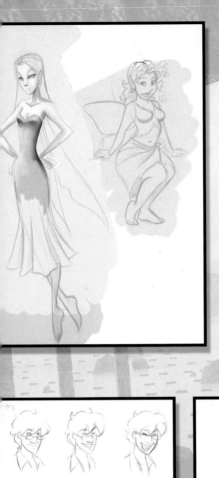

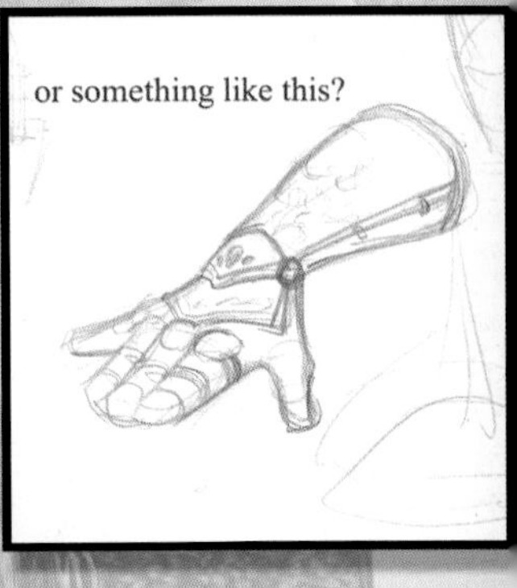
or something like this?

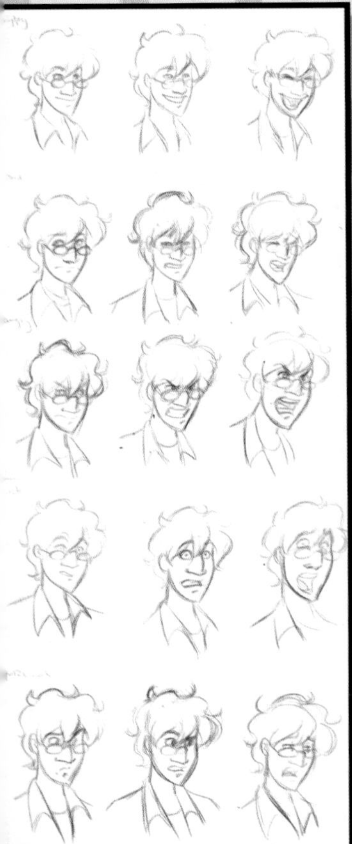

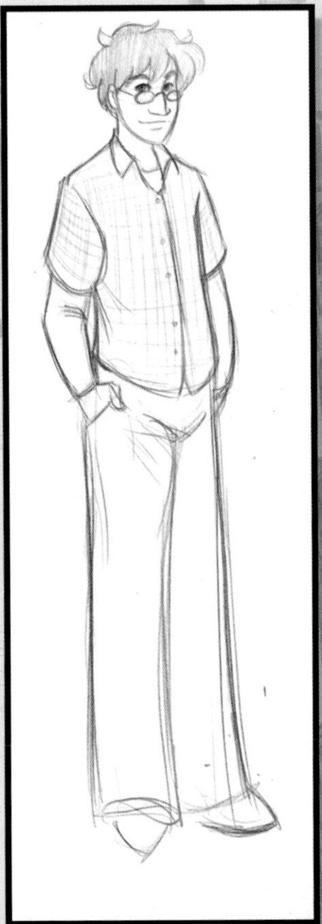

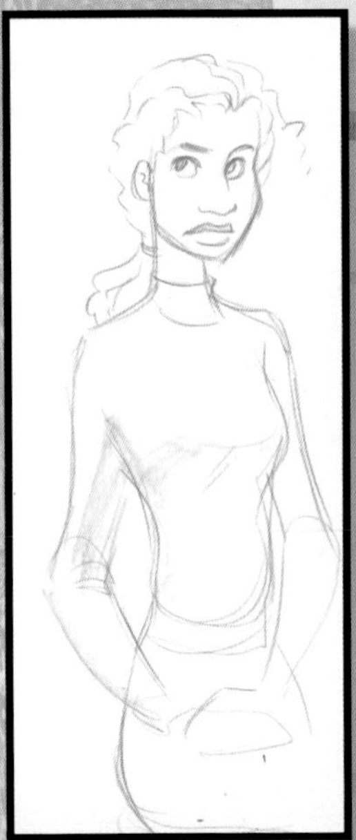

AND OF COURSE THE 3D MODELS THAT WERE SCULPTED DIGITALLY BY IVAN PEREZ.

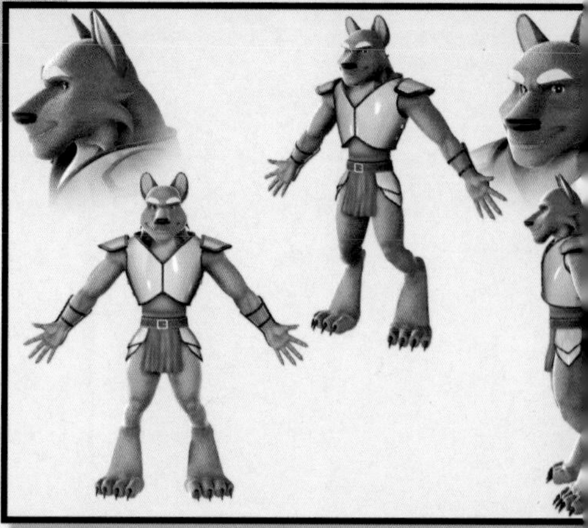

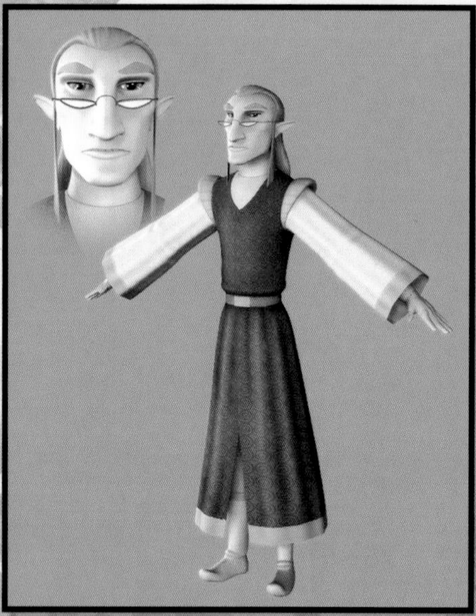

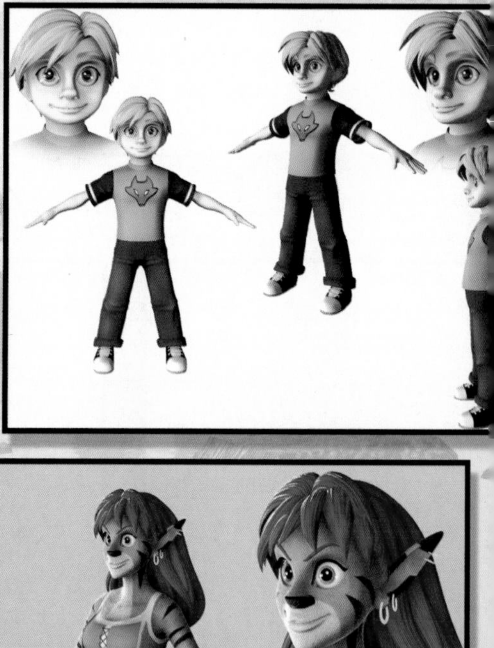

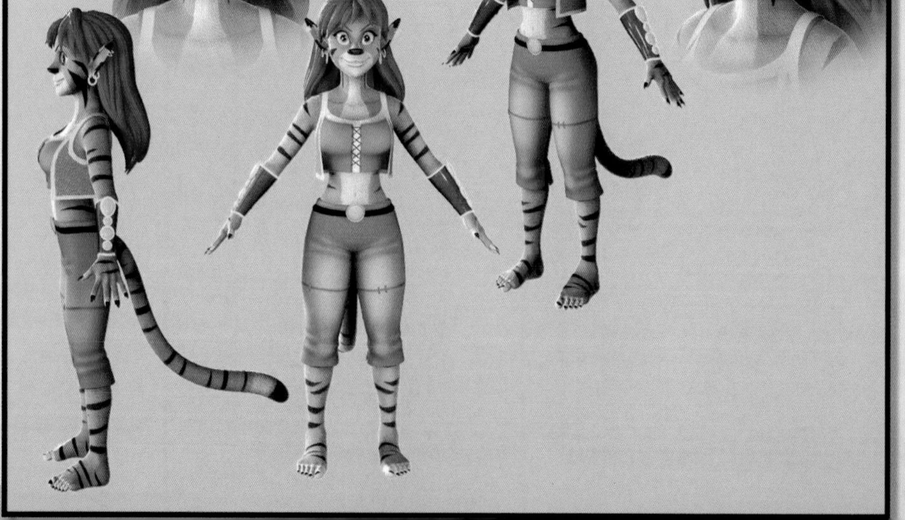

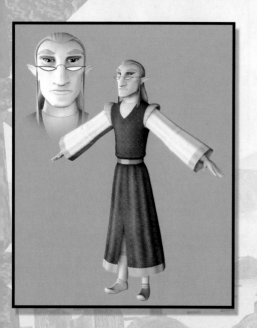

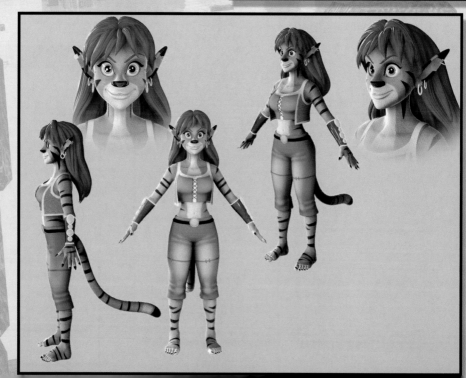

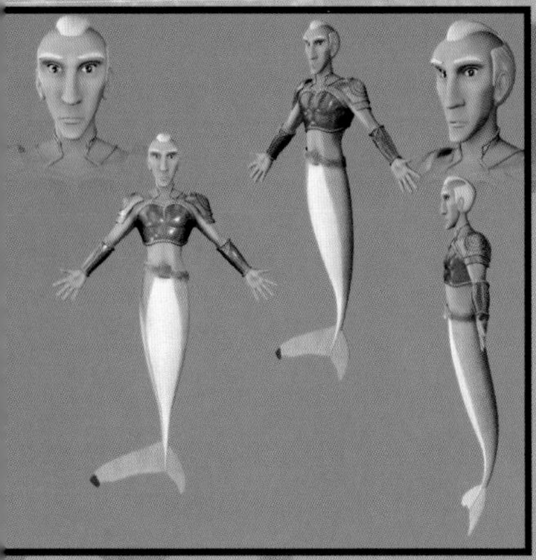
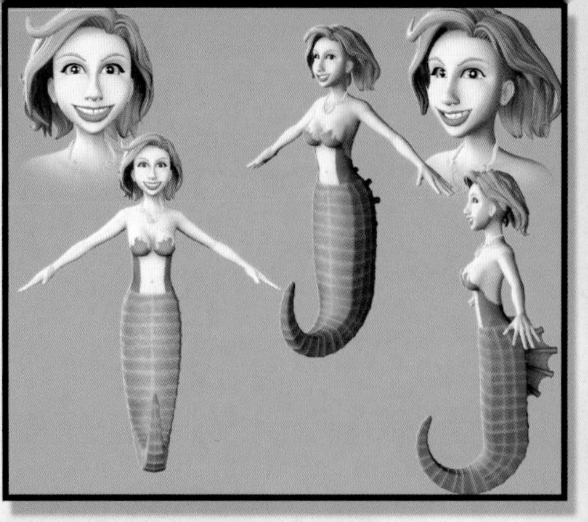
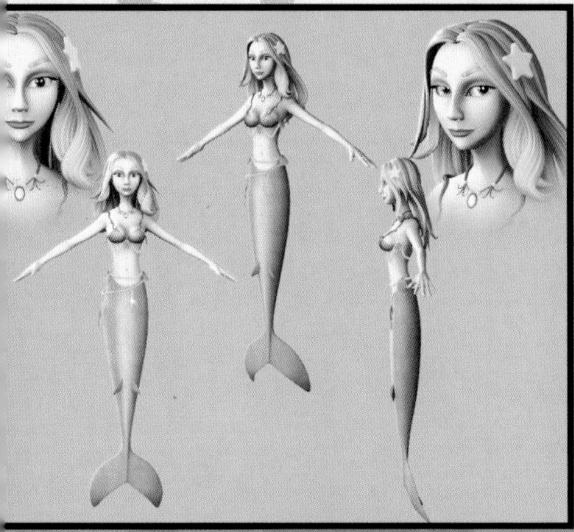
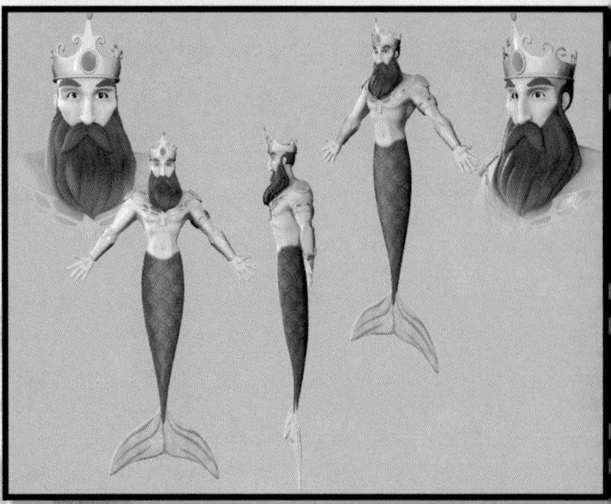
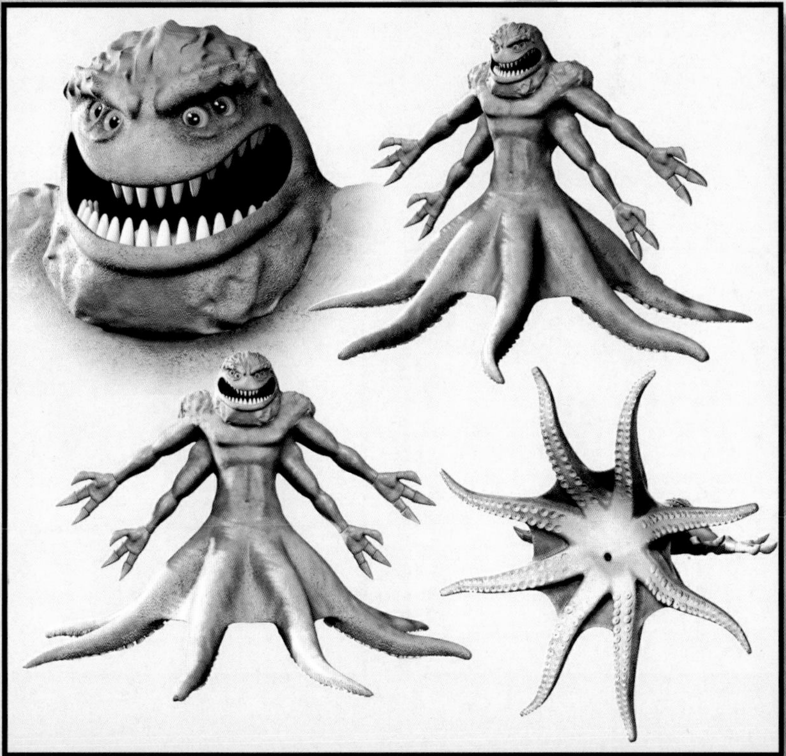

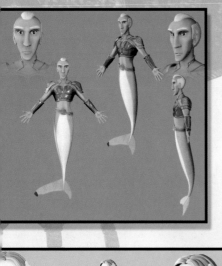

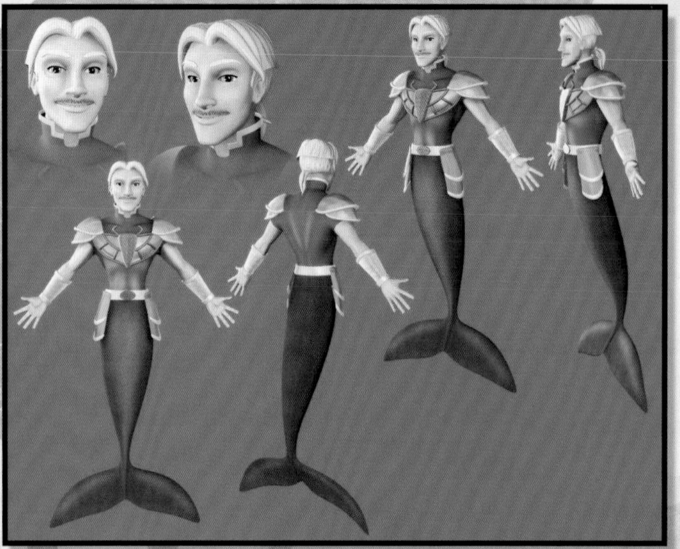
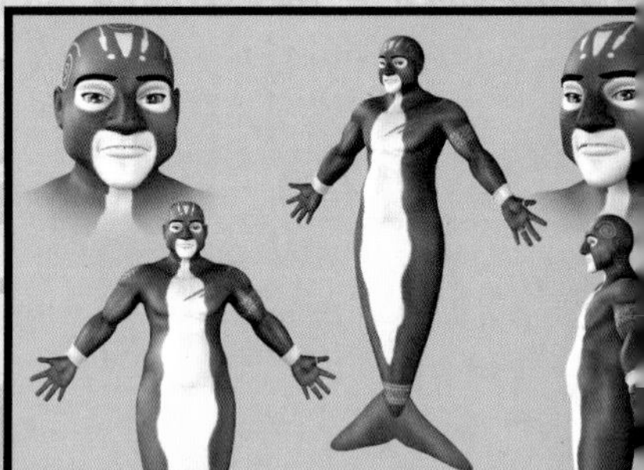
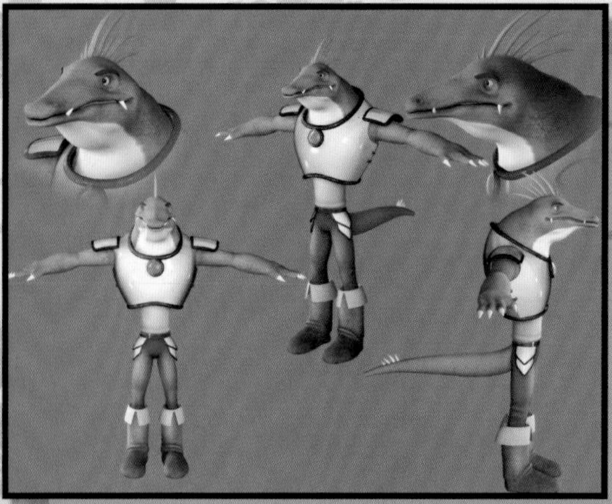
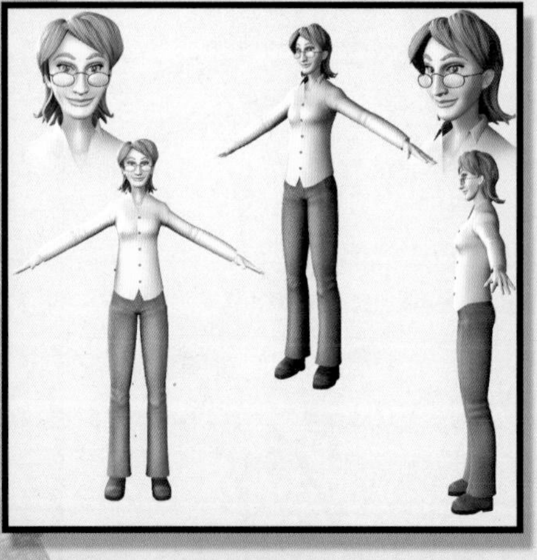
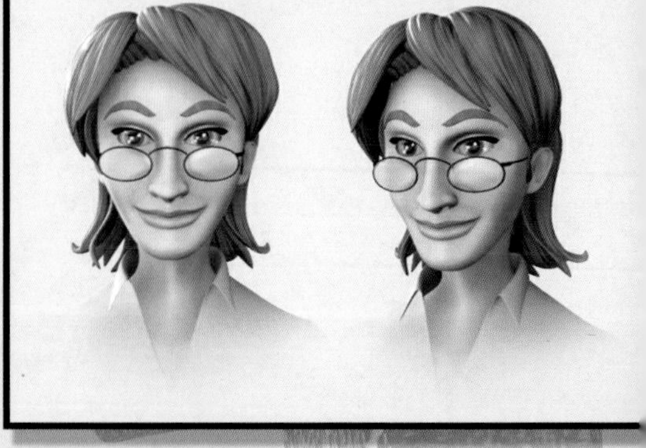

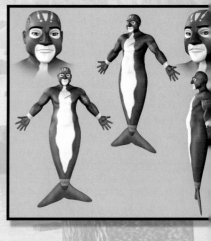

BOOK TWO SAW SOME OF THE MOST INTERESTING AND DETAILED ENVIRONMENTS TO DATE.

STEFANO TSAI AND ANTERO PEDRAS BOTH CREATED SOME INCREDIBLE SCENERY FOR THE DREAMLAND INHABITANTS TO DWELL IN.

ONCE AGAIN, STEFANO DESIGNED ALL OF THE ENVIRONMENTS AS WELL AS MODELLING WITH ANTERO.

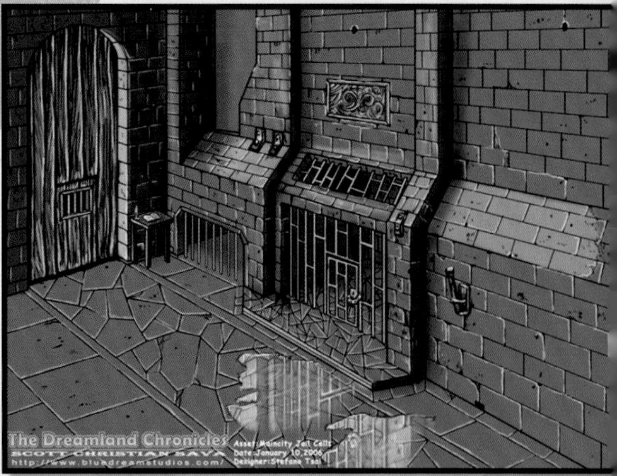

The Dreamland Chronicles
SCOTT CHRISTIAN SAVA
http://www.bluedreamstudios.com/
Asset:Maincity Jail Cells
Date:January 10,2006
Designer:Stefano Tsai

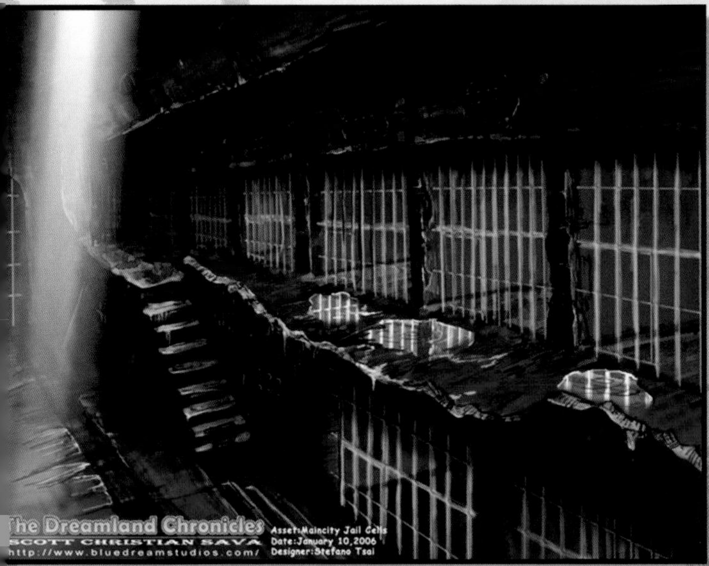

The Dreamland Chronicles
SCOTT CHRISTIAN SAVA
http://www.bluedreamstudios.com/
Asset:Maincity Jail Cells
Date:January 10,2006
Designer:Stefano Tsai

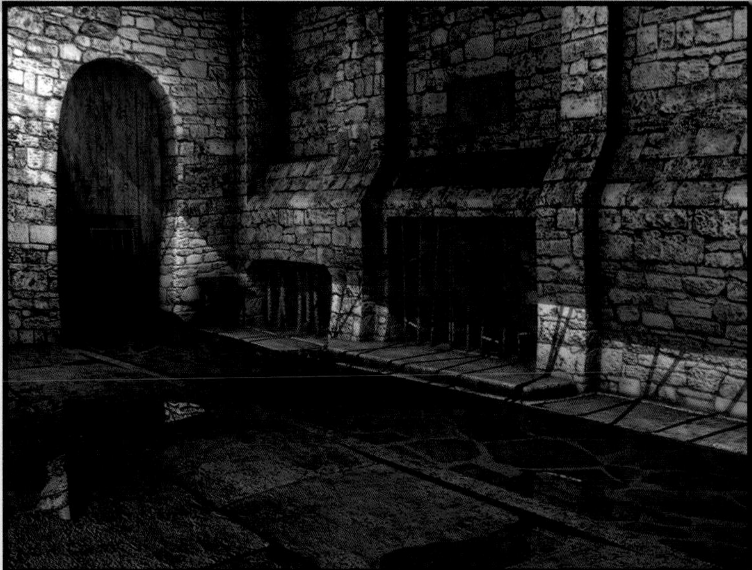

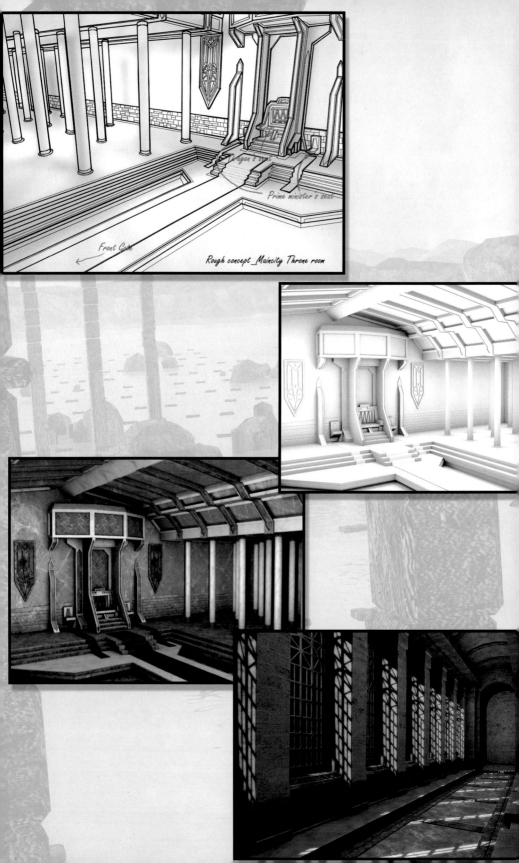

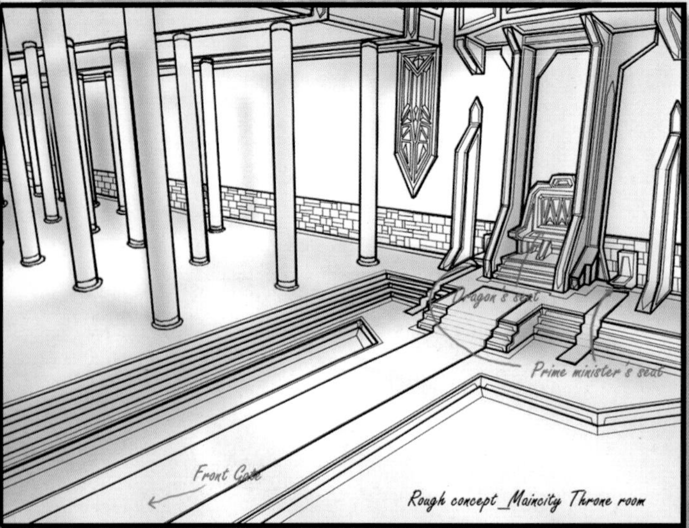
Dragon's seat
Prime minister's seat
Front Gate
Rough concept_Maincity Throne room

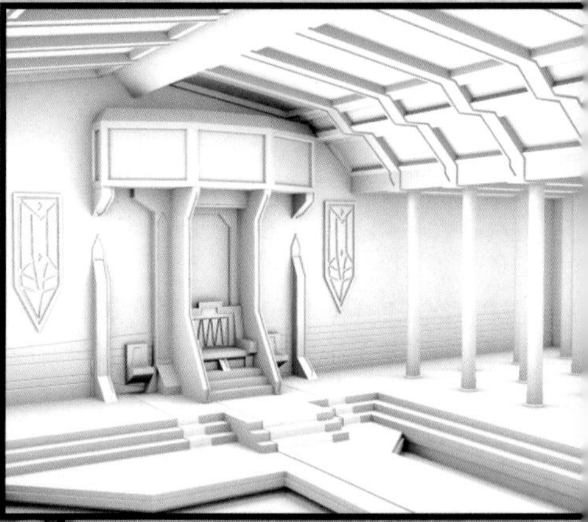

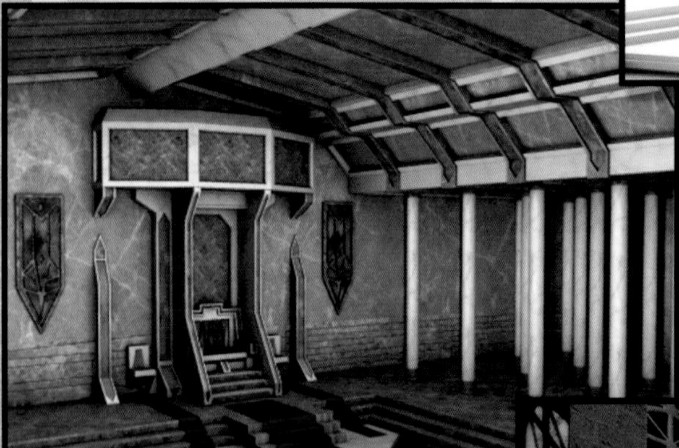

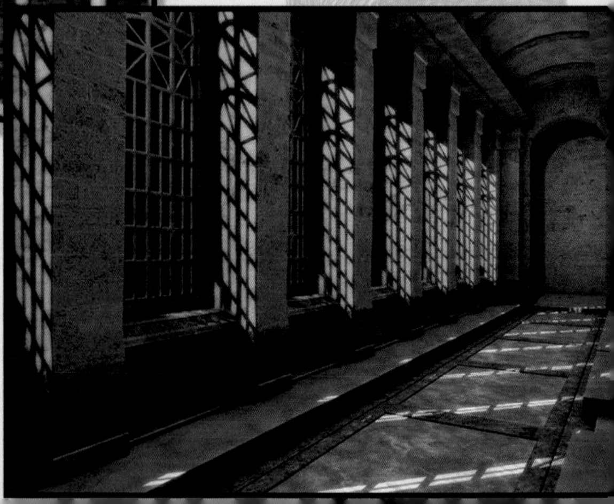

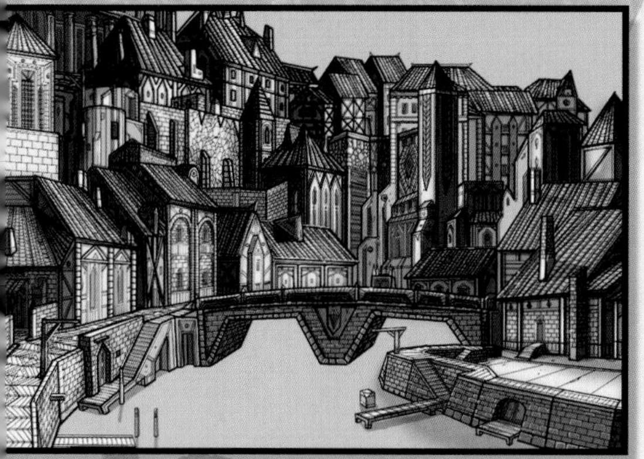

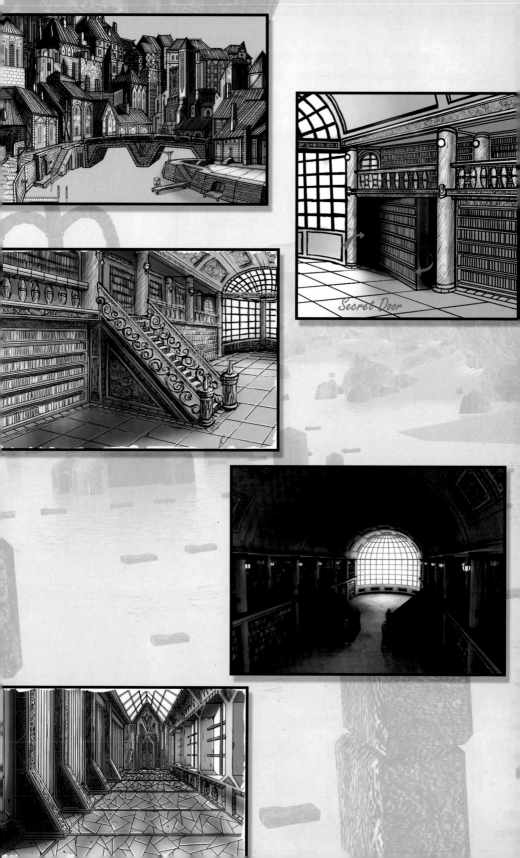

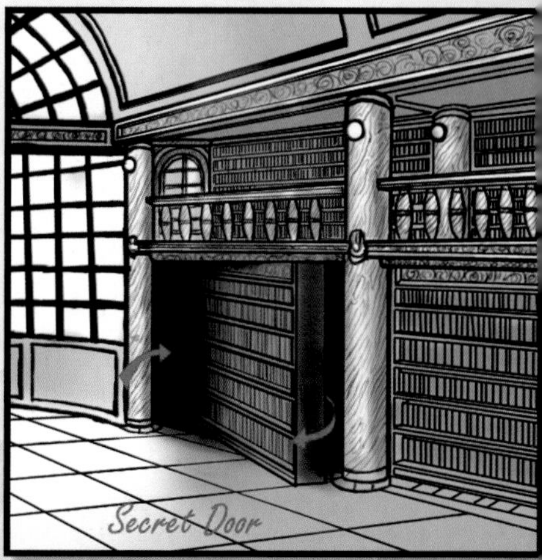
Secret Door

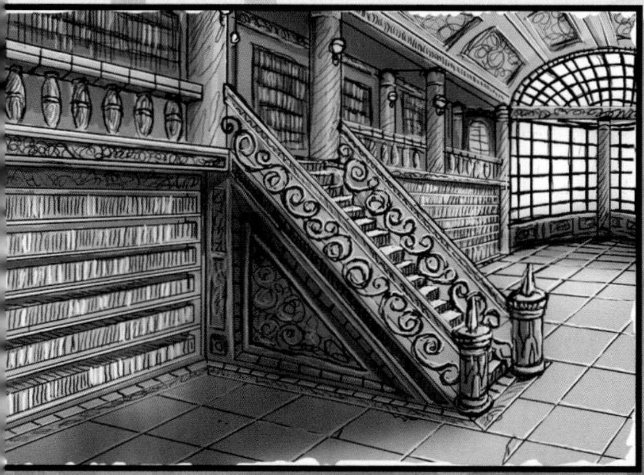

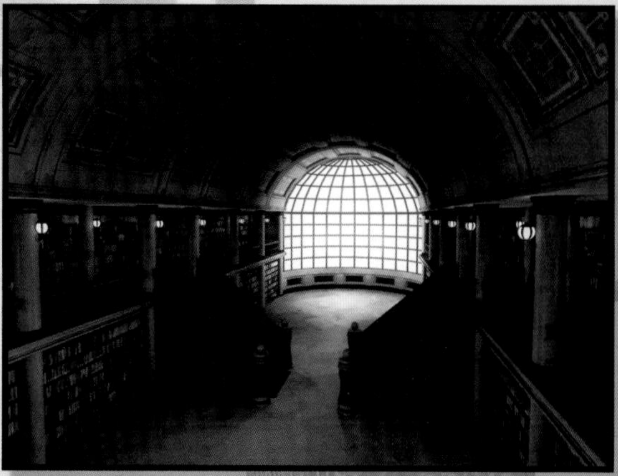

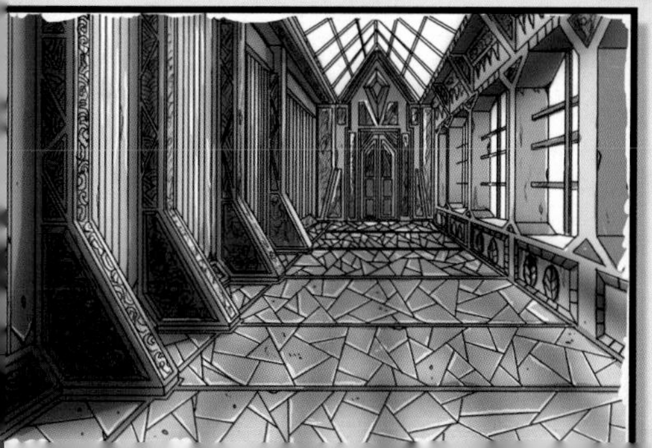

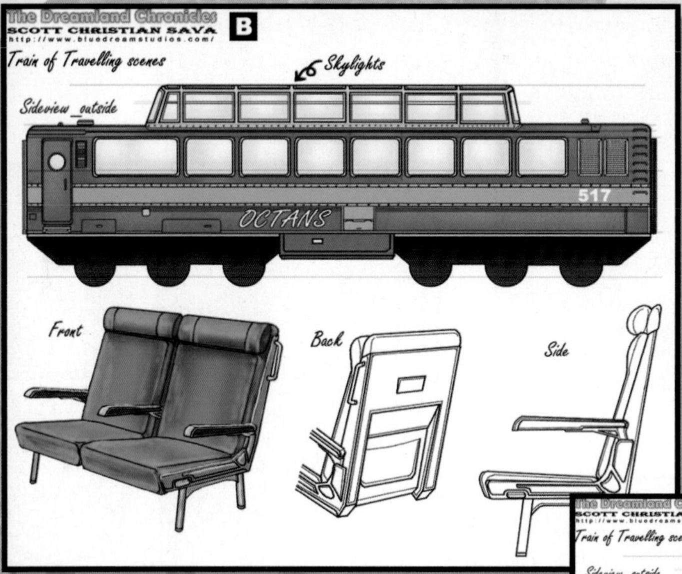
The Dreamland Chronicles
SCOTT CHRISTIAN SAVA
http://www.bluedreamstudios.com/
B
Train of Travelling scenes
Skylights
Sideview_outside
517
OCTANS
Front
Back
Side

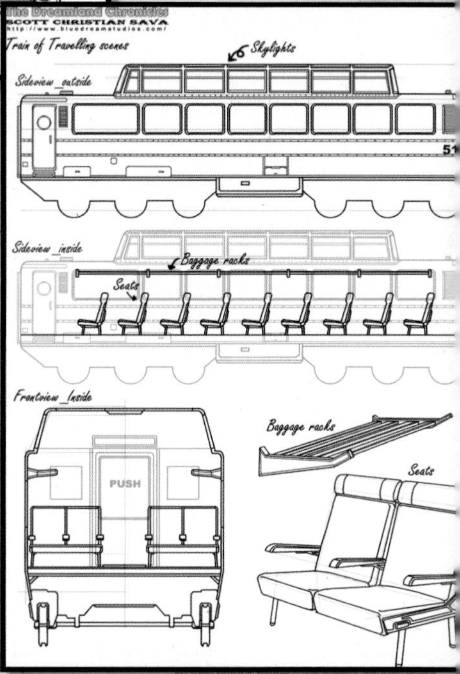
The Dreamland Chronicles
SCOTT CHRISTIAN SAVA
http://www.bluedreamstudios.com/
Train of Travelling scenes
Skylights
Sideview_outside
Sideview_inside
Baggage racks
Seats
Frontview_Inside
PUSH
Baggage racks
Seats

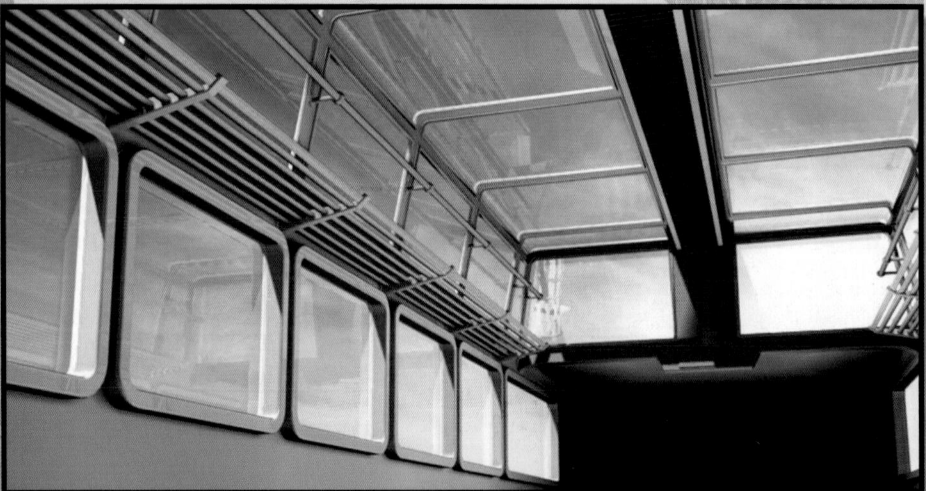

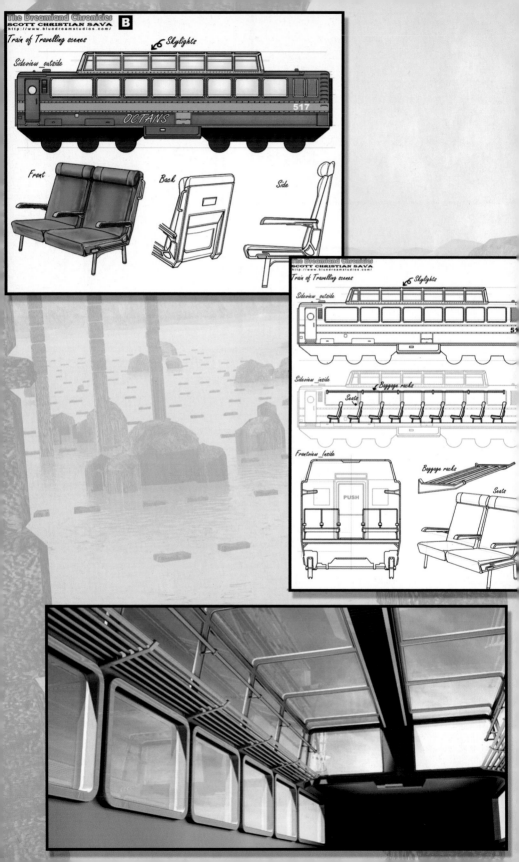

FAN ART AND SUCH

SINCE THE DREAMLAND CHRONICLES WENT ONLINE IN JANUARY OF 2006...I'VE HAD THE CHANCE TO MEET SO MANY NEW PEOPLE ALL OVER THE WORLD.

OVER 2,000,000 NEW READERS TO BE EXACT. WOW.

SO MANY SO THAT WE NEEDED A FORUM TO LET EVERYONE CHAT AND GOOF OFF AND SUCH.

ON THE FORUM, READERS POST FAN ART AND OTHER FUN STUFF.

THE FOLLOWING PAGES SHOW OFF SOME OF THE GREAT FAN ART FOR DREAMLAND FROM READERS AGE 6 TO 60.

THANK YOU FOR ALL OF THE GREAT FAN ART.

:♥? Thanks for your support! -Britt

BY BRITTANY FUERST

BY BRIANNE ROTTSPINE

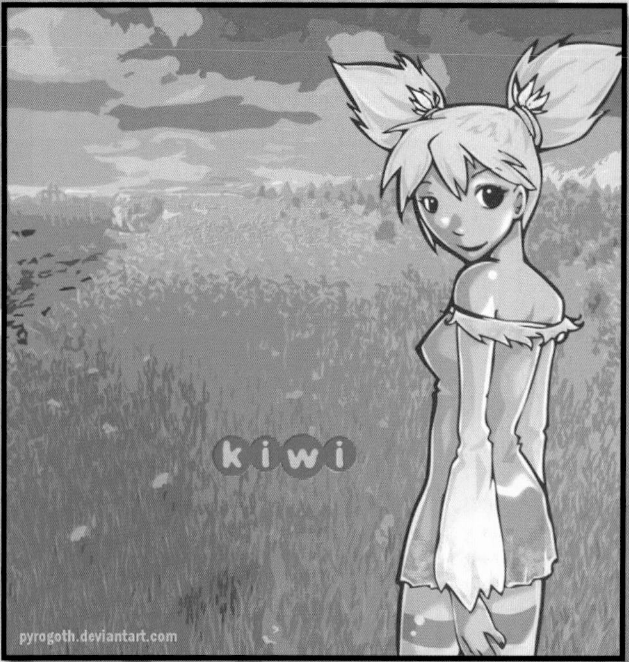
kiwi
pyrogoth.deviantart.com

BY
KIMBERLY
CHAN

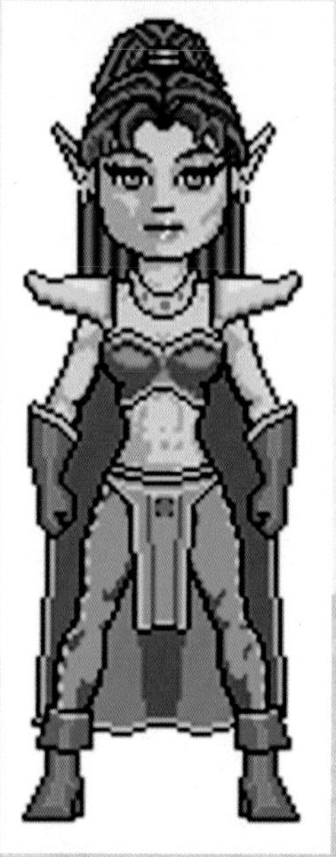

BY
ELLIOT KANE

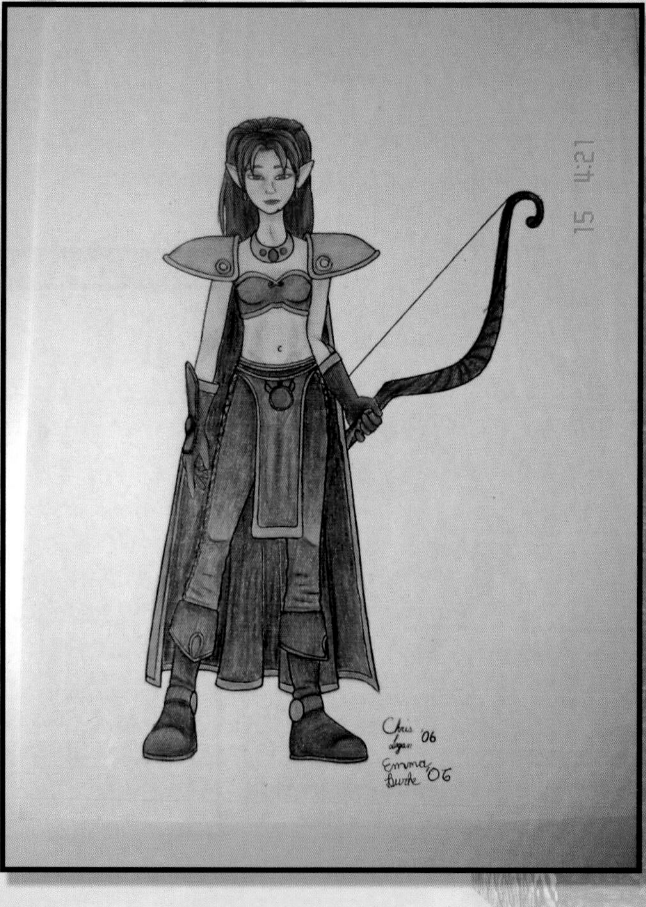
15 4:21

LINEART
CHRIS LOGAN
COLORS
EMMA THE FIRST

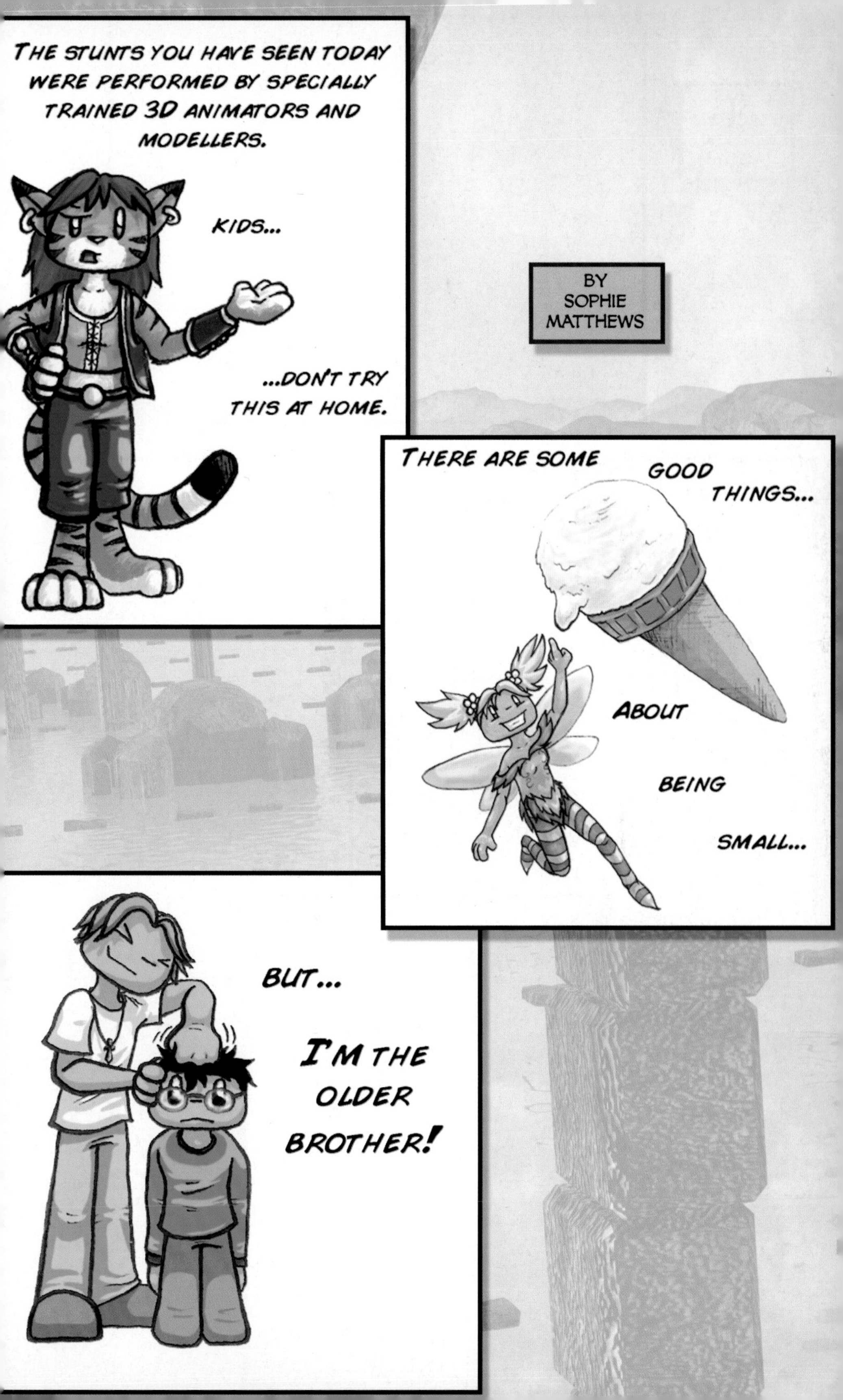
THE STUNTS YOU HAVE SEEN TODAY WERE PERFORMED BY SPECIALLY TRAINED 3D ANIMATORS AND MODELLERS.
KIDS...
...DON'T TRY THIS AT HOME.
BY SOPHIE MATTHEWS
THERE ARE SOME GOOD THINGS...
ABOUT BEING SMALL...
BUT...
I'M THE OLDER BROTHER!

BY GRACELYN DOTSON (AGE 6)

BY EMMA THE FIRST

Paddington
Humblehattem
the Third
from The Dreamland Chronicles
4/23/07   © Salt Croatian Sava

Kiwi
from The Dreamland Chronic

NASTASIA ASCHENHEART
29   4/23/07   ©2008 Sava

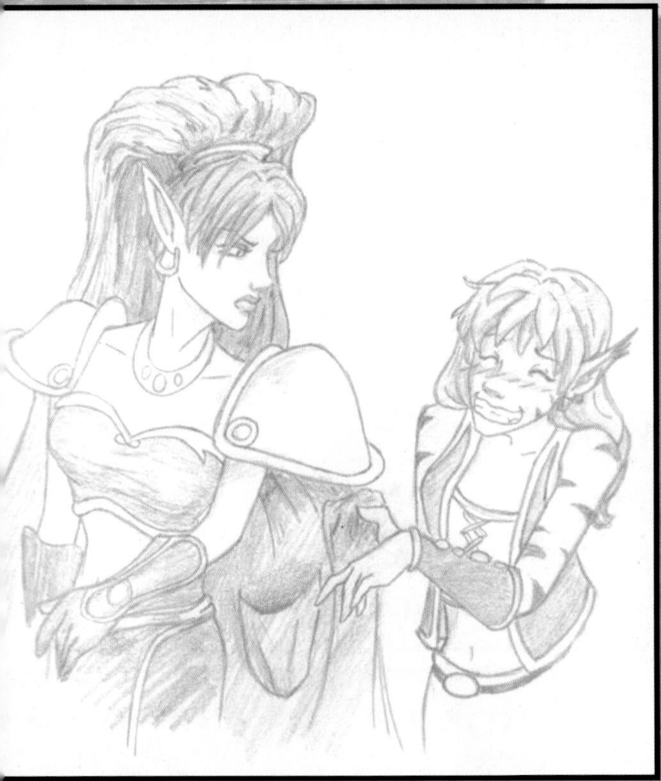

BY
ANGELA
CHRISTY

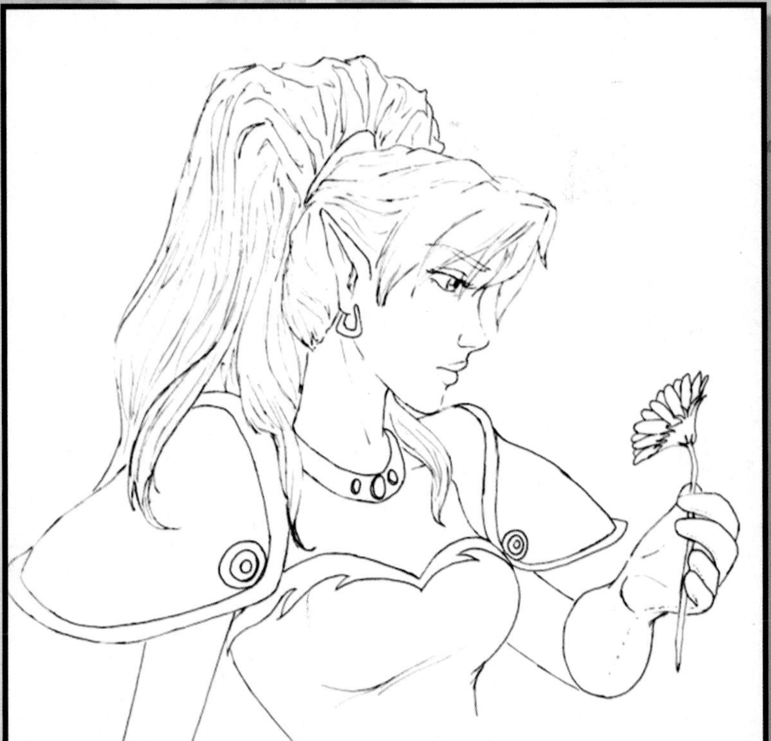

A RUNNING GAG ON THE FORUM HAS BEEN THE "PRINCESS BRIDE" GAG THAT STARTED WHEN NICODEMUS UTTERED THAT INFAMOUS WORD..."INCONCIEVABLE".

SOON...LINES FROM THE MOVIE WERE INSERTED BY FANS DAILY. THEY WERE JUST SO FUNNY...WE HAD TO TRY AND COLLECT SOME OF THEM.

SO FOR THOSE OF YOU WHO'VE SEEN THE PRINCESS BRIDE...ENJOY.

FOR THOSE OF YOU WHO HAVEN'T...GO WATCH IT!

INCONCIEVABLE!

HELLO. MY NAME IS NASTAJIA ASHENHEART. YOU KIDNAPPED MY PARENTS. PREPARE TO DIE.

AS YOU WISH.

VERY WELL. LET US BE OFF TO ASTORIA. PLEASE TAKE CARE OF MY PEOPLE ARVAMAS.

HAVE FUN STORMING THE CASTLE!

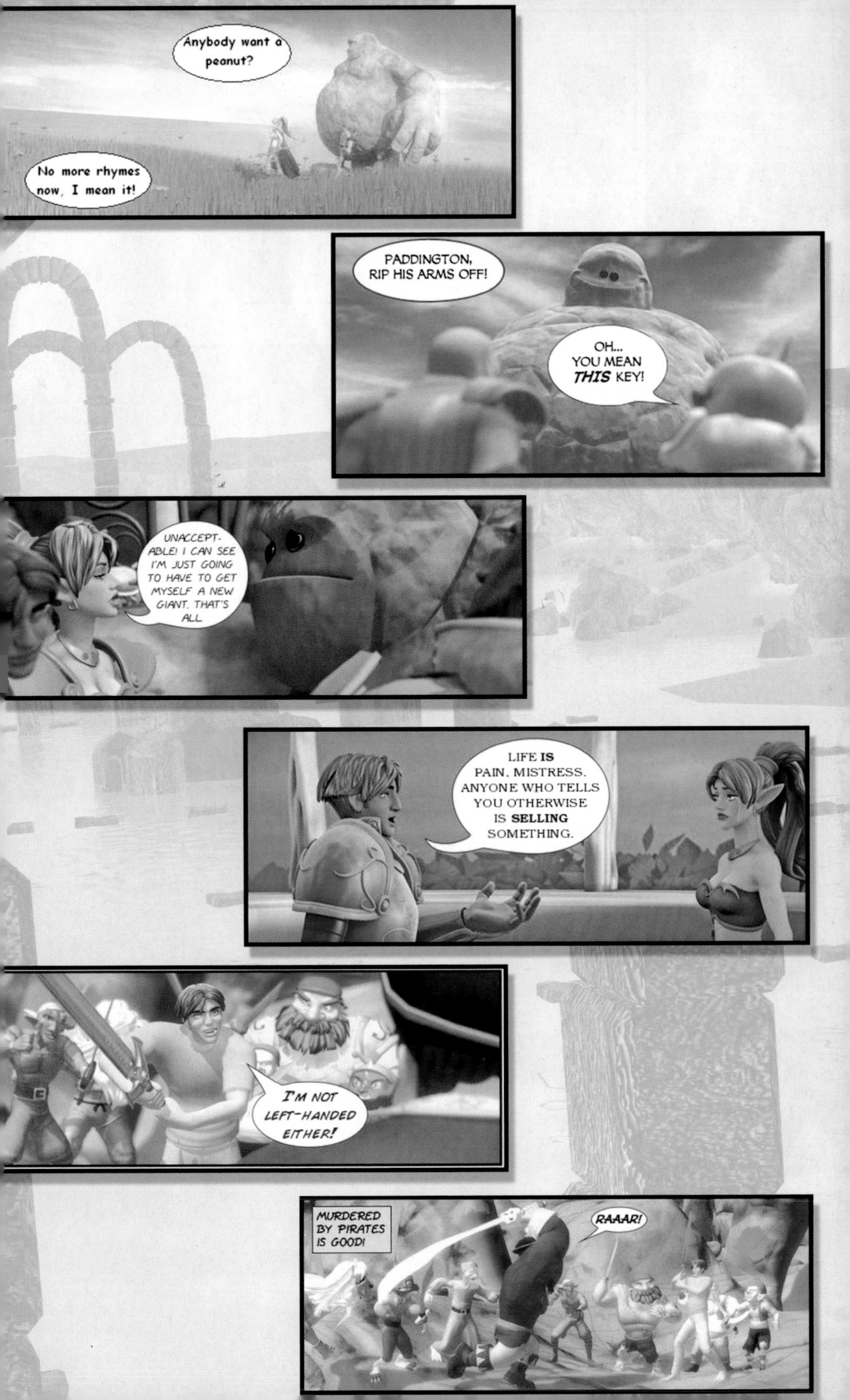
Anybody want a peanut?
No more rhymes now, I mean it!
PADDINGTON, RIP HIS ARMS OFF!
OH... YOU MEAN THIS KEY!
UNACCEPT-ABLE! I CAN SEE I'M JUST GOING TO HAVE TO GET MYSELF A NEW GIANT. THAT'S ALL.
LIFE IS PAIN, MISTRESS. ANYONE WHO TELLS YOU OTHERWISE IS SELLING SOMETHING.
I'M NOT LEFT-HANDED EITHER!
MURDERED BY PIRATES IS GOOD!
RAAAR!

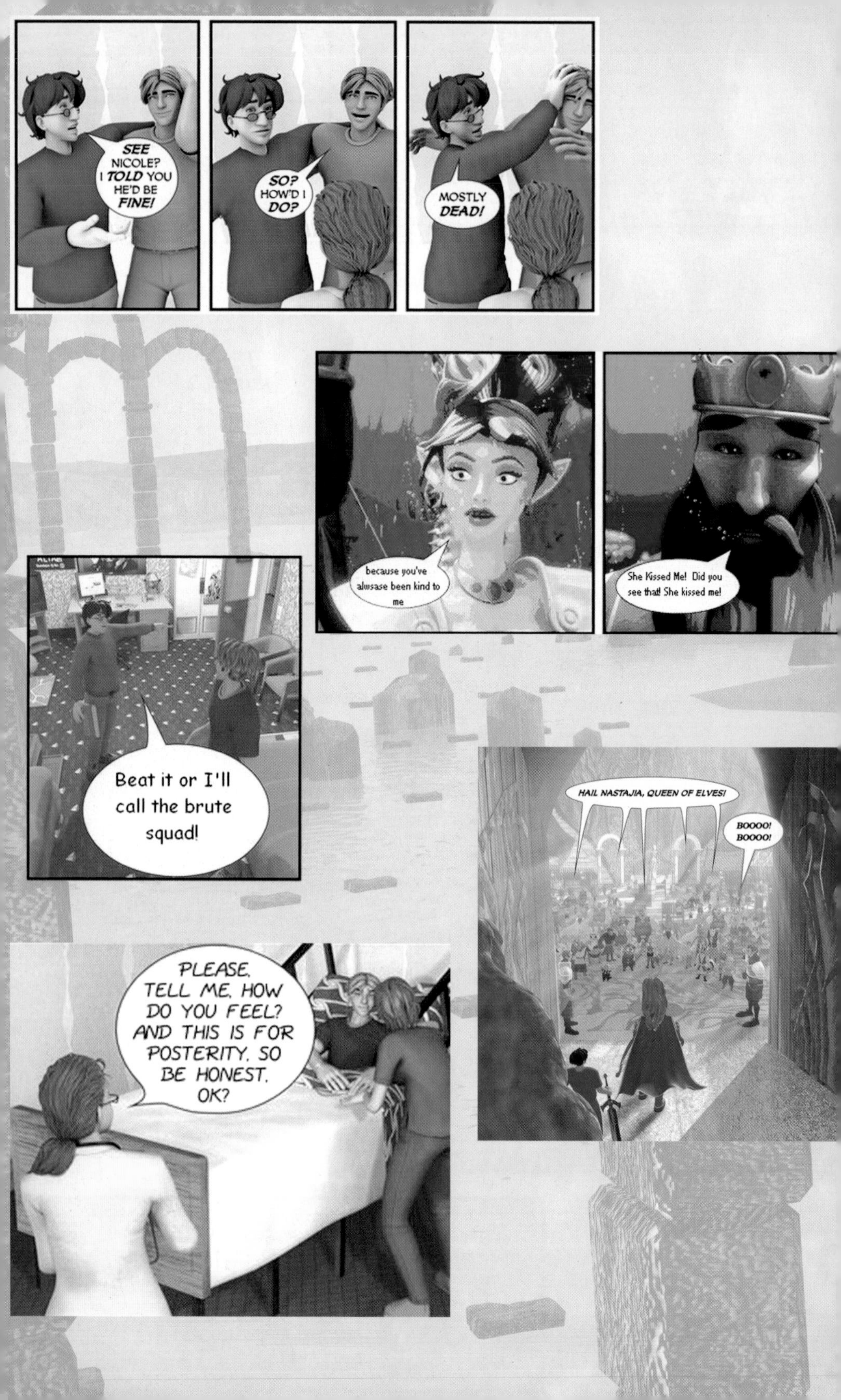
SEE NICOLE? I TOLD YOU HE'D BE FINE!
SO? HOW'D I DO?
MOSTLY DEAD!
because you've alwsase been kind to me
She Kissed Me! Did you see that! She kissed me!
Beat it or I'll call the brute squad!
HAIL NASTAJIA, QUEEN OF ELVES!
BOOOO! BOOOO!
PLEASE, TELL ME, HOW DO YOU FEEL? AND THIS IS FOR POSTERITY, SO BE HONEST, OK?

LIKE A FEATURE FILM...
THE DREAMLAND CHRONICLES
IS A TEAM EFFORT.

I HAVE BEEN VERY BLESSED
TO BE ABLE TO WORK
WITH THE MOST TALENTED
PEOPLE FROM ALL
OVER THE WORLD.

ARTISTS FROM TAIWAN,
GERMANY, RUSSIA, SPAIN,
PORTUGAL, CANADA,
AND MORE GAVE THEIR
TIME AND TALENT TO HELP
BRING DREAMLAND
TO LIFE.

CHARACTER DESIGNS:
KAREN KRAJENBRINK
ROBIN MITCHELL

CHARACTER MODELING:
IVAN PEREZ
CAN TUNCER
MARCELLO BORTOLINO
PETER STAROSTIN
ERIK ASORSON

CHARACTER RIGGING AND MORPHS:
JENN DOWNS
PETER STAROSTIN
KOBI ALONY
IVAN PEREZ
JOEL CARLSON
PETER WONG
TRUNG TRAN
JEREMY CHAPMAN
FRANK LENHARD

3D SOFTWARE:
AUTODESK'S
3D STUDIO MAX

ADDITIONAL SOFTWARE:
ADOBE PHOTOSHOP,
FRISCHLUFT'S LENSCARE,
BRAZIL RENDERER

COMIC FONTS:
RICHARD STARKINGS
AND COMICRAFT

ENVIRONMENT DESIGNS:
STEFANO TSAI
KAREN KRAJENBRINK

ENVIRONMENT MODELLING:
STEFANO TSAI
ANTERO PEDRAS

TECHNICAL AND RENDERING SUPPORT:
FRANK LENHARD
ANTERO PEDRAS

MARKETING:
BRIAN PETKASH
SPHINX GROUP

SPECIAL THANKS:
MY WIFE DONNA, MY PARENTS, MY COUSIN DR. RUSS CARAM,
AND OF COURSE THE REST OF MY FAMILY.
ADDITIONAL THANKS:
MARV WOLFMAN, JERRY BINGHAM, KEVIN GREVIOUX,
AUDRY TAYLOR, DAVID WISE, MATTHEW MARTIN,
SCOTT ZIRKEL, MIKE WIERINGO,
DEAN YEAGLE, FRANK CHO, SCOTT KURTZ, KENT SILVEIRA,
CRYSTAL YATES, SARAH ELLERTON, AND
MIKE KUNKEL.

A SPECIAL THANK YOU TO ALL OF THE READERS AROUND THE WORLD WHO'VE HELPED MAKE DREAMLAND SUCCESSFUL!

WITHOUT YOUR SUPPORT, THIS BOOK WOULDN'T BE IN YOUR HANDS RIGHT NOW.

I'VE ENJOYED MEETING ALL OF YOU AND TALKING TO YOU EVERY DAY. I LOOK FORWARD TO MANY MORE YEARS OF EXPERIENCING DREAMLAND WITH YOU ALL.

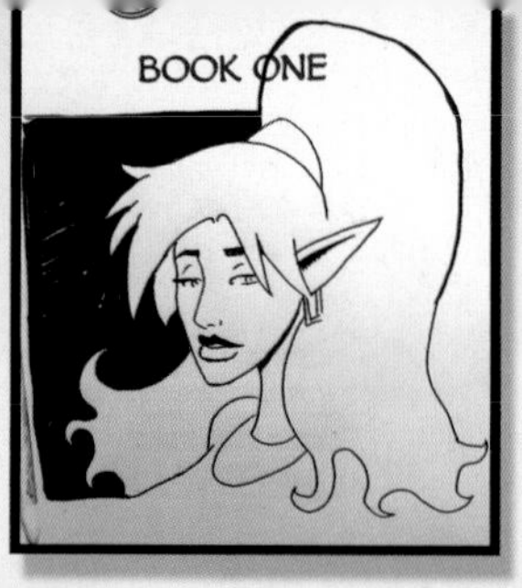
BOOK ONE

ONE OF THE FUNNEST THINGS ABOUT MAKING DREAMLAND IS MEETING ALL OF THE READERS AND DOING SKETCHES FOR THEM INSIDE THE BOOK.

HERE'S JUST SOME OF THE HUNDREDS OF SKETCHES DONE FOR READERS ALL OVER THE WORLD.

I HOPE TO GET BETTER AT IT SOON.

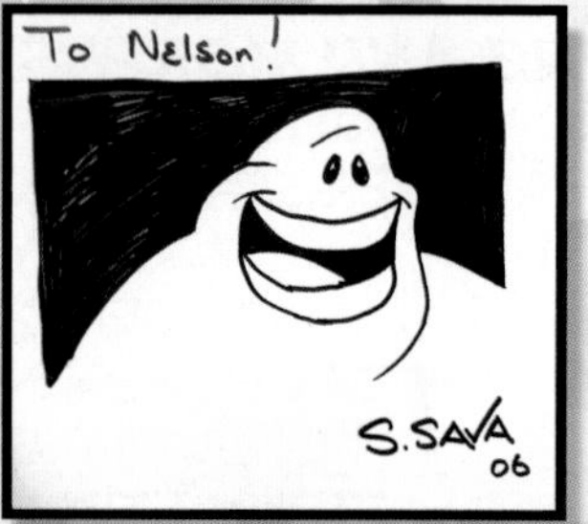
To Nelson!
S.SAVA 06

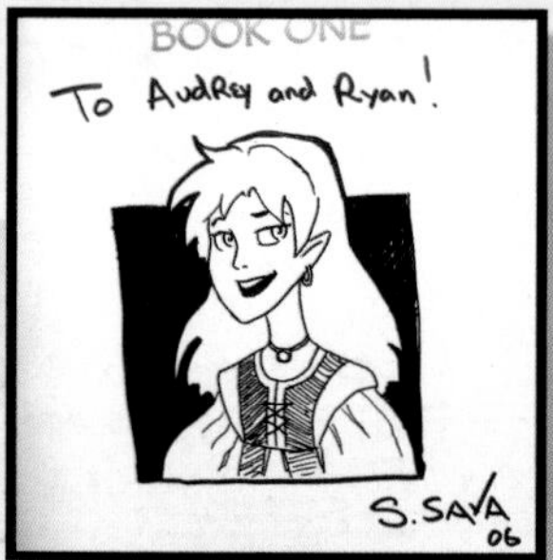
BOOK ONE
To Audrey and Ryan!
S.SAVA 06

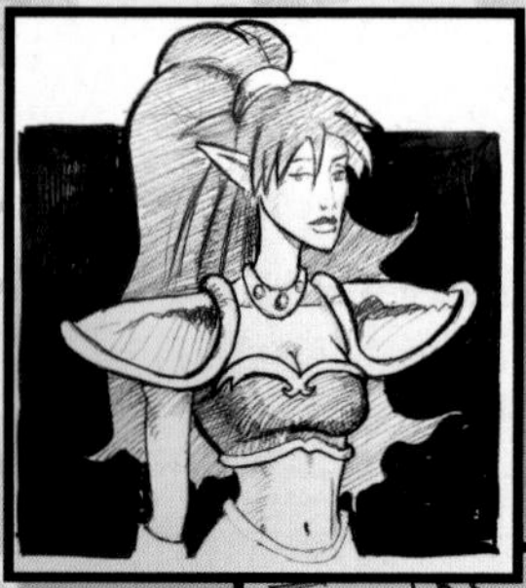

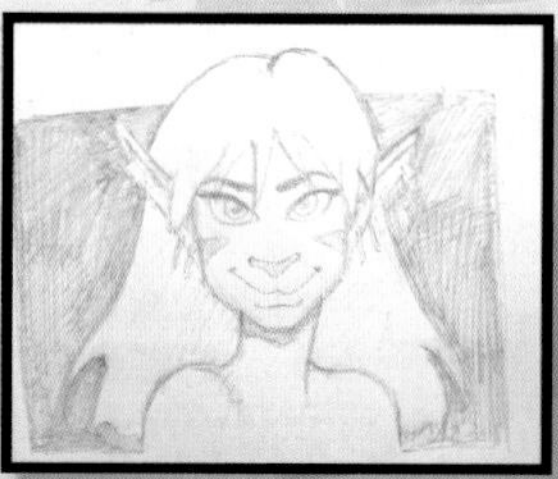

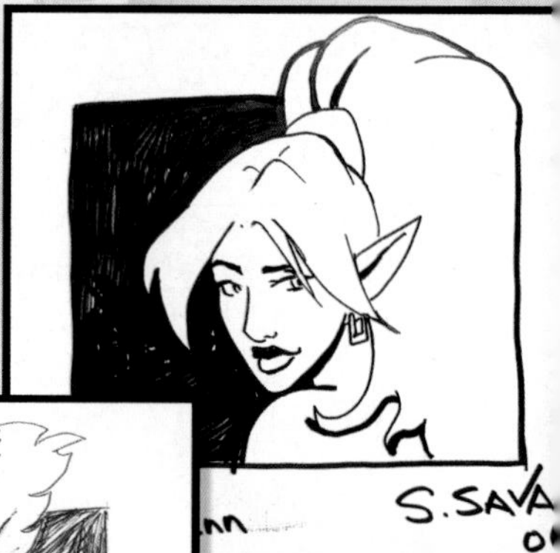
S.SAVA

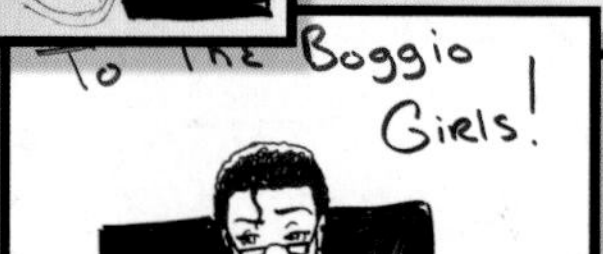
Boggio Girls!
S.SAVA 06

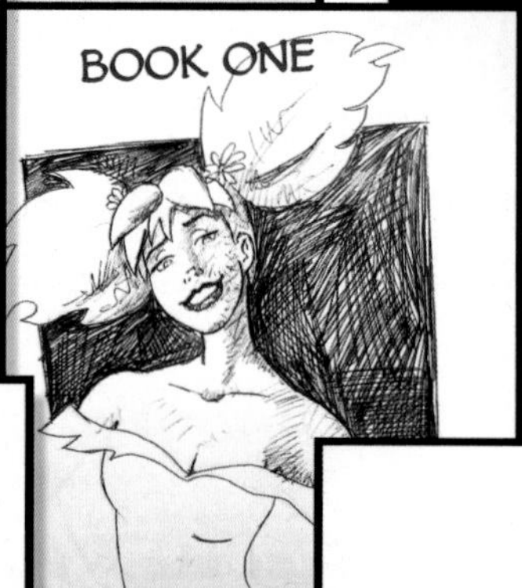
BOOK ONE

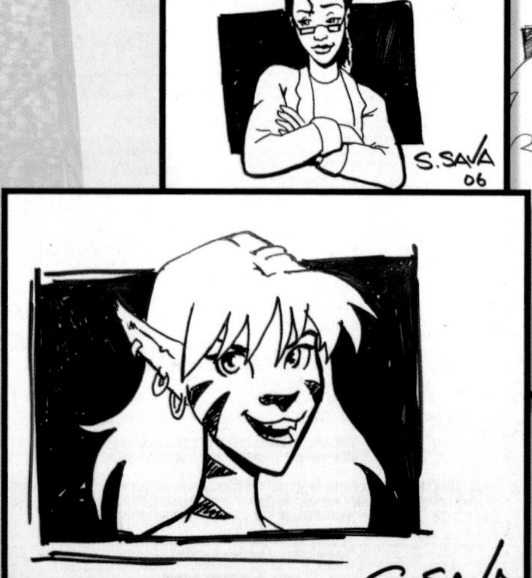
S.SAVA 06

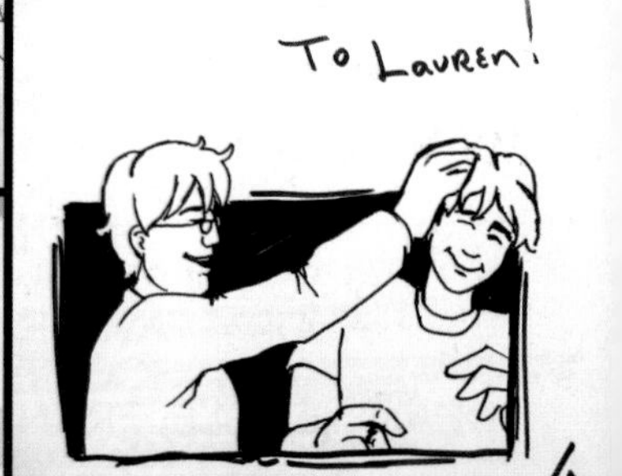
To Lauren!
S.SAVA 06

EVERY ONCE IN A WHILE I GET THE ITCH TO PAINT AGAIN.

WITH ALL THE TECHNOLOGY... IT'S SOMETIMES NICE TO SIT BACK AND PLAY WITH PAINTS.

HERE'S A COUPLE OF PORTRAITS I DID TO TAKE A BREAK FROM PLASMA SCREENS AND POLYGONS.

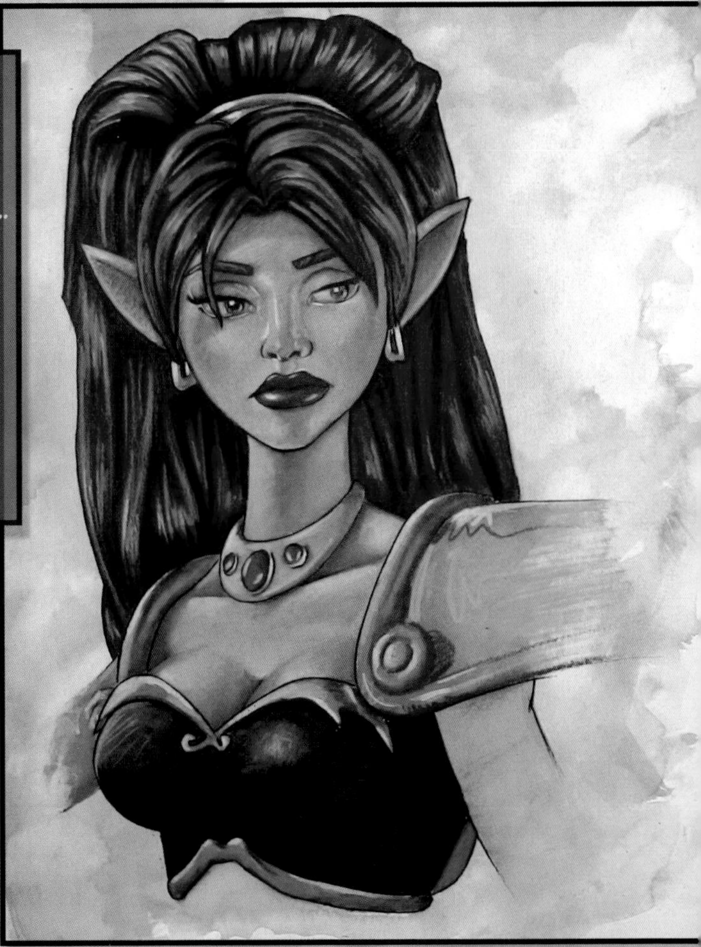

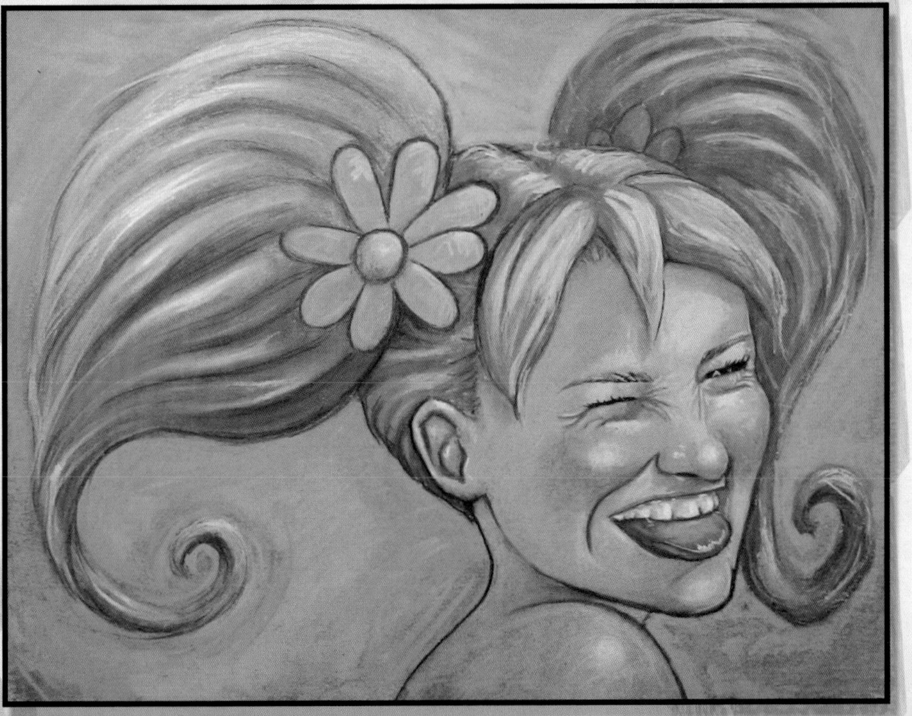

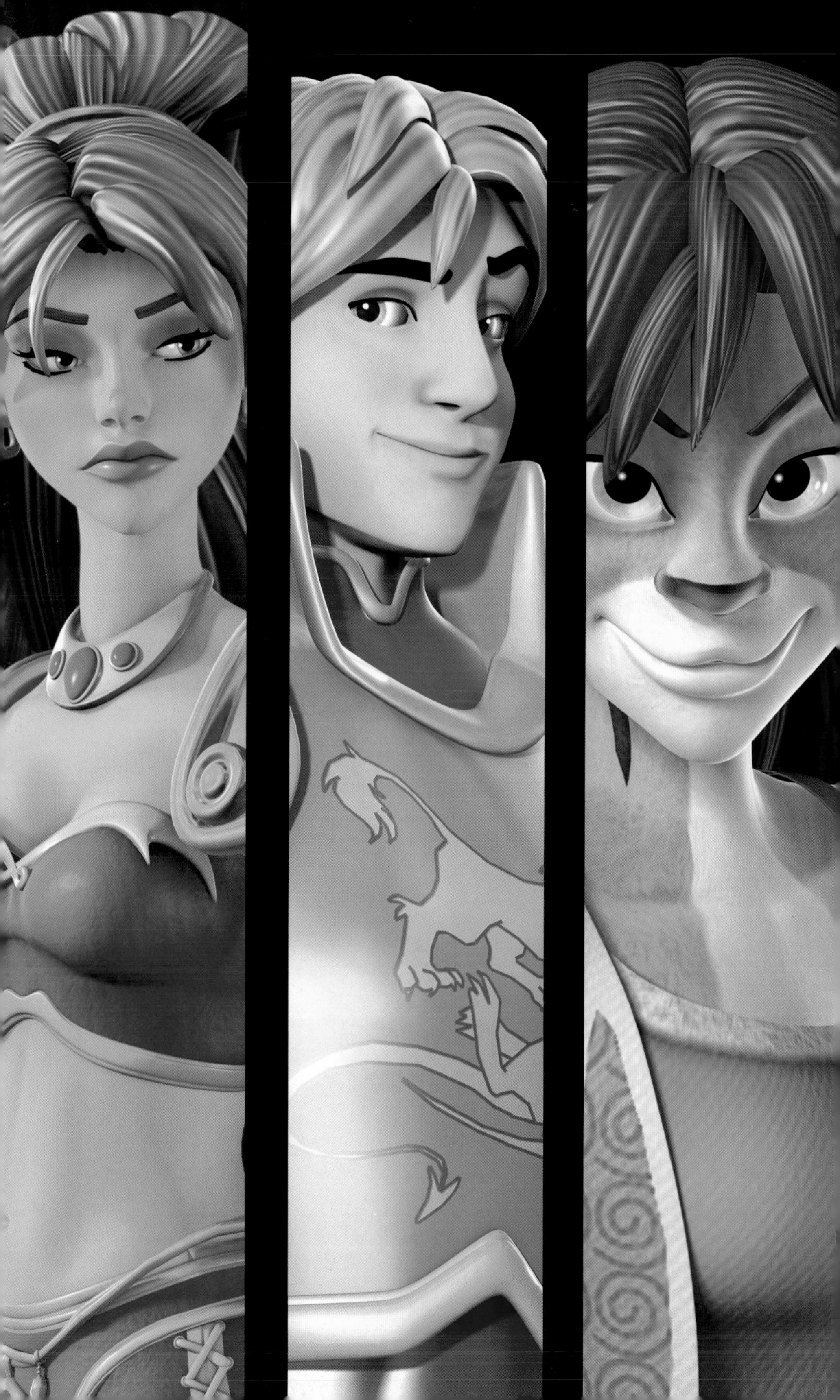

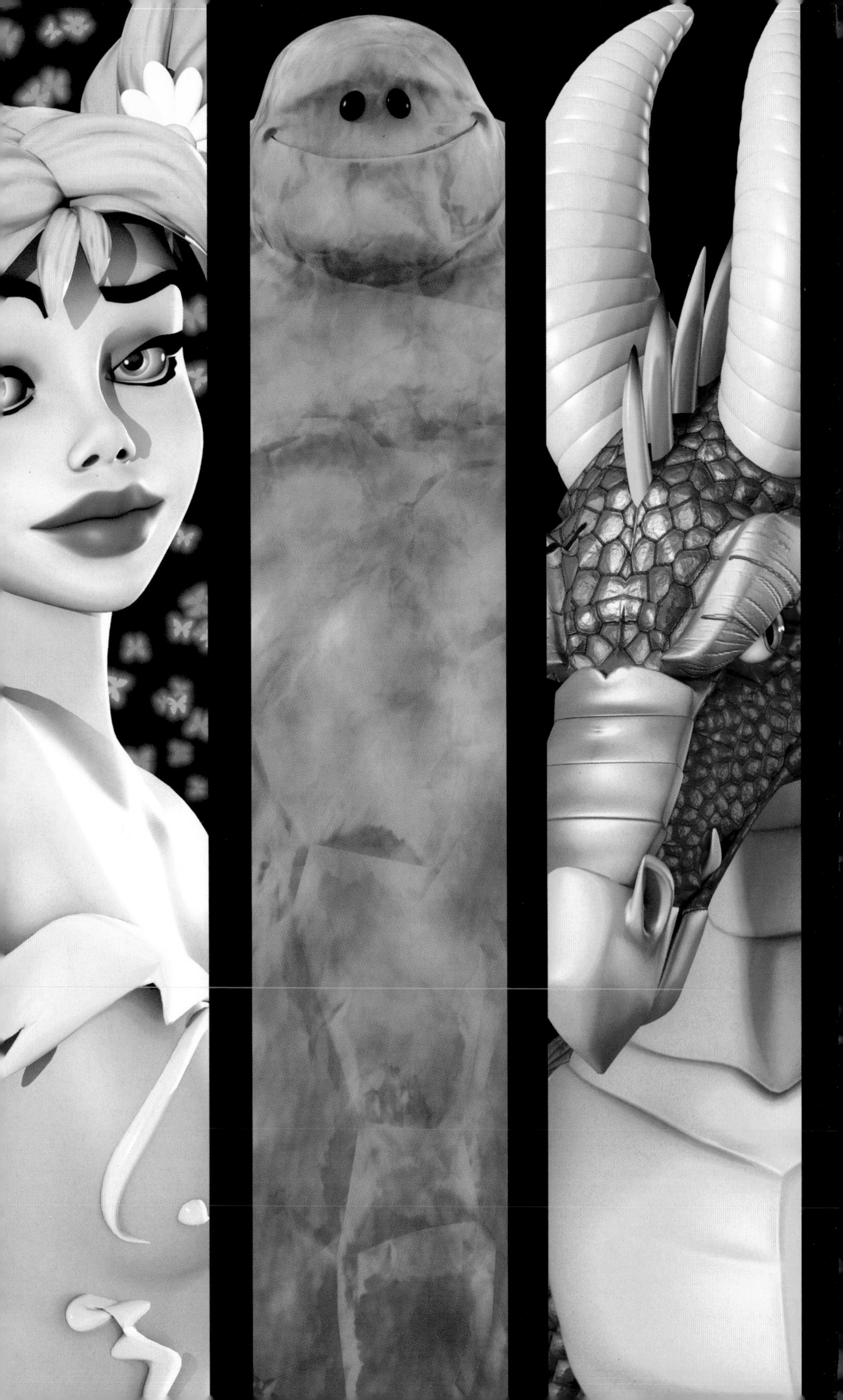

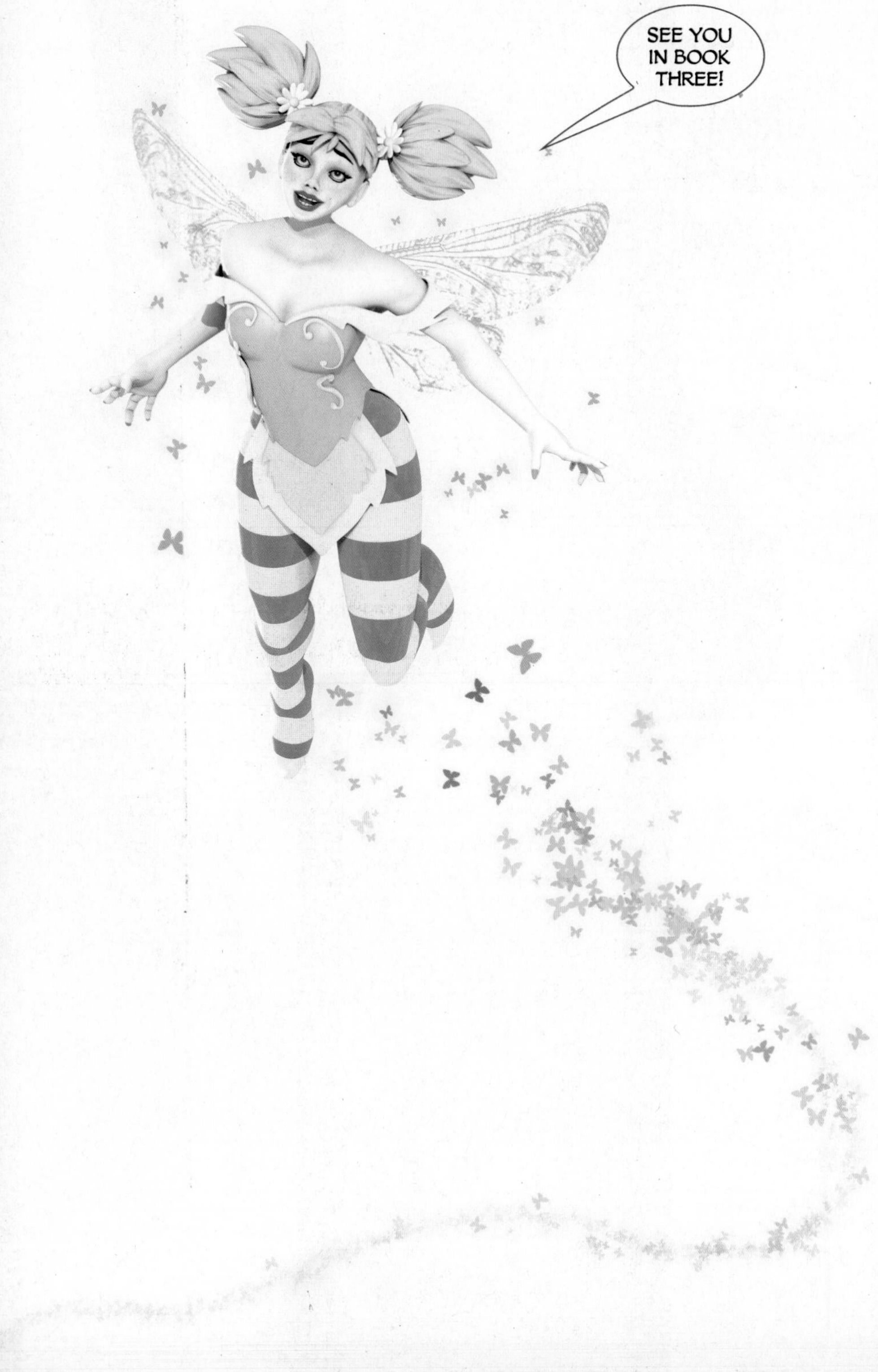
SEE YOU IN BOOK THREE!